THE PUBLIC RIGHT TO KNOW

Accountability in the Secretive Society

THE PUBLIC RIGHT TO KNOW

Accountability in the Secretive Society

JOHN CRISPO

McGRAW-HILL RYERSON LIMITED

Toronto   Montreal   New York   London
Sydney   Johannesburg   Mexico   Panama
Düsseldorf   Kuala Lumpur   New Delhi   São Paulo

THE PUBLIC RIGHT TO KNOW: Accountability in the Secretive Society

ISBN 0-07-082248-4

1 2 3 4 5 6 7 8 9 AP75 4 3 2 1 0 9 8 7 6 5

Printed and bound in Canada

To

Melba, Carol Anne & Sharon
Without Whom
the Fight for a Decent Future
Wouldn't Seem Nearly as Worthwhile

TABLE OF CONTENTS

AUTHOR'S PREFACE

This book is not intended as an academic treatise. It is much closer to a political tract. It is based on no working hypothesis or preconceived notion other than a conviction that North American society is in such bad shape that serious reforms must shortly be undertaken if everything now taken for granted is not to be completely undermined.

Through a series of experiences, I have gradually come to the conclusion that there is one key element in the restoration of individual and institutional accountability and integrity in North America consistent with maintaining the general way of life it has come to represent. This key lies in the wholesale disclosure and exposure and public scrutiny of matters which have in the past been veiled in secrecy. There is real hope for reform only if a breach can be made in the iron curtain surrounding and precluding effective surveillance of the anti-social and irresponsible activities so many groups are engaged in.

The first area in which the author came to realize the importance of disclosure and exposure and public scrutiny was appropriately enough in his own area of specialization, industrial relations. Therein, disclosure and exposure and public scrutiny have a salutary role to play — not least in the protection of individual union members' rights within the very organizations established to advance and protect their positions as employees. Hence the need for a Bill of Rights for union members, a neutral judicial system such as the United Automobile Workers Public Review Board, and other devices which are discussed later in this volume.

The importance of disclosure and exposure and public scrutiny also came to the fore when I was called upon by the now-defunct Canadian Prices & Incomes Commission to examine fee-setting and related activities of groups of professionals. Here again, I found myself calling for more disclosure and exposure and public scrutiny of what such bodies were up to — this time, among other things, in the form of public representatives on the governing councils of professional associations — representatives who would report annually to society at large on the public stewardship of the groups in question.

On another occasion, I was invited to submit a brief on the role of multinational corporations in Canada to the Select Committee of the Ontario Legislature on Economic and Cultural Nationalism. As one who generally believes that multinational corporations have, in the main, a potential for far more good than harm in the world at large, I found myself hard pressed to defend my position, because of the paucity of data available on their operations. Particularly noteworthy is the absence of accurate figures on the intercountry transfer payments within such corporations. Once again, therefore, I was struck by the need for disclosure and exposure and public scrutiny of information to ensure an accurate analysis of the effect of such institutions on the public welfare both within and between the countries in which multinational corporations operate.

In acknowledging the assistance I have received in writing this book, my first obligation is to the many authors and publications from whom I derived much of the inspiration and most of the material on which the book is based. Without their generous permission to reproduce their work, this project would never have reached fruition. My greatest personal thanks are due to my former secretary, Grace Bray, who more than generously gave of her time on and off the job to complete the first manuscript. In this and so many other respects she demonstrated good will, hard work and loyalty well above and beyond the call of duty. Nancy Ramsey and Cheryl Rovet took over from Grace to handle the many revisions in the manuscript, to help trace the original sources of many of the quotations cited, and to seek permission for their use. For assistance in digging up materials from all manner of sources the author is especially indebted to Peter Strathy, Librarian, in the Faculty of Management Studies and Jean Newman, Librarian for the Centre for Industrial Relations Information Service, both of the University of Toronto. David Fowler, a Ph.D. student in the Faculty of Management Studies, was also of much assistance in gathering data for the chapters on management and particularly for the one on "Corporate Social Responsibility."

April, 1975   JOHN CRISPO

1

INTRODUCTION

This book is based on the premise that North America is a sick society. Neither in the United States nor Canada, however, has the country, its people or its major institutions deteriorated so badly that they are beyond repair. Were this the case, it would be naive to call for reform, and revolution would be the order of the day. The danger is that the longer appropriate remedies are ignored or postponed, the more likely it is that the extremists will have their way.

THE UNDERLYING SICKNESS AND ITS POSSIBLE RAMIFICATIONS

That North America is a sick society seems to the author to be indisputable. The fact that many of the privileged among its ranks do not acknowledge it to be so is probably the most damning and serious indictment of all. Some of those who have recognized the problem in North America may occasionally acknowledge the injustices which pervade the system, but even these few are reluctant at any personal cost to do anything to alleviate or correct these injustices. Meanwhile, at the other end of the spectrum, the have-nots, the disadvantaged, and the down-trodden are becoming more prone to question the basic order in which they find themselves trapped. Indicative of the desperation of the few who have written off the existing system is the apparent kidnapping by the so-called Symbianese Liberation Army of the daughter of Randolf Hearst, purportedly primarily in order to force him to channel millions of dollars worth of food to the poor of California. That the latter in turn should be so desperate and eager to collect such spoils as to riot over its distribution is still another revealing manifestation of the rot that has set in.

The problem is that time may well be on the side of those who would resort to revolutionary ends and means. This is because of the potentially explosive combination of a society more able and yet less willing to cure its ills and the increasing awareness and impatience of the growing numbers who are its victims in one form or another. Despite and perhaps because of its supposed affluence, North America, and especially the United States, could be at the frontier among countries likely to sow the seeds of their own internal transformation as this article which appeared in *The Toronto Telegram* points out:

Jean-Francois Revel, a husky Leftist philosopher and journalist, has scandalized the French Left and created an international literary stir by writing a book arguing that the revolution of the 20th century will occur in the United States.

What then does the United States have that makes it the potential engine of world revolution?

1

"It has economic growth. It has advanced technology and a high level of basic research. It is oriented to the future instead of the past. It is undergoing an upheaval in the standards of behavior and individual freedom. It rejects authoritarianism. It broadens freedom in art and life-style and experience of the senses. Finally it permits the coexistence of many subcultures.

"The only revolutionary stirrings in the world in the last decade have originated in the United States. The one truly original revolutionary invention — the whole phenomenon called 'dissent' — has come from the United States.

"The student revolts in Berkeley in 1964-65 were a wholly new phenomenon. They have spread to Europe and the Third World. Before them were the protests against racial discrimination and the sit-ins in the south.

"America today," Revel said, "is a laboratory for revolutionary experiment because it has all the new problems of a modern society. America is the first society to have achieved a high degree of affluence and one of the results of this is that you have the highest proportion of young people in universities of any country in the world.

"You have a certain proportion of the privileged class turning on its own social class. That was the situation in France before the French Revolution. A large part of the French aristocracy were for the new ideas then. It was the educated people who read Voltaire: the peasants couldn't.

"The main condition for invention of a new type of society doesn't have to be violence. The first condition is the ability to change. Take the Vietnam War. In America for the first time in history tremendous criticism of a war has come from inside a country that is itself a belligerent.

"...I think the U.S. is building a new type solution that no society before ever had.... Americans will have to go through a very deep change in the mentality of their society. But I think that is taking place."[1]

Although the likelihood of revolution in North America is overstated in this scenario, the perpetuation of glaring disparities in the distribution of income alone could prove sufficient at some point to trigger such a transformation. As suggested in the next chapter, probably nothing condemns North America more than these persistent inequities in the distribution of its wealth. Despite years of vaunted efforts to redress these imbalances through public spending and taxing policies, the allocation of income to the top and the bottom remains as unfair as it has been for decades. That the wealthy and near wealthy in such an affluent society should continue to be able to foster and impose these disparities is reason enough to question the very nature of the present system.

Fundamental reforms may not be put off for long without drastic repercussions because of three strategic mistakes which the North American establishment has made. These have been to provide growing numbers of the relatively disadvantaged with greater access to television, the automobile and education. As unfair as the North American trickle-down system is, it has assured its disadvantaged comparatively more than the downtrodden have in other parts of the world. But this deliberate stabilizing gesture or magnanimous form

[1] Robert J. Donovan, "U.S. A Lab for Revolution?", The Toronto Telegram, October 6, 1971.

of charity — call it what you will — could in the end prove the undoing of the system. Television has given the poor a perspective on how the other half lives, the automobile has provided mobility to see that it's really true, and education has awakened the intellect to the raising of some penetrating and vexing questions. At some point, it should not take that much leadership to galvanize the deprived and discontented into a movement which could really upset the status quo.

There is another perhaps even more telling way of putting the challenges that beset North American society. At the one extreme this society is neither a communist nor a socialist system. At the other, neither is it any longer really a capitalist or free enterprise system. Instead it is increasingly becoming what might best be described as an organized society in which more and more groups are banding together to promote their own particular brand of self interest. Not unnaturally this self interest normally is reflected in the various groups' income aspirations both in an absolute and relative sense.

When it comes to income distribution, the most striking feature about present-day North America is the fact that the existing pecking order is breaking down. No longer is anyone satisfied with his or her position in the income hierarchy. Rather the old reference points are being discarded as one group after another decides it is too far down the income ladder and determines to do something to improve its comparative status. The result contributes to the explanation for the current inflationary treadmill to nowhere as different groups try to leapfrog and whipsaw each other in their never-ending vieing for position.

Combine all this with an obsolete series of checks and balances which does not begin to restrain abuses of power by any number of groups and it is not hard to see why such an uncontrollable rat race has broken out. Worse still, the process tends to become self perpetuating and inevitably self destructive when no major corrective steps are taken. This becomes all the more important as more groups organize, as the income pecking order becomes less and less acceptable, sustainable and tenable, and as it is perceived more widely that nobody is being effectively called to account for excessive accumulations of power let alone abuses of that power.

The cumulative effect of all of these corroding forces is a growing feeling that there is no longer any real commitment to equity, fairness or justice in the distribution of income or anything else in North America. As this realization spreads it intensifies the disintegrating forces, thereby setting in motion a potentially devastating vicious circle of socially destructive events.

The real question is whether the existing order can rise to the challenge which confronts it before it is too late. If, over and above everything else economic growth has to be compromised, and even sacrificed to some extent, in order to conserve energy and preserve the environment, then that challenge may come sooner than anticipated. For if growth has to be slowed, then those who have may prove less willing to allow as much to trickle down to others, thus providing even fewer leftovers for the underprivileged. To put it another way, real emphasis might then have to be placed on actual redistribution of income from the "haves" to the "have-nots." This should happen anyway, but the pressure for it will surely intensify if some de-emphasis of growth has to take place.

If North America does not respond to these legitimate concerns and needs by democratic and voluntary means, the result could be resort to more drastic measures by those at either end of the have—have-not spectrum. The right-wing establishment might be driven to more fascist measures to protect its privileged position, while the downtrodden could be persuaded by the left to adopt equally totalitarian actions to wrest a greater share of society's wealth.

THE FOCUS, PURPOSE AND LIMITATIONS OF THIS BOOK

Compared to these foregoing general, more global, and certainly more trying issues and possibilities, the challenges and problems which are the focal points of this volume may seem quite insignificant. This is not the case, however, since many of the most glaring income disparities, and other injustices and the threats to which they give rise are the result of the abuses perpetrated on the rest of society by organized interest groups whose powers remain unchecked. Until society comes to grips with these unrestrained vested interests, little more basic social reform can take place because it runs so counter to the influential positions they now occupy. So as minor and unimportant as some of the reforms advocated in this study may appear, they are essential to an assault on the more fundamental evils which plague North America.

In this book, the reform spotlight is focused on the political sphere, the business and corporate world, the professions and organized labour, and the mass media. In all of these areas, it appears that for every problem which can be identified there are possible solutions consistent with the general nature of North America's present socio-economic-political system.

Perhaps the major purpose of this book is to suggest that confrontation over most of the basic issues troubling North America can be forestalled, if not obviated, by demonstrating to those so obviously shortchanged by the system that those traditionally best able to exploit them and the system as a whole are being called to account for their abuses. This can be accomplished within the existing framework by adjusting the present system of checks and balances to induce those responsible for abuses to behave more in the public interest. This is what this book is all about — attempting to find ways and means by which to establish a new series of reciprocal rights and responsibilities so as to ensure a more acceptable and durable balance between those at opposite ends of the income distribution and, one might add, power and status, scale.

It has already been emphasized in the Preface that this volume treats the United States and Canada almost as one in terms of both the diagnoses of and the prescriptions suggested for the problems posed. Some Canadians will take exception to this on the grounds that as sick as Canada may be it hardly compares with the U.S. on this plane. Materials gathered for this volume do not support such a strong distinction, although the sources drawn upon are predominantly from the U.S., rather than Canada.

This point leads naturally to the mention of some of the major limitations of this kind of study. In the first place, no one author can claim to be anything like an expert on all the many facets of North American life. That is why such heavy reliance has been placed upon the writings of others. Indeed, more than three quarters of this book is made up of citations and quotations drawn from works other than the author's.

Some may question the author's dependence for the most part on sources other than the traditional academic outlets. This is because these outlets have ignored the underlying issues or gone at them in such an abstract and theoretical manner as to render them almost useless from an effective public policy point of view. Instead of the customary academic citations, this book is replete with references from quasi-academic publications such as *Harvard Business*

Review and *California Management Review*, such business and labour periodicals as *Business Week* and *AFL-CIO News* and such well-known newspapers as *The Globe and Mail* and *The Christian Science Monitor*, the latter two proving the most fruitful sources of all.

Articles from these and similar publications have naturally been selected because of the point of view they espouse. Despite references to counter assessments and counter arguments, the materials cited for the most part mirror the author's own position. Needless to say, however, an effort has been made to avoid irresponsible and unsupported sources of documentation. Fortunately, in spite of limited amounts of attention devoted to many of the topics featured, there is enough available to build aspects of the central themes of this volume around each of the areas examined.

AN OUTLINE OF THE BOOK

It remains in this brief opening chapter to outline the contents of those which follow. To begin, there is a lengthy chapter setting forth the characteristics of the troubles that pervade North American society. The depth and nature of the sickness as well as its signs and symptoms are highlighted. Although admittedly overstated to some extent, this account of the present condition of North American society is close enough to the truth to make anyone shudder who is concerned about its long-run viability. Those who would quarrel with an indictment such as is outlined in the next chapter or would simply prefer to ignore it may well choose to stop here, if not at that point. That is a risk which must be taken if the foundation is to be laid for the various analyses and findings which ensue.

The following chapter embodies a brief and hopefully persuasive case for working from within the existing system — for reform, rather than from without — for revolution. Too many basic institutions and values are at stake to attempt a radical departure from the basic framework of the present system. At the root of it all are those fundamental values relating to freedom of speech, assembly, et cetera, which could easily be lost sight of and sacrificed in anything but a reform of the existing order. To go beyond this would be to jeopardize too many other things as well, and probably to entail less gain than loss.

Having highlighted the nature of the challenges and problems confronting North America and the dimensions within which solutions must be found, all but one of the remaining chapters of the book are devoted to particular components of the total system. To begin, there is a chapter on "Parties, Politics and Politicians," an area in which the need for reform — at least in the United States — hardly needs stating after Watergate and all that is conjured up by that term. This is clearly the most critical area of concern within North American society. On the one hand, if North America cannot clean up its political processes, it cannot hope to clean up many of its other blights. On the other hand, if it can make headway in the political arena, there is hope in other areas, if only because a more honest political climate would be less vulnerable to the special pleadings of private interest groups and therefore more prone to pursue the public interest where the two are in conflict as they so often are.

Turning from politics to the business and corporate world, there follow three chapters attempting to point out many of the major reforms which have to be introduced in this area of society. Although a defender of the competitive system, of corporate forms of management, and so-called capitalism, the author believes all will be lost in these areas unless they are quite drastically altered.

5

Reviewed in these chapters are many steps which can and must be taken to ensure greater public accountability by directors, executives and managers without destroying the profit motive and the very essence of the existing economic structure. Among the more controversial topics dealt with in these chapters are the question of public members on private corporate boards, and ways of diminishing the growing influence and size of the public sector bureaucracy by contracting out more of its responsibilities in order to reduce its increasingly stultifying effect on the overall economy.

After the first and more general chapter on "Business, Society and Government," which attempts to cover the overall gamut of business and corporate abuses, there follows a chapter on "Corporate Social Responsibility." This chapter sets forth a spectrum of corporate social responsibility models and endeavours to select from them an appropriate amalgam or combination which makes sense in the context of the assumptions underlying this volume and other proposals advanced in it.

Perhaps of greatest concern within the business and corporate sector of the total socio-economic-political system are the socially undesirable practices which characterize the advertising and marketing sphere. Entire books have been written on these deceptive, fraudulent and misleading practices, yet space will only permit a chapter to be devoted to them in this volume. Little more is really required, however, to demonstrate why this area epitomizes how dishonesty and lack of integrity have come to be taken for granted in North America. Superficially, at least, one could argue that there is no better place to begin nor end in seeking to bring about a higher standard of ethical behaviour.

The next chapter on "The Professions and the Trade Unions" deals with two other areas of related concern to society. Most of this chapter focuses on the immense and largely unrestricted powers society has allowed to reside in various self-governing and semi-self-governing professional bodies. Traditionally, these privileges were granted only to a few groups such as doctors and lawyers. More recently, they have been extended to more and more groups who have learned by the examples set by their predecessors. Although they are not always used for such selfish pursuits, self-governing licensing and related powers can be employed in a variety of ways to restrict numbers and otherwise strengthen the economic positions of those within these self-selective guilds. Failure to curb these powers can only lead others to seek to emulate them, thus further compounding the problem.

Also deserving of attention is the place of the labour movement in the total scheme of things. Since it comes in for more than its fair share of criticism from many other quarters, the author has chosen to highlight only a few aspects of the potential for abuse which exists under its auspices. In so doing, it quickly becomes apparent that society must face up to a difficult dilemma if it wants simultaneously to promote both democratic and responsive unions and accountable and responsible ones.

Often referred to as the fourth estate, the mass media has a critical role to play in the reform of society. This is brought out in a chapter entitled "The Media and Its Message." It cannot be denied that the media has in the past played an important part in the reform of North America — if only by exposing the abuses of others, a contribution which is not to be minimized. In some instances it has also gone some way towards reforming itself through press councils and other measures. Nonetheless, much remains to be done in and through the media if its full potential as a quasi-public utility is to be exploited in the remaking of society. The role of the media in this process is so vital that its reform must receive high priority.

The final chapter of the book summarizes the basic themes of the preceding chapters and shows how these common themes could come together to form the basis for a revitalization of the existing socio-economic-political order without changing its basic characteristics.

The most fundamental theme advanced throughout is that through more disclosure and exposure and public scrutiny of what is going on in many North American institutions, much can be done to reform them by inducing them to act as much in the public interest as in their own. It will be emphasized again in the concluding chapter, as it has been here, that the challenge is to get on with the business of reform before a more drastic response is called for or imposed.

To emphasize the basic thrust of this volume, and to further set the stage for the remaining chapters, it is appropriate to conclude this introductory chapter with some thoughts on what must become "The Age of Accountability":

Out of America's political and moral turbulence is emerging the Age of Accountability.

The phrase was used recently by Lewis A. Engman, chairman of the Federal Trade Commission, at a meeting of national advertisers. He suggested they were accountable not only for accuracy in telling the good points about their products — but for disclosing additional information to the public "where failure to disclose such information would result in unfairness or deception."

But the demand for accountability, as Mr. Engman noted, does not stop with advertising. He said that the current "wrenching crisis" of confidence in government is part of a crisis of confidence in all institutions that has been building for years.

Restoring confidence is the task of the Age of Accountability.

Its success depends on the responsiveness of all to their own particular kind and degree of accountability. Parents have always made their children accountable; now children make parents accountable for acting according to their precepts. Corporations have always made customers accountable for paying their bills; now customers make corporations accountable for their products.

The Atomic Energy Commission is being made more accountable than ever for nuclear plant safety. Users of natural resources are made accountable for their impact on the environment. Disposers of waste products are made accountable for their effect on air, land, and water. Manufacturers are made accountable for their part in the safety of those on whom they profit. The press is made accountable by a national news council that tries to preserve press freedom, too. Consumers become a race of Naders.

The Age of Accountability is not a departure from, but a return to, the taproots of America. Colonists were outraged at remote rulers unaccountable to the ruled. After Lexington and Concord, a back-country county in North Carolina instructed its delegates at a provincial constitutional congress to demand a most obvious sort of accountability:

"You are instructed to move and insist that the public accounts fairly stated shall be regularly kept in proper books open to the inspection of all persons whom it may concern. If this should not be confirmed, contend for it."

Sensitized by Watergate, Americans are again "contending for it" — for accountability — with renewed determination. They are, in John

Stuart Mill's phrase of a century ago, "pushing to its utmost extent the accountability of governments to people."

Certainly campaign financing and government procedures will be subject to new accountability as long as the Watergate momentum lasts. The people want to vote on the basis of facts, not fabrications. Given the truth, they can then fully play their own accountable role in the Age of Accountability.[2]

[2] "The Age of Accountability", *The Christian Science Monitor*, November 6, 1973.

2

NORTH AMERICA AS A SICK SOCIETY

The term "sick society" is bandied about so loosely these days that some commentators hesitate to use it. Yet popularly speaking there is no better term to describe the malaise which presently afflicts much of modern-day society in North America. Although the disease may run deeper in the United States than Canada, it is present to a disturbing degree on both sides of the border.

A particularly well-informed and terribly depressing view of the U.S. situation is to be found in Richard C. Goodwin's *The American Condition*.[1] His reviewer in *Business Week* sums up this view:

For more than a decade, Richard Goodwin has been one of the best-known and most respected voices in the liberal, intellectual establishment: speechwriter to Presidents Kennedy and Johnson (he wrote the "Great Society" and "War on Poverty" speeches for Johnson) and to candidates McCarthy, Robert Kennedy, and Muskie. These credentials alone would guarantee his study of alienation in contemporary America — what he calls his "pathology" of American society — a substantial audience. Moreover, he is a pleasure to read. His mind is acute, his pen facile, and his turns of phrase mostly admirable.

What gives *The American Condition* an extra dimension, assuring that it will be widely reviewed and furiously debated in the weeks ahead, is its timing. Goodwin's pathology (the word is defined by Webster as "the study of diseases, their essential nature, causes and development, and the structural and functional changes produced by them") appears in the winter of America's deepest discontent. Watergate persists like a toothache. The oil crisis has swallowed the economic boom of 1973 and threatens the nation with both inflation and a recession in 1974.

Not in decades have so many Americans worried about their society. And here comes Goodwin — distinguished social commentator, hand-holder to the mighty, eyewitness to the drama of the past 15 years — to offer his views. Even those who do not share Goodwin's political ideology (or rather former ideology, since he plainly isn't the activist Democrat of a decade ago) are obliged to listen to what he has to say.

The question then becomes whether Goodwin has said anything worth listening to, and the answer is "yes" — with some qualifications.

The American Condition is a demanding book. This is not a criticism but simply an observation. It is an essay drawn out too long. It is a harsh, intellectually punishing book whose unremitting negativism will disturb many readers. Goodwin insists that he understands what is wrong with America but concedes that he has no concrete prescription for change. If it is a depressing book, it is because Goodwin meant it to be so. "To be

[1] Richard C. Goodwin, *The American Condition* (New York, Doubleday, 1974).

9

cheerful is to accept," he says, "and one who accepts is forever without hope." But he leaves the reader frustrated, yearning for answers that are not given.

Goodwin finds the American condition appalling, the American dream become a nightmare, the American people caught in the grip of economic and political institutions so vast and inhuman that even the men who believe they control the system are in reality more servants than masters. "Modern confusion and distress," he says, "now reveal themselves as a consequence, not of human evil, but of the process which provides material abundance. Amidst unparalleled productive power, freedom is being eroded and confined."

The existentialists saw man's individualism destroyed by society, and they reveled in acts of liberated individualism. To Goodwin it is society that has been shattered — with individualism all that survives. But it is individualism perverted, each man alone in his prison, out of touch with his fellows and with his own humanity. He no longer has a community to belong to or a national ideal to believe in. He is truly lost.

Goodwin's villains are the bureaucratic institutions of our society, especially — but not exclusively — the corporate and industrial concentrations of wealth formed in the furious growth of the postwar years. He concedes that a huge economy needs huge institutions but argues that "the extent of consolidation exorbitantly exceeds these needs. No reasons of abstract economic efficiency dictate that the needs and demands of an expanding national market can be met most productively by three automobile companies, one computer company, a single telephone corporation. . ."

Existing in symbiotic embrace with the economic bureaucracies are others. Organized labor is a bureaucracy; so is the American educational system. The growth of the economic bureaucracies has been paralleled by the growth in power and might of the central government, itself the most gigantic, unresponsive, coercive bureaucracy of all.

So our institutions, in Goodwin's view, have grown too large. More disturbing, they have grown unresponsive. He sees today's economic bureaucracies as inefficient, non-competitive, uneconomic in the use of resources, dedicated to minimizing risk and uncertainty, more interested in continuity and expansion than in human needs.

This is so, he says, because these institutions are so vast that they are no longer owned by men. Ownership is so diffuse that it is no longer possible to speak of these bureaucracies as being owned in the sense that the Rockefellers once "owned" Standard Oil. Instead, they are simply overseen today by a succession of managers, none of them with sufficient power to do more than act as temporary stewards. The managers, says Goodwin, can inhabit the executive suite as long as they do nothing to imperil the institution — "allowed," in Goodwin's words, "to command the power which they do not own as long as they don't take too much — touch the principal or impair the machine."

So man created and is now subservient to what he created, and the word for that subservience is alienation: "the dimunition of human life through man's subjection to his own creations."

Alienation is neither new nor distinctly American. The process began centuries ago with the Industrial Revolution and the forging of the modern nation-state. Community ties fell apart, scales became greater than human, society fragmented, leaving the individual to stand alone against forces that he could not control. What is new, says Goodwin, is that "modern economic relationships have hugely accelerated the social fragmentation which had seemed to be approaching the limits of possibility even before the bureaucratic ascendancy."

Alienation exists in every developed or developing country. It hurts more in America because it is so antiethetical to the American dream of freedom for all. Other nations have historical and cultural traditions and common ethnic origins to give them support, to bind their people together with some sense of community and national purpose. America has only its idea, says Goodwin, and that idea is "always in the present." To Goodwin, " 'Justice,' 'freedom,' 'opportunity,' 'model and exemplar to the world' are either present realities or the idea is dead."

This is a bleak view, all the more bleak because Goodwin cannot see how the alienating process can be halted. Man is made impotent by the increasing inhumanity of his institutions, and his very impotence insures that the institutions will grow bigger and still more inhuman. In one of the most dour conclusions since Cotton Mather, Goodwin says: "We are not the victims of perfectible weakness in the social structure. Our humanity is being consumed by the structure itself."

Alienated man by himself, says Goodwin, can do little to improve his lot. Nor can he look to government, he says, in a dramatic about-face for a man who toiled so hard for the government-can-do-it-all administrations of Kennedy and Johnson. In the final analysis, he decides, any government must reflect the realities of the society that created it. Society can change its government, but government cannot change society. Government, Goodwin concludes, can act only when its actions will not disturb the existing social structure. "It cannot act effectively," he argues, "if the source of discontent is fundamental, residing in the design of society."

Checkmate. Modern man is powerless to change his social structure. And unless the social structure changes, says Goodwin, "we can expect the political evolution of recent decades to continue — the dilution of popular control, remoteness and bureaucratization, accumulation of central authority and, increasingly, the integration of government into the economic process."

In the end, Goodwin can do little more than wring his hands over the future. His hopes for change are slight, as he himself concedes. "Economic relationships should be decentralized," he says. Perhaps the seeds of change lie within the 60-million workers who are not part of the bureaucracy or organized labor. Human consciousness does change, he acknowledges: "The germinating energies of change exist in all economic relationships." But having covered the past and present, Goodwin simply is not ready to tackle the future; that must fall to someone else.[2]

Almost as if to bear out Goodwin's disturbing underlying analysis, and drawing on a number of recent public scandals to make its point, The Wall Street Journal has editorially expressed concern about the cumulative impact of blatant corruption on a society's confidence in its ability to govern itself:

As if the widening Watergate drama and Equity Funding case were

[2] Gordon L. Williams, "A Cheerless View of Modern Man". Reprinted from the March 16, 1974 issue of Business Week by special permission. Copyright 1974 by McGraw Hill, Inc.

11

not bad enough, additional charges of scandal and corruption reverberate throughout the land:

A majority of New Jersey citizens, responding to a poll by the Eagleton Institute of Politics at Rutgers University, believe both their state and local governments are corrupt. Former Illinois Gov. Otto Kerner, a judge in the U.S. Court of Appeals, was recently fined and sentenced to three years in federal prison. The Queens district attorney resigned after being indicted on charges of covering up an investigation into a multi-million-dollar get-rich scheme. And reports from other parts of the country tell of kick-backs, funds illegally diverted and influence peddling.

All this atop what is clearly the biggest governmental scandal of this generation, and what may very well be the biggest business scandal as well. And in each of these cases, what is most disheartening is the breadth of apparent complicity.

With scandal and corruption cutting across partisan political lines and extending into the White House and the fanciest executive suites, little wonder that the revelations have prompted analogies of Augean stables and decadent civilizations of the past.

But it is probably wise not to go too far in lamenting that the nation has lost its way, or in believing that the old verities and values have been replaced with barratry and dishonor. The preamble for the Populist Party platform in 1892 declared: "We meet in the midst of a nation brought to the verge of moral, political and material ruin. Corruption dominates the ballot box, the legislatures, the Congress, and touches even the ermine of the bench." The Populists, too, were sure they were meeting amid the decline of the nation, when in fact much of America's greatness lay just over the horizon.

But if last rites are premature, and if America is not yet on its ethical death bed, it would be a mistake to minimize any of the alleged or actual betrayals of public trust. Although widespread corruption throughout New Jersey government is a matter of public record, for example, only 12% of Garden State citizens believe corruption is worse there than elsewhere. We imagine citizens of other states would share the same impression of pervasiveness.

This public demoralization is the most important effect of scandal. There is a case to be made that ethical standards have risen in general and that today's worst scandals are not as gross as some in the past. But it is today's standards that count. The way people feel about public and private leaders and indeed their own peers — their subjective assessment, as it were — is often as important as the actual situation. The scandals and corruption above have been especially damaging because they involve not just malfeasance or fraud, but betrayal at the highest level of leadership.

More important than the money or personal gain involved is the damage that corruption and scandal inflict on the bonds of trust necessary for self-government. Almost 200 years ago Edmund Burke noted that, "Among a people generally corrupt, liberty cannot long exist." And while the American people and their elected representatives are far from being generally corrupt, every new scandal helps to reinforce that notion by undermining public confidence and eroding those all-important bonds of trust.[3]

[3] "Those Important Bonds of Trust", *The Wall Street Journal*, April 30, 1973. Reprinted with permission of *The Wall Street Journal* © Dow Jones & Company, Inc., 1973.

Especially intriguing are the results of a special Louis Harris poll conducted for *Time* as long ago as 1969. This pre-Watergate survey revealed a fascinating shift in ethics and morals, perhaps mostly for the worse, but at least toward what appeared to be much less hypocrisy in moral issues. Extracts from the *Time* account of this survey are illuminating:

In his latest survey for TIME, Louis Harris has undertaken a study of moral attitudes among Americans in an effort to illuminate the changing U.S. moral climate. The results produce ample evidence that, despite considerable indignation at what they believe to be unjust, Americans in general are far more permissive about morals than they were only a few years ago.

Men and women, young and old, professionals and laborers, whites and blacks, Christians and Jews, all agree by lopsided majorities that morality in the U.S. has declined over the past ten years. Nationwide, 67% of Harris' sampling of 1,600 representative Americans take that view, while only 11% believe that moral standards have risen. Those who feel that morality has improved point to increased concern for racial and social justice and to widespread revulsion against the war in Viet Nam. The majority that finds a decline in standards attributes the trend more than anything else to increased emphasis on sex, crime and violence in newspapers, magazines, books, TV and films. Another often cited cause is that "people are more materialistic."

"Perhaps the most dramatic evidence in the entire poll on how rapidly American morality is changing," says the survey, "is the rise — and the admission of that rise — in what would surely have been considered highly serious moral infractions only a short time ago." The number of people who say that they know someone who commits adultery has risen from 24% to 36% since 1964; 15% now — v. 10% then — virtually admit to instances of adultery in their own family. In other areas, 13% know someone whose child uses marijuana, 59% know someone who drinks too much, 22% know someone who gambles too much, and 11% — or one out of every nine Americans — know someone who is a homosexual. In each instance, that "someone" is frequently a member of the respondent's own family; of the 55% who said that they knew someone with marital troubles, more than half also replied that the party involved was "close to me."

When it comes to judging themselves rather than others, substantial minorities of Americans admit to committing either illegal or immoral acts, many of which they tend to take for granted. For instance, 30% nationwide admit to having cheated on an examination; 19% admit to having taken advantage of a cashier's error (32% of the young); 16% say that they have taken an employer's supplies or equipment without his permission; 13% have ignored parking tickets (20% of the college-educated); 12% have walked out of a store with something they didn't pay for (23% of the young); and 10% have failed to return borrowed library books (18% of the young).

One striking finding is that most Americans regard the violation of traditional morality as a lesser wrong than the attempt to disguise such violation with hypocrisy. The survey confirmed this indictment by posing situations in which respondents had to pass comparative judgment on various types of miscreants, "respectable" and otherwise. Common criminals, militants and the sexually promiscuous almost always came out better across the entire Harris sample than the prototypical Establishment figure who violates a trust.

Examples:

- A politician who takes bribes is worse than an adulterer (54% to 32%).
- A manufacturer of unsafe automobiles is worse than a mugger (68% to 22%).
- A policeman who takes money from a prostitute is worse than the prostitute (81% to 8%).
- A white grocer who sells bad meat to a Negro customer is worse than a Negro rioter (63% to 22%).
- A psychiatrist who improperly commits an old person to a mental hospital is worse than a draft dodger who fakes a physical defect (65% to 20%).
- A prosecutor who railroads an innocent man is worse than an armed robber (78% to 10%).
- A doctor who refuses a house call to someone who is seriously ill is worse than a homosexual (71% to 18%).
- A businessman who illegally fixes prices is worse than a burglar (54% to 28%).
- A landlord who will not repair a firetrap is worse than a campus demonstrator (65% to 23%).
- A rich man who uses loopholes to pay little or no income tax is worse than a welfare chiseler (60% to 22%).

These answers suggest that the widely bruited public antipathy to nonconformists has been exaggerated. Says Harris: "Analysis of this list leaves little doubt that immoral acts committed by Establishment figures are viewed as much worse, by and large, than anti-Establishment figures who have caused all the recent flurries of public indignation. The results strongly suggest that the central theme of the young in protest against hypocrisy and double standards has more going for it in terms of potential public support than might have previously been imagined."[4]

Before turning to the symptoms and deeper meanings of North America's sickness, it should be mentioned that the resiliency of the system should not be ignored or minimized. Although this aspect of the situation is dealt with more fully in the next chapter, a comment by one of North America's most respected newspaper editors is useful at this point:

A couple of brief forays during the last 10 days — to San Francisco and to Detroit — confirm the impression that the American nation and the systems which hold the country together are functioning extremely well. At least, that's how it struck me. The United States is going through an exceedingly traumatic time. It is not cracking.

Certainly the tests to which American society is being subjected are the most severe in its peace-time history. The presidential crisis is unprecedented in scope and seriousness. If anybody had told us, a year ago, of the sensational shocks which would come, I for one would have said the lid would blow off. It hasn't. And the energy crunch, marked not only by great shortages but by fantastic increases in cost, was enough to send the economy into chaos. It hasn't.

[4] "Changing Morality: The Two Americas", 1969. Reprinted by permission of Louis Harris and Associates, Inc.

The fabric which holds together the American system is very strong. The nation is free from political hysteria. Shock waves have rippled across the nation. The "Saturday night massacre" under which Archibald Cox, Elliot Richardson, and William Ruckelshaus were peremptorily fired or forced into resignation produced the greatest single emotional impact of this sensational year. There were massive protests and an independent judicial investigation was restored. And when the filling stations began to put up the "No Gas" signs, people reacted — they went on the prowl for other pumps and waited in long lines — but they did not panic.

The capacity to survive shocks is a good thing, but it is not the same thing as drawing the right conclusions from shocking experiences and taking steps to prevent them in future.

There is considerable doubt whether the American nation has really learned the lessons to be drawn from either the presidential crisis or the ending of the era of cheap energy. Without such conclusions and action, we are asking for future trouble.

The United States must examine the measures which could restore the tripartite checks-and-balances system in its government, thus preventing the abuse of power by any of the branches. The abuse of executive power constitutes the present crisis, but there have been abuses — and weaknesses, which are abuses — of legislative and judicial power in recent years.

The integrity of government, as set up in the American constitutional system and as operated by professional politicians, is at stake. Confidence in the system has been deeply eroded. But practically nobody calls for any basic change in the system. They want its historic effectiveness not only restored, but significantly cleaned up.

As to the economy, profound reexamination of a way of life conditioned by cheap energy is under way. More emphasis will be placed on economy and on quality, rather than on extravagance and self-indulgence. These are the needs, as part of the total challenge of men's relationship to the fragile and battered environment in which they live.

What this all suggests is that the elements holding human society together are very profound. They come back, surely, to individual people themselves and the systems within which their daily lives fall. Aware as we all are of the need for improving these systems, skeptical as we may be of much leadership, we want to build on the basis of what we have, not tear it down and try to rebuild.[5]

SYMPTOMS OF THE SICKNESS

The troubles which plague North America are so widespread that it is difficult to distinguish between the superficial signs and the roots of the problem. What follows is, therefore, a somewhat arbitrary categorization of the two, beginning with some major symptoms in the order in which they are analyzed in more detail in subsequent chapters.

Sorry as is the picture portrayed by these symptoms, however, it should be stressed that it is far from complete. For example, it has been necessary to overlook the costs of such social blights as alcoholism and drug abuse. The

[5] Erwin D. Canham, "Stability under Shock," *The Christian Science Monitor*, March 25, 1974.

situation is dismal enough without emphasizing these problems — let alone those associated with the troubled state of such traditionally critical institutions as the family, organized religion and the public school system.

The Political Arena

Watergate and its aftermath have come to symbolize for many their worst suspicions about the political process. Such suspicions are not new, even in modern times, but they are surely much deeper now than they have been for some time.

Two examples of the nature of public concern about politicians during the 1950's will serve to illustrate how far public distrust had already moved even before the troubling events of more recent times. The first is a commentary reprinted from *U.S. News and World Report*, and by to-day's standards of political morality seems almost naive and trite:

Members of Congress, by and large, are men of honesty and integrity — but many of them are their own worst enemies.

Day by day they play a game called "politics," which constantly impugns the honesty, integrity and motives of their political opponents.

To breed suspicion of corruption and, through committee hearings and speeches, to issue veiled innuendoes about the other fellow's alleged crookedness, together with an accusatory emphasis on "big business" or "big unionism," implying that these groups and others are the constant recipients of special privileges at the hands of Government — this is the modern concept of political strategy.

Why are such tactics condoned? Somehow men who in their personal contacts of everyday life would never think of accusing their fellowmen of wrongdoing without convincing proof, are ready, for the sake of political advantage, to cry "scoundrel" and "rascal." They would make the electorate believe their opponents are deliberately betraying the people's confidence and hence ought not to be continued in office.

There seems to be no such thing as morals in politics. It's a rough-and-tumble game, dependent for the most part on the assumption that the electorate — to use a phrase of the late Harry Hopkins of New Deal days — is "too damn dumb to understand."

But is the electorate so shallow-minded, so uninformed, so susceptible to emotional prejudice as to accept smears and unfounded accusations as a substitute for reasoned debate and thoughtful argument?

The Congress and other divisions of the Government are often held in disrepute by stump speakers who seem to think that in political warfare no holds are barred.

Lately, the American people have been given the idea that temptations beset the members of Congress on every side and that lobbyists and campaign contributors lurk in hidden places, ready to transmit their bribes to influence this or that vote.

Instances are indeed rare where violations of the law have occurred. Existing laws forbid corrupt practices and are generally obeyed, but of much more concern are the violations of the fundamental code of ethics — activities not prohibited by law — which grow out of the present system of campaign contributions.

For, when Senator Case, Republican, of South Dakota revealed recently that a Nebraska lawyer had attempted to offer his campaign fund a contribution, he was quick to say it wasn't a bribe. But the would-be donor represents a producer of natural gas, and a bill concerning the federal regulation of that commodity was then pending in Congress. Was this an attempt to influence the Senator's vote? The contributor says "no strings were attached."

Yet, are not many campaign contributions given usually in appreciation of services rendered, or in anticipation of services to be rendered?

The reports filed with the Clerk of the House of Representatives show, for instance, that in the 1954 campaign the political committees of the labor unions spent a total of about $2,000,000 and that sums ranging from $5,000 to $35,000 were spent specifically to aid certain Senators who were elected and to defeat other candidates who were successful.

Also, the same records show many corporation executives as having contributed out of their personal incomes a large total to campaign funds earmarked for certain Senators and members of the House.

If some committee of Congress or national commission now were to examine, for example, every single campaign contribution made in connection with the congressional election of 1954 — and study every vote on every roll call of both Houses of Congress since then on specific pieces of legislation in which the contributors had a direct or indirect interest — would the dreaded phrase, "conflict of interest," emerge to plague some members of Congress as it has some officials in the executive branch of our Government?

Do the consciences of these individual members trouble them as they introduce or press for passage measures desired by the very organizations or groups which have given so much money to their own campaign funds?

These are practical questions which sooner or later must be faced realistically if our legislative body is to be free from all taint.[6]

Equally indicative of how political standards have changed since the fifties is a 1959 editorial from *The Globe and Mail* praising a provincial premier for disavowing any significant responsibility for preventing major conflicts of interest among his senior colleagues:

(The Premier) . . . made an extensive review of the standards which he feels should be maintained in public life — and which he himself has done everything humanly possible to maintain.

The essential point Mr. Frost made was that responsibility for the maintenance of integrity (that is, the avoidance of conflict between private interest and public duty) rests primarily with each Minister himself. It is not the function of a Prime Minister to make his colleagues disclose to him all of their private interests, and thus satisfy himself that each has a clean bill of health. It is their function, rather, to make such disclosures to him when they feel some private interest of theirs conflicts with their public duty; or, if they have doubts in the matter, to consult with him about it.

We may well imagine the consequences if a Prime Minister actually did think it his business to demand from each Cabinet member a full accounting of his private interests. The imputation would be that these were not men of integrity. Men who really did have integrity would not

[6] David Lawrence, "The Honesty of Congress". Reprinted from 'U.S. News & World Report.' February 24, 1956, p. 156. Copyright 1956 U.S. News & World Report, Inc.

expose themselves to that kind of imputation; would refuse, that is, to enter the Cabinet. As for men lacking in integrity, they, while consenting to the rule of total disclosure, would proceed to devise means of getting around it.

To sum up, if men entering a Government are honest (which certainly is the assumption, and certainly should be the case) there is no need to cross-examine them on their private interests; if, on the other hand, they are dishonest, such cross-examination will not give the Government any protection. It comes back to the individual, his own standards, his own integrity.

And it is probable (the British know a lot about this) that the assumption — by the public and by political opponents — of integrity in Cabinet Ministers is one of the factors making for integrity. Premier Frost put it thus: "Men and women in public life are entitled to be regarded, and should be regarded, as honorable persons."[7]

What is most vexing about the political sphere is its key element, the politician. For the most part, and not surprisingly, the motivating force behind the politician has become image, influence and power rather than principle and substance. Again both an American and a Canadian example will help to illustrate the seriousness of the situation. This time, however, current illustrations are more important and pertinent.

In the U.S. the focal point of attention was for some time on Nixon's degree of complicity in Watergate and all that it has come to stand for. One of the most disturbing side effects of this damaging period occurred within both the Democratic and Republican parties, neither of which could for a time be construed as being unduly concerned about the ethics, honesty or integrity of the President. On the one hand, most Democrats appeared convinced that Nixon was guilty of virtually everything with which he was being charged, but were reluctant to be rid of him because it was to their political advantage to have him around for a while, and the more so the more guilty he was made to appear. On the other hand, many Republicans, while apparently still having faith in Nixon's word, would have been ready to sacrifice him, guilty or not, because he was becoming such an acute electoral encumbrance to them. Although justice may eventually have prevailed in this appalling case, it was delayed, if not miscarried, because of the political machinations of Nixon's opponents as well as his friends.

In Canada too, there is a current example of political opportunism and pragmatism in Prime Minister Pierre Elliott Trudeau, a man who originally swept his party and his country because of the idealism he so strongly seemed to radiate. In his first term he was so true to his convictions that he might best be described as an ideologue. Partly, if not largely, as a result of his stubborn adherence to his ideals, he accomplished little and retained office in the subsequent election only as head of a minority government. In the process, however, he appears to have both lost and gained a great deal. He seems to have lost much of the sense of conscience and principle which lay behind his idealism, but to have acquired considerable political acumen and sagacity. The result is a man who has once again been swept back into office with a strong majority, but this time not on a campaign in any way based on idealism, but rather on crass and pragmatic opportunism and promises which would be the envy of the most successful ward-heeler in either Chicago or New York.

[7] "The Morals of Ministers", The Globe and Mail, Toronto, February 11, 1959.

In this sense, Trudeau has become all too akin to so many other politicians in the western democracies. Some time ago Walter Lippmann accurately but depressingly characterized both the plight of and the effects on such politicians in the following terms:

> In government offices which are sensitive to the vehemence and passion of mass sentiment public men have no sure tenure. They are in effect perpetual office seekers, always on trial for their political lives, always required to court their restless constituents. They are deprived of their independence. Democratic politicians rarely feel they can afford the luxury of telling the whole truth to the people. And since not telling it, though prudent, is uncomfortable, they find it easier if they themselves do not have to hear too often too much of the sour truth. The men under them who report and collect the news come to realize in their turn that it is safer to be wrong before it has become fashionable to be right.
>
> With exceptions so rare that they are regarded as miracles and freaks of nature, successful democratic politicians are insecure and intimidated men. They advance politically only as they placate, appease, bribe, seduce, bamboozle, or otherwise manage to manipulate the demanding and threatening elements in their constituencies. The decisive consideration is not whether the proposition is good but whether it is popular — not whether it will work well and prove itself but whether the active talking constituents like it immediately. Politicians rationalize this servitude by saying that in a democracy public men are the servants of the people.[8]

The Corporate and Government Scene

Another symptom of the basic challenge confronting North America is to be found in growing public disenchantment with those who manage its major private and public institutions. Administrators and bureaucrats of all kinds are increasingly suspect in the public mind. Corporate leaders are seen as selfish exploiters bent primarily, if not exclusively, on the pursuit of their own individual and institutional welfare. Senior government officials are viewed in a somewhat different, though equally critical, light. Success in their quarter appears to be equated with the power and size of the empire they build, regardless of its service to the community. Somewhere in between are the members of all manner of regulatory bodies who are supposed to prevent abuses of the public interest. Suspicions quite properly abound as to whose interests they are really serving.

That big business has long been in trouble with the public is not a new idea. What is different is the breadth of the assault on corporate management and the depth of public disquiet about its abuses. Some of the attacks on business are exaggerated and overdrawn but contain enough substance to contribute to general public misgivings and reservations. This is often reflected in opinion polls. *America, Inc.*[9] represents one of many recent and extreme attacks on big business. To quote from one review of this book:

> In riotous and bloodcurdling detail, authors Morton Mintz, a reporter for the *Washington Post*, and Jerry S. Cohen, formerly chief counsel and

---

[8] Walter Lippmann, *The Public Philosophy* (Boston, Little, Brown & Company, 1955). Published by Little, Brown in association with Atlantic Monthly Press.
[9] Morton Mintz and Jerry Cohen, *America Inc.* (New York, Dial Press, 1971).

staff director of the Senate antitrust and monopoly subcommittee, have made a strong indictment of the people and organizations who are characterized in their subtitle as the owners and operators of the United States. *America, Inc.* is a mind-numbing book.

Relentlessly, the authors take us on a "tour through a state of concentration," telling tale after tale of corporate acquisition and merger. They recite the familiar refrain that federal antitrust law is not sufficiently powerful to stem the dangerous tide of increasing concentration in all industries. They describe the evils that concentration can wreak. They give examples in which the federal regulatory agencies have been bought off by big business. From there, they proceed to the dismal wasteland of radio, television, and newspapers, where, they charge, the public interest is submerged in a bid for profits, and independent publishers and other news media are gobbled up by conglomerate corporations, which then suppress stories that would be detrimental to their other products. Among other things, the result of all this concentration, the authors report, is to aggravate greatly the burgeoning inflationary trends.

Next, the authors tell how some businessmen have invested in politics with the aim of purchasing the election of senators and congressmen, and what happens once their candidates are elected. Since Presidents of the United States cannot personally make all decisions relating to lucrative transportation routes, radio and television licenses, and other areas regulated by federal law, the authors thoughtfully outline numerous ways in which regulatory agencies may be corrupted.

In fact, the authors spare us nothing: What sex was to the Puritans, white-collar crime is to many businessmen, and the authors treat us to a discussion of those nether activities which may land, but only occasionally have landed, the businessman in jail. Mintz and Cohen charge that the super-concentrated industries in the United States can play God, and hold back innovations that would be kind to the environment, to minorities, to safety, to privacy, to craftsmanship, and to life itself. And, finally, as if all that were not enough, the authors plunge right in to show us how private corporations seek to play at being secretaries of state, dabbling in foreign affairs around the world.

America, Inc. is not simply a cry against vague and undisclosed evils; in the best muckraking tradition it is thoroughly documented to present a look at the seamy side of business. Examples spill across the pages, at times at such a furious pace that the reader has difficulty digesting one set of horrors before he is compelled to divert his attention to the next.

Early in the book, the authors note that "to function effectively and reliably as private governments, giant corporations must govern constitutional governments." This is both the premise and the promise of the book: The who and the how are revealed and explained. Mintz and Cohen draw on government reports and documents, published papers, articles, speeches, and books. It would be as unfair as it is impossible to single out any particular example here, for that would only serve to suggest that the book is narrower than it is.

I must note in passing that the book is mind-numbing in another but related sense: Because of its very completeness and because it is drawn almost exclusively from prior published material, the reader must be prepared for a dense and heavy journey through its pages. Like swimming through molasses, it is best to jump in, to keep going, and never to look back, no matter how slowly you think you are moving.

America, Inc. is 377 scathing pages long. Its brilliance is contained in the first 357 pages only; the last 20 pages, entitled "Conclusions and Recommendations," are unsatisfactory. Having established the capacity of the American corporation to govern at times the government itself, the authors propose to control the network of private government by creating still another governmental agency. Mintz and Cohen's "primary recommendation . . . is that federal chartering replace state chartering of corporations" to allow the government to define the role of the corporation. The charter device would be used to restrict the activities of corporations and to provide to the degree possible, a monopoly-free economy. Only one sentence in the entire book deals with what the chartering agency would be like or how it would operate. "Decisions of this kind, of course, would be made by a chartering authority, subject to safeguards, such as a special court of appeals."

This is an extremely weak proposal and delineated hardly at all. First, it utterly ignores the very great, practical, and constitutional problems involved. Almost all of the hundreds of thousands of business corporations operated today are chartered under state authority. In the famous *Dartmouth College Case*, the Supreme Court held nearly 150 years ago that corporate charters are contracts between the incorporators and the state and any attempt to revoke the charters would be unconstitutional. Thus, any attempt to transfer existing state charters to federal authority is fraught with the greatest peril.

Second, the business corporation is faced today with a formidable array of federal regulations. A schoolchild can tick off the names of more than a handful of institutions headquartered in Washington and established to regulate the economy. If corporations have captured these agencies, as the authors charge, there is no reason to believe that they would fail to capture a federal chartering agency.

Third, the existing federal regulatory agencies, including the Justice Dept., have broad power to carry out many of the reforms suggested by the authors. The real challenge is to find ways to prompt these agencies into action. I believe that vigorous personnel policies aimed at attracting energetic and brilliant people with a commitment to investigation and enforcement is a fundamental step. There are undoubtedly other steps, and the failure of the authors to consider any of them unfortunately mars an otherwise extremely thoughtful book.

A curious omission underscores the thrust of the book. The authors apparently feel that only the corporations "own and operate" the United States. They are extremely reticent about the power of unions. And, except for a passing reference relating to corporate marketing of drugs, they ignore altogether the increasing power of professional groups throughout the U.S., a power cogently demonstrated in Jethro K. Lieberman's book on *The Tyranny of the Experts*.

Finally, a dangerous suggestion lurking innocently in the last chapter points out the hazards of over-simplifying solutions to complex problems. The authors suggest that the evils of concentration in one industry — news media — could be alleviated in part through the simple expedient of "a court interpretation of the First Amendment to give access for comment and rebuttal in publications that refuse even to print letters to the editor." The danger is simply that if the government had power to command access to the press whenever "rebuttal" was required, it would ultimately lead to nothing short of government control over the press. If freedom of the press is to mean anything, it must never mean that the government has the power to decide what is fair and responsible comment.

The problems are billiantly raised by the authors. The problems are awesome. But the solutions require much deeper and more prolonged analysis.[10]

That the public in general is losing faith in business is reflected in polls going back over a number of years. One such poll, discussed in *The Christian Science Monitor*, resulted in these findings:

It is no secret to businessmen that they have lost some public respect in recent years. But the degree of that loss may be a shock to them.

"Business must stem a flood tide of adverse public opinion if it is to continue to prosper," Thomas W. Benham warned 1,500 top corporate executives this week attending the White House Conference on the Industrial World Ahead.

Mr. Benham is president of Opinion Research Corporation. Through opinion surveys, he has compiled documentation of the sharp decline in public favor of business.

Here is Mr. Benham's evidence of growing public unhappiness with business:

Some 60 percent of the public gives "little approval" to business in 1971, compared with 47 percent in 1965. Eleven percent expressed "high approval" in 1971, versus 20 percent in 1965.

Breaking down the populace, the decline in approval among younger people has been sharpest. The professional and managerial group — normally thought to be favorable toward business — also shows a sizable decline in approval of business. So have college graduates.

Reports Mr. Benham: "It is not only the enemies of business who have been intensifying their attacks; the friends of business also have been weakening in their support at the same time."

Mr. Benham's pollsters measured public sentiment by asking people to agree or disagree with various general statements about business. He found a steady decline in favorability.

For instance, about 83 percent agreed last year with the statement, "Large companies are essential for the nation's growth." But that is down 5 percent from 1965.

Fifty-one percent agreed in 1971 that "The profits of large companies help make things better for everyone." That is off 16 percent from 1965.

Similarly, fewer people disagree today with the statement, "There's too much power concentrated in the hands of a few large companies." In 1965, 31 percent disagreed; only 21 percent last year. Last year 35 percent disagreed with a statement that, "For good of the country, many of the largest companies ought to be broken up." In 1965, 45 percent disagreed.

Further, more people think big companies get cold and impersonal as they grow.

Mr. Benham also sees "a massive shift in people's confidence in competition as a mechanism to keep prices fair." Only 27 percent think

[10] Earl W. Kintner, "Big Business as All-Purpose Villain". Reprinted from the June 12, 1971 issue of *Business Week* by special permission. Copyright 1971 by McGraw-Hill, Inc.

this way now. Sixty-two percent figure government control is needed.

In the case of consumerism, Mr. Benham says, "it's not all smoke — there is some fire there." In a nationwide probability sample, his firm found 21 percent of those quizzed said they had been cheated or deceived in recent dealings as consumers. Products chiefly mentioned were groceries, meats, autos, and appliances.

The major complaints were faulty products, deceptive packaging, overcharging, misleading ads, and poor service.

Commented Mr. Benham: "Our consumer tolerance for defects and poor service has been wearing thin. And the politicians and the consumerists have been helping the erosion process."

Thus 66 percent of the public now favor federal laws to help consumers get value for their money, against 55 percent in 1967.

Mr. Benham presented a table showing a much increased sensitivity of the public to many aspects of the environment. Further, he found that the percentage of people who say companies are doing little about pollution has been rising — from 41 percent in 1961 to 53 percent with the latest poll.

And 76 percent now favor new federal laws to protect public health and safety, compared with 70 percent in 1967.

Now, 81 percent would even close plants that violate pollution laws, as against 70 percent in 1967.

Concluded Mr. Benham: "There is perhaps nothing more urgent than this tremendous problem of public dissatisfaction when we lay plans to grow and expand to meet the needs of American society in the future."[11]

Commenting on these and similar findings, Business Week editoralized:

The swift decline in the esteem in which the general public holds business is a sign of serious trouble ahead for corporate management. . . . Business management has done little to correct the wildly erroneous ideas the average person has about the workings of industry and the economy. It has too often refused to talk about its problems openly and frankly. This reluctance has convinced the public that business indeed has something to hide. . . . To reverse the disaffection the public has for business will take a lot more than public relations campaigns. It will take management willing to talk candidly about the bad as well as the good.[12]

Meanwhile, there is also growing disenchantment about government, not only because of the Watergate corruption ruboff, but also because of government's seemingly insatiable appetite for a larger share of national resources. The fact that the public demands much of what increased government services provide does not detract from its criticism of the additional taxes which are levied to pay for them. Apparently this is true largely because the public has doubts about the efficiency of government with its ever-expanding armies of civil servants who at times appear to be doing little more than shuffling paper. Not atypical of public concerns in this respect is the following commentary which appeared in Financial Times:

[11] David R. Francis, "Sharp Decline Found in Public Approval of Business", The Christian Science Monitor, February 11, 1972.

[12] "Why the Public Has Lost its Faith in Business". Reprinted from the June 17, 1972 issue of Business Week by special permission. Copyright 1972 by McGraw-Hill, Inc.

Government has become one of Canada's biggest industries, ranking with such major segments of the economy as manufacturing, the service industries, and wholesale and retail trade.

If government is treated as a separate sector, not as part of the service industries, this is how the Canadian labor force was divided last year:

	thousands
Factory workers	1,970
Service workers	1,600
Trade employees	1,500
Government workers*	1,260
Transport, communications, utilities	770
Construction workers	550
Farmers	470
Finance sector workers	410
Miners, fishermen, loggers	230
Total	8,760

*Excluding crown corporations employees.

Government is the fastest growing part of the economy in terms of people employed (as well as money spent).

In the three years ending in 1973, the part of the labor force which Statistics Canada calls "public administration" — consisting of some but not all government workers — grew by 20%. No other part of the labor force grew as fast. The rest of the service sector grew by 13%. Construction employment was 16.5% higher. Manufacturing added 10% to its work force.

Why is government growing so fast? No one knows for sure. Professor Richard Bird of the University of Toronto was asked by the Canadian Tax Foundation to try to find out after Mitchell Sharp, then minister of finance, had told the tax foundation's 1967 conference that public spending was "the chief issue in our political life" and the question was not whether it would grow but "how much it will grow and for what it will be used."

Prof. Bird's glimpse of an answer to Mr. Sharp's question was along these lines: there is no single, simple "law" which determines the level of government spending but it is a problem in supply and demand, complicated by the fact that the demand is filtered through the political process and the bureaucracy.

In this framework, here are some things that can be said about the rapid growth in the number of Canadians on government payroll:

• Public demand, or at least public tolerance, seems to have been at work. . . The number of civil servants has gone up rapidly during wars and levelled off on a new, higher plateau in the post-war period. But something new is now happening. The civil service is increasing at wartime rates but without a national crisis to relax the bounds of public tight-fistedness.

• Government services are demanded in dimes and paid for in dollars. He who wills the ends is presumed in law to have willed the means. But it is doubtful whether citizens seeking more government services are really consciously aware that they are thereby demanding higher taxation. When this newspaper, among others, demands more and better numbers from StatCan. one result is a 120% jump (to 5,500 from 2,500) in the past eight years in the number of people working for StatCan.

• Parkinson's Law ("Work expands to fill the time alloted to it.") is in operation in the Canadian bureaucracy. In 1960 there was one federal bureaucrat in the department of agriculture for every 75 farmers. But as the number of farmers has decreased, the number of bureaucrats has expanded. By 1966, there was one bureaucrat for every 64 farmers. By this year, there is a bureaucrat for every 45 farmers.

An example to the contrary — which shows that Parkinson can be suspended if not repealed — is the defence department. In 1960, when there were 120,000 in the armed forces, there was a supporting briefcase army of about 50,000. This was a ratio of two civil servants for every five men in the forces. This year, with the armed forces cut to about 80,000 there are 34,000 supporting bureaucrats — again a ratio of two-to-five.

But the general rule — apart from stern government action like the $1.8 billion spending limit clamped on defence in 1969 and not relaxed until 1972 — was stated by Prof. Bird: "Existing programs expand, they almost never fade away, let alone die (and) a creeping expansion of total government activity is thus almost inevitable."

But this does not explain why creeping has turned into a gallop nor the fact that the government share of the economy — admittedly hard to measure — now comes close to 40%. Only in one year of the "total mobilization" of the economy during World War II did the government share, including defence, top 40%.

In 1945, Colin Clark, the British economist, argued that when the level of total taxation went beyond 25% in any country, incentives to produce were fatally harmed and incentives to spend dangerously increased. The penalty would be inflation, taxpayer revolts and ultimately the collapse both of the national economy and the democratic system.

Since then, Clark's "catastrophic school" of tax-limit theorists has been ridiculed by other economists who have pointed to higher levels of taxation in countries such as Canada, apparently without either economic or political collapse.

No one can be so sure now, with inflation running at double figures, that Clark was wrong, although his 25% may have been a low guess. Prof. Bird concluded that there might indeed be a "critical limit" beyond which "social organization changes in important ways, which is not to say that the new order will be worse or better than the old."[13]

Reflecting public agitation about all of the foregoing concerns are gnawing suspicions about the efficacy of the regulatory processes which one Big Brother, government, sets up to control another Big Brother, corporate management. That there are grounds for doubts in terms of these interrelationships is suggested by what happens to conscientious regulators from time to time. One such case is described below:

Once again one of the federal regulatory agencies is under fire, this time for doing too good a job for the comfort of big business which it is supposed to regulate. The dismissal of Miles W. Kirkpatrick, chairman of the Federal Trade Commission, should be seen for what it is: an attack against the free enterprise system.

Free enterprise capitalism is probably the most efficient approach ever devised to the economic problem if we will only let it operate. It also

---

[13] Don McGillivray, "Government Expansion: Will the Brakes Work?", *Financial Times*, August 26, 1974.

scores high with respect to equity, at least as Americans see equity, attempting to distribute to each resource what it earns in the marketplace (though some may dispute this concept of equity on Judeo-Christian grounds).

But a model that is efficient and equitable within a world of simple products, with a great many producers of each, as the theory has been worked out, can easily be turned into a model for exploitation in the big business, complex-product world of today. Equal freedom for all becomes translated into freedom for the few to exploit; that is, in many little ways freedom for the many becomes effectively denied.

Consider the freedom to know. As long as free enterprise capitalism has been talked about, "complete knowledge" has been one of the ideal market conditions to be met, or at least approximated, if free enterprise could be said to exist. The buyer, and the seller too for that matter, at whatever level, whoever he may be, is entitled to know. It should not be possible to hide or conceal the qualities, quantities, and prices of products, nor engage in false advertising or make deceptive statements. Insofar as complete knowledge is abrogated, the market cannot carry out its economizing function in an *efficient* and *equitable* manner.

Since industrial firms normally buy their raw materials on the basis of technical specifications, and since they, if they are of any size at all, normally have engineering skill capable of reading and comparing specifications, a reasonable degree of knowledge is present. Their plight is not so serious. But what about the consumer? Whether one turns to the drug and cosmetic markets, TV sets, children's toys and clothing, weights and packaging, or what-have-you, the opportunities for deception are glaringly present.

According to the tenets of free enterprise capitalism, when for some reason the market breaks down and fails to carry out its economizing function in an efficient and equitable manner, there arises a case, prima facie, for government interference. If the problem is serious enough the government must intervene and enforce the conditions that would normally have been present — for example, complete knowledge — had the product been simpler and the number of producers very large. The government has found it increasingly necessary to provide the knowledge which the marketeers withhold and even distort with respect to the thousands of little articles that enter into every household, since the complexity of these products is beyond the expertise of the average householder, and the opportunities for false and dangerous advertising claims are everywhere present.

In recent years, particularly since the beginnings of the Nixon administration, we have seen the Federal Trade Commission and the Federal Drug Administration aggressively challenge the makers of patent medicines, cigarettes, television sets, automobiles, and a multitude of other items whose quality or effectiveness the public cannot assess.

The men who head the companies which manufacture these products would be among the first to protest their devotion to the capitalist system. Yet, by denying knowledge in many ways, from lack of full disclosure to outright deception, they too often undermine that system.

Big business did not like what the FTC has been doing to curtail its antifree-enterprise habits. Their dislikes apparently reached the highest levels of the Nixon administration and in mid-December last year the Los Angeles Times captioned an article with the headline, "FTC Fears Restrictions on Its Aggressiveness." The article charged that one of President Nixon's "top advisers," Joel Whitehead, the same individual who has threatened the news media, charged the FTC with irresponsibility, with "verbal stoning (of firms engaged in false advertising) in the public square." Mr. Kirkpatrick, the present aggressive chairman of the FTC, went the article, may well be replaced.

Well, Mr. Kirkpatrick has been replaced. On Jan. 10 he was fired and the job given to one of Nixon's inner circle.

What was Mr. Kirkpatrick's error? He believed in free enterprise capitalism — providing knowledge where unscrupulous business firms choose to deceive — and at least some of Mr. Nixon's top advisers apparently do not.

The actions of the FTC and other federal agencies to protect and inform the consumer, thereby promoting the economizing function of the market system, has been one of the shining achievements of the Nixon administration. It will be tragic, indeed, if we slip back into another "dark ages" of ignorance, where consumers again find themselves at the mercy of unscrupulous advertisers.[14]

The World of Advertising and Marketing

Probably nothing more forcefully symbolizes the sickness of North America than what goes on under the guise of advertising and marketing. Particularly on the advertising side — just about every conceivable strategy and tactic has been employed. Only recently has any effective policing begun to be put in place. Speaking of advertising and marketing together, the author once termed those involved "advertising and marketing hucksters purveying their false images about fraudulent products in deceptive packages." Extreme as that statement may appear, careful reflection suggests that it is still probably closer to the truth than the advertisers' and marketers' self-conception of their activities and role in society.

Even if they are fooling themselves about their part in the total system, it is encouraging to note that they are not fooling many others. Especially encouraging is the fact that youngsters have more than begun to see through the deceit and shallowness of their work:

Canadian kindergarten children, both French and English speaking 5-year-olds, have "complete faith" in the truthfulness of television advertising.

In Grade 2, the 7-year-olds "begin to have very divided opinions concerning the honesty" of commercials.

And in Grade 4 the 9-year-olds "completely distrust them (commercials) because of past experience.[15]

That the entire advertising fraternity has serious problems is effectively and succinctly spelled out in the following commentary from The Globe and Mail:

Advertising is going through the most interesting period in its history.

[14] Gerald F. Sorrensen, "An Attack on Free Enterprise", The Christian Science Monitor, January 19, 1973.
[15] "9-Year-Olds Distrust All Commercials, Study Shows", Toronto Star, April 28, 1972.

If challenge is accepted as a valid stimulant to creativity — and creativity is the core of advertising — current and recent pressures on the international advertising business should precede interesting new creative directions.

This is a question not so much of evolving improved techniques as of change — a swift and direct break with advertising's traditional laissez-faire approach to the consumer market.

It is evident that advertising must do more than stay abreast of, or adapt to, new or shifting expectations. The problem of defining these expectations — not to mention anticipating what lies ahead — is a major challenge in itself.

Consider briefly some of the factors that are keeping the Canadian and, in part, the international advertising business in ferment:

—Continuing pressure by consumer groups demanding equal time, financed by public money, to counter the effects of some types of broadcast commercials could lead to similar demands for other media.

—The varying degrees of restrictiveness of government controls and the probability of more controls are still generating uncertainty and even confusion.

—An increasing government encroachment on media generally is prompted by an assumed concern about the direction of existing and emerging communications techniques and systems. The electronics communications sector, which is subject to tough licencing and regulatory controls, is an example. Provincial and federal government squabbling about jurisdiction over broadcast communications will continue;

—Despite recent nostaglia themes, there is less general consumer preoccupation with unrealistic glamor — still a hallmark of much advertising;

—Justified or not, there is continuing disillusionment with "progress", considered by many to be as much a contributor to social ills as a panacea;

This disillusionment, which may stem from unrealistic expectations, raises the question whether progress — a word with many interpretations — in any era has been considered a cure-all for prevailing social shortcomings:

—Disparities within society are emphasized by advertising. It is highly improbable that a decline in advertising appeals to status would change the situation one iota, but that is not the issue;

—The credibility of advertising generally is low. Whether it is at record low, as some suggest, cannot be determined in the absence of acceptable data on other decades;

—The volume of advertising directed at consumers daily threatens to make advertising a self-defeating process. It is estimated the "average" North American urbanite is exposed to more than 500 advertising messages daily through print, broadcast, billboards and direct mail.

People, it is suggested, are being turned off by advertising, by the so-called clutter of commercials on television and by the heavy ad content of some print media.

But advertising — classified ads in particular — can be interesting reading. The front-page of The Times of London was all classified ads until recently, and they made some of the most interesting reading in that newspaper.

—Charges and test court cases involving false or deceptive advertising are besmirching both advertisers and advertising generally, whether or not they result in convictions;

—The move toward truth in advertising poses one of the toughest problems facing the business: untruth by omission.

These and other factors are, of course, known to many in advertising. A difficulty in coping with them effectively lies in the structure and nature of the business itself. It is segmented but national and retail advertising are lumped together by many consumers with unsightly posters, give-away sheets, unattractive neon advertising signs, and with the noise pollution that accompanies some urban sales and political propaganda.

Advertising is not a tight, homogenous entity to which effective, over-all policy approaches can be easily applied. The fragmented efforts under way to meet changing conditions reflect the structure of the business — aggressive, individualistic and competitive. Infighting and disunity are more the rule than the exception.

There is an argument for the advocacy role of advertising in the following context: advertising that produces results for clients within existing laws is justified even if the sensibilities of some sections of society are offended.

This argument could properly emphasize the impossibility of achieving 100 per cent acceptability for advertising because of differences in subjective opinions, to which advertising is particularly vulnerable. In cliche terms, the end — in this case proved results — justifies the means as long as the total process is within the law. To advance the argument further, there is no rationale for the existence of advertising but the results it can produce.

The argument implies the dependency on, and close relationship with, clients that advertising obviously must sustain if it is to exist, let alone thrive. It also raises some questions about the prevalent chatter in the advertising business about "social and moral consciousness and responsibility." This is related to the believability factor that admen desperately want to project.

The business will find that, to be believed, it will have to reflect these virtues through all its work and not through part of it or through laudable philanthropic causes. A blanket assumption by advertising of noble virtues is just as distorting as a blanket condemnation of all advertising as immoral and irresponsible.

It is incorrect to assume the profit motive or a disenchantment with business is inevitably at the basis of all criticism of advertising: the one relevant criticism of advertising in a free society is of the approaches it uses — do they make a negative or positive contribution to society, or do they even matter? A cost-benefit analysis of advertising could well confound critics. One constant danger is that of inflating the role of advertising, even if it needs surveillance.

To many people, considerable current advertising is offensive or demeaning even if it does achieve its purpose. This response may be genuine and, if so, the impact of advertising in this context should be judged against other factors in society that are probably even more demeaning to the same people. This does not excuse certain forms of advertising.

Many others think that government and other regulations on advertising have produced no more than a rehash or refinement of traditional promotional techniques. The direct-mail sector has moved toward computer-based "personalized" appeals; the technique has changed, but the message has not. A new Toronto-based television station experiments with different programming concepts, but the succession of dreary old commercials detracts to some extent from its originality.

All media that are not government-subsidized are affected by the limits within which advertising may operate. Government's ability to lower the boom on advertising is an effective instrument for possible use against media. This occurred in British Columbia under the Social Credit Government, although the expressed reasons for the elimination of liquor and cigarette advertising from all media involved health and morality, of all things.

Controls spawn their own drawbacks, a fact that seems to have been overlooked by the vigorous consumer groups that lobbied for increased regulatory action against advertising. Dealing with false or exaggerated claims, promotions aimed at children and so-called racially based ads has involved direct government action. Once into the action, governments can find almost limitless scope for continued and increased involvement.

A wry twist to the truth-in-advertising situation was the recent statement by the Canadian Advertising Standards Council, a group with representation from media, advertising, advertisers and consumers, that it would review political advertising under the same rules the council applies to product or service advertising.

This prompts the question, who is leading whom in truth one-upmanship? The answer may be that the exercise is a circular one, which has a low priority in current consumer concerns.[16]

The Self-Governing Professions

Equally discerning has become the public attitude towards both the traditional and the many new self-governing professional bodies. There was a time when the public believed that doctors and lawyers and others like them were only in the business of self-regulation to better serve the public interest. In the past, there may even have been cases where this was the truth. There may actually be some instances where this is still the case or largely so. The author, like many others, is a little more skeptical and for this reason has watched with interest the decline in public awe and reverence for those who were for so long perceived to be in such exalted positions.

Today there is a widespread realization that what is actually a matter of private interest can often be cloaked in what is alleged to be in the public interest. Consequently, like so many other organized groups, the self-governing professions are no longer above reproach. Indeed, unless it can be demonstrated conclusively that they are serving the public interests more than their own self-interests, they are likely to lose most if not all of their self-governing powers. Indicative of the trend in this direction is the following:

All professional organizations need some measure of government control, former chief justice J.C. McRuer argued today.

McRuer, vice-chairman of the Ontario Law Reform Commission, spoke at the annual convention of the Institute of Accredited Public Accountants.

"There can be no doubt," he said, "that for some professions the

[16] Nicholas Cotter, "Pressures Create Ferment in Advertising", The Globe and Mail, Toronto, November 22, 1972.

power of self-government is to be preferred. For other professions or occupations state control and state licensing is the proper form of government.

"It is essential that in all cases where the Legislature has conferred on a body power of self-government that some measure of state control be retained if the public interest is to be adequately protected."

The powers of self-governing bodies are of special interest to the accredited accountants because the 300-member group is seeking equality with the Institute of Public Accountants.

The latter group controls the accountancy profession, Emile Waitzman, a director of the accredited accountants group, told The Star.

M.S. Werger, secretary of this group, said it wants the standards and training of all accountants handled by universities.

The powers of a professional organization, McRuer said, "may be exercised for the public good, but human nature being what it is, they are far more likely to be exercised for the good of those to whom the powers have been delegated."

For a legislature to delegate powers over the affairs of others, without giving the governed a right to elect those who govern them, "is a denial of the principle of democratic government.

"Excessively high standards may produce specialists, but leave a vacuum with respect to areas where services of a specialist are not required," he warned.

Self-government, he explained, includes control over licensing, admission to a profession, education standards, and training — powers "to exclude persons even though they may be qualified to meet reasonable standards."

McRuer said the aim of conferring self-government on any group is well put in an English statement concerning the functions, procedure and disciplinary jurisdiction of the British General Medical Council.

"The duty of the council, "it says, "is to protect the public, in particular by supervising and improving education . . . The council is not an association or union for protecting professional interest. . ."

The former chief justice emphasized he was explaining a philosophy and not trying to apply it to any particular group or groups.

McRuer said the power to discipline is a grave one and involves setting standards and ethics over which the public has no control.

Whatever the means adopted, McRuer said, the line of communication must enable the government to know that the public interest is at all times adequately protected.[17]

The Labour Movement

Another symptom of the troubles which beset North America is the state of its labour movement, if such it can be termed. Trade unions have an essential and vital part to play in North American-type societies but, in the process, they often become the scapegoats for all manner of evils — evils for which others deserve to share the blame. Their vulnerability to public criticism stems in large measure from the openness with which they must display their avarice. Unlike many other organized interest groups, they must usually pursue their selfish ends in a quasi-public or public arena. This is especially the case where

[17] "Controls Necessary on Professional Bodies Law Reform Man Says," Toronto Star, November 1, 1971.

their demands are accompanied by strikes and other manifestations of industrial conflict.

Naive and simplistic reasoning leads to the erroneous conclusion that unions should take the blame for any inconvenience and hardship which may result from such conflict and also for any ensuing settlements if they are deemed in any way to contribute to inflation. The author has more than once heard unions being accused of being on an inflationery path to nowhere because of the allegedly self-defeating nature of their wage gains in real terms. It seems not to matter that most other interest groups are part and parcel of that same inflationary spiral. To their great advantage, more often than not the others do their handiwork behind closed doors and with little or no public notice — let alone fanfare.

Usually lost sight of in the customary public assaults on unions is their interrelationship with their members. Although democracy may not always function as well as it should within individual unions, union leaders are finding it increasingly difficult to keep up with the demands which their members place upon them. At best union leaders are finding it less easy to cope with the membership militancy which so often now seethes beneath them. At worst, they are losing control to rank and file elements who are showing less willingness to work within the existing system. One of the key challenges in the field of public policy as it relates to internal union affairs is to find an appropriate balance between union democracy and union responsibility.

There is no convenient and neat way to capture in words the way in which North America's sickness has affected the labour movement, but the following article may help in putting the union problem in its proper socioeconomic perspective.

The postal strike, the air-traffic controllers' slowdown, and municipal employees' strikes all have something in common. More, that is, than work stoppages.

In a few brief years, the general temper in America has assumed an unwelcome stridency. It sometimes seems as if we have become a pack of dogs snarling at each others' heels.

It wouldn't be correct to say that labor relations in this country had always been peaceful. One thinks of the Haymarket riot in Chicago in the last century, of the strikes in mining country in the West, and of the conflicts during the '30's when the industrial unions were organized.

Something even more vital than labor relations is involved today, though. It is a feeling that things aren't right any more, that waiting for "the organization" to take care of it isn't enough, that we need to take things into our own hands.

More union wage negotiations are being turned down by the union members. True, the members are younger and more militant than their leaders. But the lack of trust in organized leadership is the more basic problem.

Another one is that we live in a society that has taught us to work hard and spend hard, to want and even feel that we need more than we have. The pressures on us for individual economic performance are tremendous.

The color ads in magazines and on TV don't leave much room for realizing that in any society someone is going to be at the bottom, and that those at the bottom also need to get some satisfaction out of life, too.

Corporate managers and advertising executives who so successfully develop the wants that keep American factories busy probably don't ever stop to realize how boxed in the average man feels. He may be just as boxed in economically in other countries, but there his financial performance isn't as important a criterion in judging him as human being.

So, on the one hand, there is this malaise in the thinking about our institutions. The individual decides he should do more for himself, but doesn't really know how to be effective as an individual in a mass society. And on the other hand are the social pressures to keep up economically — pressures that many of the young are refusing to accept. The economically underprivileged don't have the luxury of making such a choice yet.[18]

The Mass Media

North America's mass media is trapped in a dilemma. On the one hand, it is for the most part as profit-motivated as any other private sector in the economy and must therefore cater to the advertisers' concept of what appeals most. All too often this means a media which aims at the lowest common denominator by featuring the sensationalistic and the violent. On the other hand, the media should serve as an effective forum for the exchange of ideas, a role which many in the media would like it to play, although its profit-making orientation makes it difficult for it to do so.

How serious the problem has been for some time is brought out in a 1966 Canadian commentary on an American assessment of the situation in the same year:

"Mass communications . . . can make more money not meeting its responsibilities than by doing so.

"American culture is marked by the compulsive consumption of trash and by the enabling of practices such as intentional obsolescence. Masscomm enthusiastically endorses such activities. . ."

"Masscomm's delight in the shoddy, the tasteless, the mind-dulling, the useless, is well-established. It is a direct consequence of masscomm's allegiance to organized rapacity. Ethical qualms about the effects of dishonest commercials disappear like morning mist in the glow of a comfortable advertising contract. . ."

"I suspect there are deep historical reasons for masscomm's non-acceptance of well-defined obligations. But I think the main reason is that masscomm is preoccupied with another responsibility, that of making money."

This collection of quotes comes from a paper published earlier this year by California's Centre for the Study of Democratic Institutions. It is affiliated with the Fund for the Republic and both have a lot of big names.

The quotations come, more specifically, from V.H. Ferry, a vice-president of the centre and the fund, formerly in both journalism and public relations.

Whatever you may think of Ferry's viewpoint, you'll have to agree with this: There are far too few thoughtful, well-informed critiques of what mass communications is doing.

Our newspapers, magazines, radio and TV are supposedly doing a vital job in a democracy — informing, educating (and entertaining) the public. More, they are supposed to help protect the public, both by cir-

[18] Richard A. Nenneman, "Time of Temper", The Christian Science Monitor, March 28, 1970.

culating information and by finding and resisting injustice. How many members of the public — or employees of masscomm, as Ferry calls it — ever think about how well this job is done?

Most criticism of mass communications is fragmentary special pleading. A politician thinks an opponent got a better break than he. A businessman wants publicity and can't get it. A soccer fan wants more soccer and less football in the sports pages. All may tell you solemnly, speaking from their own special prejudice, that mass communications is doing a crummy job . . . just crummy.

That is one big problem. So much of the criticism is not that mass communications is doing a dishonest or wholly inadequate job, but merely that it is wrong in its emphasis and its beliefs. Ferry himself sounds a little this way in his strong feelings about Viet Nam coverage.

This misses the point. It's possible to criticize a newspaper for failing in its job because it is not giving complete coverage to Viet Nam but not because it agrees or disagrees with U.S. policy there.

This is true in all issues. The question is: Is the importance of the subject recognized in fair, complete coverage by mass communications? Not: What attitude is being taken in editorials and interpretative stories?

There's an obvious exception to this rule. If an attitude is taken dishonestly, or without careful thought, mass communications can be criticized for not doing its duty.

Ferry, of course, argues, that mass communications — some of it, anyway — inevitably is going to form opinions in such a way.

Masscomm is too busy making money, in his view, to worry about its obligations to a free, democratic society.

What he is saying — and what mass communications must say — is that it is necessary to make money AND at the same time recognize a public responsibility that goes beyond profit.

This is a tall order — and a tough problem. Making money isn't always so easy. (It has been pretty tough in the newspaper business, judging by the number of fatalities.) Sometimes a combination of politicians and businessmen ranged against one newspaper can almost guarantee considerable loss — in the short run anyway, and in the long run it may be dead.

Ferry says mass communications must be prepared to give up some profits, if necessary, in order to serve the public. Any newspaper — and, hopefully, any mass communicator — worth his salt must agree.

But other, non-communicating companies don't have to do this. Why pick on mass communications? Well, because if mass communications doesn't build a sturdy, thoughtful public, what will? Certainly, few would trust government. And there is no other agency with the ear of the millions.

The clear conclusion is that if mass communications must perform a special task, sometimes costly to itself, it must have special privileges specially designed to enable it to do the job and survive at the same time. That's logical. The only trouble is that no one has yet figured out just what the privileges should be.

Because they haven't, newspapers and magazines — though with an honorable, if checkered, tradition of hell-raising independence — remain under the great pressures which Ferry outlines.

Generally speaking, radio and TV gave in long ago.

I know that you find independence and crusading journalism at times on radio and TV. But it's incidence is extremely low. Most of the time is spent in carefully controlled entertainment.

Just take one example. Red Barber, a good baseball announcer was fired recently from the New York Yankee baseball radio broadcast team. Near as could be made out, he was fired because he wasn't doing a good job — so it was felt — of packaging and "selling" the Yankees.

In other words, he wasn't supposed to be an independent reporter and interpreter. The Yankee radio broadcasts — and this applies to most radio and TV sports coverage, in degree — were supposed to be a long commercial for one product (Yankee baseball) into which were dropped other commercials for beer and so on.

In its small way, this is a betrayal of the public right to be informed.

Since we have probably lost radio and TV as important, dependable agencies of reform and impartial information, we must have the newspapers and magazines. Without them, the public has no chance of knowing what big government and big business and big labor are REALLY up to — whether it is bad or good. Even with them, understanding is difficult enough.

Canadians should think and write and talk about this far more than they now do. Otherwise they'll become animated sausages controlled by the powerful sausage-makers in government, labor, business — and education and the arts.[19]

THE DEPTH AND NATURE OF THE SICKNESS

Having delineated some of the more obvious signs of the malaise which besets some of North America's leading institutions, it is now appropriate to try to identify the underlying causes. The order in which these causes are examined is to be explained by ease of exposition rather than by any particular ranking.

Growing Individual Selfishness

Few things are more disturbing about North America than the all-consuming narrow inward-looking selfishness which so characterizes the bulk of its inhabitants. Competitive self-pursuit has proven a powerful engine for growth and productivity but it has produced some appalling side effects. The result has been a so-called affluent society in which acquisitive instinct and rising expectations in terms of both leisure time and material goods have outstripped society's capacity to provide either. Moreover, the never-ending scramble for more, both absolutely and relatively, has pitted man against man and group against group. In this ceaseless struggle for a greater share of the spoils, the end has often come to justify the means without regard to custom, decency, ethics, or law.

Considering the pervasiveness of these forces, North America stands indicted in one fundamental sense more than virtually any other part of the world. Those who have have so protected their positions vis-à-vis those who have not, despite a host of social security and tax measures which are supposed to redistribute income, that the wealthy remain as privileged as ever, while the poor are as short changed as ever. In fact, there is some evidence to suggest that the income gap is widening, especially at the extreme ends of the spectrum:

[19] Jack McArthur, "The Tough Task No One Discusses", Toronto Star, November 9, 1966.

The old adage that the rich get richer and the poor get poorer was never truer than right now, according to Rep. Henry S. Reuss (D) of Wisconsin.

Latest census figures, he says, show that President Nixon's administration is helping the 20 percent of top-income Americans increase their share of national wealth "at the expense of the rest of society."

In 1968 the highest one-fifth of the population enjoyed 40.6 percent of the nation's income. In 1970, according to Census Bureau figures quoted by Mr. Reuss, this share had grown to 41.6 percent.

This meant that Americans on lower rungs of the income ladder were dividing smaller shares of the pie — that the income gap between rich and other Americans grew during Mr. Nixon's first administration.

"But wait," adds Mr. Reuss, member of the House Committee on Banking and Currency and of the Joint Economic Committee of Congress. "Mr. Nixon's Robin Hood in reverse . . . appears in most striking form when you look at the share enjoyed by the richest 5 percent of American families."

This top 5 percent, he notes, enjoyed 17 percent of total U.S. income in 1950, but slipped to 14 percent between 1950 and 1968.

Under Presidents Truman, Eisenhower, Kennedy, and Johnson, in other words, "the poor, and particularly the fellow in the middle, greatly improved their position" vis-a-vis the rich.

This trend reversed itself as soon as President Nixon took office. By 1970 the share of the top 5 percent of earners was up to 14.4 percent.

"And for 1971," declares Mr. Reuss, "we find the Census Bureau reporting not a figure but a gobbledygook-full footnote, stating that the Census Bureau hopes to have this figure in a year or so.

"However," adds the Wisconsin lawmaker, "a Census Bureau official, who preferred not to be named, informed us that the true figure would show the top 5 percent with a staggering 16.2 percent of the total, a 15 percent gain for them since 1968."

Mr. Reuss is a highly respected expert on economic affairs, a man not given to hyperbole. He is also one of many prominent Democratic lawmakers in both houses disturbed by what they regard as the tilt of Mr. Nixon's administration toward the affluent.

In his early White House years the President gave tax breaks to business, in an effort to stimulate the U.S. economy. This worked, but a side effect, according to Census Bureau figures, was to widen the income gap between top and bottom.

White House spokesmen stress that, after years of stagnation, real take-home earnings of American workers — after the deduction of taxes and inflation — have risen during the Nixon years.

This also is true. Between 1964 and 1970, according to the Department of Commerce, real spendable income scarcely rose at all, when corrected for the cost of living rise and taxes.

Real income actually declined in the 1970 period, when a business slowdown coincided with inflation increases close to 6 percent.

Put another way, low- and middle-income people may have been narrowing the gap slightly between themselves and the rich, but they were not gaining in real income.

Then, on Aug. 15, 1971, Mr. Nixon introduced his new economic policy, characterized by a 90-day wage-and-price freeze, followed by still-existing controls. . . .

"Since August, 1971," says the Department of Commerce, "real spendable earnings for the average worker and his family have risen at an annual rate of 4.3 percent." The average American, in other words, now is beating inflation.

Nixon officials and Mr. Reuss appear to be looking at two sides of the same coin. The average American is earning more, but his income is not rising as quickly as that of the top 5 percent of money earners.[20]

One revealing and yet subtle manifestation of the extent to which the advantaged have protected themselves relative to the disadvantaged shows up in the neglect of basic public services. This appears to be a much more acute problem in the U.S., Canada having advanced much further, for example, in the provision of most forms of social security. An especially distressing and inequitable result of the reluctance to face up to the need to provide elementary public services in the United States has occurred in the field of education where the neglect of many public school systems has reached the point where it verges on a national disgrace. Only the well-to-do are able to rescue their children from this situation by sending them to private schools.

The Christian Science Monitor wrote a strong editorial condemning what was happening in the field of education:

- "Educators don't know what education should do," reads a headline in a national newspaper.
- "Missouri district to close its schools," reads the headline in another paper.
- "Survey calls U.S. formal classrooms 'grim,' " a story in The Christian Science Monitor reveals.

These are but three of a steadily growing number of reports, facts, figures and judgments which tell us that the crisis over education in the United States is already critical and becoming more so with each passing semester. And when one considers that the United States was once almost unique in its love for and dedication to education, one can grasp how urgent is the present challenge to (a) restore public confidence in the schools and (b) make them adequately interesting to young minds.

In the opinion of one educator, the loss of public confidence stems "from the stubborn unwillingness, or more probably, the tragic inability of educators to articulate a simple, compelling, and clearly understood rationale for education."

Certainly, some such failure on educators' part must lie in part behind the events in the Hazelwood district of suburban St. Louis, where all public schools, serving 25,000 children, will shut down on October 15 because voters four times refused to pass a school tax levy.

Equally certain is the fact that the financial crisis in which an evergrowing number of school districts find themselves comes from a broad backlash against the attitudes of young people, school administrators and intellectuals, all three of whom are widely looked upon as troublemakers, as permissive, and as downright un-American.

This is a tragic situation. It can only deepen and embitter whatever gaps and rifts already exist within American society. If there are two absolute, unavoidable facts of modern life, they are that the young must be well educated and that every child has a right to this formal prepara-

[20] Harry B. Ellis, "Reuss Finds Widening of Rich-Poor Gap", The Christian Science Monitor, January 11, 1973.

tion for a constructive and happy adulthood.

Voting down school funds (as distinguished from needless school frills) is self-defeating, cruel, and stupid. But so is the attitude of far too many school administrations which have neglected to maintain order. So too is the failure of educational theoreticians to come up with an adequately broad scale with pedagogical methods in tune with today's jet-speed, tension-ridden life.

A breakdown of American education is too tragic to contemplate. No other challenge has a higher priority.[21]

Even if North America's rate of economic growth does not have to be slowed because of environmental and other considerations, some means must be found to mitigate the selfishness which precludes even a modest redistribution of income to the poor and which allows the neglect of public services as opposed to the acquisition of private goods. The trickle-down theory will not forever pacify those at the bottom, nor can neglect of essential public services persist without serious social repercussions.

Indifference and Intolerance

Reflecting the individual selfishness which pervades North America is a frightening combination of indifference and intolerance. Since indifference is the more manifest of these two related problems, it merits more attention than the intolerance which accompanies and perhaps even grows out of it.

In regard to indifference, an extract from a 1972 Wall Street Journal article entitled "Aimless America: Affluent, Poor, Old and Young All Turn Inward, Grow Moody", is discouraging though instructive:

When James L. Ragland, grocer, starts talking about his troubles, it takes a lot of listening.

First off, he's black, and his customers are black. And everyone is poor. Mr. Ragland's medium-sized, Spartan store, called Pantry One, is located in the heart of North Hartford, a section of town thrice convulsed by riots, pillage, burning. The scars are everywhere. The front of Pantry One, once solid glass, now is built of concrete block.

Second, Pantry One has never been profitable since it was bought by Mr. Ragland and 10 associates from a white owner 18 months ago. "The discount stores are eating us alive. People will come in here to get their eggs and a bottle of milk, but they go to the big discount stores to do their real shopping," says Mr. Ragland.

Moreover, "unemployment in this neighborhood is close to 50%, and a lot of people are pretty desperate," says Mr. Ragland. Indeed, in just the past six months, three vendors have quit servicing his store. "When they would get out of their trucks to make a delivery, somebody would break into the trucks." Even inside the store, thievery is a constant problem. "Why, there are 10 or 15 people who live right in this neighborhood that I can't even let come in the store because they steal so much."

With problems like Mr. Ragland has, not knowing from month to month how much longer Pantry One can continue to operate, it's small wonder that he devotes almost all of his time and attention to his business. He's hardly even aware that 1972 is a presidential election year, that the city of Hartford is making significant strides toward easing many of its

[21] "School Breakdowns", The Christian Science Monitor, October 13, 1970.

38

ills in minority and low-income areas, that countless jobs formerly closed to blacks or browns or women or older workers now are opening up. "I've got more than I can handle just looking after my own affairs," says Mr. Ragland.

If Mr. Ragland is tuned out and turned off, withdrawn and oblivious to matters that don't have an immediate impact on his personal situation, he's only typical of citizens across the country. From New England to the West Coast, the average taxpayers, the men and women who make the economy and the country tick, are backing away from the plans and programs, the causes and crusades that they had enthusiastically jumped into in recent years.

Instead, they're devoting their time and energies to personal matters, to carving out better niches in the world for themselves and their families, often closing their eyes and covering their ears to anything that doesn't have an immediate and quite personal effect on them.

That's the conclusion emerging from a rather leisurely cross-country trip, generally following U.S. Highway 6, which stretches from Rhode Island to California. Along the way, in big cities and in little towns, in country stores and in corn fields, surprisingly similar sentiment crops up. Possessed by almost a quiet desperation, residents of America are disregarding the larger issues. They're turning inward.

Says Delbert S. Elliott, a professor of sociology at the University of Colorado in Boulder, just north of Route 6: "People are frustrated, They're especially frustrated with institutions — from the top of the federal government on down. They've learned from some very real experiences. They've come to understand that the institutions are running things, and that they're beyond the control of individuals. So people are just giving up. They're directing all their efforts toward influencing the things that, rightly or wrongly, they think they can control."

Such Americans are to be found everywhere along Route 6. What follows, in more or less chronological fashion, are brief accounts of chats with some of those people. The people are chosen for no special reason except that they seem to have something to say.

Brewster, N.Y.

Richard G. Allen, 55 years old, lives with his wife, a teen-aged daughter and a son just back from Vietnam, in an aging, two-story brown-shingle house at the foot of peaceable Hill Lane, where it intersects with U.S. Route 6. One thing sets it apart from other houses in this mountainous village of 12,000. Mr. Allen's front yard is full of bird houses — stacks and heaps and rows and piles of them. Thirty or more hang in a single tree. Mr. Allen, who answers the door, is obviously in ill health. His right foot seems to drag, and when he moves about, he's stooped, his arms folded across his stomach, as if he's in pain.

"I had a stroke last August. Before that, I was a kind of handyman, mostly a carpenter. Now I can't do much of anything. I just build bird houses for something to do. Different people come by every once in a while and see them and buy one. I sell them for any thing I can get — maybe $2, maybe $50. In the last year, maybe I've sold a dozen."

Inside Mr. Allen's house, the table is set for lunch, with big white coffee cups turned upside down in the center of the plates. In the middle of the table stands a small jar of honey, a carton of milk, a bottle of ketchup. Lunch will consist of bread and honey.

"We don't live very well. All there is is my Social Security. It ain't enough to live on, but it's all there is. It doesn't seem like the government gives anybody any special consideration — you know, really looks close at their individual case. It doesn't matter what President is in office. I'll tell you one thing. Social Security is so low that I always spend more than I get. I keep thinking I can make it up if I ever sell any bird houses. But I've about decided it won't ever be a profitable business. It's just something to do until I die."

Joliet, Ill.

Central High School, an aging, three-story stone structure dating to 1901, occupies almost two square blocks on the eastern edge of this city of 78,000. Four years ago, racial tension among its 2,500 students — about 25% black, 8% Spanish speaking, and the remainder from white families of all income levels — was dangerously high. At one point, about 50 police roamed the hallways dealing with limited disorders, and for two years after that police were called in periodically. Today, says Harold Miller, who taught at Central 11 years before becoming principal four years ago, the picture is just the opposite.

"We have, of course, many problems. But the major one is apathy. There is such a large number of students, maybe 25% or more, who are utterly aimless. They aren't turned on or excited by any of the traditional things, not the traditional values anyway. They aren't saying anything, and they aren't doing anything. They just aren't interested. They're like zombies.

"A lack of direction has always been there, but in the last year, it's gotten bad. The kids just don't care about school. We see it especially in our absenteeism. It's 10% to 12% a day. That's average. And our special programs, those aimed at helping just this kind of student, don't seem to be working. Basically, we try to help them find a vocation. We set up job-related interviews and even help arrange for them to get jobs. We'll line up an interview, or a job, for somebody, and they won't even bother to show up.

"To these kids, the emptiness of graduation is very, very real. It means nothing to them. I keep telling them that they're right. It isn't so important to graduate from high school. What is important is to fit into our society as a useful and productive person. But it's all lost on them. I don't think we've got a single program in the U.S. dealing effectively with this disaffection, this aimlessness and alienation."

Artinez, Calif.

Grace Episcopal Church sits atop a hill in this town of 18,000, about 30 miles northeast of San Francisco. A visitor finds the Rev. Ellis E. Peterson, the 59-year-old rector, a much troubled man. In many ways, he speculates, the feeling, the mood and the outlook of his church's 200 families typify the attitude of the whole country. Sitting in his office, surrounded by books on religion and philosophy and psychology, stroking his beard, he's bewildered.

"My people are simply frustrated. They've given up on everything you can name — their church, their religion, education, government of all levels. It all seems to be coming apart in little pieces. To them, nothing is solid any more. The result is that they've withdrawn, built a shell around themselves and crawled into it. The war, poverty, the despised, they mean nothing to them unless they touch them personally. Their attitude is, if it's going to affect me, then I'm terribly concerned about it. Otherwise, I'll stay in my shell. . . .

"People are indifferent. They've had so much change so fast, now they just want everything to stop and hold still for a while. They want something they can rely on, something that is solid in their lives. We had a long discussion just yesterday on a little change — just a few words — in the Lord's Prayer. But they want no part of it. They're frightened of this whole business of change.

"I've been in the ministry for 35 years, and I've never seen people as withdrawn and selfish as they are right now. When I preach on our responsibility to mankind, our responsibility to the lost, the unfortunate, the minorities, they just turn off their hearing aids. They don't want to hear it. They don't want to hear about the real problems and what we ought to be doing. I feel like I've never been needed so much, but at the same time, I've never been so lonely and alienated from my parishioners."[22]

More frequently the problem of indifference shows up in the conscious neglect of a fellow citizen's distress whether he be a victim of a criminal offense or other misfortune. In this area it seems appropriate to cite a recent case in Toronto, partly because that city, on the whole quite legitimately, boasts of its relatively crime-free and safe streets.

An elderly cripple lay unconscious in the slush of a downtown Toronto street for 20 minutes last night, three canes at his side, while passers-by ignored him.

"People were actually stepping over him" said Ann Krane of Etobicoke. "How could they do that to a helpless old man?"

Mrs. Krane, her daughter and a friend driving to a church choir practice, spotted the unidentified man lying in the gutter at Queen and Bathurst Sts.

"We just couldn't leave him lying there." Mrs. Krane said, so the three women dragged the man to the sidewalk and hailed a passing Metro Police cruiser.

One man told The Star he had "hung around to see what would happen" when he noticed the unconscious man at 8 p.m. He said he counted 100 people who passed by during a 20-minute period.

The man gave his name to a Star reporter, but asked that he not be identified.

Police took the crippled man, estimated to be about 75, to Toronto Western Hospital where he was x-rayed for a possible concussion and held overnight for observation.

"How could everyone just let him lie there like that?" Mrs. Krane wondered in an interview last night.

"Maybe he was drunk, but he still needed help. He's still a human being."

With Mrs. Krane were her daughter, Connie Choptiany of Bloor St. E. in Mississauga and Elsie Mazur of Etobicoke. They saw the man from

[22] Everett Groseclose, "Aimless America: Affluent, Poor, Old and Young All Turn Inward, Grow Moody", *The Wall Street Journal*, October 16, 1972. Reprinted with permission of *The Wall Street Journal* © Dow Jones & Company, Inc., 1972.

their car and decided to help, though they knew they'd then be late for choir practice at St. Vladimir Ukrainian Greek Orthodox Church.

A couple of passers-by told them to mind their own business.

"If we had minded our own business," Mrs. Mazur said, "that man might still be lying in the slush."[23]

Sometimes North America's indifference and intolerance show up in forms which surprise even the most cynical. Take the following account of the New York subway workers who decided to expose the worst elements of the system in which they were formally employed as inspectors:

When Bert Schussel and Daniel Stone first decided to blow the whistle on worker abuses and corruption on the New York City subway system they had no idea they would end up victims in a miniature trial.

Now in a courtroomlike atmosphere — American flag standing stiffly, legal counsel poring over papers, and a television artist sketching a profile of the referee — they are appearing as defendants at a transit authority (TA) disciplinary hearing. The charge: making a film showing co-workers drinking, sleeping, and playing cards on the job.

As they sat "in the dock," the former New York City subway inspectors looked as if the world weighed on their shoulders.

They have lost their jobs. They are flat broke. Their former colleagues shun them. Their families have been subjected to threatening anonymous telephone calls. And during those days on the payroll their lives were endangered.

Mr. Schussel just missed being hit by a large steel bolt.

Mr. Stone declares he almost certainly would have been electrocuted had he not noticed the subway car under which he was working was hooked up to the live 600 voltage third rail. . . .

As bad as these experiences were, there was an even deeper hurt.

It was the anguish of knowing that even after they had reported widespread abuses — and been suspended without pay in the process — the public was so apathetic.

"I am completely disturbed by the apathy of the public," says Mr. Schussel, a burly, bearded man casually dressed in a knit, zippered shirt and dark corduroy trousers.

"We tried to show the public was being robbed and how the trains were unsafe, all for the good of the people. And this is the way we end up," he said.

For Mr. Schussel and Mr. Stone this was the supreme irony. They had started out as complainants. Now they find themselves defendants in an action they started.

With the city transit authority instituting its own disciplinary hearings against them with its own appointed referee, neither they nor Councilman Robert Postel, a candidate for Mayor of New York who was defending them free of charge, feels they could get a fair shake.

The disciplinary hearing was invoked because of the TA charge that Messrs. Schussel and Stone "rigged and contrived" the film apparently showing workers loafing on the job. A further charge was removing official records.

Why did the two subway inspectors on the world's busiest subway system go to such lengths as borrowing a television camera from

[23] Pat Brennan, "Cripple Lay in Slush, Ignored", Toronto Star, February 13, 1974.

WNEW-TV in New York to prove their point? Because, they said, nobody would hear them out when they made their complaints. Not the union, nor management, not city hall.

The TA produced more than 30 signed affidavits from workers at the 240th Street inspection barn in the Bronx in support of its claim the film was rigged.

Since then a lie detector test revealed no flaws in the suspended inspectors' testimony, while one prosecution witness has been arrested and charged with perjury.

An examination of these signed statements revealed that the card games which violated regulations were not staged as charged.

The suspended inspectors further charge extensive overtime abuses, and the selling of whiskey, radios, and jewelry on the side during work hours.

One worker allegedly spent his workday on his cabin cruiser, punching in in the morning and then leaving for the day. He could be reached when needed by shortwave radio. Another, a long-distance runner, worked until 11 a.m. before reportedly changing into his running shorts and jogging around Van Cortlandt Park.

Taking advantage of a late start to the TA disciplinary hearing, Mr. Stone, a lean, quiet-spoken man, recalled how he shared his initial concerns with his companion Bert Schussel.

"Gee, Bert, the way things are being run at this location, I have never seen the things done here that are done in other places. The overtime is being distributed completely wrong. A select group is getting the "lion's share."

When pressed as to why no other workers had come forward to corroborate their testimony, Mr. Schussel just shook his head.

"You must realize," he said, "that no man doing two hours a day and getting paid for 40 hours a week, who has a pension after 20 years, and who can come and go as he pleases, and who can engage in private enterprises during the course of the day, is going to make any complaints. A common phrase of the men was 'how sweet it is.' "[24]

To highlight the problem of intolerance, one could cite numerous examples of racial and other minority group bigotry. Equally, if not more compelling evidence of this phenomenon was to be found in the reaction of many "hard hats" to those they perceived as student radicals. One student's account of his temporary return to his old hard hat role epitomizes the extensiveness of the intolerance North America has bred:

In January, 1966, I left college, frustrated with education and went out into the world. I became a construction worker in Manhattan and met a unique brand of people — proud, hardworking and dedicated to the proposition that their children would not sweat as they had. We worked hard together and slowly our mutual respect grew. After a stint in the U.S. Army, I returned to college. Needing money, I had already made the decision to return to construction work last summer; then the developments of the spring — especially the attack on a Wall Street peace rally — added new goals to my summer work. I wanted to see what prompted such rage. On April 15 I phone Mr. Y, the president of my local. He

[24] David Winder, "Transit Sleuths Become Victims", The Christian Science Monitor, January 31, 1973.

remembered me well. He would gladly give me a job, starting July 6. I'm at the job a full hour early. My full beard and long mop of hair are still with me. I'm eyed by everybody there with a mixture of hate and fear. I find the little dirty room where 25 laborers change, eat and talk. The silence is deafening. Finally a small dark man snarls: "What do you want?" I reply that my name is Andy Waldron. He is incredulous. He checks my union book with disgust and seems unhappy to find that it is in order. Most of my co-workers don't talk to me. Al, the group loud-mouth, asks me to put a flag in my helmet. I agree, but add a peace symbol to the other side.

It's my second week. I show up one day and as I'm changing a boom-ing voice shouts: "Waldron, you no good punk, what are you doing here?" It's Big John, the foreman on my old job. I'm so happy to see him that I almost cry. He mentions, loud enough for everybody to hear, that I was in the service. Everybody is looking at me now. Big John's acceptance has changed everything.

This Thursday night is our local union's meeting night. I go to see Mr. Y the night before and ask permission to hand out attitude question-naires. He doesn't know who I am and is horrified when he finds out. He admits that he wouldn't have put me on had he known what I look like now. I explain my questionnaire and ask to distribute it at the meeting. He becomes enraged, and threatens to have me fired the first time he hears of any trouble. So much for that idea.

Tonight I have my regular rotation at closing windows, which is worth an hour of overtime. I'm alone. As I enter a room I'm jumped from behind. I'm pummelled to the floor, and somebody starts yelling, "Let's shave off his beard." Loudmouth Al. Suddenly I hear someone yelling my name. It's Big John. With one huge shout he stops the proceedings and clears them out. Big John calms me and asks me if I'll quit now instead of the end of next week. I try to explain that whatever they think of me, they can't think that I'm a quitter, they can't think they've beaten me. He agrees, but warns that he may not be around next time.

The rest of my time is uneventful. They say nothing to me, and I nothing to them. The last week is over. I leave, but I know now I was wrong; hate and fear have driven these men beyond the reach of logic. I've failed, and would go on failing, no matter how long I stayed.[25]

More frightening than the actions of groups such as the hard-hats have been those coming from officials at the highest levels of government. As indi-cated earlier, Canada had the implementation of its *War Measures Act* with all the curbs on civil liberties which that entailed. Even before Watergate burst on the American scene, there were similar signs of an infringement on individual freedoms in that country, with little or no justification:

Mrs. Kay Worden is a Weston, Mass., housewife who feels deeply about the Vietnam war. During the Republican National Convention she put a mildly phrased advertisement in the Miami Herald asking people to write to President Richard Nixon about the war. She also took a room in the Hotel Fontainebleau and said in the advertisement that she would be there to talk to anyone interested.

[25] Waldron, Andrew (a pseudonym for a student at college in northeastern United States). © 1969 by The New York Times Company. Reprinted by permission.

Funny things happened when people tried to telephone Mrs. Worden at the Fontainebleau. Some were told that there was no such person in the hotel. Others were asked whether they were calling in response to the advertisement, and told they could not be connected unless they answered the question. Somehow, not many callers got through. A hotel official, when asked about the business, spoke of "security."

Mrs. Worden has had legal advice since then, and she plans shortly to bring a suit against the hotel, the Republican Party and the Federal Bureau of Investigation. Her claim will be that they monitored her telephone calls and harassed the callers. When she talks about the affair, she sounds more puzzled than angry. She says she just wants to find out who was doing what: "If asking people to write to the President is a danger to security, then somebody around here doesn't want democracy."

If officials of the Government or the Republican Party were in fact involved in the Kay Worden episode, it would hardly be surprising. One of the most significant qualities of the Nixon Administration is its insensitivity in matters of personal liberty.

The outlook for individual liberty in the United States must be regarded as a fundamental issue in the election campaign. It is not one that is much articulated, or perhaps that can be, but many people are nevertheless aware of its implicit significance.[26]

The Rejection of Authority

Institutions and leaders of all kinds are suspect today as perhaps never before. Authority, however exercised, whether legitimate or illegitimate, is being challenged. The result is a society in which everything established is being "Called Into Question":

If we glance about us today, we see that almost every human institution, every compartment and discipline of society, is being called into question. Hardly one of them escapes the demand for self-examination or reform. This demand, which amounts to a reassessment of all kinds of values, is a central happening of the times in which we live.

Is the institution that of politics? The parties in America are called upon to reform their nominating conventions, perhaps to institute national primaries, certainly to truncate the overlong campaigns.

Religion? The Roman Catholics wrestle with church authority and birth control; the Protestants with the question whether the clergy shall be activist street-marchers, or minister primarily to the parish flock.

Industry? Businessmen are being challenged to think beyond profits to community service and the hiring of the unemployable, and to the quality and usefulness of their products.

Television? A government-financed network is projected, which shall have less violence and more social purpose and cultural programs, but whose uniqueness so far seems to lie, for one thing, in its articulation of leftward viewpoints.

Racial attitudes? Militants are demanding full civil rights and equality of opportunity — at once. And all mankind is being summoned to

[26] Anthony Lewis, "The Growing Corrosion of U.S. Personal Liberties", *The Globe and Mail*, Toronto, October 9, 1972. © 1972 by The New York Times Company. Reprinted by permission.

ponder whether people, blacks as well as whites, regard their fellow-beings through racial spectacles or in the clear light of God's impartial vision.

Natural science? Researchers begin to probe the genetic structures and to ask whether it is possible — and whether it would be ethical and moral — to "retailor" human beings, or build a so-called master race by chemically tinkering with the chromosomes.

And so on and on. Not a very settled time in which to live. . . . Surely the duty confronting responsible individuals, as the winds sweep down this unsettled century, is to see, to make sure, that the hurricane does not over-throw society, does not wreck what has been so arduously achieved over the decades — does not put a discount on righteous conduct, does not devalue constitution and courts, parliaments and congresses, the discipline of dedicated work, and the worth of law and order.[27]

That there can be good as well as bad sides to the breakdown of a society's standards of discipline is brought out in this article from *The Globe and Mail* which assesses the continuing impact of the Vietnam War on the United States:

The United States is moving out of Vietnam after the longest and most divisive conflict since the Civil War, but Vietnam is not moving out of the United States, for the impact of the war there is likely to influence U.S. life for many years to come.

It is probably too early to distinguish between the temporary and enduring consequences of Vietnam, but one thing is fairly clear: there has been a sharp decline in respect for authority in the United States as a result of the war — not only a decline in respect for the civil authority of Government, but for the moral authority of the schools, the universities, the press, the church and even the family.

There was no ceasefire on this front. Vietnam did not start the challenge to authority, but it weakened respect for the executives who got the nation involved in the war in the first place, for the Congress that let it go on for more than a decade, and for the Democratic process of debate that failed to influence the course of the war for years and finally declined into physical combat and sporadic anarchy.

Even after the ceasefire, there is considerable dissension in the country over whether this challenge to authority was good or bad. Many Americans argue that it was precisely this dissent and defiance that forced social reform at home and the ceasefire abroad.

Others argue that the war produced a whole new revolutionary climate in the United States, which encouraged the Communists to prolong the war, and disrupted the unity and previously accepted attitudes, standards and restraints of U.S. public and private conduct. But very few Americans challenge the proposition that, for good or bad, something happened to U.S. life that they didn't yet understand or agree about, but that it was different, important and probably enduring.

The imponderables — the changes in attitudes and assumptions, and the decline in truthfulness and self-confidence, for example — promised to be even more significant for the future than the actual financial strain of the war.

Among other things, Vietnam changed the nation's way of looking at

[27] William H. Stringer, "Called Into Question", *The Christian Science Monitor*, October 2, 1968.

itself and the world; reduced U.S. willingness to get involved in distant continental land wars for ambiguous reasons; and envenomed the relations between the political parties and between the President and the Congress.

After Vietnam, the U.S. people seemed less sure about many things they had previously taken for granted. They were not so sure, for example, that the United States always prevails in foreign conflicts, that big guys always like little guys, that money and machines are decisive in war; and that small states would rather surrender than risk the military might of the United States.

The tone of John Kennedy's first inaugural address in 1961 at the beginning of the nation's deep involvement in Vietnam, and the tone of Mr. Nixon's second inaugural address during the last phase of the ceasefire negotiations, illustrated the change in the U.S. mood and commitment.

"Let every nation know, whether it wishes us well or ill," Mr. Kennedy said in his oft-quoted promise, "that we shall pay any price, bear any burden, meet any hardship, support any friend, oppose any foe to assure the survival and the success of liberty. This much we pledge — and more."

After the disappointments and disillusionments of the ensuing 12 years, Mr. Nixon was more prudent and modest in pledging what the United States would do.

"We shall do our share in defending peace and freedom in the world," he said, "but we shall expect others to do their share. The time has passed when America will make every other nation's conflict our own, or make every other nation's future our responsibility, or presume to tell other nations how to manage their own affairs."

Moreover, the disillusionments of Vietnam not only led to a more modest estimate of what the United States could or should do to help maintain freedom and order in the world, but seemed to encourage a downward reappraisal of what Government could do to maintain the health and welfare of the poor at home.

In short, after Vietnam, the emphasis was not on what Government could do but on what it couldn't and shouldn't do; the emphasis was not on welfare but on work; not a compassionate society, but on a competitive society in which the comfortable majority would pay less tax and everybody would rely more on himself and less on the federal Government in Washington. . . . It will take some time to restore the self-confidence of the pre-Vietnam years in the United States, but it may be that the destruction of many popular misconceptions in Vietnam will produce a more mature, if sadder, nation.[28]

The authority of established institutions and leaders must often give way if any kind of social progress is to be made. The danger is that in the process, authority itself may become the issue, thus threatening order and leading to anarchy. Although North America is hardly yet on the verge of chaos, there are sufficient signs of such a possibility to give rise to real concern.

[28] James Reston, "There is No Ceasefire in U.S. Revolt Against Authority", *The Globe and Mail*, Toronto, January 24, 1973. © 1973 by The New York Times Company. Reprinted by permission.

47

Alienation

Not to be neglected in this catalogue of current North American disorders is the phenomenon of alienation which can take many forms. At least five types of alienation can be delineated:

Melvin Seeman has identified five alternative meanings of alienation that represent the major ways in which the concept has been used in traditional sociological analysis. The first and perhaps most common of these usages is in terms of *powerlessness*. It is this type of alienation with which Marx was primarily concerned in his analysis of the working class. As was noted above, however, loss of control over the important events that affect our lives has become an almost universal experience in complex mass societies. A second major usage of the term alienation may be labeled *meaninglessness*. Various writers have noted the increasing difficulty in rapidly changing segmented societies in finding appropriate standards for judgment regarding courses of action or patterns of belief. Meaninglessness refers, more specifically, to the difficulty in making accurate predictions about the behavior of others or about the outcome of our own actions. Situations have meaning to us to the extent that we are able to anticipate their outcome. Industrialism has increased the incidence of social situations that are meaningless in this sense. A third type of alienation, according to Seeman, is *normlessness*. This type is based upon Emile Durkheim's concept of *anomie*, which refers to a situation in which there are no effective norms or rules for behavior. As the term has been used in contemporary sociology, it has come to mean a circumstance in which there are no legitimate means to achieve socially prescribed goals. In industrial societies, for example, emphasis upon the goal of economic success is more pervasive than are the legitimate means for attaining this goal. The expectation that it is necessary to use socially unapproved means to be successful illustrates normlessness in Seeman's sense. *Isolation* represents a fourth way in which the concept of alienation has been used. According to Seeman, "the alienated in the isolation sense are those who, like the intellectual, assign a low reward value to goals or beliefs that are typically highly valued in the given society. The hippie who rejects prevailing middle-class values, the political extremist who advocates the destruction of current political institutions, and the hermit who completely renounces the contemporary way of life all share this form of alienation. The final variant of alienation found in sociological writing is *self-estrangement*. Both Marx and Fromm use the concept in this way. A person is self-estranged when he engages in activities that are not meaningful in themselves but are simply means to other ends. We can describe the person as being alienated from himself under these circumstances because what he is doing is not something that he regards as being important. "The worker who works only for his salary, the housewife who cooks only to get it over with, or the other-directed type who acts 'only for its effect on others' — are instances of self-estrangement."[29]

Some of the causes and consequences of alienation are showing up most acutely in the workplace although its manifestations are to be found throughout society:

[29] William A. Faunce, *Problems of An Industrial Society* (New York, McGraw-Hill, © 1968), pp. 88-90.

There are two parts to the problem of employee alienation: (1) the productivity output of work systems, and (2) the social costs associated with employee inputs. Regarding the first, U.S. productivity is not adequate to the challenges posed by international competition and inflation; it cannot sustain impressive economic growth. (I do not refer here to economic growth as something to be valued merely for its own sake — it is politically a precondition for the income redistribution that will make equality of opportunity possible in the United States.) Regarding the second, the social and psychological costs of work systems are excessive, as evidenced by their effects on the mental and physical health of employees and on the social health of families and communities.

Employee alienation *affects* productivity and *reflects* social costs incurred in the workplace. Increasingly, blue- and white-collar employees and, to some extent, middle managers tend to dislike their jobs and resent their bosses. Workers tend to rebel against their union leaders. They are becoming less concerned about the quality of the product of their labor and more angered about the quality of the context in which they labor.

In some cases, alienation is expressed by passive withdrawal — tardiness, absenteeism and turnover, and inattention on the job. In other cases, it is expressed by active attacks — pilferage, sabotage, deliberate waste, assaults, bomb threats, and other disruptions of work routines. Demonstrations have taken place and underground newspapers have appeared in large organizations in recent years to protest company policies. Even more recently, employees have cooperated with newsmen, Congressional committees, regulatory agencies, and protest groups in exposing objectionable practices.

The acts of sabotage and other forms of protest are overt manifestations of a conflict between changing employee attitudes and organizational inertia. Increasingly, what employees expect from their jobs is different from what organizations are prepared to offer them. These evolving expectations of workers conflict with the demands, conditions, and rewards of employing organizations in at least six important ways:

1. Employees want challenge and personal growth, but work tends to be simplified and specialties tend to be used repeatedly in work assignments. This pattern exploits the narrow skills of a worker, while limiting his or her opportunities to broaden or develop.

2. Employees want to be included in patterns of mutual influence; they want egalitarian treatment. But organizations are characterized by tall hierarchies, status differentials, and chains of command.

3. Employee commitment to an organization is increasingly influenced by the intrinsic interest of the work itself, the human dignity afforded by management, and the social responsibility reflected in the organization's products. Yet organization practices still emphasize material rewards and employment security and neglect other employee concerns.

4. What employees want from careers, they are apt to want *right now*. But when organizations design job hierarchies and career paths, they continue to assume that today's workers are as willing to postpone gratifications as were yesterday's workers.

5. Employees want more attention to the emotional aspects of organization life, such as individual self-esteem, openness between people, and expressions of warmth. Yet organizations emphasize rationality and

seldom legitimize the emotional part of the organizational experience.

6. Employees are becoming less driven by competitive urges, less likely to identify competition as the "American way." Nevertheless, managers continue to plan career patterns, organize work, and design reward systems as if employees valued competition as highly as they used to.

Pervasive social forces: The foregoing needs and desires that employees bring to their work are but a local reflection of more basic, and not readily reversible, trends in U.S. society. These trends are fueled by family and social experience as well as by social institutions, especially schools. Among the most significant are:

The rising level of education — Employees bring to the workplace more abilities and, correspondingly, higher expectations than in the past.

The rising level of wealth and security — Vast segments of today's society never have wanted for the tangible essentials of life; thus they are decreasingly motivated by pay and security, which are taken for granted.

The decreased emphasis given by churches, schools, and families to obedience to authority — These socialization agencies have promoted individual initiative, self-responsibility and -control, the relativity of values, and other social patterns that make subordinacy in traditional organizations an increasingly bitter pill to swallow for each successive wave of entrants to the U.S. work force.

The decline in achievement motivation — For example, whereas the books my parents read in primary school taught them the virtues of hard work and competition, my children's books emphasize self-expression and actualizing one's potential. The workplace has not yet fully recognized this change in employee values.

The shifting emphasis from individualism to social commitment — This shift is driven in part by a need for the direct gratifications of human connectedness (for example, as provided by commune living experiments). It also results from a growing appreciation of our interdependence, and it renders obsolete many traditional workplace concepts regarding the division of labor and work incentives.[30]

What happens when alienation and anomie become wide-spread is not altogether clear. But one possible answer is to be found among some of North America's young people who have been driven to all manner of social aberrations — presumably in an effort to either destroy or find themselves:

"The leading cause of death for persons under 35 [in New York City] are: drug abuse, suicide, murder." So writes the New York Post in a current series on some of the problems of life in the nation's largest city.

Should we not all take a moment to think on what such a statistic means? Do we fully realize the condition into which society has allowed itself to fall when the three leading causes for death among young people are traceable — not to health conditions, not to accidents — but to social and personal tensions? Are we adequately aware of the degree to which we have failed to help youth make the difficult transition into the adult world?

[30] Richard E. Walton, "How to Counter Alienation in the Plant", *Harvard Business Review*, November-December 1972. © 1972 by the President and Fellows of Harvard College; all rights reserved.

Any society, which becomes aware of a fact such as this, and does nothing about it, is both morally and intellectually delinquent. Only by facing up to the disgraceful neglect and shortsightedness which have produced such a situation can society become straight with its conscience.

We acknowledge that all of society, of whatever age-group, is more or less the victim of today's deep social, moral, spiritual, and intellectual disorientation. There are millions of grown-ups to whom today's conditions seem just as hard as they do to younger generations.

Yet, notwithstanding this, the main burden of action lies upon the adult community. This latter may not have either purposefully or actually created the conditions which produce youthful drug abuse, suicide, and murder. But it can certainly be said that the adult community has on the whole fallen tragically short of its obligation to try to end such conditions. Here, at least, youth has much justification when it asks its elders: "why have you permitted such a world to exist?"

Nothing would be more mistaken than to imagine that youth, because of its exuberances, its sometimes recklessness, its search for novelty, its quick emotionalism, has a predisposition towards drugs, suicide, or murder. The opposite is true. Youth starts out buoyantly and with high ideals, with a bent towards warm social intercourse, and full of hope. Only outward conditions which slowly but steadily grind down these qualities would lead any large number of young folks to the degradation of drugs or the taking of one's own or another's life.

It is far from pleasant to read of these conditions. But they must be faced, and faced honestly, if they are to be met and healed, and all youth is to have the joy, security and achievement which are youth's rightful heritage.[31]

Crime and Violence

Last but not least in this list of social blights, is the potential breakdown in law and order as crime and violence spread. Crime takes many forms. One of the most rapidly growing is that which North Americans refer to as "white collar crime." Indicative of the toll of this and related types of crime perpetrated solely by employees against their employers is the following article from *Cost and Management*:

Crime in business has reached alarming proportions, says Norman Jaspan, president of the New York-based international management consulting firm that bears his name. . . .

Right now there is a better than 50 per cent chance of sizable dishonesty in any firm, and a 75 per cent chance of costly malpractice. "Generally," Mr. Jaspan emphasized, "fraud in a company is a good barometer of the quality and integrity of its supervisors." In fact, 62 per cent of the dollar losses sustained by business is attributable to employees at the supervisory level — and the very fringe benefits and incentive programs designed to promote loyalty and honesty often cause employees to become dishonest.

"Retailers, as a result of employee dishonesty, are showing declining profits in the face of rising sales, and they will continue to do so until they

[31] "A Tragic Situation", *The Christian Science Monitor*, November 4, 1969.

learn to control inventory shortages," asserted Mr. Jaspan.

Industrial firms are sustaining even higher losses which are particularly dangerous because they are concealed by their methods of accounting. Millions of dollars are lost as a result of cheating on the incentive plan, yield manipulations, falsified scrap reports, excessive waste, sabotage, improper work performance, kickbacks, destruction of records and theft of confidential information.

Many companies are victimized by opportunistic service men and technicians who frequently become their firm's most serious competitor by setting up prosperous businesses of their own — on company time, using their employer's tools, materials, equipment and resources.[32]

France's national past time, tax evasion, is also on the upswing in the United States, if not in Canada as well:

Tax return "fudging" has become, in the words of one government official, "the new national pastime."

The number of American wage earners who file dishonest income tax returns, or none at all, is growing, says Johnnie Walters, internal revenue commissioner — and "the trend is frightening."

Walters told a congressional sub-committee this week that complex tax laws, the age of protest, tax evaders and persons who believe tax laws are inequitable are driving up the number of non-filers each year.

If not checked, he said, the current $2.5 billion to $3 billion lost through noncompliance will rise to $6 billion a year by 1976.

The Internal Revenue Service has estimated that perhaps as many as 50 per cent of all taxpayers do some kind of cheating on their tax returns. Since the agency in recent years has been auditing only about 2 per cent of all returns, chances are fairly good that a well-concealed fudge or two by an average taxpayer will sneak through.

No figures are available for the number of tax cheaters in Canada, where the filing deadline is two weeks later than in the United States — April 31. However, tax investigators with the Toronto district taxation office uncovered $1,733,000 in evaded income taxes in Metro alone in the year ending March, 1972.

Most serious cheating, they found, was by operators of small businesses, professionals and other self-employed people. And it was well hidden.

The days are gone when the most common phony items on tax returns were things like a 3-year-old dependent named George who turned out to be a Springer spaniel.

These days, it's things like the housewife in California who placed a wig in precarious niche above the toilet in her bathroom. An earthquake hit in February, 1971, causing the wig to plummet into the toilet bowl. The housewife, claiming earthquake damage, deducted $100 — the price of the wig — from her tax return.

The government, however, disagreed.

A school teacher in El Centro, Calif., who for several years had claimed an exemption for her child, was discovered to be a spinster living alone with a parakeet.

She was prosecuted on tax fraud charges. . . .

[32] "Employee Dishonesty Rampant in Business", *Cost and Management*, September-October, 1972.

And the list goes on.[33]

Common every day garden variety crime is so prevalent in many large American cities that it is almost taken for granted. Detroit has an especially bad criminal record and has been compelled to take numerous steps to try to alleviate it:

As Christmas shoppers swarm across Woodward Avenue from one department store to another, a policeman's voice booms down at them from a loudspeaker attached to a street lighting standard.

He watches from the window of an upstairs stockroom and he tells the pedestrians how to cross the intersections safely and to watch for turning cars. Then he warns all the women to hold their purses tightly in front of their bodies while they are in the stores and never to leave parcels on car seats where they are visible to people passing by.

Once inside the stores, the shopper is again confronted with this constant reminder that purse snatchers, pick-pockets, muggers and shop-lifters are on the prowl.

Signs are posted prominently in some of the stores warning the customers never to place their purses or shopping bags on counter or on chairs while trying on hats or shoes. The signs warn that if a purse is snatched or a purse stolen the owner should not resist.

"Your life is more important than the contents in your purse," notices read, "but if you are determined to try and apprehend the thief, be sure you have a chance to scream, kick, bite, scratch, or use any other means you have of attracting help."

In many of the stores, such as Woolworth's and Kresge's, armed guards in blue security uniforms partrol up and down the aisles swinging three-foot-long billies and packing pistols at the hip.

In the larger department stores, such as J. L. Hudson Co. and Crowley's — which are comparable to Eaton's and Simpsons — the guards are not as noticeable because they are in plain clothes.

They are there though, just the same, and in even greater numbers. . . . This year, Hudson's security chief, Wesley Meuir, doubled his detective staff in an effort to reduce shoplifting losses which two years ago reached the staggering sum of $3-million from the downtown Detroit store.

All of this security and the attempts to educate the ordinary citizen in the ways of the criminal, is a direct result of efforts being made by the Greater Detroit Chamber of Commerce to make downtown Detroit a safer place for people to come and shop.

Crime in Detroit's inner city, and the area outwards for about 10 miles from the downtown section, has been increasing at an alarming rate since the race riot of 1967. This area is almost totally black and a crime of some type — a homicide, a burglary, a mugging, a car theft, or a purse-snatching — happens here every 10 minutes day in and day out.[34]

Much more frightening to most than crime per se is the resort to violence which often accompanies it. Worse still, violence itself has in some ways be-

---

[33] Harry Anderson, "Tax Fudging: It's the New U.S. Pastime", *Los Angeles Times*, March 14, 1973. Copyright, 1973, *Los Angeles Times*.

[34] John Scott, "Detroit: Shoppers Guarded and a Crime Every 10 Minutes", *The Globe and Mail*, Toronto, December 12, 1970.

come as much an end as a means. On this subject, a 1971 editorial from *The Globe and Mail* on the situation in the Province of Quebec is worth citing:

It used to be said, there is safety in numbers. Today in Quebec it would be more accurate to say, there is danger in numbers.

Those who have a sense of responsibility, or claim to have a sense of responsibility, must now know that any large demonstration in the volatile atmosphere which exists is almost bound to end in violence. Violence feeds heartily upon the breakdown in Quebec's social structure, needs only the least invitation to go into the streets and explode.

This breakdown has come close to being complete. Those professions and authorities and leaders that in a stable place build stability have almost uniformly abdicated their duty.

The teachers went out on strike. The teachers led the children into the streets and to the doors of the Legislature to protest the language bill.

One group of doctors struck, and stayed out for months, ignoring the needs of their patients. Specialists of the medical profession planned to strike, and were only prevented by extraordinarily punitive legislation proposed by the Government.

The Montreal Police struck, and a man died in the riots that ensued.

The Quebec Provincial Police struck. The Hull Police struck. The University of Quebec at Montreal and the University of Montreal were closed down by strikes, and violence has taken place. . . .

It was the month of October, when the whole province was remembering the kidnappings of the last month of October, the threat of greater violence which hovered then and was depressed only by the authoritarian War Measures Act and the Public Order (Temporary) Measures Act and the Armed Forces. There were murmurings about a violent anniversary of the violence, and the groups of violent ones were beginning to surface, the separatists, the Maoists, those of many stripes, who share nothing but a desire to see anarchy in Quebec.

The Quebec Government offered no firm lead, swinging between timidity and tyranny.

What then did Louis Laberge, president of the Quebec Federation of Labor, Marcel Pepin, president of the Confederation of National Trade Unions, Yvon Charbonneau, president of the Corporation des Enseignants du Quebec, think would happen when they marched 10,000 people on the strife-torn Montreal newspaper, La Presse?

Mr. Laberge knew. He had discussed it with the Montreal Police earlier. He had said it would be violence. . . . There was violence. There were 15 minutes of violence before the police reacted. There were many hurt and many arrested, and a woman died.

Those who lead in Quebec must know now how uneasily they sit. A demonstration, any demonstration — for St. Jean Baptiste Day, on the campuses, in labor disputes — all can end in violence.[35]

Despite many reports and studies on such an elementary crime- and violence-fighting measure as gun control, little or no progress has been made on this front, either in the United States or Canada. On this subject, two editorials, the first American, and the second Canadian, are illuminating:

Nothing short of the registration of every privately owned, commer-

[35] "Rich Soil for Violence", *The Globe and Mail*, Toronto, November 2, 1971.

54

cially stocked and publicly assigned firearm in the United States can provide a gun control worthy of the name. To such a law must be attached drastic penalties for disobedience. If the Senate and the House of Representatives do not pass such legislation, they will be playing false with the safety of every man, woman and child in America and will be dishonoring the memory of those national leaders who, in recent years, have been brutally assassinated.

Notwithstanding reports that a wave of public sentiment is now increasing congressional willingness to pass strict legislation, we believe that only unremitting voter pressure can lead to any worthwhile remedial action. Congressional dislike of offending powerfully organized lobbies (in this case the National Rifle Association) is too well known to allow of any complacency on this score.

We do not believe that the present administration bill now before Congress is enough. Primarily, it forbids the mail-order sale of rifles and shotguns. While this may be better than nothing, it is only barely so. What is absolutely required is a law requiring every last gun-owner and gun-buyer to register every old and new firearm. This would at least bring some measure of control over guns bought locally and not through the mail.

To this, as we mentioned above, must be attached severe penalties for the possession of any unregistered or incorrectly registered firearm. This law is necessary since it would place upon the gun-bearer or the gun-possessor the obligation of proving that he had come by the weapon lawfully. Failure to prove this would be prima facie evidence of guilt, subjecting one to the penalties which such a crime deserves.

For years, there has been an almost unanimous demand on the part of law enforcement officials, from the Federal Bureau of Investigation chief, J. Edgar Hoover, on down, that the gun traffic be brought under control. It is a national disgrace that only a series of assassinations has been able to move Congress to the point where it was willing to bother with firearm legislation.

The ridiculousness of the opposition to strict controls can be seen from the statements of Harold W. Glassen, the rifle association's president. He termed efforts to control guns childish and nonsensical, and then went on to say that Americans were being deceived on this issue in the same way that the Nazis deceived the German people.

If this is the level of the association's thinking, we cannot think of a better reason for disregarding its views.[36]

And in Canada:

Metro Police Chairman C.O. Bick may not have expressed himself with classic elegance the other night when he said that federal authorities "better get off their big fanny" and do something about gun legislation if they are serious about keeping Canada's streets safe. But his worries are shared by a great many people today.

Canadians have long heard horror stories about some of the great American cities, where guns of all descriptions are casually bought and sold. This abundance of deadly weapons is undoubtedly a major element in the appalling rate of homicide and other violent crimes in these cities.

But are Canada's gun laws all that much better? True, any Canadian

[36] "Register Every Last Firearm", The Christian Science Monitor, June 15, 1968.

who wants to buy a pistol or revolver must obtain a permit from the police and register his weapon. But these restrictions have not stopped people acquiring weapons. Recent statistics indicate there are 200,000 registered handguns in Ontario — 90,000 in Metro Toronto alone.

There are no restrictions at all on the purchase of rifles and shotguns. Anyone over 16 can walk into a sporting goods stores and buy a high-powered rifle or a 12-gauge shotgun with no questions asked.

And there is a direct relationship between the availability of firearms and violent crime. Bick noted that four Metro police officers have been shot to death in the last two years. Within the past 10 days revolvers or sawed-off shotguns were used in seven hold-ups in the city. The police report, in fact, that 90 per cent of the robberies in Metro in the last year were performed with handguns or sawed-off rifles and shotguns.

To save the comparative peace in Canada, the federal government should adopt three measures at once.

First it should follow the recommendation of the Canadian Bar Association in 1972 and prohibit the private possession of handguns, restricting them to police officers and others who have an official duty to protect the public. The only exception should be for members of target shooting clubs, with the weapons to be kept securely on the club premises.

Second, it should establish a system of permits and registration for rifles and shotguns. This would give the authorities a chance to restrict hunting weapons to farmers, sportsmen and others who have a legitimate reason for owning them, and to keep them out of the hands of criminals and maniacs.

Finally, it should require sporting goods stores to record all sales of ammunition, with the name and address of the purchaser. This is done now in the sale of poisons — which are no more deadly than bullets.

Restrictions of this type would not end violent crime in Canada. But they would go a long way toward keeping it under control.[37]

For a constructive overview on crime and violence, it is useful to turn to a review of *Crime in America*,[38] a book written by Ramsey Clark, a former Attorney-General of the United States:

If Simon & Schuster had published Ramsey Clark's *Crime in America* just before the fall elections, rather than just after, this book by the former Attorney General might have qualified for the rare accolade conferred last month on the Report of the President's Commission on Obscenity & Pornography — a formal vote of disapproval by the U.S. Senate. For Clark's book, like the obscenity report, seeks to speak facts in a place where, under the 1970 Approved Rules of Political Dialogue, facts are off limits.

The 1970 Approved Rules do not forbid discussions of crime. They simply require the discussants to follow certain well-established guidelines:

FIRST: Crime is a function of "permissiveness" (an endemic disease, the most virulent form of which is "creeping permissiveness").

SECOND: Permissiveness is primarily the fault of the Supreme Court.

THIRD: College administrators, the media, and the "no win" crowd generally (and see especially Messrs. Gore, Goodell, Lowenstein, Tyd-

37 "Tighter Gun Control is Needed Now", Toronto *Star*, March 4, 1974.
38 Ramsey Clark, *Crime in America* (New York, Simon & Schuster, 1970).

ings, Yarborough, and their ilk) are also to blame.

FOURTH: If you like busing and smut and pot and gun controls so much, why don't you go back to Hanoi where you came from?

Clark's book doesn't follow these guidelines. His are more complicated, and less fun:

Take the map of any city — your city — and mark the parts of town where health is poorest. Now mark the parts of town where education is poorest. Next mark the parts of town where unemployment is highest. Then mark on your map the areas where the oldest buildings and houses stand. Now look at the map of your city. You have marked the areas where there are slums, poor schools, high unemployment, widespread poverty; where sickness and mental illness are common, housing is decrepit, and nearly every sight is ugly — and you have marked the areas where crime flourishes.

Behold your city — you have marked the same places every time. Poverty, illness, injustice, idleness, ignorance, human misery, and crime go together. That is the truth. We have known it all along. We cultivate crime, breed it, nourish it. Little wonder we have so much. What is to be said of the character of a people who, having the power to end all this, permit it to continue?

Ramsey Clark does not pretend to be giving us new information. Quite the contrary, it is an essential part of his message that "we have known it all along." We heard it from Attorney General Katzenbach and his colleagues on the President's Commission on Law Enforcement & the Administration of Justice. We heard it again from Governor Kerner and Mayor Lindsay and their fellow members of the President's Commission on Civil Disorders. The data were confirmed by Dr. Milton Eisenhower and his colleagues on the President's Commission on Violence. And former Governor Scranton and the other members of the President's Commission on Campus Unrest have told us only two months ago why, given the skills and resources at our command, the gap between the nation's preaching and its practice has led so many young Americans to doubt our society's capacity to fulfill its democratic promises.

The first great merit of Ramsey Clark's book is that he has the patience to assemble the data, lucidly and concisely, once again. Its second great merit is that he has not lost faith in our capacity to do better. Nor does he merely prescribe more jobs, new houses, better schools, adequate medical care, and an end to racial discrimination; or content himself with reminding us how little we know about narcotics, where our legislators would have the law intervene with such assurance, or how much we know about guns, where our legislators will scarcely permit the law to intervene at all.

Clark tells us, for example, how to give police officers a new sense of professionalism and purpose; and those familiar with the plans of New York's Commissioner Patrick Murphy, or New Haven's Chief James Ahern, or Dayton's Chief Robert Igleburger, will know what Clark means. And, to take another example, Clark pitilessly rivets our attention — as Chief Justice Burger is also seeking to do — on that structured wretchedness of prison life that we choose to characterize as a "correctional system."

But the greatest merit of Ramsey Clark's book is not the information it imparts, nor yet the persuasiveness with which this good advocate urges his fellow countrymen to make the modest investments that can pay the measureless dividend of a peaceful community. What really marks the book is Clark's insistence that law — the law of the American Constitution — is the necessary instrument for building a free society.

The Bill of Rights, scorned by hard-hats and Weathermen alike, is for Clark a statement of process and of purpose. While he served as the nation's chief law enforcement officer, Attorney General Clark would not countenance those short cuts that marginally ease the prosecutor's task but imperil the liberty of the citizen: Witness his hostility to wiretapping — a hostility shared, it is right and proper to note, by his President, Lyndon Johnson. Nor did Attorney General Clark bemuse himself into thinking that a man's worthy motives provide exemption from the law's imperatives: "If, in his judgment, the facts indicate that a Dr. Benjamin Spock has violated the law, a prosecutor has a duty to indict — or resign — even though he may believe the person to be morally right."

The 1970 elections are done. The bumper-stickers and the 30-second spots have served their biennial purpose. The Democratic Congress and the Republican President have returned from the hustings to find that the real issues — the issues identified by Ramsey Clark — are still at the top of the real national agenda. The upward curve of crime is not likely to be blunted by laws requiring lengthy minimum prison sentences, or cutting back on the Supreme Court's *Miranda* rule on confessions, or encouraging preventive detention. But positive results can reasonably be expected from laws upping the pay and training of policemen, or making it harder to buy a gun. And so too, in the longer run, from laws hospitable to President Nixon's proposals to civilize and rationalize the welfare system, or laws enabling the Equal Employment Opportunity Commission to fashion effective remedies for discrimination in the building trades or in white collar employment.

What we must now decide is whether we will continue to treat the war on crime as a public relations game of cops and robbers or finally recognize that it is in fact a modern aspect of the continuing and harder and more prosaic job — the job the Constitution long ago directed us to undertake — of "insuring domestic Tranquility."[39]

The appalling outcome of North America's failure to take effective action on gun control and other crime- and violence-fighting measures is suggested by one vision of the future which provides a depressing and discouraging but nonetheless fitting note on which to conclude this chapter:

That time has arrived. Eighteen miles southwest of Houston is a 1,000-acre, limited-access, electronically fortified walled "city," where every one of the $40,000-$200,000 homes is equipped with a mandatory $500 security package. The city's name is Sugar Creek. By the time it is finished, Sugar Creek will be entirely surrounded by a 6-ft. brick wall. At the only two entrances there will be guard posts containing police or closed-circuit TV. Every house will have electronic sensors on the downstairs doors, and many will have them on the windows. And optional "panic buttons" will turn on lights, sirens, and bells, and summon private police.

"We didn't have to sell security," says Jake Kamin, one of the owners

[39] Louis H. Pollak, "A Soldier of Justice in the War on Crime". Reprinted from the November 21, 1970 issue of *Business Week* by special permission. Copyright 1970 by McGraw-Hill, Inc.

of Sugar Creek. "The nation knows it's looking for security."

Kamin, president of American Mortgage Co., joined two other Houston businessmen — lawyer David Searls and Stewart Morris, operational head of Stewart Title Co. — to develop the community.

Poor neighbors. The site they chose is surrounded by the homes of low-income Mexican-American families, many of whom speak only Spanish and some of whom work in Sugar Creek homes. "There are a lot of Mexican-Americans in the neighborhood," says one of the 14 home builders. "The people who come out here know that, and the security system makes them feel better."

Kamin got the idea for a super-secure community from his work on a subdivision near the Manned Spacecraft Center, south of Houston, where he collaborated with National Aeronautics & Space Administration contractors.

He hired the Apollo Systems Div. of General Electric Co., which does contract work for NASA, to design the home-security systems for Sugar Creek. GE decided to use components that were already available — off-the-shelf sensors, controls, wiring, and a new $4,500 minicomputer. They came up with a mandatory security package which "makes the whole community tough, not just a few homes in it," says Robert Taylor, a GE systems analyst.

The minicomputer installed by GE plays a dual role. It not only provides a link in the intruder-alarm system, but will also eventually be tied to a larger computer that homeowners can use for chores such as budgeting and income-tax calculations. Soon, the site will have a golf course and a development of shops and offices.

Safety first. But it is security that has attracted many buyers to Sugar Creek. The sixty homes already built have been snapped up. "The first thing that brought us out was that we read about the security system," says Mrs. James C. Davis, wife of a retired Air Force officer, who now works as a meteorologist. The Davis family was accustomed to the security of bases protected by military police.

So many people feel the need for security that builders can hardly put up houses fast enough, says Kamin. Plans call for erecting about 2,000 homes on the site, but the owners have options on another 8,000 acres, and Kamin says Sugar Creek could house 200,000 people in another 15 years.

The Sugar Creek concept is spreading. Another Houston builder has just announced plans for a 650-unit super-secure apartment house in St. Petersburg, Fla., which will cost $5.5-million. Like Sugar Creek, it will be surrounded by a 6-ft. wall.

The social implications of the "walled city" have gone unquestioned in Houston, where crimes against property — including burglary and theft — have risen 21% over the past year. The only doubters, in fact, are those who wonder if the system will work. Larry Sondock, of McCane-Sondock Protection Systems Co., calls the devices "more of a gimmick than protection."

But there is no doubt in the minds of the buyers. Don Marquardt, a motorcycle dealer who bought a $75,000 French Mediterranean home, says: "Nothing has been left to chance." And his wife adds: "It's going to be a perfectly elegant community."[40]

[40] "The U.S. Gets Its First Walled City". Reprinted from the March 6, 1971 issue of *Business Week* by special permission. Copyright 1971 by McGraw-Hill, Inc.

3

THE REFORM OF NORTH AMERICA

The message in the previous chapter may have appeared so disheartening as to suggest radical or even revolutionary change as the only solution to the problems confronting North America. Although major change is of the essence and is urgent, it need not be radical or revolutionary unless it is put off too long. Reform is a more appropriate term for what is required, and it is more likely to preserve what is worthwhile in the existing order. The difference involved is more than a matter of degree, given the institutions and values which are at stake.

WHAT'S AT STAKE

The very nature of North America's socio-economic-political system is what is at stake. This system is based on an hierarchy of interrelated institutions and values which the vast majority of citizens still seem to cherish. Whether they will continue to do so depends largely on society's ability to grapple successfully with the many challenges that beset it. Failure to do so could lead people to look for any number of other alternatives, regardless of the risks they might entail.

At the base of North America's prevailing hierarchy of institutions and values is what are normally termed fundamental Western values. In the report of a task force, of which the author was a member, some insight into the history and importance of these values was provided:

In any society there prevail values fundamental to it and to the goals it pursues. These values are often enshrined in the concept of fundamental human rights, or "natural rights". Relating mainly to freedom of the person, property rights, and freedom of thought and political action, they compose the liberal democratic traditions of western society designed to enhance the free development of the human personality. The concept of natural rights implies that they exist in the natural order of social intercourse, for man to perceive as he will or as they are revealed to him. Whatever their metaphysical source, they are the product of great moments in history, of the hot fire of human conflict. As such, they are the product of historical accident, because circumstances dictate the kind of right or freedom that society is concerned to recognize and defend. They are also the product of human perceptiveness, or lack of perceptiveness, and of re-evaluation over a long period of time. The historical events may thus be viewed as dramatic moments in a continuing search for the identification and protection of fundamental human values as means to human fulfillment.

The *Great Charter* of 1215 is a foundation of the rule of law — the right to be judged by one's peers and by the law of the land. The *Bill of Rights* of 1689 established the supremacy of Parliament and the principle of free elections, paving the way for a constitutional monarchy and eventually for democratic government, as the principle of universal manhood suffrage was gained in the 19th and 20th centuries. The subordination of governments to the governed inheres in the *Declaration of Independence* of 1776, as does the recognition of the inalienable rights to life, liberty and the pursuit of happiness. Much the same values are reflected in the *Declaration of the Rights of Man* of 1789, with the additional recognition of property rights. To these are added, in the First Amendment to the *United States Constitution* of 1791, freedom of religion, speech, the press and assembly; the Fifth Amendment adds the right not to be deprived of life, liberty or property without due process of law, a reaffirmation not merely of freedom but of freedom under the law. The *Canadian Bill of Rights* of 1960, in section 1, declares the right of the individual to life, liberty, security of the person and enjoyment of property, and the right not to be deprived thereof except by due process of law; the right of the individual to equality before the law and protection of the law; freedom of religion, speech, assembly and association, and the press. The Bill reflects not history itself so much as the lessons of history.

The foregoing instruments are national in scope. In addition, there are some seventeen international declarations and covenants which, because of their contemporary nature, add profoundly to the principles of the protection of fundamental human freedoms under the rule of law in an environment of democratic government.

Two documents bear special comment. The preamble of the United Nations Charter reaffirms faith in fundamental human rights, in the dignity and worth of the human person, and in the equal rights of men and women. Most of the rights of the person and of freedom to think and act under the law, as set out in the 1948 Declaration of Human Rights, were gained or recognized long before in the western democracies. But the Declaration is a landmark in the assertion of economic rights and the pursuit of economic justice as a means of enhancing the free development of the human personality. The Declaration includes such rights as the right to work, to protection against unemployment, to form and join trade unions, to social security, to rest and leisure, to an adequate standard of living, to education, and to participate in the cultural life of the community.

In brief, fundamental human rights today embrace as ideals the political rights of freedom of speech, religion, association and assembly; the egalitarian right of freedom from discrimination on the basis of race, national origin, colour, religion and sex; the economic right to a decent standard of life; and, for Canada at least, the linguistic right to the use of the mother tongues of French and English.

These rights are supported by the rule of law in a democratic society. The rule of law itself constitutes a fundamental human right: to security of life, liberty and property, security of the person and personality, and the assurance of procedural fairness — due process of law — in the determination of rights and obligations. Section 2 of the *Canadian Bill of Rights* articulates many of these procedural safeguards to the administration of justice according to law.[1]

Too often there is precious little appreciation of how important the freedoms enjoyed by North Americans are. Excerpts such as the following from the essay, "Let Us Enjoy Our Freedoms," serve to remind U.S. and Canadian citizens of the benefits which accrue from North American democracy:

Our civilization is the first one in history that has not been based on slave labour. This is unquestionably a great advance, not only morally but in its contribution to our self-respect and welfare. Dr. Albert Schweitzer told the story in *African Notebook* about a well-to-do woman who visited his hospital accompanied by four slaves. The next day Dr. Schweitzer met her while she was gathering wood, and asked her why she had to carry her own firewood, since she had four slaves. She replied: "Having slaves does not mean that one is well served." So not only are the slaves free, but we are free of having slaves: to depend upon our own efforts is to develop ourselves and to be free.

The word "freedom" has many shades of meaning. Depending upon its context it stands for political liberty, personal liberty, non-slavery, independence, or the power of self-determination. It implies more than mere liberty, for it demands insurance and protection by provident institutions such as governments which secure us from arbitrary subjection. Thomas Hobbes said in his great treatise *The Leviathan:* "A freeman is he that, in those things which by his strength and wit he is able to do, is not hindered to do what he has a will to do."

The Rule of Law is a great ideal, with the will of the people as the source of its authority. Freedom is not liberty for everyone to do what he pleases without being subject to any law. It is freedom of man to have a standing rule to live by, common to everyone in his society. It is freedom within bounds rather than wholly anarchic freedom. It consents to curtailment of some natural or savage liberties so that the human spirit may rejoice in greater, wider freedom.

The Rule of Law means that there is one law for all men, that all men are equal before it, and that no man can be punished except for the breach of it. It reconciles social order with individual freedom and initiative. It means that the government itself is not above law, and that it respects the independence of the courts and the safeguards of the citizen's liberties. Only Parliament can alter law, and Parliament is the people.

Democracy is that system of government which more than any other is predicated upon the dignity of the individual. This is not a dignity imposed by law, or conferred by learning or implied by status. It is the dignity of self-respect and self-development, for self-control is the essence of democratic living. It is the dignity of people who manage themselves so that they do not require outside coercion.

Our forefathers, although failing here and there in some points in the administration of free institutions, were pre-eminent for the time in

[1] A.W.R. Carrothers, et al., *Canadian Industrial Relations: Report of the Prime Minister's Task Force on Labour Relations* (Ottawa, Queen's Printer, 1968), pp. 9-12. Reproduced by permission of Information Canada.

which they lived. We cannot with impunity set aside the institutions and authorities which for a thousand years have inspired and guarded and dignified our freedoms, but we can improve them and add to them.[2]

To date these freedoms or values have found their greatest implementation in what might best be described as liberal democratic political systems. Whether congressional or parliamentary in form, or utilizing some combination of the two, this type of political framework has provided the fullest protection for such freedoms as those pertaining to speech, assembly and so on. As suggested in such expressions as "government of, by, and for the people," the liberal democratic political process depends on several underlying principles. First and foremost, there are, under a universal franchise, regular elections of the governing assemblies, legislatures or parliaments through a system of freely-created political parties. Second, and in keeping with the concept of responsible government, there is a cabinet and executive branch of government dependent either directly or indirectly upon the support of a majority of the elected representatives. Third, there is a court system with an independent judiciary which bears much of the responsibility for the maintenance of a rule of law rather than a rule of men.

Needless to say, this brief outline of the nature of the liberal democratic political process does not begin to do it justice. Important as well for example, are the increasingly significant roles played by that awesome bureaucracy termed the public service, by the host of regulatory bodies which have been created, and by the mass media. All of these important facets of the present system will be dealt with at greater length in later chapters. For the moment, it must suffice to acknowledge their place in the system, while suggesting that as vital as their roles may be, they do not detract from the fact that the cornerstones of the liberal democratic political process still remain the legislative, executive and judicial branches of the government.

Where an appropriate interplay between these various branches of government has been well established, the resultant advancement and protection of the fundamental Western values has been unequalled. This is the first, and perhaps least controversial, link in the chain which can be built between the series of institutions and values which are the focal point of this chapter. Far more debatable is the next link, that between liberal democracy and modified capitalism or mixed free enterprise.

History bears out the contention that there appears to be an indisputable link between the nature of a country's political process and that of its economic system. Despite the fact that history is misleading at times, it is noteworthy that no country has sustained a liberal democratic political process, and the fundamental Western values which cannot survive without it, except in combination with a modified capitalistic or mixed free enterprise economic system. There are a variety of other kinds of economic systems available but so far no other has persisted in conjunction with the basic political freedoms North Americans take for granted.

Before pursuing this point, it is well to be clear on the meaning of modified capitalism or mixed free enterprise. Certainly nothing like the early laissez faire days of capitalism is intended. Nonetheless, there is a range of economic systems which falls under the rubric of capitalism or free enterprise. At one extreme is what one might term "capitalism with a vengeance" as still practiced in its most ravaging form in the United States and, to a somewhat

2 "Let us Enjoy Our Freedoms", The Royal Bank of Canada Monthly Letter, Vol. 50, No. 6, Montreal, June 1969.

lesser extent, in Canada. Dog-eat-dog capitalism is still very much alive in North America despite increased government regulation supposedly designed to contain its worst abuses. The point is that the "haves" still retain most of their privileges because of tax loopholes and other gimmicks designed to protect their positions, while the "have-nots" remain unprotected by either a decent floor under their incomes or sufficiently comprehensive social security programs. The result is a society riddled with inequities and unable even to approach one of the basic tenets of its *raison d'etre:* equality of opportunity — not in terms of education, health, or anything else.

Close to the other extreme is what has been termed "capitalism with a conscience" as still probably best exemplified by Sweden. There the public sector is smaller than in either the United States or Canada, so that private enterprise has even more scope to operate. On the other hand, at a not insignificant cost in terms of incentives and motivation, a major and sustained effort has been made to ensure that those at the bottom of the income ladder do not suffer as harshly as they do either absolutely or relatively in other modified capitalistic or mixed free enterprise countries. Sweden therefore demonstrates, as do a few other countries, that the advantages of capitalism can for the most part be preserved while at the same time ridding it of its worst defects.

Regardless of its position in the spectrum, a modified capitalistic or mixed free enterprise system's essential features are likely to be the same. To quote again from the aforementioned task force:

The motivating force within this general framework is economic self-interest. Within the limits of various laws designed to protect the public interest, decisions are permitted to be made on the basis of individual or institutional gains. These decisions set in motion economic forces that effect the distribution of available resources among competing ends through the interaction of capital, labour, and other markets.

It is not hard to discover why western societies have, with varying degrees of doubts, reservations and constraints, accepted the institutions and incentives of the modified capitalistic or mixed enterprise framework. Despite its faults and shortcomings, the system has so far provided a greater opportunity for individual and social fulfillment and achievement than any viable alternative. No effective substitute for the relatively free market has yet been found to ensure optimum allocation of resources. Nonetheless, it has its deficiencies and detractors.

State involvement in the mixed enterprise system has increased. Although it is still basically a decentralized market-oriented system, the role of the state can be seen in an increasing number of areas. In some cases government has intervened because of imperfections in the operation of the system. In other cases intervention has been brought on by inequities growing out of its unrestrained operation.

Cyclical fluctuations have forced the state to intervene in an effort to smooth out the growth rate of the economy. The early classical economic notions about the self-correcting nature of the system have been proved unsound. As a result government has had to employ fiscal, monetary and related policies when the economy proved unable to produce socially acceptable results.

Of more immediate interest have been the efforts by society to curb the worst abuses of the system. Although state intervention in industrial relations began, in effect, before the industrialization process, such intervention abated for a time after its introduction and later reappeared in a variety of forms. Government had to take cognizance of the hardships created by unemployment, underemployment, sweated labour, low wages, long hours, brutal supervision and unsafe and unhealthy working conditions. The result was a gradual introduction of protective labour standards legislation to prevent the harsh social consequences that arose from unimpeded economic determinism. Thus the force of law was put behind what were considered to be minimum standards of pay and working conditions. Politically determined criteria of equity were substituted for the terms of employment that would have been produced by unrestrained market forces. Government thereupon became party to the employment relationship.

At the same time, workers began to join unions and to engage in collective bargaining with their employers. Although employers resisted this development with all resources at their command, it eventually became apparent that unions and collective bargaining were natural concomitants of a mixed enterprise economy. The state then assumed the task of establishing a framework of rights and responsibilities within which management and organized labour were to conduct their relations.

Government has consequently come to play an integral part in the prevailing economic system. It is government's expanding role that has made it a "modified" capitalistic or "mixed" enterprise system. Yet despite this growing state involvement, the economy remains largely governed by competitive and institutional forces created by individuals and organizations pursuing their own economic and social goals.[3]

Aside from considerations from history, there is a logical basis for the view that liberal democracy is best linked with modified capitalism or mixed free enterprise. However defined or practiced, such a democratic system is almost invariably characterized by less centralized decision making than any alternative. This being the case, there is usually less at stake in the political decision-making arena and consequently more room for give and take. Where, in contrast, the state is at the centre of everything, takeovers by one major interest group or another, or some combination of them, is likely to become more attractive and compelling. Furthermore, once in power such blocs are unlikely to prove very tolerant of any kind of dissension, let alone opposition.

Whether or not one accepts a logical link between capitalism and democracy, where they have been combined certain outgrowths have proven inevitable. Because of the growing size of markets and the increasing complexity and costs of modern technology, among other considerations, capital has invariably become more concentrated. In so doing, it has acquired great power which it has often abused in its relations with other groups, especially labour. Not unnaturally, this eventually has produced an organized response in the form of trade unions and collective bargaining. These institutions have now become such an accepted and integral part of North American society that it is hard to conceive of it without them. Indeed, undermining these instruments would, in the end, also undermine the total system.

Other groups have also found it advantageous to organize to advance and protect their self-interests. Many of these groups have had organizations of one kind or another for decades, but it is only comparatively recently that they have

[3] A.W.R. Carrothers, et al., *Canadian Industrial Relations: Report of the Prime Minister's Task Force on Labour Relations* (Ottawa, Queen's Printer, 1968), pp. 12-13. Reproduced by permission of Information Canada.

taken on the trappings of trade unions and have engaged in their own forms of collective bargaining. Among these groups are associations, institutes and societies of professionals, such as doctors and lawyers, be they employed or self-employed. As earlier inferred, these groups are little more than high-class unions. Producers' organizations, particularly in agriculture, have similar aims and aspirations.

In terms of influencing the present situation, last, but hopefully not least, among those who are organizing under one guise or another are consumers. Although they may never prove powerful enough as a group to offset those whose primary interests lie in the receipt of income, various types of consumer groups are essential to the maintenance of a proper balance between the many contending interest groups which are bound to persist.

The point is that society is becoming organized in the fullest sense of the term. This is probably inevitable, and it may even be sound. That remains to be seen. Be that as it may, an organized society is quite different from a collectivized or socialized society and is undoubtedly more compatible with the general socio-economic-political order which has been established in North America.

THE LACK OF ALTERNATIVES

Those who want to dismantle or tear down the existing order either have nothing to offer in its place or offer something of which the consequences are too uncertain to risk. In the first category are those who have so given up hope in the current system that they would try anything else. Having no clear cut alternative they usually give up the struggle or drop out into a commune or some other less desirable form of escape such as the drug cult.

More persistent and serious, and therefore more frightening, are those who believe in one brave new world or another. Well-intentioned as most of these groups may be, the outcome of their efforts would be a much more centralized and powerful role for the state. Whether in the name of planning, state capitalism or just plain ordinary socialism or communism, their goal is to reduce the power of the private, and particularly the corporate, sector by either further regulating or eliminating it. Then, through some grand overall design, democratically arrived at, of course, the state would guide society through a better way towards a greater end.

The trouble with all of this lies in the fact that it is creeping statism. Some would argue that the state is already too powerful. Although that may not yet be the case, there is a trend in that direction which must be resisted. This does not mean that the state should not play a more active role in many areas. But it may mean that the state should play a less active role in other areas. Even more important is the form which state intervention should take. The way in which government intervenes is as important as the reasons for its intervention. Improving the rules and regulations of the capitalist or free enterprise game is far more sensible and far less dangerous than attempting to take more of it over.

Doubtless the state could ultimately take over everything if it wanted to. The question is whether it should, and if not totally, how far down that treacherous path should it go? Few would advocate a total takeover, but more than is healthy would support the kind of gradual takeover which invariably leads to further intrusions and ultimately to complete statism.

Creeping statism, and by that it is meant that the state subsumes more and more activities which previously lay in the private sector, is inimical to a free society. The reason for this incompatibility lies in the power which would build up in the public sector. No society known to man has permitted that kind of build-up of state power without paying a terrible price for it. Although the examples of history may not be infallible, it is worth reiterating that no society has remained free, either in terms of its citizens' rights or its political processes, while transferring all significant powers to its government.

A POSSIBLE WAY OUT

North America is a sick society but it is not so sick that it cannot be reformed. Moreover, bad as it is, it still has a lot going for it relative to most, if not all, other societies, except perhaps a few other western industrialized democracies such as Sweden. North America may not represent the best of all possible worlds, but it's still one of the least of the evils.

The question is how urgent is the need to improve it and how does one go about doing so. As for the first question, it has already been answered by the previous chapter. The signs of trouble are so many, varied and pervasive that improvements must be made soon if public disenchantment and disillusionment is not to increase beyond recovery. If the public is not soon to turn to those with more drastic remedies — if remedies is the appropriate term for such solutions — then those who believe in reforms consistent with North America's existing institutions and values must make their move soon.

As for the answer, there is, of course, no easy or single solution. Instead, the existing systems of checks and balances designed to keep society in some semblance of order must be reassessed. This system is now so obsolete that it is in danger of collapsing. Unless it is updated, that is exactly what will happen.

It is the theme of the remaining chapters of this volume that no matter how sick the part of North American society in question, it can be made to perform better by rearranging the checks and balances within which it is intended to operate. Central to this theme, as already enunciated, is the need for more disclosure and exposure and public scrutiny of what is going on within many of society's leading institutions. In and of itself, disclosure and exposure and public scrutiny will lead to the cessation of many undesirable practices. Equally important, however, will be the assistance this approach can render to the effective erection of new checks and balances as they are required to ensure proper activities in the institutions in question.

Although the state has a major role to play in this process, it is largely as regulator and rule maker and not as an all-encompassing octopus embracing more and more of the total system. That distinction is vital if society is to avoid statism in a form completely incompatible with the host of freedoms North Americans have thus far enjoyed.

In keeping with this basic thrust, it is perhaps appropriate to conclude this chapter with three editorials, the first from The Globe and Mail, and the others from The Christian Science Monitor. The first draws heavily on some recent commentaries concerning the malaise which afflicts U.S. capitalism:

The future of capitalism in the United States has been questioned of late in an interestingly academic fashion. One of the diagnosticians is John G. Gurley, professor of economics at Stanford University. Writing on The Future of American Capitalism in Economics and Business, he said:

"My main conclusion is that there are some powerful, adverse forces operating against U.S. capitalism . . . The deteriorating environment derives primarily from the continuance of revolutionary movements against international capitalism, from the intensification of rivalries among leading capitalist states for investment outlets, trade advantages, and access to raw materials, and from labor's growing ability to exert pressure on capital's share of the national income. . .

"However, these adverse forces against capitalism are far from being unopposed. International capitalism, led by the United States, is a powerful force in the world and is capable of many more victories against world proletarian movements. Still, my judgment is that, on balance, the tide is running against capitalism on a worldwide basis. . .

"If this is so, the response of the capitalist class is most likely to be a call for increased state intervention in the economic life of the nation . . . We can expect state intervention to be intensified for the purposes of tightening the bonds of labor discipline at home, mobilizing national resources against revolutionary activity abroad, and defending U.S. capitalists' interests in an increasingly competitive and hostile environment of global capitalism . . . Capitalism will survive as an increasingly state-directed monopoly capitalism. But many elements of democracy will not."

Another questioner is Robert L. Heilbroner, whose article Capitalism Alive or Dead was excerpted from World magazine for the December edition of Intellectual Digest:

"Had anyone in the 1930s been told that the U.S. gross national product in the early 1970s would surpass a trillion dollars — effectively doubling the real per capita income within the lifespan of the majority of the population then alive — I am sure he would have felt safe in predicting for the United States an era of unprecedented social peace and goodwill. Yet that enormous economic change has taken place and social harmony has not resulted. . .

'I think it is fair to say that among the new evidences of social unrest — the drug culture, the cry for participatory democracy, the alienation of students, the new sexual morality, the retreat to the life of the commune — none is congenial with or supportive of those attitudes and behavior patterns on which capitalism has traditionally rested. It is possible, in other words, that we stand at the threshold of an era in which deep-seated changes in lifeways will undermine capitalism in a manner as fatal as the most dramatic proletarian revolution might do, although perhaps less rapidly or romantically."

The two views see different results, and they see them for the United States. Yet Canadian prosperity has risen with U.S. prosperity — in economic tandem with it — and could decline with it. These men are not prophets, but the choice they postulate is founded in realities we see ourselves.

What Canadians may have to prepare themselves to decide is whether they will drift toward state capitalism minus democracy, or a new kind of society not oriented to profits but, according to Mr. Heilbroner, operating under "a degree of social control . . . that far exceeds anything now known in any capitalist country".

If we are to preserve individual freedom, it must be made central to all our considerations, not handled as a by-product. Capitalism has so far permitted more freedom than communism. But Canadian capitalism, less successful than U.S. capitalism, has permitted more freedom, and of late years we have recognized it: we are proud of the peace and safety of our streets as compared with that of U.S. streets, to take but one comparison.

These are long-term things; but probably shorter long-term things than those of any other century. If we want freedom and prosperity, in even a modest package, our best minds must begin preparing the package now. To let things ride is to invite the extremity of left or right, neither offering freedom and, quite probably, neither offering the great majority of Canadians prosperity either.[4]

That there is hope for serious reform rather than a dramatic revolution is reflected in a *Christian Science Monitor* editorial calling for "The Orderly Revolution":

By sharing the word revolution with radicals, moderates are acknowledging that change — breathless change — is the new tradition. Bad semantics, right instincts.

Who will be the leaders of the '70's? Those who anticipate and direct the energies of protest that are the troubled by-products of change. These men won't necessarily hold office or even be political. In fact, they will tend to depoliticalize issues. For their aim will be to talk the protesters down from the barricades and convert them to a different kind of revolution — to a new due process of change.

Ralph Nader is one such orderly revolutionary. In effect, his Center for the Study of Responsive Law is a strategy for opening a sort of hot line between a government and its citizens before old, ever-more-tangled lines of communication, anger and demoralize both parties.

John Gardner, former Secretary of Health, Education, and Welfare, is another such revolutionary. His simple insight is that every special interest is superorganized and lobbying madly — except people. He hopes that, by serving as a continuous, reasoned voice of protest, his people's lobby, Common Cause, will be able to insist upon priorities to which American money and energy should be dedicated.

Saul Alinsky is still another private-sector guerrilla — a self-styled radical himself but one whose methods are more revolutionary than his credo. He dreams of a breed of organizers — roving grievance committees who can "sit down with the Canadian Indians on Monday night, help the Chicanos in the Southwest on Tuesday, be in a blue-collar suburb in Chicago on Wednesday, spend Thursday with white steelworkers in Pittsburgh, move Friday to a black ghetto."

These are just three faces of the new revolutionaries — pragmatists rather than ideologues, problem solvers who promise to be as various as the challenges of the '70's. At times, their unorthodox ways are bound to irritate. But insofar as they provide expression to public will — insofar as they ease the frantically increased demands upon the government — these new revolutionaries will be doing as much as anyone to prevent the old-fashioned sort of revolution from happening.[5]

[4] "Put Freedom First", *The Globe and Mail*, Toronto, March 19, 1973.
[5] "The Orderly Revolution", *The Christian Science Monitor*, February 22, 1971.

4

PARTIES, POLITICS
AND POLITICIANS

No more serious problem confronts North America than the decline in public confidence in its political processes. So low has this confidence sunk that the credibility of politicians seems at an all time low. Although this situation is far more critical in the United States than in Canada, the American Watergate scandals have had an impact north, as well as south, of the border. If nothing else, they have induced Canadians to take a closer look at their own political machinations, scrutiny of which does not lead one to be encouraged.

After reviewing the general malaise which clouds all parties, politics and politicians in North America, this chapter turns to major manifestations of this malaise in the United States and to some similar, although less disquieting, manifestations in Canada. To conclude, a section is devoted to the more positive aspects of Watergate and related experiences. Some long-needed fundamental reforms are already emerging, something which must happen if credibility is to be restored in the liberal democratic political process in North America.

Perhaps the leading question now is what will happen as a result of the Nixon resignation and pardon. While this clearly removes an unparalleled blight from the political scene, Nixon's unrepentant departure may lead to a pronounced slowdown in the movement for reform. Should this happen, he may well go down in history as little more than a dangerous and deceitful scapegoat who was sacrificed by other politicians while they avoided much needed reforms affecting themselves.

THE DECLINE IN PUBLIC
CONFIDENCE AND CREDIBILITY

Although parties, politics and politicians may be no more immoral today than in previous eras, they are perceived as such. A few years ago when Americans were asked to rank 20 leading callings, professions and trades in terms of honesty and integrity, politicians came second to last — today they would probably come at the end of the line. Reflecting the public's view of its politicians are several recent polls in the United States which reveal that for the first time a majority of Americans no longer trust their federal government.

The causes of this decline in public faith in the political process are manifold. Topping the list, of course, is Watergate and the blatant forms of corruption which that name has now come to represent. Under the name of Watergate has fallen virtually every dirty trick in which the most despicable of politicians might engage. Bombarded for almost two years by one exposé after another, it is no wonder the American public has become so disillusioned that it would rather not hear any more about it. Worse still is the fairly widespread view that Nixon's biggest mistake was to be caught at it, since in varying degrees all politicians are thought to engage in the same kind of intrigue, albeit less extensively and with more finesse. Accurate or inaccurate, such an attitude can completely undermine all faith in the democratic process.

Already at the operational level of the present system there are signs of deep trouble. Nixon's abortive tax-evasion cannot help but undercut the efficacy of the U.S. tax system which, like that of Canada, is based to a large extent on individual taxpayer honesty and integrity. There is also a growing feeling that politicians are in politics solely for a combination of what they and those who back them can get out of it. In this self-aggrandizing process, it is easy to gain the impression that there is no real concept of the public interest, let alone any attempt to further it. Instead, in the name of "the art of the possible," or some other rationale, politicians simply play off their own individual interests against the various power blocs with which they have to contend. As these power blocs vie for position, the role of the politician becomes little more than that of protecting his own position while making compromises which satisfy enough of these interests to keep them in reasonable balance. In fact, this may be all that democracy is about, thus suggesting that the only hope for championing the public interest is to ensure more organization of public interest groups, such as consumers, relative to producer interest groups with which the system is replete.

One effect of all of this, as was brought out in an earlier chapter, is the portrayal of leading politicians as little more than opportunistic, pragmatic and unprincipled individuals who stand for little or nothing, and thus blow along with the latest gust of political wind, regardless of whether it is good or bad for society. A case in point is to be found in the radical transformation of Canada's Prime Minister from a sincere idealogue to a blatant politician in the basest sense of that term. Whether driven to this transformation by public pressure, his own changing disposition, or some combination of these and other forces, is difficult to tell. The most charitable view is doubtless that the system drove him to amend his ways. In any event, there seems to be no resemblance between the sincere idealist he once was and the crass politician he became:

Apart from speed, the difference between a tactical withdrawal and a retreat is a matter of commitment. If you believe in what you're fighting for, you withdraw in order to be able to fight again. If you don't, you bunk out.

The Trudeau government is not in retreat from the social battlefield. It is in rout. One could write that brave ideals were being abandoned, except that to give something up you must first have possessed it.

A government which substitutes pragmatism for ideology and the pursuit of power for its own sake for belief in principle is by no means a bad thing. Those were Disraeli's standards and he was probably Britain's most effective prime minister in the last 150 years. The point instead is never to take seriously what such a government says, as opposed to what it may do.

In 1971, youth and "the quality of life" were trendy. The Trudeau government gave us Opportunities for Youth and the accompanying rhetoric: "The government believes that youth is sincere in its efforts to improve society." In 1974, the "work ethic" is fashionable. The government gives us a Student Summer Employment and Activities Program

71

(SSEAP) and defensive prose: "The matching of jobs and students . . . balanced work opportunities . . . the work ethic . . . close co-operation between the private and public sectors."

The retreat affects all the social sectors. The "community employment" program proposed almost a year ago is bogged down in interdepartmental wrangling and is going nowhere. A proposed daycare centre program has been shelved in the Department of Health and Welfare. A leader of one of the native organizations in Ottawa told me the other day, "The wind has been blowing in our faces for about six months. The word is through the bureaucracy: Indians are out."

Some policy changes are overdue. Despite high unemployment, 100,000 jobs are going begging. The public plainly is in no mood to subsidize welfare freeloading. What needs to be recorded, though, is how easily the government gave up.

OFY provides the best example. Except in name it has been killed. What began as a hopeful program to help youth "improve society" has become a conventional make-work scheme. This happened without a single voice of dissent in cabinet.

Secretary of State Hugh Faulkner took the first step last fall when he asked that OFY, which he judged a political liability, be transferred from his department to Manpower. Just after the New Year, Manpower Minister Robert Andras got cabinet's approval to cut back OFY from $42 million last year to $18 million.

Three weeks ago Andras took his plan to the national Liberal caucus and to his astonishment, as he later described it, was given "the worst time I've ever had in caucus." One after another the backbenchers, mostly from Ontario, attacked what one of them called "the way we give in the moment anything we do that is worthwhile is attacked."

The MPs were largely responsible for restoring the OFY funds to the $30 million finally announced (mostly achieved by cuts in departmental summer hiring). But pressure came also from another direction, and for a quite different reason. A week earlier the Quebec caucus had also debated OFY and had also demanded an increase in funds. The Quebec MPs, though, were less concerned with the quality of life than with the quantity of patronage.

Cabinet's role was crucial, precisely because it played none at all. "The public isn't in a mood to accept increases in welfare," Welfare Minister Marc Lalonde told me in a recent interview. "We will have to stress the work aspects of our programs." Faced with that mood of pragmatism, the cabinet's left has given up the struggle.

Prime Minister Pierre Trudeau, of course, could have made the difference. After the last election he made a tactical withdrawal on bilingualism in the civil service. Trudeau, though, made it quite plain where he stood, and pushed a special resolution on bilingualism through the House.

Social programs are something else. About a year after OFY was created Trudeau said, in private, "This is one of the programs I am proudest of." This time, when the spirit of OFY was buried in the work ethic, Trudeau had nothing to say. He couldn't: He was in Switzerland, skiing.[1]

Hope of restoring some sense of the public interest to the political process

[1] Richard Gwyn, "Trudeau Is Not Retreating, He's Fleeing", Toronto *Star*, February 12, 1974.

is further reduced by the extent to which that process is subject to manipulation by the monied interests who back the different parties and politicians. Call it what you will, money still counts for a great deal in the North American political process, thereby ensuring a continuing advantage to those who have, over those who have not. Sometimes money is used in a most crude way to buy parties, politics and politicians. More often, the influence is more subtle, but no less effective. Regardless, this is a now well-publicized facet of North American politics which had added to the public's cynicism and disgust about the whole business.

Last, but not least, although not yet fully appreciated, is the growing complexity of issues which have to be considered in conjunction. Even without the obvious immorality which has come to characterize so much of North America's political life, democracy would be in some difficulty as the realization spreads that modern-day problems do not lend themselves to any easy answers. That this could become the root problem has thus far been hidden by the more superficial reasons for a breakdown of public faith in democracy. Combine the two and the effects could be disastrous. On a more hopeful note, if the most corrupt elements of the political process can be cleaned up, it may well be that it will have a better chance of coping with the serious socio-economic challenges which are now facing it.

The net result of all of these trends is indecisive and ineffectual leadership which cannot help but attract public attention, misgivings and reservations. All of this adds a sense of urgency to the need to get on with the business of political reform, for which the solutions are not difficult to perceive once one appraises what has gone wrong.

AMERICA'S WATERGATE

Watergate has come to represent so much of what is wrong with the American political process and, indeed, American society, that it is hard to know what to include in its broad sweep. Perhaps, therefore, it would be best to start with the brighter side. As also reflected in the ongoing civil rights struggle in the United States, the real strength of the U.S. would seem to lie in the fact that it all comes out in the end. America is still such an open society that even the most corrupt and evil of men in the highest of offices cannot hide their filth forever. The judicial and legislative checks and balances are still such that, despite attempts to subvert virtually every aspect of the executive branch of the government, the wrongdoing which was being perpetrated could not be hidden forever. Nixon's longstanding record as a politician is not such as to lead one to be surprised at the nature of the men he surrounded himself with, let alone the corruption they have presided over from their high places. Despite the Nixon resignation, the appalling thing is that he and the men around him got away with it for so long and are likely to suffer so little for it if, as and when, they are all called to account. Nixon's pardon would appear to prove the old adage that the higher one's place or station in life the less one suffers for even the worst of wrongdoing.

The crisis of confidence and credibility which has resulted from Watergate is to be explained by the variety of misdeeds which have come to be associated with that term. Relatively early in the crisis, a *New York Times* editorial indictment of Nixon indicated just how many charges could be laid against him even at that point:

The visible disintegration of President Nixon's moral and political authority, of his capacity to act as Chief Executive, of his claim to leadership and to credibility, leads us to the reluctant conclusion that Mr. Nixon would be performing his ultimate service to the American people — and to himself — by resigning his office before this nation is forced to go through the traumatic and divisive process of impeachment.

The doubts about Mr. Nixon that have gathered an ominous momentum over the past 12 months have arisen, basically, from three different sources — constitutional, political and personal — and they are now flowing together in a surging torrent.

Every President comes under attack from the political opposition, as is normal in a democracy; and every President makes misjudgments and administrative errors. If that were all that could be said about Mr. Nixon, the possibility of his resignation or impeachment would never arise. The gravity of the case against him rests instead on his deliberate violations of the letter and the spirit of the Constitution and, flowing out of this, the collapse of public confidence in the integrity of the man who only one year ago was elected to the Presidency by the largest popular majority in American history.

In an obsession with secrecy, in reliance on the blanket of "national security" to cover virtually any action, Mr. Nixon has at least twice given his approval to projects that would violate the law and his oath of office. In 1970, he endorsed a secret plan involving concededly illegal acts against domestic radicals. Although this plan was soon rescinded, Mr. Nixon later established a White House investigative unit, the notorious "plumbers," that did engage in illegal acts. Revelation of White House involvement in this kind of activity, including attempted subversion of both FBI and CIA, was what first shook public faith in Mr. Nixon's understanding of the proprieties of his office.

In his management of the Vietnam War, Mr. Nixon compounded the secrecy, deceit and unconstitutional practices that had already grievously harmed the Presidency under Mr. Johnson. The secret bombing of Laos and Cambodia and the invasion of Cambodia were the acts of a President with scant regard for the authority of Congress and for the will of the people.

In an entirely different area of public policy, the President has abused his power in respect to the impoundment of funds. Mr. Nixon has tried to convert the implied, discretionary power to impound into an absolute item veto. In his exercise of that power, Mr. Nixon has acted as if he regarded his re-election as a mandate to do as he pleased in administering the budget.

The deceitful manipulation of the Presidential war-making powers, the deliberate violations of the law in the national security investigations and the abuse of the impoundment authority have all created in the minds of the people the enduring conviction that Mr. Nixon has little respect for the restraint of the law and no real understanding of constitutional checks and balances.

The character of the President's political leadership has aroused profound distrust that goes far beyond the sentiments normally engendered by party politics or philosophical disagreements over public policy. There is now substantial evidence that the President's men, in their effort to build up political power for President and party, have engaged in a lawless and corrupt style of politics and political financing.

It is unnecessary to review the many ramifications of the Watergate scandal. One need only note that for the first time in 50 years, two Cabinet members — John N. Mitchell, the former Attorney-General and the former campaign manager, and Maurice Stans, former Secretary of Commerce and former chief political fund-raiser — have been indicted. John W. Dean III, formerly the President's legal counsel; Jeb Stuart Magruder, formerly his deputy campaign manager, and Frederick Larue, formerly one of his White House assistants, have pleaded guilty to obstruction of justice. John D. Ehrlichman, formerly the President's chief domestic adviser, and two lesser White House aides have been indicted on other charges. H.R. Haldeman, another of the President's closest assistants, has been forced to resign. Still others formerly in high office in the Nixon Administration have publicly conceded that they committed perjury, destroyed evidence, obstructed justice, or committed other crimes but have not yet been indicted. Could these men have so acted without the President's knowledge?

In addition to the Vesco case in which Mr. Mitchell and Mr. Stans have been indicted, there is documentary evidence that:

The milk producers promised the Administration $2-million in campaign money while seeking the favorable rulings that they obtained with regard to milk prices and import quotas on foreign milk products;

ITT offered $400,000 to defray the cost of the 1972 Republican National Convention while the White House was actively intervening — despite denials subsequently shown to be false — to force the Justice Department to settle an antitrust suit on terms acceptable to ITT;

Howard Hughes transmitted $100,000 in cash to C.G. Rebozo, the President's closest friend, while seeking favourable antitrust rulings from the Government.

Vice-President Agnew is a case apart. According to the Justice Department, bribes had been paid to him not only when he was an official in Maryland but throughout his first term as Vice-President. This is the man whom Mr. Nixon twice chose as his highest associate in Government.

President Nixon's personal leadership has served to increase rather than relieve the gathering doubts about his fitness to remain in office. Mr. Nixon has inflicted upon the public for 14 months a bewildering series of complicated and evasive explanations of his conduct in the Watergate scandals. His firing of Archibald Cox, his acceptance of Attorney-General Richardson's resignation, and his abolition of the office of Special Prosecutor served to convince many Americans, once and for all, that their President was determined not to have a thorough and independent inquiry into the charges against him and his associates.

The President's truly astonishing conduct with regard to the Watergate tapes has aroused even deeper uneasiness. First, Mr. Nixon seemed about to provoke a constitutional crisis by refusing to obey a confirmed court order that he turn over nine tapes to Judge Sirica for inspection. Then he abruptly reversed himself and announced that the tapes would be made available. And now he has informed the court through his attorney that two of the tapes — probably the two most critically important — never existed.

Other personal actions by Mr. Nixon have fed public distrust. It is dismaying to millions of ordinary taxpayers to learn that their President, during part of his first term in office, paid almost no Federal income tax because he claimed a huge and legally dubious deduction. It offends the instinctive sense of fairness of ordinary citizens when it is finally disclosed that their President has surreptitiously burdened the public treasury with major expenditures affecting his two private estates quite apart from the two provided by the Government. It offends the sense of propriety of most citizens that their President should live beyond his means by borrowing heavily from two millionaire friends. . . . In the almost daily rush of revelations, it is not easy for the numbed citizen to keep in mind the full enormity of Watergate. Despite ample instances of past government corruption, nothing can be found in U.S. history even remotely approaching the skein of events that the word Watergate no longer defines or contains. . . .[2]

Few of the allegations against Nixon were new to the American political scene. The shocking thing is that one man's administration should be the focal point of so many abuses at one time. How thoroughly the Nixon administration exposed the American political process for what it is is suggested by a review of a few of the major commissions and omissions with which it has been associated. Fund raising for election purposes is a good place to start. Although campaign funding has doubtless always been a source of one degree of corruption or another in the U.S., the Nixon entourage brought more of this corruption to the surface by the brazen manner in which it used various pressures to solicit funds, whether in an illegal or legal form. Two articles on this subject are worth citing. The first from The Christian Science Monitor, indicates the kind of tactics which were apparently regularly employed to extract large donations from America's leading corporations:

The Senate Watergate committee is disclosing what looks like a pattern of secret $100,000 contributions by big corporations to the Committee for the re-election of the President in the campaign of 1972.

Some corporations also made lesser contributions to Democratic candidates in the primaries. Except for the Watergate inquiry, these donations would not have been disclosed.

Companies so far that have pleaded guilty are American Airlines, Braniff Airways, Goodyear Tire & Rubber Company, Gulf Oil Corporation, and Ashland Oil Company. Corporations are given a nominal fine of $5,000, with individual fines of $1,000 on the top executive. Phillips Petroleum Corporation executives have acknowledged illegal contributions but have not appeared in court.

Put on the stand under oath, corporate executives used expressions like "extortion," "blacklist," and "no option" for the contributions. They went along under pressure, they implied. They "laundered" gifts by paying them in $100 bills, or having them contributed by corporate subsidiaries outside the country.

Republicans in 1972 raised the largest presidential campaign fund in history, amounting to over $40 million. Subsequently some corporate donations have been returned, witnesses said.

Contributions to Democrats were relatively modest. Claude C. Wild Jr., vice-president for government affairs for Gulf, said that $10,000 went to Sen. Henry M. Jackson (D) of Washington and $15,000 to Rep. Wilbur D. Mills (D) of Arkansas in their primary campaigns.

[2] Editorial, The New York Times, November 5, 1973 © 1973 by The New York Times Company. Reprinted by permission.

Maurice H. Stans, while Secretary of Commerce, solicited the donations, witnesses said. Mr. Stans subsequently became chairman of the Nixon finance committee.

Did such methods border on "extortion"? Sen. Sam J. Ervin (D) of North Carolina, committee chairman, wanted to know. Orin E. Atkins, chairman of the Ashland Oil Corporation, replied "very much so."

Committee counsel asked why gifts were made. Mr. Wild, like Mr. Atkins, said they felt they had no option. The multibillion-dollar Gulf Company did not want to "be on a blacklist, low man on the totem pole" if it did not respond. Mr. Wild implied that the donation would mean he would get somebody in the administration "to answer my telephone calls once in a while." Latest witnesses are George Spater of American Airlines and Russell D. Young of Goodyear Tire.

Mr. Atkins agreed that Mr. Stans, as Commerce Secretary, did not directly ask for corporate funds as a contribution, which are forbidden by law. But he said that an amount of $100,000 could not come from an individual within the corporation and Mr. Stans must have known it.

The Gulf and Ashland Oil companies laundered their contributions in different ways.

According to Mr. Wild for Gulf, a member of the Nixon finance staff, Lee Nunn, called him twice for a $100,000 contribution and "the implication was that this was a quota expected from large corporations." Mr. Wild got the money to Mr. Nunn in two separate donations of $50,000 each through a Gulf subsidiary, Bahamas Exploration, Ltd. The cash appeared in the bookkeeping account as "miscellaneous expense." The Watergate investigation brought it to light.

Mr. Atkins used a Swiss bank, funneling funds to the Republicans from an Ashland subsidiary in Gabon. The $100,000 was given in the form of $100 bills and entered on the books as a "capital expense." Clyde Webb, vice-president of Ashland, delivered the money to Mr. Stans, who by that time had moved over to the Nixon finance committee, said Mr. Atkins. "He [Mr. Webb] dumped it in his desk drawer," witness testified.[3]

That in some mysterious fashion government concessions are made in return for corporate financial generosity is not surprising. Sometimes, however, the links are so badly hidden from public view that their blatancy is sickening.

The International Telephone and Telegraph Corp. (ITT) had a problem: The U.S. government had filed three anti-trust suits against this largest of the multi-national conglomerates and was aggressively trying to limit its growth.

ITT took action: Well-orchestrated lobbying with top Nixon administration officials and a timely pledge, perhaps for as much as $400,000, toward the costs of the 1972 Republican national convention.

ITT got results: The government, in a sudden reversal, agreed to an out-of-court settlement favorable to the company after President Richard Nixon personally ordered his justice department not to appeal one of the anti-trust cases to the U.S. Supreme Court.

[3] Richard L. Stroug, "Pattern of Corporate Gifts to Nixon Campaign Emerging", The Christian Science Monitor, November 19, 1973.

The White House now says Nixon later permitted the appeal, but the effect of his order was to delay the appeal, a delay that pleased ITT very much.

For seven weeks in March and April, 1972, the Senate judiciary committee explored the details of the government's settlement with ITT in 1971, but there was a lot of information that it did not uncover. All during the summer and fall of this year, however, more pieces of the puzzle have been put in place, enlarging but not completing the picture.

Two weeks ago, Vice-President Gerald Ford said that papers proving the president innocent of wrong-doing in the case would be released "prior to the first of the year."

However, information obtained from congressional hearings, from ITT and White House documents and from other sources shows that the White House was more actively involved in the case than had been known previously, and that some officials may have lied under oath to hide that involvement. Specifically:

— Nixon, who was not known to have played any role in the case, intervened at a crucial point by telephoning the man in charge — deputy attorney-general at the time, Richard Kleindienst — and bluntly ordered him not to permit an appeal. Kleindienst threatened to resign if he could not press the appeal.

— The attorney-general at the time, John Mitchell, may have perjured himself when he said under oath that he had never discussed the ITT case with Nixon and had not learned of ITT's convention pledge until after the out-of-court settlement had been reached.

A memo written in March, 1972, by a White House aide at the time, Charles Colson, warned other aides that there were documents contradicting Mitchell's testimony before the Senate judiciary committee and that they "directly involve the president."

— Kleindienst may have perjured himself when he told the judiciary committee under oath that he had never discussed the ITT case with Nixon or anyone else at the White House except in the most casual way.

— The White House may have been involved in moves to hinder investigations of the scandal. Colson noted in his memo that one document in ITT files "suggests that Kleindienst is the key man to pressure (Richard) McLaren (the head of the justice department's anti-trust division), implying that the vice-president would implement this action." He added: "We believe that all copies of this have been destroyed."

Colson was wrong. All the copies had not been destroyed, and one of them was uncovered this summer with a memo written directly to former vice-president Spiro Agnew that suggested that Agnew would help ITT undercut McLaren's anti-trust efforts.

Memos from ITT files have also been made public in recent months showing that as far back as mid-1970, key ITT officials were meeting with Mitchell, Agnew, Colson and others, including Nixon's former domestic affairs adviser, John Ehrlichman, trying to persuade them that McLaren's anti-trust policies bordered "on the fanatic," were contrary to the president's, and should be reversed.

When McLaren took over the anti-trust division in 1969, his views on conglomerate mergers were well known. He felt that some conglomerates were too big and too powerful, and that they posed the same threats to free competition as monopolies did.

His chief target was ITT, the eighth largest company based in the United States and the largest of the multi-national conglomerates. ITT had nearly 400,000 employees, operated in 67 countries and manufactured products ranging from satellite communications equipment to bread.

By April, 1971, three of the division's four anti-trust suits involved ITT.

The suits were intended to force ITT to get rid of three recently acquired companies: The Hartford Fire Insurance Corp., the country's fourth largest writer of property and liability insurance, the Canteen Corp., one of the country's largest distributors of vending machines, and the Grinnell Corp., the largest producer of fire-alarm systems.

The Hartford case had not yet gone to trial. The Canteen case has been tried, but the judge has not yet handed down his decision. The Grinnell case had been won by ITT, but the anti-trust division was set to appeal it to the Supreme Court.

The division has not lost a merger case in the Supreme Court in more than 20 years; and ITT lawyers conceded that there was a "high probability" that, if the Grinnell case was appealed, the government would win.

That was the situation on April 8, 1971, when ITT president Harold Geneen summoned his lawyers to a meeting in New York city to plan ways of stopping the anti-trust suits. He set in motion a major lobbying effort among high-level administration officials designed to force McLaren to relax his opposition to conglomerate mergers.

On April 16, top company officials descended on Washington, meeting with such ranking administration officials as John Connally, then the treasury secretary, and Peter Peterson, then a White House adviser on economic affairs.

Two ITT agents separately contacted the justice department. Both spoke to Kleindienst, neither spoke to McLaren.

On April 19, Nixon phoned Kleindienst and told him not to appeal the Grinnell case. It is not known exactly what prompted the president's call, but it is clear that it came at a crucial point in the case.

As reconstructed from a number of sources, this is the sequence of events:

First, Kleindienst phoned Lawrence Walsh, an ITT lawyer and a personal friend, and gave him the bad news — the justice department probably would go ahead with the appeal.

Then Ehrlichman phoned Kleindienst and told him that Nixon wanted him to stop the appeal. Kleindienst has said that he replied that he could not agree because the decision to appeal the case had already been made. Ehrlichman is reported to have snapped: "Oh, we'll see about that."

Minutes later, the president called. According to Kleindienst, he said: "Listen, you son of a bitch, don't you understand the English language? Don't appeal the goddamn case, and that's all there is to it." Another version has Nixon saying much the same thing but using considerably stronger language than "son of a bitch."

Kleindienst then summoned McLaren and Erwin Griswold, then the solicitor-general, and asked if they could delay the appeal. Griswold said it was nine days past the deadline for requesting delays but that he probably could do it.

Kleindienst then phoned Walsh and told him the good news — the appeal would be delayed for a month.

Kleindienst and the White House maintain that the delay was insignificant because the case eventually was appealed but settled before coming to trial.

The White House explanation is that Nixon did not know all the facts of the case when he called Kleindienst. After they were explained to him, a White House spokesman said, Nixon reversed himself and permitted the appeal.

ITT officials, however, considered the delay very significant. In the next few weeks, the thrust of the justice department effort in the Grinnell case turned from prosecution to negotiation, and by the time the appeal was filed, ITT was well on its way to obtaining a settlement that would allow it to keep its most valuable possession, the Hartford company with its $2 billion in assets.

On July 31, 1971, the out-of-court settlement was announced. ITT was forced to rid itself of the Grinnell Corp., the Canteen Corp. and the Avis Corp. within three years, but it was allowed to keep Hartford, which had about three times the earnings of the other companies combined in 1971.

Although Kleindienst and the White House spokesman say Nixon did not influence the outcome of the case, it is clear that the direction of the justice department's prosecution of the case changed significantly at about the time of the president's phone call.

During the secret negotiations leading to the out-of-court settlement, ITT officials dumped large blocks of their personal ITT stock. The significance is the stock, that had sold for between $78 and $83 a share during the negotiations, immediately dropped to $69 a share after the settlement was announced.

Ruben Robertson, a lawyer for consumer advocate Ralph Nader, estimates that the insiders avoided losses of nearly $1 million by selling to an unsuspecting public during that time.[4]

On a more personal plane, Nixon and his accounting and legal advisors were working on his own private financial fortunes. Although a modicum of justice has eventually caught up with him on this front, he must be given credit for trying just about everything in the tax evasion game before being called to account:

— It's called Form 1040-U.S. individual income tax return — and no matter how the figures come out by the April 15 deadline date they hurt.

As millions of Americans sit down to fill out their Form 1040s this week, wondering if they'll get away with writing off the car for business use, they are reading that President Richard Nixon took the tax man for at least a cool $300,000.

That, in effect, will be the message a team of staff experts delivers to a Congressional committee today.

What can a New York truck driver or a California grocer think when they read that in 1970, Nixon paid $783 in taxes on an income of $200,000? Or that in 1971, Nixon's tax bill was only $792, and in 1972 a mere $873?

[4] Anthony Marro, "The ITT Case: How Lobbying and a Little Cash Get Results". Copyright 1973, Newsday, Inc. Reprinted with Permission.

In fact, in four years — from 1969 to 1972 — Nixon paid just $78,650 in federal income taxes on an income of $1,122,264. That's an average of $19,662 a year on an income of $282,556 — or just about what a Kansas city dentist would pay if he was making $67,000 a year.

It didn't take the canny old Arkansas Democrat, Representative Wilbur Mills, long to make the calculations and flatly predict that Nixon's tricky tax returns will force him out of office before November, and never mind about Watergate.

Certainly millions of Americans are sick and tired of Watergate, but equally certain is the fact that they're sick and tired of the annual tax bite.

And now they are going to get a detailed look at Nixon's Form 1040.

Here's what the American taxpayer is likely to hear about Nixon's tax return — considered by some committee staff members as almost a guideline on how to beat the tax man:
• The San Clemente, Calif., real estate deal, considered by critics as a clumsy attempt to beat capital gains taxes.

In 1970 Nixon sold some of the land on his estate to his buddies Charles (Bebe) Rebozo and Robert Abplanalp. It was Abplanalp who lent him the money to buy it in the first place.

It was this $1.2 million deal that Nixon contends left him with no capital gains at all. Later, however, an audit by an accounting firm at Nixon's request reported a capital gain of $117,370. The committee is expected to find the gain considerably higher.
• The vice-presidential papers deal.

The reason for Nixon's tiny tax payments in his early years in the White House was largely based on $576,000 in deductions he claimed against his income by donating these papers to the National Archives.

However, Nixon's former tax lawyer Frank DeMarco has admitted that he drew up and back-dated a deed transferring the papers almost a year after a law went into effect prohibiting such tax write-offs.

DeMarco claims the deed was actually a copy of one that had been prepared before the cut-off date, but subsequently lost. The committee is expected to disallow the write-off completely.
• Nixon's business expense claims, which according to committee sources are approaching the bizarre.

Nixon apparently went so far as to claim for the cost of flowers sent to funerals and in one item deducted $244 for California gasoline tax payments in fuel used in a truck at the San Clemente estate.

At that rate, the committee staff has concluded, the truck would have had to be driven 47,000 miles around the 28-acre property.

But there's more. Nixon didn't pay any California state income tax, citing his residence in Washington — a technical loophole that's legitimate but considered so politically inadvisable that not one of California's 26 congressmen dared take advantage of it.[5]

Not content with his efforts at tax avoidance, Nixon also derived full advantage from the "executive privileges" which he took to be part of his high office. This abuse is brought out most forcefully in the following article which compares Nixon's life style with that of Ralph Nader:

— All comparisons of Richard Nixon with other presidents are in-

[5] Bruce Garvey, "Nixon's Tax Trickery Shows Americans How to Finish Ahead", King Features, April 2, 1974.

vidious, but people insist on making them. It is pointed out, for instance, that while Thomas Jefferson went $20,000 in debt occupying the office that President Truthful now honors, Nixon has spent his time in the White House becoming a millionaire.

A more immediately instructive comparison might be drawn, however, between our presidential tax loopholer's manner of living off the public purse and Ralph Nader, a man whom a small minority of us would like to see in Nixon's job. The exchange would be like putting a tourniquet on the U.S. Treasury.

Fortune magazine (The Imperial Life Style of the U.S. President, by Dan Cordtz, in the October issue) says that the White House staff under Nixon has probably tripled since the Johnson years. The adverb "probably" must be used since the actual White House budget is a more closely kept secret than the details of national security items.

If it came from an anti-administration source I wouldn't believe it, but Fortune says: "One aide walks beside the president to tell him in advance whether to turn left or right at a corner or warn of the number of steps in a staircase. The ranks of such courtiers have increased at an unprecedented rate during the Nixon administration."

The magazine has counted 75 maids, butlers, cooks, and caretakers attending Mr. N in addition to five Boeing 707s (up two from Johnson), 16 specially soundproofed helicopters, and a fleet of 11 Lockheed Jetstars needed to transport him and the rest of the czar's entourage around.

"Ladybird Johnson rode the Eastern Airline shuttle on shopping trips to New York," Fortune informs us, "but the Nixon family, including his daughters and sons-in-law, habitually travel by government plane. Even Ron Zeigler has been known to use an official helicopter to fly from San Clemente to a party in Hollywood . . ., an official car (transports) Mr. Nixon's Irish setter, King Timahoe, to Camp David in solitary grandeur."

Compare this to Nader, who lives in an $80-a-month furnished room and has no servants, no cars and no airplane. His gross annual living expenses are about $5,000 a year, or roughly what it costs the public to support Nixon for a morning.

Nader operates out of a small pedestrian office. Nixon has no fewer than nine different offices, including one set up at his friend Robert Abplanalp's house, and two each at San Clemente and Camp David. Why a man needs two private offices in the same place has yet to be explained.

Speaking of Camp David, Fortune, which has grown accustomed to the luxurious life of the world's most powerful executives, reports in tones almost shocked that "since Nixon became president, several of the lodges (at Camp David) have been rebuilt and others redecorated. A heated free-form swimming pool has been installed to go with the existing bowling alley, archery and skeet ranges, pool table, tennis courts, pitch-and-putt golf green, and nature trails."

All of this is government-owned and maintained at public expense and you would like to think it would be enough, but he has to have four houses, counting San Clemente, which even Fortune says was bought through a "sweetheart loan."

No wonder he has no time to run the country. Just getting to and using all those facilities must be an all-consuming operation. Nader, on the other hand, puts in an 18- to 20-hour day, or a 126-hour working week, which means if the U.S. elected him president he'd be too busy to collect houses. Anyway, he's too stingy.

Thomas Whiteside, in a New York magazine profile, says: "To save stamps and stationery, Nader states in his ads that the money sent in by contributors won't be acknowledged." If only Nixon had confined himself to written thank-yous with his illegal oil contributors.

Moving about with a manilla folder and nobody to tell him when to turn right or left, Nader is given at least partial credit for a list of legislation that goes far beyond automobiles, among which are the Natural Gas Pipeline Safety Act, the Radiation Control Act, the Wholesome Meat Act, the Wholesome Poultry Products Act, the Occupational Safety and Health Act, and on and on, and all done without the service of a single butler.

It is crazy. People say that America is too old and too crooked to take an honest president, but a Nader inauguration would be a gas. Can't you see him, after getting himself inaugurated, going over to the rooming house and packing his other suit in his beat-up bag, and then walking over to the White House and telling the guard at the gate that Nixon's fanfare blowers can go home because he's just signed the lease.[6]

Far more serious than Nixon's blatant resort to questionable sources of campaign funding and his personal financial finagling was his administration's attempted, if not successful, subversion of critical agencies of government long felt to be exempt from political intrigues. Aside from the abuse of the CIA (Central Intelligence Agency) and FBI (Federal Bureau of Investigation), there was the threat to the independence and integrity of the IRS (Internal Revenue Service). This has led to widespread demands for a thorough investigation of the purported misuse of the latter:

The American people now must be given a thorough congressional investigation of the Internal Revenue Service. This is said with reluctance, because the IRS has given an impression of integrity and independence that appeared to be well founded. Indeed, White House memos publicly presented to the Senate Watergate committee expressed frustration over attempts to make the IRS "politically responsive" — as Nixon aides asserted it had been under Democratic administrations.

Now, however, the gravest doubts have been cast on IRS relations with the White House. Attorney General Saxbe has just told reporters the Justice Department may investigage the IRS — which, if done without fear or favor, might help Justice's Watergate-damaged reputation.

The doubts have come to a crescendo in the combination of the IRS treatment of Mr. Nixon's taxes and the evidence of alleged politicizing of the IRS offered by Republican Senator Weicker at Senate hearings. An IRS spokesman has reportedly admitted a deficiency in previous examination of Mr. Nixon's tax returns, which failed to uncover the enormous underpayments he is now required to make up. But apparently those responsible have not been disciplined. Neither the IRS nor the White House, despite Mr. Nixon's waiver of privacy on his taxes, will answer the question of whether a penalty for negligence is included in the amount he has agreed to pay.

What needs to be disclosed is whether the President was and continues to be treated with a forbearance or outright favoritism not granted to his fellow taxpayers. This should be examined by the House impeachment inquiry in any event.

6 Nicholas van Hoffman, "The Prince and the Pauper — Washington D.C. — Style", King Features, January 3, 1974.

The other side of the coin is the question of whether the IRS was manipulated by the White House in regard to taxpayers other than the President. Here Senator Weicker's evidence raises an image of White House access to tax records of the favored and unfavored that suggests the Nixon administration was more successful in politicizing efforts than the earlier Watergate committee public testimony suggested. Were White House aides, in fact, effective in memoed efforts asserting that the IRS head "should make personnel changes to make IRS responsive to the President" and "should be told that discreet political action and investigation are a firm requirement and responsibility on his part"?

Such questions are part of the whole matter of how far the Nixon administration succeeded in aides' stated aims of using its incumbency for political purposes — and thus preparing the ground for Watergate. The resulting impetus for reform must be sustained however numbing the ordeal of disclosure becomes.[7]

The cumulative effort of one sordid disclosure after another led the House of Representatives to commence an impeachment inquiry which eventually decided to zero in on five areas:

The House Judiciary Committee was told by its staff yesterday that the panel's impeachment investigation has been narrowed to focus only on the most serious charges of wrongdoing against President Richard Nixon.

Of 56 original allegations against Mr. Nixon, the staff, headed by former assistant attorney-general John Doar, reported that nearly a score of those charges have been dropped and that the final phase of the six-month-old probe will concentrate on the five main areas:
— The possible involvement by the President in the alleged coverup of the White House role in the 1972 burglary and bugging of the Democratic National Committee's Watergate headquarters.
— Possible fraud in the preparation of Mr. Nixon's federal income tax returns during his first term in office.
— Allegations that in return for a pledge of campaign contributions the President ordered diary import quotas to be lowered and price support levels to be raised.
— Allegations that an anti-trust suit against International Telephone and Telegraph Corp. was settled in return for a pledge of financial help toward the cost of conducting the 1972 Republican national convention and that the President had knowledge that perjury about the matter may have been committed by several of his key aides.
— Allegations concerning the activities of the White House special investigative unit, the so-called Plumbers, including the burglary at the office of Dr. Lewis Fielding, former psychiatrist of Daniel Ellsberg.[8]

While the House Judiciary Committee was proceeding with its impeachment inquiry, the Senate Watergate Committee released its final report, which together with the other evidence and findings it had already filed, provided more than ample grounds for removing Nixon from office. The Toronto Star reported:

[7] "Investigating the IRS", The Christian Science Monitor, April 10, 1974.
[8] "Impeachment Inquiry Is to Focus on Five Areas", The Globe and Mail, Toronto, April 1, 1974. © 1974 by The New York Times Company. Reprinted by permission.

The Senate Watergate committee released its final report Saturday night, saying that the Watergate scandal was characterized by corruption, fraud and abuse of power.

The three-volume report, based mainly on last summer's televised hearings, concludes that Watergate, described as "one of America's most tragic happenings," developed because some in the White House viewed the president's power as almost without limit.

Although the committee said it drew no conclusions as to guilt or innocence because of impending trials and the presidential impeachment proceedings, the report's 2,216 pages were laced with rebukes for the White House and members of President Richard Nixon's re-election campaign.

The committee, presided over by Chairman Sam Ervin, made a sweeping series of legislative recommendations to try to ensure there will be no repetition of what it called the most serious scandal in U.S. history. . . .

On the cover-up, the report said that the president and his aides never really gave serious consideration to making the facts public, even after former White House counsel John Dean warned Nixon there was a "cancer on the presidency."

It said the president did not follow up warnings about the cover-up as early as July 6, 1972 — only three weeks after the burglary at the Democratic national headquarters.

The report gave some new details of White House efforts to use government agencies to keep the president in power, of plans to punish White House enemies and reward political friends and of campaign dirty tricks.

It also disclosed the results of investigations into the "sale" of ambassadorships and illegal use of campaign funds.

"This characterization of Watergate is based not merely on the fact that the Democratic national committee headquarters at the Watergate was burglarized in the early-morning hours of June 17, 1972," the report said.

"Rather, it is also an appraisal of the events that led to the burglary and its sordid aftermath, an aftermath characterized by corruption, fraud and abuse of official power."

It said the Watergate affair reflected an alarming indifference to concepts of morality and public trust.

"Indeed," the report said, "the conduct of many Watergate participants seems grounded in the belief that the ends justified the means, that laws could be flaunted to maintain the present administration in office.

"Unfortunately, the attitude that the law can be bent where expediency dictates was not confined to a few government and campaign officials."

The report said this trend extended to some of the most prominent U.S. corporations which gave illegally to the 1972 Nixon campaign from their corporate coffers. . . .

The committee said evidence showed that from the earliest days of the administration "the power of the president was viewed by some in the White House as almost without limit."

"Especially when national or internal security was invoked," it said, "even criminal laws were considered subordinate to presidential decision or strategy."

If the report declined to take sides, some of the committee members did not.

North Carolina Democrat Ervin, while saying he is not attempting to judge whether Nixon is impeachable, wrote a vivid indictment of the conduct of the White House during the Watergate period and made it clear he believes the president must take responsibility.

Citing the evidence of the report, Ervin said the president's men had as their objective the destruction of the integrity of the process by which the president is elected.

Their second objective, he said, was to cover up their own wrongdoing.

Although the final report deleted a conclusion that campaign funds had been used to buy the silence of the original Watergate defendants, Ervin said exactly that happened.

"They made cash payments totalling hundreds of thousands of dollars out of campaign funds in surreptitious ways to the original seven Watergate defendants as 'hush money' to buy their silence and keep them from revealing their knowledge of the identities and activities of the officers and employees of the Nixon reelection committees and the White House aides who had participated in Watergate" Ervin said.[9]

Throughout the process of trying to account for his administration's many criminal activities, Nixon resorted to every tactic in the book. Delay and evasiveness were the hallmarks of his strategy and they did, if nothing else, serve to postpone the inevitable. Appropriately *The New York Times* characterized the President's response as one of defiance:

The position of the Senate Watergate committee has been left in a cloudy never-never land by the on-again, off-again agreement between the White House and the committee's leaders, Senators Ervin and Baker, concerning the tapes. Whatever promises were made originally by the President and his lawyers were quickly rendered meaningless by a seemingly endless series of devious shifts in subsequent White House interpretations.

The weekend debacle has brought to light for the first time some indication of the multitude of ways in which the President has been seeking to obstruct the inquiry into the Watergate scandals. Mr. Cox disclosed that his efforts to get at the facts were frustrated on a much broader front than the disputed tapes of presidential conversations. Documents of presidential aides were placed beyond his reach by transfer to the shelter of "presidential files." This cover of executive privilege was used after Mr. Nixon had personally assured the American people: "Executive privilege will not be invoked as to any testimony concerning possible criminal conduct in the matters under investigation."

These behind-the-scenes deceptions have now been followed by open defiance of Congress, the courts and the ousted special prosecutor. Using the Federal Bureau of Investigation in the manner of a totalitarian police force, the President directed its agents to swoop down on the special prosecutor's offices and to deny Mr. Cox and his staff access to

[9] "Corruption, Fraud Assailed in Report on Watergate Affair", Toronto *Star*, July 15, 1974. Reuters.

their files or even to their personal papers. One Cox associate, confronted by this gross abuse of police power, commented aptly that "one thinks in a democracy this would not happen."

Commenting on the implications of these tactics, the article continues:

No crisis transcends in seriousness contempt for the law by a President, charged under the Constitution with executive responsibility for insuring enforcement of the law. . . . Chief District Judge John Sirica warned in his decision on the tapes that Mr. Nixon's intransigence would set the White House apart as "a fourth branch of government" and place the President entirely beyond the reach of the law.

The desperation of President Nixon's moves this weekend to block the Watergate investigation makes it plain that neither law nor orderly governmental process now stand as obstacles to the exercise of his will.

The constitutional confrontation, which the courts and the special prosecutor tried so hard to avoid, has been precipitated by a President who considers himself sole judge of the law and who uses the power of his office to purge independence from the executive branch and to supersede the mandate of the courts by arbitrary exercise of his will.

This espousal of absolute rule has thrown the country into a governmental crisis of fearful dimensions.[10]

The Watergate saga dragged on and on and became more degrading and demeaning for the entire political system, for all those involved, and for Nixon himself, a man seemingly so void of anything approaching honesty, integrity or morality that at times he seemed oblivious to it all. To say the least, it was a sad spectacle:

Watergate has made superlatives risky. There has always been worse to come. But few utterances, surely, will be more memorable than President Nixon's advice to his staff, as quoted in the House Judiciary Committee version of the White House transcripts: "I don't give a shit what happens. I want you all to stonewall it, let them plead the Fifth Amendment, cover up or anything else . . ." Mr. Nixon, it may be recalled, was the pious (almost sanctimonious) young vice-presidential candidate who in 1952 voiced a burning concern about the importance of restoring "proper language" to the White House. Still, Mr. Nixon's habit of loading his talk with expletives, to the point of tedium, is the least shocking aspect of this sordid story.

What is shocking, and worse, frightening, is the record of massive, misleading, misguiding, misdirecting manipulation practiced by the man who holds the highest office in the most powerful nation on earth. No Western country in memory has gone through so humiliating a public degradation as the United States has done under President Nixon. Decency would dictate that he resign. But decency does not appear to be in charge at the White House. So the sordid story goes on.[11]

[10] "Defiant Nixon Takes a Reckless Path Towards Absolute Rule", The Globe and Mail, Toronto, October 23, 1973. © 1973 by The New York Times Company. Reprinted by permission.
[11] "The Degrading Catalogue of Watergate", The Globe and Mail, Toronto, July 16, 1974.

There are two sides to Nixon's eventual capitulation — albeit with no real admission of guilt — and his abrupt exit from office. On the one hand it is undoubtedly true that the whole sordid exercise did eventually prove to be what *The Christian Science Monitor* called a "test and triumph" of the American system of government, although a very belated and costly one. Moreover, as the same newspaper pointed out in another editorial, there is much to be learned from the whole Watergate episode:

Certain fallacies and falsities are tending to shape public attitudes toward the Watergate mess. These are dangerous. The final outcome of the tragedy — whether it proves to be just a weakening disaster or actually a healthy surging of national life — depends largely on whether the American people identify and repudiate these falsities. Here are some of them:

1. *That the American system is a failure, rotten to the core, and should be replaced.*

It is not a failure. The very disclosures and pending prosecutions show the essential soundness of the American political system. The system is working. Under the kinds of autocratic governments most peoples have had throughout history — and a good many political systems today — such disclosure and prosecution would be impossible.

Nobody should demand replacement of this governmental system without a convincing answer to the question: With what?

2. *That corrupt practices are normal to the political process – that Watergates have happened under previous administrations.*

It is true that any human political system is a mixture of good and evil elements — and the United States has had its share. But the great achievement of the American system is that governmental processes based on honesty and trust, measured by noble ideals, subject to moral standards which are written into law, and open to scrutiny by the governed — processes in which political leaders are answerable to the governed — are the norm. All this is, historically, a remarkable achievement. It is the basis of a free society. If the opposite — corrupt practices — were to be accepted by the people as the norm for political conduct, a fundamental change in American society would ensue. Demoralization, weakness, and government by conspiracy would result.

3. *That nothing can be done about corruption in government because everybody is doing it.*

Wrong. Much can be done. It's already obvious that the stream of shocking disclosures will make most politicians and government servants more careful in future. But correction by legislation must be insistently demanded, backed, and sustained by public sentiment. Where such sentiment has existed, reform has been proved possible and governmental practices have been cleaned up. It exists nationally today. But it must be channeled and crystallized into action. This is a job for Congress, the media, national leaders, and the people at large. It is urgent now.

4. *That stability and national prosperity do not necessarily depend on a return to better standards.*

They do depend on it just as surely as the future of the Nixon administration depends on it. Our economic and political system is built on trust. Trust requires honesty. It involves the governing of economic and political processes by laws and ethical standards that call for honesty.

Trust and honesty are the only cement that exists for a free society. This fact is not and never will be obsolete.

5. *That exposure of Watergate is enough.*

It is not enough. Reform is necessary. There is need for the media to explore not only the anatomy of wrongdoing but also the prime question of what practical steps the United States can take to pull itself out of the mess and the moral laxness and lassitude that produced it. Americans face an unusual opportunity for progress. Will a people shocked and appalled at the disclosures translate their indignation into corrective action?

6. *That Watergate is a partisan matter.*

It is not. It was produced in part by a prevalent, and impersonal, moral blindness. It may also have been part the result of the pressures on a President and his staff from trying — at one and the same time — to end the Vietnam war, organize a "generation of peace," arrange a detente with both China and Russia, protect the delicate and crucially important SALT talks from failure, and cope with domestic turbulence.

In the atmosphere of an upcoming election, these and other pressures bred bad judgment and grievous overreactions based on fear. These pressures, and this underlying fear, led to a state of mind in which wrong seemed right and the end seemed to justify the means. To say all this is not to excuse anything or anybody. It is simply to stress that in a world of unimaginable complexity and nuclear dangers, the tremendous pressures bearing in on the White House are not just the President's problem — they are everybody's problem and he and those assisting him need our prayers.

7. *That the end justifies the means.*

Not so. This is a central issue of the whole Watergate situation. The administration and the nation are being forced to face up to the implications and consequences of this false and deceptive assumption. Watergate did not happen in a vacuum. There is need to root out corrupt attitudes and practices from government, business, labor, and the relations of individuals to each other.

The end does not justify the means. The sooner the White House, national leaders, business, the media, and the public generally see through this self-defeating fallacy — and resolve to act accordingly in private and public affairs — the sooner American society will return to sanity and stability.[12]

On the other hand, regardless of the personal outcome for Nixon himself, it is still highly questionable whether the real lessons of Watergate will be learned:

The danger of post-Watergate political reform is not that it will go too far, but that it will pull up too short.

Have no doubt about it, there are members of Congress who want to substitute the appearance of reform for its substance. They want to look like all-the-way reformers while acting like halfway reformers.

A very visible and dismaying example of this is the recent action of the House Administration Committee, which has just completed its redraft of the strong measure enacted by the Senate to take money corruption out of federal elections.

[12] "Watergate: Fact vs. Fantasy", *The Christian Science Monitor*, August 15, 1973.

After long resistance the committee finally accepted that section of the Senate bill which would provide a mix of private and public financing of presidential primaries, national conventions, and presidential elections. It didn't dare stand out too totally against the voter demand.

This satisfied the wish of the committee majority for something which looked like reform but simultaneously it inserted provisions in the House bill which took care of its wish for nonreform.

And how did they do it? They provided feeble enforcement.

After adopting some of the stronger provisions of the Senate bill, they pulled its teeth. They did this by putting enforcement in the hands of officials who take their orders and hold their jobs subject to the will of those who could benefit by nonenforcement; namely, the clerk of the House, the secretary of the Senate, and the comptroller general (who is an agent of Congress) plus four members of Congress.

And even that wasn't enough to satisfy the halfway reformers. They carried halfway reformism still further. They not only put enforcement in the hands of their own agents, they retained for themselves a continuous veto power over the way they do their job.

In the near future the whole House will vote on whether it will stomach this kind of thing.

I would put some of the Ervin committee recommendations on how to prevent future Watergates in the same category of pretty good but not good enough.

On balance it seems to me the committee has produced welcome and valuable recommendations but they don't go far enough.

Take its central proposal for a permanent office of public attorney to investigate and prosecute cases within the executive branch where there is a real or apparent conflict; that is, those cases which the executive might prefer not to investigate.

The committee makes a good case for doing this. Teapot Dome and Watergate are sufficient reason. But the committee makes no case at all for giving the public prosecutor jurisdiction over cases within the executive branch and denying it jurisdiction over cases within the legislative and judicial branches.

Why limit the jurisdiction of the public attorney to only one branch of government? Is there any good reason why Congress should exclude itself from the same scrutiny which it would apply to the executive?

Surely the conflicts of interest and the abuses over which the public attorney could well have jurisdiction are not all within the executive branch. There are abuses, illegal ethical practices and conflicts of interest by congressmen. Bribes through the device of big political donations get into the hands of congressional candidates as well as presidential candidates. Illegal "dirty tricks" are perpetrated in congressional campaigns as well as in presidential campaigns.

Since the Ervin committee deems it sound — and with good reason — to give the public attorney jurisdiction to handle criminal cases affecting the personnel of part of the federal government, why isn't it equally sound to give it jurisdiction over cases affecting all federal personnel?

One of the reasons for creating a public attorney is that this very action would begin to help restore public confidence in the executive branch. But why not do the same thing to help restore public confidence in the Congress, which is a little less esteemed than the President, and the judiciary.

Shouldn't the three coequal branches of government — executive, congressional, and judicial — be treated equally and put on the same scales of justice?

Congressmen are constantly intervening with the regulatory agencies. Shouldn't the public attorney be looking over their shoulders as well as over the shoulders of the executive?

Why this omission? Could it be that Congress likes to reform everybody but itself?[13]

CANADA'S WATERGATES

As has already been indicated, Canadians tend to pride themselves on being a cut above their American neighbours when it comes to political morality. Canada has not experienced anything quite like a Watergate and all that that episode has come to epitomize, but it does not follow that the country has a great deal to be proud of in terms of its own standards of public conduct. Although some critical aspects of Canadian life, such as the judiciary, have been more free from political intrigues than their American counterparts, others are just as susceptible to abuse, if not more so.

That Watergate-like developments are not inconceivable in Canada has been acknowledged in a number of quarters. Not unnaturally, the press in Canada has commented often on its need to remain as vigilant as its American counterpart proved in unearthing political scandals. The following article from *The Globe and Mail* considers this question and calls the problem:

... a premise that is very much in vogue in Canada at the moment. This is the view that the Canadian parliamentary system makes it impossible for a Watergate to happen in this country.

This argument is probably sound, if it means that a Canadian head of government would be quickly toppled from office by a public scandal of comparable proportions to Watergate. Dependent on the support of Parliament or Legislature, he has none of the defences that shore up an independently elected president when he is under attack by a large segment of his own party as well as the opposition.

But the difference between parliamentary and presidential systems applies only to what may happen after a scandal has reached, and aroused, public attention. It applies only to the differing abilities of the two types of leader to hang tough in the face of informed and angry public opinion.

What appears to be forgotten by those who say it can't happen here is that the bugging of the Democratic National Committee headquarters was not intended to reach, let alone arouse, public opinion. Neither was the cover-up that followed it. But for the digging of two unusually persistent junior reporters with the Washington Post and an unusually determined judge, the name "Watergate" would still mean nothing more than an innocuous Washington hotel complex.

Is there anything in the Canadian character, any innate incorruptibility in our politicians, to suggest that an equally vigilant press is unneeded here? The record over the years of scandals involving ministers of the

[13] Roscoe Drummond, "The Halfway Reformers", *The Christian Science Monitor*, July 24, 1974.

91

Crown and other elected political figures in this country offers no such assurance.

Having a system that makes it easier to remove a government leader once a scandal becomes public knowledge does not relieve Canadians, any more than Americans, of the need for press vigilance that will make citizens aware of how public figures and institutions are performing.[14]

In July, 1973, *Maclean's* warned of some of the safeguards which remain to be built into the Canadian system in order to avoid a Watergate on this side of the border:

All during the Watergate outpourings, I've been thinking about a story an American newspaperman once told me about Richard Nixon. It was during the late Fifties and he was touring the Middle West as Eisenhower's vice-president, trying to boost the soggy fortunes of obscure Republican congressmen, building up the party credits that would eventually lead him to the presidency. As he landed at Toledo a crowd of banner-waving young Republicans surged up around the aircraft and Nixon responded with one of his characteristic victory waves. Accompanied by a small press contingent, he switched to the DC-3 of a small feeder airline for a side trip to a place called Defiance, Ohio, where he spoke about "all the old-fashioned virtues," raised a little money and shook a lot of hands. It was late at night when his party got back to Toledo and the airport was deserted. Nixon, his face set in a concentrated frown, strode up the ramp of the larger plane that would fly him back to Washington. Then, just before ducking into the cabin, in pure reflex action, he turned around, flashed a smile and waved at the empty tarmac.

The story of that wan gesture at Toledo so long ago has stuck in my mind's eye as an indication of the man's essential emptiness. He has always seemed to me like some self-invented plastic figure, with the smile and the wave sheltering a banality of truly imperial proportions. There was never any new Nixon. From Checkers to Watergate has been a perfectly straight line. Still, the Watergate scandal has revealed a whole new dimension to the Nixon phenomenon. His loyalists (and at this writing the extent to which they were acting on Nixon's orders still isn't clear) seriously distorted the democratic system of the United States to gain the President's reelection. This was corruption of a very special kind.

While we watch it with a mixture of fascination and disgust, there is no way that Canadians can feel the total impact of Watergate. It's not only that Watergate is unlike any political scandal in Canadian history (and we've had our share), what's more important is that the Americans' response to the transgressions of a political leader is completely alien to us. For them, their President is not only a politician and the chief executive officer of the governing administration: he is a symbol, a hero, something close to a deity. To us a Prime Minister is a political leader. We expect a high moral standard from him; but if he should be involved in a scandal, it would be his shame not ours.

That's why under the stress of scandal, the difference in our political system works to Canada's advantage. "Few Canadians," wrote historian Ken McNaught recently, "know how many distinguished Americans have envied the system by which it is possible to hold the head of government

14 "Apprehended Watergates", The *Globe and Mail*, Toronto, February 15, 1974.

responsible for the misdeeds of his administration without at the same time appearing to attack the head of state."

Even so, at least two safeguards are required immediately to make Canadian federal governments less susceptible to the dark side of the temptations that accompany power. The first is a fundamental revamping of an electoral slush fund system that all but forces the parties to take on political debts they must redeem once they reach power. The Barbeau Committee, which reported on electoral practices in 1966, made some urgent and useful recommendations but nothing has been done since — even though Pierre Trudeau called it his "top priority" in the spring of 1968.

The other equally important, reform is to guarantee the long term independence of the Auditor General of Canada. . . . Now, it's a long, long way from the $17-million Bonaventure boondoggle to the uglinesses of the American scandals. But Watergates don't develop overnight. They grow out of small compromises, "forgivable" oversights, bureaucratic arrogance and politicians who forget that they are supposed to represent public and not their own interests. The way to prevent a Watergate North is to bring in the necessary reforms in Canada *before* they are needed.[15]

In terms of a more detailed analysis of the Canadian political scene, it is instructive to start with the country's oldest political chestnut of all, the Senate. Although a second legislative chamber doubtless could play a useful role in the Canadian political system, that potential cannot possibly be realized given the form of Canada's present upper chamber. Years of attempts to abolish or reform that body have now given rise to a great deal of apathy. This is unfortunate as it reflects a degree of futility which must be undercut if serious efforts are to be made to improve the country's political processes.

The most disturbing feature about the Canadian Senate is not its role within the total system or even how ineffectively it pursues that role, but rather the nature of its membership and the basis of its appointment. With few exceptions, Canadian Senators are financial bagmen or former elected representatives for the party in power when they were appointed. Occasional selections are made which run contrary to this general pattern but these can only be perceived as the exceptions which prove the rule.

Worse still, for a body which should be reasonably representative of a cross section of the Canadian public, most Senators retain one or more directorships on the country's leading corporations. A recent article in the Toronto *Star* revealed just how far these links extend and what they imply:

— Eight of the 22 members of the Senate banking committee hold 130 company directorates, according to public records.

There now are 91 men and women in the 102-seat Senate, and 11 vacancies. Together the 91 hold 220 corporate directorships, as recorded in the Parliamentary Guide and two financial directories.

Directorates are concentrated mainly in the Senate banking, trade and commerce committee. The 22 committee members, half of them lawyers, hold 75 per cent of the reported directorates in the Senate — 165 of 220.

Members of the committee are executives or directors of a variety of businesses, including banking, investment and insurance, mining, real estate development and manufacturing and retailing of soft drinks, pulp

15 Peter C. Newman, "The Dark Side of Temptation and What Watergate Means to Us", *Maclean's*, July 1, 1973.

and paper products, aircraft parts, food products and clothing.

This apparent concentration of corporate power in a group charged with examining legislation in such areas as tax reform, corporate control, foreign investment, consumer protection, customs tariffs and anti-dumping laws makes the committee a prime target for those who would limit the extent of Senate business connections or abolish the Upper House altogether.

Heading the list of eight senators who hold 130 directorships is Montreal businessman Louis-Philippe Gelinas, a Liberal from Quebec, with 24.

Liberal Senator John Aird, a Toronto lawyer, has 14 directorships recorded in the Parliamentary Guide and the Financial Post Directory of Directors.

Liberal Senator Paul Desruisseaux, a Montreal businessman, has 18 and Liberal Harry Hays, an Alberta rancher, 11. Liberal Alan Macnaughton, a Montreal barister and former House of Commons speaker, has 20.

Senate Opposition Leader Jacques Flynn, Quebec city lawyer, is listed as having nine and Progressive Conservative Louis-Philippe Beaubien, another Montreal businessman, 16.

Liberal Senator Salter Hayden, a Toronto corporation lawyer and chairman of the banking committee for 19 years, holds a reported 18 directorships.

The fact that senators are appointed on recommendation of the Prime Minister and have no fear of being ousted by voters has brought their business connections under heavy criticism. Until June 2, 1965, senators were appointed for life. Those named after that date must retire at 75.

Gelinas argues it is important to his role as a legislator to hold directorships, to enable him to be "appraised of what's going on in the economy."

"It's been my whole life. . . . I didn't get all these directorships only since I was appointed a senator," he said. "You declare your interests and you don't vote. . . . I've never had any problems."

Flynn said the banking committee votes "only about once a year."

The Senate spent 10 months in 1970 examining proposed income-tax legislation and proposed a raft of amendments, none of which were implemented at the time. During its study, the committee served as a forum for business interests that voiced opposition to the government bill.

Flynn maintains the proposed government legislation aimed at controlling conflict of interest among senators and members of the Commons will do more to reassure the public than change the face of the Senate.

The draft legislation, tabled last July, would bar senators and MPs from sitting on boards of companies that do $1,000 or more contract business annually with the government. It also would force disclosure of all directorships, clamp down on paid lobbying activities and restrict the proportion of a company's stock a parliamentarian could own. Infractions could result in removal from office for MPs and stiff fines for senators.

Disclosure of directorships is voluntary at present. Senators with no directorships listed in the Parliamentary Guide often are shown by other sources, such as the Directory of Directors, to hold several.

Senate Government Leader Paul Martin say: "There's nothing sinister in being a director in itself. . . There's no obligation, no law which says a man can't be a director of a company."

He agreed directorships and business connections are a public matter. "I think the public does have a right to know."

.The public generally mistrusts all politicians, Flynn says, and the proposed legislation will help to polish their tarnished image, "but little else."

"It's the whole social attitude of people who are directors of corporations," argues Stanley Knowles, New Democratic Party House leader in the Commons and long-time proponent of Senate abolition. "Their basic concern is for the success and profitability of business. They just don't have the viewpoint of ordinary Canadians."

On the other hand, the danger of corporate directorships held by members of the Commons can be counterbalanced by the need for MPs to win re-election, he says.[16]

More than once in the past, the loaded nature of the Canadian Senate has led to obvious questions about the validity of the judgment it brings to bear on issues relating to its members' corporate linkages, as this item from the Toronto Star points out:

"Our job was that of a jury," said Senator Salter Hayden, explaining to the press yesterday how he chaired the Senate committee on banking, trade and commerce through its examination of the government White Paper on tax reform.

"We had all the evidence submitted to us by people we regard as creditable; responsible people. We made our best assessment."

Hayden, 74, beneath his wispy white hair and benign, baby-pink smile, is a Toronto corporation lawyer, director of the Bank of Nova Scotia and a score of other companies.

His deputy chairman is Senator Lazarus Phillips, 75 next month, director of the Royal Bank and a dozen other companies, poor boy who worked his way through McGill to become a wealthy Montreal tax lawyer and is today more attached to middle-class business values than any son of riches.

These two tough, clever men spent much of the summer writing the commitee's 20,000 word report, aided by staff expert Arthur Gilmour, a Montreal accountant who seems to suspect that senior civil servants are touched with socialism.

The other 28 members signed the report after deleting some of the more colorful language about the oppression of decent, law-abiding, middle-class Canadians by taxes.

The 30 members of this jury are hardly average Canadians. Among them they hold about 150 company directorships and uncounted millions in shares, bonds and mortgages.

The evidence before them was dominated by business views. As Phillips put it yesterday, they heard ". . . the best possible evidence we could get from people who know their business."

The alphabetical list of briefs and witnesses printed at the back of the report bears him out:

Ad Hoc Committee of British Insurance Companies.

Alcan Aluminum Limited.

Anglo American Corporation Limited.

[16] "Senators' Ties to Firms Listed", Toronto Star, October 18, 1973.

Aquitaine Company of Canada Ltd.
Association of International Business Corporations. . .
And so on through 342 names. Occasionally there is a non-business name, but few.

With such a jury and such evidence, the verdict was never in doubt.

The government's White Paper proposes to make a major change in the tax system under which most of the senators have prospered. It suggests shifting a substantial share of the tax burden from the poor to the middle and upper income groups — the groups from which the senators are drawn and which they represent.

The senators are not, of course, opposed to easing taxes on the 4,000,000 Canadians at the low end of the income scale. Indeed, they say they are enthusiastic about the idea, and heartily endorse the White Paper.

They think it splendid also to cut the rate of income tax on the very richest people, as the White Paper suggests.

But the senators see no need at all to make up the loss of revenue by raising taxes on the middle-income Canadians and by imposing a sharp tax on capital gains. And they can see special reasons for aiding farmers and apple growers — good Canadians, all of them, said Senator Phillips.

Such a pity, added Senator Jacques Flynn, Conservative leader in the Upper House, that they could not, for technical reasons, extend the helping hand to fishermen also.

It all works out happily in the report anyway. The poor get the concessions proposed by the government, the middle class are left to enjoy their hard-earned income; the tax on capital gains is cut back to manageable size.

When the newsmen tried to find out yesterday just how the senators balanced their books, with tax increases on the rich to pay for tax decreases on the poor, they were soon left floundering by Hayden and Phillips.

For one thing, the Senate report uses 1967 figures while the White Paper uses 1969 estimates. For another, the senators say they just could not find out in some instances how the White Paper estimates were prepared, and in other cases they simply disagreed. And finally, said the senators, after all, they were not finance ministers drawing a budget which had to balance.

Tax experts can probably find hours of enjoyment comparing the Senate figures with the White Paper estimates, and rummaging through the mountains of evidence and stocks of analysis which lie behind yesterday's Senate finding.

But no matter, for because the Senate itself is basically incredible, a club of rich men with vested interest in the financial establishment, the report cannot have much influence.

That's a pity, because the senators put a lot of effort, intelligence and experience into their review and they should be worth hearing.

The Senate was intended by the Fathers of Confederation to be a place for sober second thoughts, the House of Parliament in which sensible men of property could exercise a check on the extravagant democrats in the Commons.

If the role is now outdated, don't blame the senators. Blame the prime ministers who appointed them, who have failed to legislate against conflict of interest, who have flinched from real reform.

Blame, for example, Pierre Trudeau, who has allowed 18 vacancies to accumulate in the Senate presumably because he is afraid to disappoint political supporters expecting his patronage.

Eighteen senators drawn from the low end of the income scale might have written quite a different report on tax reform.[17]

That, like his predecessors, the allegedly reform-minded Mr. Trudeau has no serious intentions of doing anything very basic about the imbalanced political monstrosity that is the Canadian Senate, is suggested by some of his most recent appointments, as discussed in this *Globe and Mail* item:

Shrewdly noting that the Liberals had only 70 representatives in the Senate to 17 for the Conservatives, Prime Minister Pierre Trudeau decided that what the Upper House needed to restore a proper balance was three more Liberals. So our new senators are: Raymond Perrault, former Liberal leader in British Columbia; John Godfrey, a Toronto lawyer and party fund-raiser; and Maurice Riel, chairman of Montreal Metropolitan Corporation.

Ah (we hear you ask) but what about their other credentials — the non-political ones? Impeccable, by the standards that tradition has established for the house of sober second incomes, at least as far as Mr. Godfrey and Mr. Riel are concerned. Mr. Perrault seems to have been too interested in practical politics, advertising, and television to have acquired the customary string of directorships, but he walks into the Senate flanked by two who have.

Mr. Godfrey views the world with a perspective that can only come from being a lawyer, a former president of United Accumulative Fund Ltd. and director of a number of companies, including Montreal Trust Co., and Canadain Admiral Corp. Ltd.

Mr. Riel weighs in as a past director of the Bank of Canada and its subsidiary, the Industrial Development Bank, and has served as a director of several corporations, including the Royal Trust Co. and Panarctic Oils Ltd.

There's nothing like a good solid business background to give a senator a grip on the nation's affairs — a point that came up the other day in connection with the Senate's banking committee and the fact that eight of its 22 members could count 130 company directorships among them. Assuming they could remember all of them.

The argument was advanced that a senator might have some difficulty maintaining scrupulous objectivity while studying legislation that might affect the profits of one of more of the companies whose affairs he helped direct. It was, we thought, a point worthy of a considered answer, but the best that Senator Louis-Philippe Gelinas (24 directorships) could manage was that it was important to his role as a legislator to hold directorships. Apparently it enabled him to be "apprised of what's going on in the economy" and he had "never had any problems".

The notion that the important indicators of the economy are all piped through the boardrooms of the country will be of great interest to all those Canadians who have never seen the inside of a boardroom but can tell you of the strange things that are happening to the price of hamburger meat.

Is this idea responsible for the dire straits in which the economy now

[17] Anthony Westell, "Senators Form 'Packed Jury' on White Paper", Toronto *Star*, October 1, 1970.

finds itself — this weighted corporate input, this specialist viewpoint? You wonder, in fact, how they can gather their thoughts for debate with the burden of so many company problems bearing down on their poor shoulders.[18]

Unless we are to abolish the Senate, there must be a drastic overhaul of its composition. As a beginning it would be useful to try to achieve at least a better inter-party balance of political has-beens and fund-raisers. Beyond this it would be useful to secure a number of Senators without pronounced past political leanings. One specific possibility would be to have a Senate made up of 10-year appointees, one third each to be named by the federal government, the provincial governments and a mixture of private groups including farmers, labour, management and the professions. The Senate would then be far more representative than is now the case and might even undertake some meaningful reviews of the legislative efforts of the House of Commons as well as take more initiative of its own. In any event, just about anything would be an improvement on the present situation.

The fact that Canada has put up with the Senate in its present form is only one manifestation, and some would argue a trivial one, of the extent to which crass political opportunism, if not corruption or immorality in the broadest sense of those terms, is taken for granted in the country. Turning to more insidious matters, it is intriguing to note that the financing of at least two major political parties in Canada has traditionally been handled in much the same way as in the United States. Aspects of this situation are brought out in the following 1972 article from the Toronto *Star*:

The paragraph was buried near the end of the report in a recent edition of the Montreal Gazette.

It stated that discussions between Judge Claude Wagner and federal Conservatives relating to Wagner's possible candidacy in the coming election were rumored to have involved a $300,000 guarantee.

The report was unusual in a number of respects.

It gave publicity to allegations of financial negotiations between a party and a prospective candidate before the individual had identified himself with the party and while he held a position which supposedly isolated him from active politics. Usually this type of story reached the public long after the event. And it gained credence by being linked to a statement about Judge Wagner by Opposition Leader Stanfield.

It's quite a difficult decision for such a man to make. "There's a question of security," Stanfield was quoted as saying.

Stanfield would not have made this unusual public admission were he not under the impression that dealings of this kind are so routine today that they surprise no one. And the total absence of reaction to the Gazette report indicates that he was right in this assessment. Despite the fact that the report cited a specific sum of money and a considerable one by any standards no attention was paid to it.

It didn't even rate a routine denial.

The episode illustrated the close relationship between money and political power in our system, the large amounts of money which can be involved and public apathy and scepticism about the system. It also threw light on an aspect of the system which is often ignored by reformers.

Much attention has been paid in recent years to the sources of politi-

18 "Where Background Counts", *The Globe and Mail*, Toronto, October 9, 1973.

cal funds. Official investigations in Canada have revealed to no one's surprise that the two largest political parties receive the bulk of their funds from a relatively small number of corporate donors. The New Democratic Party obviously receives much of its money from organized labor. Every investigation has resulted in proposals for compulsory public disclosure of the sources of party funds.

Where the money comes from, however, is only part of the story. It is just as important to consider where the money goes.

Most discussions of party financing deal with the obvious party expenditures on conventions, travel, publicity and the costly apparatus of modern electioneering. Relatively little is known about the "dark side" of spending by parties, except that it exists and consumes prodigious amounts of money.

The practice of "purchasing" candidates, although it is far from universal, is certainly not limited to isolated figures of major importance. In Montreal recently, a prospective candidate was known to be shopping among the two major parties for the best financial deal before declaring his candidacy. He wanted his annual salary for two years deposited in his account before he would make a move in public.

It would be naive to pretend that political parties have not always tried to take care of their own or that the pay-off cannot assume a variety of forms. But that is no argument for condoning it, particularly when it threatens to become a common and costly feature of the system.

The successful candidate in a leadership or electoral campaign hopes that victory will ensure his independence within his party. This is a dangerous gamble. If the basic discussions between a party and a prospective candidate are in terms of money and the candidate's own security, it probably will be difficult to change this basis at a later date.

Reform can come from two directions.

The most efficient is reform from the top: legislation covering disclosure of political contributions and election spending.

But when a party is in power the system works in its favor, and reform demands an extraordinary degree of political enlightenment. Despite his protestations in 1968, Prime Minister Trudeau has shown no originality in this respect.

This still leaves room for initiative by individual candidates.

In Edmonton West, publisher Mel Hurtig campaigned for the Liberal nomination this month with a pledge that his campaign in the election would be governed by a set of personal voluntary ground rules. These could include complete disclosure of the source of all campaign funds, a limit of $1,000 from any individual or corporate contributor, refusal to accept campaign funds from corporations owned or controlled outside of Canada and a spending limit of 50 cents per elector during the campaign.

Describing Canada's present election laws as "among the least effective of any of the western democracies," Hurtig promised to work for a more open system in Canada allowing much greater participation by Canadians "of all income levels."

He said that "even the present ineffective laws are frequently violated and the average Canadian would be appalled by the manner in which campaign funds are normally obtained.[19]

[19] Peter Desbarats, "The Dark Side of Campaign Financing", Toronto Star, April 15, 1972.

Another 1972 account from the *Star* discussing the Canadian campaign fund situation makes for even more disturbing reading:

Liberal party organizers say they will be knocking on the doors of about 1,200 corporations across Canada in the next few months in the hunt for money they'll spend trying to win the next federal general election for Prime Minister Pierre Trudeau.

Until a few years ago, the Liberals and Progressive Conservatives, by their own testimony, appealed to only about 300 large companies at election time.

This time the governing party's corporate supporters in Ontario alone will hopefully number about 500, said the Liberals' chief federal fundraiser, Toronto lawyer John Godfrey.

But an Ottawa political science professor, Khayyam Paltiel, author of the recent book Political Party Financing in Canada, is sceptical of those figures.

"You could put all the corporate contributors (to both major parties) in one not-very-big room," he told The Star.

While Godfrey and Paltiel may disagree on the numbers involved in the game of election financing, both are advocates of reform of the system.

It is an unhealthy state of affairs in a democracy, Godfrey said, when a government and its major opposition must depend almost solely on the financial support of "one segment of society."

Even in the community of corporate contributors there are those who would like to see drastic changes.

William Osborn Twaits, chairman and chief executive of Imperial Oil Ltd., a company which gives regular financial support to both major parties, said grass-roots funding of political activity is vital if Canadian governments are to become more efficient and more responsive to the wishes of ordinary people.

Yet in recent months Trudeau has sounded far less enthusiastic about the campaign financing reforms he promised four years ago, and his critics are beginning to say the Prime Minister doesn't really want any meaningful changes in the system.

For a century, under that system, the old political parties have depended almost exclusively on large, unidentified corporations to stock their election war chests.

The New Democratic Party — which opens its books to public examination — looks for support to the big trade unions, although leaders insist the party's reliance on organized labor is not as great as critics claim.

While politicians differ on the extent of influence wielded by those who pay the bills, all parties are worried about the soaring cost of elections in an age when campaigning depends so much on image and style.

Paltiel predicted that the three main federal parties will among them spend about $30 million in the election expected this year (compared with an estimated $16 million seven years ago).

The business of raising most of that money, needed to bombard voters with television commercials, newspaper advertisements and leaflets, will be, as it always has been, a highly secret one.

Do the big-money contributors exert any control over political parties and their policies?

The suspicion is always present but a definite answer could be provided only through full knowledge of fund sources and amounts, coupled with an examination of government appointments and policies, said Paltiel.

But this kind of disclosure has been strongly resisted both by the two old parties and their benefactors for decades.

Organizers concede, however, that corporate contributors sometimes seek special access to the decision-makers on Parliament Hill.

They will attempt on occasion to use the office of the fund-raiser — or "bagman" — to lobby against a government decision or get a hearing from a cabinet minister — a channel of communication not available to the ordinary voter.

It is a persistent NDP charge that the old parties preserve the secretive political financing system for the benefit of certain groups with special interests.

"Of course the corporate contributors are getting favors," said Clifford Scotton, federal secretary of the NDP. But his claim cannot be documented, because Canada has no law requiring any kind of financial disclosure by the parties. . . .

When regulations do exist they are often ignored, as the article goes on to discuss:

With each passing election more candidates ignore the statutory requirement to report their expenses. Of 967 contestants in the 1968 election, 700 filed reports. In 1965, 758 observed the law.

Today, said Paltiel, spending declarations are "unreliable, incomplete and partially false."

They're enough, however, to convince some analysts that for all the multi-million-dollar hoopla of the American election circus, Canadians may be paying more on a comparative basis to elect their representatives.

The result is that the parties must turn more and more to the big corporations and the big unions.

That state of affairs, almost anybody in the political organizations will agree, is unhealthy.[20]

The next section of this chapter reveals that some real progress is being made in the field of electoral campaign fund reform in Canada. At the same time, however, the country remains as vulnerable as its southern neighbour to the kind of skullduggery that led to the resignation of the American vice-president, as this article from The Globe and Mail points out:

The events leading to the resignation last week of Spiro Agnew as vice-president of the United States, however agonizing for the individuals concerned and the nation itself, have wider implications that affect all governments, people in public life, contributors to political candidates and those who do business with government.

It is almost a national sport for Canadians to greet each new assault on the conscience of the American republic with an air of unwarranteed smugness — as if it could not happen here. It could — not because of any lack of honesty among politicians, but because our tax laws are as uncertain and our election finance procedures as archaic as those to the south.

Consider the Agnew case, as presented to the court. Putting the best

20 John Doig, "Everyone Wants Election Financing Reform — But It'll Be a While", Toronto Star, April 18, 1972.

face on it, it would appear that he received funds, however solicited, from corporations doing business with government. He takes the position the money was a campaign fund contribution, and thus not his personal income. The Government characterizes it as a payoff for a political favor, making it income that was taxable even though earned through an illegal act.

Mr. Agnew was charged with tax evasion for failing to report and pay tax on the contributions Revenue Department officials regard as payoffs and which he treated as campaign funds. He in effect refused to contest the case, and by so doing tacitly admitted guilt.

To begin with, the tax law ignores the existence of contributions to political parties or candidates. Are they gifts? If so, should they be taxed under the gift tax laws in effect in each province? If they are gifts, who is the beneficiary — the candidate, or his party?

If they are gifts to the party, should the party be treated as a non-profit community service organization? The fact is that generally political parties are unincorporated associations that have no legal existence for tax purposes.

If it is argued that political donations to a candidate should be treated as income to him, then it must be remembered that tax law does not permit a candidate for office to deduct his campaign expenses. Without a doubt, the vast majority of candidates for elective office finish their campaigns in the red.

Because the money they spend in an effort to get elected is money laid out in pursuit of a job that pays taxable income, it can be argued that the campaign expenses should be deductible and campaign contributions taxable.

The problem is equally aggravating from the contributor's point of view. He is exhorted by campaign workers on all sides to do his duty to encourage good people to stand for public office — by supporting them financially. When he contributes to community service organizations the expense is deductible, but a contribution to public service is not deductible.

Then there is the person doing business with government. He is asked to make, or voluntarily makes, a contribution to the governing party or one of its candidates. Is that a payoff, a criminal bribe, even though there are no conditions attached to the gift?

There are many many such questions, and it is conceded that finding answers cannot guarantee that the system will be free from human corruption. But we can and must vastly clarify and improve the rules of the game to restore public confidence.[21]

In various ways, Canadian politicians find it possible to reward their friends and financial backers. The ultimate reward, at least in terms of supposed honour and prestige, is appointment to the Senate. Unfortunately, and worse still, judgeships may also go to the party faithful regardless of the availability of more qualified candidates. More rewarding financially are appointments to operating commissions and regulatory bodies. Some contracts, especially in the field of advertising, are let without tender to political favourites. This article from *The Globe and Mail* suggests that in the latter area, at least, no attempt is even made to try to cover up what is going on.

[21] I.H. Asper, "Agnew Affair Holds Lesson for Canada", *The Globe and Mail*, October 18. 1973.

The growth of provincial and federal advertising accounts brings up the question of the appointment of advertising agencies for government departments on a basis of political patronage.

The Institute of Canadian Advertising, an association of agencies including Canadian-controlled and foreign-controlled members, has no official viewpoint on political advertising or political patronage in the selection of an agency.

Bruce Johnston, president of the institute, questioned the need for an ICA policy on the matter, adding that the institute has no policy with regard to the work done by its members for private industry.

Mr. Johnston's own agency, McKim-Benton and Bowles Ltd. of Toronto, lost the Ontario Department of Health account when a new minister, Thomas Wells, was named to head the department.

Mr. Johnston was quoted (but not identified) in the Task Force on Government Information report on the subject of political patronage in the selection of an agency:

"The practice of awarding assignments on the basis of political patronage is, at best, archaic and, at worst, an open invitation to inefficiency."

The royal commission on government organization concluded seven years ago that it was time for Canada to abandon the patronage system, and it recommended: "Advertising accounts (should) be awarded on the basis of competitive proposals in the manner of other government contracts."

Bryan Vaughan, president of Vickers and Benson Ltd. of Toronto, said that. . . . [he] believes that the federal Government is generally observing the recommendations of the Government Information Task Force in its appointment of advertising agencies, but added that he was not sure that political partronage does not still play a part at the provincial level.

George Sinclair, president of MacLaren Advertising Co. Ltd. of Toronto, said that political patronage is not desirable in the selection of government agencies.

His agency has handled the federal Liberal Party in the past three elections, and he thinks it likely that MacLaren will again be the party's agency for the next election.

The agency has the accounts for the Canadian Government Travel Bureau and the Bank of Canada, but Mr. Sinclair said these appointments were not based on political patronage.

"I dare say there is still some political patronage," said Mr. Sinclair, but he added that if there were none, his agency would have more government accounts rather than fewer.

The subject of political patronage in the selection of agencies is one that merits close examination in light of the fact that governments are becoming — if they are not already — the largest source of advertising revenue in the country.

And that development is likely to continue rather than abate.

The patronage game is one that many major agencies say they would rather not play, but the business is there to be had and the rules of the game are set by government. The agency that wants that government business must be willing to play by the rules.[22]

[22] John Simpson, "Issue of Political Patronage is Intensified as Government Advertising Budgets Increase", *The Globe and Mail*, Toronto, April 19, 1972.

In Quebec, patronage tends to be more open and taken for granted than in most other parts of Canada. Even in that province, however, concern is now being raised about practices that go back many decades.

People here are asking questions about how the former premier, Jean Lesage, who has amassed an impressive string of directorships since he retired from politics in 1970, can act as a legal adviser to the Government on the one hand while doing legal work for companies that do business with the Government on the other.

Unobtrusive listings in the recently released public accounts of the province show that Mr. Lesage's law firm, Lesage, Cote and Lesage of fashionable Grande Allee Est, was paid $22,876.84 by the Department of Agriculture during the last fiscal year for "professional, administrative and other services."

Another listing, this time under the Roads Department expenditures, shows the firm was paid $21,168.60 for the same type of services as rendered to the Agriculture Department during the same year.

That adds up to $44,045.44 for the 1972-73 year.

Mr. Lesage operates a thriving private legal practice, which has included representing several hospital corporations in their dealings with the Government as well as the Montreal developer who tore down the Van Horne mansion last summer after it had been declared a historical site by the Quebec Cultural Properties Commission.

The question put to Premier Robert Bourassa, the man who inherited the Liberal leadership from Mr. Lesage, was whether this arrangement doesn't constitute a conflict of interest.

It did not, Mr. Bourassa said. "Mr. Lesage's role in advising the Government was limited to helping with the editing of certain bills. His private practice certainly doesn't conflict with his work for the Government."

Still, the Liberal administration's failure to institute clearly defined conflict-of-interest regulations has left Mr. Bourassa in the embarrassing position of having to explain away some entries in the public accounts.

One such example is the $252,534.22 in Government contracts from six departments paid to Paragon Business Forms, a company partly owned by the Premier's wife, Andree Bourassa, and his brother-in-law Claude Simard, Quebec's Minister of Tourism and Fish and Game.

That sum was for the year 1972-73. Further research showed that since the Liberals came to power under Mr. Bourassa in April, 1970, Paragon has received $760,000 in Government contracts. The company is controlled by Clauremiand Ltee., a holding company in which both Mrs. Bourassa and Mr. Simard own 23.7 per cent of the outstanding shares.

Again Mr. Bourassa said he saw no conflict of interest in this instance because the transactions between the Government and the company were all "normal and regular." In fact he praised his brother-in-law for having taken the risk of investing in a Quebec company instead of bonds, for instance, which would have turned him a higher profit.

Mr. Simard defended his position by pointing out that he had resigned as Paragon's vice-president in 1970, the year he was first elected to the National Assembly. And since then the company's activities have been directed by a trust company, Trust General du Canada.

'I have had nothing to do with the transactions between the company and the Government," he said.

But Mrs. Bourassa has been more directly involved. She signed the company's 1972-73 annual report and her position as a major shareholder gives her room to influence the company's affairs.

All this is causing some bad moments for Mr. Bourassa and his team, who say they have brought a tightly controlled and cost-trimming fiscal administration to the province after years of Union Nationale slackness.

It's no help in that respect either when an item crops up that shows Mr. Bourassa and his party ran up a $20,000 hotel bill at the London Hilton in early 1973 when the Premier was in England to drum up investments for Quebec.

However, a great deal of that seemingly lavish outlay can be accounted for by the fact that the Premier and his travelling staff of 10 stayed five days in London and played host to a champagne banquet for 500 of the United Kingdom's top financiers.

As far as conflict of interest is concerned, Mr. Bourassa says his staff is trying to deal with the question. He has designated Jean-Claude Rivest, one of his bright young advisers, to draw up a complete report and submit regulations to limit such conflicts.

But it's taking time, he says. "Finding definite formulas and workable rules is a bit of a problem."[23]

In Nova Scotia, another province long famous for its corrupt political practices, dump truck drivers have been forced to consider strike action to put a stop to political patronage affecting them, as reported in *The Globe and Mail*:

Representatives of Nova Scotia truckers say they are prepared to strike to end a system of political patronage that can mean a man's livelihood if he doesn't support the party in power.

"Why on election day should your family's survival depend on what happens in the voting booth?" asks Gerald Mosher, president of the Pictou County Truckers Association.

Mr. Mosher said that getting work with the Department of Highways does not depend on a trucker's ability "but on the politics of the person behind the wheel." He said local party groups, patronage committees, decide which truckers get work.

"Different areas have committees and they are knowledgeable about who voted how. Since the Liberals took over from the Conservatives, some trucks are idle. I believe it was the same with the Tories."

The Liberals have been in power in Nova Scotia since 1970 and Mr. Mosher said in one case "a Tory had road work done in front of his house and was told his truck couldn't be used."

Donald Cameron, Conservative member of the Legislature for Pictou East, said he knows of cases where truckers are not getting even an hour's work with the department because they voted the wrong way. "It's quite a system when we're supposed to be civilized, isn't it? I'm sorry to say it's happened in both parties in the past."

Mr. Mosher said voting the wrong way can mean the difference between a trucker's earning $20,000 a year or $200. He also said that when elections are called favored truckers are expected to make campaign donations.

"On March 18 at 7 p.m. two people came to my door and said they

[23] Hubert Bauch, "The Benefits of Nearness to Power", *The Globe and Mail*, Toronto, April 11, 1974.

had a dirty job to do." That job was to get money for the April 2 provincial election campaign that returned the Liberals to power.

Mr. Mosher said the two men represented the Liberal Party and that if an inquiry into the patronage system is called he will name them, but not before.

Mr. Mosher said he has no politics and that his offer to give money to the Liberals, Conservatives and New Democrats was turned down. He said truckers "will try anything" to end the patronage system.

Gordon MacLean, secretary-treasurer of the Nova Scotia Truckers Association, said he thought if the Government does not agree to do something about it at a meeting with truckers later this month it could lead to a province-wide strike.

"I think every truck in the province will be tied up," said Mr. MacLean, a Conservative supporter.

He said he knew of one case after the 1970 election where two trucks belonging to a Conservative "sat in the yard for 14 months without a job."

He estimated about 2,000 truckers, mostly involved in hauling gravel throughout Nova Scotia, are caught in the patronage squeeze if they hope to get jobs with the Department of Highways.

Lloyd Webster, president of the provincial association, said "probably a lot of things go on that the higher-ups in Halifax don't know about. There's probably other things they know and close their eyes to."

He said local roads superintendents and foremen are told who to hire. "I'm not in a position to say who gives the orders, but it appears to me to be the patronage committees. Politics can make or break a trucker." He believes the patronage system could be broken by turning the hiring procedures over to the association.

"We just about had patronage all out and when the Government turned over (in 1970) they kicked the feet out from under us," Mr. MacLean said.

Mr. Webster said the man who did the kicking was Garnet Brown, Minister of Highways from November, 1970, to September, 1972, and at present Provincial Secretary.

"He made no bones about patronage. We were told in no uncertain terms that he agreed 100 per cent with patronage. At least you can say he has been honest about it."

He said the present Highways Minister, Leonard Pace, has "more or less indicated he would give us a chance for the association to do the hiring."

Mr. Mosher, who is in the gravel business and also has a truck, said he has done work for the Highways Department "and patronage has never hit me." He thinks it might be a case of mistaken identity, in a sense.

He is from Halifax and he went into trucking and the gravel business three years ago in the Pictou County area. "I bought a truck while the Liberals were in power and I guess they thought whoever would do that is a Liberal." He also drives a snowplow for the department but he expects that job will disappear next winter. But most of his work, he said, does not involve Government jobs.

He has been president of the Pictou County association since March 7 and he decided to make an issue of patronage "after a couple of nights without sleeping. People call me and say, 'I've a family and I can't get work' — what would you do?

"At election time you wouldn't believe the tension involved in a village. It puts neighbor against neighbor and relative against relative. Four years of income totally depends on how you vote."

Mr. Mosher, who lives in the hamlet of Bridgeville, about 100 miles northeast of Halifax, said in rural areas committee members could be 98 per cent sure of the way a person voted. And he added: "That's a low estimate really."

For one thing, he said, in the villages there are regular meetings to which members of only one party are welcome and those who attend are known. For another, rural people tend to follow their parents' voting pattern "If for no other reason than the gifts that the Department of Highways can give away. Children sitting around the dinner table can hear their parents talking and saying things like 'Boy, if the other party gets in we're in trouble.' "

In bigger communities such as New Glasgow, 10 miles away, you don't get that, he said, but in the hamlets and villages "the department can touch maybe 30 per cent of the community and you don't want to be on the wrong side. You can't afford to be."

He said it is possible to change your party, but only once, if you do it a second time, you're finished with everyone.[24]

Returning to the federal level, one discovers that politicians can always find new ways of looking after their friends. The Ottawa establishment's network is so old-boy oriented that those at the top of the system never lose out. Aside from the Senate, there are, as has already been mentioned, appointments to judgeships, government operating commissions, and regulatory bodies. Because of improved civil service regulations it has, until recently, proved more difficult to place favourites at the lower end of the political pecking order. But then, admittedly for quite different reasons, the government came up with its Local Initiatives Program designed to reduce the incidence and impact of unemployment while furthering worthy local causes. Not surprisingly the funds available under this program have been dispensed far more generously in government ridings, as *The Globe and Mail* reports:

Constituencies represented by Liberals received Local Initiatives Program grants totalling $106.7-million in 1972-73 while Conservative-held ridings received $59.6-million.

The information was tabled in the Commons yesterday by Mark MacGuigan, parliamentary secretary to Manpower Minister Robert Andras, in answer to a written question by Tom Cossitt (PC, Leeds).

The answer to an accompanying question by Mr. Cossitt showed that $26.9-million of the LIP grants to the Liberal ridings went to those held by Cabinet Ministers.[25]

Canadian politicians also have yet to resolve conclusively the problem of personal conflicts of interest. A few, such as the Senators, appear for the most part to be oblivious to the problem. Others, hopefully the majority, are uneasy about the present lack of clarity on the subject and would probably welcome some clear-cut guidelines. In the meantime, there is ample room for suspicion that many politicians do not draw a firm and proper line between their own

[24] Cecil Jennings, "N.S. Truckers Ready to Strike over Political Patronage", *The Globe and Mail*, Toronto, May 10, 1974.
[25] "LIP Grants to Liberals' Ridings Almost Double Those to Tories", *The Globe and Mail*, Toronto, March 21, 1974. By permission of The Canadian Press and The Associated Press.

private interests and the public welfare. Because of this problem, there are attempts being made at various governmental levels in Canada to draw up comprehensive codes of conduct for both politicians and public servants. That some of these attempts represent only a beginning has been suggested on more than one occasion:

There are two ways in which a leader of government can transmit to all around him the disciplines he expects to apply in conflict-of-interest situations. He can bring his guidelines down on the table with a wallop that will jerk everyone upright and make them take him seriously; or he can slide them, half hopefully and half apologetically, toward those who may be concerned.

Prime Minister Pierre Trudeau, for all the reputation he carries of dealing firmly and confidently with most people he meets, leaned distinctly toward the latter method as he introduced in the Commons the Government's policy on conflict of interest in the public service.

It is really a wild exaggeration to classify this as a statement of policy. Mr. Trudeau seemed to be telling the public service that, while it was an institution in which Canada could take pride, there were certain things he *hoped* its members would not do. It was a statement wreathed in principle, tinselled with high hopes, and surmounted by a sugar-plum fairy of pure naiveté.

This is not to malign the public service, whose integrity we would match with any in the world. But if the institution itself is to benefit by Government action, that action should surely take firmer shape than the vague series of guidelines that were inflated to a philosophy by Mr. Trudeau.

The rules, such as they were, were planted in a soggy mass of self-evident objectives. Thus: "Public servants must not place themselves in a position where they are under obligation to any person who might benefit from special consideration or favor on their part or seek in any way to gain special treatment from them." (Can anyone imagine a less-than-pure civil servant suddenly feeling that he had been cornered?)

Again, from the "policy" statement: "Public servants will be expected, as are Ministers of the Crown, upon appointment to office, to arrange their private affairs in a manner that will prevent conflicts of interest from arising if there is any risk of that occurring."

Only an utter cad would let us down.[26]

Worth considering are the dire warnings of some politicians that conflict of interest legislation could itself be carried too far. It is not surprising that one such warning should come from one of the Maritime Premiers where patronage and other forms of political intrigue are virtually an accepted way of life.

Too-stringent legislation against conflict of interest could have a detrimental effect on the political system, Premier Richard Hatfield of New Brunswick suggested last week.

He made the comment during a week in which various allegations about conflict of interest, patronage and misspending were due before the Legislature or courts.

All were postponed but a report on the indirect dealings with the

[26] "In This Permissive Age", *The Globe and Mail*, Toronto, December 20, 1973.

Government by the firm of a Cabinet minister and Government back-bencher is due again this week.

Mr. Hatfield said that "some of the things that have happened on the continent" have contributed to the need to elaborate on and restate confict-of-interest legislation.

"What used to be quite acceptable in politics is no longer acceptable," he said in an interview. "What used to be not even questioned is now extremely difficult to defend."

But conflict of interest is a difficult question, he said. "What kind of standard do you want from the point of view of people in politics and government? If we're going to say that any person must give up their business to go into provincial politics and pay some kind of price for it I think we're effectively cutting off a needed input into the Government and into the Legislature.

"What about people in government who are practicing law, people who practice medicine, dentistry and so on? You know, if it can be shown that somehow the Government looked after those people, other than ways they always have, you know law firms get business. . .

"Doctors get paid by the Government. People in the retail business receive money from the Government in the form of welfare cheques."

Mr. Hatfield, a 43-year-old bachelor describes himself as a professional politician. The family potato-chip and potato-marketing firm, of which he used to be sales manager, has been sold since he entered the Legislature in 1961.

"Do we want our political system to be made up entirely of professional politicians?" Mr. Hatfield said, referring to the possibility of stringent conflict-of-interest legislation ruling out all others.

There has to be a standard that politicians can be measured by, he said, and New Brunswick's standard of ethics is "that you can't directly benefit from being in Government."

Mr. Hatfield was asked about the case of Thermofoam Manufacturing (1972) Ltd. The president of that company is Supply and Services Minister Carl Mooers and the secretary is Reginald Mabey, Conservative member of the Legislature for Sunbury.

Their firm produces insulation materials that have wound up in Government buildings after being sold to contractors, but not directly to the Government. Building specifications put out by Mr. Mooers' department specify Thermofoam products as being among several that can be used on Government buildings.

A report on how much has been used on Government buildings was sought by the Liberals and was to have been tabled in the House last week. It was not ready but Mr. Mooers said yesterday he thought it would be tomorrow.

Mr. Hatfield said Mr. Mooers has taken steps to remove himself from his business and "the question is should he abandon his company, should he make a sacrifice? Should he set up a blind trust and dissociate himself entirely from it? I think that effectively he did but the question is whether that's enough any more."

Mr. Mooers said he has taken no active part in the company's decision-making since he entered the provincial Cabinet on July 18, 1972. He has also been thinking of getting out of it entirely. "Negotiations have been going on for some time, based strictly on a business decision," he said earlier this month.

Mr. Hatfield said that "everybody knew that (Mr. Mooers) was in that business. The people who elected him knew he was. I knew he was."

As for the specifications: "It specifies the kind of material they can use, it doesn't say they have to buy them."

Mr. Hatfield then asked: "Should we buy outside the province?"

Mr. Mooers' company is one of two in New Brunswick that produce a plastic-foam insulation and provincial policy is to buy locally whenever possible.[27]

It seems unlikely, however that reforms in this matter will be carried too far. Patronage, at least in some forms, unfortunately sometimes seems a cherished practice which is unlikely to disappear from the scene.

ESTABLISHING A BASIS
FOR POLITICAL MORALITY

This, the first of a series of chapters on specific problem areas, is probably the most important, since political morality is clearly the most fundamental ingredient in restoring public confidence in the total socio-economic-political system. It is clear that both North American political systems are in need of basic reforms the extent of which has only been partially conceived to date. To conclude this chapter, therefore, there is offered a list of significant steps which should be taken to ensure a strong basis for moral behaviour in the political sphere.

To begin, it is useful to point to some of the general lessons which one can glean from the Watergate fall-out. Encouraging is the impact of Watergate on current election campaigns and on new and old candidates for high office. Pressure on politicians to prove themselves persons of honour and integrity may not only result in candidates of higher calibre, but may lead to commitments to basic electoral reform.

The benefits of Watergate and more localized recent scandals include not only a new interest in campaign finance reform, reaching down into state and local levels — but actually a new, healthy competition by candidates for the title of campaign Mr. Clean. In turn, this competition is enhancing the chances of reform itself.

This is the case in Massachusetts. Incumbent Gov. Francis Sargent and his Democratic rival Michael Dukakis have been trying to outdo one another both in backing progressive state campaign legislation and in setting the ground rules of their personal campaigns.

At the moment Mr. Dukakis may have a thin edge: he has offered to disclose monthly his campaign finance position instead of at six-month intervals, and he has offered to make public his personal net worth as well. The latter may not be a wholly fair offer, since Governor Sargent is from a well-heeled family and Mr. Dukakis's net worth may be very modest. But it is at least politically astute and illustrates how Watergate's ripples are penetrating American politics for the better.

Seven states already have acted this year to close campaign finance

27 Cecil Jennings, "Tough Legislation on Conflict Could Hurt Political System, Hatfield Says", *The Globe and Mail*, Toronto, April 23, 1974.

loopholes. This does not mean, however, that the forces that have resisted the pre-Watergate reform are suddenly and wholeheartedly embracing post-Watergate proposals.

In Massachusetts, for instance, the Sargent/Dukakis Mr. Clean competition is giving leadership strength to the fight for reform. Massachusetts proposals parallel federal reforms already passed by the U.S. Senate and pending in the House. The state versions would include dropping the present ceiling on an individual's contribution to $500 from the present $3,000; require transactions of over $25 to be made by check; ban contributions by lobbyists and public employees; require full disclosure of campaign income and outlays before election day; and boost fines and prison terms for campaign finance law violation.

It is welcome to see a competition for integrity and voter confidence strengthen the prospects for essential campaign finance reform in state and local races as well as on the more prominent national scene. The real winner of a competition to run a scrupulously honest campaign has to be the American people.[28]

Turning to some major specifics in the electoral reform area, it seems appropriate to first consider both the attractiveness of a political career and the financial sacrifice which many highly-qualified potential candidates have to make if they choose to enter politics. Presently, Canadian members of Parliament receive a salary of $18,000 and a tax-free allowance of $8,000. As for the base salary, at least $50,000 would be more in order provided they are compelled to drop all outside activities and to devote full time to their demanding responsibilities. The following article from The Globe and Mail shows that such a proposition is bound to be opposed — sometimes on the basis of the most convenient rationale to be found extant at the time:

The latest figures on unemployment showed that 7.8 per cent of the Canadian labor force was out of work. In some of the more unfortunate categories — such as laborers — the percentage of jobless stood at 24.3 per cent. Many of them have been out of work for months.

They have been out of work because the Liberal Government of Prime Minister Pierre Trudeau has deliberately depressed the economy to throw them out of work because, he said, he was fighting inflation. No wage increase, he insisted, should be larger than 6 per cent.

Yesterday Mr. Trudeau announced that the salaries of members of Parliament would be increased, retroactive to October 8, by 50 per cent, from $12,000 a year to $18,000 a year. Their tax-free expense allowances would rise from $6,000 a year to $8,000 a year. Senators would also receive a 50 per cent increase in salary, from $12,000 to $18,000, and their tax-free expense allowances would go from $3,000 to $4,000.

These raises are not just or unjust fair or unfair, they are simply indecent.

We do not oppose reasonable remuneration for members of Parliament. But to introduce such massive increases at this time, when hundreds of thousands of Canadians are suffering want and the loss of security and dignity as a direct result of Government action, is arrogant and heartless, is disgusting.

[28] "The Mr. Clean Winner Is. . .!", The Christian Science Monitor, November 16, 1973.

111

Moreover, it has been done in the most irresponsible way. The Beaupré committee, which examined the salary situation, recommended that the salaries of MPs be increased to $23,000 immediately and to $25,000 after the next election, and that the tax-free expense allowance be eliminated in favor of an accountable expense system.

But Mr. Trudeau has gone for a total of $26,000 ($30,000 if the MPs paid taxes on expense money) and retained the disreputable tax-free allowances.

These members of Parliament, who will be setting the tax for their fellow Canadians, will have no notion of the weight of the burden, because Mr. Trudeau will allow them to escape a great part of it.[29]

Another argument against much more generous salaries for politicians is that it would tend to entice some candidates interested in higher remuneration alone. That would, of course, be harmful, but the major purpose of the reform would be to attract more candidates into the political arena. Hopefully those who appeared to be in it for the money alone would be rejected. Related to this concern, however, there is the very distinct possibility that higher salaries would simply serve to induce many unqualified incumbents to seek to hold on to their positions at all costs. That is an inevitable risk that can be reduced by bringing in the proposed salary increases over one or two elections. Certainly, as a general principle, no salary increases should ever come into effect until after an election has been held to determine who the voters deem most worthy of the higher rates.

Allowances for the basic expenses of office should probably be raised at least as much as the salaries. As well as some allowance for research and secretarial expenses, funds should be provided to ensure an office holder ample opportunity to travel back and forth to his constituency and to perform services for his constituents. Without such allowances, any salary increase is likely to be dissipated to some degree, especially for many who have to rely on part of their own incomes for these purposes.

Once the salaries and basic expense allowances of politicians are raised to an adequate level, elected representatives should not only have to drop all other outside work but should be under some compulsion to devote their full time to their duties. That this is a problem, and that there are possible remedies has been brought out in items expressing concern over congressional absenteeism in the United States:

Congress' bid to reassert its responsibilities has provided the opening for some lawmakers to deal with an old problem — congressional absenteeism.

Calling absenteeism "a thorn in the side of Congress," Rep. Clarence E. Miller (R) of Ohio has introduced a constitutional amendment providing for expulsion of members who miss 40 percent of the votes during a term.

"There could be no better way of promoting public confidence in our abilities and commitment to move America forward than a high level of congressional attendance and voting participation," Mr. Miller says in introducing his bill.

The Ohio congressman, who has not missed a vote since coming to Washington in 1967, noted that a 5 percent absentee rate in private indus-

29 "Greed in a High Place", The Globe and Mail, Toronto, April 27, 1971.

try is considered high, yet the 11 percent rate in Congress this year is its best record since 1959.

According to his count, the House was unable to form a quorum on 330 occasions last year because members were absent.

"The place to start in reasserting congressional responsibilities in this government is by doing the job we are elected and paid to do," Mr. Miller says.

Mr. Miller is hopeful of getting positive action on his measure in time for the 1974 congressional elections when absenteeism is expected to skyrocket.

Some members argue that their elective responsibilities sometimes require their presence elsewhere during congressional votes. They explain that whenever relatively unimportant issues are being debated, they may fulfill more important engagements that have direct bearing on their jobs.

Sen. William Proxmire (D) of Wisconsin, who has not missed a vote since 1966, does not buy that argument. Every roll call is important, he says.

According to statistics compiled by the Congressional Quarterly, several members would be expelled today if a 40 percent absenteeism rule were in effect.

Mr. Miller contends that members cannot do the job they were elected to do "if you are off globe-trotting or campaigning."

One member who remains cool to that type of rhetoric is the chairman of the House Judiciary Committee, Rep. Peter W. Rodino Jr. (D) of New Jersey.

Mr. Rodino says that the committee "has so many important matters before us" it would be some time before it gets to the absentee question — if it ever does.[30]

Besides the financial disadvantage there are other problems tending to reduce the number of those choosing to enter politics. Relatively few individuals are wealthy enough to risk leaving their present jobs for a venture into the tenuous and uncertain world of politics without the assurance that a commensurate job will be awaiting them upon their return. The major exception to this rule is lawyers who often derive personal and professional advantages for themselves and for their firms through the contacts they develop while in politics. This explains why politics has become so much the preserve of the lawyers, with very mixed results from the public point of view. Because of their training, lawyers have a natural and useful head start in politics, but they also have an almost unavoidable vested interest in making laws more complex than the common man can understand without aid, which could conceivably involve the legislature in the greatest make-work project that any group could ever dream of devising.

To make it possible for a wider spectrum of citizens to participate more fully in the political life of the country, provision should be made for unpaid leaves-of-absence for those wishing to run for public office. In effect this is what was done for members of the armed services during two world wars and it is standard practice for those on jury duty. Except perhaps for small firms, this should be mandatory for all employers with some provision for a compensatory

[30] "Congressional Absenteeism — New Interest in Old Problem", *The Christian Science Monitor*, December 7, 1973. By permission of The Associated Press.

tax write off where undue hardship can be demonstrated. Such leave should also be made available for a reasonable period prior to an election for campaign purposes. Finally, those taking advantage of such leave and later returning to their jobs should be assured not only roughly equivalent work but at least the average increase in wages or salaries since they left. Costly as these provisions might prove, they would be insignificant compared to the advantages which could flow from recruiting a broader range of political candidates.

Aside from measures to attract more qualified persons into politics, there is the difficult question of campaign funding. First priority should be given to the eventual realization of complete public funding of all political campaigns. In keeping with this proposal the AFL-CIO has come up with an interesting assessment and conclusion, which they report in *AFL-CIO News*:

The idea of government financing of federal campaigns has been around a long time. President Theodore Roosevelt first proposed it, and the AFL-CIO has consistently supported the concept since 1956.

We realize there are many problems that must be worked out — such as funding for primaries, elimination of capricious candidates. But, we submit, these problems are less overwhelming than piecemeal attempts to make the present corrupt system workable.

The Congress has already tried the piecemeal approach, and the events of 1972 proved that approach won't work. As soon as the Congress passed the 1971 act, a nest of political vultures found the weak underbelly — the time between the signing of the 1971 act and its effective date. They tore holes in it — large enough to drive millions of dollars through.

The AFL-CIO wholeheartedly supports complete federal campaign financing for all offices and a complete bar on any private contributions to such candidates. We know there are many grave problems that may take time to solve but there are some actions which can be taken without delay. They are:

1. Provide for sole federal financing of the 1976 presidential campaign with a clear mandate for strict enforcement of the law to prevent any contributions from any other source. In view of the politicizing of the Justice Dept. by the present administration, enforcement of the law should be taken out of the hands of the Justice Dept. by creating a special commission with enforcement powers answerable only to the people's elected representatives, the Congress.

2. To reduce the cost of campaigns require that television and radio stations, which use the public's air waves, provide equal, free air time for federal candidates. It is ironic that the air waves — the property of all the people — have become the most costly medium for reaching the people.

3. Establish a special election frank permitting postage-free mailing by legitimate candidates for federal office.

4. Establish and strictly enforce ceilings on the total, aggregate contributions to congressional candidates or their political committees. Every contribution must be reported in full and reports supplied to the public before Election Day.

We repeat, the goal is federal financing of elections.

If federal financing of elections is not provided soon and if the costs of campaigning continue to spiral, then America will be plagued by a succession of Watergates.[31]

[31] "Watergate Fallout Demands Federal Funding of Campaigns", *AFL-CIO News*, September 29, 1973.

Private support of political parties and their candidates is at present so complex that even analysis of its sources does not suggest who would benefit most if it were subject to significant reform:

At the end of the first three months of this year, special interest groups — including business and environmental groups and labor — had already set aside more than $14 million for this fall's federal elections.

This is clear evidence that the simple fact of Watergate will not alter the basic political practice of depending on special interest money. Laws will have to be changed — on federal as well as state and local levels — before the system that helped produce Watergate is changed.

But changing laws means altering the status quo. And this causes many, in government or not, to be on guard against changes in the system that may undermine the basic balance of power between parties or between other camps such as business and labor.

Would the Senate bill for campaign finance reform, now being taken up in the House, give labor an advantage over business? It is hard to see how it would. Labor would have to live with a $6,000-per-candidate ceiling as would industry lobbies. Under the developing House bill, the ceiling may be lowered to $5,000. Industry and labor both could cover as many races throughout the country as they wished, whereas individual givers could give no more than $25,000 in all, and only $3,000 per candidate. "In kind" contributions — the lending of computers, say, or desks — would have to be appraised and would count against the total dollar support labor and business could give.

It is often said that labor gives Democrats a manpower advantage over Republicans. What is meant, perhaps, is that in certain regions such as Chicago a Democratic machine can wield a manpower advantage effectively. But the facts suggest little advantage exists nationwide. Recent surveys have shown that business individuals and union individuals have been working on campaigns at about the same levels.

Actually, in areas of significant special interest legislation, labor groups are often closely allied with their business counterparts. This is true in the case of the auto industry where labor would favor protection against imports because such protection means jobs.

At the state level too the issue arises which side, business or labor or Republican or Democrat, would get an advantage under campaign reforms. In Connecticut last week the state general assembly voted an outright ban on all special interest giving for state and local races — whether by business, public interest, or labor groups. Further, a limit of $5,000 would be imposed on individual giving. A Republican introduced the bill and Democrats objected that it would cut labor power.

It is hard to see a pattern in the support of campaign reform or opposition to it which would suggest it favors the prospects of Democrats or Republicans, or business or labor, or any other group.

Generally, incumbents of either party or of whatever backing stand the most to lose — a two-to-one historical advantage over rivals in attracting campaign funds.

Meanwhile, this fall's national legislative elections will be run with special interest money as usual.[32]

If private financial support cannot be eliminated from the political scene,

[32] "Campaign Reform — Who Gains", *The Christian Science Monitor*, April 29, 1974.

it must be made subject to far more stringent laws for publication and regulation. Highlights of a recent Canadian bill demonstrate that progress can be made in this area:

Major points in the election expenses bill approved by Parliament yesterday are:
* Candidates limited to spending $1 for each of the first 15,000 voters in their riding, 50 cents for each of the next 10,000 and 25 cents for each over 25,000.
* Parties limited to spending 30 cents for each registered voter in ridings in which they have a candidate.
* Names of donors of more than $100 must be disclosed publicly.
* Contributions tax deductible on a sliding scale — with a maximum deduction of $500 — that gives smaller contributors a better tax break.
* Radio and television stations required to provide a total 6½ hours of prime time during the campaign.
* Violaters convicted of an offence under the act liable to a maximum fine of $25,000.
* Each candidate required to file an audited statement of his expenses, on which government reimbursement will be based.
* Reimbursement of postage will cover cost of one first-class mailing to each voter plus 8 cents for each of the first 25,000 voters and 6 cents each for the remainder.[33]

Although there are deficiencies remaining, these reforms are encouraging. This *Financial Post* article provides an analysis of their impact and import:

Since the election was the last to be fought under the "bad old rules" governing campaign expenses, can we expect a remarkable change for the better in future federal elections, after the new law comes into effect on Aug. 2?

Certainly there should be some real changes for the better in campaigning but the old political leopards are not going to change their spots entirely. Nor can we expect short, snappy elections.

One of the first things that comes to mind, both among politicians and ordinary voters, is the excessive length of the campaigns. The new law has not set out to limit this, as such, but has put time limits on certain major activities through prohibiting advertising. Candidates and parties may not advertise, whether by radio, television or newspapers, between the date of the election writ and the 29th day before polling date. However, this does not apply to nomination meetings or meetings for the party leader.

What we are therefore likely to get hereafter is a twilight period of about a month when the election is definitely in progress, but considerably under wraps, followed by a big blast of noisy activity for the last four weeks before polling.

This should offer some relief but not a radical change. Short, snappy elections, as in Britain, will not become possible unless a continuing, up-dated voters list is maintained — a very expensive process in Canada.

Limitation of campaign expenditures is not too drastic under the new law, set out in Bill C-203, which was passed in January. Parties will be

33 "Highlights", Toronto *Star*, January 4, 1974.

allowed to spend 30c per elector on the preliminary lists, for ridings where they have official candidates.

In the 1972 election there were 13,000,778 electors. Major parties fielding a full slate of candidates would therefore have been allowed to spend a total of something like $4 million. In Monday's election over 13.5 million were expected to be on the final lists of registered electors. By the time the next election comes along spending may be around $4.5 million. This is considerably less than the major parties are reputed to have spent in the past, but it is certainly not barebones austerity.

Similarly, the limitations on campaign spending by individual candidates are not drastic. The formula allows expenditures of $1 per capita for the first 15,000 electors and lesser amounts thereafter. This works out at a range of from about $17,500 for the smallest constituencies to about $32,750 for the largest.

Critics complained that this is no real limitation, at all, but in fact much larger sums have been spent in the past in some of the more expensive ridings.

These limitations on parties and candidates will not rule out whirlwind campaigns by jet for the party leaders, but they will inhibit them and cut out a lot of trimmings.

However, really radical changes in Canadian politics — not just in campaigns — are likely to be brought about by a combination of factors arising from Bill C-203.

Tax credits for contributors to parties and candidates, as well as compulsory disclosure of the names of those contributing over $100, may produce a mild revolution in political practices.

The new law on disclosure is Watergate's gift to Canada. In the feeble bill introduced by the Trudeau government into the 28th Parliament, but never passed, disclosure of contributions was required only by categories, such as corporations, trade unions and individual contributors.

After Watergate, the 29th Parliament put through a much tougher bill requiring the names to be published of all donors of over $100, whether individuals, corporations, trade unions or organizations.

This will undoubtedly reduce the amounts given in large sums — particularly in cases where the donor customarily contributed to both government and opposition parties.

It will cut off considerable funds, especially from the Liberal and Conservative parties.

At the same time, the tax credits will encourage all parties to build up a large cadre of "card-carrying" contributors, not only at election time but during the intervening periods.

Under the new law, individuals will be able to deduct for income tax purposes 75% of contributions of $100 or less to registered parties or candidates. The formula allows a smaller percentage for gifts above $100, setting a top figure of $500 tax credit for contributions exceeding $1,150.

This means that regular individual contributors will hereafter be able to increase their donations very substantially above previous levels, not merely in election years, at no extra cost to themselves.

The NDP has hitherto been conspicuous for relying heavily upon individual party member subscriptions. Hereafter, the Liberal and Conservative parties, facing lower subscriptions from big donors, will be tumbling over themselves to enlist regular contributors.

The new law should make for more lively participation by party members, both between election periods and during campaigns.

It should help to increase popular interest in party affairs and make parties — including ruling parties — more responsive to their members' views. It should also greatly reduce the dependence of parties upon corporations and trade unions and make for greater democracy in political affairs.

In sum, federal campaigns in the future should be less extravagant in format, which is all to the good. As for content, until the millennium arrives we cannot hope to be free of lavish promises.[34]

That there is hope for U.S. reforms similar to those introduced in Canada is suggested by this *Christian Science Monitor* analysis of the post-Watergate prospects:

Campaign reform, made daily more imperative by the continuing flood of disclosures of massive abuses during the 1972 campaign, is not moving ahead through the Congress as fast as we would like. But it is moving. And prospects are reasonably good for a healthy reform bill.

The legislative situation is as follows:

The Senate has before it a comprehensive reform bill which was approved by the Rules Committee last month. . . .

The House is considering two bills. The first, the Anderson-Udall bill which was submitted to the House last year, embraces most of the Senate bill's desirable campaign reforms. The second bill is that emerging from the House Administration Committee under Chairman Wayne Hays. The Hays bill appears to be shaping up as a version asking the least change — but unfortunately it, not the Anderson-Udall bill, will be the basis for House action. Thus the task in the House will be to beef up the eventual Hays bill in the three areas it appears likely to be weak — in providing for a strong enforcement arm under an independent Federal Election Commission; in making sure campaign spending limits are set high enough so that rivals will have a fair chance to unseat incumbents; and in providing public financing for congressional as well as presidential races. . . .

What are the campaign finance reforms it is now hoped Watergate will bring?

Reform advocates put them into four main groups:

1. An independent enforcement body. Both the Senate bill and the Anderson-Udall bill would create a Federal Election Commission (FEC) with its own power to prosecute offenders. The Hays bill would omit the FEC and would leave enforcement in the Justice Department. The Nixon proposal would create an FEC, but would follow the Hays bill in leaving enforcement to the Justice Department. A conflict is posed by having the Justice Department — a Cabinet department within the executive branch shown vulnerable to political pressure by Watergate — police election finances. Reform advocates think the Senate/Anderson-Udall provision for independent enforcement will likely be passed.

2. Limits on contributions. The amount individuals or interest groups could contribute to campaigns varies in the Senate, Anderson-Udall, Hays, and Nixon versions. But limits appear likely to pass. The Senate bill would allow individuals to give a candidate $3,000 for a prim-

[34] John Bird, "End of an Era — The Last Election Splurge is Over", *The Financial Post*, July 13, 1974.

ary race, another $3,000 for the general election, for a total of $6,000 per candidate. An individual could give no more than $25,000 for all campaigns he wanted to cover. In the various versions, interest groups — such as the political action committees of business, labor, and public interest organizations — could be limited to a ceiling ranging from $2,500 to $6,000 in contributions to single candidates. But they could give in all House and Senate as well as presidential contests, without the $25,000 aggregate limit individuals would face.

The purpose of campaign finance reform is to reduce the influence of special interest money-givers to tolerable limits.

Reducing the amount an interest group can give any office-seeker to, say, $2,500 in a $100,000 campaign should keep politicians from being pocketed by big givers. When contributors can give as much as $20,000 or more as they do now, it is much harder for office holders to ignore their wishes.

The purpose of campaign finance reform is not to do away with influence groups, however. Lobbies presenting the views of business or labor or of the environmentalists should have the right to petition congressmen openly and to present their cases to the public. This is democratic procedure.

Nor is the purpose of campaign reform to weaken the present political system and eliminate entirely such rites as the fund-raising dinner. Abuses should be stopped. Interest groups should not be able to buy up seats at party dinners or earmark gifts for specific candidates. Functions like dinners help in rallying the faithful. But with such events as the $1,000-a-plate Republican and $500-a-plate Democratic fund-raising bashes in recent days, with most giving coming from interest groups, rallying the voters seems less the goal then raking in the dollars.

Nor need parties be weakened because candidates would be less dependent on them for financial support. The two major parties have been losing voter allegiance as it is, under the present system. They could perhaps regain influence among thoughtful voters if the parties stressed platform and policies more, and financial power less.

Again, the purpose of campaign finance reform is to hold the influence of money-giving to tolerable limits. When 90 percent of campaign contributions come from only 1 percent of the people, as is now the case, too much influence is clearly in too few hands.

3. Limits on campaign spending. The Nixon administration is against limits on campaign spending; the Hays and Senate versions include them, using different formulas. The Hays bill would set a $20 million limit on a presidential race, which appears a sufficient sum. But it would set a low House race ceiling, say of $50,000 or $60,000. Since in most recent tight House races spending passed the $100,000 mark, the low ceiling has been dubbed an "incumbents protection act" by reform advocates. Ironically, then, reformers want to keep campaign spending high enough so that incumbents don't swap the 2-to-1 advantage they now hold in attracting funds, for a law that would keep challengers from mounting a viable campaign.

4. Public subsidies for primary and general elections. Emerging proposals vary on this issue. The administration opposes any mandatory or voluntary public financing for any election. The Hays bill would make public financing of presidential general elections mandatory, the revenue to come from the existing tax checkoff system; but it would skip public

financing for presidential primaries or for congressional races. The Senate bill would allow full public funding for presidential and congressional general elections, plus public funds in primaries on a matching basis. Some compromise is likely to develop.[35]

Intriguingly, leadership in the political reform movement in the U.S. has come from the state level where some noteworthy advances are being made because of grassroots pressure. This has led more than one commentator to take heart despite the signs of a hesitant and painfully slow reform movement in the nation's capital:

There seems to be a vague but growing impression in this country that somehow the political system has reached its nadir of possibility. As the torpid days of summer move upon us, as the droning procedures of the great American political crisis become clogged in minutiae that is all but incomprehensible, we approach once again that public state of mind so dangerous to democratic systems — a belief that, since the possibilities of reform are withering, the system is in danger of becoming a parody of itself.

That impression, growing at the moment as it has so often in the past, rests on a basic assumption — that the possibilities for political reform lie only in Washington.

Such an assumption is simply not warranted and that is the basic reason why the current all-is-lost pessimism of the nation is nonsense.

Against all historic odds, a reform movement is rumbling through the states, creating a new tradition which, in turn, elevates interesting new politicians into national notice.

The passage of Proposition 9 [California's campaign finance reform measure], the enactment or voting for similar measures in other states, the emergence of new, young, or untried candidates in this summer's primaries, all seem to imply several things: an activist revulsion against the tawdry revelations of Watergate and a refocus of public attention upon the reforming possibilities of state politics.

That revival of visible promise in state politics is against all historic odds because the state, as an administrative and political unit, is really most logical in an agrarian society.

The power and prestige of the states withered as America became more and more industrialized with all the concentration of urban populations which industrialization implies. The annual budget of New York City, for instance, is larger than the budgets of most states.

Yet as our system grows older, those functions of government which bear most immediately on people's lives have flowed more and more to the states — matters like education, land use, campaign finance reform, property law, and the like are today state functions, by and large. That is the new tradition.

That new tradition and some of the new politicians it is producing as governors and state legislators have revived public hope in the possibilities for reform. Yet the effects and application of that hope are expressed on a regional basis. Nationally, the public attention is fixed upon

[35] "Campaign Finance Reform", The Christian Science Monitor, April 3, 1974.

the scandals and torpidity of Washington and the result is a natural pessimism.

If that is a paradox, it is also a promise. Washington is not the sole source for the possibilities of reform. There are many sources — 50 of them — and from many of them the spirit of reform is flowing as an antidote to the shabbiness of Watergate. All, in other words, is not lost.[36]

Although reform in campaign funding and related areas would doubtless do much to clean up North American politics, that alone will not solve the problem. As this piece from The Financial Post points out there is something to be said for the argument that the only solution lies in personal morality.

The Watergate investigation in the U.S., and the Ontario government's investigation into an Ontario Hydro construction deal in Toronto, are certainly making a mark upon the never-never land of political morality. The federal government, which has already introduced a bill requiring disclosure of campaign donations, last week brought down two more stone tablets: A Green Paper and a statement from the Prime Minister telling Members of Parliament and the cabinet to (and how to) avoid conflict of interest situations.

The Green Paper is a thoughtful document that picks a careful path through obvious pitfalls that beggar attempts to legislate morality. The working paper will enhance Allan MacEachen's growing reputation as one of the more astute and skilled House Leaders. Parenthetically, it could be added that when the Liberal government ignores for a moment its pretensions to divine rule, it is remarkably capable of responding to changing public expectations.

Under the proposals, MPs would be required to dispose of any significant interest they have in a company awarded a government contract. They would also be required to disclose their interest in companies dealing with the government and should not accept compensation of any kind for representing members of the public before government bodies. Since the rules would also apply to Senators, who frequently retain extensive business interests, nonparliamentary lobbyists could find themselves enjoying a windfall of new business.

Yet what to do about MPs who legitimately represent business interests?

The Green Paper suggests a number of ways of avoiding an appearance of conflict in such situations. These include resigning directorships in companies doing government business, disclosure, and strict limits on the amount of stock a Member of Parliament can hold in companies doing government business.

These rules, of course, also apply to cabinet ministers, and the Prime Minister's statement, released the day after the Green Paper, adds more restrictions. Ministers are expected to resign all directorships, sever all active business, commercial or professional associations, and dispose of investments where the link between the cabinet post and business may be too close. The remaining holdings must go into either a blind trust, or a frozen trust. The latter arrangement would allow a minister to retain holdings (such as land) that he wants to keep. If these were in a blind

[36] Roderick MacLeish, "50 Sources of Reform", The Christian Science Monitor, June 21, 1974.

trust, the Prime Minister explained, the trustee might see fit to dispose of them.

Quite obviously, and as the Prime Minister noted, these rules will not solve completely the problem of conflict of interest or the appearance of it. But at least they provide, in the Prime Minister's words, that "a clear standard will be in place against which the conduct of members of the government can be measured." And, as Trudeau added, the policy "leaves each minister with a heavy onus to conduct his personal affairs in a manner which must not conflict or appear to conflict with his public duties and responsibilities."

It is difficult to see how the government can do more — either in legislation or in guidelines — to make sure that parliamentarians avoid conflict of interest. In the final analysis, it is a sense of personal morality and his leader's expectation of it that will determine whether or not a member violates his public trust.[37]

How far one should go to encourage individual morality in politics is debatable. At a minimum however, there would seem to be the need for mandatory disclosure of all personal and family holdings and interests in order to force potential conflicts of interest into the open. The American state which has probably gone furthest in this direction is Washington, where the repercussions have been striking. Despite the alleged costs involved, as brought out in the accompanying article from *The Wall Street Journal*, it is to be hoped that the long-run effects will be beneficial.

Lobbyists in this state capital are lying low. "Why, I hear that legislators are buying drinks for each other," says former state Sen. Francis Holman of Seattle. "That's unheard of."

In Vancouver, Wash., the port commission is becoming more accommodating to its critics. It suddenly decided, for example, to make available to an environmentalist its plans for dredging and cleaning Vancouver Lake. A few days earlier it had refused him the documents.

And throughout this state, some 1,000 elected officials are threatening to resign or not seek reelection. They represent fully one-third of the state's school board members and similar low-level elected officialdom. A number of others, including a judge and several city councilmen, have in fact resigned recently. All of these angry politicians are citing problems in letting the public know all about their business connections and financial dealings.

These are just some of the signs that Washington's new "open-government" law, known as Initiative 276 and passed by a whopping 72% of voters last fall, is beginning to have a major impact. The measure was prompted by scandals in local government and foot-dragging by the legislature in suggesting reforms, observers say. So a public initiative, led by a telephone company attorney with help from groups like the League of Women Voters, was put on the ballot. The result "is the toughest open-government law in the United States," says John Gardner, chairman of Common Cause, the national citizens-lobby group, which backed the law.

Washington's new law creates a public disclosure commission with wide powers to subpoena witnesses, take testimony and publicize wrongdoing. The law also provides for suits to be brought by state or local

[37] "Personal Morality is the Basic Test", *The Financial Post*, July 28, 1973.

prosecuting attorneys to force compliance. One remedy under the law: Elections can be set aside and a new election called if any candidate or political committee violates the disclosure rules. "It is intended that this remedy be imposed freely in all appropriate cases," the law reads. Fines of up to $10,000 and injunctions are also provided.

The law, as upheld by the trial court, requires enormously detailed reports on campaign spending of every state and local candidate and on financial and business ties of every elected official in the state except precinct committeemen. Campaign reports, for example, must list every donation over $5 by name, address and date. Financial reports of elected officials must show every creditor to whom more than $500 is owed and the source and nature of each portion of income above $500 yearly.

Lobbyists here for the first time are required to name the legislators or other officials whom they entertain. Each expense above a low minimum of $15 must be itemized, and for the first time spending on a year-round basis must be reported by lobbyists. Previously, they filed spending reports only when the legislature was in session. Although a court injunction has halted enforcement of lobbyist reports pending appeals, the heightened sensivity to wining and dining of legislators already has caused a semidrought in bar and restaurant spending here, observers say.

When and if the law is fully effective, it's likely to have even broader impact. "The heavy lobbyist spending is between sessions, when the lobbyists sponsor vacations such as fishing trips and the like," says one lawmaker.

The law also grants the public access to nearly the entire paperwork output of any state or local government unit and requires every agency to adopt clear rules for opening its files and operations to public scrutiny. An early test of that provision came in Vancouver when the port commission there refused Dr. Russell Maynard, a conservationist, its plans to dredge Lake Vancouver. He filed suit under Initiative 276, and the commission promptly supplied the documents.[38]

Other logical steps which must be taken to rid North American politics of the corruption which persists lie in the extension of already tried and true principles. Only two need be mentioned here. First of all, virtually no public monies should be spent on any contracts which have not been subject to proper tendering. This stricture should obviously include advertising since it is such a lucrative area and is so close to the heart of modern-day electioneering. In addition, the merit principle should be extended throughout the entire public service, except for high-level positions where it is set out by law that the incumbents are expected to resign in the event of a change of administration. Otherwise, all full- and part-time government employees should be subject to strict civil service standards based on the merit principle alone.

Another area of concern relates to the growing use of confidentiality and secretiveness in government circles. A special case in point is revealed in the following article from The Globe and Mail, an article which also deals with the broader issues involved:

The broad and unchecked powers open to federal Cabinet ministers, under the Federal Court Act, to withhold documents from production in

---

38 " 'Open Government' — In Washington State, a New Era of Frankness Upsets Many Politicians", The Wall Street Journal, July 6, 1973. Reprinted with permission of The Wall Street Journal © Dow Jones & Company, Inc., 1973.

any court, are excessive, dangerously open to abuse and in urgent need of revision.

The section of the act was brought to public attention when Justice Minister Otto Lang, in the capacity of acting Solicitor-General, invoked it to withhold from production in the Federal Court of Canada certain documents related to an appeal by two former Royal Canadian Mounted Police officers against their dismissal from the force.

(The two officers have since withdrawn their appeal. According to their counsel they did so to prevent public release of other documents the production of which was not opposed by the Government.)

The disturbing subsection of the act is 41 (2). It provides that: "When a Minister of the Crown certifies to any court by affidavit that the production or discovery of a document or its contents would be injurious to international relations, national defence or security, or to federal-provincial relations, or that it would disclose a confidence of the Queen's Privy Council for Canada, discovery and production shall be refused without any examination of the document by the court."

No paranoid fear of a Canadian Watergate is required to find this sweeping power of unsupervised secrecy alarming. Conservative justice critic Gordon Fairweather, a former provincial attorney-general, regards it as dangerous. So does Alan Borovoy, general counsel of the Civil Liberties Union in Toronto. And Mr. Lang himself, according to a spokesman, regards the powers as too broad and flexible and believes the act should be amended.

As written, the subsection appears to give any member of the Cabinet the power to withhold from a court any document merely by certifying that this is necessary for any of the reasons listed. Since disclosing a Cabinet confidence is one of the reasons provided, the contents of virtually any document could be covered merely by making them the subject of a brief discussion in Cabinet.

And although, according to Mr. Lang's office, Government practice is that such affidavits are filed only by the Solicitor-General, the wording of the act leaves this power open to any minister of a Cabinet.

There is nothing in the act to ensure at least that the power be used only by Cabinet decision.

There is nothing in the law to prevent this unchecked power being used by any minister for any purpose that suited him, to prevent the production of a document politically or personally damaging to himself, for example.

To say this is in no way to imply that any member of the present Cabinet would consider such abuse of the available power, or that any official would obey instructions to carry out such an abuse. But the power is there.

Certainly there may be instances in which disclosure of a document would genuinely damage the national interest, as distinguished from the political interest of a particular government. But the national interest requires an impartial check on the validity of any attempt to invoke the power to prevent such disclosure.

Subsection 41 (1) of the Federal Court Act provides a model that might be adapted to provide this essential check. Under this subsection a minister may certify to a court that a document should be withheld in the public interest, but the court, after examining the document, decides whether this claim is justified, or whether the "public interest in the proper administration of justice outweighs in importance the public interest specified in the (government) affidavit" opposing the document's production.

The validity of a government claim under subsection 41 (2) should also be subject to a court check. And since this subsection is intended to deal with possible injuries to such matters as national security, the Federal Court of Canada, from which there is a right of appeal to the Supreme Court, would be the most appropriate referee.

To close the door effectively to abuse, both subsections should be amended to impose on the full Cabinet, rather than any single minister, the responsibility for any effort to invoke this form of Crown privilege.

The case of the two dismissed RCMP officers raises a number of disturbing questions. But the government powers the case has brought to public attention are not merely disturbing. They are clearly dangerous. They demand urgent reform.[39]

If one is to err in one direction or the other in this area, it should surely be in the direction of more openness in government. One reason for taking this position is to force into the open the subversiveness of some government operations whose undercover efforts might not otherwise ever surface. A major case in point is the CIA, which recently fought a long, but fortunately unsuccessful, battle to suppress an intriguing exposé of some of its more sordid activities.

In 1972, Victor Marchetti, a former CIA analyst, proposed to write a book that would make a mockery of the CIA myths and expose its operatives as bureaucrats with delusions, dangerous in spite of themselves, living off an undeserved reputation for derring-do. Only if the agency were made human, he believed, could anything ever be done. . . .

Apparently this idea struck a sensitive spot somewhere in the CIA, for the agency stole a copy of Marchetti's book outline from a New York publishing house. The agents retired to CIA headquarters in Langley, Va., and scoured the law for a way to keep the book from seeing the light of day. They found one.

In April, 1972, the U.S. government sought and obtained a permanent court order enjoining "Victor Marchetti, his agents, servants, employees and attorneys, and all other persons in active concert or participation with him" from disclosing any information, "factual, fictional or otherwise," without the prior consent of the CIA. The order was upheld by the U.S. court of appeals, and the Supreme Court declined to review the case. If Marchetti now speaks out from his classified mind, he faces instant imprisonment for contempt of court — no juries, no show trials.

Marchetti, outlawyered in Round 1, vowed to go on. After signing a contract with Alfred A. Knopf for a critical, non-fiction book on the CIA, he took on a co-author — John Marks, a 30-year-old ex-Foreign Service officer — and drafted a 500-page manuscript. It was dutifully handed over to the agency in August, 1973, and the book came back from the scissors shop riddled with 339 national-security delegations, excising more than a fifth of the text.

A new legal challenge to the censorship began last week in U.S. district court in Alexandria, Md. For the American Civil Liberties Union

[39] "Dangerous Crown Privilege", *The Globe and Mail*, Toronto, September 30, 1974.

lawyers who represent the authors, it is the first legally sustained exercise of prior restraint on national security grounds in the history of the United States.

For the CIA, the principle at hand is nothing less than the government's right to conduct its business without internal subversion. If people like Marchetti are allowed to blab incontinently about matters of state, the government's executive arm will be paralyzed, it believes.

The Marchetti-Marks manuscript shows that the CIA has trimmed away its intelligence functions so completely that it can justify its existence only on the basis of the clandestine ju-jitsu it tries to practise on foreign governments — the bribes, the coups, the surgical removal of unfriendly political strains abroad.

Although much of the material in the Marchetti-Marks book is available in newspapers and in the CIA books, the agency censored it anyway, on the ground that Marchetti's former status would authenticate what is now only rumor.

There is a reference in the manuscript, right after several pages that have been decimated by CIA censors, to "the CIA's ties with foreign political leaders." The obvious inference to be drawn is that the authors had identified foreign leaders with past or present CIA connections, and several sources have identified this kind of material as the most explosive in the book.

If the government wins again, Marchetti and Marks will have unwittingly helped create the legal tools to make a vassal of every government employee who enters the sacred chambers of national security.

In effect, Americans might then become divided into two basic types — those sufficiently gulled by the state's alleged need for privacy as to sign its contract of omerta, and those who refuse. The robots of the first group would run the government, protected by the courts against the public. The second group would lose interest in the government itself.

The agency would be left free, in the name of military defence, to expand its covert missions in the global fringes of the Third World — the only places where, especially to the bombed peasants of Southeast Asia, it is clearly no joke. The CIA is drawn to the Third World like a lonely derelict to a porn shop, where the salve for dreams is cheap and available.[40]

A final and vital ingredient in any effort to cleanse North American politics of its greatest evils is a watchdog of some kind. To a very large extent this is a role which logically falls upon opposition parties and the media. To an increasing extent, however, private public interest groups of one kind or another are making their presence felt. This is one area in which the U.S. is far ahead of Canada where there is nothing like Common Cause or the Nadar Movement. Even at lower levels in the U.S., some fascinating public lobbyists are having a marked impact. One such body is the Center for Analysis of Public Issues, in New Jersey, a state which in the past has more than exemplified the need for such a watchdog.

How can you stop cheating and defrauding of taxpayers? Expose greed and fakery in government offices? Is there a way to play gadfly to sting legislators to action?

[40] Taylor Branch, "The CIA: U.S. Spy Agency Fights to Suppress Book by Insider", Toronto Star, January 12, 1971.

126

"Yes," says John Kolesar, director of the Center for Analysis of Public Issues. He should know. The center is New Jersey's version of Nader's Raiders, but instead of exposing flaws in new cars, or the unsavory contents of hot dogs, the Princeton group pulls the cover from government malpractice.

In three years, with eight book-length reports and a chain of newsletters, the center has taken on the state consumer agency on grounds that it did not prosecute shysters, farmers who don't want to preserve agricultural land, the injustices of the juvenile-justice system, and cable-television companies who paid off "the guys who knew the guys" for franchises.

"We don't have Nader's name or prestige," Mr. Kolesar regrets, "so just because we say something is rotten doesn't mean anybody is going to do anything about it. We have to rely on the creditability and content of our reports.

"We try to find specific failures and name the people in charge of them so that the guy under the gun either has to disprove what we're saying, or change what he's doing.

"It takes a lot of research to narrow it down to 'Where's the failure? Why doesn't anything happen?' But if you do it that way, it works. People in public office, whether elected or appointed, don't like to be pointed out as falling down on the job in a specific way, so they move."

In addition to legislation which includes a law to regulate cable TV, and another to prevent lawyers from charging huge percentage fees for bond issues, the agency has made headway in "tidying up the old, slap-dash way of paying lawyers who work for New Jersey's municipalities, school boards, and autonomous authorities," Mr. Kolesar said. "A taxpayer's suit was brought against the Bergen County Sewer Authority on the basis of those fees we reported, asking for repayment of overages."

The center also listed offenders in a report on health services in Newark, "The Doctor Is Out." It named people who were working short hours; agencies where the staff was idle; and dentists who were not showing up at clinics.

But the report's greatest impact was on restaurant inspection.

During the course of the investigation state health officials had admitted they had made a survey of restaurants which had been printed but never circulated. A copy of the report was released after a long hassle.

It revealed that many restaurants throughout the state did not meet minimum sanitary standards. And neither the state health department, nor any of the county health departments which operate almost totally with state funding, would reveal the identities, much less close, the substandard restaurants. Health officials claimed their inspections were not public records.

Much hullabaloo in the press and pressure on the governor's office finally forced the department to reverse its policies. Beginning Dec. 15, 1972, New Jersey started the most rigorous inspection system in the nation. It provided for mandatory posting of inspectors' ratings near the entrance of all restaurants, supermarkets, and other food establishments, and made available full inspection reports at the establishments, with copies available at state and local health offices.

The center is effective in making positive suggestions as well as pointing the finger. It may reprimand an agency [or individual], but it also describes how their jobs should be done.

Interns investigating records in New Jersey's consumer-protection office did just this when they found the office acting more like a complaint bureau than a law-enforcement agency.

They suggested, after counting numerous complaints of "switch and bait" swimming-pool deals, that the bureau prosecute companies which offered the public cheap portable swimming pools and then signed them up for $2,200 jobs.

"Don't just deal with each complaint individually," the bureau was advised. "Put a stop to the practice so that you don't get 100 complaints every summer. Get injunctions. Set penalties. Get some priorities. You can't handle all the cases, so pick the important ones — the most unconscionable — and start deterring."

"Now," Mr. Kolesar claims, "the Consumer Protection Bureau is an aggressive organization, not the timid, placid thing it was when we first took a look at it."

There is no shortage of investigations to be made or projects to be undertaken, so the center must take its own advice to set priorities. In choosing which studies to do, Mr. Kolesar noted that, "We try to represent a cross section of general public interest. Then we pick things which are not being given enough attention."

Not yet, that is.[41]

Hopefully it has been demonstrated here that ethical standards of behaviour can be encouraged and perhaps even sustained in the political field. What is demanded in order to achieve this is evident. First and foremost, there is a need to make politics a far more attractive option for a much broader spectrum of the general public; second, to move towards more and more public funding of political campaigning while enforcing measures for full disclosure and careful regulation of private sources of support; third, to instill a higher level of morality in the average politician by imposing more strictures designed to reduce actual and potential conflicts of interest; fourth, to rid government of whatever forms of business and personal patronage are still left open for manipulation by shrewd politicians and their bureaucratic underlings; fifth, to force more openness in government. Finally, there is a need for more citizen vigilance, especially through private watchdog agencies in whatever form they can be organized.

[41] James L. Walker, "A Growl from New Jersey's Watchdog Agency Carries Much Weight", The Christian Science Monitor, October 1, 1973.

5

BUSINESS, GOVERNMENT AND SOCIETY

Reform of the business sector is central to any meaningful effort to reshape North American society. There must be a comprehensive assault on the unethical practices which pervade many facets of the business and corporate world. Entire books have been written on particular aspects of this challenge, but in this volume only the basic elements of the total program required will be highlighted. Even then it will require three chapters to begin to do justice to the subject. This chapter provides an extensive overview of the problem, and the next one bears down on the concept of corporate social responsibility. A third chapter is devoted exclusively to advertising and marketing, primarily to advertising, which epitomizes some of the worst features of North American capitalism.

Chapter five begins with a brief resumé of the position of business in today's society as seen from within the corporate sphere as well as from outside of it. A number of public-interest issues raised by the activities of today's corporations are then taken up. These issues include, among others, directors and their duties, audits and what they hide, and various forms of government regulation of business. There follow individual sections on four focal points of current public concern: the multinational corporation, the stock market, the public service, and consumerism.

THE MODERN CORPORATION

Today's corporations — private, quasi-public or public — are in transition and trouble. As they evolve, debate rages on about the general advantages and disadvantages of corporate forms of business, about the separation of ownership and control in corporations, about their managers' roles as trustees, and about their public image. A brief examination of these fairly broad questions will set the stage for the more detailed assessment of specific public-interest issues which follows.

Corporations – Their Pros and Cons

Corporate forms of business organization have yielded many advantages without which North American society could not have reached its present stage of affluence, however unfairly that affluence may be distributed. Through the concept of limited liability, corporations have proven able to command and concentrate great masses of capital. This in turn has permitted them to bring together vast amounts of resources, both human and material, to engineer impressive technological advances, to sell their products and services in immense markets, and to realize great cost economies because of the size of their production runs and sales. The result has been the most efficient, innovative and productive economic system yet known to man.

Against these advantages must be weighed the actual and potential disadvantages which flow from today's corporate enterprise. The concentration of capital which has made possible North America's impressive economic progress has also put enormous influence and power at the disposal of those in control of that capital. Economically that influence and power is magnified through interlocking directorships and many other forms of corporate interaction. But such influence and power does not stop at the corporate door or in the economic sphere. It permeates the political world and is to be reckoned with in just about every other area of society as well.

Perhaps these linkages, as much as anything else, help to explain the mixed feelings of North Americans about big business and those who control it, mixed feelings which are hardly new to the scene. This attitude is examined in the following extract from *California Management Review*.

America has an historical ambivalence toward its business corporations and their leaders. On the other hand, it admires the productivity, efficiency, responsiveness and technological advances of the industrial system which has provided the majority of Americans with a standard of living unequalled elsewhere. Society has, consequently, bestowed substantial wealth, status and power upon corporate managers as recompense for the important contributions their activities have made to American life. At the same time, however, a second current has persisted in the public's view of corporations and the men who run them — one of deepseated distrust, dissatisfaction and even fear concerning the underlying motives, social utility and consequences of our corporate political economy. *Business Week*, reporting a 1972 survey conducted by a national research organization, recently wrote of "America's growing anti-business mood." The article indicated big corporations "face the worst climate in a decade," not merely among the more radicalized young, but among upper middle class managerial and professional persons who traditionally have been the staunchest supporters of business. In a related editorial ominously headlined, "Why the Public Has Lost Its Faith in Business," the publication admonished business leaders that management has to face the fact that today our society "has become disenchanted with the way business operates." While some of the current antipathy toward business may be primarily ideological, that is, directed against capitalism per se rather than against the performance of corporations and their leadership, such a distinction between the "system" and its most essential actors is precious. Large business enterprises are the basic structural components of the contemporary American variant of capitalism and are properly considered as synonomous with it.

Historical attitudes toward business reveal an almost cyclical fluctuation between admiration and antipathy. For example, although during the past decade criticism of the American economic order has been particularly widespread and strident, a mere thirteen years ago, David Chalmers noted the social and political importance of the post World War II acceptance of the business community by the middle classes. Similarly, waves of general business popularity (the 1940s, the 1920s, and the 1880s) have alternated in the past with unpopular periods (the 1930s, the era 1890-1915 and so on). Just as it is now apparent that the rapprochement of the 1950s was not nearly as complete as Chalmers suggests, the public's current disaffection with business is probably not as severe as *Business Week* indicates and, indeed, may well decline in the near future. The fact remains, however, that while most Americans do not favor a radical re-structuring of our current socio-economic institutions, chronic tension remains between the business sector and the rest of the society.[1]

That the corporate sector of North American society is in deep trouble with the public is acknowledged by business executives themselves. A recent Conference Board survey of such executives revealed a number of reasons why they felt their organizations were vulnerable:

- Shoddy products or services which do not live up to business claims for them.
- Inaccurate, misleading, or "unexplained" financial reporting.
- False, misleading or excessive advertising.
- Poor service, unnecessary repairs.
- Meaningless warranties or guarantees.
- Arbitrary treatment of employees.[2]

Among senior executives in industry, there is a wide range of opinion as to how business should respond to criticism coming either from within or beyond their ranks:

. . . A tenth of the sample believe that the sole business of business is profits. At the other extreme 17% believe that business should assume public responsibilities even at the cost of reduced profits. A fifth believe that business should concentrate on profits but pay more in 'taxes and human resources' to solve social problems. Another 8% believe that busi-ness should develop know-how in solving social problems and make its skills available to the government at a profit. A final 42% believe that business must first make an adequate profit and then assume public re-sponsibilities which may not be profitable.[3]

Ownership and Control

The onus of responsibility for the present state of affairs in the corporate world is not as debatable as it once was. Ever since the classic work by Berle and Means on *The Modern Corporation and Private Property*,[4] it has been recog-nized that there is a wide separation between ownership and control in most large corporations. Even a special study group of the Chamber of Commerce of the United States recently accepted this distinction:

[1] Edwin M. Epstein, "Dimensions of Corporate Power, Pt.1", © 1973 by The Regents of the University of California. Reprinted from CALIFORNIA MANAGEMENT REVIEW, Vol. XVI, No. 2, pp. 9—10, by permission of The Regents.
[2] Douglas N. Ross, "Business Confronts Itself at the 'Credibility Gap' . . . and Agrees There's Reason for It to Look Before Leaping to a Conclusion", The Conference Board RECORD, July, 1973, Vol. X, No. 7, p. 24.
[3] "Conscience & the Corporation", *Management Today*, September, 1970, p. 109.
[4] Adolf A. Berle, Jr. and Gardiner C. Means, *The Modern Corporation and Private Property* (Chicago, Commerce Clearinghouse, Inc., 1932).

Gradually the Federal government delegated to the states its former close control over the corporation, a process that was completed with the enactment by states such as Delaware, Maryland and Nevada of general incorporation laws giving great latitude to management. The functions of the entrepreneur were at that point clearly delineated: the stockholders supplied the capital, took the risk of losing their capital and had legal title to the profits. But control of the corporation rested with the management, which in practice chose the majority of directors. This control could be magnified, at first through the voting trust and later, when this device was declared to violate the Sherman Antitrust Act in the 1911 Standard Oil case, by a holding company. Even in the absence of a holding company, diffused ownership of voting shares and use of proxies by management enabled it to elect its own slate of directors. Control could be wrested from management only through purchase of a majority of the voting stock (which in a large corporation could be extremely expensive) or through a proxy fight in which non-management interests established a committee to solicit proxies from stockholders in competition with management. The larger the corporation and the more widely distributed its stock, the more easily could management maintain its position.[5]

That this applies to Canadian Crown corporations as well as to their private equivalents should not be surprising. Whether one refers to the new Canada Development Corporation, the long-standing Canadian National Railways, or the equally long-established Ontario Hydro, the same pattern emerges. The surprising feature, at least in the latter instance, is that the Government of Ontario and its people, who are the real owners of Ontario Hydro, only recently became aware that they had relatively little direct control over it. The major outcome of this realization was the creation by the Province of a rate review board to pass judgment on increases proposed by its own public utility.

Corporate Managers as Trustees

As this and the ensuing chapter will suggest, there are various roles which corporate managers can assume. One possible role is that of trustee, although this raises the question as to whom they are acting for in that capacity. Narrowly speaking, one could argue that they are basically trustees for the shareholders. This is the traditional view. At the other extreme, one might argue that they enjoy and should be responsive to a kind of public trust. This is one outgrowth of the corporate social responsibility school about which much more will be said later. In between is the notion of corporate managers at the vortex of a host of competing interests: those of employees, suppliers, customers, neighbours, and the public at large. In this view, it is the job of the manager to reconcile the conflicting claims of all of these groups.

The problem with the latter point of view is that it so complicates, confuses and even obviates the manager's job that it in fact probably dilutes his accountability. No matter what managers do under these circumstances, they will be able to claim responsiveness to one group's interest or another's. Worse still, to avoid trouble on any front, they may become risk averters rather than risk takers, thus subverting one of the fundamental aspects of enterprise management. Mere survival, both of the institution and of the individual manager, could become the only objective, an objective which is incompatible with the

[5] The Corporation in Transition: Redefining Its Social Charter (Washington, Council on Trends & Perspectives, Chamber of Commerce of the United States, 1973), p. 3.

kind of dynamism and growth one commonly associated with corporate management. One observer in the *Journal of Contemporary Business* has put the result in an equally disturbing way:

This is the reading or, to my mind, the misreading of some of the modern organization theory which treats the firm as a coalition (managers, workers, stockholders, suppliers, customers), whose members have conflicting demands that must be reconciled if the firm is to survive. The managers, according to some theories, then operate the firm largely in their own self-interest, keeping the other coalition members quiet by paying them what becomes necessary. With the shareholders, in particular, management does not try to maximize profits but merely "satisfices" — that is, it tries to make satisfactory profits the way a student in pass-fail grading might try merely not to fail rather than try to get the highest grade in the class.[6]

The Corporate Public Image

As confusing as the results of the search for a new corporate managerial role may be, the quest for such a redefined position is quite understandable. In an earlier chapter it was emphasized that business is in as much, if not more, trouble with the public as any other leading institution in North America. One way of capturing the essence of the increased difficulty business is in in the public mind, is to review the major popular books shaping opinion in this area over the last decade or so. A summary of one such effort, from *Management, Business and Society Review*, suggests some intriguing shifts in public perceptions and values relative to the corporate sphere:

The sixties opened with the popularity of books which suggested a general, but as yet undefined, sense of moral uneasiness with the accomplishments of our business-oriented society. *The Waste-Makers*, *The Status Seekers*, and *The American Way of Death* all sought to confront the excesses of salesmanship and consumption. They articulated a popular suspicion with "marketing" which persisted throughout the decade. *Unsafe at Any Speed* focused not on business's threat to the people's pocketbooks and psyches, but rather to their health and safety. Nader's exposé of the automobile industry was only one of a frightening series of corporate horror stories concerning products which ranged from drugs to children's pajamas, from meat to tires. The stuff of many of the decade's headlines, the consumer scandals served to reduce public respect for the integrity of many of America's most well-known economic enterprises. Carson's *Silent Spring* broadened public awareness of the scope of the corporate influence on American society by documenting the dangers of involuntary consumption of corporate products.

With respect to the scope of "consumerism," Galbraith's *New Industrial State* marked a significant turning point. Formerly, consumer advocates had generally restricted their concerns to business production which involved either threat to the public's physical well-being or outright fraud and deception. Galbraith, however, challenged the ideal of consumption itself. The public was being inundated by a flood of goods

[6] Eli Goldston, "Corporate Social Responsibility and Management Behavior", *Journal of Contemporary Business*, Winter 1973, p. 68. Reprinted with permission of the *Journal of Contemporary Business* © 1973.

and services not to satisfy consumer needs, but rather to stabilize the profits of producers. Consumer sovereignty was a myth. Galbraith's book signified a serious escalation of criticism of the corporation. The corporate system was attacked not for the inadequacy of its performance, but for its success. By questioning the primacy of "economic" values, Galbraith struck at the root of business's justification for its existence.

A clear indication of the growing hostility to business which marked the beginning of the seventies was the publication of *America Inc.* by Morton Mintz and Jerry Cohen. Its somewhat simplistic indictment of business's "bigness" did not endear it to critics from either the business community or the Left. Yet the evident attraction of its populist appeal suggests a marked heightening of the political content of criticism, a sharp contract with the more culturally oriented critiques that characterized the beginning of the sixties.

A comparison of *The Pyramid Climbers* with *Up the Organization* yields a somewhat more subtle distinction between the decades. It does not seem that the ethnic homogenity of the corporation has undergone any marked change. Packard criticizes the exclusion of blacks and Jews from the boardroom. Eight years later, Townsend writes, "Most of us come from good solid European stock whose record of rapacity, greed, cruelty and treachery would make Genghis Kahn look like Mahatma Gandhi." In their discussion of the treatment of women, however, we begin to note some contrasts. Packard admonishes the corporation not to discriminate; but Townsend, writing in a considerably less passive age, lays out a strategy for women to scale the corporate ladder, in spite of, or perhaps along with, their sex. Which approach will prove more productive is still an open question. In any event, the ladder still remains.

A more serious distinction between Packard and Townsend concerns the relationship between the corporation and the individual. Both authors perceive a clear antagonism. Packard is concerned that the integrity of the individual executive is threatened by the corporation's obsession with conformity. Townsend also perceives the banality of much of corporate life, but his concern is different. He worries lest the corporation not take full advantage of the talents of its executive employees and thus suffer a decline in efficiency. Has the spectre of the "organization man" finally been replaced by the ogre of the organization?[7]

A recent survey by Louis Harris, reported in the Conference Board RECORD, is even more revealing since it gets at public reaction concerning the performance of business as business.

The cross section of the public was asked to give its impression of the job that American business is doing in each of 18 areas of business activity.

Here a dramatic drop in public approval appears for almost every activity pursued by American business in running its day-to-day affairs. This decline in business reputation may, I think, be one of the major results of the economic reverses the country has experienced since 1966.

In only four areas do majorities still give business a passing mark: in developing new products through research, in installing the latest improvements in machinery, in building new plants to make the economy

[7] David Vogel, "The Books That Shaped the Public's View of Business", *Business & Society Review*, Summer 1973, No. 6, p. 63.

grow, and in developing new markets and growth opportunities. There is, in fact, fairly solid support for new plant investment and economic growth, despite public concern for ecology and the environment.

One of the most serious declines, however, is the number of Americans who are prepared to give business high marks for "bringing better quality products to people" — from 75% in 1966 to 42% in 1973. People have come to be skeptical about American "know-how," worried that it might pollute, contaminate, poison, or even kill them.

Another serious drop is in the public's feeling that business does not care for people as human beings and does not offer them an opportunity to use their full creative abilities. Combined with this is a worry over workers displaced by automation.

Today, 61% of the public feel that business is not helping take care of workers displaced by automation; the figure was only 18% in 1966. Seven years ago an overwhelming 73% of the public gave business credit for "offering young people a chance to get ahead." Now 58% criticize business for failing to create such opportunities for youth.

The survey shows a slight improvement since 1971 in public regard for the way business provides "enough steady jobs" and "job openings for blacks and other minorities," but only 34% of those interviewed say business allows people to use their full creative abilities. Yet in 1966 business was applauded for providing an atmosphere conducive to personal fulfillment by a thumping 62%.

In the overall rating of how business runs its business, product quality and the human dimension are even more critical than profits in shaping public opinion. It may, indeed, even be futile to discuss profits with the public at large. We still report, however, that our survey of January 1973 found that only 10% felt that business is "keeping the cost of living down," and only 19% believe profits are being kept "at reasonable levels." And this was at the same time when, for the first time in a year, more than half those interviewed thought inflation was coming under control.[8]

Responses to the rising credibility gap confronting corporate management cover a wide gamut. Advertising and public relations campaigns designed to boost the image of business represent the most superficial response to the problem. Variations on the corporate social responsibility theme represent another possible approach. Yet the only answer probably lies in a serious assessment of what ails North American business in terms of legitimate public concerns about its performance, and an honest, down-to-earth effort to come to grips with the problems that emerge from such an assessment. What follows in the remainder of this and the next two chapters is an attempt to establish a frame of reference within which to try to achieve those objectives.

CORPORATIONS AND THE PUBLIC INTEREST

This section considers a number of continuing and recent concerns about the state of corporate management, issues which are receiving some attention, although clearly not enough.

[8] Louis Harris, "The Public Credibility of American Business", 1973. Reprinted by permission of Louis Harris and Associates, Inc.

Directors and Their Duties

Regardless of whether they are basically responsible to the shareholders or to the shareholders combined with other groups, it is clear that, except where they own the company, corporate directors should not be working for themselves. Only insofar as they have a trust relationship should they be thinking of their own personal obligations. Yet North American corporate history is replete with examples of directors who seem to be motivated largely, if not solely, by self-aggrandizing considerations.

How irresponsible corporate directors can become when the circumstances permit is suggested by a recent exposé entitled: "Missing: a Company That Everybody Walked Away From," printed in The Financial Post:

Whatever happened to Dairy Barn Stores of Canada Ltd.?

That was the Toronto-based, Quebec-incorporated company that raised some $280,000 from a public issue in 1971, largely on the strength of "future plans" that somehow never materialized.

It signed contracts with a number of other companies that, in most cases, were never followed through. It left a string of unpaid debts, perhaps as much as several hundred thousand dollars, owing money to just about every company it dealt with.

It issued to the public what seems to have been a series of misleadingly optimistic statements, which probably helped push the value of its shares to nearly double the issue price. (The public relations agency through which these statements were issued seems to have been the one company that was paid in full.)

And then, incredibly, it just quietly disappeared. All directors and officers simply resigned, apparently disclaiming further responsibility.

All of which leaves a number of important questions unanswered:

• What is the status of the company now? Although all directors and officers have resigned and all company operations apparently ceased, the company has not been declared bankrupt.

• What is the position of the shareholders? Trading in Dairy Barn shares was suspended July 3, 1973, by the Quebec Securities Commission and almost certainly will not be reinstated. Shares were issued to the public, in 1971, at $2.65 each. A year later, they had risen to a high of $5. At that price, the company had a market value of more than $3 million, but its net book value was still only $230,000.

The QSC has made a number of attempts to obtain information on the company, but so far without success. One of its problems is that the company head office, books and the main individuals involved are in Ontario — outside QSC jurisdiction.

The Ontario Securities Commission, on the other hand, also seems to have no jurisdiction because the company was incorporated in Quebec.

There seem to have been three main factors that attracted investor interest.

First was the emphasis Dairy Barn placed on its association with Dairy Barn Stores Inc. — the company that successfully operates 56 Dairy Barn stores in the U.S. (all on Long Island). Dairy Barn Stores of Canada was, however independent of its U.S. namesake, although there was a licensing agreement between the two companies that gave the Canadian company the right to draw on U.S. knowledge and experience.

Second was the line-up of Dairy Barn Stores of Canada's board of directors, which included George Cohon, president of McDonald's Restaurants of Canada Ltd., and well-known Toronto lawyer Alan Eagleson.

Both Cohon and Eagleson say they were invited to sit on the board by H. Wayne Tanenbaum, a member of Toronto's wealthy Tanenbaum family, and chairman of the board.

Tanenbaum was one of the promotors of Dairy Barn, and when it went public, held 166,100 company shares. When contacted by FP, he initially said he did not want to discuss Dairy Barn, and did not want his name associated with the company.

He did claim, however, that although he was chairman of the board (and one of the two principal shareholders of the company), he was not consulted on major company decisions. Also, he implied he had been told a number of "falsehoods" about Dairy Barn, and that the company had been "badly managed."

He then refused to talk further until he had consulted his lawyer. Later, through his secretary, he said he would not meet an FP reporter, but would consider a list of questions submitted to him in writing, and answer those "that his lawyer thinks are within his purview."

The second major shareholder in Dairy Barn was Seymour Aaron Aronoff, company president and chief executive officer, who also held 166,100 shares.

The son of a rabbi, Aronoff studied theology, but later opted for a business career. He successfully established (and later sold) Dominion Photo Services, and now heads two private companies in Toronto — S'Arnoff Holdings Ltd. and Globetrotter Management Ltd. Globetrotter operates from the same offices used by Dairy Barn, where all Dairy Barn records are apparently stored.

Aronoff says Tanenbaum was fully aware of Dairy Barn's activities; otherwise he would not have put money into the company. Both Aronoff and Tanenbaum personally guaranteed some of Dairy Barn's debts at Bank of Nova Scotia, and, according to Aronoff, they lost "upwards of $100,000 each" in the company.

The third major shareholder in Dairy Barn was Toronto businessman Joseph Byck, who held 82,800 shares at the time shares were offered to the public. He was instrumental in obtaining Canadian rights for the Dairy Barn name — through an organization called the Byck Syndicate — and, although he was not an officer or director of the company, was responsible for selling many of the Dairy Barn franchises.

Altogether, Tanenbaum, Aronoff and Byck owned 415,000 Dairy Barn shares, held in escrow for three years by Guaranty Trust. They received their shares for selling the company all the assets of the Byck Syndicate, in effect assignment of the license agreement with Dairy Barn U.S.

The third major appeal to an investor in Dairy Barn stock, would appear to have been the company's future plans, which unfortunately were never fulfilled. . . . [In August, 1972], in spite of its claim that "Dairy Barn is developing a fast-growing chain," the company had opened just three stores. And in its two years of operations, it managed to open a total of seven.

Although the report for the year ended April, 1972, said "progress has been slower than originally conceived" and showed a loss for the year of $182,080 (gross revenues were $56,000, cost of sales, operating and administrative expenses were $232,000), the impression was still that of a company well on its way to "exciting growth ahead."

In fact, the company was then in the throes of a financial crisis, and was desperately trying to refinance.

Dairy Barn's efforts to refinance took many shapes. The one that was apparently adopted was one that required the careful co-ordination of agreements reached with a number of other corporations.

The first agreement — announced in August, 1972, the same month the annual statement was released — was with Neal Petroleum Ltd., whereby the two companies would develop combined Dairy Barn store/gas bar outlets.

Neal, a subsidiary of Ultramar Co., London, at that time operated 750 gas stations in Eastern Canada, and, according to Dairy Barn, was to have made these sites available to Dairy Barn for evaluation.

At the same time, Dairy Barn announced it was negotiating to develop similar store/gas bar outlets with BP Oil Ltd., Imperial Oil Ltd. and Sun Oil Co. Subsequently, it announced an agreement whereby 12 such outlets would be established. . . . The second part of Dairy Barn's refinancing involved an agreement whereby Glendale Mobile Homes Ltd. would build prefabricated Dairy Barn stores. The stores would be paid for, under another agreement, by Borden Co., the company that supplied Dairy Barn with its dairy products.

What Dairy Barn seems to have been trying to arrange was this: Dairy Barn would lease suitable gas-station sites from the oil companies; Glendale would build the stores to go on the sites; Borden would pay for the stores and then lease them back to Dairy Barn.

If Dairy Barn then sold the whole operation as a franchise, so that site and store rentals were paid by the franchisee, it would have set up a store at very little cost to itself.

Or, to put it another way, it seems Borden was being used to refinance Dairy Barn's ailing operations.

The arrangement, however, fell through, and none of the agreements was ever followed up. Glendale, and particularly Borden, both lost money on the deal.

The flurry of press releases announcing the various agreements, however, does seem to have had some impact, in that the value of Dairy Barn shares increased. By October, 1972, they reached a high of $5.

Dairy Barn's end finally came in mid-1973, when all officers and directors simply resigned from the company. (George Cohon had resigned Jan. 1, 1973; Alan Eagleson resigned in May, 1973.)

The last officer to leave the company — on Aug. 17, 1973 — was the secretary-treasurer, who tersely informed the Quebec Securities Commission that Dairy Barn had closed all its retail outlets, laid off all its employees, and, as of 5.00 p.m. that day, closed all its offices.

With that, the company essentially just disappeared. And as far as FP can determine, none of the ex-directors or officers feels he has further responsibility.

Meanwhile, Robert Stevens of Bowmanville, Ont., continues to operate the two Dairy Barn franchises he bought for $12,500 each.

Early in 1973, he says, Dairy Barn "threatened to close my door," so he bought out the company's interest in his stores. Altogether, he estimates he paid Dairy Barn some $150,000.

He continues to use the Dairy Barn name, however, and since the company is still officially in business somewhere, he feels he is still bound by the franchise agreement.

Part of that agreement says he must pay Dairy Barn 4% of gross sales. So for the time being, he continues to set aside his 4%, wondering: who does it belong to? And wondering too, no doubt: whatever *did* happen to Dairy Barn Stores of Canada?[9]

A fundamental challenge confronting the large North American corporation is to discern the appropriate role for its board of directors. Since such boards can seldom hope to scrutinize the day-to-day operations of the corporations over which they preside, their role is more that of general overseers than managers. This distinction has led to some intriguing rethinking of the duties of today's corporate directors. One such effort led to the following redefinition of the board of directors' role:

. . . Boards of directors do not and should not run major corporations. Their role is that of direction, and the distinction is vital — it's the management executives' job to do the day-to-day decision making and risk taking.

The image of a group of directors arriving at momentous decisions that will be passed on to hired managers is absurdly outmoded in any company with modern professional management. And certainly, no company today that lacks effective professional management will be saved by the directors trying to do management's job.

What kind of contribution, then, can directors make to organizations run by managers who are more talented, better trained, and more highly motivated than they used to be, and who face more challenges than ever from without? The question confronts us with a paradox: the increasing competence of management appears to make the board of directors both more of an anachronism and potentially more useful and more necessary than ever before.

It would seem that the increasing competence of management must further diminish the board's potential contribution, but recent developments suggest just the contrary. Progress in management skills lessens the possible contribution of directors *only within the sphere of operating decisions*.

The job of a board with incompetent managers is simply to replace them with more competent people. The challenge to the growing majority of boards blessed with good management is to identify those things that management cannot do for itself and structure the board's role accordingly. Then it will be in a position to make real contributions, which will be all the more welcome because they do not infringe upon the responsibilities of the men charged with getting today's work done and planning tomorrow's use of the resources entrusted to them.

No management has the capacity for impersonal and objective self-appraisal. It cannot evaluate objectively its own management philosophy, its own structure, its use of decision-making techniques, or its allocation

9 Richard Starks, "Missing: A Company That Everybody Walked Away From", *The Financial Post*, January 26, 1974.

of resources and people. It is a prime responsibility of the board, therefore, to audit periodically the organization structure and the processes of management to ensure that the corporation is healthy in these respects.

Such an audit has two parts. The first, which is primarily quantitative, concerns goals, strategies, and performance measurement. The second, which is primarily judgmental, concerns managers' ability and the policies and procedures that enable them to work as a successful team.

Faced with the complexity of today's multi-product, multi-division and even multi-industry corporations, the part-time director requires much more than past statistical data if he is to exercise judgment. Directors must understand the significance of the key factors for success of each of the corporation's businesses, and goals must be set aimed at improving these factors. The director needs to know how management expects to achieve these improvements and then measure performance against them.

The second, judgmental part of the management audit is more difficult. In addition to an appraisal of the quality and style of the company's executives, it calls for a review of the organization's structure, policies, and procedures. Here the directors will make use of one of their principal assets — their objectivity.

By concentrating on resource allocation, the directors are concerning themselves with problem definition, rather than second-guessing management's operating decisions. As Dean William F. Pounds of the Sloan School of Management at MIT has observed, much progress has been made in sharpening our problem-solving and decision-making skills, but little has been added to our ability to decide where these skills should be applied.

Accordingly, a second major contribution that directors can make is to serve as an early warning system. There can be little doubt that such a system is needed. Men who began their careers with an organization decades ago, and who have devoted their skills and their experience ever since to immediate functional and operating needs, cannot usually be expected to be *au courant* with changes taking place outside their sphere of interest and expertise, however relevant these might be to the future. That explains why so few industries seem capable of major innovations from within, and why so often the innovative opportunities are grasped by outsiders. Directors who could alert management to such opportunities would be of inestimable value.

Moreover, the gap between the demands of change and the ability of organizations to respond to change is growing. The reason is simple enough: the more complex organizations become, the more they have to depend on established patterns of behavior to maintain stability. To populate organizations with people who have mastered the requisite skills requires some orderly basis of tenure and promotion. Yet these very systems of order and stability reduce the organization's ability to identify and deal with change. That is why the agent of change often has to be someone from outside the organization — an independent director who has no reason to favor the status quo. . . .

In recent years, the directors' greatest failure to act in an independent, informed and objective manner has been in the area of diversification. The wave of massive write-offs of director-approved projects, even by better-managed companies, has contributed heavily to the erosion of confidence in the US corporate system. There is ample evidence that once management steps outside the technologies and markets it has mastered, decision-making becomes increasingly risky. As one chief executive stated in announcing a major write-off, "We over-estimated our ability to manage a business in which we had no direct experience." Clearly, in these areas of diversification that lie outside the special experience of operating management, the objectivity and competence of the board must be brought to bear.

Acquisitions and mergers require particularly sophisticated decision-making on the part of directors. Not only are they outside management's direct experience but they have their own unique characteristics, cash flows, and capital needs. Also, a vital element is an evaluation of management's plans for integrating the acquired company into the ongoing management process. By the time an acquisition is brought to the board, management has become an advocate. Hence it is essential that the directors have access to independent and informed analysis of the proposal.

In these activities, the relationship between the executive and outside board members is highly sensitive. To change it along constructive lines calls for a thoughtful review by both parties of the role of the board, to enable it to make its valuable and vital contribution without putting it in conflict with the prerogatives of management.

Jack Rathbone of Standard Oil of New Jersey (now Exxon) once expressed this relationship in telling terms: "A man who is in a tough executive post has got to be able to call together a group of his associates, his colleagues, his subordinates, and sound out his plans, thrash them out when they are in half-baked form. But in addition, I believe very strongly that he needs one more step if you are going to have the proper safeguards, and that is the job of proving his point to an independent group who have not been participants in the plans, but who stand aside and judge. They interfere in no way with management, but they are damn good judges. I think if that element is lacking, you are always in danger. Any chief executive should have full authority, but he should also have the privilege of going before a board and defending his practice."

The word "privilege" is significant here because it carries the idea that every chief executive has both the right and the responsibility to be judged. It also implies that while failure to use the board as a free constituency may appear to buy time and protect the executive, his real strength in difficult times lies in being sure that the independent board has all the facts and shares in the basic decisions.[10]

Another reassessment of the duties of a modern corporate board led to five guidelines directed at improving their effectiveness:

1. *All insiders on the board other than the chairman and the president should be asked to resign.*

[Many] seemingly plausible arguments for having insiders on boards are essentially specious. The same objectives can be accomplished through other means:

- If one functional role of the board of directors is to provide advice

[10] E. Everett Smith, "The Goldberg Dilemma: Directorships", *The Wall Street Journal*, February 7, 1973. Reprinted with permission of *The Wall Street Journal* © Dow Jones & Company, Inc., 1973.

and counsel, do insider officer-directors have to be on the board in order to advise the president?

- If the board is to serve as some sort of discipline, how does an insider on the board serve as a discipline on himself?
- If the board is to be available in the event of a leadership crisis, can insiders objectively conclude that their president's performance is so unsatisfactory that he should be replaced?
- If the board's role includes the determination of objectives, strategies, and major policies, should inside office-directors recommend objectives and strategies that they themselves have recommended?
- If directors should ask discerning questions at board meetings, can an insider officer-director do this without jeopardizing his working relationship with the president?
- If the board should evaluate the president, how is an officer-director with aspirations of continued employment to do this except in favorable terms?

2. *The specific functions of the board should be discussed and agreed on by the chairman, the president, and the outside board members, and put into writing as a charter for board activities.*

3. *Criteria should be established which the board is required to use in a formal annual evaluation of the president's performance.*

Recommendations as to the distinctive factors by which the president's performance is to be measured can be constructed on (a) the criteria used by the president in evaluating his subordinates and their operations; (b) the company's annual operating budget; (c) the company's annual capital budget; (d) market data, when available, such as share of market; (e) performance data of competitors with comparable product lines; and (f) financial tests such as return on investment, profit margin, earnings per share, cash flow, and inventory levels.

4. *Directors should ask presidents at board meetings the same questions as they would if they owned a substantial part of the company.*

The sorts of questions a director would ask in the management of his personal business affairs, in other words, should be the sorts of questions he poses to the president. In my judgement, directors unwilling to accept this standard of liability and to fulfill their legal responsibility of representing the shareholders — the owners — should resign.

5. *Compensation rates should be established for outside directors which motivate them to take an active and responsible role.* One reason for outside directors' passivity and lack of involvement is their relatively limited monetary incentive to devote time and energy to another company's problems. Outside directors, in my judgment, are today generally overpaid for what they *do*, and underpaid for what they *should do*. Significantly higher directors' fees would, I believe, motivate able and responsible directors to devote the time and energy they should to the affairs of the corporations they serve.[11]

Recently, controversy over the role of corporate board members has focused, to a considerable degree, on the issue of inside vs. outside directors. The

---

[11] Myles L. Mace, "The President and the Board of Directors", *Harvard Business Review*, March-April 1972

term "insiders" means those working for the corporation and normally embraces only those in senior executive positions. "Outsiders" usually include board members and senior officers from other companies, professional board members and retired executives. The term "outsiders" can also embrace so-called public members; that possibility is dealt with on a separate basis in the next chapter. An article by Stanley C. Vance reviews the pressures leading to a gradual increase in the number of outside directors defined in the narrower sense. Among these forces are the gradual disappearance of the family firm, the force of government regulatory bodies, shifts in equity-to-long-term borrowing ratios, stress on representativeness of boards, growth of multinational corporations and the role of conglomerates. After weighing all the pros and cons, Vance concludes:

Thus the boardroom directorate continues to seesaw inside and out. If at first these ups and downs appear inconsequential, it may well be that the direction of movement has a more profound influence. While "inside" and "outside" are perhaps inadequate terms, we must admit that they do indicate differences which are real.[12]

A recent Canadian twist to the insider-outsider issue is the development of legislative requirements for majority Canadian representation on the boards of foreign-owned corporations operating in Canada. These requirements have provoked at least two recent commentaries which relate to the broader issue as well. The first from *Industrial Canada*, was appropriately headed "Wanted — Canadian 'Dummy' Directors."

On December 15, 1972, Ontario passed an amendment to its Business Corporations Act requiring that a majority of directors of Ontario incorporated companies be resident Canadians as of October 1, 1973. Many foreign controlled Ontario companies are now scrambling about looking for resident Canadians who they feel confident will vote and act as expected on their "boards". Corporation lawyers often refer to this type of appointee as a "dummy" director.
British Columbia recently introduced amendments to its Companies Act that will also require Canadian citizenship for a majority of the directors of B.C. companies. The federal government likewise intends to get into the act shortly, and announced its intention to introduce similar amendments to the Federal Corporations Act later this year. Since most foreign subsidiaries operating nationally are federally incorporated, this will trigger a new demand for resident Canadians to fill out the boards on a very extensive list of large companies. This very impressive list of companies will no doubt exert considerable caution in looking for their "dummy" directors. After all, a multinational corporation may not want corporate policy affected by some maverick sitting on the board of his Canadian subsidiary.
With this growing demand for "dummy" directors, many Canadians will be receiving invitations to sit on boards of foreign subsidiaries within the next couple of years. Although the function may appear cosmetic and simply a matter of fulfilling a nominal legal requirement we should issue a word of caution.
There has been a trend towards increasing the responsibilities of

[12] Stanley C. Vance, "The Seesaw in the Boardroom", The Conference Board RECORD, January 1974, Vol. XI, No. 1, p. 33.

directors in Canadian corporate law. It is no longer sufficient to attend directors' meetings and not "rock the boat". The law will presume liability in many instances if the director remains silent. For example, in Ontario he must disclose an interest in a contract or transaction and not vote on such a matter. If a company redeems or acquires its own shares in contravention of the Act or the articles of incorporation, a director who voted in favor of it would be liable to the corporation to the extent of the amount paid. Also in Ontario, if a dividend is declared when a company is insolvent the directors who voted for it will be liable.

In fact the director who fails to have his decision recorded in the minutes will be deemed to have consented. Even if he was not at the meeting his consent will be presumed unless he forwards his dissent by registered mail within seven days of his becoming aware of the board's decision. He may even be liable for unpaid wages to employees under certain circumstances.

The recently proposed "New Business Corporations Law for Canada" extends directors' liability, even further — to situations where commissions, discounts, allowances, loans, guarantees or financial assistance are given contrary to law. In most cases the consenting directors will be jointly liable to restore to the corporation any amounts illegally distributed. Furthermore, most legislation today now sets out a general statement of duty and care for directors. The recently introduced B.C. legislation, for example, states that "every director of a company in exercising his powers and performing his functions shall (a) act honestly and in good faith and in the best interests of the company and (b) exercise the care, diligence and skill of a reasonably prudent person."

With these increasing responsibilities one should not take his duties as a "dummy" director too lightly. Some corporations may have no objection to "dummy" directors who are uninterested and apathetic but beware — the responsibilities are not as nominal as the name suggests.[13]

The naive thinking which lies behind insistence on a majority of Canadian citizens on the boards of directors of Canadian subsidiaries was brought out in a *Globe and Mail* article entitled "Residence Law Means Return to Artificiality."

. . . These new provisions must have been enacted in the naive hope that the new majority of Canadians on the board of directors would be able to overrule or somehow modify to Canada's benefit the wishes of foreign owners of Ontario corporations.

There are various kinds of foreign-controlled Ontario corporations.

In a public corporation whose shares are widely held by the foreign, and probably to some extent the Canadian public, effective control usually rests with management. Even though the majority of the shareholders may be foreign, the Canadian management is probably already responsive to the Canadian situation and brings a Canadian perspective to management. It should not be difficult for such corporations to comply with the new rules, and some may already have a majority of resident Canadian directors. However, control probably will remain with the management and not with the directors.

In some public companies, voting control is tightly held by a small

[13] "Wanted — Canadian 'Dummy' Directors", *Industrial Canada*, March 1973, p. 7.

group of foreign shareholders or perhaps one foreign shareholder. In this type of corporation the controlling group always ensures that the directors will comply with its wishes. The new provisions will not change this.

Most private corporations are owned by one or a few shareholders, and if they are not themselves the directors they have nominee-type directors who will comply with their wishes.

The new rules will create a problem for public and private companies, whether publicly or privately controlled by one or a few foreign shareholders. How can they have a majority of resident Canadian directors and still retain firm control over the company? The directors, after all, are required by law to manage the corporation.

Conceivably, a majority of resident Canadian directors could make decisions contrary to the controlling shareholders' wishes before they can be removed. The answer is that the shareholders will seek out Canadian directors who are willing to follow orders.

Practicing lawyers are beginning to realize that they will be the first targets for the new job of nominee resident Canadian director. But there are problems for lawyers and other persons wishing to fill this role. The Business Corporations Act has imposed new liabilities on directors and prevents Ontario corporations from providing a comprehensive indemnity to such directors in case they suffer losses through being directors.

The act contemplates that anyone who is appointed a director will actually be involved in the management of the company and will be aware of all important decisions. If he does not provide a certain standard of care in acting as a director he may be subject to various liabilities under the act.

The new provisions ensure that in many companies controlled by foreign shareholders the majority of Canadian directors will not be so involved and aware of the companies' problems, since they will be nominee directors obediently following the orders of foreign shareholders.

One result will be that the nominee directors will seek broad indemnities from the foreign shareholders to cover any losses suffered by them in the course of their duties.

Since Jan. 1, 1971, practicing lawyers have enjoyed the absence of nominee directors and nominee shareholders who had prevailed under the previous Companies Act. In this period, many closely held corporations have been operating with one or a few shareholders who are also the directors; nominee directors have been eliminated to a great extent.

But for foreign-controlled corporations, the resident Canadian director rules will take Ontario back to the artificiality of the old days. There will be nominee directors who have no real power and artificial directors' meetings at which the real controllers are not in the majority.

Could the good intentions of the drafters of these new provisions have been realized in any other way? It is naive to assume that resident Canadian citizens are going to gain any significant degree of comprehensive control over foreign-owned corporations without the enactment of much more significant laws, which would probably border on expropriation.

A reasonable objective for legislation of this type would be to require foreign-owned corporations to employ certain Canadian management personnel. Control would remain in the hands of the foreign shareholders, but the management might be able to bring more Canadian perspective to the day-to-day operation of the company. Many foreign-owned companies in Canada operate with only foreign key personnel. Surely this does result in disregard for Canadian customs, policies and objectives in some cases.

It might be possible to provide that within a certain number of years, all foreign-owned Ontario corporations shall have a Canadian as chief executive officer. This would result in some artificiality in that figurehead Canadian presidents would be controlled by foreign assistant secretaries carrying secret messages from the foreign owners. But at least such provisions could give Canadians a chance to show they can handle top management jobs for foreign-owned companies.

There is convincing evidence that Canadians can handle such jobs. If such rules were enacted, however, Canada would probably need to concentrate more funds and attention on business schools and other management training facilities.

The new provisions for resident Canadian directors cast the legislators in the role of a fairy godmother waving her wand at foreign-controlled Ontario corporations and magically turning them into good Canadian Cinderellas. Those who have thought about the problem will realize that it will take hard work and careful planning to achieve useful objectives for Canada in this area.[14]

There is growing recognition of the need to pin down precisely the responsibilities of corporate board directors whether they are insiders or outsiders. One important aspect of this process is to more fully clarify the rights of shareholders in relation to the actions of directors when these actions are deemed improper or inappropriate. Finding a proper balance in this area is difficult as is suggested by the fears aroused by recent legislative proposals at the federal level in Canada.

. . . Businessmen, their lawyers, and securities analysts will want to look closely at some of the features that eventually will be written into the law governing the 25,000 federally incorporated companies.

The new bill [Canada Business Corporations Act] contains new responsibilities for directors and new powers for shareholders. The combination could be dynamic. Directors have already expressed concern about a legislative drift toward greater shareholder rights, which, it is felt, might lead to frivolous lawsuits.

In general terms, the new legislation will charge directors with dual responsibilities: to "act honestly and in good faith with a view to the best interests of the corporations and (to) exercise the care, diligence and skill of a reasonably prudent person."

A director must act in the best interests of the corporation and not his own interests. A director cannot "exculpate himself by employment contracts, broad indemnity clauses, or shareholder ratification, particularly where he is also a majority shareholder," background papers to the bill explain.

The duty of "care, diligence and skill" is largely new law, department officials note. Although these duties are presumed to exist in common law, "in fact in the corporation law context those duties have some-

[14] Peter R. Hayden, "Residence Law Means Return to Artificiality", *The Globe and Mail*, Toronto, September 25, 1973.

times been qualified to the point where they are now almost meaningless," the background papers comment.

The "Canadian content" rule for foreign-controlled companies (a majority of directors of federally incorporated companies must be Canadian,
or Canadian resident) will take effect in five years. The new law adds that
this majority of directors must be resident Canadians "who are not employees of the corporation or any of its affiliates."

The intent of the sections of the bill dealing with shareholders is to
create a better balance between shareholders and management.

Shareholders would have power to initiate by-laws and amend or
repeal existing bylaws, remove directors at any time by ordinary resolution, amend the company's articles of incorporation, and submit proposals to shareholders meetings.

Those who dissent from the decision of a shareholders meeting
would have the right to require the company to buy their shares for fair
value. If the shareholder is not satisfied with the company's valuation, he
may apply to the courts for another valuation.[15]

As this *Business Week* article points out, only one thing is certain: searching questions will continue to be asked about the role of directors:

There was a time when a corporate director could regard his appointment as just an agreeable tribute to his wealth and his connections, a
sign that he had entered the inner circle of the business community. If any
director still thinks of his job that way, the proliferation of stockholder
suits, the drumfire criticism of the militant consumerists, and the mounting complaints of minority groups should make him think again.

If corporate management is to survive in anything like its present
form, directors will have to take on new responsibilities. They must make
sure that corporate goals are consistent with the larger goals of U.S. society. And they must monitor management to see that it pursues these goals
effectively.[16]

Conflicts of Interest

Within the corporate sphere, conflicts of interest can take many forms and
involve many individuals other than members of boards of directors. Specific
problems result from the pervasiveness of interlocking directorates and the use
and abuse of insider information. Beyond these problems there is a need for a
general code of ethics involving all sorts of business activities.

The challenge in the case of interlocking directorates is to ensure that
they are not used to pursue anti-competitive practices and other behaviour
contrary to the public interest. That this is difficult, to put it mildly, is suggested by a *Financial Post* report of a recent Canadian survey which draws on
U.S. as well as Canadian experience:

A cobweb of interlocking directorates links many of Canada's largest
corporations. Between industries and within industries, leading firms

[15] Stephen Duncan, "Directors Worry New Act May Bring Frivolous Lawsuits", *The Financial Post*, July 28, 1973.
[16] "What Are Directors For?" Reprinted from the May 22, 1971 issue of *Business Week* by
special permission. Copyright 1971 by McGraw-Hill, Inc.

and their suppliers, customers and competitors are tied together through boardroom connections.

The fact that these interlocks exist is well known. What is not known, however, is their structure and their effects on competition.

For the first time in Canada — through the mechanism of Canada's proposed competition act — interlocking directorates are to come under the scrutiny of federal-government investigators.

Generally speaking, interlocking directorates are the concern of anti-trust authorities because such arrangement can be, and have been, used as devices for lessening competiton. They provide a unique means of inter-corporate communication.

As the management of various companies becomes inter-twined, there is a greater likelihood of "co-operation" among them instead of arms-length bargaining and active rivalry. Through the use of interlocking directorates small groups of businessmen have been known to extend their sphere of power and their control in the marketplace.

Interlocking directorates are basically of two kinds: A *horizontal* interlock connects companies engaged in the same line of work; a *vertical* interlock is one which exists between, say, a customer and a supplier.

Interlocks can be either "direct" — where directors of competing companies are members of each other's boards — or "indirect," where instead they each serve together on the board of a third company.

Besides interlocking directorates there are other kinds of interlocking relationships which can also affect competition. For example, an officer of Company A may serve as a director of competing Company B, and an officer of Company B may be a director of Company A. Technically this is not an interlocking directorate but the possible anti-competitive effects can be the same.

To anyone studying the subject of interlocking directorates two obvious questions come to mind: how common are they and what forms do they take?

Reliable information on interlocks in the Canadian economy is almost non-existent. Consequently, with the aid of a university research grant, we recently conducted an inquiry of our own — on a modest scale and strictly on an experimental basis.

We utilized two different approaches. . . . Between the two studies there were scores of interlocking directorates. The results gave an idea of the structure of these relationships and the identity of the individuals who provided the links between companies. Vertical relationships significantly outnumbered horizontal. In the case of indirect interlocks, commercial banks provided the vehicle for the majority of them.

What we achieved in our research can be compared analogously to the "tip of an iceberg." It is one thing to identify the interlocks — it is quite another thing — and much more difficult — to try to determine their effects on competition.

It would be singularly misleading to suggest that just because an interlock exists competition has automatically been affected adversely, or that the interlock was created for that purpose. Not at all.

It is widely acknowledged that many directorships are honorary — the individuals concerned may take only a minor part in the affairs of the companies. Even in the case of directors who provide active leadership, while some may have been sought out for their company connections, probably just as many were elected because of their judgment and business acumen. Anti-competitive motives or effects may be non-existent. Clearly, any legislation dealing with interlocking directorates will have to be applied selectively.

Interlocks are to come under government scrutiny — in section 36 of the proposed competition act — for the first time since combines legislation was introduced 84 years ago. The new legislation will apply to both vertical and horizontal interlocking directorates, in all sectors of the economy, to large and small companies alike — there is no minimum-size criterion.

It will not apply in the case of "affiliated" companies, e.g. where one is a subsidiary of another, nor will it cover interlocking "relationships."

Interlocking directorates will be dealt with by the Competitive Practices Tribunal, not the criminal courts. The Tribunal will have the power to prohibit an interlock if it is "satisfied" that the interlock "has had, is having, or is likely to have the effect of significantly lessening competition."

It is highly unlikely, except in rare instances, that the Tribunal will be able to demonstrate in some tangible way that an interlocking directorate has affected competition or might do so. Occasionally there may be flagrant examples of boardroom pressures or of directors acting in conflicting roles. But in most cases it will probably boil down to the Tribunal having the difficult task of trying to measure or speculate about a certain director's influence.

It would not be surprising if, in time, the Tribunal — in an effort to make the section workable — gravitated toward something in the way of a *per se* approach based on clear-cut guidelines, e.g. categorically prohibiting horizontal interlocks.

It is difficult at this point to predict how the structure of directorships will be affected when the proposed Act becomes law. If the Tribunal takes a tough stand there could be some major reshuffling and an accompanying increase in the number of directors in the country.

All things considered, however, including the nature of the problem and the difficulty of determining in some tangible way the effects on competition — to say nothing of the Tribunal's anticipated crushing work load — it is more likely they will take a soft line on interlocking directorates. Certainly in the early stages, it is highly probable that only in the most conspicuous and extreme cases will the Tribunal take any action.[17]

Turning to the matter of insider trading, the challenge is to ensure high standards of ethical behaviour among all the individuals privy to significant information not yet made available to the shareholders and the public. In the final analysis, those at the top of the corporate heirarchy who lack integrity will probably find some way around any code, guideline or law designed to prevent them from exploiting confidential data. The problems involved in trying to curb improper insider trading were well brought out in a 1973 *Fortune* editorial:

Among the numerous morals that might be extracted from the Equity Funding scandal, one is surely worth special attention: there is still no

[17] Dr. James A. Sherbaniuk, "Can You Put a Gauge on Boardroom Interlocks?" *The Financial Post*, October 13, 1973.

generally agreed upon understanding of the rights and responsibilities of stock-market "insiders." Indeed, there is no agreement about who insiders *are*. Four decades after passage of the Securities Exchange Act, almost a decade after the sensational Texas Gulf Sulphur case, in which the Securities and Exchange Commission broadened and extensively elucidated the rules applying to insiders, the law remains murky.

Its murkiness will be evident to anyone who has followed the controversies enveloping the Equity Funding case. One controversy has to do with the behavior of Raymond Dirks after he received the now famous telephone call from a former employee of Equity Funding, tipping him off to the fraud. Dirks is an insurance analyst with Delafield Childs, Inc., a New York Stock Exchange member firm. After he got the report, he proceeded to verify it — which is, one might suppose, what a serious researcher should do when he hears an important rumor about one of the companies he follows. Along the way, Dirks told his institutional clients about it — which also sounds reasonable.

Dirks says that he was acting, all during this time, under the impression that his behavior did not violate any of the insider regulations. He argues that he was not himself a corporate insider and neither was his original informant. And, of course, when he took his suspicions to the executives who really were insiders at Equity Funding, they denied everything (although toward the end, it seems clear, they were not very convincing). Neither Dirks nor his firm, so far as is known, sold any Equity Funding stock after he was tipped.

The New York Stock Exchange has nevertheless contended that Dirks flagrantly violated both its own regulations and the SEC's. Dirks was, in fact, among the first to be prosecuted in the Equity Funding case. He has been charged with fraud by the Exchange, which contends that he should have come to it with his information, that he should not have circulated "rumors of a sensational character," and that he should not have informed his clients about matters of such importance that were not generally known to investors.

The reasonableness of these contentions will be argued at length during the disciplinary proceedings now under way. The Exchange can plausibly argue that its regulations were unambiguous and that the SEC's ban on passing along material nonpublic information was equally clear. But Dirks can fairly respond that he was simply following the powerfully entrenched customs of Wall Street. Analysts routinely supply clients with material information not generally available to the public, and clients expect them to do precisely that. Why else were so many institutional investors on the phone to Dirks after word about his information began spreading through Wall Street? The proposition that an analyst who learns something important about a listed company should bring it to the Exchange will strike many analysts as hilarious.

There is no doubt that the SEC has been reasonably consistent about some aspects of the insider issue. The commission has said for many years that no investor may trade on the basis of material information not generally known to the investing public. The commission has also prosecuted brokers who passed on such information, expecting to be rewarded with some business from grateful customers. Thus the SEC views about tipping may present some serious legal problems for Dirks.

Yet there are difficulties about taking these views at face value. The main one is that they have so little correspondence with the everyday reality of Wall Street. Almost every day's business-page report on the stock market includes evidence that some investors have foreknowledge of major corporate announcements; over and over, one observes, the price movements take place *before* the announcements. Much has been made of the fact that Equity Funding stock fell during the period when Dirks was informing his clients. But it had also been slipping for many months before then: when trading in the stock was suspended, the price was less than one-third of what it had been early in 1971. This would seem to be a strange phenomenon in a company about which outsiders heard little but good news.

Another difficulty is that the SEC's rules rest upon distinctions that seem unrealistic. The SEC has repeatedly proclaimed that research is the lifeblood of the securities business. But what is the research to consist of if it excludes information not generally available?

The SEC has tried to make a distinction between raw data and interpretation of the data. In a speech a year ago, William J. Casey, who was then Chairman of the SEC, argued that "the real nature of securities analysis . . . is the sifting and investigating of *disclosed* financial information." (Emphasis added.) Without this "invaluable" effort, Casey went on, "the individual . . . would have to swim for himself in an ocean of financial data."

What makes this distinction unrealistic is that most corporations nowadays go a good deal beyond disclosing raw data. Most of them go to considerable lengths to make the data meaningful to their stoockholders. Analysts who simply work with published data are not apt to be performing a very useful service. (They are also not apt to get much business from serious investors.)

What the SEC keeps talking about as interpretation inevitably involves the obtaining of "information." Most interpreters of financial data do much more than merely observe certain logical relationships between bits of the data. To have any serious understanding of the data, they must understand the strategic concepts that govern corporate behavior, and it seems reasonable to think of any briefing they may get about these concepts as "information" — perhaps the most important information of all. Many people would be better off today if some such information about Equity Funding had been developed earlier by analysts.

The new Chairman of the SEC, G. Bradford Cook, has said that he wants to clarify the laws pertaining to insiders and has acknowledged that "maybe the existing law [is] somewhat unclear." It is hard to believe that the commission will have much success in clarifying things until it perceives how remote from reality some of its past formulations have been.[18]

That tougher criminal as well as civil sanctions should be in force to deal with unscrupulous insider traders is more than suggested by a report on a proposed new British law that was in the legislative mills in late 1973.

In Britain, the use of confidential information — withheld from the public — for a quick killing in stocks, is soon to be made a criminal offence.

Proposed legislation prepared by the Department of Trade & Industry

[18] "Insider Trading and Stock-Market Realities", *Fortune*, May 1973, p. 178 © 1974 Time Inc.

is about to be presented to Parliament to give teeth to the generally accepted business principle equating improper insider dealing on the stock exchange with common theft.

Lord Shawcross recently warned publicly that the net to catch offenders would be cast very wide. It is believed by sources close to the lawmakers that the definition of "insiders" would cover all directors as well as employees of a firm and all its professional advisors with access to confidential information.[19]

That stiffer criminal as well as civil penalties are even more necessary in North America than in Britain is suggested by the results of a comparative survey of American and British directors and executives. The survey revealed their own opinions on the prevalence and propriety of taking advantage of inside knowledge, and the opinions they hold on their colleagues' activities in this area:

... The question was: "Imagine that you are a member of the board of directors of a large public company. At a board meeting you learn of plans for an impending merger of your company with a smaller public company which has had an unprofitable year, and whose shares are currently selling at a price so low that you are certain that it will rise when any news of the merger becomes public knowledge. What would you (others) do?"

In the US survey and UK Directors' survey, half the respondents were asked what *they* would do, the "personal" response; and the other half were asked what they thought *the average managing director* would do, the "other" response.

There appears to be a wide divergence of opinion on this subject, especially between the US and UK. Three out of four directors consider their colleagues would not take advantage of any information, and it is clear that UK directors take their responsibilities more seriously in this matter than do executives in UK or US (indeed, in the US one in two seem to have no scruples in this matter). Some difference between directors of large and small companies was noticed; for instance, more than 20% of the 170 answering this question, who were directors of UK companies employing less than 1000 people, thought the average managing director would buy shares, compared with only 5% from larger companies. On the apparent difference in attitude between directors and managers, it might be argued that one reason some managers do not reach board level is because they cannot be trusted with confidential information. But it is perhaps a cause for concern that such a high proportion of managers see little wrong with the use of confidential information for personal gain.[20]

Britain also provides a useful starting point for a discussion of the degree of reliance which can be placed on self-regulation. The final report of a series of special reports on corporate behaviour prepared under the auspices of the Confederation of British Industry has received a mixed though largely positive reaction.

"A company should behave like a good citizen in business. The law

[19] Thomas Land, "In Britain, Improper Insider Trading May be Treated Like Common Theft", *The Financial Post*, May 26, 1973.
[20] Simon Webley, "Business Policy & Business Ethics", *Journal of Business Policy*, Vol. 3, No. 3, 1973, pp. 6—7.

does not (and cannot) contain or prescribe the whole duty of a citizen."

So says the Confederation of British Industry (CBI) in its final report on corporate behavior.

Published as *The Responsibilities of the British Public Company* (CBI, 21 Tothill St., London SW1), the 48-page study goes a long way toward upholding the heavy moral dictum uttered by Prime Minister Edward Heath during the hottest days of the so-called "Lonrho Affair". . . .

The report states:

"Where abuse of proper practice is established," it says, "such as in the case of 'insider dealing,' the task of regulation must be undertaken by the government."

There's no doubt that the uglier manifestations of the ambiguities present in existing company law — ambiguities that allow the practice of insider dealing to flourish — can be dealt with effectively through the type of legislation proposed in the government's white paper on company law (the Companies Bill is to be introduced in the new session of Parliament), but the Companies' Acts cannot provide what the committee calls "moral imperative." This, the report says, is the duty of the companies and their boards.

We are now presented with the crux of the report: moral responsibility. A vastly different — but equally problematic — situation to that very tangible business of making money.

"Within its own field of knowledge," the committee asserts, "skill, geographical concern and financial capacity (these are important limitations), a company has the duty to be responsive to the movement of informed public opinion as well as to the requirements of authority. A company should, as is indeed the practice of the best companies, pay proper regard to the environmental and social consequences of its business activities, and should not sacrifice the safety or efficiency of goods and services in the interests of expediency of competitiveness."

The report has a great deal to say about the ability of private enterprise to adapt to the new circumstances in which it has to operate, but much of the onus is placed on the shareholder:

"As a company is a 'company of shareholders,' it is at least arguable that those who own the equity of the business have corresponding duties both to the community which has made incorporation possible and created conditions in which trade may be carried on, and to those categories of persons with whom the company deals at arm's length."

That is: creditors and suppliers (with whom, the committee suggests, better relations should be forged); and in some cases even employees and customers. The committee has a special word with regard to the latter:

"It should never be forgotten that it is those who have least to spend whose money problems are most acute and who are least well equipped to cope with them."

The shareholder is then encouraged to take a more active role in determining policy decisions; in exercising an effective discipline over the board by attending annual meetings, scrutinizing accounts, and questioning directors on any matters they think affect the interests and conduct of the enterprise. "Obligations, additional to the specific requirements of the law, undertaken by the company, become one of the terms on which shareholders accept membership of the company."

The committee, however, has no useful comment to make about the particular and peculiar functions of the international company and its shareholders — except to state that, so far as the responsibilities of such companies relate to their operations in Britain, they are within the ambit of the report.

Institutional shareholders are in a special position. They are the pension funds of local authorities and nationalized industry, the insurance companies, the investment trust companies, the unit trusts, and the large charitable trusts. Between them, they own approximately one half (this is a growing proportion) of the equity of British quoted public companies.

The report suggests that institutional shareholders, because of their strong position and greater expertise, must take a leading role and set an example to the whole body of shareholders.

It has been suggested that the authority of a large body of shareholders might be more effective if focused by the existence of a supervisory board with powers of ultimate control over the management.

The answer to these questions and others (concerning the structure and responsibilities of the board, the responsibilities of the company to its employees, etc.) will no doubt come in the next few months as the Companies Bill is debated in Parliament. But in a country where attempted voluntary schemes are almost a national pastime, the CBI seems to be relying too heavily on the willingness of business to adapt to what are perceived as new moral and social responsibilities. The rallying cry to a new awareness hasn't yet been heard above the shouts of the jobbers on the floor of the stock exchange — and one rather doubts that it will.

Although the report speaks of noble ideals and ethics beyond Christian reproach, it does not — alas — explain how this can be achieved while the mainspring of private enterprise is still: profit. [21]

Business Week and other leading business publications have, for some-time, featured articles on the changing moral climate of North America and the consequent need for an improved code of ethics among managers. One article included a list of suggestions designed to ensure ethical standards of behaviour both at the individual and institutional corporate levels, "Rules for Avoiding Conflicts:"

• Establish a conflict-of-interest committee, with representatives from top management, to consider and implement rules governing the conduct not only of employees but of the company itself.

• Insist that key managers and employees in sensitive positions complete questionnaires at least once a year disavowing conflicts and disclosing associations that could lead to conflicts.

• Forbid employees to use inside information for personal profit, or to disclose it to such outsiders as banks, brokers, and institutional investors. Require executives to report periodically on any dealings in the company's stock.

[21] Jocelyn Thompson, "How Britain Plans to Run Its Insider Trading Rules", The Financial Post, August 18, 1973, p. 18.

• Avoid transactions between your company and any of its officers, directors, or major stockholders. Have any such deals scrutinized by impartial outsiders.

• Exercise caution in dealings between affiliated companies. At the least, have a committee of outside directors pass on transactions between a parent company and a subsidiary that has some public ownership.

• Appoint some alert, energetic outside directors. They can help you spot conflicts in the making.

• Steer clear of directors who serve on the boards of companies that compete with your company, even if the competition is in a minor, remote area. Some experts advise flat out against putting a broker or investment banker on your board.

• Set up an audit committee of outside directors. It is good insurance against top-level internal conflicts.

• Warn employees that paying bribes to secure business is as much against company rules as accepting them.

• Do not sweep conflict-of-interest problems under the rug. If a law has been broken, turn the matter over to the proper law-enforcement authorities. [22]

That too much reliance should not be placed on corporations and their directors, executives and officers to put their own houses in order is not only suggested by the absence in most corporations of codes of behaviour such as the above, but also by their reaction to government attempts to legislate improved standards of performance as this *Financial Post* article reveals:

Some provinces, led by Ontario, have already passed amendments to their companies acts spelling out a code of conduct for directors. The draft Canada Business Corporations Act, which eventually will replace the present Canada Corporations Act governing federally incorporated companies, also contains a section stipulating how a director should discharge his duties.

Basically, the new laws say that a director must act honestly and in good faith with a view to the best interests of the corporation, and exercise the care, diligence and skill of a reasonably prudent person.

Furthermore, if a director fails to conduct himself as directed, the legislation specifically empowers a shareholder to sue him on behalf of the company.

It is not surprising that a question in the survey relating to this legislative trend drew the sharpest and most detailed response from company chairmen and presidents.

The thrust of their views was that there is potential danger in spelling out a code of conduct with legislative sanction to sue, because it may encourage frivolous shareholder suits, thereby dissuading competent people from serving on boards.

Here, for example, is the view of A. Bruce Matthews, chairman, Canada Permanent Trust Co., Toronto:

"Directorship is a position of trust. It would be difficult, if not impossible, to define in detail, a code of conduct for directors. Legislation or

[22] "Conflict of Interest: The Moral Climate Changes". Reprinted from the April 14, 1973 issue of *Business Week* by special permission. Copyright 1973 by McGraw-Hill, Inc.

regulation sanctioning shareholder suits to enforce a right of the company is partly in effect in the U.S. The results have been chaos in the courts, with serious abuse in subjecting companies to unwarranted expense.

"In many cases, frivolous charges are made which have to be heard. The right of shareholders to change the board is sufficient."

"As a facet of 'consumerism' such legislation is probably inevitable, albeit unnecessary as to the great majority of corporations," said W. F. Griffiths, chairman, Canada Safeway Ltd., Winnipeg.

"In their program to attempt to correct faults and abuses created by a very small percentage of directors and companies, I feel they have over-reacted," responded F. H. Sherman, president, Dominion Foundries & Steel Ltd., Hamilton.

"Legislation is justified only if needed. No need is apparent in these areas," said C.D. Shepard, chairman, Gulf Oil Canada Ltd., Toronto.

"Subject to adequate protection for the directors against frivolous suits and the development of adequate case law based on Canadian conditions rather than those of foreign countries (i.e., the U.S.), it is probably a good thing," commented J.H. Moore, chairman, John Labatt Ltd., London.

"As far as public companies are concerned, the legislative trend in specifying a code of conduct will, in the long-run, severely hamper sound, forward-thinking directors' actions," said W. R. Clerihue, president, Celanese Canada Ltd., Montreal.

"Conscientious directors have always acted responsibily in the discharge of their positions of trust. Legislation which unduly exposes such directors to frivolous shareholder actions will result in fewer qualified persons being willing to accept the risks attached to such exposure and the overall quality of boards will suffer," was the view of J. V. Clyne, who just retired as chairman of MacMillan Bloedel Ltd., Vancouver.

James A. Pattison, chairman, Neonex International Ltd., Vancouver, said he is in favor of the new legislative trend.

Edmund C. Bovey, president, Northern & Central Gas Corp., Toronto, welcomed a code of conduct as a general guide. He disapproved of legislative sanctioning of shareholder suits because the common law already recognizes such actions.

Robert Hendricks, chairman, Cominco Ltd., Vancouver, considered the new trend "a lot of nonsense."

None of the companies surveyed has reacted to agitation by consumer and similar groups by appointing board members to represent the "public" interest, or any particular racial, economic or other group. As Raymond A. Rich, chairman, Canadian Hydrocarbons Ltd., Calgary, put it:

"Every director represents *all* stockholders — whether black, white; rich or poor; any race or politics. We're running a business, not a welfare agency."[23]

The greatest hope for eliminating some of the worst abuse by corporate directors, executives and officers — such as taking advantage of inside information — may lie in giving shareholders and other interested parties ample legal recourse with which to correct and remedy any such improprieties. Grounds for such recourse are now well established in the United States:

[23] Robert Catherwood, "Directors Cool About Conduct Code", *The Financial Post*, July 14, 1973.

What the Texas Gulf case did was to extend liability to insiders and their associates who trade on the basis of nonpublic information, thereby "getting the jump" on shareholders and potential shareholders who are not privy to this information. Liability for this behavior has now been developed under law in favor of outsiders who make disadvantageous stock transactions either in dealing with the insiders or while the insiders are trading. Insiders also may be liable to the corporation, on the theory that the information used by the trader is the property of the corporation. Inside trading activity has been castigated by the courts, in strong terms, as fraudulent behavior.[24]

Protecting the Honest Insider

The problems pertaining to ethics and integrity which persist in the North American corporate realm necessitate the protection of the honest insider who reveals improper corporate practices. More often than not, such individuals can bring these activities to the public attention without identifying themselves. If they cannot do so, the price they pay can be very high indeed. Despite the risks involved, as this *Wall Street Journal* item shows, more people seem to be informing on their employers for all manner of illegal and/or unethical doings:

In January 1971, the world champion whistle blower, Ralph Nader, gathered a group of associates and admirers together at the Mayflower hotel in Washington to talk about the fuzzy lines between corporate loyalty and public duty.

The question of the day was: At what point should an employee's obligations to society take precedence over his employer's well being and move him to publicly blow the whistle on defective products, concealed hazards, pollution, public waste and corruption?

From those discussions has come a new book, "Whistle Blowing", by Mr. Nader and two colleagues, Peter J. Petkas and Kate Blackwell (Grossman Publishers Inc., 398 pages, $6.95). It's dull and dated in places, a bit too shrill in others, but it probably deserves far wider readership at all levels of the corporate ladder than it is likely to get.

It's the middle of the book that makes the whole thing worthwhile, 142 pages of brief, fascinating case histories of 33 whistle blowers detailing their motives and methods, their gains and suffering. They are mostly conscience-stricken persons with little in common but a strong sense of individual responsibility and a determination not to be ignored.

A sampling of some who spoke out against corrupt, illegal or otherwise harmful activities of their organizations:

— Dr. A. Dale Console, former medical director at E.R. Squibb, who started a public outcry over worthless drugs and misleading pharmaceutical advertising in 1960. "I reached a point where I could no longer live with myself," he says.

— Christopher Pyle and Ralph Stein, ex-Army intelligence men, who brought to light the Army's massive clandestine civilian surveillance operations in 1970. So thoroughly had they thought out and documented

---

[24] John A. Hetherington, "Corporate Social Responsibility, Stockholders and the Law", *Journal of Contemporary Business*, Winter 1973, p. 51. Reprinted with permission of the *Journal of Contemporary Business* © 1973.

their "responsible dissent" that when the Army lied and clamped a tight lid on the affair they blew it right off again.

— Charles Pettis, a crack civil engineer at Brown and Root Overseas, who exposed fraud, waste and unsafe construction on a Morrison-Knudsen road project in Peru in 1968. He was fired, blackballed from the engineering field and hounded out of South America. He's still unemployed, in Spain, but he says: "You've got to stand up against pressures on that kind of thing to live with yourself."

— Seven employees of Colt Firearms, who, in 1971, disclosed massive tampering with test results on Colt M-16 rifles to conceal poor quality and frequent malfunctions. The seven testers whistled, not because troops were going into combat carrying faulty weapons, but because the testers themselves were being forced to work in unhealthy conditions — on indoor firing ranges choked with lead-filled dust. Soon after the brief public outcry, new ventilation systems were installed.

— Edward Gregory, a senior quality control inspector for General Motors in St. Louis, who forced a 1969 recall of 2.4 million Chevrolets with built-in faults that allowed carbon monoxide to seep into passenger compartments. He started trying to get the fault fixed in 1966, and kept beating management over the head with its own rules while doggedly sticking within the routine GM channels. He was bullied, ridiculed and downgraded before he finally won. Then, without admitting it should have heeded his early warnings, GM awarded him $10,000 for previously ignored suggestions he made for sealing the cars. He spent $2,700 of it on an 18-foot boat and Polaroid Camera which he uses on weekends to patrol the polluted Mississippi near his home. So far, complaints he has filed against a railroad, a steel plant and a glass company have brought crackdowns and cleanups.

— A. Ernest Fitzgerald, one of the Pentagon's top civilian cost reduction specialists (with a Civil Service rank equivalent to major general) who revealed to congressional investigators in 1969 the $2 billion cost overrun on Lockheeds' C5A transport for the Air Force. He became a pariah overnight and was shunted off to study cost problems of bowling alleys in Thailand. Air Force sleuths probed his private life, but found nothing more damning than that he was a "pinch-penny type person" who drove an old Rambler. With cruel irony, they finally abolished his job in an "economy move". He's trying to build a small consulting business now, similar to the one he abandoned for the Pentagon in 1965.[25]

The question remains as to what should be done to protect the honest insider from retaliation. In his fascinating article "On Muckrakers and Whistle Blowers," Timothy M. Ingram concludes with a reference to the discouraging response of even so liberally and reform-minded an individual as Robert Townsend. Ingram then offers his own alternatives.

Many who might offer a sympathetic ear to a corporate tattletale still feel there is a price for conscience. Even Robert Townsend, that liberal-minded proponent of controlling corporate might, says he would discourage giving a dissenting employee the privilege of immunity from reprisal. The sensitive employee should attack the problem by disagree-

---

[25] Richard Martin, "Why People Inform on Their Bosses", The Wall Street Journal, October 17, 1972. Reprinted with permission of The Wall Street Journal © Dow Jones & Company, Inc., 1972.

ing with the head man inside the shop, argues Townsend. If he's over-ruled, he can either swallow hard and accept the decision, or quit. There are certain business manners and hierarchy which must be respected.

What Are the Alternatives?

Agreed, management effectiveness depends upon quick, independent judgments about the worth of staff, and managers have to be able to depend on work being carried out as directed. Too often, though, the firing power of corporations is used to muzzle things it doesn't want to hear or wants others to hear. As it stands, the whole area of employee rights is a legal wasteland. Outside the realm of labor unions, the law has done little to protect the wage earner from abusive and overreaching exercises of employer power. At the very least, there should be protection against reprisals for workers who report the unlawful acts of their company, or testify before a court or government agency. Perhaps also there should be a right to refuse to do certain tasks or assignments found morally repugnant, much as a conscientious objector.

As more water-cooler carping reaches outside ears, executives may decide it's cheaper to listen. Permitting a climate in which workers feel free to criticize may avert the damaging publicity or agency investigation brought on by the outburst of a disgruntled, stifled employee. Many mild-mannered men now put the whistle to their lips because there is no ombudsman or in-house inspector general to investigate and act on their problems.

One of the most constructive and least publicized efforts to prod company presidents to formulate an intelligent policy respecting employee free speech took place during the height of mass antiwar demonstrations, by the Ad Hoc Committee for Working Americans and Responsible Dissent. Based at Stanford, in the heart of the San Francisco Peninsula's aerospace and electronics industry, the committee convinced a number of firms to endorse a statement, recognizing that management had a responsibility to its work force to establish a policy which would not smother dissent, "whether that dissent agreed or not with organizational objectives." Of importance, it stressed that "an atmosphere where people are uncertain of their right to speak out is inherently political and stifling."

The emotion-laden issue, creating the twitches and the crackdowns, is the pilfered memo. This gets to the deepest level of the company's "proprietary interests," the notion that all sensitive information is company private property and not to be divulged. Now, custom is fighting law, as leaks, whistle blowing, and underground papers become partial antidotes for corporate lockjaw. In a day when the paper shredder is replacing the gold washroom key as the symbol of importance, these sporadic exposés, though annoying to business, will never open to public view the day-by-day dealings. Most chief executives can outsit an intermittent Senate investigation. But what they raise — and this has received increasing attention to the point of cliché — is that corporate actions affect all of us, so we all have a right to know. As mammoth concerns are seen more and more in terms of political and social enterprises, more corporations will either institute voluntary disclosure policies or be compelled to by SEC rules and state corporation codes. As sleuthing for hidden facts and the tricks of the trade becomes more of a full-time profession, one suspects that demands for a Freedom of Information Act for corporations may not be too far off.

It was thought that government information should be shared with private individuals only upon proof of need. But the Freedom of Information Act legislates that the contents of federal files are part of the public domain, and open to inspection. If a person's request for internal agency data is denied, he can petition the court to order it released. The premise is that the citizenry has a right to know what its government is doing for it, and to it. That same premise might well be extended to corporations. It would posit that the public has access to figures showing how much a firm is polluting the waters, contributing to political campaigns, perhaps paying in taxes. The ownership rights of information giving a competitive advantage — formulas, customer lists, and the like — would be protected and treated as property. At minimum, it's a safe guess that demands will continue for future "fishbowl" laws requiring detailed annual reports.[26]

If ethics and integrity are to be instilled throughout the corporate world, honest insiders must be protected. If they produce evidence of fraudulent, dishonest or illegal behaviour from the inner recesses of the business world, their positions should at least be protected — worthless a gesture as this may prove, especially in terms of any possibility of future advancement and promotion. Where the circumstances are such that it appears that informers will be too disadvantaged to remain, adequate and even generous compensation should be forced from the corporation if their employee's revelations do lead to evidence of corrupt practices. It may even be that society should develop a system of rewards to induce concerned individuals to bring to the attention of some public office, activities which they believe to be contrary to the public interest.

Audits and What They Hide

A major explanation for the lack of information about so many corporate practices is to be found in the superficiality of traditional auditing procedures. Historically, it appears that auditors have done little more than check on the accuracy of the corporation's profit-and-loss statement and balance sheet in accordance "with generally accepted accounting principles." As shareholders and other interested parties have discovered to their chagrin, that dictum can cover a multitude of omissions and commissions. As one well informed individual has put it:

But, any experienced corporate manager knows that net profit figures can be managed as often for reasons of accuracy as for reasons of deception. Most important, the exactness of any quantification is limited by the arbitrariness of the accounting period. For enterprises with long-lived assets, deferred taxation, and complicated and even convertible capital structures, net profit per share in terms of quarters or even years is a pretty delusive figure. Management has more discretion with figures than most C.P.A.'s will readily admit. Most publicly held firms would regard themselves as imprudent if they did not have "up the treasurer's sleeve" items which could raise or lower net profit by the equivalent of at least a quarter and, preferably, 6 months' earnings. There are many instances in which accounting judgements have altered earnings far in excess of that. The

26 Timothy H. Ingram, "On Muckrakers and Whistle Blowers", *Business & Society Review*, Autumn 1972, No. 3, pp. 29—30.

more complex the company, the more controllable the reported profit for an arbitrary time period.[27]

Given the latitude available to accountants and auditors acting on their own discretion, it is not surprising that business and corporate officials should begin to feel that they can produce any figures and results that they desire:

But perhaps more insidious is the influence . . . on the manager who has not had training in the morality of financial reporting. The engineer or sales-oriented executive who reaches the top more likely will think of accounting standards in the same way he views tax regulations: something we must comply with, but let's see if we can't find a loophole or at least pick the alternative that gives us the greatest advantage.[28]

To be fair to the auditing profession, it must be acknowledged that it is caught in a dilemma. On the one hand, the auditor is reporting to the management of the corporate client that hires him, a management which is interested in the most favourable portrayal possible on the financial statements. On the other hand, there are many others, including investment analysts and investors, as well as shareholders, who rely on those statements for an honest and thorough idea of the actual performance of that management. What one group considers a full and proper presentation may be considered quite deceitful and misleading by the other.

That the auditing profession has hardly begun to reconcile these conflicting responsibilities is suggested by recent legal opinions as well as contemplation of reform in its own ranks. From outside the profession, the most rude awakening has come from courts confronted by negligence suits filed against auditors. In one landmark United States case, the judge included the following passage in his ruling:

The first law for accountants was not compliance with generally accepted accounting principles but rather full and fair disclosure, fair presentation and, if principles did not produce this brand of disclosure, accountants could not hide behind them and make whatever disclosures were necessary for full disclosure. In a word "present fairly" was a concept separate from "generally accepted accounting principles" and the latter did not necessarily result in the former.[29]

This and similar decisions have led to a good deal of discussion about the concept of a two-part audit opinion. One Canadian commentary on this possibility, although a little technical, is instructive:

Finally, one must question a concept which is fundamental to the Canadian position; what does it mean for statements to "present fairly," if it does not mean accordance with GAAP? If they present fairly, that presumably means that they are presented in a manner consistent with some set of criteria which has been explicitly defined for this purpose. Since,

[27] Eli Goldston, "Corporate Social Responsibility and Management Behaviour", *Journal of Contemporary Business*, Winter 1973, p. 67. Reprinted with permission of the *Journal of Contemporary Business* © 1973.

[28] W. Warren Brown, "A Businessman Talks About Accounting Standards", *Financial Executive*, November 1973, p. 58.

[29] Cited in "Accounting: A Crisis Over Fuller Disclosure". Reprinted from the April 22, 1972 issue of *Business Week* by special permission. Copyright 1972 by McGraw-Hill, Inc.

theoretically in the CICA position, statements could be in accordance with GAAP but still not present fairly, then there must be another, perhaps "higher," set of principles to support the fairness judgment. What are these principles? Is not the basic idea of GAAP that those principles gaining acceptance are those whose use ensures "appropriate results"? Are not these "appropriate results" the conceptual equivalent of fairness of presentation? Perhaps the answer is not to require both accordance and fairness of presentation, but, in fact, to improve the definition and specification so that accordance with GAAP does ensure fairness of presentation. Does the CICA view the two-part opinion as an interim measure, to be discarded when GAAP have been adequately established?[30]

At issue basically is the question: "Should the auditor tell all?", which is the title of one recent *Financial Post* article indicating to what depth some commentators feel an audit should probe:

The troubles of one small company — Shully's Industries — raises a much bigger issue about disclosure of corporate information.

The issue, by no means a new one, is this: if the auditor thinks a company has little chance of continuing as a going concern, shouldn't he say so by qualifying his opinion?

Shully's went into receivership two weeks ago. Its serious financial difficulties came to light three months after the date of the auditor's report — which gave the company a clean bill of health.

The auditor's report was qualified — but on the grounds of a possible adjustment for goodwill, which had nothing to do with the company's cash position.

Not all the facts in the Shully case are known yet. And even if it transpires that the auditors, Laventhol Krekstein Horwath & Horwath, did know that the company couldn't survive, they were under no legal obligation to say so.

And there are many who would say that accountants do not even have a moral responsibility for warning shareholders of probable disaster ahead. There are some, in fact, who argue with reason that it would have been wrong to draw attention to the company's basic problems.

The argument in favor of an auditor not qualifying his opinion in these circumstances is essentially two-fold:

• The auditor's responsibility rests with ensuring that *the financial statements present fairly the financial position of the company* as at Dec. 31, 1972 (or whenever).

• To qualify the opinion on grounds other than the accuracy of the financial statements might well have an adverse impact on the ability of the company to continue as a going concern (the self-fulfilling prophecy).

One additional argument often thrown in, is that if the company is in serious financial difficulty, this will probably be evident from the financial statements anyway, and that to qualify the opinion would be a superfluous act. But if it is superfluous, why should the qualifying of the opinion be held responsible for having a potentially adverse impact upon the company's business?

There are other considerations, too. What of the possible adverse impact on suppliers, customers, and shareholders, both present and pros-

[30] Leonard G. Eckel, "The Two-Part Audit Opinion", *CA Magazine*, June, 1973, pp. 42—43.

pective, if a qualified opinion is *not* given? Aren't they entitled to know that something may be amiss, and that they may be in danger of not receiving payment for their supplies, or proper servicing of products which they have purchased, or of suffering a loss on their investment?

True, not everyone reads annual reports and financial statements. It might well be asked, therefore, what effect qualifying the opinion will have anyway.

But if the auditor gives a qualified opinion — or denies an opinion, or gives an adverse or piecemeal opinion — he is thereby putting everyone "on notice" that a closer examination ought to be made of the financial condition of that company.

In this way, the regulatory agencies and the financial press are more likely to note the event than if a so-called clean opinion of the statement were offered. The financial difficulties of the company, in short, are more likely to become a matter of public record.

This in no way says that the operations of the company should cease. But it is important that everyone associated with the company concerned has an opportunity to reassess his relationship with it.

In large measure, the auditor's responsibility rests with the financial statements and whether these, in particular, state fairly the value of the company's assets.

But just how much do the financial statements by themselves reveal?

There is nothing magical about any company's given yearend (the balance sheet date). It just happens to be a particular moment in time when it's convenient to stop the clock, and to attempt to give an accounting of the company's financial position.

Although any given set of financial statements tells the experienced reader a great deal about the business, it cannot hope to give an accurate portrayal of the ongoing and thoroughly dynamic nature of the business over a period of 365 days.

Obviously the average shareholder can glean, far less from reading the statements than the auditor, who has an intimate understanding of his client's financial affairs. And since even the best annual report is a gross simplification of reality, surely the auditor should at least share some of his intimate knowledge with the shareholders, to whom he is responsible. Isn't this especially so when the company is in real trouble?

The heart of an annual report is the balance sheet, the income statement, and the funds flow statement. In other words, figures.

But what of the quality of management? The company's marketing programs? Its market share? Its research and development? Its staff turnover?

These are just a few of the questions which pertain, in effect, to the making of the financial statements. And they are not always evident in an annual report, although naturally these will be of great interest to the auditor during his audit.

None of this means that the auditor should be responsible for auditing, for example, the effectiveness of marketing programs. His concern is only with how these matters show up in the financial statements. But, after all, the auditor does know his client's business. Because he is ultimately responsible to the shareholders, surely he should warn them about a possible failure of the business.

The accounting profession itself seems to be of two minds. The Canadian Institute of Chartered Accountants handbook is not clear on the subject, and its recommendations permit an interpretation either way. So, some auditors have qualified their opinion when they considered a company was in financial difficulties, and others, perhaps a majority, have not.

The argument for not qualifying is probably summed up by Robin C.W. Logie, partner of Coopers & Lybrand. He says the auditor's prime responsibility is to be "satisfied with the value placed on the company's assets," and that it is not, in fact, the auditor's responsibility to qualify his opinion if that requirement had been met.

On the other hand, "I would have thought that part of the auditor's responsibility is to draw this to the attention of the shareholders," says A.J. (Pete) Little, executive partner of Clarkson, Gordon and current president of the CICA.

Little recognizes, nevertheless, the danger of qualifying an opinion. "It's a very serious matter . . . and the auditor must be very careful."

To Shully's credit, it should be noted that both president Maurice Shully and general manager R.C. MacGillivray were fairly open about the company's financial problems in their comments which appeared in the recent annual report.

Still, since presidents' statements are generally optimistic, the responsibility of the auditor remains a vital consideration. Perhaps the auditor should comment on the president's report as well as the financial statements.

The crux of the matter really is this — no matter how fairly the financial statements or president's report present the financial position of a company, they do so only on the assumption that the company is a "going concern" and will continue to be.

But how much sense does it make for an auditor to adhere strictly to the assumption of the "going concern" and the need to assess the "going concern value" when the "going concern" may soon cease to exist — and its "value" will therefore change?[31]

To the author there can only be an affirmative answer to the question "Should the Auditor Tell All?" The only really debatable issue is what "all" embraces. Some idea of what is required in terms of full disclosure is brought out in excerpts from a *Business Week* article entitled "Disclosure is the Weak Spot in Audits."

■ Break down inventories according to the way in which they are expected to be sold. . . .
■ Summarize fixed-asset acquisitions by year and depreciation method. . . .
■ Disclose management's justification for the capitalization of major intangibles, such as research and development expense. Explain the basis for the realization period selected.
■ Provide a summary of the aging of account receivable at each balance sheet date.
■ Disclose certain nonaccounting information that could have drastic effects on future operations. . . .
■ Present comparative industry statistics and management's commentary on them.

[31] Brian Roger, "Should the Auditor Tell All?" *The Financial Post*, September 8, 1973.

- Present information on business segments. I suggest, as a partial solution to the present controversy surrounding the definitional aspects of this disclosure, that consideration be given to presenting the information according to the managerial units in which the enterprise conducts its business.[32]

The role of corporate audit committees is also worthy of consideration. Such committees are not new although their role is receiving some renewed attention. These committees are usually composed of a subcommittee of the board of directors — often with a majority of outside directors — and it is normally their responsibility to carefully scrutinize and pass judgment upon the auditors' findings, particularly where they are at any variance with the corporate financial officers' viewpoint. That audit committees can play an extremely constructive role is being more widely recognized, as this *Financial Post* article suggests:

Both the Lawrence Report (of the Select Committee on Company Law, Ontario, 1967) and the Hughes Commission (on Atlantic Acceptance Corp.) recommended that companies should establish audit committees. Consequently, the Business Corporations Act, 1970, of Ontario made an audit committee a statutory requirement for any public company incorporated in the province. The new Companies Act of B.C., effective Oct. 1, 1973, also has a provision for audit committees. And with a similar requirement now part of the proposals of the new Business Corporations Act of Canada — which, after its first reading several weeks ago, will probably come to debate in the fall — the majority of companies in Canada may be required to have an audit committee within a year.

However, while the audit committee has been part of the Ontario business scene for the past 30 months or so, just what the committee should be doing is still being determined.

The Ontario act itself says little. It specifies that the committee should consist of a minimum of three directors (two of whom should be outside directors), and that, "The corporation shall submit the financial statement to the audit committee for its review and the financial statement shall thereafter be submitted to the board of directors."

The problem is two-fold: no body of knowledge exists as yet as to how the audit committee should function; and many directors are finding themselves faced with responsibilities in an area which is essentially new to then. (This comes at a time when the liabilities of the director are being made more explicit than ever before.)

Although the auditors are not responsible for ensuring that their clients comply with the act (if it applies), they do, nevertheless, advise their clients if their actions contravene the act. Also, many of the auditing firms have been attempting to advise their clients on how to set up the committee, what it should do, and what benefits will result. . . .

Since the auditor's position will be strengthened by the committee, it isn't surprising that auditors favor the system.

As the Lawrence Committee noted in 1967: ". . . one of the most serious threats to the independence of the auditor is the close relationship which frequently (and naturally) develops between management and the auditor."

[32] Robert A. Kleckner, "Disclosure Is the Weak Spot in Audits". Reprinted from the June 30, 1973 issue of *Business Week* by special permission. Copyright 1973 by McGraw-Hill, Inc.

However, the audit committee assures the auditor his independence from management and offers him better access to the board of directors. Directors, too, benefit, because they get a clearer idea of their responsibilities.

Although the audit committee may concern itself with a variety of corporate matters, its essential task is to review, in depth, the financial statements constituting the company's annual report. This, and all matters surrounding the financials, including the actual audit itself, are its prime concern. So the audit committee would probably meet at least twice a year — just before the annual audit starts and when it is finished, to review the financial statements.

Beyond that, there is some difference of opinion over what else should concern it.[33]

An issue of grave concern to the public interest is the ease with which some corporations have changed their auditors when the auditors came up with assessments not to the liking of the current management. The auditing profession itself has shown some consternation about this practice but not enough to stop it, even if it could do so. In the United States some restraints have been placed on the practice by forcing firms to explain publicly why they are changing auditors.

Although relations usually are close between a company's management and its outside auditors, disputes over accounting principles and public disclosure requirements aren't unusual. And while the link between a company and an accounting firm usually is long-lasting, changes in auditors aren't unheard of. But the accompanying battles are fought out behind the closed doors of the executive suite and rarely become known to either shareholders or the public.

But now a sizable crack has opened in this traditional wall of secrecy. With the strong backing of the American Institute of Certified Public Accountants, the auditors' professional association, the Securities and Exchange Commission has begun requiring disclosure of disputes between auditors and their clients that end in divorce.

The new SEC rule requires not only that a company report on an 8-K, a change in auditors and an explanation of the dispute but also that the ousted auditor write a letter confirming the management's recital. The purpose is to strengthen the hand of an auditor in a dispute with a corporate client and to discourage companies from shopping around for accomodating accountants.[34]

Finally, of course, there is the matter of liability for erroneous statements and misleading information verified by auditors. Provided auditors are protected when they insist on proper standards — as, for example, standards making it more difficult for firms to switch to more accommodating auditors — there is no reason why they should not be held fully responsible for mistakes they make or sanction. Otherwise the degree of faith and trust shareholders and

[33] Brian Roger, "What Those Corporate Audit Committees Are All About", *The Financial Post*, August 18, 1973.
[34] Charles N. Stabler, "Now, When Auditors and Clients Split Up After Feud, the Public Must Be Told Why", *The Wall Street Journal*, February 23, 1972. Reprinted with permission of *The Wall Street Journal* © Dow Jones & Company, Inc., 1972.

others can place in auditors' statements is minimal at best. If accurate and complete accounting records are to be maintained and published, and if auditors are to place their stamp of approval on them, they must also stand behind them to the fullest possible extent under the law. That they are so responsible under U.S. law is now clear. That also seems to be the trend in Canada, as it quite obviously should be.

Corporate Social Responsibility Audits

Quite apart from the conventional financial audit, there is the concept of a corporate social responsibility audit. Since the question of corporate social responsibility is the focal point of the next chapter, the issue of a special audit to measure this aspect of corporate behaviour requires little more than mention at this point. It will suffice to highlight the pressures leading to such audits, comment on their intended purpose and allude to some of the problems they raise.

As to the forces inducing the adoption of such audits, one article in *Harvard Business Review* has cited seven variables:

1. Executives generally desire to acquire both an individual and a corporate image of social responsibility, one that harmonizes with a public concern which they (and we) do not believe is going to subside.

2. Businessmen, like everyone else, are caught up in the changing mores and priorities of the society and are concerned today about matters which only a few years ago did not worry them. The level of this concern should not be under-estimated. Pollution, the disadvantaged and minorities, clarity and directness in advertising — issues like these have moved rapidly onto (and higher and higher on) the agendas of corporate executives.

3. Another influence is commercial. A number of consultants, sensing the possibility of a new source of business and inherently curious about the whole complex area, are trying to develop ways of performing social audits.

4. Then there is the stimulus of the outside "auditors" — the Naders, the Council on Economic Priorities, the new mutual funds, the recently established journal called *Business and Society Review*, minority groups, ecologists, and so forth, all of whom have a stake in making public almost anything that a company may want to hide. Obviously, such stimuli encourage managements to present their cases in ways they think accurate and proper; but, perhaps even more important, managements want to know what is in store for their companies if they are attacked. This second motivation has obtained in some of the companies with which we are acquainted, where managements actually do not (or did not) know what or how well they were doing, although they may have had some suspicions.

5. Nonprofit organizations such as churches and educational institutions have spurred the idea of social auditing. Urged by their constituents to establish a "social portfolio," to sanitize their holding of paper from companies adjudged irresponsible, or to influence the policies of those in which they have investments, these organizations have been seeking (usually with painful unsuccess) to establish some way of determining if Company X is or is not socially responsible.

6. Investment houses which, for a variety of reasons, are establishing

funds specializing in "clean" securities are also generating interest. These houses face the problem of identifying companies that both act responsibly and promise to be good long-term gainers. This is not a simple matter: it begs a gaggle of questions turning on what is "good social performance."

7. The social activists themselves have an obvious stake in some kind of measurements. If they expect to have significant impact on corporate behavior, they need some yardsticks to use in advising the general public of the social health of this or that company.[35]

Turning to the purposes of corporate social responsibility audits, one author has identified at least five:

1. As part of the strategic and operational planning process, to examine systematically on an organisation-wide basis the existing policies and practices relating to social responsibilities, internal and external to the organisation.
2. To analyse strengths and weaknesses, threats and opportunities in these policies and practices.
3. To prepare an improvement plan, short and long term, concentrated on a limited number of identified priorities. This improvement plan for social responsibilities to be balanced with other objectives and integrated into the overall organisation's planning and control procedures (not left as an 'optional extra'), so that the plan gets implemented.
4. To review progress regularly and to reset priorities at least annually.
5. To involve in the audit and implementation those able to make the best contribution.[36]

Turning to the problems posed by corporate social responsibility audits: they are many and varied, as later sections of this chapter and the next will reveal. First and foremost there is the problem of accessibility to and quantification of pertinent data. Since a kind of cost-benefit analysis is called for no matter which aspect of social responsibility is to be examined, all the facts available must be mustered to avoid overly impressionistic appraisals. Related to this first problem is the issue of who is to conduct the audit. If it is to be insiders they will have the advantage of familiarity with the situation, but their views will naturally be suspect. In contrast, if outsiders are involved they will doubtless be less well-informed, although presumably more detached and objective. There is no easy answer to this dilemma except perhaps to assign a mixed group of insiders and outsiders to the job. Nor is there an obvious solution to the issue of whether the entire audit should be made public. If not at least partially made public, it may prove little more than an exercise in self-delusion. To make it all public, however, might prove not only embarrassing, but damaging from a competitive point of view. Perhaps it is best, therefore, to conclude this section by simply noting that there are many problems associated with corporate social responsibility audits, problems which go a long way towards explaining why they have not yet made much headway either qualitatively or quantitatively.

[35] Raymond A. Bauer and Dan H. Fenn, Jr., "What *Is* a Corporate Social Audit?" *Harvard Business Review*, January-February 1973 © 1973 by the President and Fellows of Harvard College; all rights reserved.
[36] John Humble, "Getting Ready for the Social Responsibility Audit", *The Director*, February 1973.

Government Regulation

Historically, the failure of corporations to put their own houses in order has led to a vast accumulation of government rules and regulations designed to compel, or at least induce, them to behave more responsibly. The government's progress in this regard has been mixed for reasons which will become apparent in this and subsequent sections. For the time being, attention will be concentrated on the record to date. At later points in this volume, attention will be focused on the means by which this record might be improved.

Government regulation of business has a long history. Initially much of this regulation was business-inspired. Specification of weights and measures and tariff protection provide two illustrations. Beginning around the turn of the century, however, North American governments began to look with less favour upon many business practices. The antitrust movement in the United States and the companion, but less effective, anticombines movement in Canada, represented major turning points in the evolution of government attitude toward business.

Today the range of public regulation of business is so great that it would take volumes to begin to describe and evaluate it. For present purposes, it must suffice to highlight some of the dilemmas, issues and problems involved. In doing so, no pretence is made of anything more than a cursory review of the challenges inherent in the regulatory process. It should be obvious that these challenges are immense, at least partly because government rulemaking now embraces everything from the setting of minimum standards for all sorts of things, through regulations of the terms of trade at all points in the flow of transactions, to traditional anticompetitive practices, both domestic and foreign.

One wonders where all this regulation has led. Are business practices any more responsible than they were before governments got so deeply involved? A subsequent chapter on advertising and marketing would hardly seem to suggest this. Perhaps those in business who choose to be other than honest are so determined that no one can stop them. In this depressing sense it may be that regulation simply begets more regulation as unscrupulous businessmen hire more accountants and lawyers to find loopholes in existing laws, thereby forcing governments to try to close them through further enactments — only to see the process start all over again. As in the case of government efforts to keep up with individual attempts to get around the intent of the income tax system, this could prove a futile and never-ending task contributing little except to the coffers of accountants and lawyers and others paid to find a way around the best of public intentions.

Then there is the related question of how effective the regulators really want to be. All too often it would appear that the regulators and the regulated become so attached that one wonders who is regulating whom.

Charging that government regulation often contributes to inflation, the chairman of the Federal Trade Commission urged a complete reexamination of federal regulatory policy with an eye toward eliminating some agencies.

While he didn't call for abolishing any specific agency, FTC Chairman Lewis Engman told a Detroit meeting of financial analysts: "Most regulated industries have become federal protectorates, living in a cozy world of cost-plus, protected from the ugly specters of competition, efficiency and innovation."

He promised the FTC would fight anticompetitive proposals in proceedings before the agencies involved.

Mr. Engman's harshest criticism was for the Civil Aeronautics Board, which regulates airlines, and for the Interstate Commerce Commission, which regulates truck lines and railroads. But he also criticized the Agriculture Department and the Federal Communications Commission as protectionist.

"Our airlines, our truckers, our railroads, our electronic media and countless others are on the dole," he said. "We get irate about welfare fraud but our system of hidden regulatory subsidies makes welfare fraud look like petty larceny."[37]

Of late, however, at least in the United States, there has been some encouraging evidence of regulatory bodies truly attempting to serve the interests for which they were intended, as this *Christian Science Monitor* article reveals. It concerns the nomination of a consumer specialist who won out over the already well-represented oil interests on the Consumer Product Safety Commission.

Consumers are watching the federal regulatory agencies more closely than ever before.

They look the nominees for agency positions over both as regulators and as persons concerned with the board public interest. They keep reminding the White House and the Congress that Congress delegated its regulatory power to independent agencies; this power was never an executive-department function.

The President has the right to name the regulators who must be confirmed by the Senate. By law, a political party may hold only a one-vote majority on each commission.

By the end of the year, President Nixon will have named 34 of the 38 posts on the Federal Power Commission, the Federal Trade Commission, the Interstate Commerce Commission, the Consumer Product Safety Commission, the Civil Aeronautics Board, and the Federal Communications Commission — the agencies most involved with issues affecting consumers.

Each of these regulators will serve a six- or seven-year term. Needless to say, the public has a major stake in their selection.

One of the more recent of these regulatory appointments is that of R. David Pittle as the fifth commission member of the Consumer Product Safety Commission. His selection marked a significant victory for consumers.

The selection of Mr. Pittle, a man fully qualified to serve on a commission whose job it is to set safety standards on consumer products, is a successful case in point.

In addition to being an engineer, he has taught at Carnegie-Mellon University and the University of Wisconsin and worked under a National Science Foundation grant to analyze consumer attitudes toward safety and develop a safety-oriented high-school level consumer-education curriculum.

[37] "Federal Agencies Are Anticompetitive and Should Be Revised, FTC Chief Says", *The Wall Street Journal*, October 8, 1974. Reprinted with permission of *The Wall Street Journal* © Dow Jones & Company, Inc., 1974.

He was one of the founders of the Pittsburgh Alliance for Consumer Protection and was its president at the time President Nixon named him to the Consumer Product Safety Commission.

To continue to have an impact, consumer groups must find the experts, support them wholeheartedly and endlessly urge their appointment.

To do less is to turn the commission over to the politicians and the regulated.[38]

Particularly encouraging is the fact that even one man of integrity dedicated to the public interest can shake up an essential regulatory body and almost single-handedly infuse it with new life and vitality.

Much to the dismay of the broadcast and telephone industries, Federal Communications Commissioner Nicholas Johnson's term won't expire until 1973.

This rangy Iowan with the long, cornersdown moustache may well hold the distinction of being the one Washington regulatory commissioner business would most like to remove from office.

It's not his decisionmaking power that nettles. Often he is the lone dissenter among the seven commissioners on a license renewal or in a case in which misleading advertising is charged; he has no veto power.

It is all those blatantly proconsumer speeches, articles, and books he puts out and the jibes he takes at business in the process. His theme is the great gap between theory and practice in the corporation and free enterprise and in the government and democracy.

This is a man whose position may be more clearly distinguished by the foes he's made than by the friends he keeps. A year or so ago five state broadcaster associations tried to have him impeached.

This fall American Telegraph & Telephone Company, the world's largest company, became sufficiently incensed to accuse the commissioner of "deep-seated bias and prejudice against the Bell System" and to formally petition him to disqualify himself from taking part in future FCC decisions involving Bell.

The straw in this case was a lively speech entitled "For Whom Does Bell Toil?" which the commissioner gave in October at a Chicago digitronics conference. It minced no words in charging AT&T with blundering in missing opportunities to increase its business and reduce costs.

Specifically, Mr. Johnson said the company had overpaid its taxes by "perhaps billions," failed to borrow money at cheap rates years ago, and only grudgingly conceded to offer discount rates in off-peak hours.

Ordinarily a giant corporation weathers such storms in silence but the thunder in this one proved too much for AT&T. In two weeks time it issued a sharp rebuttal and formally presented Mr. Johnson with a petition.

The commissioner, now preparing a reply, refuses to comment on the issue other than to say, at the least, he is glad to have secured Bell's attention.

To some, Mr. Johnson's working chambers might seem as refreshingly unorthodox as his views. The visitor shuts behind him an FCC door

[38] Erma Angevine, "A 'Declaration of Independence' for Federal Regulatory Agencies?" *The Christian Science Monitor*, October 15, 1973.

171

bearing a Bill of Rights poster with a "void where prohibited by law" stamped across it in red. Rock and roll music wafts through the offices inside as young aides scurry about, papers in hand.

The commissioner, after greeting you with a friendly "Howdy" and an extended hand may settle back in his office rocker, one foot propped on a low table, to tell you what he's been thinking about. At the start he warned that 95 percent of his views, he has already written and spoken about.

He summons an aide who brings in an impressive stack of speeches. The commissioner's recent article, he says, is in the new Playboy. It deletes his comments on the demeaning role of women in TV programming, he notes.

The visitor soon realizes his range of targets is as broad as Ralph Nader's. Mr. Johnson unhesitatingly takes on anything from sanitation conditions in fish-processing plants and the destructiveness of strip mining to the antiballistic missile, and women's liberation.

But the stress and statistics are reserved for the Federal Communication Commission's special province: the communications channels of radio and television, newspapers, and telephones. His message, that there is neither competition nor effective regulation in these areas, is not new, as he is fond of saying, but his method of delivery — statistic packed and a tongue-in-cheek variation on the hard sell — is very much "today."

He professes amazement that his "common sense" philosophy should be considered so out of the ordinary.

"It's a kind of a sad commentary of our times that anybody who talks about reality is dubbed as a radical and that anyone who sets out to serve the public is considered 'outspoken' and 'controversial,' " he argues.

"What is this? I'm just doing my job, and I would hope enough others would do the same that 'public official serves public interest' wouldn't be considered headline material. It's kind of a 'man bites dog' story."[39]

Even with the best of intentions, however, regulatory bodies are often at a distinct disadvantage in relation to those institutions over whose conduct they are supposed to maintain a close watch. Once again, U.S. experience, as related in this article from *Business and Society Review*, seems far more instructive than Canadian experience:

Public demands to stem corporate abuses have resulted in the haphazard development of the federal government as watchdog, spawning a bewildering array of agencies and subagencies. Although the massive federal bureaucracy which regulates business may seem to be overkill, in fact, the small research and enforcement sections of most agencies are often no match for the money, staffs, information systems, and influence of major corporations or industry groups.

For example, in 1971 the Federal Communications Commission announced a study of the rate structure of the nationwide telephone conglomerate, the American Telephone and Telegraph Company. The object was to investigate charges of excessive rate increases by the company and the enormous profits of AT&T's unregulated equipment subsidiary, Western Electric. Soon after the study was under way, the FCC concluded it did not have the resources to analyze the telephone giant, and suspended

[39] Lucia Mouat, "FCC Member's Proconsumer Jibes Nettle Business", *The Christian Science Monitor*, November 30, 1970.

the project. Only after an avalanche of protest from the public and the Department of Defense (which felt cramped by AT&T's frequent rate increases), did the FCC receive sufficient funds from the Office of Management and Budget to resume the study. To do this the FCC's staff has been enlarged by over 30 percent, but it is still unclear whether the agency can effectively evaluate, and regulate, the huge firm.

Even though the government does require information from business on a wide range of topics, its data is often so incomplete in terms of the totality of a problem that overall assessments are impossible, or so general they are meaningless. Many federal agencies were crippled from the beginning by legislative compromises which gutted their information-gathering and enforcement powers.

For example, the Justice Department's Antitrust Division keeps plugging along, but to assert that it prevents monopoly is absurd. The agency has no administrative enforcement powers and must gain its few victories through lengthy and costly court battles. Virtually no agency information about monopolistic practices is available to the public until the agency has filed formal charges, which it seldom does, and the evidence is a matter of public record.

The federal antidiscrimination apparatus, the Equal Employment Opportunity Commission (EEOC) and the Office of Federal Contract Compliance (OFCC), has made unprecedented gains in the last five years but again, unless formal charges are filed against a company, you cannot find out what they are up to. The EEOC requires nearly all employers of over 100 persons to report the racial, ethnic, and sexual balance of its workforce. However, it has no administrative enforcement powers, and must resort to the courts in order to stop any discrimination. It would seem a simple enough matter for an individual outside the government to use the EEOC's data to determine a corporation's equal opportunity status, but, unfortunately, it is confidential. (In order to pass the Civil Rights Act of 1964, congressional supporters agreed to the confidentiality of this data as part of a compromise.) The agency may release the data only for entire industries or in other aggregate form. It should also be noted that such data from companies is never verified by the government.

The fact that figures from the companies are not verified by the government is significant. Often the bureaucracy simply does not have the staff (or the power in some cases) to verify the numbers even on a selective basis. This is not to suggest that deliberate deception is the rule, but anyone who has dealt with corporate-reported figures on oil or natural gas, for instance, realizes that such figures often raise more questions than they answer.

Many critics also charge that in the course of attempting to regulate industries, government agencies become buffers between the public and the industries, and take on the additional role of protector and promoter. This conflicting role not only decreases the agencies' effectiveness as a regulator, but also inhibits the flow of critical information.

Thus the problem of making corporations accountable is compounded. Not only are government agencies not adequate in preventing big business from abusing its power, but they often prevent what little hard information they generate from reaching the public. Also, a strong case can be made that the federal government will remain ineffective in corporate regulation so long as the business community retains its disproportionately powerful effect in lobbying with, and political contributions to, the executive and legislative branches.[40]

In pressing for more effective regulation of undesirable corporate practices, one eventually comes up against the question, "Even if in the public interest, what price vigilance?" This question is now to the fore in Canada because Canada fell so far behind in setting effective rules of the game for business that the catch-up process was bound to produce an anguished outcry. Commenting on one version of Canada's proposed new Competition Act, for example, the Toronto *Star* had this to say:

No honest citizen questions the need for legislation to eliminate misleading advertising, ban on-the-shelf price increases (the practice known as double-ticketing) or prohibit various kinds of fraudulent sales techniques. To halt such practices are some of the appealing objectives of Herb Gray, consumer affairs minister's revised Competition Act, which the Commons approved in principle yesterday and sent to the Finance Committee for detailed examination.

What is repugnant about the bill are the methods by which it proposes to achieve these objectives, specifically the arbitrary authority it proposes to give the appointed officials of a new Restrictive Trade Practices Commission and a lack of protection to ensure that businessmen accused of misconduct get a fair trial.

No businessman will know what the law requires him to do or not to do until, over a period of years, the commission has applied its own interpretations. This is an abdication by Parliament of its responsibility to spell out the rules by which it expects society to operate; instead, power is conferred on appointed officials out of the public's reach.

In addition, many sections of the bill offend against rights that are basic to a fair trial.

To start with, the accused person does not have a right to be tried in a criminal court but instead may be tried in the federal court, which ordinarily deals with such matters as patents, trade marks, taxes and custom duties. Surely if a jail sentence is a possible outcome, an accused has the right to be tried by judges who are experienced in criminal matters.

Many sections of the bill impose a strict liability in criminal matters, the effect being to deprive the accused of the excuse that the act in question occurred because of events beyond his control, or that he took all reasonable precautions to avoid committing an offence. It is unreasonable to make a man subject to imprisonment for two years for matters beyond his control.

Other amendments allow statistical evidence to be introduced without providing the opportunity for cross-examination to challenge its reliability. If the statistics come from private persons the commission may allow cross-examination; no such right would apply concerning statistics from government sources.

But statistics have no claim to greater accuracy than any other form of evidence. In fact, on many occasions departments of government have been unable to agree about their own statistics; in other cases, statistics have proved to be wrong. A person's freedom should not be placed in

[40] Lee Stephenson, "Prying Open Corporations: Tighter than Clams", *Business & Society Review*, Winter 1973-74, No. 8, pp. 44-45.

jeopardy because he is not allowed to question the basis on which statistics have been prepared.

There is no doubt that trials can be expedited by limiting or denying the right to cross-examination, and it is easier to enforce laws if an accused is not allowed to put forward as his defence that the acts involved occurred because of events beyond his control.

But one requirement for a fair trial is to give the accused a meaningful right to defend himself, and ease of enforcement is not the only test to be applied to a criminal trial.

Administrators are naturally concerned with achieving results and are not necessarily concerned with fundamental rights. Nevertheless it must be possible in a free society to legislate while respecting the fundamental rights that make a free society possible. Gray's bill, desirable as its objectives may be, offends against these rights, and should not be passed in its present form. [41]

Indicative of how fast things are moving now in Canada and of why questions are being raised about where the regulatory process will end, is a brief summation from a January, 1974 issue of The Financial Times, of the plethora of new regulatory laws then being considered across the country.

Business can brace itself for a raft of new legislation and proposals on consumer protection in 1974. Across the country, it is already clear that most governments are planning new initiatives in this area, and this spring's Throne speeches may well bring promises of even more.

Last week the Times conducted a cross-country survey to find out what is now known about the prospects for this year. Here are the results.

Federal

• A major target for 1974 is an overhaul of the Bankruptcy Act to remove loopholes in both commercial and personal bankruptcies. Standards will be set to eliminate the kind of quick-and-easy bankruptcy that one official says "has gotten to be a game" in certain areas, particularly in Quebec.

• New regulations will be proclaimed under the Packaging and Labelling Act. Draft rules were published last year to control open-date marking and labelling of perishable goods; these will be proclaimed shortly, possibly amended to take industry comments into account. These regulations will be phased into application, once proclaimed, over 24 months.

• New regulations also will be issued under the Hazardous Products Act.

• Further ahead, possibly for 1975, lies a revision of the federal Interest Act. This will affect interest terms and disclosure.

British Columbia

The province's new Department of Consumer Affairs is just getting established; it eventually will have three branches — community programs, legal and trade regulation. Some legislation is already in the works.

• This spring the government will introduce an omnibus trade practices act patterned more on precedents abroad (in the U.S., Britain and Au-

41 "The Wrong Way to a Good End", Toronto Star, April 2, 1974.

stralia) than on anything done so far in Canada. It will govern all "unfair, deceptive or unconscionable" practices in retail trade, and will apply to any party guilty of such practices — including finance companies, advertising agencies, manufacturers and wholesalers, as well as retailers. Emphasis will be placed on guaranteeing redress for consumers, rather than simply on policing business.

• The department is investigating the mobile home industry, which looms large in B.C. A bill is likely to regulate what one official calls the "incestuous relationship that exists between some manufacturers and some mobile home park operators." Also under study are moves to ensure that homes are built to meet the standards necessary for winter living.

Alberta

No new legislation is currently expected this spring. But the government is studying warranties and guarantees, no-fault insurance and revisions of the real estate act — policy decisions may be taken this year.

Saskatchewan

Like all provinces, Saskatchewan is planning a major look at warranty legislation. Apart from that, this year's efforts involve only housekeeping amendments to laws already in force.

Manitoba

Most attention this year will go to a working paper published last week by the Manitoba Law Reform Commission which proposed abolishing the principle of "caveat emptor" in the sale of homes. In essence, the commission suggests a warranty system for houses "so that the burden of incompetent or negligent work and services will not rest upon the purchaser but rather where such burden belongs, upon the incompetent and slipshod themselves. . . ."

Ontario

• Regulations are expected this spring under a new bill to make credit reporting companies accountable for the accuracy of their information and provide consumers' access to the files. The files may contain no information more than seven years old, and the contents may not be exported (i.e. to the U.S.).

• A fair practices act, still to be drafted, will provide the government with general powers similar to those planned in B.C. Courts would be empowered to rule that merchants had inflated prices unnecessarily or were speculating. Consumers would have the right to enforce guarantees on the basis of what is called "true information." The province is considering "cease and desist" orders to prevent an individual from engaging in business for a fixed period if it can be shown that he repeatedly contravened the act.

• A green paper on warranties has been published, and legislation may be introduced this fall. The idea is to require a basic warranty on "most consumer products" that the retailer or manufacturer would or could supplement as they saw fit.

• Condominium act amendments have had second reading and will be back before the legislature this spring. The idea is to protect condominium buyers from sudden price increases after they sign an offer to purchase and make a down payment. There is also a clause providing the consumer with the right to decide who shall manage the building.

• Insurance act amendments are being delayed until agreement is reached with the other provinces on a common policy. The plan is to force insurance companies to pay whatever a court awards in an auto accident case to the limit of the driver's policy, even though the driver may have been impaired at the time of the accident.

Quebec

• A revision of the Consumer Protection Act is planned. It probably will include new laws on warranties and retail sales.

• Advertising by banks and finance companies is to be controlled.

• A new code is planned for rugs and floor coverings.

Detail of some of these changes will be clearer when the Consumer Protection Council releases its report and recommendations this week.

New Brunswick

A commission established by the provincial justice department to examine consumer law will report this spring. Its proposals are not yet known, but they are expected to set the stage for a thorough overhaul of all branches of consumer legislation. The government probably will decide on policy this year and present legislation early next year.[42]

The trend is clearly in the direction of more and more regulation despite a realization in some quarters that regulation alone simply will not solve everything. The field of securities regulation is illustrative of that frustrating limitation, as this *Financial Post* article points out:

"I'm going to sue!" is an exclamation that is rarely heard in the Canadian financial community. Yet billions of dollars of transactions are effected on the telephone every year — giving substantial backing to the motto of English brokers, equally applicable here: "My word is my bond."

This practice of ethical business is a long tradition and certainly in the best interests of the brokers who wish to attract public business. Investors have long memories and any firm that deliberately acted against its clients' interests would soon lose its clients. So this is the first and most basic protection given to Canadian investors.

In every group of people there are some who do break the rules and in the past, following the British tradition, the investment people themselves dealt with such problems. Right from the earliest days to the 1960s, this was the structure of investor protection — those who transacted business would regulate themselves. Those who approached the public for new money would issue to all who purchased the security a prospectus which was "full, true and plain disclosure." These two principles constituted an admirable structure because they worked well, were flexible and the cost to the public was negligible.

But times have changed and heavy criticism has been leveled at the old system. Can any group engaged in seeking profits ever give sufficient weight to the public's interest? What are the restrictions on getting into the "club," and are they fair? The business itself has become so complicated that there are at least half a dozen subdivisions — brokers, bond

42 Joan Fraser, "Lots of New Laws Coming Up", *Financial Times of Canada*, January 14, 1974, p. 18.

dealers, short-term money specialists, mutual funds, etc. Who is to decide on conflicts between them?

The answer of government was that the securities industry must become more regulated, and the two main regulators are: the provincial securities commissions and the stock exchanges.

As a result, there are now some several hundred people engaged in security regulation in Canada, and that is without any significant federal government regulatory structure. The Securities Act in Ontario is about 100 pages in length and there are at least 100 pages of regulations. If any of these regulators were asked, they would probably reply that the number on their staff is quite insufficient to meet the mounting demands of the public.

The proliferation of regulation leads to bigger staffs, higher costs, and greater inflexibility. Our regulatory system will become more like the American method, with countless rules — which in time will lead to only one winner: the lawyers and other specialists who argue as to which rule prevails.

This complexity might lead to a much more frequent use of that standard U.S. phrase: "I'll sue you."[43]

Other Considerations

Beyond the possibilities mentioned, there may be others useful in the attempt to balance corporate private interest and the public interest. For example, although some may consider this merely a matter of terminology, government incentives and disincentives astutely deployed to redirect corporate efforts can often prove more effective than straight regulation. The idea of speedier tax write-offs for pollution abatement facilities is a good example of a worthy incentive. To illustrate the role of disincentives, one need only cite the threat of class-action suits directed at producers of defective products to indicate what can be done in this area. Such incentives and disincentives are now in force in a variety of forms, but much more could doubtless be accomplished through such devices.

Other considerations worthy of further study include the naming of truly public members to corporate boards of directors, a more forceful consumers' movement, and even greater public disclosure of the activities of the corporate world than has already been suggested. These matters will be treated separately in this and in the next chapter because of their importance. Before turning to them, however, there are a few special areas which call for comment.

THE MULTINATIONAL CORPORATION

Of special concern is the need for regulation of international corporations of which Canada has more than its share. Even the United States, long the world's major home base for many of the largest multinational corporations, is now showing signs of concern about American subsidiaries of companies with headquarters in other countries. What is particularly interesting about the regulatory problems associated with these corporations is that the requirement for disclosure and exposure and public scrutiny probably has an even more important role to play in their case than in that of purely domestic companies.

[43] C. Warren Goldring, "Investing for Bigger Profits in the 1970s: Regulation Doesn't Solve Everything", *The Financial Post*, September 22, 1973.

Given their rapid growth, their huge size, and their significant power, it is not surprising that multinational corporations have become the focal point of so much attention. They have become extremely controversial institutions with arguments concerning their pros and cons heard around the globe. On the plus side it is generally agreed that such entities do tend to bring to host countries capital, entrepreneurship and technological advances which might otherwise have been delayed for some time. One can summarize the case made against the multinationals by citing the allegedly truncated branch-plant nature of many of their foreign operations, as well as the threat they sometimes pose to the socio-economic-political sovereignty of countries which become overly dependent upon them. Despite the endless debate about the advantages and disadvantages associated with such ventures, they seem unlikely to disappear, nor even to diminish in significance in the near future.

Given the pervasiveness of the multinational corporate phenomenon, it should not be surprising that it is now the focus of careful examination by two leading international bodies. Both the United Nations and the Organization for Economic Cooperation and Development have embarked on major investigations of the activities of multinational corporations with a view to ascertaining what kinds of international regulation may be required to ensure their proper behaviour on a worldwide basis. What may ultimately emerge from deliberations and studies of the problems of multinationals has been described in *Business Week* as "A GATT for Investments."

There is a decisive, new factor in international economic relations for which no provision has ever been made in the existing framework of world rules and regulations. It is one that today touches all elements of the world economy. I refer, of course, to the rise in importance of transnational investments.

In the late 1950s, total U.S. direct investment in manufacturing facilities abroad amounted to approximately $31-billion. By latest count, the corresponding figure now stands at about $90-billion book value, and several times as much on a market value basis. Annual sales from all of these plants probably approach $180-billion, something like twice as much as the total value of annual U.S. exports and imports combined. Neither seven years of limitations imposed by the Office of Foreign Direct Investments nor any other past or present foreign restrictions have been able to stem the tide, and there is little evidence that the trend will alter its upward thrust in the foreseeable future. Furthermore, what has heretofore been largely a U.S. phenomenon now shows every sign of becoming highly multilateralized, with Europeans and Japanese alike increasingly active in stepping up their direct foreign investments in the U.S. and around the world. Even Middle Eastern oil billionaires are now said to be girding to join the parade.

Let it be said at once that, notwithstanding the cries of alarm of our own Messrs. Burke and Hartke — and of their soulmates in other lands — this evolution toward a world economy marked by substantial multilateral direct investments among the major nations can be a very good thing for everyone. It certainly need not be a zero-sum game, where one country must lose if another gains. Quite the contrary. Just as the years of trade-barrier dismantling have shown that all can gain from a fair and open trading world, so an analogous system of open foreign investments can equally benefit the world as a whole, with none winding up the loser. What is involved in both instances, after all, is a better allocation of world resources, leading to an increase in the total level of material well-being for all.

A new framework. To businessmen who have gone "multinational," this proposition will seem self-evident. But the point here is not to argue the direct investment case pro or con.

The plea, rather, is that we recognize reality and adjust world rules and institutions to take account of it. This requires more than a mere tinkering with the old rules of the General Agreement on Tariffs & Trade (GATT) and the old International Monetary Fund system. A new framework of rules and institutions, capable of coping with transnational investment as well as with world trade and monetary relationships, is now imperative.

To illustrate the present anomalies in world economic affairs, one need only compare the situation regarding trade relations with the situation regarding investment in today's world.

Trade relations are still governed by GATT rules. Though weakened and much in need of overhaul, they continue to provide necessary, if not indispensable, understandings about the dos and don'ts of national behavior in international trade. GATT rules define the limits on discrimination against foreign goods in home markets to which nations are willing to commit themselves. They are reciprocal, so that one nation's commitments are the quid pro quo for analogous commitments made by another; they are multilateral, in that a large number of countries participate in the process.

Most important, GATT is the forum for discussing and negotiating changes and deviations from existing commitments in an orderly manner and according to an accepted set of rules. In this way, as it has been for more than two decades, GATT gives to world exporters an element of predictability as to the way nations will behave on trade matters and a measure of assurance against arbitrary discrimination. By providing an accepted means of adjudicating disputes, it substitutes negotiation and compromise for confrontation and self-escalating trade wars. Simply put, GATT rules have put a measure of law and order into trade.

Arbitrary actions. Some businessmen have been critical of GATT rules because of their relative ineffectiveness in certain situations. No one, however, has seriously advocated scrapping law and order in trade matters, or going back to a world in which every nation is free to do as it pleases.

Paradoxically, this is precisely today's situation as regards transnational investment. Although such investment has become much more important than exports alone, there is no predictability as to national behavior, no firm assurance against arbitrary actions, no real inhibitions against competitive discriminatory moves by individual nations. In sum, there is no accepted system of law and order in the growing international investment world.

A U.S. corporation exporting its products to an EEC member country knows what to expect. But when the company commits considerable investment capital within the borders of that same EEC country, protection against arbitrary discrimination becomes considerably more fuzzy. In competing with local companies, it may or may not have the same access to favorable government-guaranteed credit as its competitors. Tax breaks may be given to the domestic competitor but not to the foreign-owned company. If additional stock interests are to be acquired, special permission has to be sought, and the basis for receiving it is often murky and uncertain. Equal access to government contracts may or may not be available. Rules for the treatment of employees, for plant location, or — heaven forbid — for shutting down an operation, may differ between national and foreign-owned plants.

The issue is not that foreign-owned plants are always discriminated against. Frequently, indeed, they are not. The point is, rather, that in the absence of international understandings, the possibilities for arbitrary action remain entirely open.

If the present situation is unsatisfactory, it is clear that things are likely to get worse rather than better. Heretofore, it has been largely American investment that has been open to arbitrary pressures and discrimination. As European and Japanese direct investment becomes important in the U.S. and elsewhere, the chances of serious friction increase accordingly. What used to be the threat of an old-fashioned trade war now assumes the added dimension of an investment war as well.

Anyone who considers this view of the future unduly pessimistic is referred to a recent bill introduced in the House by those stalwart defenders of the protectionist faith, Representatives Dent and Gaydos, Democrats of Pennsylvania. Noting an increase in foreign investment in the U.S., their bill would limit foreign voting control of any U.S. corporation to 5% or less. True, this sort of thing doesn't stand much of a chance under present circumstances. It does provide an interesting glimpse of what could happen around the world unless some rules of the game are worked out.

Setting up a code. There are many possible approaches, and there is plenty of room for study, reflection, and — to be sure — negotiation, before coming up with the right answer. The plea is not for a particular course of action but rather for the need for concerted action per se.

One solution could lie in negotiating a kind of "Investment GATT" for the developed world; that is, to model a set of investment rules on what has worked well in the trade field. The objective would be to reduce the range for arbitrary national action against foreign investors by making explicit the limits on their freedom to discriminate against foreign capital that nations are willing to assume. A means might be set up to arbitrate disputes, and a set of rules adopted to govern the right for compensatory relief when the code is violated.

Any number of possible subjects might be covered in such a code. The obvious ones involve commitments regarding access to favorable credit, tax treatment, government contracts, repatriation of earnings, stock purchase and sale, regulations regarding listing on public exchanges, treatment of employees, opening and closing of plants, and the like.

Nations would make specific commitments regarding the treatment of foreign investors on each of the subjects covered, with due allowance for deviations in national security industries or other special circumstances. The commitments of one nation would be balanced by analogous commitments from others. Moreover, since some countries have felt threatened by the uncertainty of foreign investors' behavior within their boundaries, the code might also contain a specific statement of behavior expected of foreign investors.

No one likes more involvement by governments in economic relations than is absolutely necessary. As in the trade field, however, governments are already intimately involved in investment decisions. An Investment GATT, far from creating a new set of restrictions, would have as its purpose the liberalization of the world investment environment. By setting the framework within which private investors as well as traders can operate securely and free from the threat of arbitrary action, it would broaden rather than restrict freedom for all. Few people today question this proposition as regards trade; the analogy to the investment world should be easy to see.

First step. Once all this has been done, what remains is to relate an Investment GATT to a rejuvenated Trade GATT and to a revised monetary system among the world's principal economic powers. Perhaps one general world economic organization should be substituted to deal with these three separate though interrelated problems. On the other hand, it may be simpler to retain separate organizations in each of the three major fields and to determine only by what means close coordination between them is to be achieved.

For practical purposes, we will probably have to begin by attempting an agreement among the world's developed nations alone. While the need for protection against arbitrary treatment of foreign investment is perhaps greatest in the developing countries, their capability for assuming meaningful commitments is correspondingly slight. Perhaps these countries may at first become associate members, subject to special rules, as in the trade field.

We are living in an age in which economic interrelationships among the world's principal nations have grown more intimate and more complex. A complex world abroad, as at home, requires rules and institutions to govern behavior and to resolve controversy.

Traffic regulations designed to deal with a bicycle economy cease to be relevant when more and more people switch to auto and truck travel over superhighways. International economic relations likewise require institutions and rules suited to the problems of today and tomorrow rather than to those of yesterday.[44]

None of these proposals make any sense, however, unless there is much greater disclosure and exposure and public scrutiny of what takes place within multinational corporations, particularly in terms of their intercountry transfer payments and pricing policies and practices. When debating the pros and cons of multinational corporations, one constantly comes up against the fact that insufficient information is available on their activities to permit a full account, or even proper airing of the issues they raise. Consider the question of whether multinational corporations manipulate their intercountry transfer payments and pricing systems in order to avoid countries with relatively high tax rates or even price controls. Clearly, such companies have the ability to operate in this manner and therefore must eventually be compelled to prove they are not doing so. At the very least, this requires that multinational companies be forced to reveal both the amounts involved in, and the rationale for, their intercountry financial arrangements. Otherwise, no intelligent assessment of the allegations so often raised against them can take place. Assuming they have nothing to hide, such corporations have everything to gain and nothing to lose from this sort of approach.

[44] W. Michael Blumenthal, "Needed: a GATT for Investments". Reprinted from the August 18, 1973 issue of *Business Week* by special permission. Copyright 1973 by McGraw-Hill, Inc.

In the latter spirit, this section can be concluded on the reasonably encouraging and optimistic note sounded in this *Harvard Business Review* article:

In his interesting new book, *The Multinationals*, Christopher Tugendhat compares the position of the MNCs with that of the Catholic Church in medieval times. Kings and emperors did not like to be over-shadowed by the Church's international organization, strength, and influence. Some reacted by negotiating concordats with the pope defining their respective spheres of action and specifying ground rules for harmonious coexistence. Other political rulers broke with Rome and set up their own independent churches.

Conceivably, the same could happen today, with some nations planning to live with the MNCs, others deciding to go it alone. Judging from the studies that I have reviewed in this article, however, it seems doubtful that the second alternative is realistic. The likelihood, therefore, is that countries will try increasingly to work together and, in Tugendhat's words, "establish a new industrial concordat between themselves and the companies."

Despite the possible losses of flexibility for MNCs, such a trend would almost surely work in their interest in the long run. For one of the reasons that MNCs are on trial today appears to be the lack of a legal framework in which to rationalize their actions. The sooner such a framework begins to take shape, the sooner the MNCs can look forward to doing business in a more stable world environment.[45]

STOCK MARKET ABUSES

The stock market is another area in the business arena that deserves attention. Although it has been in the doldrums for some time and has become a less and less significant source of capital over the years, what goes on under its auspices cannot be written off lightly. Perhaps one of the reasons why the stock market has become a less important institution in the total scheme of things is that so many abuses have occurred under its jurisdiction. In saying this, it should be emphasized that what goes on in the stock market should not be equated with business policies and practices in general. Except perhaps for the field of advertising and marketing, there is little in the general corporate domain which competes with what goes on in the stock market in the sense of breach of trust, lack of integrity and unethical behaviour.

Historically the stock market has been so replete with abuses of all kinds that it is a wonder that it has survived at all. The fact that it does survive, albeit with declining significance, reflects the failure of public authorities to rid the market of many of its abuses, despite strenuous efforts, and a fatalistic acceptance by all concerned of the fact that, within fairly broad limits, it is not unlike a fixed horse race. After highlighting the abuses which persist and dealing with the regulations which have been imposed or are proposed, this section concludes by stressing the most fundamental change required.

When it comes to documenting the abuses which still permeate the stock market, one could begin almost anywhere. It might be best to start with a

[45] David W. Ewing, "Keeping Informed: MNCs on Trial", *Harvard Business Review*, May-June 1972 © 1972 by the President and Fellows of Harvard College; all rights reserved.

Business Week review of a second book in the subject by a commentator who in some quarters would be classified as a highly successful muckraker:

Here comes Richard Ney again, astride his white charger, leveling his lances of self-righteousness and hyperbole at the dragons of Wall Street. And, it must be added, drawing some real blood here and there.

In his 1970 book, *The Wall Street Jungle*, Ney shed valuable light on the secretive practices of New York Stock Exchange specialists, those men on the floor who are charged with maintaining "fair and orderly" markets for stocks but who often rake in considerable profit for themselves while the public takes a bath. The specialists, in Ney's polemic, are the center of a widespread "conspiracy" to swindle ordinary investors. His accusations — some apt, some overly impassioned — won him a lot of enemies in the financial community. But they also won him friends elsewhere in the country — most notably Senator Lee Metcalf (D-Mont.), chairman of the Joint Committee on Congressional Operations and member of the Migratory Bird Conservation Commission, who has written a laudatory foreword to Ney's new book, *The Wall Street Gang*.

Ney's earlier book made the best-seller lists for weeks, and the ensuing publicity and talk shows generated considerable interest in Ney's Bel Air (Calif.) investment advisory operation. So, casting himself as a kind of Galahad of the Capital Gain, the former actor has decided to repeat his act.

It's a melodrama that might better be titled "Innocence Betrayed." The stock market represents, in theory, a free interplay between supply and demand, which in turn reflects economic events and trends. But like many another player, Ney begins to suspect that Something Else Is Going On. Economic and corporate analysis, he now feels, is only so much "pseudo-knowledge" designed to "hypnotize" investors into buying near the top of a market rise, so that savvy insiders can bail out.

The market is really manipulated by the specialists, Ney insists, who work off inventories at market tops, sell short on the way down, then cover their shorts and build up inventories at the bottom in an endless cycle of larceny reminiscent of the bull-and-bear raids of the 1920s. The specialists, in Ney's script, control the New York Stock Exchange, which in turn controls the flow of information that suckers the public in and out at the wrong times. The way to beat the insiders at their own game, Ney argues, is to ignore information and study stock charts, which can give clues about what the specialists and their friends are going to do next.

In 1970 Ney held that the big banks, the Securities & Exchange Commission, the Federal Reserve Board, and Congress were all in the NYSE's pocket and party to the "conspiracy." Now he has broadened his view to include many major U.S. corporations; the financial press, which obediently purveys the NYSE's propaganda; the courts, many of whose judges see their self-interest aligned with Wall Street's; and the White House, whose current denizen is closely tied to such financial figures as Maurice Stans, John Mitchell, and Peter Flanigan.

On the last score, one example that Ney cites was President Nixon's 1971 announcement of wage-price controls, after the Dow-Jones industrials had sunk 123 points in three months. "There is no sure way of knowing whether he timed his announcement at the Stock Exchange's signal or whether the Exchange scheduled its drop to the August low to conform to Nixon's schedule," Ney writes. "But that there was conspiring between the White House and the Stock Exchange, I have not the slightest doubt." Investors subsequently plunged into the market, but the rally quickly aborted. Ney's explanation: The specialists' heavy short selling kept prices from rising very far. The market then tumbled another 130 points.

Ney's chief error of judgment is in labeling as "conspiracy" what is more a fortuitous confluence of self-interests. Beyond that, he torpedoes his arguments time and again by priming them with overstatement, egotism, and pretentious philosophy. And that's a shame, because behind his posturings is a wealth of provocative research, culled mostly from SEC and Congressional studies, NYSE rules, and the much-disparaged press. It is information that often falls shy of proving his points but that nonetheless raises good issues. Some highlights:

■ The biggest shareholders in many U.S. companies are outfits such as Kane & Co., Carson & Co. and Cede & Co. These are code names for interests that wield immense influence over corporate managements, including publishers and TV networks, through the power to vote proxies. Kane & Co., for instance, is one of the many code names for Chase Manhattan Bank, while Carson & Co. is one of Morgan Guaranty Trust's. The Prudential uses as many as 18. Cede & Co. is the code for the NYSE's Stock Clearing Corp., which holds most of those shares that investors leave in "Street name." In 1972 Cede was the largest shareholder in 36 major corporations, and in most cases held far more than the 5% that designates an "insider." Why are the institutions and the Big Board so secretive about these code names and voting power?

■ Investors are not supposed to be able to sell short except on upticks. But through a loophole in NYSE regulations, specialists can short heavily on downticks — a maneuver that facilitates bear raids — and report their sales as long sales instead of short.

■ Ney outlines an excellent scenario of how unscrupulous brokers can manipulate a stock up and down at will when they underwrite secondary offerings — large blocks of stock sold by insiders — and merchandise them to the public.

■ Ney devotes five chapters to the ins and outs, perils and satisfactions, of suing brokers or the NYSE, together with some interesting precedents. But, he notes, "regrettably, most investors sign margin agreements . . . stipulating they will submit all disputes . . . to arbitration. This, of course, is a form of evasion (and fraud)." For one thing, such a stipulation is in violation of a Supreme Court ruling; for another, argues Ney, the arbitration process is rigged in favor of the stockbrokers.

It is a very murky, greed-ridden, and paranoid world that Ney describes. The book's only comic respite lies in a portfolio of photos showing the sun-tanned Ney surrounded by the attributes of affluence: his Rolls-Royce, his Afghans, his swimming pool, his champagne, and his lovely 27-year-old Oriental research assistant, Mei-Lee. They give us the image, all in all, of a man who owes everything to the "conspiracy" he shrilly deplores.[46]

That Canada is far from free of stock market abuses should not be surprising in view of the weaker regulatory framework which persists in the country.

[46] William G. Shepherd, Jr., "Our Hero Returns for a Second Act". Reprinted from the June 15, 1974 issue of *Business Week* by special permission. Copyright 1974 by McGraw-Hill, Inc.

A Toronto *Star* newspaper account of the trial of one character involved in the fraudulent practices which persist is most illuminating:

A self-confessed "stock manipulator, deal man and rounder" told an Ontario Supreme Court jury yesterday how stock promoters and distributors can control and manipulate the Toronto, Vancouver, Montreal and Canadian Stock Exchanges for profit.

James Colby Danielson, 44, who told of his brushes with the law as a stock dealer throughout the United States and Canada, was testifying against two Metro men charged with conspiring with others to defraud the public of money between Jan. 1, 1972 and Dec. 31, 1972.

He claimed to have dealings with the accused, Howard Mondrow, 42, of Sandfield Rd., Willowdale, who had 400,000 shares of New Dimension Resources Ltd. (NDR) and Bertram Wilkes, 49, Rushton Rd., a public relations consultant who is alleged to have helped Mondrow with his promotional work.

Danielson told the five-woman, seven-man jury that he met Mondrow in October, 1972 through Wilkes who, as a financial writer, had been helpful in deals in the past.

Danielson at the time had Maple Film Corp., which dealt with old westerns for television, and he needed stock to pledge so he could get some money. He testified that Mondrow wanted to unload all his NDR stock because he needed $200,000, but he wanted to sell the stock without depressing the market. An agreement was reached whereby Danielson would distribute the stock and Mondrow would help him with his company, the Crown witness said.

"There are about 90 distributors in Canada," said Danielson. "They make a deal with the promoter to get rid of the stock without depressing the market. The promoter wants to turn the stock into money so he retains a distributor who sells it. He (the distributor) does the dirty work. He gets rid of the stock.

"The distributor gets between 20 and 30 per cent. He gets as much as he can and pays out as little as possible. If I can bribe someone for 10 per cent I get more profit.

"The reason brokers will take a bribe is because it far, far exceeds the regular commission or broker's fee from a legitimate sale," he continued.

"I discussed with Mondrow about bribes or secret commissions," Danielson told assistant crown attorney Clay Powell, "and I said I wouldn't give in to this inflation. I said I would not pay more than 10 per cent to a stock salesman."

He said when a bribed broker made an NDR sale he would phone Danielson immediately, tell him how many shares were bought and at what price. Danielson would immediately call Mondrow, pass on the information and Mondrow would put that amount of stock up for sale within seconds. By the time the deal was listed on the rolling tape at the Toronto Stock Exchange, it had been completed, the money had switched hands, the price of the shares hadn't changed and the public didn't know about it.

He peppered his five-hour testimony with names of brokers who had been bribed and well-known brokerage houses across the country. One stock salesman, Frank Bryan, of Frank S. Leslie and Co. Ltd., made in excess of $25,000 in security commissions from Danielson between April 1971 and Oct. 1972 the witness testified.

Bryan is one of six co-conspirators named in the indictment who were working in brokerage houses at that time.

The trial continues.[47]

That these sorts of practices continue despite increased securities regulations in both countries is testimony to the ingenuity of those nefarious individuals who manipulate the securities industry. However numerous they are though, it should be acknowledged that the decent and honest element in the industry has periodically attempted a thorough house cleaning. Of late, for example, some elements of the New York Stock Exchange have been questioning the specialist system, and several general reform measures have also been suggested:

• The elimination of fixed commission rates on all orders, concurrently with:
• A requirement that all trades of listed securities be made on registered national securities exchanges operating under similar rules and regulations.
• A requirement that exchange member broker-dealers must do 100 percent of their business with unaffiliated public customers.

The SEC has already gone ahead with the first part of the NYSE's proposal. But two other important areas — the adoption of similar rules and regulations and the requirement that broker-dealers do 100 percent of their business with the public — remain open for discussion.

That much remains to be done in the field of exchange regulations is suggested by the following summary of some of the key issues with which the SEC is still in the process of coming to grips:

Commission rates	The New York Stock Exchange wants increases of 10% to 15% on commissions on orders under $300,000. The move is opposed by key Congressmen and some members of the industry.
Exchange membership	A new SEC rule limiting exchange membership rights of financial institutions is being challenged in the courts. Congress may legislate tougher rules independently
Portfolio disclosures	Congress wants SEC to draft a bill forcing bank trust departments and other institutions to disclose stock holdings and trading information. Casey resisted, but Cook urged the staff to get to work on it. Resolution will depend on Garrett's leadership.
Accounting	The staff is revising proposals that companies explain their accounting practices and reconcile differences in reports to IRS and to stockholders
Profit forecasts	New rules on forecasting are promised. If com-

[47] Wendy Darroch, " 'Dealer' Tells of Bribes to Push Sale of Stock", Toronto *Star*, May 23, 1974.

	panies make public forecasts, they may be required to put forecasts in reports filed with SEC
Insider trading	The staff is working on guidelines to define insider trading for companies and investors. Clarification is long overdue in this murky subject[48]

There is a basic problem pertaining to the stock market with which few want to deal: the matter of trust. Anyone who advises, counsels or in any other way provides service for a client interested in buying or selling financial securities is in a trust relationship with that client. Yet in most cases that same individual can be trading on the market on his own account or through some dummy account. That builds in an automatic conflict of interest which hardly anyone would be able to avoid if the circumstances or opportunities were drastic or enticing enough. Nothing short of a complete ban on the buying and selling of securities, either directly or indirectly, by anyone having an official relationship with a broker, any other intermediary, or the stock market itself, will rectify this situation. Until such a ban is introduced, the public cannot have and should not have any confidence in the loaded casino-type operation which now confronts it in the stock market. The fact that such a ban would meet with widespread resistance by those involved is indication enough of where their primary and true interests lie.

THE PUBLIC SERVICE

Often overlooked in analyses of the present state of North American society is the role of the public service. Admittedly, many commentators bemoan the fact that the bureaucracy seems to have a never-ending tendency to grow at all levels of government, but that is where the criticism usually ends. This proliferation in itself is frightening enough when one considers the vast numbers already employed in the governmental juggernaut. At the federal level in Canada, for example, almost 100,000 were added to the payroll within five years of the Prime Minister's pledge that he would hold the line on further expansion of that already mammoth, and to a large extent unmanageable, body.

The surprising thing is that government seems to get away with so much without even a public whimper. One observer in *The Financial Post* has suggested that a disproportionate amount of public attention is devoted to financial accountability in the private corporate sector in comparison to that devoted to it in the governmental sphere:

Without getting too involved in the merits of private enterprise vs government, it is worth pointing out that the private sector comes in for far more comprehensive public scrutiny in its financial affairs than does the government.

Annual and quarterly financial reports from public companies get timely and widespread scrutiny from both the press and the public. The quality of financial disclosure is continually improving and there is a highly respected accounting profession in Canada which is responsible for independently assessing the fairness of the financial presentation.

---

[48] "Some Key Issues for the New SEC Chairman". Reprinted from the July 14, 1973 issue of *Business Week* by special permission. Copyright 1973 by McGraw-Hill, Inc.

As a result, Canadian public business gets a prompt, effective scrutiny from everyone. Corporations with excessive profits hear the public outcry and see the emergence of competitors. Unsuccessful companies are required to take immediate action to get into tune with the needs of the customers. The result is that, over the years, private enterprise has made a substantial contribution to the efficient mobilization and use of Canada's people and resources.

There is not the same good financial reporting and comprehension about government financial affairs. There are massive financial reports on government activities but for the most part the public has little or no notion of their significance. The amounts are too large for the layman to understand and the form of disclosure is archaic.

. . . The public does not have any idea of the financial disclosure used by government bodies . . . and ends up either confused or apathetic about government expenditures.

In the absence of good clear financial reporting for government, what happens? Everybody assumes the worst. The public and opposition alike fling abuse, much of it unwarranted and without substance, on the government in power.

The accountants could help if they were to start thinking about the financial disclosure requirements of government. In addition, new ways are needed for interpreting expenditures in terms of social values rather than profit, but at the same time devising a means of measuring efficiency in the same manner by which profits reflect the efficiency of private enterprise.

With so much of the country's spending now going through the public sector, clearer and prompt financial reporting is required. This will help rather than hinder, any party in power because attention can then be focused on matters of importance, rather than on the whole system.

So what is in store for accounting? To protect itself from unfair criticism, business should start publishing supplementary price-level financial information.

This will show more realistic figures for investment, rates of return and profits. Hopefully this will enable business to retain a larger share of its resources in recognition of its need to maintain capital for developing the country and contributing to the prosperity of Canadians.

At the same time, governments must be held accountable, and this is possible only through much better and more timely financial disclosure. The mystery and confusion that now surrounds government reporting must be eliminated.[49]

Indicative of the growth trend in the government establishment in Canada and of some of the reasons underscoring it is the following commentary from the Toronto Star:

The other day, . . . CMA President Keith Rapsey hit a large nail square on the head. Canada, he said, is headed toward "one-boss economy" in which everyone, directly or indirectly, works for government.

No doubt for effect, Rapsey exaggerated. But only just. Federal, provincial and municipal spending added up to 28 per cent of the gross

[49] David C. Higginbotham, "Fuss Over Business Profits Obscures Need to Look at Government Books", The Financial Post, July 13, 1974.

national product in 1960 and to 32 per cent in 1968. It's 40 per cent today.

The trend is toward 100 per cent; more to the point, there's nothing in sight to stop it or to slow it.

Ottawa's estimates for 1974-75 are, at $22 billion, almost one-fifth higher than last year's. The civil service has grown from 43,000 in 1971 to 320,000 today.

Ottawa attracts attention because of its size and because the statistics are conveniently available. But the provinces are much more expansionist. The budgets of British Columbia and Alberta are, respectively, higher by 29 per cent and 27 per cent than for a year ago. The provincial civil service is growing at 4.5 per cent a year, compared to 3.5 per cent at Ottawa for the federal civil service — both far faster than for the total labor force. In two decades the provincial share of total government spending has jumped from 20 per cent to 40 per cent.

Government establishments have become, in author and businessman Richard Rohmer's phrase, "a civil self-service which grows by feeding upon itself."

A commission of inquiry, as proposed by the Conservatives, might curb some of the more flagrant abuses; departmental reorganization used as a device to increase the number of senior officers; "grade up-creep," by which officials do the same work but are reclassified upwards; contract personnel used to evade manpower ceilings; research done as make-work.

The civil service, quite plainly, is out of control. It has learned how to guarantee its endless expansion by manufacturing new demands for its own services. But that is only part of the problem, and the lesser part at that.

Most Canadians want, or have a vested interest in, increased government spending. As individuals most Canadians in theory want economy in government. But in practice, as members of particular interest groups, almost all of us want more money spent on ourselves, whether as artists, academics, welfare workers, farmers (who as Agriculture Minister Eugene Whelan notes "are free-enterprisers when times are good and socialists when times are bad") or, for that matter, Rapsey's manufacturers.

A second explanation lies in a profound shift in public expectations. The private sector can produce goods and services in abundance. But the public today is searching for something more — for quality, for Canadian control, for a peaceable environment.

"People feel," says R.C. Frazee, vice-president of the Royal Bank, "that government institutions are more likely to give them what they want than private institutions."

This trend is self-evident. Newfoundland is taking over part of Brinco; British Columbia will take over B.C. Telephone, and the CPR may be nationalized. All governments have moved massively into the resource field. Housing costs are causing comparable pressures for government land banks and for control of real estate speculation.

It's easy to heave rocks at bureaucrats for empire-building. But the real issues lie elsewhere. Do Canadians really want a totally state-run society? If not, which interest group will step forward first to suggest that its funds be frozen?

As government endlessly expands, who is left with the credibility and independence to criticize it?

Finally, since governments in some dim past were supposed to be for the people, what happens when there are no people left, only governments.[50]

Complaints about the multiplication of public servants are mounting in Canada, but few are coming up with concrete suggestions about what can be done about it. Nonetheless, some intriguing diagnoses and prescriptions are being advanced, such as the following by Richard Rohmer:

... When Sir John A. Macdonald formed his first Cabinet in 1867 he appointed 12 ministers to head 12 departments. The number of federal civil servants reported on staff in 1867 was 330 and the population of Canada was 3,463,000.

By 1900 the number of ministries had increased by one to 13. The number of civil servants had increased 1,000 per cent to 3,344, while the population increased 64 per cent to 5,301,000.

Now we move ahead 50 years to 1950 when the number of ministries was 18. The growth of the civil service was over 40 times compared to a three-times increase of population. The civil service was up to 127,196 from 3,344 in 1900 while the population went to 14 million from 5 million at the turn of the century.

Let's look at where we are today. The number of ministries is 27 and the civil service has increased 150 per cent.

From 1950, while the population has grown only 60 per cent, the civil service is up to 320,003 (with another 13,000 to come this year) from 127,196 and the population went to 22½ million from 14.

I visualize each ministry or department as a pyramid.

If each ministry was a pyramid you would have at the top of it (apart from the itinerate ministers who come and go) a deputy minister and, under him, his assistant deputy ministers and from there the pyramid spreads down to a very large base.

In 1900 the average number of bureaucrats in each department was 257; in 1974 the average number of civil servants per ministry has gone to 11,851.

Even so there is still only one minister, one lone and lonely politician at the pyramid's peak.

The minister of the day in any department has little opportunity to obtain assistance and counsel from his colleagues in the Cabinet.

They are overloaded with their own problems and, in any event, they don't want to have interference from or involvement in any other ministry. Perhaps a minister can talk with a trusted fellow Cabinet member when they gather at the Cabinet table or sit on the odd committee together.

But effectively every minister must operate by himself. He must rely almost exclusively upon the advice of his deputy minister.

The deputy minister usually is an expert in the work of the ministry. He may have seen several ministers come and go. He has at his command in the pyramid under him a growing army of experts and non-experts upon whom he can call. The deputy minister has power, especially staying power.

The system is designed to make the minister (who, as a rule, is a man

[50] Richard Gwyn, "The Biggest Boss Is Growing Even Bigger", Toronto *Star*, March 30, 1974.

191

with no expertise in the department to which he is assigned) the captive of the deputy minister and his staff.

Virtually all policy proposals to the minister are formulated, researched and prepared by the civil servants, except when an inventive minister or a creative Cabinet decide on a matter of policy in principle and then direct the bureaucracy to research it and bring it back.

The system is also such that the entrenched federal civil servants find it totally unacceptable that any concepts outside their own mandarin class and outside Ottawa are automatically rejected because they do not come from within their own structure. They give the appearance of believing that any citizen beyond the moat around the Ottawa ivory tower is really a second-class person who couldn't possibly have an idea or an opinion.

Ottawa is characterized everywhere in Canada as "remote." It is remote and, in my opinion, it is the arrogant aloofness of the all-powerful bureaucracy which makes it so.

When you come back to the position of the minister he is, after all, only one single human being with the power to assimilate only so much information and to make only so many decisions. He must make those decisions in isolation. And he must assess what the public viewpoint would be simply from his own point of view.

The only other point of view which he has access to on a day-to-day basis is that of his civil servants. How they read what is best for the public in British Columbia, Alberta, the Maritimes or Manitoba or the Northwest Territories while sitting on their seats in Ottawa has always been a mystery to me, but obviously a matter of power and pleasure to them.

The minister's political input into the decision-making process is usually the last and therefore the least because all it is is the making of a decision — yes, or no, or amend. There is rarely an opportunity for the insertion of the politician's point of view during the processing of any proposal on its way up from the bowels of the pyramid.

Let's look at another result of the massive growth of the departmental pyramids.

If you set all the pyramids side by side, some would be tall and some would be short. Their lines of communication run vertically — that is to say information can flow from the bottom of the pyramid to the top. Sometimes it can even flow from the top to the bottom. It may flow slowly and in an unco-ordinated fashion or it may flow quickly. Nevertheless the flow is vertical, usually in an upward direction to the deputy minister, then to the minister and, if appropriate, through him to the Cabinet.

However, the horizontal flow of information between ministries is extremely limited, impeded as it is by jurisdictional jealousies, lack of liaison and co-ordination and failure to comprehend or understand the programs which other ministries are embarked upon. Therefore it is not uncommon to find serious overlapping of projects or research being carried on by different ministries.

As the self-generating pyramids grow larger the communications gap between them also grows larger.

Of course there are those who would argue that there are now many interdepartmental committees such as the Advisory Committee on Northern Development, which is made up of senior civil servants from the various ministries having a piece of the action in the Arctic. Such committees at least go part way to overcome the communications gap. But, again, they're committees of bureaucrats, not politicians.

Another phenomenon occurs as the pyramid grows larger and larger carrying the minister heavenward as he is wafted upward on an ever-increasing pile of problems and decisions. The phenomenon is that day by day he becomes more remote from the public, the people whom he serves. The higher and bigger the pyramid, the more impossible it becomes for any member of the public to reach the minister personally, to talk with him on the telephone, or to see him to express a point of view. Even backbenchers have an extremely difficult time putting the arm on their own ministers.

What about the man or woman, the taxpayer, the public who want to see the minister? Rarely do they get to see him unless they have some particular "in" or influence with somebody.

No, the Canadian who wants to deal with his Government must deal with the bureaucracy because there is no one else to get at and the civil servants know it.

This is power. It is power which is in the hands of the civil servants, not the politicians. The civil servants make the decisions. It is they who deal with the public.

Those who have had the experience of dealing with the bureaucracy at Ottawa must have some understanding of the point I am attempting to make.

What about limiting the growth of the civil service? Evidently it is impossible.

In 1969 the Prime Minister gave a pledge to the Canadian public that there would be a freeze on the growth of the civil service.

At that time there were 235,000 on the payroll, not including the CNR, Air Canada, Atomic Energy of Canada Ltd., the Canadian Wheat Board or the Canadian Armed Forces.

Notwithstanding the pledge of the political arm of the federal Government the civil service will grow this year alone by 13,000 to 333,003 — an astronomical increase of 98,003 in the short period of just five years since the Prime Minister's promise.

This is runaway growth. It is runaway on two counts.

The first is in terms of growth in numbers. The second is that there is no way the Cabinet or the current Prime Minister — that is the political arm of Government — can stop it, at least not under the present structure.

When you see, as we have, the enormous number of civil servants in the pyramid beneath each minister and the incredible power which the bureaucracy has acquired through the mass of its own weight of numbers, the conclusion is irresistible that the political arm of the Government of Canada is powerless in Canada to stop the growth of the civil service because the bureaucracy has overpowered the politicians.

With this runaway growth of the federal bureaucracy (which really now could be called the "civil self-service" because it grows by feeding upon itself), our society is both witness and victim of an escalating invasion of government into every facet of our lives. Obviously there is a happy willingness on the part of the bureaucracy to find more and more fields of human endeavor to investigate, regulate, control and manipulate.

The final matter to be discussed is this: What would a prudent and reasonable voter in Canada expect the political arm of the federal Government to do if it once again accepted the principle that the growth of the bureaucracy in Canada is runaway and then took action to stop it?

While there are those who will disagree with the proposition that I am either reasonable or prudent, I am at least uninhibited enough to put forward a handful of suggestions. I do this with every confidence that those in power in Ottawa — that includes the political as well as the bureaucratic arms of the federal Government — will never hear or see them. For, after all, I am one of those second-class citizens on the far side of the moat around Ottawa's ivory tower.

So, in the comfortable belief that I will not be responsible for influencing anyone in a position of power, I turn to my respectful suggestions.

The political arm of the federal Government should:

(1) Forthwith decree a maximum limit to the number of people that can be engaged in the civil service and should roll back the permitted number to the number originally set by the Prime Minister in 1969 plus a per annum increase proportionate to the growth of the population; and to give effect to this cutback the Treasury Board should set a budgetary limitation for the pay and allowances to be permitted to the civil service. This technique has been effectively used by the civil service to reduce the Canadian Armed Forces both in men and the amount of money available to it. Now it should be used on the bureaucracy itself.

(2) Restructure the Cabinet system in such a way that associate ministers are created with at least one in every major department — so that each minister has a colleague of ministerial rank with whom to consult and to assist him in his day to day confrontation with the bureaucracy.

(3) Give prompt and favorable consideration to altering the Cabinet structure into a two-tier system comparable to that used in Britain.

(4) Investigate and inquire into the need and desirability of substantially increasing the number of seats in the House of Commons so that the number of members of Parliament more adequately reflects the growth of the population and so that the House of Commons may be given a better opportunity to oversee the control and development of policies and their implementation.[51]

The underlying problem may be the failure to distinguish between the provision of goods and services for which the government should accept ultimate responsibility and how those goods and services can best be delivered. There is, in the view of many, a desirable long-term move in the direction of government's assuming more obligations with respect to basic human needs. In large measure, of course, this duty can be met through transfer payments to those who are disadvantaged, leaving it to them to purchase the package of goods and services they need most. Even in this area, costs could be drastically reduced while benefit levels were raised if a viable way could be found to implement a guaranteed minimum income in place of the variety of overlapping social security systems which now exist.

Transfer payments aside, there are an increasing number of goods and services being provided by all levels of government. This is where a basic distinction is required. The fact that the government should ensure that a given product or service is available to all citizens does not mean it should provide it

51 Richard Rohmer, "Canada's Runaway Growth in Bureaucracy", The Globe and Mail, Toronto, March 19, 1974.

itself. To stem the tide of further growth in the public service, it would probably be more desirable to introduce incentives to ensure that these goods and services are produced by the private sector. No-fault auto insurance is a case in point. This cost-saving and otherwise sensible approach is gradually spreading from province to province across Canada. So far most of the governments which have gotten involved in the promotion of this concept have chosen to set up their own insurance company for this purpose. Perhaps it would make more sense to simply order the existing private carriers to make such insurance available on a universal basis or get out of the business. Competitive forces being what they are — even in the insurance industry — most, if not all, companies would probably respond in short order, thus obviating the need for another large government department. As far as existing government activities are concerned, contracting out has a large role to play. Before turning to that possibility, however, another distinction should be made.

There is a difference between the effectiveness and the efficiency with which public funds are expended. Effectiveness of government spending really relates to the determination of the right kinds of government allocations and the setting of priorities for all manner of government undertakings. Although governments sometimes appear to act as if there is no limit to the public purse, taxpayer resistance is rising, and more attention is going to have to be paid to proper division of the more limited funds likely to be available in the future. Fortunately or unfortunately, this is essentially a political decision-making process, with the elected representatives and their advisors making the decisions subject to their replacement by the voters next time around. When it comes to the question of efficiency, it is a matter of how well government expenditures are made in the sense of getting the most value for the least cost. Here again there are inevitable political overtones involved, especially where one degree or another of patronage still prevails, as in the case of much government advertising.

Nonetheless, it is in the area of government spending in general that the greatest hope lies for at least testing the efficacy of the present public service. It is in this context that the role of contracting out is not to be minimized. One brief and reasonably well-balanced account of this solution appeared in the *Saturday Review Special Business Supplement.*

. . . [One] policy tool for mobilizing the energies and resources of business for social tasks is to "contract out." For example, city governments may hire (or contract) private firms on the basis of competitive bids to take over any of a number of municipal services, such as garbage collection. In some American cities this is already being done, with substantial benefits in the form of lower costs and better service. Even fire-fighting might conceivably become "private enterprise." Again, there are some experiments already going on — in some Texas communities, for instance. We are experimenting with "voucher systems" in education that, in effect, create competition — both among educational philosophies and among different educational efficiencies. We have been experimenting, with mixed results, with "performance contracts" in a number of school systems that turn over some activities, such as the teaching of reading, to outside private contractors whose fee is based on how well the children do on standard tests.

One area in which "contracting out" is likely to be tried on a large scale is the training of the young "hard-core" unemployed. Nobody has done very well in this area, but business has done less poorly than most.

In some such training programs, a full one-third "make it"; few government programs are even half as successful. If we should decide to employ the private sector to tackle this fundamental problem in our society, what incentives would be needed? What standards should be set? Is training enough, or should we also "contract out" the creation of jobs for the graduates of the training programs?

"Contracting out" has been around for a long time. Large parts of the American health-care system, Blue Cross, Medicare and Medicaid, are in effect "contracting out" programs in which an independent contractor, physician, or hospital is being paid on a fee-for-service basis.

These examples show, however, that "contracting out" is by no means a panacea. This policy requires clear standards and controls; their lack is probably the greatest weakness in Medicare and Medicaid programs. It also requires that there be actual competition between contractors, on price as well as on performance. But it provides choice and competition and thereby holds out the promise of efficiency. Above all, the contractor is paid only if he performs at the minimum standard, whereas a government service, as all experience shows, tends to double its budget if it fails to deliver.[52]

That contracting out can result in substantial savings to the public purse is indicated by examples which can be cited at every level of government. Not unexpectedly, one of the most extreme illustrations to be found emerges from the chaos that is New York City.

In New York, for example, private carting companies pick up garbage at a cost of $18 a ton; pay federal, state and city taxes; and make a good profit. On the other hand, the City of New York's Sanitation Department picks up garbage at a cost of $50 a ton, pays no taxes, and makes no profit.[53]

A recent Toronto experience, also relating to garbage collection, shows the many political as well as other obstacles standing in the way of using contracting out to keep parts of the public service competitive.

According to City Hall expertise, it is impossible to evaluate the comparative efficiency of private and municipal garbage collection without first eliminating the private competition. That's the oddest notion Toronto Works Commissioner Ray Bremner has come up with in a long time.

In a report supported by Toronto Executive Committee, Bremner wants to terminate the garbage collection contract inherited by the city when Forest Hill Village was taken over in 1967.

With his budget increased by the $190,000 now paid the private contractor, he says, the city will collect Forest Hill's garbage for a trial period of a year, while two independent consultants — to be paid a total fee of $8,600 by the city — figure out which system is better.

It doesn't seem to matter that Forest Hill residents are generally content with their collection service as it is — for one thing, they still get

[52] Peter F. Drucker, "Can the Businessman Meet Our Social Needs?" Reprinted from Saturday Review Special Business Supplement.
[53] David B. McCall, "Profit: Spur for Solving Social Ills", Harvard Business Review, May-June 1973 © 1973 by the President and Fellows of Harvard College; all rights reserved.

back-door collection which most of the rest of the city does not — or that Superior Sanitation Services, the contractor, is ready with figures to show it can do the job more cheaply than the city.

In fact it already has provided figures. The issue came up a year ago and the outcome then was to extend the contract for a year, during which costs were to be audited. Superior Sanitation supplied statements for July, August and September, then was told they were no longer needed. Now the city Works Department says it can't find a basis for comparison in its own overall garbage collection budget of $5,615,717.70.

The intent a year ago was to make a comparison with costs in the Moore Park-Rosedale district, where the city provides the service in a roughly equivalent area. In his present report, Bremner does not bother to say what went wrong with that idea, but simply asserts that the only solution is for him to take over the Forest Hill job, back-door collection and all.

This is nothing more than the blind march of bureaucracy, accompanied by its own referees, unsure where it is going, but determined that nothing will stand in its way. It's a safe bet that once the city is in, there'll be no more talk about handing back to the private contractor.

A case can be made for keeping the Forest Hill system as a means of checking the relative efficiency of the public system elsewhere. Perhaps even there would be merit in contracting out garbage collection in still other areas to see if experience elsewhere is right in suggesting that this can be the cheaper and more efficient way. If City Hall really wanted to find out if the case applies here, it would take some publicly served area and turn it over to private contractors on a trial basis for comparison, not destroy an operation which by all accounts is working efficiently.[54]

Despite the foregoing examples, all is not hopeless when it comes to testing public service efficiency in comparison to that of private enterprise. At the federal level in Ottawa, there is a pilot project taking place under the auspices of the Department of Public Works and the Public Service Alliance (the predominant union representing Canadian federal civil servants) designed to compare the housekeeping costs of government-employed cleaners with those of a private contractor specializing in such work. Regardless of the outcome of this particular project, it would seem desirable to have on-going comparative yardsticks of this kind in force in every branch of the public service at all levels of government to ensure that they are performing at a competitively high standard. The caveat which must be added, of course, is that the public service should not be expected to perform as cheaply as contractors providing poorer conditions of employment.

This raises still another public service problem to which only passing reference can be made. Now that collective bargaining is becoming the order of the day among public employees, particularly in Canada, there is a danger that their unions may become so strong, both economically and politically, that their wages, benefits and conditions of employment will outstrip those in the private sector. There are already signs of such a trend in the United States where the impact of negotiations is only beginning to be felt, as this item in The Christian Science Monitor suggests:

With more than 5 million workers on its payrolls, the U.S. Govern-

[54] "As Usual You Can't Beat City Hall", Toronto Star, March 18, 1974.

ment is the nation's largest and some say most generous employer. Critics charge this generosity comes at taxpayer expense. They wonder:

• Can the taxpayer afford the constantly rising bill for government salaries and benefits? It has doubled in a decade, says the nonprofit Tax Institute, Inc., a research organization.

• Are government employees overpaid and overpensioned? The average federal pay is $9,900 annually for blue-collar employees and $13,200 for white-collar workers; in each case above the national average.

Pensions, after 40 years of service, are 80 percent of the last three years' average pay. That is four or five times better than social security, but payroll deductions are nearly the same.

One of the inflationary factors, on the federal level, is the civil service system of pay increases, sometimes referred to as "a raise within an escalator within an elevator." One secretary went to work for the federal government in 1962 at $4,565. Since then, she has earned the normal five grade promotions, each with a pay increase. She also received raises for longevity and merit — she's entitled to 10 over 18 years — and more raises to keep base pay even with that paid to secretaries in private industry. The result: She now earns $19,246 annually, a jump of more than 400 percent.

Pensions are another matter.

Many state and local governments have adopted the federal system of paying a retired employee 70 to 80 percent of his average wage the last years on the job.

At the top of the federal pay structure is the 2,500-man executive staff. Its wages range from $60,000 for Cabinet officers and Supreme Court justices to $36,000 for heads of minor agencies.

In the middle is the $42,500 paid to congressmen and senior judges, $40,000 for undersecretaries and lower-level federal judges, and $38,000 for assistant secretaries.

The next level is the most controversial. It covers 1.3 million white-collar workers. The maximum for top managers, including 150 admirals and generals, is $36,000. The maximum can not by law go higher because it would invade the executive staff pay schedule. The minimum is $5,017 for the lowest clerk in his first year.

The third bracket covers 489,000 blue-collar workers. By law, they are to be paid the same wages as their privately employed counterparts in the same city. In fact, their average pay of $9,900 annually is well above the $8,440 average for all blue- and white-collar workers in the private sector.

Civil Service Commission experts say that, generally speaking, lower echelon white-collar jobs pay better than their counterparts outside government, but top federal salaries are lower than the pay for similar work in private industry. Senior clerks, for example, are lumped in a GS category — $8,055 to $10,467 — with college graduates, and that tends to push up clerical salaries beyond pay in the private sector.[55]

As a general rule, government employees should be paid neither better nor worse than comparable workers in private industry. If they are paid more, they are being rewarded more generously than those who ultimately pay part of

[55] "Are Government Workers Paid Too Generously?" Reprinted by permission of The Associated Press.

their bill for doing precisely the same kinds of work, which is clearly unwarranted. If they are paid less, then they are really subsidizing the public, which is even more unwarranted. In addition to wages, benefits and conditions of work, there is still another feature of the private sector which should be adopted in the public service. That is the matter of incentive systems. As the following article from *Business Week* reveals, there is ample scope for effective incentive systems designed to encourage public employees to get the job done more efficiently:

In Detroit, sanitation workers recently collected extra paychecks averaging $100, their first bonus under an incentive plan set up last summer to improve garbage collection. In Tacoma, Wash., firemen have won a two-hour reduction in their workweek by agreeing to a city plan that redeploys men and equipment and yet maintains fire protection services without extra manpower. In the city of Orange, Calif., policemen signed a pact last July that provides extra pay when and if the reported rates of robberies, rapes, burglaries, and car thefts decline.

These agreements are typical of a growing trend among American municipalities to try to get more and better performance for the tax dollars they pay their employees. Saddled with rising budgets, escalating public demand for services, limited sources of revenue, and resistance to higher taxes, mayors, county executives, and public managers nationwide are looking for, and slowly finding, ways to increase the efficiency and productivity of public employees. As new mayors in large cities like New York, Detroit, and Atlanta move into office this week, higher costs for limited gasoline and fuel oil supplies during the energy crunch are lending new urgency to the need for innovation.

The National Commission on Productivity estimates that about 800 local governments, including most major population centers, now have formal programs to improve productivity. A score of public and private groups, including federal government agencies, the business-supported Committee for Economic Development, the International City Managers Assn., the Urban Institute, and the Ford Foundation have joined the search for ways to upgrade municipal performance. "In local government circles productivity is a magic word," says Sam Zagoria, a municipal labor relations expert.

The economics. Businessmen who have wrestled with productivity improvement are familiar with its potential for increased profit. Local politicians have jumped on the productivity bandwagon because public tolerance of rising budgets and taxes is ebbing while services as basic as garbage pickup seem to be getting worse in many cities.

Says William Grinker, a local government specialist at the Ford Foundation: "For a lot of reasons — high taxes, corruption, outrageous union demands, lousy services — people are sick of the way the public sector operates, and they want to see change." A politician's view comes from Edward K. Hamilton, former deputy mayor of New York and chief architect of the city's 15-month-old productivity-improvement program: "Productivity is really the means by which both elected officials and union leaders in the future will be able to account for themselves to their constituencies. In those terms, productivity is coming to mean electability."

Whether to save political skins or tax dollars, the economic implications of the productivity push at the local level of government are vast.

Each year local and state governments are adding 450,000 employees. That is an annual net increase equal to more than half the number of workers in auto plants. From 1967 through 1972, total local spending jumped 80%. As a percentage of the gross national product, local government expenditures grew from 8.7% in fiscal 1967 to 11.1% in fiscal 1972. With economists forecasting continued growth in state and local government spending through the 1980s, the NCOP projects that a 1% annual productivity improvement could cut expenditures by almost $50-billion by 1985.

While the potential payoff is huge, achieving it will be difficult, for the state of the productivity improvement art in local government lags far behind industry. "In the two main skills used to upgrade productivity in industry, financial control and industrial engineering, local governments are decades behind," says the NCOP's executive director, John M. Stewart. "Still, there are some very sophisticated cities, and progress, while it's coming slowly, is coming."

The dividends. In Detroit, the city's productivity plan for sanitation workers brought a saving of 46¢ per man-hour from July through September last year. Sanitation workers agreed to meet performance standards, including cutting overtime, in exchange for 50% of the costs saved by their work. The result was the $100 average bonus. Peter Jason, Detroit's labor relations director, says that the city's yearly savings could come to $2-million in reduced overtime alone. "And last summer," he adds, "we got the garbage picked up. Before then we didn't."

In Tacoma, Wash., City Manager William Donaldson turned a demand by firemen for a two-hour reduction in the workweek into a yearly cost saving of $160,000 for fire protection services. Because they agreed to manpower and equipment deployment changes, Tacoma's firemen are now working 48 hours a week instead of 50. The changes included closing one fire station, taking one man off each fire truck, and creating a special five-man fire fighting team that answers each alarm. Says Donaldson: "We're pleased with the idea of working productivity into labor costs. The key was the firemen's willingness to try something new."

Since Orange, Calif., agreed to increase its police force's pay when and if reported rapes, robberies, burglaries, and auto thefts declined, the rates of those four crimes have dropped 22%, according to George F. Johnson, former president of the Orange Police Assn. Productivity bonuses could go as high as 6% during the two year contract. The precise amounts will be set this spring, when the first official crime statistics are released.

There is a potential bug, however, in the Orange experiment. Linking pay to the crime rate creates an incentive for the police not to report crimes. "There's a real chance to fudge the numbers," says the Ford Foundation's Grinker. "I can just imagine how something like that would work in a big city." Orange officials contend that comparing calls to the police with individual officer reports will keep the numbers clean.

The city with the most advanced productivity improvement effort is New York. For the past 15 months, the city has been publicly reporting quarterly progress toward meeting 300 productivity targets set for 16 city agencies. Edward K. Hamilton estimates total savings in excess of $200-million. He credits changes in manpower deployment, scheduling, and technological innovation with most if it.

The problems. For most cities, though, work on productivity is only beginning, and the problems to be solved remain enormous. Simply defining productivity is difficult, and measuring it is a mind-bending job of enormous intellectual subtlety. The traditional definition of productivity used in manufacturing industries — the number of units produced (output) divided by the man-hours to produce them (input) — is not really applicable to local government, which provides specialized services but does not "produce" anything tangible. "What is a unit of safe streets?" wonders Karen Gerard, urban economist for Chase Manhattan Bank.

Just how knotty the problem is shows up in a number of the 300 indexes used to measure productivity in New York. For example, one measure reported by the city's Health & Hospitals Corp. is "number of emergency room visits." "The problem with that," says John Tepper Marlin, executive director of the New York-based Council on Municipal Performance, a nonprofit group trying to measure and compare the quality of municipal services, "is that knowing how many people visited emergency rooms says nothing about the quality of treatment or the cost of service."

As Marlin implies, hard-to-measure quality of service is as much a part of productivity measurement as the "number of cases processed" or "number of violations issued," two other typical measures used in New York's program. But quantifying quality leaves most experts scratching their heads. Says Edward K. Hamilton: "You cannot measure the smell of garbage *not* in front of someone's house because it was picked up on a collection day."

Along with the subtleties of definition and measurement, the realities of local government conditions frequently discourage productivity improvement by pitting local managers against hard-to-budge bureaucrats and municipal employee unions. The National Commission on Productivity lists several key roadblocks to real productivity gains in local government: short tenure of local officials, "crisis management" techniques, and lack of data to permit the public to relate specific costs to specific services. "For instance, the typical department manager's salary and status are based upon the size of his budget and the number of people he manages," says NCOP's Stewart. "So the incentive is to increase staff and budget size."

The unions. Experts stress that municipal union cooperation is crucial to meaningful productivity gains. They point out that while some union leaders are aware that future wage gains will have to be tied to productivity increases, that realization has yet to filter down to the rank and file. The problem is that to most workers in both government and industry, productivity is still a scare word often associated with work speedup and job loss. "Everyone is for productivity," says William W. Hamilton, Jr., public affairs director for the American Federation of State, County & Municipal Employees, the nation's largest public employee union. "It's like motherhood, But when you touch Joe Worker in Cleveland, he screams like hell." Adds Edward K. Hamilton: "Nirvana comes when a union leader sees it's politically profitable within his union to be for productivity."

Nassau County, New York, is not nirvana. But there the 30,000-member Civil Service Employees Assn. is actively cooperating with County Executive Ralph G. Caso in a unique labor-management productivity effort. The two-year program is funded by the Labor Dept., the NCOP, the Ford Foundation, and Nassau County itself.

Now a year old, the productivity push in the county has labor leaders and local officials huddling to work out hoped for cost-cutting changes in work practices, schedules, and the use of equipment. What brought labor on board, says Irving Flaumenbaum, the county's top labor leader, "was the promise of sharing any savings equally with the county and the realization that we couldn't keep bargaining away as we had until now."

Labor's attitude gives Nassau County a running start. County officials, while optimistic, caution that dramatic gains won't come overnight. And they are aware that correctly conceptualizing their problems is crucial to any real productivity improvement. "The key mission," says Vincent J. Maeri, the county's productivity project director, "is to think adequately."[56]

Since the underlying theme of this book is disclosure and exposure and public scrutiny, it would not be proper to conclude this brief section on the public service without a reference to the problem of secrecy in government. For reasons which are usually unjustifiable, politicians and senior civil servants seem to have an almost unbelievable proclivity to stamp every document they get their hands on "confidential," "privileged," "top secret," or some other such sacroscant term. Those who have had experience with such documents are often amazed at how much trivia gets so labelled. Granted, there are certain cabinet and other top-level advisory and diplomatic memoranda which should not be made public until well after their intended use, but this does not excuse the extension of this usage to the vast majority of materials to which it has been applied.

To see the ridiculous extremes to which governments often go to hide certain facts from the public, one need only cite one recent Canadian example of contempt for the public's right to know what its representatives are up to. The article is from The Globe and Mail:

Back on September 2, 1969, when he was still Minister of Justice, John Turner made an important and excellent speech to the Canadian Bar Association.

Mr. Turner's topic was, Twin Freedoms: the Right to Privacy and the Right to Know. In the first part of his speech, Mr. Turner discussed the importance of individual privacy and promised legislation to protect it. Then he turned to what he called the "companion" freedom, the public's right to know — specifically, the right of public access to government information.

"Government secrecy," Mr. Turner told the Bar Association, "is sometimes legitimated as the state's right to privacy, but it may well be a denial of the public right to know. If individual privacy is a foundation of democracy, the citizen's right to know is fundamental to any participatory democracy. The public cannot be expected to dialogue meaningfully — still less decide — if it is refused the very information which would make such a dialogue and decision-making possible."

Although no one could accuse the Government of rushing headlong into reforms, it did eventually enact protection of privacy legislation. Having done that, the Government chose to rest on its laurels, ignoring Mr. Turner's companion freedom, the right to know.

[56] "Boosting Urban Efficiency". Reprinted from the January 5, 1974 issue of Business Week by special permission. Copyright 1974 by McGraw-Hill, Inc.

Ignoring if not quite forgetting. On March 15, 1973, the Government announced a new set of rules to govern production of documents in Parliament. All papers were to be made public unless they fell into one of 16 categories specifically exempted from production. They covered such things as: legal opinions provided for the use of the Government; papers, the release of which would be detrimental to the security of the state, to international relations or to federal-provincial relations: Cabinet documents, and internal departmental memoranda. Then, there was Number 16, a catch-all: "Papers requested, submitted or received in confidence by the Government from sources outside the Government."

These exemptions were unnecessarily broad, but the new rules seemed to be a start in the right direction. The trouble is the Government has made absolutely no effort to follow the guidelines.

There have been periodic complaints in the Commons, most recently by Conservative frontbencher Paul Hellyer (Trinity) this week.

Mr. Hellyer had motions on the order paper requesting the production of applications and correspondence related to four grants made by the Minister of State for Multiculturalism, Stanley Haidasz — $18,000 to New Canada, of Toronto; $8,000 to the Cross-Cultural Communications Centre, Toronto; $5,000 to Centre Chinois de Quebec, and $6,500 to the Black Youth Television Workshop, Montreal.

Each motion was rejected — on the grounds of confidentiality — by Dr. Haidasz, and Mr. Hellyer's protests to Speaker Lucien Lamoureux were to no avail.

There is no reason in the world why Mr. Hellyer should not have been given the information he sought. The grants involved do not come to a great deal of money, but it is public money all the same, and groups applying for public money should expect their applications to be scrutinized by the public and by Opposition MPs, not just by sympathetic Cabinet ministers.[57]

To get some idea of how this menacing threat to responsible government in a free society can be met, even in such a sensitive area as that of national defense, it is instructive to include a recent commentary on American progress in this area:

Government *of, by,* and *for* the people ought to be open *to* the people. In the slow process of opening up government in the United States, the Freedom of Information Act of 1966 has provided a plateau of access to documentary information. Now further progress is imminent, unless opponents of new legislation are successful in threats to seek a presidential veto.

Fortunately both the Senate and the House have now passed bills by more than the two-thirds necessary to override a veto. Such majorities seem an encouraging recognition of the need for increasing public and press access to documents not legitimately "classified" for national security purposes.

It is in the national security realm where the Senate has recently passed an amendment bringing its bill into line with an important House provision. This provision would establish a legal basis for federal judges

[57] Geoffrey Stevens, "Twin Freedoms", *The Globe and Mail*, Toronto, April 26, 1974.

to examine classified material in camera in order to decide whether it could be released. Earlier the Supreme Court had ruled that existing law did not give judges this power.

Senate legislation had threatened to undercut the proposed new authority for judges to examine the material, by setting up guidelines "so weighted in favor of classification markings as to make it almost impossible for judges, even after conducting in camera review, to overrule any secrecy stamp the government wishes to keep in place."

The quotation is from Senator Muskie, who offered the amendment to delete such guidelines while maintaining "protection for sensitive military or diplomatic data."

Passage of the Muskie amendment appears to mean one less obstacle to House-Senate agreement on the new Freedom of Information legislation. This ought to include the House's provision that government agencies must make records available within 10 days, rather than the longer period permitted in the Senate version.[58]

CONSUMERISM

Last, but hardly least, in this lengthy list of issues pertaining to business, government and society, is the matter of the consumers' movement. In one form or another, this movement has existed for a long time. It may have had its beginnings in the cooperative movement but more recently has become manifest in the form of groups such as the Consumers' Association of Canada, and in publications such as the U.S.-based *Consumer Reports*. In the United States especially, the scope of consumerism has broadened immensely in the last five years. There has been a truly remarkable proliferation of organized groups to promote the point of view of the consumer:

The discontented consumer found many more effective ways to express feelings and press for change during the 1960s than ever before. The development of means of translating discontent into effective pressure distinguishes recent consumer efforts from those of the 1910 and 1935 eras.

The consumer has been more ably represented by advocates such as Ralph Nader, Senator Warren Magnuson, and a number of journalists who pursue similar interests. These men are able to identify and publicize problems, and to follow up with workable programs for improvement. In a real sense, they are self-elected legal counsels to a typically unrepresented constituency. Many consumer problems would have remained smoldering but unfocused discontents without their attention. New product researchers have frequently found consumers do not seem to know what is bothering them or realize that others are similarly troubled until the extent of the problem is publicized or an alternative is provided.

The institutional framework has also been expanded and strengthened in recent years. Traditional bodies, such as Consumers Union and Consumers Research, Inc., have now received support from permanent bodies in the government such as the Consumer Advisory Council and the Office of the Special Assistant to the President for Consumer Affairs. These agencies have been specifically developed to avoid

---

[58] "More Freedom of Information", *The Christian Science Monitor*, June 17, 1974.

the problems of excessive identification with regulated industries which plague some of the older regulated bodies.[59]

The lengths to which some new consumer groups are willing to go and the tactics they are prepared to adopt are also noteworthy, as this *Christian Science Monitor* item points out:

First, consumer boycotts, Now, consumer "trials."

Handing out "people's subpoenas" to public officials and food corporations, the California Food Action Campaign (CFAC) held a one-day "trial" here aimed at the Del Monte Corporation, world's largest canner of fruits and vegetables.

Charged with "corporate irresponsibility, advertising overkill, and too much concern for profit at the expense of the consumer," Del Monte was rendered "guilty on all charges."

The company was "subpoenaed" but said it chose not to respond at the "trial" because the forum "was not concerned with facts."

"We singled out Del Monte," said Kay Pachtner, campaign coordinator, "because they are no better or no worse than other food manufacturing corporations."

CFAC, a coalition of consumer activists affiliated with former Sen. Fred Harris and his New Populist Action, prededed the "trial" with five weeks of workshops up and down the state "to educate consumers where their food dollars go."

Del Monte, through corporate Chairman Alfred W. Eames Jr., said the company resents "being singled out as the scapegoat for the rise in the cost of living by individuals and groups whose motives, if not political, certainly aren't altogether clear. . . ."

He defended Del Monte by pointing out that during fiscal 1973 the company earned a 10.3 percent profit increase "but we took a smaller profit bite than we did the year before. . . . We increased profits by increasing sales volume, not our profit margin."

CFAC said that less than 1 percent of the 32,500 food manufacturing firms in the country gained 61 percent of the industry profits last year. This concentration works against consumers, small farmers, and food industry workers, said CFAC.

Mrs. Pachtner cited a 1972 Federal Trade Commission report which insisted that if there had been more competition in just 13 food lines, shoppers nationwide would have saved $2 billion in grocery bills.

"That extra $2 billion," she charged, "went to pay exorbitant executive salaries, advertising over-kill, corporate waste and inefficiencies, and excessive profit margins."

CFAC wants to draw attention to the "concentration of power in the food industry because consumers are being overcharged, food supplies are being manipulated, food quality is on the decline, more than a thousand family farmers a week are squeezed out of business, and meanwhile food middlemen are enjoying soaring corporate profits."

The "trial," the first of its kind, drew some state legislators and federal officials, including Raymond Lloyd, regional director of the FTC. He

[59] George S. Day and David A. Aaker, "A Guide to Consumerism", *Journal of Marketing*, Vol. 34, July 1970, p. 17. Reprinted from *Journal of Marketing* published by the American Marketing Association.

said that since 1967 enforcement of anti-trust laws and trade laws have cut into corporate concentration in agriculture.

Mr. Eames, speaking the following day at Del Monte's annual stock-holders meeting, said "too many shoppers believe that profit is the difference between what a retailer pays for a can of peas and what he sells it for." He singled out "operating expenses" as the "greatest portion of the markup."

"The amount of each food dollar," he said, "that winds up as profit is an insignificant fraction after costs are paid for processing, packaging, transporting, storing and distributing a product."

CFAC charged that Del Monte priced its own red-shield label food at 14 percent higher than the same food produced by the company under different labels. "The company says this reflects the shoppers' faith in Del Monte products," said a housewife. "I say the shoppers are the victims of advertising."

Suggestions to decentralize the food industry included government changing its emphasis from protecting big business to the small farmer and consumer, increased consumer representation on state food and agricultural boards, perhaps "family farm bills" which encourage more family farming, more farmer's markets in cities, and turning small plots of open land into mini-farms on the outskirts of cities.[60]

Responses to consumerism have been forthcoming both from business and government. Attempts are being made to revitalize some of the traditional links between business and the consumer such as The Better Business Bureau. At the level of the individual firm, some companies are making sincere efforts to cope with legitimate consumer complaints. At least one American firm has found such an effort highly rewarding. *Business Week* reported the efforts of Joseph B. Danzansky, officer of Giant Food, Inc.:

With considerable fanfare, Danzansky's company became one of the first major supermarket chains to adopt unit pricing, open-dating of perishables, and ingredient labeling of private-label foods, cosmetics, toiletries, and over-the-counter drugs. These practices now have become standard operating procedure with many other food marketers as well.

These and other Giant reforms were bound to pay off in customer goodwill, and they have. But it is still not quite so clear-cut on the bottom line. . . . There is, however, one measure of Giant's success: its increasing share of the market. . . .[61]

Despite numerous other examples of similar endeavours, the impression remains, as the title of one 1973 *Business Week* article put it, that there has been "more talk than action on consumer complaints":

Sherry Chenoweth, state director of consumer services for Minnesota, pulls no punches on her favorite subject. Pillsbury, General Mills, and several other major Minnesota companies have set up corporate consumer affairs departments. "They are almost a consumer fraud in themselves,"

[60] David Holmstrom, "Consumer Group Hands Out 'People's Subpoenas' to Hearing", *The Christian Science Monitor*, October 2, 1973.
[61] "The Shoppers' Friend at Giant Supermarkets". Reprinted from the April 6, 1974 issue of *Business Week* by special permission. Copyright 1974 by McGraw-Hill, Inc.

she says. "They are an easy out and a stop-gap measure to make the public believe they are involved in and concerned with consumerism. I am not impressed. It is primarily public relations puffery."

Such sentiments — shared by many consumerists and even by some corporate executives themselves — will confront more than 300 consumer affairs directors next week when they meet in Anaheim, Calif., to form a national association. Many of the country's largest corporations will be present, ranging from Du Pont and RCA to Pan American, J.C. Penney, and Hunt-Wesson. Says one corporate consumer affairs type: "The meeting will provide a good opportunity for people responsible for consumer affairs to learn how other companies are handling problems of consumer education, response, and warranties."

While some consumerists view the meeting as just another public relations ploy, a few are at least encouraged by what it symbolizes. As Erma Angevine, executive director of the Consumer Federation of America, puts it: "You might say we've hit the mule over the head and finally gotten its attention."

Rhetoric. Even the most firebrand consumerists are willing to admit that some companies have made important strides in consumer affairs. Among those most often singled out: General Foods, Sears, Motorola, and General Electric. "Yet far too many other companies settle for paper consumerism," says Fran Lee, consumer reporter for radio station WPIX in New York.

To consumerists, the big stumbling block is often the people put in charge of consumer affairs. "Frequently, he or she is just some second-rate executive with a new title who can't or won't go to bat for the consumer," says Laura Horowitz, former complaint coordinator for the Virginia Citizens' Consumer Council.

As one example, consumerists cite Byron Nichols, former marketing executive at Chrysler Corp., who suddenly surfaced as "Your Man in Detroit." In a saturation ad campaign, Chrysler owners were told to send their complaints to Nichols. The trouble was that many called instead of writing, and Chrysler's switchboard in suburban Highland Park nearly buckeld under the load. So Chrysler backed off, and the only current reference to "Your Man in Detroit" is in an information packet given to new car owners. There is no phone number or street address — just a box number.

Lowell Dodge, director of the Center for Auto Safety, a Washington-based Nader organization, claims that Nichols can never be reached by telephone, does not answer letters, and is himself the source of growing consumer irritation. "We now get more complaints about Nichols than we do about Chrysler cars," Dodge says. In fact, Dodge's center has filed a complaint with the Federal Trade Commission, charging that Chrysler's "Your Man in Detroit" program is deceptive promotion.

Ford Motor Co. and its "No Unhappy Owners" program has similarly produced plenty of unhappy owners. When Ford first announced the program, the CFA's Mrs. Angevine relayed a bundle of owner complaints. They all came back with a letter saying owners should contact Ford's regional representatives — "which proves," says Mrs. Angevine, "they hadn't even read the letters. We'd already done that."

Ford and Chrysler, of course, defend their programs. In fact, a Chrysler executive became indignant this week when a reporter asked,

207

"Whatever happened to my man in Detroit?" "He's still here," the executive snapped.

The only auto industry program that draws high marks from consumerists is American Motors Corp.'s "Buyer Protection Plan." It promises 1972 and 1973 AMC owners virtually "no-questions-asked" repair on anything during the first year or 12,000 mi. and offers a second-year option — at $149 — that includes two years or 24,000 mi. of total coverage, including routine maintenance. While even this program has a few problems — for instance, dealers who are slow to make repairs — it has still paid off. "AMC just reported its best six-month period in 13 years," says Louise Duffy, assistant to Presidential consumer adviser Virginia Knauer. "I'd even bet the 'Buyer Protection Plan' was the reason."

Form letters. In Minnesota, Sherry Chenoweth claims that such programs succeed because of top-level corporate commitment. More often, she says, there is no commitment — only "corporate hypocrisy." She cites General Mills. "It makes a big play for consumer respect," she says, "yet the company was one of the prime lobbyist against open [freshness] dating when it came up in the state legislature. Apparently, General Mills feels everyone but the consumer is entitled to know when a package should be pulled from the shelves."

General Mills Vice-President Mercedes Bates, who runs the Betty Crocker Kitchens, claims that is not so at all. She says simply, "There is no good consumer benefit from open dating of longlife products" — such as Betty Crocker cake mixes. She also feels that unit pricing — another "must" among consumerists — does not necessarily produce "wise shoppers." In her view, the consumer is not entirely interested in learning to be a better shopper. "A course on consumer buying, which Betty Crocker Kitchens sponsored with the federal government, had to be dropped because of lack of interest," she says. She views the primary function of the company's 18-month-old Office of Consumer Response as answering complaints in the mail "in a warm, friendly fashion."

WPIX's Fran Lee claims too many companies settle for letter-writing. "I recently wrote to Kitchens of Sara Lee about two frozen meat dishes that the company sells: Beef Burgundy and Beef Stroganoff, both priced at $1.39. My husband and I placed the tiny portions on our plates, and when we counted the pieces of meat and vegetables, it came to mostly gravy, and 50¢ worth of meat, if that." Sara Lee answered with a form letter, beginning "We very much regret that the Sara Lee entrees you tried did not meet your expectations," then went on to give a pitch for Sara Lee quality. "Sure, companies are spending a lot of money hiring letter writers," says Fran Lee, "but is a form letter like this an adequate response?"

Product misuse? On their side, consumer affairs directors concede that industry has far to go, but note that many of the complaints arise from misuse of products. Alberto-Culver Co., which answers 1,300 complaint letters a month, recently received a frantic note from a Nebraska housewife who said she had ruined her hair by washing it with a combination of Alberto-Culver's VO-5 shampoo and Kraft's Miracle Whip salad dressing. "Apparently, it's all the rage in the Midwest to condition your hair with Miracle Whip," says a somewhat bemused Alberto-Culver spokesman. "But this woman was the first to combine it with our VO-5."

Corporations also complain that consumerists emphasize what is wrong in consumer affairs and seldom acknowledge what is done right. In an effort to "balance the record," Senator Frank Moss (D-Utah), chairman of the Senate Commerce Committee's consumer subcommittee, gave the country's 300 largest companies a chance to answer their critics. Late last year, his subcommittee released a 466-page compendium of corporate good deeds, entitled *Initiatives in Corporate Responsibility*. Though he was obviously pleased with the report, Moss nevertheless appended a disclaimer: "Without desiring to minimize the achievements noted herein, a brief caveat is in order. The staff was not able to evaluate the activities described by the respondents, nor to determine which of the industry responses represented actions taken only under the pressure of external demands."

Minnesota's Sherry Chenoweth adds her own cautionary note. "Corporations that are genuinely concerned see consumerism as not being an evil but as a deep-seated concern on the part of their customers. The consumer doesn't want to take over control of companies. He wants to be a part of the decision-making process." Business, she adds, should not treat consumerism with fear. "What's happening in consumerism now," she says, "is a mere token compared to what will be going on in five years if companies don't show a greater concern for their buyers."[62]

Government reaction to the consumer movement has been more encouraging than the reaction of business, if only because politicians seem to be more sensitive than corporate executives to consumer concerns. In Canada this trend has been marked by the formation of the Federal Department of Consumer and Corporate Affairs and a spate of federal and provincial consumer protective legislation. In the United States, similar, but often more far-reaching, proposals have been forthcoming, as discussed in this *California Management Review* article. One such proposal calls, among other things, for a special department of consumer affairs.

I am convinced that we must establish a strong Department of Consumer Affairs whose mandate would be to represent and promote the consumer interest in national policy. Such a department would be able to encourage the research and develop the data required to analyze and promote the consumer interest. Presumably, it would itself develop expertise to represent the consumer interest in such matters as standards formulation, the development of transportation and communications policies and the implementation of our fiscal and monetary policies.

Such a department could have the responsibility for developing the social indices which are so much needed by all decision-makers in both the private and the public sector if we are to define our goals and measure our progress in attaining them. In the long run, such a department could be the leader of fundamental discontinuities in our economy resulting from our failure or refusal to recognize and identify the areas in which consumption may be shortchanged by labor or business. Presumably, the force and stature of this department would compel and assist not only government but also business and labor to appreciate and take the aggregate interest of consumers into account in their decision-making.

In order for such a department to be able to discharge its responsibilities effectively, it is essential that it be accorded affirmative operational powers. This could be done in one of two ways. The department could be empowered to intervene directly in the proceedings of other

---

[62] "More Talk Than Action on Consumer Complaints". Reprinted from the May 19, 1973 issue of *Business Week* by special permission. Copyright 1973 by McGraw-Hill, Inc.

government departments where the interests of consumers are affected, or, those government agencies whose decisions directly affect the consumer interest could be required to submit to such a department a statement — comparable to the environmental impact statement — of the type of decision or action contemplated by them and the nature of and extent to which the consumer interest will be affected with full opportunity for the department to submit comments.[63]

This is clearly the direction in which events are moving in the United States, and it is possible that Congress will eventually pass legislation creating a meaningful consumer protection agency which, among other duties, would engage in the following activities:

• Request any agency to take up a consumer complaint in its area.
• Seek judicial review of federal agency proceedings.
• Seek information from industry to carry out investigations if the agency handling the problem finds no serious reason to object.
• Request the National Bureau of Standards or other testing agencies to test consumer products in specific cases and make results public.
• Serve as a register of consumer complaints and company responses and make both available to the public.[64]

That support for this kind of measure is widespread is indicated by the endorsement it has received from a broad cross-section of the business press.

Businessmen understandably are somewhat nervous about the drive to create a federal agency charged with looking out for the interests of the U.S. consumer. But the legislation taking shape this week in the House deserves the support of business as well as the various groups that now speak for the consumer.

There is a danger, of course, that another agency would simply multiply the red tape and increase the delays that already frustrate businessmen when they deal with the government. But it is also possible that the new agency could help speed the regulatory process by improving input and clarifying issues.

Beyond that, a consumer agency could improve the level of debate between business and the consumerists. By putting a sharp focus on the vague charges the consumer groups now feel free to make, it could show business where its real problems are. And by equalizing the balance between well-financed, well-organized business groups and the often disorganized consumer spokesmen, it could help restore public confidence in the regulatory process.[65]

One significant form of consumer retaliation against irresponsible corporate behaviour is now running into trouble in the United States just at a time

[63] Mary Gardiner Jones, "The Consumer Interest: The Role of Public Policy". © 1973 by The Regents of the University of California. Reprinted from CALIFORNIA MANAGEMENT REVIEW, Vol. XVI, No. 1, p. 23, by permission of The Regents.
[64] "The Consumer Agency's Targets". Reprinted from the March 30, 1974 issue of Business Week by special permission. Copyright 1974 by McGraw-Hill, Inc.
[65] "A Consumer Spokesman". Reprinted from the April 6, 1974 issue of Business Week by special permission. Copyright 1974 by McGraw-Hill, Inc.

when it could be emerging as a remedy in Canada. Class-action suits have been gaining strength in the United States as an effective way in which consumer groups can seek collective recourse on behalf of all those affected by a corporation engaging in illegal or unethical conduct. While Canada's Minister of Consumer and Corporate Affairs has been promising to facilitate the use of such a remedy in Canada, the U.S. Supreme Court has been removing its legal underpinnings in that country. The concern this has occasioned in the U.S. was captured in a recent editorial in *The Christian Science Monitor*:

In terms of basic justice it would seem that the United States Supreme Court ought to facilitate rather than inhibit what Justice Douglas called "one of the few legal remedies the small claimant has against those who command the status quo" — namely, class actions. Such facilitation would be in line with an encouraging, but by no means complete, trend in the American courts to minimize disparities of wealth and influence in seeking to ensure the equality before the law promised to all citizens.

Yet in the past several months, for one reason or another, the Supreme Court has been making class actions more difficult on legal grounds. And its latest decision is seen as a key setback to consumers, environmentalists, and others who may have small individual claims adding up to large claims when lumped together in class actions.

This ruling, in *Eisen v. Carlisle & Jacquelin*, said that all identifiable members of the plaintiff class had to be individually notified of the suit so that they would have the option of disassociating themselves from it — and perhaps suing individually. Also, the cost of notification would have to be borne by the plaintiff. (A lower court had accepted the alternative of notification mainly by newspapers, with defendants bearing 90 percent of costs.)

In the Eisen antitrust case, brought on behalf of small investors against two huge trading firms, the class amounted to some 6 million persons, more than 2 million of them identifiable. To notify them, just the postage would daunt most plaintiffs.

And it is reasoned that many potential class actions will now prove too expensive to be pursued. Consumer and environmental groups can still sue on behalf of themselves and their members, which has been a familiar practice. Unorganized citizens with hopes of joining in class actions appear to be hardest hit.

Interestingly enough, Justice Douglas and his two fellow dissenters went along with the main thrust of the majority opinion. But he suggested that the case be returned to a lower court for division of the large class group into something more manageable. Perhaps it is in this realm that the usefulness of class action can somehow be retained. It is hard to disagree with Mr. Douglas's impulse to "strengthen his (the small claimant's) hand with the view of creating a system of law that dispenses justice to the lowly as well as to those liberally endowed with power and wealth."

Congress's increasing concern for consumer interests ought to include consideration of class-action legislation. But the eight-year record of the Eisen litigation — and Justice Douglas's comments — suggest that the legal profession and the judiciary at the trial court level may well need to make better use of the rules and procedures already available to implement effectively the class-action concept.

211

Wiser handling of these cases in the lower courts or corrective legislation, or perhaps both, are needed. We hope they will be forthcoming.[66]

Aside from fighting such retrograde steps as the foregoing, it is not entirely clear where the consumer movement will head now. Some possibilities are suggested in an account of likely future developments in Canada. These considerations appeared in The Globe and Mail:

Canada has achieved one international distinction that many businessmen would be glad to forgo. It is well in the forefront of the "consumerism" movement.

Consumerism is, of course, often used as a term of disparagement. Proponents of the movement prefer to call it the consumer protection movement. Under either name, the consumer movement has gathered a great deal of strength, durability and government support over the past decade. It is a development that business probably will have to learn to accommodate to a far greater extent than anyone could have foreseen in 1960.

In the view of Professor Jacob Ziegel of Osgoode Hall Law School, York University, consumerism already has won some important victories, but many more battles lie ahead.

"In a sense," he writes in the current issue of The Canadian Banker, "they will be more difficult struggles because they will challenge more strongly entrenched interests and require a much more sophisticated examination of our communal structures."

What has given impetus to consumerism on this continent, apart from (or perhaps because of) the leadership provided by such dramatic disturbers of the peace as Ralph Nader, is the decision of government to play a more active role in protecting what it conceived to be the interests of consumers in the marketplace.

Prof. Ziegel describes several reasons for the burst of activity in this area in recent years. One is the rapid urbanization of Canadian society in recent years, and the proliferation of household products.

Before the Second World War, the typical grocery store stocked about 1,500 different items, compared with at least 7,500 items at present. Each year, more than 1,000 new items are brought to the market — prepackaged, prelabelled and with no assurance other than the producer's statement that the contents will live up to the claims made for them.

Also, increasing affluence and the ready availability of consumer credit have enabled millions of Canadians to become owners of automobiles and household appliances. There is, according to Prof. Ziegel, a great and growing consumer dissatisfaction with the quality of some of the new durable goods, particularly automobiles.

But the most important cause of the rise of consumerism, and the unifying factor, he says, is the "overwhelming disparity in sophistication and bargaining power between the consumer and the professional supplier of goods and services."

Written agreements are usually standardized, and are to the disadvantage of the consumer. "The businessman relies on a battery of experts to counsel him in his affairs; and the consumer is expected to fend for himself, and by himself. Such an unequal confrontation can have only one result."

[66] "Class Action and Justice", The Christian Science Monitor, June 7, 1974.

Prof. Ziegel, who is an active consumer advocate and a former member of the Canadian Consumer Council, may in some respects overstate his case. Business can no more be thought of as a monolithic power, always acting against the interests of consumers, than the fragmented, individualistic consumer movement can be considered to be a single force in the marketplace, enforcing honesty on the business community.

It has always been the case that the buyer who believes he has been treated unfairly by one supplier can take his business elsewhere. If he is not satisfied with the product of one manufacturer, he can switch to another brand. This is, of course, no protection against fly-by-night operators or the unscrupulous few whose primary interest is a quick and transient profit.

Several of the most successful, long-established manufacturing and retail organizations in Canada built their success on recognition of the fact that business survival is likely to be short-lived unless the consumer is satisfied. This business ethic is not yet dead, despite the critics, and there are still many responsible executives who understand clearly that when a company loses its reputation for honesty and fair value for the price charged, it is nearing the end of the road.

At the same time, it must be acknowledged that the options open to consumers have been reduced since the war, with the increased domination of the retail market by a relatively small number of giant chains, and with the disappearance of many independent producers of such consumer products as automobiles. But new retail outlets have appeared, such as the discount department stores, and import competition exerts a considerable discipline on domestic manufacturers.

The confrontation between business and consumers is not quite as one-sided, nor is the outcome as predictable, as Prof. Ziegel suggests.

Where difficulties do arise is, for example, in the use of package sizes that make price comparisons almost impossible, and in the problems consumers have in learning the relative merits and proper applications of different types of synthetic fabrics and plastics. It is not by any means clear how far it is necessary for governments to go in enacting legislation to correct abuses and to give consumers more effective representation at the government level.

The recent trend has been for governments to go rather a long way in this direction. In Prof. Ziegel's view, the critical breakthrough in Canada — which has put this country in the "forefront of consumer progress" — came when the Ontario Government in 1966 set up its Consumer Protection Bureau and when the federal Government in 1967 established the Department of Consumer and Corporate Affairs.

The Ontario initiative has since been followed in most other provinces, and the federal department has acted as a catalyst in promoting change at both the federal and provincial levels in what is thought to be the best interests of consumers.

These actions have given consumerism considerable status and respectability, and lead Prof. Ziegel to the conclusion that "the future looks much more promising than it did even 10 years ago."[67]

Perhaps the only thing that can be said for sure is that consumers are no longer going to remain one of the few unorganized groups in North American

[67] Ronald Anderson, "Consumerism and the Struggles to Come", *The Globe and Mail*, Toronto, December 11, 1971.

society. Individuals have become much more aware of their place as consumers and much more attuned to the need to respond to their problems as a group rather than on an individual basis. Although the consumer movement has not reached massive proportions in an organization sense, it has in terms of awakening more and more people to their stake in the things which various elements in the total movement are trying to accomplish.

In the survival of North American society, this is all to the good, despite some excesses, as it promises to establish a more effective realignment of checks and balances within the overall system. If looked upon in this light, most of the developments highlighted above should be welcomed by businessmen as well as everyone else:

In the American corporate state, the citizen's relationship to government is somewhat like that of the consumer's relationship to industry. Both the citizen and the consumer want an honest product, honestly advertised. When they insist on this, they are not opposing the system but helping to make it work.

The parallel comes to mind in the light of a remarkable speech from a voice at the top of American business — Edward B. Rust, president of State Farm Insurance Companies and of the United States Chamber of Commerce. Discussing the various social obligations of the business manager, Mr. Rust says that "he should need no instruction at all in bringing to the marketplace a product or service that meets whatever claims he is willing to make for it."

This is a basic demand of consumer advocates like Ralph Nader, Mr. Rust adds. "His primary insistence is on products that perform as they are supposed to, on warranties that protect the buyer at least as much as the seller, on services that genuinely serve. . . ."

Challenging some businessmen's notion that "consumerism and its spokesmen" are enemies of the free-enterprise system, Mr. Rust says:

"The whole point of Nader — so obvious that it is often overlooked — is his single-minded dedication to making the free-enterprise system work as it's supposed to — to make marketplace realities of the very virtues that businessmen ascribe to the system. . . ."

As in the economic system, so in the political system. What the citizen-consumer wants the government to do is make realities of the virtues that leaders ascribe to the system.

The parallel seems especially pertinent during an administration oriented toward the interests of the business community. It is an administration which itself sometimes conveys an image of a certain kind of corporation — tightly held, taking for granted the provision of executive perquisites for the hardworking boss, and more interested in staying in business than in supplying the product as advertised.

When citizens and their representatives try to keep this administration up to the mark, to restore its damaged credibility, they are not working against the system but as a partner in it.[68]

DISCLOSURE & EXPOSURE & PUBLIC SCRUTINY

To conclude this lengthy chapter, a brief resumé of its underlying theme is in

[68] "Citizen Consumers", *The Christian Science Monitor*, October 10, 1973.

order. Although many other measures are required, none of them will amount to anything unless they are based on much more disclosure and exposure and public scrutiny of pertinent data. To appreciate the basic point, one need only consider the many forms of corporate information that are not available to the public:

The public has no way of learning the following basic things about a corporation from any source whatsoever:

• How much a company spends to lobby on federal, state, or local legislation. Current lobbying and election laws are so riddled with loopholes that corporations can effectively conceal from the public millions of dollars spent for such activities. It has also become clear from investigation of the 1972 presidential election that millions of dollars in illegal corporate campaign contributions can be concealed.

• How much a company has invested in foreign countries and what impact such investment has on domestic prices and jobs, and on the politics and economy of the other countries.

• Who owns a company, other than those owning 10 percent or more which must be reported to the Securities and Exchange Commission. (Even this is not entirely revealing — ownership of large corporations is often concentrated among family individuals or members of boards of directors. A number of family members or directors, or both, may each own 10 percent or less of a company but the aggregate ownership may be a controlling interest.)

• Whether advertising claims made by a company are true. The Federal Trade Commission requires the manufacturers of a handful of products — such as automobiles, televisions, and tires — to file proof of their advertising claims with the Commission. However, these products are only a small percentage of those on the market.

• How seriously most companies' products pollute the environment and what they are doing about the pollution they create. Data on air and water pollution from manufacturing processes is compiled at many regional, state, and local agencies, but the information can be difficult to obtain, even though it is normally public by law. The new National Pollutant Discharge Elimination System which according to the 1972 Federal Water Quality Act amendments replaced the Refuse Act permit system, has simplified this problem by making data on company water pollution readily available at regional Environmental Protection Agency offices. However, high duplicating costs may be encountered, and data is supplied by the companies and generally unverified.

As long as such gaps remain in the information pried from companies by government or other groups, American corporations will be truly accountable to none but themselves. Perhaps the Council on Economic Priorities' fair treatment and analysis of voluntarily disclosed social data presents a new and potentially effective alternative for both the companies and the public. [69]

In the absence of public availability of more corporate data, there is every reason to be skeptical not only about what business is up to but also about how effectively it is being called to account for any abuses to which it is party:

Given the limited resources typically available to competent resear-

[69] Lee Stephenson, "Prying Open Corporations: Tighter than Clams", *Business & Society Review*, Winter 1973-74, No. 8, p. 49.

chers, the great secrecy in which much of the pertinent data concerning business behaviour at every level is typically enshrouded, it is generally difficult to obtain the necessary information to make intelligent appraisals of business power in the specific context. For every Congressional hearing regarding ITT's activities in Chile, or corporate campaign contribution to Watergate, or trial concerning price fixing in the electrical industry, or FTC study of market concentration in the oil industry, the large majority of situations raising questions of corporate power have little by way of essential material which is a matter of public record. Even in the above mentioned instances, our information was incomplete.[70]

As emphasized in this item from *Business and Society Review*, greater disclosure and exposure and public scrutiny are clearly part of the price which business must pay if it is not to fall prey to far more drastic action in the name of social reform:

Disclosure of more corporate information is badly needed. The impact of corporate decisions on the public generally escapes public notice. . . . Obviously some information must be protected, but no doubt less than management claims. The present SEC rule requires management to furnish only data which has profit implications. The rule should be broadened to include details bearing on social questions.

Disclosure also carries an indirect advantage like any unwelcome publicity, the disclosure of unflattering information imposes a high cost — embarrassment. In the case of a corporation, this could quickly turn into the cost of consumer retaliation. Disclosure could thus lead to the hiring of more blacks, the reduction of pollution, or the production of safer automobiles. Are not the Pentagon Papers a grim warning of the evil that can be done when a powerful political institution manages to operate in unjustifiable secrecy?. . . .

The public is beginning to realize that some corporate practices are at odds with the welfare of society and it is starting to understand the political character of corporate activities. But this is not reason enough to restructure corporations along government lines or to politicize corporate structure and risk making the corporation effective for no task at all, economic or social. We cannot afford to cripple the corporation. Serious as its faults are, continued economic activity and growth are vital as long as distress and privation remain the lot of many people in this country and abroad. Moreover, reduced economic activity will hardly be permitted by the poor or the upward-bound middle class.

Rather than seeking political transformation of the corporation, reformers would be wise to make the corporate system which now exists work in society's behalf. This can be accomplished by economic measures, invigorating corporate democratic forms, establishing self-critical voices inside the corporation, and requiring greater disclosure of corporate social conduct. These measures would give shareholders a degree of control over management decisions and make corporate thinking more social-minded. Above all, the single most potent vehicle for change could be through the market itself — altering the market mechanism so that it advances society's social as well as economic goals.[71]

[70] Edwin Epstein, "Dimensions of Corporate Power, Pt. 1". © 1973 by The Regents of the University of California. Reprinted from CALIFORNIA MANAGEMENT REVIEW, Vol. XVI, No. 2, p. 12, by permission of The Regents.
[71] Donald E. Schwartz, "Reforming the Corporation from Within", *Business & Society Review*, Spring 1972, No. 1, pp. 67-68.

6

CORPORATE SOCIAL RESPONSIBILITY

To summarize and draw together many of the matters raised in the previous chapter it is useful to explore the concept of corporate social responsibility. People have wrestled with this concept in one form or another for years. In their famous encyclicals, for example, the Popes of the Catholic Church attempted to come to grips with such inter-related topics as those of fair profits and just wages. In regard to the social responsibility of corporations, one can pose a series of questions which gradually raise the stakes in terms of public accountability.

One such series of questions with reference to any number of corporate actions runs as follows: Is it profitable? Is it consistent with the corporation's target market share or other such measure? Is it legal? Is it good for public relations? Is it good for the corporation's people — e.g. managers, shareholders, employees, customers, etc.? Is it ethical? Is it the "right thing" to do? One can build quite a hierarchy of issues out of a series of such questions.

This chapter presents brief synopses of twelve possible models of corporate social responsibility ranging from "business is business at any price" through "business is business but there are some priorities" and "business is business but it should have a broad social conscience" to "business is business and therefore it should be nationalized." After highlighting each of these potential approaches, the chapter concludes with the author's attempt to bring some of the more valid of them together into a cohesive and meaningful package.

It is helpful to note that the term "social responsibility" is not always considered a useful one when discussing the issues being tackled here:

Few phrases are so bandied about today as the "social responsibility" of business. It has been used so widely and in so many situations, however, that it has lost much of whatever meaning it may have had. It is now little more than a propaganda instrument. The term never has described corporate behaviour, but is used primarily as a weapon in the combat between corporations, regulators, and consumer groups. Old weapons may be sold to developing countries, but old phrases never die — they stay on to dilute the quality of public discussion.[1]

A commentary from *California Management Review* captures the essence of the challenge implied by the use of the term "corporate social responsibility," however valid or invalid the term may be:

---

[1] Robert Rutherford Smith, " 'Social Responsibility': A Term We Can Do Without", *Business & Society Review/Innovation*, Spring 1974, No. 9, p. 54.

We are witnessing today an important paradox. On the one hand business is being roundly attacked and condemned, not only as an institution but also for specific actions. David Rockefeller puts it this way: "It is scarcely an exaggeration to say that right now American business is facing its most severe public disfavor since the 1930s. We are assailed for demeaning the worker, deceiving the consumer, destroying the environment and disillusioning the younger generation."[1] Yet at no time in our history has business been a greater beneficial force in society. At no time in our history have businessmen thought more about the consequences of their actions.

The underlying cause of this paradox is that there are important changes taking place in what the public expects business to do. So far, business is responding to these new demands without major problems. Most observers predict however, that in the future the demands which the public will place on business to do things in the social area not traditionally assumed by business will accelerate. If this takes place without very careful consideration of the consequences, the results could be catastrophic for business and the community.

Unfortunately, the forces at work are moving without a clear understanding of or agreement upon what responsibilities business has or should assume in the social area. It is about time that we tried to get specific about underlying policies which should govern businesses' assumption of social responsibilities. It is also time to develop concrete policies and actions which may be used by an individual company in its pursuit of social responsibilities.[2]

To appreciate the controversy which surrounds the question of social responsibility, it is obviously important to understand the differing assumptions and contexts within which the various protagonists in the debate are operating:

Anyone who is disturbed by the bewildering array of definitions and conceptions with which the subject of "social responsibility" is burdened should seek his peace, not in the principles and practices of lexicography, but in the basic assumptions on which each author builds his perceptions of this slippery concept. Differing perceptions of social responsibility are not the primary cause of the problem; instead, the many divergent perceptions of the context within which the issue of social responsibility is raised is the issue. How one perceives the social system as a whole and the relationship between the whole social system and its subsystems and among those subsystems is the primary variable. Depending on these perceptions, social responsibility might be seen, for example, as an imposition, an opportunity, an act of charity, a liability, a subterfuge, an exercise in public relations, an excuse, an ideology, an historical imperative, a biological phenomenon, an impossibility, a social expectation, a means of communication between system and subsystem, a search for respectability or legitimacy, a part of the process by which the techno-structure attributes social purpose to its own goals, the performance of basic chores, a subversive doctrine, a mode of conduct, the conscience of business (or of society), an adjustment mechanism for change, social con-

[2] George A. Steiner, "Social Policies for Business", © 1972 by The Regents of the University of California. Reprinted from CALIFORNIA MANAGEMENT REVIEW, Vol. XV, No. 2, p. 17, by permission of The Regents.

sciousness or awareness, enlightened self-interest, a duty to maximize profits or protect shareholders, an expedient response to temporary social change, propaganda, a manifestation of status anxiety, or a part of a cultural revolution.

Each view proceeds from a different set of assumptions with regard to reality and to the context in which the social responsibility issue is to be discussed. A couple of years ago, Milton Friedman wrote:

"In a free-enterprise, private property system, a corporate executive is an employee of the owners of the business. He has direct responsibility to his employers. That responsibility is to conduct the business in accordance with their desires, which generally will be to make as much money as possible while conforming to the basic rules of society, both those embodied in law and those embodied in ethical custom."

Professor Friedman's basic assumptions are clear, and once the corporate executive is perceived as an employee of the owners in a private property system, there is little uncertainty involved in forecasting Friedman's perceptions of that executive's social responsibility. Although the qualification, "while conforming to the basic rules of society" would appear to leave the door open for more flexible perceptions, we know from additional reading in Friedman's works that the "basic rules" were intended to mean only "free and open competition without fraud or deception." Many commentators would say today that society has changed its rules and that Professor Friedman has not noticed or is unwilling to recognize the changes.

Paul T. Heyne explicitly disavows one of Friedman's underlying premises when he states that ". . . it is no longer possible to believe that the public good will by some mysterious alchemy emerge from universal selfishness," but does not avoid an even more basic one:

"The conclusion of our arguments is that the businessman's primary and overriding responsibility is to use the resources of society in the most *economical* way . . . we cannot conceive of an argument which would make of *economy* anything but an unqualified good."

Daniel Bell, who starts from a very different set of premises, does find an argument that makes economy something less than an unqualified good and uses it to reach a very different perception of social responsibility.

"Corporations are institutions for economizing; but they are also ways of life for their members . . . To think of the business corporation, then, simply as an economic instrument is to fail totally to understand the meaning of the social changes of the last century . . . When one uses the phrase the 'social responsibility' of the corporation, one is not indulging in rhetoric (though many corporate officials are), or thinking of *noblesse oblige* (which fewer corporate officials do), or assuming that some subversive doctrine is being smuggled into society (as some laissez-faire economists suggest), but simply accepting a cardinal sociopsychological fact about human attachments."

Bell's assumption is set forth clearly when he writes that: "a corporation, while producing things, is made up of people" and that "one cannot treat people . . . as things." Bell suggests also that a society may operate in a "sociologizing" or "politicizing" mode as well as an "economizing" mode. He believes that American society now is shifting strongly from the economizing to the sociologizing mode.

Hazel Henderson manifests a different package of assumptions —

219

some of them shared with Friedman or Heyne — and argues for a narrow construction of social responsibility on the ground that a broader concept would create the risk that well-meaning corporate leaders might gain more power than they already have. She assumes the importance and relevance of changing social expectations but regards them as something "capricious" and "unexpected," interrupting something else which is "established" and "normal":

Increasingly, a private enterprise is finding itself caught in a bind because society, which laid down the traditional ground rules for private enterprise, has now decided to change them in midstream. No wonder, then, that business leaders are left with a philosophy gap."

R. Joseph Monsen sees changing social expectations as the norm and, thus, avoids such metaphors as "midstream." He builds an involved and aggressive concept of social responsibility on this assumption and on certain perceptions of the characteristics of pluralistic and capitalistic societies.

These examples could be multiplied endlessly, but multiplication and repetition would add little to the conclusion that how one perceives social responsibility is dictated largely both by ways in which our society as a whole and some of its more important parts are perceived and by the basic assumptions that are made regarding them.[3]

Some authorities have attempted to bridge the gap between the extreme points of view which exist on corporations assuming a broad social conscience. Not surprisingly, however, their efforts have met with a mixed reception:

There are two theories about the social responsibility of business. First is the durable thesis of the 18th Century libertarians — largely associated today with Professor Milton Friedman and the Chicago School of Economics. It holds that business will best serve the society when it concentrates exclusively on maximizing profits.

But these days it is bad form to make public statements against spending money for corporate good works. So most of the hard-line free traders are still in the closet. Whenever they emerge, however, they hold fast to the philosophical underpinnings of enterprise capitalism. Of course, under their libertarian view, buying government contracts from officials with flexible ethics and paying cash for favorable antitrust settlements is definitely out. The free enterprisers insist that the businessman owes absolute obedience to public laws against larceny, fraud, burglaries from the offices of competitors, and any other pernicious activities that the government forbids. But free enterprise economics does not rely solely on a concerned and militant legislature to protect the society. For undeniably there is lawmaking power in the marketplace itself.

The second school of thinking about corporate responsibility is made up of all those mushy-headed social tinkerers who, like myself, are making most of the noise these days. We concede that the idea of a democratic marketplace, so painstakingly constructed by Adam Smith, was splendid for a nation of small English merchants competing with each other in 18th Century Berwick-upon-Tweed. Today, we argue, the free pursuit of indi-

[3] Dow Votaw, "The Nature of Social Responsibility: 'You Can't Get There from Here' ", *Journal of Contemporary Business*, Vol. 2, No. 1, Winter, 1973, pp. 1-3. Reprinted with permission of the *Journal of Contemporary Business* © 1973.

vidual cupidity simply does not work out for the society at large. Concentrations of economic power in combination with collective economic and social injustices of the past have put whole groups in the society — as well as the society as a whole — in a permanently weakened and powerless position.

In the view of the liberals, the idea of corrective backlash in the marketplace becomes nonsense if all the school buses are made by one manufacturer, or even by a handful of manufacturers who make decisions in unison. What's more, the ethical corporation is undercut because, if it slows down on its profit, somebody else will be dumping garbage into streams, stinking up the air, or otherwise using — without personal cost — a priceless natural resource.

Neil W. Chamberlain (who is Armand G. Erpf Professor of the Modern Corporation at the Graduate School of Business, Columbia University) takes a stand that is certain to draw fire from both sides. In *The Limits of Corporate Responsibility*, he dismisses the idea that the public will can bend corporations to its purpose, but he does not agree with Professor Friedman that socially responsible activity is a seditious act of giving away the stockholders' money. Nor does he agree with the most intelligent thought ever expressed by the departed Spiro Agnew that corporate good works are a private usurpation of the legislature's job of setting public policy. Rather, the author's theme, which he documents skillfully and pragmatically, is that in any large industrial economy, the maximization of profit or the search for growth is inevitable, even though they will most certainly produce side effects that most of society will regard as harmful to the public interest.

The author proves his doleful theme. Much of his book is devoted to showing the hopelessness of expecting Gulf Oil and General Motors to deal with racial discrimination, product safety, environmental and consumer exploitation, and just plain boring work. Sure, there is room in the system for funding of mini-capitalism in urban ghettos and *mea culpa* ecology advertisements being run by many corporations. But this is propaganda, cosmetic change at best. So long as the system relies on competition for gain, says Chamberlain, structural change is well nigh impossible. And don't look to Washington for help. The author cites case after case where government regulation has failed.

Perhaps the most important contribution of Professor Chamberlain's book is to set out a contemporary, carefully reasoned and documented exposé of the myth of corporate responsibility. The argument he develops is the best that has appeared in print so far: that under present conditions we can expect very little from an uninformed marketplace, an insouciant federal government, and large economic institutions that stand to lose — in the short run or in the long run — by being good guys.

But the gap in the author's clear and sometimes brilliant work is his failure to examine adequately the potential of those still tentative efforts to restore countervailing power to the marketplace.

What potential, for example, is there in the idea of public directorships — people who are funded and staffed within large business institutions to raise new questions, look for defects in old arrangements, and reach new conclusions? Through Watergate we have discovered the enormous clout of public opinion.

But we still don't know what GM would in fact do if its black public director, Reverend Leon H. Sullivan — who is nationally honored among both whites and blacks — were to call a press conference and suggest that in all good conscience GM should stop buying 50-million new tires a year from corporations that pollute the city of Akron and treat its black population as economic expendables.

And what of the hoary old ideas of self-regulation? Suppose, for example, (as that financial giant William McChesney Martin has urged) 50% of the directors of the New York Stock Exchange had been chosen from the public instead of from industry? Suppose those public directors had insisted that the exchange make serious public noises about suspending the stock listing of Detroit Edison Co. when a federal judge in Detroit recently fined the company $4-million for "deliberate and invidious racial" discrimination (the largest award of punitive damages in the history of the Civil Rights Act of 1964)? And suppose the stock-listing department of the exchange issued some serious warnings of potential delisting to Abbott Laboratories, whose record of drug recalls for adulteration and mislabeling, according to a careful study of government statistics, is 19 times as bad as Smith Kline & French, and almost twice as bad as any other drug company in America?

Finally, Professor Chamberlain doesn't really touch on the potential of restoring power to the consumer. How did it come about that Ralph Nader, and a few other little public interest groups, with nothing going for them but the forces of the press, put an end to Corvair cars and dozens of other acts of corporate malfeasance endangering the public? The doomsayers, who are wailing with Professor Chamberlain, have also overlooked the remarkable achievement of the underfunded Reverend Jesse Jackson, head of Operation PUSH. Using time-honored capitalistic practices of selective buying and lawful pickets, he has put more black people into construction jobs in Chicago than the combined efforts of the government-sponsored Chicago Plan, Philadelphia Plan, and the federal Equal Employment Opportunity Commission.

So perhaps Adam Smith was right. Real controls do lie in restoring the sovereignty of the consumer. Maybe we simply have been unfaithful to his scheme. Certainly nothing that is happening so far in the USSR or in East Germany has challenged his thesis.

Dozens of academics are getting their thoughts together on corporate responsibility. Those like Neil Chamberlain who are depressed, should learn more about the toilers in the vineyards who are seeking to repair the confidence of a submissive and neurotic marketplace. They are the people who are really dedicated to capitalism![4]

A SPECTRUM OF CORPORATE SOCIAL RESPONSIBILITY MODELS

Like any such spectrum, the following range of models involves considerable overlap and cannot be organized in a precisely sequential manner. Nonetheless, it does serve to bring out the distinguishing characteristics of the many variations which can be identified in this area.

[4] Theodore Cross, "The Corporation and Social Change". Reprinted from the January 19, 1974 issue of Business Week by special permission. Copyright 1974 by McGraw-Hill, Inc.

1) Business Is Business at Any Price

The mere mention of this category quickly brings to mind "the robber barons" of the last century, many of whom continued their nefarious, but highly profitable, activities well into the present century. Some of these wealthy characters were kind enough to express their thoughts in words which have not been lost to posterity. In 1882, for example, W.H. Vanderbilt offered this honest and revealing remark: "The public be damned. I'm working for the shareholder." Others claimed that the sanctity of God was behind their efforts. Perhaps the most famous of these utterances was that made in 1902 by a company president in the course of a serious strike. He claimed that men like him were:

Christian men to whom God in his infinite wisdom has given control of the property interests of the country.[5]

The basis of this approach is simply that anything goes. There are no ethics. There is no integrity. About all there is by way of restraint is some interfering law which the successful executive is expected to circumvent. The name of the game is profit maximization, and it doesn't matter how one attains that exalted goal. That this philosophy is not yet dead can be inferred from much of the material presented in this volume. It is instructive, however, to look at this cavalier attitude at two levels. It is one thing to find a lack of ethics and integrity and even blatant fraud and dishonesty at the alley or bucket-shop level where survival is the order of the day. Among marginal contractors in the construction industry and in all sorts of enterprises in the service sector of the economy, those involved are operating with a short line of credit and virtually on a hand-to-mouth basis. In such frequently desperate circumstances, who is to say whether it is possible to resist the temptation to manage at a gutter level in order to get by, let alone begin to prosper?

It is quite another matter, however, when some of North America's leading corporations are found to be engaged in the kinds of practices documented in this work and so many others like it. Nonetheless, they have their apologists and defenders, some of whom can find it possible to rationalize just about anything. A critical reviewer for *Business Week* discussing one recent book dedicated to upholding the current business establishment had this to say about the kind of thinking that supports the "anything goes" attitude:

■ No one acquainted with current economic analysis of pollution problems, for instance, can agree with Jacoby's shallow conclusion that "because the poor stand to gain most from environmental enhancement, an attack on pollution is one battle in the war on poverty." If local property taxes are increased to finance sewage treatment for central cities and electric rates are raised to pay for lower-sulfur fuels, these regressive levies will mean that only those of the poor who water-ski and prefer less sulfur in the air to fewer rats in the ghettos will be given for their money what they really prefer. Some war on poverty![6]

2) Business Is Business but It Should Do a Better Job

According to this view of business, its biggest failing is not to have done a better job of business. The task of the corporation is to be creative, innovative,

[5] Cited in L.H. Canfield et al, *The United States in the Making* (Boston: Houghton Mifflin, 1940), p. 552.
[6] Review by Eli Goldston reprinted from the July 21, 1973 issue of *Business Week* by special permission. Copyright 1973 by McGraw-Hill, Inc.

productive and ultimately profitable. Instead of concerning itself with wider social concerns, business should concentrate on this primary responsibility. Such a point of view was well expressed in a dissent from the report of the Committee for Economic Development on "Social Responsibilities of Business Corporations," a report which put a lot of emphasis on business meeting wider public obligations.

What society wants from business is clearly indicated by examining a few typical cases. In the case of the railroad industry, for example, which is in deep trouble, what society wants and has not received is an imaginative modern system of transportation supplying both passenger and freight service. For many years what the railroad industry has been furnishing has not even approached that standard.

If the New York telephone communication system is in trouble today, it is not due to changing conditions or requirements, but primarily because what had been for decades the best telephone service in the world haś over a period of recent years deteriorated so badly to where it is perhaps no better than third rate.

Once more, if many of the elective utilities of the country are in trouble, it is not because of new requirements but because they have not taken care of their basic responsibility to give an adequate power supply, always reliable and not subject to sudden cataclysmic failures. That they have also been careless of their obligations to do so with minimal adverse effect on the environment has not helped them to get public absolution of their failure to discharge their primary responsibility.

And if our automobile manufacturing industry is in difficulty, it is due to the fact that for too many years the manufacturers and purveyors of automobiles have, *for competitive reasons* (my underlining) failed to realize that they could not continue to build the same automobiles, making them larger and more expensive, with more chrome plate and more horsepower under the hood, while at the same time neglecting safety and the Frankenstein of environmental pollution they were raising.[7]

Put another way, one can still make a strong case for the profit motive as a major stimulant to society's economic advance and welfare, as opposed to the notion of profit as a crass form of exploitation.

Broadly stated, the role of business is to help achieve an optimal allocation of society's resources. This entails an *obligation* to maximize the profits of the enterprise. While profit is often sheathed with an unfavorable connotation which suggests that profit maximizers are squalid individuals who rob widows and beat small children, a more realistic view of profit would be to view its role in the general decision-making system.

Economically, profit is the quantity of resources remaining when all factors of production have been paid a fair share of the proceeds from operations. To some economists, this implies that profits can be generated only by underpaying the factors of production, or by overcharging the consumer. However, if profit is viewed as a means of providing for future

[7] Phillip Sporn, "Memoranda of Comment Reservation or Dissent", in *Social Responsibilities of Business Corporations* (New York: Committee for Economic Development, June, 1971) p. 63.

productive capacity, through investment in plant, equipment, research and development, it becomes far more realistic as an evaluative concept. If profit can be defined as essentially an accounting concept, it can perhaps be replaced for evaluative purposes by the concept of economic efficiency, or seen simply as the degree of apparent confidence society places in the actions of various organizations and segments of the decision-making system. What remains is a measure that can be applied to any institution considered appropriate for making societal decisions. If economic efficiency provides a means for evaluating actions, the most appropriate system for future decision-making is the one that can provide the best return by this standard.[8]

3) Business Is Business but There Are Some Priorities

Consistent with the previous model, and overlapping with some of the later corporate responsibility models outlined in this spectrum, is the view which holds that while the prime role of business is as stated above, it has no right to earn a profit until it has done fairly well by the other major segments of society affected by it. Thus, to put this view in its simplest form: the corporation should be a fair employer, deal with its suppliers on a reasonable basis, provide its customers with reliable products or services at competitive prices, pay its share of taxes and be considerate of the community within which it operates. Only after meeting all these obligations can the corporation justify a decent return for its shareholders.

One corporation in Canada which at one time proclaimed a variation of such an order of priorities is Dominion Tar and Chemical Company. Several years ago it agreed to the following statement in concert with the many unions representing its employees:

A) To attain an economically sound, competitive and profitable operation which will make possible:
   1. The satisfaction of consumer needs with quality products and services;
   2. Improved wages and salaries and other conditions of employment; and
   3. Improved returns to shareholders.
B) To increase job satisfaction through measures such as:
   1. Full recognition by all concerned of the rights and dignity of employees;
   2. Opportunities for employees to confer with Management through their representatives on matters of policy and proposed policy changes which affect employees, including matters beyond those covered in the applicable collective agreement; and
   3. The development of informed interest and meaningful participation by employees in the success of the enterprise.
C) Over and above the foregoing objectives, to recognize the promotion of the national interest and the growth of the Canadian economy as an overriding obligation.[9]

[8] Paul Preston, "The Future: Prospects and Alternatives for a Business Role", Business & Society, Vol. 13, No. 2, Spring, 1973, pp. 8-9.
[9] Annual Report, DOMTAR, January 26, 1965, p. 1.

4) Business Is Business but It Should Police Itself

This model argues that the legitimate position of business in North America would be much enhanced if it were to clean up more of its undesirable practices on its own. The idea is that there should be better codes of ethics and more guidelines governing standards of individual and institutional conduct. At the individual firm level, such standards can be used in an effort to discourage acceptance of gifts from interested groups, gifts which really amount to bribery. At the industry level, they can be implemented to dissuade all manner of undesirable competitive practices. Such approaches may even be tried on an international basis to regulate the behaviour of multinational corporations or to preserve the balance of nature and resources.

As appealing as it sounds, business self-regulation often leaves much to be desired; as this article from *Business and Society Review/Innovation* points out:

The concept of self-regulation is usually influenced by the models offered by the legal and medical professions, in which admission to the profession is controlled by the profession itself and in which practitioners can be expelled by the professional organization with no recourse to the courts or other outside authority.

Both medicine and law are practiced on a small scale, by the individual or a small group. Attorneys and physicians can be controlled by their professional association, which not only can introduce economic sanctions (appointments to hospitals, referrals, etc.), but also can withdraw accreditation, eliminating a member from the profession entirely. Given these powers, an attorney or physician can afford to alienate his professional group even less than he can his law firm or clinic.

Can an association of *corporations*, be they in the broadcasting, electronics, or construction industry, be comparably "self-regulating"? The film industry's attempt is worth consideration. The motion picture rating system, often considered a model of industry self-regulation, is notable for two reasons: first, it was adopted due to outside pressures, and second, it has been made more ambiguous under the economic pressure of foreign film competition.

In 1923, the American Society of Newspaper Editors adopted the canons of journalism, statements concerned with the public's right to know; this code has had a relatively conflict-free existence. Broadcasting has a somewhat similar self-regulatory history. The National Association of Broadcasters created a code of ethics in 1929 in response to the interest in programming shown by the Federal Radio Commission. Revised periodically, the code for television is enforced by a five-member board whose sole authority is to remove the code seal from a station's advertising. The radio code has no enforcement provisions.

Numerous other groups have similar codes, notable for the ambiguity of their standards. For instance, the Public Relations Society of America Code says, "A member shall conduct his professional life in accord with the public welfare," and "A member shall not engage in any practice which tends to corrupt the integrity of channels of public communication." Of those mentioned only the motion picture group has considerable economic power, since the failure to get an appropriate rating may exclude certain audiences.

In sum, self-regulation usually is the consequence of external pressure, typically has limited enforcement provisions, complies with economic necessities and may really serve as a status symbol for the industry concerned. Clearly, such corporate self-regulation is different from and less effective than that exercised by the law and medical associations whose codes served as models.[10]

The challenge inherent in corporate self-policing codes and guidelines obviously does not lie in their promulgation, but in their enforcement. This fact helps to explain the rationale behind the next alternative in this spectrum. It is obvious that real teeth are required of any self-regulatory mechanism unless it is to prove little more than a public relations sham.

5) Business Is Business but It Should Have Government Help to Police Itself

Some corporate leaders want to tidy up their back yards but feel unable to do so as long as major competitors do not follow suit because of the costs involved. This is particularly true in the environmental field where the cost of pollution abatement facilities may be prohibitive to the individual firm if its rivals fail to introduce the same equipment, and by that failure gain a market edge. It is in this context that many top business executives look upon a limited amount of government regulation with some favour.

The role of the state in fashioning business behaviour can of course be approached at several levels. On the general plane, the government's role can be quite pervasive. It can establish guidelines and rules inducing, and where necessary, compelling industry to employ its resources in a manner consistent with society's interests, while still making a profit. Through a series of incentives and disincentives, the profit motive can actually be tapped to use the corporation to solve social problems. A classic example of one such set of incentives and disincentives in Canada are the various inducements which have been put into effect to try to attract industry to depressed regions instead of only to prosperous ones. When wisely employed, government strategy in matters of industrial behaviour can be utilized to avoid some of the usual problems caused by industry, and to ameliorate and eliminate other social difficulties not necessarily caused by industry.

At the level of the firm or of a specific industry, there are all sorts of codes and guidelines for behaviour which government may be called upon to help implement at the request of those most affected by its intervention. Not atypical of this kind of request is the one which followed a recent case of food poisoning which showed negligence in the food-canning industry in the United States. So disturbed was the industry about possible adverse consumer reaction to this case that it publically proclaimed itself in favour of more stringent government regulations of its business.

Before leaving the question of the government's role in helping to put the corporate house in order, it is worth noting that there are major risks involved in some forms of government do-gooding in this area, as a *Michigan Business Review* article states:

The benefits of using government contracts to promote basic social policies are quite clear. Important national objectives may be fostered without the need for additional, direct appropriations from the Treasury.

[10] Robert Rutherford Smith, " 'Social Responsibility': A Term We Can Do Without", *Business & Society Review Innovation*, Spring 1974, No. 9, p. 54.

To a congressman, this may seem a painless and simple approach. Because restrictive procurement provisions seem to be costless, the government has been making increasing use of them. Any disadvantages, being more indirect, receive less attention.

Yet, upon reflection, these special provisions are all burdens on the governmental procurement process. They cannot help but increase overhead expenses of private contractors and federal procurement offices alike. Many of the provisions also exert an upward pressure on the direct costs incurred by the government. Supposedly, the basic concern of governmental buyers is to meet public needs at lowest cost. Yet, special provisions such as the Davis-Bacon Act have tended to increase the cost of public construction projects through government promulgation of wage rates higher than would have resulted if the market were allowed to operate without impediment.

The greatest shortcoming of the use of government contract to foster unrelated economic and social aims is the cumulative impact that they have on the companies themselves. Forced to take on so many of the concerns and attitudes of government agencies, it should not be too surprising that the more government-oriented corporations have come to show many of the negative characteristics of government bureaus and arsenals. The advantages of innovation, risk-bearing, and efficiency may be lost to the public and private sectors alike. That is a high price to pay for legislating social responsibility.[11]

6) Business Is Business but It Should Support Worthy Causes

Probably the oldest, and still most prevalent, form of so-called corporate social responsibility is the support of worthy causes of one kind or another. Traditionally, such support has taken the form of donations to the arts and to cultural, educational and sports activities of a wide variety. More recently, one might include in this category funds for assistance to the disadvantaged and the ghettos. There are few aspects of the public accountability of business that have raised more heated debate than the use of corporate funds for non-business causes deemed worthy by executives.

To begin on a rather cynical note, there is the view that corporate philanthropy reflects anything but altruistic ends. As one knowledgeable executive writing in *Harvard Business Review* has put it:

American corporations give away a lot of money — almost $1 billion a year. Most of it goes in traditional channels — United Funds, hospital drives, and so forth.

A very small amount goes to urban affairs. Of that amount, all too little is accompanied by an equal donation of time and thought to make sure the money is given to a useful program that actually touches human beings' lives. As once concerned corporation president said to me, "The question to me is how long the blacks will be willing to accept payoffs instead of programs."

I served as president of a fairly well-known urban charity for a while, and it was easy to raise money for it. And then I found that virtually all the money was used to maintain the staff of the charity and almost none of it for what was contemptuously referred to as program.

[11] Murray L. Weidenbaum, "Social Responsibility is Closer Than You Think", *Michigan Business Review*, Vol. 25, No. 4, July, 1973, p. 35.

We almost lost the assistant director of the project one day because he was told he couldn't have two secretaries. I told him I didn't know anyone among the many large corporations we served who had two secretaries. He replied that he, on the other hand, didn't know anyone in the charity world who didn't have two secretaries.

But the evidence seems to be pretty conclusive that most companies give in accordance with what is good for the company. An Eastman Kodak executive said, "The company's expression of its good corporate citizenship should not be explained in terms of blind altruism." And a Bethlehem Steel spokesman said, "Our giving is always in response to a need that exists and is somehow related to our business interest."[12]

To put it even more boldly:

Much of this behaviour is simply public relations . . . contributions by corporations to local community chests, churches, Boy Scouts, hospitals, and similar enterprises bear as much resemblance to true charity as does my income tax. No businessman in his right mind would blatantly refuse the importuning of these charities. He would surely incur the enmity of powerful citizens.[13]

Speaking less cynically, it is not easy to find a logical rationale for corporate philanthropy, except that it serves as a form of insurance against further government intervention in society and against the development of social ills so deep as to invite such intervention — if not topple the entire system. But, with the possible exception of the United Appeal and the United Way, these rationales hardly apply to the most conventional forms of business aid to so-called worthy causes. Such donations may reflect little more than the latest whim of the top executives or their spouses. Worse still, a coterie of these executives from different firms may simply end up having their respective corporations support each other's favourite causes. In the absence of suitable explanations, one keeps being driven back to the advertising or public relations motive — a factor which has to be uppermost in some areas of sports promotion and the like.

It is difficult to explain the rationale behind corporate giving to worthy causes, but there is a strong case to be made against it. In effect, the practice of business philanthropy allows a select few executives to use other people's money to support their own or their spouses' favoured social priorities. The funds they use may derive from a variety of groups. Most directly hit are the shareholders and other taxpayers, both of which groups lose out, at least financially, in the process — shareholders because the money comes out of the company coffers, and other taxpayers because the company's taxable income and taxes are reduced by such donations. Indirectly, any number of other groups may help to bear the burden of executive do-gooding, from suppliers and workers who may receive less, to customers who may pay more. And all this perhaps only so that top corporate executives can assuage their own consciences as well as that of their firm, if institutions can be said to have such things.

Milton Friedman has been the most effective critic of corporate philanthropy, and it is appropriate to end this section by quoting him:

[12] David B. McCall, "Profit: Spur for Solving Social Ills", *Harvard Business Review*, May-June 1973, p. 52. © 1973 by the President and Fellows of Harvard College; all rights reserved.
[13] H. Manne, "The Myth of Corporate Responsibility", *Business Lawyer*, November, 1970.

Take the corporate executive who says "I have responsibilities over and above that of making profit." If he feels that he has such responsibilities, he is going to spend money in a way that is not in the interest of the shareholders. Where does he get that money? Perhaps from the company's employees. If he can pay his employees lower wages than otherwise, he'll have some extra money to spend. It may come from the company's customers, if he can charge them more than they would otherwise pay. Or it may come from the company's stockholders. The crucial question is: What right does the executive have to spend his stockholders' money? To spend his employees' money? Or his customers' money? Who gave him the right to decide how their money should be spent? If "socially responsive" business executives would stop and think, they would recognize that in effect they are acting irresponsibly. [14]

7) Business Is Business but It Should Have a Broad Social Conscience

Because of, or perhaps despite, the valid criticisms which can be levelled at corporate philanthropy, many would urge much more upon industry, but in the form of a broader and more meaningful concept of corporate responsibility. The following is one such appeal from an article in the *California Management Review*.

If the leaders of business continue to conceive of social responsibility as a mere euphemism for charity, a surrogate for the corporate image, a concern only for the public relations department, or simply a passing fad, they will fail to meet what may be one of mankind's great challenges, and will, as a price for their failure, lose their own leadership roles in society and bring about the fall of the very organizations with which they are identified. They will make the wrong decisions, using irrelevant data, inappropriate criteria and anachronistic goals, and will find inadequate solutions to the wrong problems; they will take actions which can only aggravate the real problems while producing misleading feedback for their decision-making systems.

Growing both in size and persuasiveness is a body of evidence which compels the businessman seriously to consider the possibility that social responsibility is more than an expedient response to temporary conditions. If, as now seems very likely to be the case, social responsibility appears in the eyes of future historians to have been one of the important manifestations of profound social change, leaders of business must immediately begin to see it as such and to orient their words and actions around a better view of reality. As never before in our history, it has become necessary for the private economic sector to concern itself in a major way with its own view of its role in society. If it cannot adapt itself to its new, less central, but nonetheless important role in society, it will find itself replaced by other institutions and society may also be the loser. [15]

[14] Milton Friedman, "Milton Friedman Responds", *Business & Society Review*, Spring 1972, No. 1, p. 6.
[15] "Genius Becomes Rare: A Comment on the Doctrine of Social Responsibility, Pt. II". © 1973 by The Regents of the University of California. Reprinted from CALIFORNIA MANAGEMENT REVIEW, Vol. XV, No. 3, pp. 16-17, by permission of The Regents.

That some corporations have taken this broadest form of self-induced corporate social responsibility to heart is suggested by the attitude of major banks in the United States. The significance of a change in attitude taking place in those institutions is evident in this brief excerpt from *Business Week*:

Banks are highly visible symbols of the U.S. economic system — all the more so as they have grown huge, gone into more fields, and sought the business of consumers as well as giant corporations. So the protests against the system during a decade of social upheaval have increasingly come in the form of pressure on the banks: sometimes peaceful, sometimes violent, but invariably forceful enough so that bankers have had to listen. Men schooled to weigh each loan and investment for its soundness and return, and conditioned to measure subordinates by the color of their school ties, have had to learn some new rules. A critical facet of the new banking is the growing awareness of its obligation to society.[16]

8) *Business Is Business but Its Associations Should Assume a Broader Social Conscience*

The not undeserved public image of most business and trade associations is of a group of corporate executives conniving together to better enable them to take advantage of the consumer. That this image is not undeserved is borne out by the few studies which have been made of these associations. One such study concluded that the following episode was not atypical of their activities:

The Association of National Advertisers, Inc. recently considered a campaign to approach its membership to increase financial contributions so that the Association's Washington operations could be expanded. The excerpt in the draft memorandum provides an excellent example of the trade association mentality:
"During the past year, the A.N.A. Government Relations Committee, along with the full Board of Directors, has given intensive consideration to the resources we as advertisers have to represent us in Washington. Our conclusions and recommendations are spelled out in this memorandum.
"In essence, we fear that we are already late. In our judgment, if we do not act now, every advertiser's ability to communicate:
What he wants and as he wishes . . .
Through the media of his choice . . .
In amounts he determines . . .
Will be seriously eroded . . .
"Our proposal is confined to Washington because to our opponents—
"*Government is Seen as the Solution*
"The active critics of advertising, with *good will or bad* (italics added) and whether they be the Consumer Federation, the burgeoning 'public interest law firms' or politicians riding a bandwagon, see regulatory and legislative action as their means and lever for change. To them it is axiomatic to:
"Use the F.C.C. as their instrument to bring about change in television, rather than tuning out their sets;

---

[16] "How a Social Conscience Shapes Banking". Reprinted from the September 15, 1973 issue of *Business Week* by special permission. Copyright 1973 by McGraw-Hill, Inc.

"Call on Mrs. Knauer, rather than charging a foolish purchase to experience;

"Suggest legislation banning all hazards, rather than individually playing it safe.

"We, in contrast, and at the risk of over-simplifying, have looked to the traditional marketplace for products and ideas as the arena for discussion and decision."

Caveat emptor rides again! To this association, consumerism is a conspiracy to deprive industry of its rightful profit. Yet, industry continues to support A.N.A. — and other trade associations with a similar philosophy — at the same time that its leaders swear allegiance to good consumer practices.[17]

Fortunately the same article does reveal considerable disenchantment within important business circles about what is going on in many trade associations. As a result a partial backlash has set in, although not without potential problems of its own:

Many trade associations are faced with the lowest common denominator problem. The broader the constituency of the trade association, the more difficult it is to develop an industry consensus. The lowest common denominator factor also opens the way to two forms of tyranny: tyranny by a small number of neanderthal companies which threaten to withdraw unless their voices are heeded, and tyranny by small companies which dominate the association with their numbers while large companies pay the bulk of the association's dues. Inability of trade associations to overcome these barriers is partly responsible for the large increase in corporate Washington offices in the past five years.

Another indication of industry's impatience with trade associations is the greater use of ad hoc informal groups to accomplish legislative objectives. One of the more important of these groups is the "March Group."

Triggered by a speech by Dr. Arthur Burns to the Business Council, twelve corporations (since expanded to about fifty corporations) organized in March of 1972 to evaluate corporate presence and potency in Washington. Some of the original companies which participated in the March Group were General Electric, United States Steel, Reynolds Metals, Procter & Gamble, and TRW. Other companies which have since joined include J.C. Penny Co., Southern Pacific, Westinghouse, AT&T, Goodyear, Gulf, Ford, Alcoa, Carolina Power & Light, Standard Oil (N.J.), American Cyanamid, TWA, Armstrong Cork, Libby Owens Ford, and Eli Lilly.

Four areas were designated as initial points of focus: tax reform, international investment, labor law reform, and pension reform. These areas have since changed to environment, tax reform, international trade and consumerism. Each committee is chaired by a chief executive officer, with Washington corporate representatives providing legislative input. One of the first projects of the group was to make a preliminary evaluation of the effectiveness and utility of major Washington-based organizations.

Eleven of the twelve original members of the March Group were jointly supporting some 319 Washington-based organizations. For their preliminary review, twenty-two organizations were examined for their

[17] Larry Finkelstein, "The 'Consumerist Conspiracy'", *Business & Society Review/Innovation*, Summer 1973, No. 6, p. 22.

effectiveness, as perceived by the Washington representatives of the participating companies. Not surprisingly, organizations such as the Brookings Institution and the Committee on Economic Development received strong criticism, while trade associations such as the American Petroleum Institute and the American Mining Congress received such praise as "enjoys fine reputation in Washington".

The "fine reputation in Washington" that the trade associations enjoy is true only in the conservative business constituency. By what standards does business determine that trade associations such as API are in its self-interest, while "liberal" organizations such as Brookings and CED are "deserving of serious scrutiny"?

The March Group has recently merged with another little-known organization, the Business Roundtable. Member companies, largely those which comprised the March Group, will support this joint effort to the tune of $3 million per year for an initial three-year period.

Another important aspect of the March Group is its lack of public visibility. I have mentioned the difficulty of obtaining information from the formally constituted trade associations which receive tax-deductible funding. Information about ad hoc groups such as the March Group will be even more difficult to acquire. Should the business community choose to become more secretive about its involvement in the legislative process at a time when institutional credibility is at a low point, then it must be prepared for the public reaction when its involvement becomes known.[18]

What perhaps is needed most is a fundamental change in the attitudes and approaches of business associations, especially in those at the aggregate levels such as the Canadian Manufacturers Association and the National Association of Manufacturers in the United States, as well as the Chamber of Commerce in both countries. Instead of almost always representing the conservative and entrenched vested interests to which their members naturally incline them, these bodies might better consider the broader welfare of society — which is not always to be equated with what is good for business, despite what Charlie Wilson said some years ago about what is good for General Motors being good for the country. If business is to concern itself with social problems, it would probably be well advised to concentrate its efforts at the association level. This would have several advantages. In the first place, more resources might be mustered to assess the situation. It would also tend to get business thinking away from the narrower inclinations which usually pervade the individual firm or industry. Finally, if the problem of social welfare were responsibly and sensibly handled, the credibility of these associations might be improved in other areas where they must by their very nature take more selfish positions.

The need for an effective champion of the business cause is strong in the United States and Canada and, if anything, is likely to become stronger. To meet this compelling requirement, corporations must not only reform and update their existing associations but also think in terms of more all-embracing aggregations of business interests:

For some time now the political face of American business has been caught and held in a spotlight, revealing in particular the corporate contributions to electoral campaigns.

[18] Larry Finkelstein, "Some Tough Questions About Trade Associations," *Business & Society Review/Innovation*, Summer 1973, No. 6, p. 25-26.

Virtually everyone agrees that a stringent reform of campaign financing must be secured. This would tend to obstruct direct access to administration decision centers on the basis of past favors and so circumscribe special treatment and influence on terms inimical to or careless of the public interest.

But it is not generally realized that such a reform would need to be buttressed by a marked improvement in American business's own representative institutions. If one asks leading British industrialists how often they visit Victoria Street (home of that new giant, the Department of Trade and Industry) or Whitehall, one is told: "seldom." And their recollection, although it might be imperfect, generally is borne out in interviews with ministers and senior civil servants.

In Britain even the large industrial company is likely to reach out to government through its representative body, the Confederation of British Industry (CBI). In the United States such a company would be less likely to make use of the National Association of Manufacturers (NAM), the nearest analog of the CBI, generally preferring to go it alone.

But if this individualistic path to government is to be even partly closed off, the more roundabout but also in principle more legitimate path ought to be improved. "More legitimate" because more conducive to just and effective government, which depends in part on the conversion (in all sectors) of multitudinous demand into a relatively small and so more manageable set of arguable policy alternatives.

This is the process technically known — after Prof. Gabriel Almond, of Stanford — as "the aggregation of interests." As applied to business at least, it is much less effective in the United States than in Britain, West Germany, and a number of other Common Market countries.

The reasons are complex, but the immediate explanation begins to emerge from a brief cross-national comparison. For aggregative purposes the NAM is hampered by its low density (that is the ratio of actual to potential membership). The CBI and the Federation of German Industry have densities at least two or three times as high.

Even now that the NAM has spread itself beyond manufacturing, the CBI's coverage is wider. It brings in, as its predecessor, the Federation of British Industries, did not, 19 publicly owned corporations (utilities, transport, coal, steel, etc.), and even extends into that arcane realm, the City of London.

The CBI also has an intermediate level made up of nearly 200 trade associations and employers' organizations. It is by no means as effective as many close observers, even in government, would wish, but it does assist aggregation. The NAM has only the bottom level (the companies) and the top.

If the NAM's structural deficiencies inhibit the effective aggregation of business interests, do other structures take up the slack? The services rendered by the Business Council are confidential but can hardly be of the aggregating kind.

The Chamber of Commerce of the U.S. is a far more powerful body than the Association of British Chambers of Commerce, which up to now has played impoverished king to some rich and independent-minded (not to say imperious) barons, such as the Birmingham Chamber and London's. But although it supplements the NAM, it cannot make good the general deficiency.

Since that requirement is also ill served by American political parties, one concludes that a new structure is needed, a "Federation of American Business (FAB)." Like the CBI (1965), it would have to come from a merger of the existing peaks. This would be the more acceptable if the legitimate career expectations of their staffs were to be at least substantially met in the new body.

It is all very well for outsiders (like me) to see the FAB rising like a Phoenix from the ashes: the professionals would want to be reasonably sure of following the bird as it soars, not left behind with, or, worse in, the ashes.

An FAB would be more acceptable to the big corporations if it provided for direct company membership as well as that of trade associations, as the national chamber and the CBI now do but the Federation of German Industry and the Federation of Belgian Industries do not. It would be more acceptable to smaller companies if their place in the new order of things were assured.

Beyond that, much truly educational work would have to be done, of businessmen by businessmen, raising eyes to new horizons. But the administration and Congress could help. A real reform of campaign financing would provide incentives for building other roads to Rome.

That tendency would be reinforced if other departments extended what justice has initiated — keeping a close record of comings and goings — into active discouragement of individual company "inputs" where the public interest requires a broader, more aggregated contribution.

But that presupposes a new, more aggregating structure to which public officials can point and businessmen usefully turn. If the NAM and national chamber of commerce are not yet ready to innovate, they might at least emulate their British counterparts in 1971 by initiating an independent commission of inquiry into the overall system of industrial and commercial representation in the United States. Failing that, a foundation or research institute should take on the work.

It is worth making a great effort to improve the aggregation of business interests in the U.S., and the time to make a start is now when other, congruent reforms are on the agenda.[19]

Assuming industry does reorganize itself more effectively along association lines, the question will remain, of course, as to what purposes it will pursue. Although business' own selfish interests and objectives cannot be expected to disappear from the scene, they may be sublimated by sounder considerations. Furthermore, the broader the corporate aggregations involved, the more ideal they may be to take more reasonable positions on the whole corporate responsibility issue.

9) Business Is Business but Its Employees Should Have a Voice in Its Affairs

This model for the conduct of business affairs really has very little to do with corporate social responsibility, but does involve workers in the corporate decision-making process. The extent to which this would increase business accountability to the public is debatable, although the concept is now gradually spreading by law to a number of developing countries, with Western

[19] "Professor Says Public Interest Needs Business Spokesman", The Christian Science Monitor, October 31, 1973.

Europe leading the way with many experiments in the area of worker representation on corporate boards. A review of Western Europe's experience is instructive, especially in view of the fact that in one form or another it is likely to become a hallmark of corporate practice within the European Economic Community. *Business Week* investigated this new approach in Sweden which has only recently adopted it:

A carefully chosen group of carpenters and cabinet-makers returned to school in Sweden this week to learn all they could in a hurry about business organization, market research, and production planning — not to mention the theory of corporate decision-making. The woodworkers will need all the instruction they can get. Along with 2,000 other workers, most of whom have been enrolled in the same cram course, they will assume the unfamiliar role of directors this fall in some of the largest companies in Sweden.

Workers representation on boards is now a matter of law in Sweden for companies with at least 100 employees. The statute became effective last April, but most of the worker-directors are only now beginning to claim their places in the board room. Businessmen, workers, and politicians all over Europe will be watching closely, because as often happens with Swedish social experiments, this one may soon be sweeping the Continent. Norway, Britain, and Denmark already are considering similar legislation, and workers in other countries are starting to take notice as well.

Germany, of course, has had worker-directors for 20 years. But Germany's two-tier board system sometimes seems to have prevented the unionists from effectively participating in making the decisions that affect them most. The Swedish experiment, some observers say, will be a far better test of how the idea really works.

The classroom. The first hurdle to overcome has been preparing the workers for what they will face in the board room. That is why the giant Swedish Trade Union Confederation is sponsoring its crash course for blue-collar worker-directors at its training school outside of Stockholm. Some white-collar unions are offering individual courses of their own. And classes provided by the Swedish Management Institute are briefing other workers for their duties on the board.

"Students who come from large companies, who are accustomed to union contract negotiations, have no worries about taking their place alongside other board members," says Britt Sweno, who heads the blue-collar union's training program. "But those who come from small companies and who are not full-time union officials worry that they might not be able to fully participate."

To help conquer such fears, one course demands the worker's participation. Using a fictional electronic company as a model, the "board gaming" class requires students to solve serious problems in an important department of the company. The solutions lie in information the students have gleaned from other courses that range from export trade to research and development. The $2.5-million training program, financed by the union and the government, will be modified later when workers are polled about their actual experiences in the board room.

The worker-director law is technically a three-year trial, but no one doubts it will be extended and expanded. As part of a larger concept of "industrial democracy" espoused by the ruling Social Democratic Party, the worker-director law is also supported by opposition parties, except the Communists, who cast the only votes against it.

More influence. Not everyone is happy, though. Industry associations, while claiming to support the concept, fought hard to keep it voluntary. As Ingmar Eidem, chairman of Sweden's largest chemical company, Kema Nord, and former head of the Swedish Federation of Industry, put it: "This is starting at the wrong end. Workers certainly should be given greater responsibility, but in those areas where they are working. Industrial democracy should be built up starting at the shop floor."

To a degree, trade union leaders agree. "Board representation is not the royal highway to industrial democracy," the Trade Union Confederation admits in a recently published handbook on the new law. The main thrust of industrial democracy, the unionists argue, should be to gain workers' influence in matters that involve them daily.

Gert Gunnarsson, an employee representative at Volvo, Sweden's largest company and one of a handful of corporations that placed workers on its board before the law was passed, says: "Board representation is only a small step. The next one must bring consultations and employee influence down to lower levels."

Companies that have tried worker directors are mostly cautious in their appraisals. Volvo, for example, declines to call its experiment either a success or a failure. Gotaverken managing director Hans Laurin calls his shipyard's experience with worker board members "nothing very sensational."

Laurin, while generally positive about the worker-representative concept, predicts that results will vary widely from company to company. "There will be some clashes due to routine distrust and because of personalities," he says, "but I expect these will be in the minority."

Boosters. Some executives are more optimistic. Sven Widen, former head of the Liberal Party and board chairman of F.E. Lindstrom, a 115-year-old family-owned manufacturer of industrial pliers, was criticized by some of his fellow industrialists when he put two workers on his board. But Carl-Olof Lindquist, the company's managing director, says that "there have been no negative effects, only positive."

Another enthusiastic supporter is industrialist Tore Browaldh, chairman of Svenska Handelsbanken and several other corporations, including Sweden's largest forest products company. As a board member at Volvo, he was so impressed by the performance of the workers on its board he is now one of their biggest boosters.

"I personally regard them as a real asset," says Browaldh. "The employee representatives at Volvo know more about the actual problems on the shop floor than the rest of us. They are politically and economically awake. They are good intellectually and they have both wit and humor."

Browaldh sees no signs that the workers are intimidated by the other members, either. "As union leaders they have been accustomed to dealing with management. It's not an overwhelming step for them," he says.

For those less assured, Browaldh offers his own advice as a frequent lecturer at seminars for worker-directors. His tips could make Sweden's managers cringe. "Ask the managing director how much money is tied up in stocks," he advises, "and then order him to reduce it by 35%, which is almost always possible despite the protests that are made." Or: "Don't waste time on current problems. These are the result of decisions made long ago. Concentrate on the future."

Browaldh also warns worker-directors not to let the managing director drown them in statistics. "And remember," he adds, "the board's duty is not only to name a managing director, but also to fire a managing director if necessary."

Barriers. Not surprisingly, problems already have cropped up and not all of them have been solved. One involves payment of director fees. Board members, who may meet no more than once a month, often collect fees substantially higher than a skilled worker's total wage. Paying the same fees to the worker-directors could create jealousies among fellow employees that would wipe out the benefits of the program. Management and workers agreed that worker representatives would receive only their normal wages, plus payments for extra time devoted to board business based on their regular rate of pay.

Another problem was language. Many Swedish companies, operating multinationally or with some or all their shares foreign-owned, hold their board meetings in English to accommodate their non-Swedish members. Unfortunately, some of the workers are not sufficiently fluent to use English effectively in the complicated business that comes before a board, even though English is the "second language" in Swedish schools. One suggested solution is to hold meetings of such boards in both languages.

A more basic question to be resolved is how much of a worker-director's loyalty should be to his fellow unionists and how much to the company. Banker and industrialist Marcus Wallenberg, for one, says of the new worker-directors: "We understand they want to attract our interest. We say, 'You must remember you are sitting on the board and must take into consideration the total interests of the company, not just one side.' To make the company as successful as possible is the basis for their own security."

Britt Sweno, who conducts the blue-collar training school, disagrees. "If the worker representatives forget their fellow workers' interests, this reform will be a failure," she says. "After all, men sitting on boards always represent special interests — banks, finance groups, stockholders. Why should it be different with the workers?"[20]

Writing about the possibility of corporate board reform in general in the United States, one observer in Business and Society Review/Innovation, has drawn the following conclusions about the likelihood of American employees and their representatives serving on such bodies:

Until the proposal for employee representation is adopted and vigorously pursued by American trade unions, it is a purely academic idea. Nevertheless, there are three powerful forces at work which could, in time, make employee representation a reality.

The first factor is the changing attitudes of workers. The attitudes of both blue- and white-collar employees toward their work are a matter of growing concern. Job alienation, increased absenteeism, increased labor turnover, declining productivity, low morale, resistance to dull and repetitive work, and hostility to the production line — all are familiar fea-

[20] "When Workers Become Directors". Reprinted from the September 15, 1973 issue of Business Week by special permission. Copyright 1973 by McGraw-Hill, Inc.

tures of the current scene and have made business aware of the importance of increasing job satisfaction.

The second factor is the developing interest in federal incorporation of major corporations. The increasing abdication of control by various states over the internal conduct of corporate affairs, and growing concern with the role of the large corporation in society, makes enactment of a federal incorporation statute within the next 15 years quite possible.

The open question is the content of such a statute. We have little idea of what to expect. Clearly, however, consideration of so fundamental a departure as a federal incorporation statute would inevitably involve a serious inquiry into possible areas of corporate reform. Proposals for employee representation on the board, and for public or government directors, would be given high priority on such an agenda.

The third factor is the strength of the movement for employee directors outside the United States. The world grows smaller and smaller and the experience of other nations increasingly significant to us. The widespread acceptance in Europe of employee representation is bound to influence American business attitudes. In addition, the multinational experience of many large American corporations will make a great deal of difference. Firsthand experience with employee representation in practice can only increase understanding of the proposal.[21]

10) Business Is Business but All of Its "Stakeholders" Should Have a Voice in Its Affairs

This variation on the previous model calls for widening representation on corporate boards of directors to include other constituent interest groups besides employees and their representatives. Among those embraced by such an umbrella approach could be consumers, suppliers and dealers. Referring to these categories in an article in Business and Society Review/Innovation, it has been said:

There is little or no support for proposals to include these representatives; such proposals are purely theoretical or symbolic. Furthermore, there are serious practical problems in determining the constituency to select such directors: Who would be entitled to vote? How would votes be allocated between, say, major and incidental suppliers? What procedures would ensure the conduct of a contested campaign?

The case for adding consumer directors to the board receives little support from the history of consumer-owned enterprises in this country, such as the mutual insurance companies owned by policyholders, or the mutual savings banks owned by depositors. These companies invariably possess self-perpetuating boards, and have shown no greater concern for consumers than their stockholder-owned competitors. If possible, they have even less public accountability because of the absence of the stock market as a measure of performance — and there is no takeover bid as a possible discipline.[22]

Regardless of which interest groups are chosen to be represented on corporate boards, a number of problems are bound to arise:

[21] Phillip I. Blumberg, "Who Belongs on Corporate Boards?", Business & Society Review/Innovation, Spring 1973, No. 5, pp. 46-47.
[22] Ibid., p. 43.

The proposals for special interest representation on the board present serious problems. The first of these general problems is the lack of American experience with such solutions. While the European experience may give us some insight, European models cannot be expected to function in the same manner in the different political, economic, historical, and cultural setting of the United States.

Second, it is doubtful how effective special interest directors could be. The imposition of a minority of such directors upon the board may accomplish little in the face of the hostility of the majority of the board. If decisions are made in caucus prior to the board meeting, reducing it to an empty formality; if there is an inadequate flow of information; if there is limited cooperation from management — the special interest director will be unable to function effectively.

Third, to whom would the special interest director owe primary loyalty? Under traditional corporation law, the director owes undivided loyalty to the corporation and to the stockholders; further, such loyalty runs to all stockholders, not merely to those who elected him or her. The special interest director representing the interests of a particular group would face a fundamental conflict of interest.

[They] are bound to face a conflict of interest, unless their addition to the board is accompanied by far-reaching corporate changes. If the present purely economic objectives of the corporation were broadened so that the advancement of stockholder interests were no longer the primary goal, then of course the obligation of undivided loyalty to stockholders would disappear. New fiduciary standards for directors would have to be fashioned, which would reflect the changed composition of the board and the revised objectives of the corporation — and almost inevitably the new criteria would have to recognize the paramount loyalty of special interest directors to their constituencies.

However, this development would transform the board into a political institution, a microcosm of the community. *All* the directors would become, in effect, special interest representatives (whether for an outside group or simply for the shareholders), working to satisfy their particular constituency. The problem of conflict of interest for the individual board members would be replaced by the problem of *conflict among* all the directors. It is extremely doubtful that such a board could manage a corporation effectively. Board decisions would involve shifting alliances between the constituent groups, with log-rolling deals (for the exchange of support for respective proposals), all of which would lead to a condition aptly described by Beardsley Ruml decades ago as "gangsterism."

... The board, in short, could be reduced to a battleground of competing interests.

Last, special interest representation presents the fundamental problem of assuring adequate representation on the board for all the groups in society affected by the corporation. Even if so awesomely difficult an objective were somehow achieved, with appropriate degrees of recognition for all interests, the adverse consequences of transforming the board into an arena of conflicting forces would remain.[23]

[23] *Ibid.*, p. 45-46.

11) Business Is Business but It Should Be "Socialized"

Still another approach is the socialization of business as opposed to nationalization, which will be the last choice to be examined in this spectrum of possibilities. Socialization is to be distinguished from nationalization in the sense that the former involves making business more responsive to the public interest without actually taking it over. Socialization may be attempted through private or public channels. Privately, for example, General Motors has set up a five member subcommittee of its Board of Directors, called the Committee on Social Responsibility to monitor the corporation's policies and practices in terms of their social impact. Commendable as this initiative may be from the point of view of recognizing the need for this kind of monitoring, it is still an inside operation and vulnerable to the charge of tokenism and window-dressing. Even where those on the internal monitoring body are outside directors they are still executive, or at best, shareholder appointees which in no way necessarily qualifies them to represent the public interest.

Another alternative is to place truly public directors at least on leading corporate boards of directors. One of those who has advocated this approach on a fairly refined, sophisticated and well thought-out level, is Robert Townsend, former president of Avis, and as author of *Up the Organization*, one of the corporate world's most biting critics, although at times it would almost seem that he speaks tongue-in-cheek:

There's a lot of talk these days about protecting the public from corporate power and corporate abuse by putting guardians of the public interest on boards of directors, and I think the idea makes a lot of sense. Now, John Galbraith says that boards of directors don't really do anything — that all the real decisions are made further down the line. This is quite true. The average company director spends only forty hours or so a year in the boardroom. And the meetings sound like those at the Augusta National Golf Club: name-dropping, discussion of salmon fishing in Norway, some superficial talk about the state of the economy and the goddamned unproductivity of labor; and then they adjourn with two $100 bills or more in everyone's pocket! The directors don't really know what's going on, who the players are, what attitudes, relationships, and problems govern the company's actions. How can they, in forty hours a year? How could the prestigious outside directors of Penn Central, for example, possibly know what was going on when they spent only a few hours once a month in a room on the eighteenth floor of the Transportation Building in Philadelphia? They couldn't, and when it went bust, they were as surprised as everyone else.

So why bother to put a public director on a board like this? Because the proper person, making the directorship a full-time job and given adequate resources, could avoid this trap and be very effective in serving the public interest.

To begin, I feel that all manufacturing companies with over a billion dollars of assets should be required by federal law to seat full-time public directors on their corporate boards. Although only 110 industrial-sector companies currently fall into this category, these are the companies that have the power. It's very difficult to argue against public directors for these monsters.

Each public director should be given a yearly budget of a million dollars of the company's money. Peanuts — much less than one cent per share of stock. With it, he could pay himself a maximum of, say, $50,000 annually, and have enough to support a staff — scientists, accountants, lawyers, engineers — to develop answers to questions which he felt were important and which hadn't been answered to his satisfaction. Moreover, he should have an office in the company headquarters and receive notice of *all* meetings conducted throughout the company, automatically open to attendance by him or one of his staff members. This is an important point, because the first ploy the company might use to decoy him would be to hold four meetings simultaneously. In addition, he and his staff must have access to all files. No doors should be closed to them.

The public director, in turn, would be required to call at least two press conferences a year and report on the company's progress or lack of progress on issues of interest to the public. It will be argued that he will reveal company secrets. Let us pray he will. Secrecy is one of the most overrated and abused of corporate privileges.

Many companies, of course, will attempt to corrupt the idea of public directorships by choosing their own directors or by determining the kind of people chosen: the old routine — a blob in every job. So the question is: Who would select, approve, and assign public directors? One possibility is to form an ad hoc committee of senators and representatives who have occupied at least vice-presidential offices in nonfamily-owned businesses. Let them screen and approve candidates as Supreme Court nominees are approved by the Senate.

And they should choose people who meet, at a minimum, four criteria: They must be (1) knowledgeable about large-corporation behavior, with at least ten years' experience — some of it in line jobs as opposed to staff or expert jobs; (2) wealthy enough and/or disinterested enough in corporate power to be utterly uncorruptible; (3) energetic; and (4) reasonably intelligent. Within the space of a month, I think I could find 110 people who might well qualify, and I'm sure there are another thousand or so who would qualify and be available to the government.

Once a pool of eligible public directors is created, specific directors should be chosen by blind draw and assigned to corporations at random. They should also be rotated every four years to mitigate against corruption and co-option and reviewed prior to reassignment by the congressional committee to see whether they've taken the shilling or lost their energy.

Since I believe that all the top managements of this 110-company group are engaged, whether they know it or not, in short-changing their employees, customers, stockholders, and, if possible, the general public, while living off the fat of the land themselves, they will not greet this proposal with great cries of glee. Some might even find it so distasteful that they would choose to spin off enough subsidiaries to fall below the billion-dollar mark rather than permit a public director on the board. That's OK. A lot of people feel that this in itself would be healthy for the country.

The big companies would still try a variety of diversionary tactics. They would, for example, try to swamp the public directors — to tie them up with meaningless, dead-end assignments, task forces, all sorts of projects. They would attempt to deluge them with the mountains of meaningless data which all large corporations have in abundance, to fill their offices with so many computer printouts, they couldn't get in to answer the phone. The corporations would try to plant phonies and ringers on the director's staff. They would try to transfer such business as has been conducted by executive committees, finance committees, and at board meetings to other informal, nameless underground committees.

But if the public director were really experienced, intelligent, and energetic, he would be aware of these efforts and able to overcome them. My guess is that he would get help from a lot of people in the company — people below the top-management level who are turned off by what top management is doing or not doing. He would find a lot of friends and a lot of sources of informal and valuable information if he were there all the time, and especially if he gave out his home phone number to enough people.

By way of contrast, consider the plight of the twenty or so blacks who are currently on big company boards of directors, without budgets and without staffs, and who are expected to have real impact on the companies' behavior. Consider the difference between Leon Sullivan, who has tremendous demands on his time, and a public director who has an office in the headquarters building, a million-dollar budget, and who makes this a full-time job. Consider the catalytic effect of a dedicated, informed, full-time outsider on what is now a farce — a charade.

Public directors could completely transform board meetings. Out of sheer shame, other directors would be compelled to help him pursue relevant questions, criticize the answers, and discuss important matters.

Professor Andrew (End of the American Era) Hacker has concluded that since economically and politically we're all on the Titanic, we may as well go first class. If we can make the public-director concept a matter of law for giant corporations, and then get qualified people in the slots, I'm not persuaded we'll have to settle for a bad trip, first class or tourist.[24]

Reactions to Townsend's proposal and a similar one by Arthur Goldberg have been forthcoming from many sides. Fairly typical of the more critical comments put forward is the following one by Neil Jacoby:

I wholly agree with former Associate Supreme Court Justice Goldberg's criticism of the board of directors of the typical large, publicly held American corporation. Membership on such boards and observation of their operation have led me to conclude that there is a wide divergence between the legal theory of the board — that it is the ultimate architect of corporate policy and auditor of management — and the actual function of the board — which is that of advisor to management and "legitimator" of management decisions. De jure, the board is the governing body of the corporation, and appoints and dominates its management; de facto, the management usually dominates the board.

Professor Myles Mace has documented the fact that few corporate boards truly carry out their classical legal functions. The bankruptcy of the Penn Central, and the subsequent investigation of this debacle by the House Committee on Banking and Currency, revealed disquieting faults in the railroad's board of directors. The Committee's staff report censured the Penn Central board for the narrow range of backgrounds of its members, their ignorance of the condition of the company, and their subservience to the interests of financial institutions, of which many were officers.

[24] Robert Townsend, "Let's Install Public Directors", Business & Society Review, Spring 1971, No. 1, pp. 69-70.

Unfortunately, these criticisms have a rather wide application to corporate business.

Yet, I must demur from Mr. Goldberg's remedy. He would establish a committee composed of all of the outside (i.e., non-officer) directors. He would equip this committee with an expert staff of auditors and experts, with access to all of the company's records, to advise it.

We may be sure that this would have the practical effect of splitting the board into two factions — inside and outside directors. Experience proves that factionalism on a corporate board in this fast-moving world is dangerous, and may even be lethal. Even a wrong decision is often better than one delayed by the acrimonious debate of contending groups.

The Goldberg proposal would also blur the line of responsibility of the corporation's management. It would create uncertainty: which faction of the board should management look to for direction? The existence of dual teams of auditors and accountants, both with access to corporate information, would inevitably cause frictions and conflicts. And, of course, the duplication of corporate personnel would impose large additional overhead costs.

The proposal for the appointment of "public interest" directors to corporate boards, presumably by a governmental agency, can be opposed upon many of the same grounds as the Goldberg proposal. Their presence on corporate boards would necessarily compromise the character of the corporation as a task-oriented, efficiency-seeking, profit-motivated institution, operating in an unstable environment of rapid social and technological change.

There is a way to reestablish the board of directors as policy maker and auditor of managerial performance, to free it of domination by management, and to equip it with wider perspective while avoiding divisiveness within the board. *The key to better corporate government is to increase the power, independence, range of competence, and compensation of outside directors* in large public corporations. Specifically, corporation laws should require that a majority of the directors of all such corporations shall be *outside* directors. The laws should require boards to establish standing committees — a majority of whose members shall also be outside directors — on nominations, management and financial audit, and public affairs. The per diem compensation of outside directors should be no less than that of the chief executive officer of the company.

By putting nominations in the hands of a committee dominated by outside directors, it is likely that a greater diversity of backgrounds and competencies among board members would be attained, along with greater sensivity to social problems. By requiring a committee dominated by non-officers to audit the performance of executives, the task is sure to be performed more competently than at present. By giving outside directors a plurality in a committee on public affairs, the corporation is likely to become more attuned to its relationships with society. Finally, by raising the compensation of outside directors, the company will be able to command enough of the time of highly competent persons to enable them to keep on top of the corporation's business problems. Outside directors of big companies should be expected to spend a quarter or more of their time at their directorial tasks. They will then be prepared to do more than "legitimate" the decisions of management.

A corporate board in which the balance of power is held by active and able outside directors is likely to be socially more sensitive — and a better steward of the shareowners' interests — than one dominated by executives preoccupied with the company's internal affairs. And when outside and inside directors in such a board have access to the same information, and work with the same corporate staff, they will avoid the factionalism that frustrates good corporate government.[25]

The author believes there is much to be said for public representatives on major corporate boards of directors but recognizes that there are problems in terms of their selection, the resources made available to them, and their accountability to the public at large. Some possible solutions to these vexing challenges will be dealt with in the concluding section of this chapter.

12) Business Is Business and Therefore It Should Be Nationalized

Those most disillusioned with North America's present corporate system would doubtless like to see more of it nationalized. Except in terms of its ideological appeal to some political groups, it is hard to see why nationalization would receive much support. Admittedly, there are certain services so vital to the public and so inherently monopolistic that if they are to be effectively delivered, they must be either taken over or closely regulated by the state. In either event, the record of nationalized enterprises has hardly been so encouraging in terms of efficiency or other criteria as to induce many to get on the bandwagon. In itself, nationalization accomplishes very little. The Ontario government, as was indicated earlier, apparently became so dubious about the rate setting policies of its own long-standing and relatively well-regarded electricity utility that it set up another board to pass judgment on its policies. Many other illustrations could be cited to indicate that nationalized industries do not necessarily exhibit any more responsiveness to the public interest, however one chooses to define that concept, than private enterprises.

A possible compromise lies in the area of the so-called public corporation as espoused by John Kenneth Galbraith and others. Although it does not come to grips with all the problems involved and is potentially replete with deficiencies of its own, it is worth considering.

There are two disparate views of the modern, large corporation — two very different views of General Electric and General Motors and General Dynamics and General Mills and General Foods. These and the other generals — something less than a battalion, about a thousand in all — contribute close to half the production of goods and services in the United States. The distinction is between what may be called the "traditional" and what may be called the "evolutionary" view of the large corporation.

In the traditional view, a deep and, indeed, unbridgeable chasm divides the state from the firm. The differentiation between the government on one side and private enterprise on the other is fully accepted. Regulation of private enterprise by the state may be necessary, but such control as there may be is subject to a heavy burden of proof. The general right that the corporation be free from interference is deeply imbedded in our history and tradition. The right is further protected by what might be called corporate privacy. You can't regulate what you don't know about.

[25] Neil H. Jacoby, "Responses to the Goldberg Proposal on Public Directors", *Business & Society Review/Innovation*, Summer 1973, No. 6, pp. 38-39.

The government can ask for information only after establishing a specific need to know. It is almost as though there is a broad presumption that what one does not know about corporate behavior does not hurt anyone.

The corollary of this view is that the corporation is kept honest and its operations are kept aligned with the public interest by the fact of competition. It is the market, not the state, that serves as the ultimate regulatory force. The market is an expression of public will, manifested in everyday purchases of goods and services; and since the public cannot be in conflict with itself, the corporation must respond to public needs. This is what puts the burden of proof on state intervention and makes such intervention necessary only if, somehow or other, the orders and signals of the marketplace have failed.

Admittedly, many who hold this view concede that the market can, indeed, fail. Firms can become too large, monopoly and oligopoly can replace competition, the state can be influenced or even suborned by the great corporations. It's quite possible, to paraphrase Marx, that the state becomes, in fact, the executive committee of the corporate bureaucracy. But in this view, the solution lies not in controlling corporate power, but in dissolving it — in reviving the market and in restoring competition. The conditions under which private business can truly be private must thus be reestablished. At this point, there is always an appeal for the rigorous enforcement of the antitrust laws and the breaking up of the giants.

The evolutionary view of the corporation is sharply at odds with the traditional one. It says that the development of General Motors, Jersey Standard, and General Dynamics invokes, at some stage in growth and in power, a clear, clean break with the economics of the private firm in the classical market. At some point, these over-whelming large firms become, and I emphasize this term, *public institutions*. The cliches of private enterprise serve primarily, at this point, to disguise the essentially public character of the great corporation, including its private exercise of what is in fact a public power. Such a corporation fixes its prices, controls its costs, integrates backwards so as to control the supply of its raw materials, and influences, persuades, and, on occasion, bamboozles its customers. The giant corporation has powerful enough leverage in the community that getting what it needs from the government becomes pro tanto sound public policy. It has, on frequent occasions, a hammer-lock on the Pentagon.

The most striking example of such a corporation, or the one on which one can take the strongest position, is the highly developed and fully specialized weapons firm — Lockheed, for example. Lockheed's physical plant is extensively owned by the government and leased to Lockheed. The company's working capital comes from the government in the form of progress payments. Its business comes all but exclusively from the government. Its cost overruns are socialized. Its capital needs — even those resulting from the mismanagement of its civilian business — are guaranteed by the government. Only its earnings and the salaries of its executives are in the private sector. Is such a firm private? Well, under the Constitution I am reminded that a man is entitled to believe anything!

The line between private and public enterprise in cases such as Lockheed is so exotic as to be ludicrous. This demarcation is, in fact, a device for diverting the attention of the public, the congressional committees, and the Comptroller General from what is in fact managerial error, executive perquisites, lobbying for new expenditures (including new weapons systems), profits, and political activity by executives and employees — all of which in a de jure public bureaucracy (or a full-fledged public corporation like the Tennessee Valley Authority) would be subjects of the greatest concern. Thus is public business hidden behind the cloak of corporate privacy.

But the specialized weapons firms, in this view of the corporation, are only the obvious case. General Motors, a different example, both sets the prices for its cars, and, in conjunction with the other automobile companies, foreign and domestic, does so for all cars. This has great effect on the public. General Motors negotiates wage contracts, and this likewise has great public effect — such public effect as has persuaded the President of the United States, in one of the more radical of his several recent radical moves, to place the price system in abeyance — a plank not part of the 1968 Republican platform. (I'm not criticizing the act, mind you.) General Motors also designs cars and incorporates or rejects safety features, also with public consequence. Its emphasis on engine design has public effect, as does the level of emissions therefrom. And General Motors powerfully influences highway construction. Few, if any, of our state legislatures make decisions that have greater impact on the public than are made annually by this one corporation. And its decisions as to what it will make, where it will produce, and what and from whom it will import have considerably more international impact than those of the very important men — my one-time colleagues in the State Department — who preside with no slight rancor over the affairs of, let us say, Chad or Mali.

The evolutionary view of the corporation therefore accepts its tendency to become assimilated to the state and regards this tendency as essentially irreversible. This view no longer presumes that the corporation has private affairs that should be protected from public scrutiny. It follows that while autonomy in the corporation's operations may have practical merit, there is no longer a presumption against public regulation. While there remains the danger that the firms will regulate their regulators, it is precisely such regulation — not the rehabilitation of market constraints nor, parenthetically, voluntary virtue — to which one must look for the protection and advancement of the public interest.

While I have presented two opposing views of the corporation with strict impartiality, it should not come as a surprise that I believe the evolutionary view has far more going for it than the traditional view.

The antitrust laws — basic to the traditional view — are eighty years old, approaching their centenary. The last really important dissolution occurred sixty years ago. This is not prima facie an encouraging record. Each new generation of reformers has held that only the feckless ineptitude and cowardice of its predecessors has kept the market from being restored. And then each new generation, its bravery notwithstanding, has also failed. I believe we can safely and however sadly conclude that if these laws were ever going to work wonders for anyone but lawyers, they would have worked them by now. And I argue that confidence in the efficacy of these laws has provided considerable support for irresponsible corporate power, in that the laws sustain the hope and perpetuate the myth of the all-powerful marketplace. These laws keep alive the illusion that public business is private, and they keep the burden of proof on those who propose regulations or even call for disclosure. And these laws totally suppress the possibility — many would say the specter — of the ultimate development of public ownership. I suggest that no one could do more for General Motors than this.

I do not object to according autonomy to the corporation. It is necessary for effective administration and effective production. There is no doubt that the independent entity, the autonomous corporate organization, is a highly useful device for undertaking and conducting complex industrial tasks. The fact that such an organization has emerged where steel must be manufactured in megatons, automobiles made in the millions, and chemicals processed on a vast scale, added to the fact that something very like the corporate entity has appeared in societies as diverse as those of the United States and the Soviet Union, indicates the utility of the autonomous corporate device. But in the evolutionary view of the corporation, autonomy is not a right by matter of principle; it is merely a pragmatic decision.

Accordingly, where there is a clash between corporate goals and the public interest — as with the safety of products, industrial effects on the environment, the effect of price and wage settlements on the economy, the equity of profits, or the appropriateness of executive compensation — there is no natural right of the corporation to be left alone. And I come here to a very important point: There is no barrier — in the developed case of specialized weapons firms like Lockheed or the incompetent ones like Penn Central, for example — to stripping away the purely artificial facade of private enterprise and converting such corporations into fully publicly owned enterprises. The one thing worse than a General Motors whose public character is recognized is a General Motors whose public character is denied. And the one thing worse than a General Dynamics that is publicly owned and publicly controlled is a General Dynamics that is publicly owned but privately controlled.

There is no magic in stripping away the myth that the market controls the modern corporation, and no magic in stripping away the hope that it sometime could be made to do so. I am quite convinced that divesting the corporation of these cloaks is the very first step toward any useful program for reform.[26]

That some type of new public corporation may emerge is reflected in the views of those on the right as well as the left. Thus Peter Drucker, like Galbraith, has written:

Finally, there is the autonomous "public service corporation," which may be employed for specific tasks. Such a corporation may be privately owned, privately run, and run for "profit," and still be "semi-governmental." One example is Comsat, which was created by an act of Congress in order to run satellite telecommunications, but whose shares are quoted on the stock exchange. Or, such a corporation may be "private," but still have its debts guaranteed by the government, which enables it to be provided for above and beyond the figures reported in the federal budget — a characteristic that has always made these corporations particularly attractive when government deficits are running high. Or, such a public-service corporation may be totally governmental like the Tennessee Valley Authority. Or, finally, it may have mixed ownership. In

26 John Kenneth Galbraith, "The Emerging Public Corporation", Business & Society Review, Spring 1972, No. 1, pp. 54-56.

fact, this latter "interface" institution, which is neither completely governmental nor completely private, but a true hybrid, has been developing rapidly in all industrial countries. One can predict that such interface institutions will play an even bigger role in this country in the next few years.

Unless we shift to complete nationalization as Senator Edward Kennedy has been proposing, a public-service corporation is almost certain to be central to health care. The main burden will then be carried by private institutions, whether insurance companies or cooperatives such as Blue Cross, yet there will also be a need for a "reinsurer of last resort," and that will have to be a public service corporation, whether set up and run by the federal government or, as in the case of Workmen's Compensation Insurance today, by the individual states.

But, and the "but" should be emphasized, there are many of society's tasks that cannot be "privatized" in any form. Mass transportation is one of them. And, even in areas where we expect private business to do the main job, government policy is needed. Energy is an example. We are not, in other words, going to go into a period in which government "shrinks." At the most, we are going to enter a period in which government mobilizes the resources of nongovernment institutions, especially of business, to help carry what is rapidly proving to be an unbearably heavy load for the taxpayer.[27]

SUMMARY AND CONCLUSION

Several conclusions emerge from the discussions in this and the previous chapter. First and foremost is the paramount need for more disclosure and exposure and public scrutiny of pertinent corporate information so that all of the many interested parties can better assess what individual businesses are really up to. Beyond this there is the equally pressing question of how far business should be driven in the direction of assuming more self-defined corporate social responsibilities. Reviewing the spectrum of possibilities outlined in this chapter, it is possible to adopt various facets of many of them.

The author's preferences are an amalgam of several of the models, and they are neither neat nor precise. In the first place, it seems hard to deny that the prime responsibility of business must still be that of generating a profit for its shareholders by outperforming competitors in terms of creativity, innovation, productivity and service. The real question concerns the nature of the constraints under which the corporation should have to operate in striving for this overall objective. Clearly there should be some prerequisites in the sense of fair and reasonable treatment of employees, suppliers and customers, and it would be commendable if business would operate on a high ethical plane and with complete integrity. In keeping with these desiderata, there is no doubt a place for codes of ethics, standards of good conduct and other self-policing devices.

It would be fallacious, however, to leave it to industry alone to put its own house in order. To begin with, government should probably preclude corporations from engaging in some of their more shallow and superficial efforts as though they were a true response to the clamour for more public accountability. At this point, the tax deductibility of many forms of corporate philanthropy should be reassessed with a view to eliminating much of it.

[27] Peter F. Drucker, "Can the Businessman Meet Our Social Needs?" Reprinted from *Saturday Review Special Business Supplement.*

Otherwise corporate leaders will doubtless continue to spend other people's money to decide on social priorities for which they have received little or no mandate. On the broader social welfare front, if there are activities engaged in by business which don't comply with the public interest, it should not be left to corporations to eradicate them even though, in the long run, they may in fact do so as part of a defensive strategy to forestall further state interference in their affairs. Rather, where publicly detrimental practices are discovered, realistic time-tables for eliminating them should be put in place and business should be compelled to adhere to them. Ultimately, of course, responsibility for deciding upon and enforcing these measures must rest with the appropriate level of governmental and political authority.

Turning to the composition of corporate boards of directors, there is no strong case to be made for employee, let alone other special interest group representation, until these boards better reflect the public interest. As distinct from so-called outside directors — often selected by the inside directors as part of an interlocking system of directorates — there is a strong case to be made for truly independent public directors. As already mentioned, however, the attainment of this end presents many problems. Their selection clearly cannot be left to governments, judging by their past practice of appointing insufficient numbers of competent and qualified individuals — often because their first choice is party bagmen and hacks — to far too many bodies where they have the right of appointment. Perhaps the appropriate government should be allowed to name one public member to each major corporate board, but it should be limited to that. Other sources of appointment could well include consumers' associations, the labour movement, churches, and post-secondary institutions of learning. At least one member should also be appointed by an appropriate business group such as the Chamber of Commerce, although no member should ever have any direct link with the corporation in question.

Corporate public board members should be paid out of the public purse and should be provided with a competent staff of their own choosing, also funded by public monies. To carry out their mandate they should also have access to all company records, except specific formulae and trade secrets not germane to their needs and of high competitive value. Regrettably, some sort of a special tribunal might have to be set up to decide on access to disputed information.

As for the duty of these public members, it should be to assess the social stewardship of the corporation with which they are associated, not in terms of their own values but solely in terms of government laws and regulations and any self-policing codes and guidelines to which the corporation has become a party. Once a year the public members should prepare and publish a general report reflecting their judgment and view of the public accountability of the business in question. This responsibility would in no way require that the public members of corporate boards be allowed to vote, and there are a variety of reasons why they should not be. For one thing, given the vote, they would be in the position of second guessing their own conduct. Thus they should have full voice but no vote.

Although corporate leaders will be opposed to this kind of approach for a number of reasons, they might well ponder the alternatives. Public criticism of and expectations for the business community are both now so inflated that more drastic remedies may be put into effect unless something more than a gesture is introduced soon. North American society has prospered under a corporate free enterprise economic arrangement and it can continue to do so, but only if the public has confidence in the social accountability of its leading business enterprises, at least in terms of certain basic rules of the game.

To be fair, however, it might be worth concluding this chapter with two notes — the first, from *Business and Society Review*, cites one authority who feels the answer can be found in a variety of techniques, all of which fall short of the public membership concept:

Rather than seeking political transformation of the corporation, reformers would be wise to make the corporate system which now exists work in society's behalf. This can be accomplished by economic measures, invigorating corporate democratic forms, establishing self-critical voices inside the corporation, and requiring greater disclosure of corporate social conduct. These measures would give shareholders a degree of control over management decisions and make corporate thinking more social-minded. Above all, the single most potent vehicle for change could be through the market itself — altering the market mechanism so that it advances society's social as well as economic goals.[28]

The second observation, from *Harvard Business Review*, suggests that no matter what is done, the only real answer lies in the hands of the thousands of individuals who populate the managerial hierarchy of the corporate realm:

Nothing will happen, either inward or outward, to further advance the doctrine of social responsibility unless those in charge of the corporation want it to happen and unless their associates share their values and put their backs into solving the organization's master problem. There must be desire and determination first. It must be embodied in a strategy that makes a consistent whole of private economic opportunity and public social responsibility, planned to be implemented in an organization which will be humanely and challengingly led and developed.

A few good guys cannot change the course of a large corporation by their personal influence, but they can arrange that the systems of implementation are appropriate in scope to the breadth of corporate economic and social purpose. Now that enlightened chief executives have made this commitment, it would be tragic to have their will subverted, their determination doubted, and their energy dissipated by bureaucratic organization.

The giant corporation, which in small numbers does half the work of our economic system, is here to stay. It is the dominant force of our industrial society. In its multinational forms it has no higher sovereignty to which it reports; in its national forms it is granted wide latitude. Thus it is important to all of us that its affairs be responsibly conducted and that limited knowledge of the art of managing a large organization not be permitted to thwart us.

If organizations cannot be made moral, the future of capitalism will be unattractive — to all of us and especially to those young people whose talents we need. It is not the attack of the muckrakers we should fear but the apathy of our corporate citizenry.[29]

[28] Donald E. Schwartz, "Reforming the Corporation from Within", *Business & Society Review*, Spring 1972, No. 1, p. 68.
[29] Kenneth R. Andrews, "Can the Best Corporations Be Made Moral?", *Harvard Business Review*, May-June 1973, p. 64. © 1973 by the President and Fellows of Harvard College; all rights reserved.

7

ADVERTISING AND MARKETING

There is no more outwardly degenerate, dishonest nor insulting form of corporate behaviour than some of that engaged in under the name of advertising and marketing. There is an old adage which suggests that there are lies, damn lies and statistics. To that list should be added advertising, if not marketing as well.

Advertising in particular has become a social blight in so many ways, shapes and forms that one hardly knows where to commence an indictment. Perhaps as appropriate a place to begin as any is with its enormous costs, an aspect revealed in this article from *Business and Society Review/Innovation*. The U.S. data on this score, for some products especially, is staggering:

A fundamental public policy question of the 1970s may well be: "Does advertising cost too much?" Like its 1930s cousin, "Does distribution cost too much?" it represents another point of concern about the marketing efficiency of an advanced industrial society.

The question in the thirties was whether the wholesale-retail structure and margins of middlemen unduly increased costs to consumers. The question in the seventies is whether the substantial expenditures of business on advertising are all in the public interest. Has advertising become a social expense that produces not economic growth but simply shifts in brand shares that lead to very little overall gain for consumers?

Current annual advertising expenditures in the United States amount to $20 billion, or approximately 2 percent of the gross national product. If we add the $5-$10 billion spent on consumer and trade promotion, the total cost of informing and persuading buyers may well amount to 3 percent of GNP. Thus the consumer apparently pays about three cents on the dollar to support the cost of obtaining product information and promotion. This would not seem too excessive.

However, this figure conceals the high level of expenditures on advertising and sales promotion for particular consumer products and brands. Products which exhibit a high advertising-sales ratio include soaps (11%), perfumes and cosmetics (11%), and drugs (10%). Certain companies in these fields invest a considerable percentage of their sales revenue in advertising: J.B. Williams (36%); Block Drug (30%); Noxell Corp. (30%); and Colgate-Palmolive (22%). Many brands of toiletries, cleaning agents, and cold remedies are essentially made up of a few pennies of ingredients, a few more pennies of packaging and many pennies of advertising per unit sold.[1]

Given the resources devoted to advertising, it is no wonder that it has

---

[1] Philip Kotler, Fred C. Allvine, and Paul N. Bloom, "It's Time to Cut Down on Advertising Waste", *Business & Society Review/Innovation*, Winter 1972-73, No. 4, pp. 9-10.

become a leading pollutant. By every means of communication known to man potential customers are barraged by a seemingly endless series of blandishments of one kind or another. Hopefully, the result will be a strong public backlash, something of which the advertising people are now most fearful as this Toronto *Star* article indicates:

We'll probably hear a lot during the coming months about a new form of pollution. It's called advertising pollution.

Indeed, we are beginning to hear the phrase already. Adman Jerry Goodis told a Toronto audience the other day that "toothpaste, mouthwash, cigarettes and those creepy new enzyme detergent commercials poison the airwaves just as surely as some industries poison the air."

What's beginning to worry a lot of people is not only the quality, or otherwise, of advertising but its sheer volume. A New York expert reckons that advertising pollution is a very real possibility by 1980.

Today's average consumer is exposed to something like 1,500 advertising messages a day. If statistics run their apparent course, by 1980 the total will have risen to something in excess of 3,000 per day. And that kind of overkill, say the experts, can only result in an overtaxing of the public's tolerance for advertising and, ultimately, to governmental regulation of advertising volume.

It's at least encouraging to see that our admen are themselves beginning to admit the dimensions of the problem. Robert Oliver, president of the Canadian Advertising Advisory Board, admitted the dilemma when he spoke to broadcasters in Ottawa last week.

Said Oliver: "I don't know how a mass-marketing, highly productive and highly innovative society can function efficiently without mass communication. But, unfortunately, outstanding creative talent is just as rare in advertising as it is in any other creative art.

The government's answer is legislation. It maintains that while Ottawa may have no place in the bedrooms of the nation it certainly has a role to play in the living room and the larder.

The admen, naturally, have a different answer. They can't see why it can't be done by voluntary action on their part and by better rapport between the advertiser and the consumer.

"Personally, I think women are quite justified in resenting the fact that so many advertisements present the average housewife as a pin-brained ding-a-ling," comments the advisory board's Oliver. ". . . Now the audience wants to talk back to us. What is so surprising about that? In the public-relations field we have always emphasized that communication is a two-way street. Perhaps it's high time we did more listening — and in the process we will learn to communicate more effectively."

To demonstrate that it believes in putting its money where its mouth is, the industry has reissued its Code of Advertising Standards and is currently running a series of advertisements inviting consumers to submit an official complaint if they consider that any advertisment breaks the rules.[2]

Also to be considered are the blatant deception and fraud which characterize so much advertising copy. Although this aspect of the problem is dealt

[2] Thomas Wynne, "Pollution by Advertising Becoming Tough Problem", Toronto *Star*, November 6, 1969.

with at more length later, it is worth underscoring at the outset. In this vein, a recent report on "Advertising and the Advertising Industry", by a Select Committee of the Ontario Legislature, reveals just how fed up some influential elements in society are becoming with common every-day advertising procedures:

The Ontario government should force advertisers to make "complete, factual and balanced" commercials, a government committee said today.

It called for an end to commercial endorsements by celebrities and it said sex should not be used as a sales gimmick.

On advertising content, the committee said: "Consumers are not presented with factual, complete, critical and comparative information about products, their properties, use, maintenance, and useful life.

"Instead they are subjected to subtle and sophisticated attempts to develop product association or loyalties with a desirable sexual or social life, instant personal or social status, or a variety of pleasant states of mind, few of which are really capable of being induced or accomplished by the product itself".[3]

Finally there are the likely adverse effects of advertising on the value systems of society. Although a few diehards might care to debate the point, it is hard to believe that an area of the economy so flagrantly abusive of any kind of standard, and so effectively aimed at the public at large, can help but have a deletrious impact on a number of critical groups and important variables in society:

Of all the social issues involving advertising, the broadest have to do with its impact on values and life styles. Unfortunately, as one might suspect, it is in this area that value judgments are most rife, and hard data are least in existence. Hence, rather than review the rather flimsy evidence in detail, let me lay out the major issues and questions involved.

The overriding question in this area is whether advertising *creates* or *reflects* the values of society. Most observers implicate advertisers and marketers, to some extent, not as creators of values but as exploiters of values which exist at or just below the surface. Hence they perceive that advertising not only tends to reflect values, but that it also is one of the leading edges that can reinforce and accelerate them. Unfortunately, there are virtually no specific examples cited that can be linked demonstrably to advertising-marketing alone. Thus, although advertising has certainly played a part in the growing usage of new feminine hygiene products by helping to make their use more acceptable, the existence and success of such products seem to reflect general social trends toward more openness about one's body and its sexual functions.

Attempts to connect advertising with materialism seldom recognize anthropological evidence that analogies to our society's use of products for ego-enhancement have existed in almost all primitive cultures. Likewise, there are many opinions as to whether advertising adversely affects our moral-ethical-aesthetic standards, but there is no empirical evidence. Once again, different views of what those standards are and should be, and the wide variety of institutional influences that affect them make it highly unlikely that advertising's effect on them can be isolated.

[3] "Ontario Urged to Bar Sex and Celebrity Ads", Toronto *Star*, October 4, 1974.

The same problem pertains when we consider conformity and diversity: much opinion and lots of value judgments, but no data. A marketer might argue that product proliferation offers greater opportunity for diversity. A critic might argue that having products with large shares of the market creates conformity.

In the area of interpersonal and group relationships, there seems to be more substance than in some of the other areas just cited. The portrayal of women and of ethnic groups in ads has been a topic of concern and complaint. For example, ads in which women are portrayed in a particular manner may individually be defensible in terms of management's view of the majority of its market.

Yet the cumulative effect of all such ads (for a given brand, product, or in general) may not reflect present-day roles of women. Value judgments are distinctly involved — e.g., should ads show society as it is or as someone (the advertiser?) thinks it should be? However, this is an area where notions of fairness can be brought to bear and where research can presumably help identify the impact of such ads on the "learning process" of those exposed to them.

The subject of the learning process leads to my final area of questioning of advertising's social impacts — namely, its impact on special groups, including among others the poor, the less educated, and children. In all cases, the key issue seems to be whether or not advertising exploits the relative lack of sophistication of these people. (For children there is the added question of whether advertising teaches them socially unacceptable values — whatever those may be.)

Inexperienced buyers, especially children, are typically in the process of acquiring rather than changing their ideas and values. Thus far this kind of learning — or, in the critics' view, perhaps narcotization — has unfortunately been the subject of too little research. At this point, however, it should be clear that the impact of advertising on special groups is a matter of great concern and seems to lend itself to empirical research more so than most issues in the area of values and life styles.[4]

SOME BASIC BUT BLURRED DISTINCTIONS

With some important distinctions as background, it seems best to divide the discussion in this chapter into two sections, the first diagnosing the advertising problem, the other offering some potential prescriptions for it.

To begin, it is important to understand the case to be made for both advertising and marketing, if one can distinguish between the two. Advertising is perhaps best described as the informational or persuasive side of marketing if the latter term is employed in its widest sense. In that sense marketing can be defined as covering the entire process involved in trying to lower the cost of delivering goods and services from their point of production to their point of consumption. In the case of goods, this usually means getting them from the factory door to the retail outlet at the lowest possible charge. In the case of services, it is usually more complicated, since the service must move to the

[4] Stephen A. Greyser, "Advertising: Attacks and Counters", *Harvard Business Review*, March-April 1972, p. 140-142. © 1972 by the President and Fellows of Harvard College; all rights reserved.

consumer at its point of use. In any event, advertising and marketing are ultimately supposed to reduce the cost of providing goods and services to the final user.

Historically, the major means by which advertising and marketing have attained this objective is by broadening the market for particular products, thereby enabling larger production runs and the economies of scale which go with them. In this sense, advertising and marketing have made an immense contribution to North America's general economic progress and well-being. Indeed, without their help, few of the accomplishments which North America has realized in economic terms could have been achieved — unless by centralized state planning which would have to have been on a much more effective basis than it has thus far been exhibited to be elsewhere.

Thus, it should not be surprising that marketing, in the wider sense of that term, has assumed a bigger and bigger place in the corporate sphere of things. Some would suggest, and not without reason, that marketing is gradually becoming more important than production in the business scheme of things with clearly debatable results. The *California Management Review* reports:

In recent years the emphasis of American business has shifted from production to marketing, with the latter occupying an increasing role in the total job of producing and delivering goods and services. The change reflects the fact that ability to produce products was mastered earlier than was the ability to detect new needs and then to design, distribute, and promote new products. But many people see production as an honest activity while marketing is a nonproductive activity — virtually by definition. This is not the place to analyze this assumption, but rather to record its persistence into an era in which marketing has assumed enormous importance. This negative evaluation of marketing represents an essential ideological difference between much of today's consumerism movement and current business practices.

To the modern businessman the detection and serving of new and subtle needs is a legitimate and challenging activity. The businessman sees himself as improving the quality of American life, but to his critics, many of these activities are suspect. To the critic, these subtle needs are nonexistent until the marketer creates them. A characteristic reaction is that of Dorothy Sayers: 'A society in which consumption has to be artificially stimulated in order to keep production going is a society founded on trash and waste, and such a society is a house built upon sand.'[5]

Having outlined the traditional case which can be made for the advertising and marketing fraternity, most of the remainder of this chapter will be devoted to the shortcomings in this field and what should be done about them. The topic will be dealt with almost exclusively in terms of the role of advertising, rather than marketing; however, it is well to be aware that many corrupt practices pervade the field of marketing. The role of kickbacks, for example, is fairly extensive, judging by the following article from the Toronto *Star*:

Kickbacks — ranging from color TVs to Caribbean trips — are used to

[5] William J. Wilson, "Consumer Reality and Corporate Image". © 1973 by The Regents of the University of California. Reprinted from CALIFORNIA MANAGEMENT REVIEW, Vol. XVI, No. 2, p. 86, by permission of The Regents.

induce supermarket managers to push certain products, says a former chain store manager.

"It happens all the time, it's not unusual," Alex Lauder, 31, charged yesterday on the John Gilbert hotline show on CHUM radio.

Later in an interview at Checkout Food Mart on Gerrard St. E., the store he now owns, Lauder talked about payoffs he's received in his 17 years in the food business.

"I've gotten watches, shirts, a color TV, patio furniture, a beautiful poker table in my basement and an eight-day trip to Nassau," said Lauder, who has worked for all the major chains and managed a Dominion store from 1968 to 1971.

"The suppliers offer these premiums because it gets them good display space and keeps them on good terms with the store manager.

"Of course, the head offices are always telling the managers not to do it, but it goes on anyway."

Payoffs in cash rebates are also given to supermarket head offices for special displays and co-operative advertising, Lauder said.

"The cost of these displays is built into the manufacturer's cost, and I don't doubt the cost is passed along to consumers."

Dominion executives were unavailable for comment yesterday, but an Oshawa Group official reacted angrily to Lauder's charge that IGA store managers get a free vacation once a year — paid for by food suppliers.

"Yes, the IGA managers to do get a free trip every year to Jamaica and other places. We've had an incentive program like this for the last 12 years," said Sam Crystal, public relations vice-president for the Oshawa Group, which supplies IGA and Food City stores.

"But it contributes absolutely nothing to the cost of consumer purchases in the store. It doesn't result in higher costs by one penny," said Crystal.

Loblaw's president William Sherman also denied that incentive programs add to food prices.

"Manufacturers obviously want their products promoted, and supermarkets offer them a co-operative effort to do that," he said.

"Many suppliers work out their prices in such a way as to cover the costs of the promotion, but you can't take these figures out of context."

Sherman said it is company policy to refuse gifts from suppliers, but managers caught taking gifts may or may not be fired, depending on the situation.

"Sure, supermarket managers take gifts," says a Scarborough man who until recently was national sales manager for a major canned goods supplier. "But the eleventh commandment is don't get caught."

Bill Ewart (not his real name) defends the payoffs as "a very legitimate method of influencing the retailer to promote your goods in his store."

He said in an interview yesterday that he has offered store managers everything from a hockey stick or lawn chair to radios and TVs — depending on how much they bought.

But even more costly, he says, are the co-operative advertising deals worked out with head office, which can cost the manufacturer up to $100,000 for one product.

"The chain stores demand a total of 6 to 7 percent of their sales on the product rebated to them in the form of promotional allowances, and it's the consumer who ultimately has to pay for it."

Ewart, who wouldn't give his real name even though he's now in business for himself, said that most manufacturers won't discuss it openly: "They don't dare. It's a real can of worms."

The subject of kickbacks, however, has come to light in several government inquiries into the food industry.

Maryon Brechin, who participated in a 1968 Ontario inquiry into greenhouse vegetables, said the amount of under-the-table deals discovered was "a real eye-opener."

She said she doesn't understand how the chain stores can say it has nothing to do with food prices. "I've been around too long. . . I know it comes out of my pocket."

And Ron Atkey, a former Toronto MP who was on a 1973 parliamentary inquiry into food prices, said, "We felt suspicious enough about the deals to have Beryl Plumptre of the Food Prices Review Board look at the situation."[6]

Another distinction aside from that between advertising and marketing which should be made at the outset results from the dilemma which confronts those interested in cleaning up advertising, particularly in terms of its truthfulness. There is often a fine line between factual information and distortion, a line which is not easily drawn nor defended. This dilemma will haunt the remaining sections of this chapter, and it is well to be aware of it. This requires an appreciation of the various graduations which exist between perceptions of the truth and outright deception and fraud, as this *Harvard Business Review* essay points out:

Information content: Any consideration of advertising content leads us directly to the matter of truth and deception. While we know that the public has a high tolerance of puffery in advertising, the atmosphere in recent years has become one of increasing public skepticism in regard to whether advertisements generally present a true picture of the products advertised. This growing skepticism is shared by the business community. This background, typified by the frequently heard phrase, "That's just advertising," is best reflected in the Admiral Corporation's headline for its recent campaign: "Admiral is having a *real* sale."

Nonetheless, at the same time that we have seen growing skepticism, we have also consistently seen evidence that the public thinks the standards of advertising are improving. The explanation: the public is asking for higher and higher (absolute) standards in commercial communications.

Where can public policy bite in? By recognizing various subcategories of truth, each of which calls for a different level of concern. Here is an array:

Literal truth — Is the claim substantiable?

Although on the surface the matter of claims substantiation seems straightforward enough, in fact it is far from clear-cut. For example, there are research questions about the kinds of tests (the size of a test sample of

[6] Ellen Roseman, "Kickbacks Given to Push Products Former Chain Store Manager Says", Toronto *Star*, November 14, 1974.

a product or of people) that warrant results to be considered definitive, how much "more" or "better" constitutes a valid claim, and so forth. There are also questions about whether claims central to the product's performance should have stronger (methodological) and statistical support than minor claims, and under what conditions design modifications call for retesting of a claim.

My argument here is not to shrink from seeking to have advertising claims substantiated (in fact, 90% of businessmen agree on this). Rather, it is to point out some of the difficulties associated with even such an ostensibly straightforward matter.

True impression — Despite literal truth, is the impression true?

Here we are in much deeper water, for "impression" raises questions of what goes on in a "reasonable" person's mind. Nonetheless, some useful dimensions of this subcategory can be identified, most notably that of the suppression of relevant information.

For example, does the claim pertain to all models? Is the advertised "special" in only very limited supply? Yet in considering "true impression," should we ask the advertiser to reveal — at his own expense a host of reservations and caveats about his product? (Rare indeed is the brand which is not stronger than competition on some dimensions and weaker on others.)

Traditional adversary procedure, as in the law, would argue that an advertiser should not have to subsidize the dissemination of information counter to his own interest. In the instance of health warnings about cigarette smoking, public policy has deemed otherwise.

Discernible exaggeration — Aside from the absence of literal truth, is the exaggeration or puffery discernible as such? Here, again, we must concern ourselves with the notion of a reasonable man. All of us presumably would agree that people who actually believe a specific soap power can truly "make their washing machine ten feet tall" need a different kind of help than can be provided by the FTC. But where does one draw the line?

False impression — Whether deliberately, or not, does the ad actually include material that suggests a false impression (in contrast to suppressing information) — i.e., material that has the capacity to deceive?

Ads which imply uniqueness, ads with distorted demonstrations, ads which present unsupported "best buys," and the like fall into this territory. Substantiation can help. But it is in this territory that the creative freedom to develop imagery via words and pictures clashes with literalness. Allusions and romanticization are the core of advertising for many mundane products. (After all, how legitimately excited can one get over a floor wax?)

Advertisers see regulatory efforts in this area as presaging external dictation of which selling points (not just how to express them) may be used. Indeed, some critics see regulation here as a wedge to attack the promotion of psychological differences (rather than just functional differences alone) between brands. Drawing the line between "discernible exaggeration" and "false impression" is to me the toughest judgment in the zone of advertising content.[7]

[7] Stephen A. Greyser, "Advertising: Attacks and Counters", *Harvard Business Review*, March-April 1972, pp. 137-138. © 1972 by the President and Fellows of Harvard College; all rights reserved.

Some advertisers do not even think about most of the above distinctions because to them distortion and embellishment and the like are not only legitimate but desirable. This *Globe and Mail* excerpt considers the question:

There is nothing wrong with distortion in advertising, says Gerald St. Denis, president of Publitheque, a Montreal subsidiary of McConnell Advertising Ltd. of Toronto.

In a panel discussion yesterday at the Canadian Advertising and Sales Association convention in Toronto, Mr. St. Denis suggested advertising has the same sort of literary licence as poetry.

Poetry is designed to "convince and seduce" and uses all the tools of distortion that the literary mind can devise.

"Keats doesn't offer an engineering description of his Grecian Urn."

Marketers do the same thing as poets in their advertising and in the design of their products and packages.

He said embellishment and distortion in advertising is a legitimate and socially desirable function.

Truth, said Mr. St. Denis, is more philosophic than pragmatic. It is silly to call advertising techniques "gimmicks."

"If sex must be perfumed, powdered and shaped to command attention, it is ridiculous to condemn the more modest embellishment of the world of commerce. . . ."[8]

Others have become so frustrated about trying to make these distinctions that they would advocate an assault only on really misleading ads:

What is the difference between "harmless puffery" in advertising and messages which are genuinely misleading or even untrue?

When it comes to where the line should be drawn, we'll probably never know for sure. Nor will the argument ever end.

But Ottawa and Washington, in their increasingly tough laws and regulations — accompanied by frequent stern warnings — are fighting their way toward working definitions.

"It's the greatest!" Is that harmless puffery?

How about "fast relief?" What is a definition of "fast?" Or of "relief?"

What if some one gets no relief at all? Should the ad be barred even if most buyers of the product to get speedy reactions? Surely not.

It comes down to trying to decide what is genuinely misleading and — from the government's view — being able to PROVE that it is misleading.

In this particular area of advertising control, Ottawa, Washington and advertisers have a long way to go before their ideas have been refined.

The danger is that they will spend so much time on it that they won't recognize that it is, in part, a red herring.

The first job, logically seems to be to look hard at the more concrete claims and insist that they are accurate and can be proven.

This, it seems, is what Ottawa and Washington may be doing in their latest efforts.[9]

---

[8] John Simpson, "Advertising Distortion, Embellishment Called Legitimate, Desirable", *The Globe and Mail*, Toronto, June 4, 1971.
[9] Jack McArthur, "Ads That Really Mislead Should Be Probe Target", Toronto *Star*, February 10, 1972.

A DIAGNOSIS OF THE ADVERTISING PROBLEM

There can only be one explanation for the fact that standards of ethics and integrity have fallen so low in advertising: advertisers for the most part seem to have arrived at the conclusion that the end — pushing the product — justifies the means fair or foul. In this context, it is not unworthy of note that former President Nixon began to run into his worst difficulties when he surrounded himself with advertisers and marketeers besides the usual coterie of lawyers.

Well, what has gone wrong with advertising? Just about everything, if one is to judge by the totality of the criticism erupting both within and beyond the advertising fraternity. To put today's attacks on advertising in perspective, however, it is well to be aware of how such criticism has evolved over the years:

An extensive review of historical critiques of advertising leads me to four observations:

First, as we have already noted, questioning of advertising — and indeed of the whole selling process — is not new. Centuries of commentary from economists, businessmen, philosophers, and others have treated its uses and abuses, its virtues and vices.

Second, assessments of advertising, particularly its social aspects, have deep ideological roots. And, as with all ideological matters, the debate is often very heated. One's conclusions are closely linked to one's subjective value judgments about how the marketplace works and what kind of a society ours should be.

Third, as knowledgeable advertising and marketing executives realize, any appraisal of advertising must recognize that it cannot be viewed in total isolation. After all, it is but one — albeit to the consumer the most common — of numerous forms of marketing communications, including personal selling, packaging, point-of-sale materials, and sales promotion (such as coupons and premiums). Further, "advertising is but one in the constellation of elements that constitute the familiar marketing mix — including price, product policy, distribution, and others — which every successful marketer must develop and adjust for his products and brands.

Fourth, the bulk of the positive commentary on advertising has its foundation in its economic accomplishments, while the bulk of the criticism of advertising has been based on its social impacts. For example, in studies of the public's and businessmen's attitudes toward advertising, its economic roles receive generally strong approbation (even from those who are unfavorable to advertising), but its social consequences are criticized and aspects of its content are questioned. Thus it should not be surprising that my comments addressed primarily to advertising's social effects will focus on issues wherein advertising may often be portrayed essentially in a rather negative cast.[10]

But let's let those who know the advertising industry and its failings best speak for themselves. For openers, take this 1969 account of "Admen Under Fire — From Admen — And They're Listening," from the Toronto *Star*:

[10] Stephen A. Greyser, "Advertising: Attacks and Counters", *Harvard Business Review*, March-April 1972, p. 23. © 1972 by the President and Fellows of Harvard College; all rights reserved.

The healthy wind of self-criticism is beginning to blow through the ranks of the advertising profession.

Advertising has always had its critics within the industry — but in the past they have been few and their pronouncements have generally been dismissed by the admen as being prompted by self-interest and damaging to the profession. Not quite in good taste, you know. After all, enough shots were being fired by the public without having to put up with sniping from insiders.

But nowadays it seems that scarcely a week goes by without some respected figure connected with advertising launching a public broadside against his colleagues. And, what's more, these critics are being listened to.

About a month ago Rothman president Wilmat Tennyson, invited to speak at the annual meeting of the Institute of Canadian Advertising, blasted the admen for providing old-fashioned, unimaginative service, for bowing to political pressure and for selling "unmitigated rubbish" to advertisers as new, creatives ideas.

And he hinted darkly that there were other ways other than traditional advertising for reaching the consumer. "Present creativity." Tennyson went on to say, "is often a senseless pursuit of newness, cleverness, wittiness and artiness — instead of a simple and understandable way in which to tell the consumer in a persuasive manner the reasons why he should buy the product."

Strong stuff but there was worse to come from closer to home. Toronto agency president John Straiton told a life insurance meeting in the Montreal area the other day "Advertisements are written in apparent ignorance of reader or viewer behavior — or deliberate rejection of them.

"We're rewitnessing an explosion of mannerisms and postures that have practically nothing to do with consumers. Advertisers don't seem to be aware that content is more important than technique."

"But technique doesn't impress the public. The public does not appreciate lovely photography, with multiple exposures, with slow motion, etc. They want to see it plain and they want to hear it clear."

This is the kind of stuff that admen are becoming to expect to hear from their colleagues these days. A top agency executive warns that "Unless we can become a great deal more specific in supporting our recommendations to clients, advertising could be relegated to a minor role. . ."

The president of another major agency allows that the upcoming generation of consumers is demanding more believable and convincing advertising. (And a senior researcher warns that three-quarters of English-speaking housewives in Canada regard advertising as misleading.)

Does all this plain speaking and soul-searching suggest a change of heart on the part of the adman? Does it suggest that advertising is going to get better? It probably does.

Certainly, never before has there been so much expressed dissatisfaction from within the industry at the state of advertising. It really does seem that, at last, admen are beginning to wonder whether, after all, there may not be some substance to a lot of consumer criticism.[11]

A more recent Canadian advertisers' seminar heard more of the same sort of thing:

[11] Thomas Wynne, "Admen Under Fire — from Admen — and They're Listening", Toronto Star, October 23, 1969.

. . . Joseph B. Doyle, vice-president, General Foods Ltd., Toronto, told the seminar that "business is faced with gnawing public discontent with the free enterprise system, the social value of business, and what [the public] perceives as economic inequities generated by the profit motive." He advocated a program of education for consumers.

William Erskine, marketing vice-president, Labatt Breweries of Canada Ltd., London, Ont., blamed advertising managers for many of their own, and of their companies', problems.

"There was a time," he said, "when it was the accepted practice for the corporation to work on the principle of being responsive to the consumers' wants. Today, however, . . . increasingly the corporation is expected to be responsible for establishing proper values for the consumer society itself."

David Gillespie, president, Comcore Communications Ltd., Toronto, later expanded that point: "People need not purchase new cars every two or three years. They can quite readily purchase one every 10. But think of the massive unemployment that would result in our country if we all bought an automobile every 10 years.

"It is the advertising and promotion that creates consumer desire and because consumer desire causes purchases of goods, this creates jobs. That's what advertising is all about."

Comcore is Canada's largest advertising-public relations-marketing company.

Earlier in his address, Gillespie had said that "never before has our industry been so maligned to the public at large" as it had in a recent unsponsored CBS television show entitled "The Commercial and You."

Those who saw the program will remember that noted American psychologist, Eric Fromm, concluded that advertisers are manipulators, conscious or unconscious, as well as persuaders of society.

In addition, a spokesman for the ad agencies was caught by the interviewer telling people a breakfast drink had more "food energy," when he meant calories.

Surveys conducted in Chicago and Toronto by Gillespie's firm showed that people who saw the program were in general agreement with its critical tone. Gillespie noted that "there is no complaint about advertising per se. The complaints are how we execute our commercials."

As a matter of interest, "Canadian-created commercials on an average are more factual in their execution; American ones tend to be more emotional in their claims."

Two kinds of clutter also came up for discussion: out-door advertising and the number of television commercials played back to back.

Gillespie called for the development of a whole new system for outdoor advertising — one that "enhances the environment," before outdoor advertising is banned altogether, as it has been already, almost, in Hawaii and Oregon.

As for commercial clutter, "we know it has a marked effect on commercial effectiveness and we know it offends the viewer."

Robert Marker, chairman, McCann-Erickson, Inc., New York, offered his suggestions to the seminar in regard to a change of attitude on the part of advertisers:

Marker suggested that advertisers "approach the creation of advertising with the goal of achieving agreement, not winning an argument."

"This is not a game we're in — a game in which we must win out over the consumers. This is a negotiation. And in successful negotiations, everybody wins. Negotiation is not a game. It's a cooperative enterprise."

Marker went on to say that one of the reasons for today's credibility problem in advertising is that it appears full of contradictions. "Each marketer is saying . . . my brand is best and he delivers a demonstration, test or testimony to prove his point."

Another problem arises when you try to sell something that is genuinely insignificant. "While a new floor polish may be the biggest thing in the life of its brand manager and the agency with the account, it has doubtful significance to the housewife who feels her floors are pretty shiny already."

Although advertising ethics did not play a very large role at Seminar '73, perhaps because of the large picture drawn of today's sharp-eyed consumers and their governments, ethics did come out as still a hot topic at a recent meeting of the American Marketing Association.

Seymour Lieberman, president, Lieberman Research Inc., New York, presented the results of a study into deceitful advertising. In four out of six tests with two panels of 100 middle-income consumers each, a commercial designed to deliberately mislead the prospective buyer came out well ahead of an honest version of the same ad in its ability to coax the audience into a buying mood.

Most people, for example, were persuaded to buy a mythical plant fertilizer containing protein, although protein is of absolutely no use to plants.[12]

Even more significant than the practicing advertisers' self-criticism is the criticism of those who ultimately decide which way advertising will go, that is, the senior executives of American's leading corporations. In their quarters there is, to say the least, some disenchantment, as this Toronto *Star* article shows:

A reflection of the striking change in executive attitudes [toward advertising] is found in the May-June edition of the Harvard Business Review in an article by Stephen A. Greyser and Bonnie B. Reece.

It analyses the results of a survey of 2,700 subscribers to the magazine, the great majority of whom are executives.

The findings are little short of sensational.

In general, they suggest: most businessmen see a striking need for improvement in advertising standards; they see it as their responsibility to make sure the changes are made; and they welcome consumer activism, with some reservations, as an ally in seeing that they are successful.

This means that the moving force in the reform of advertising is not people such as Canada's Consumer Affairs Minister Ron Basford, or U.S. consumer advocate Ralph Nader, or even various legislative restrictions on the quality or quantity of advertising. It is the businessman himself.

The survey finds that 57 per cent of those replying feel some advertising insults their intelligence more seriously than it did 10 years ago, while 18 per cent feel this had become a less serious problem. Comparatively large groups also felt that in the past 10 years, advertising had

12 John Bradshaw, "We're Facing Flak from All Sides", *The Financial Post*, May 19, 1973.

become a more serious offender in terms of bad taste, the sale of objectionable products, lack of information and sheer irritation.

This probably doesn't really mean that ads have actually become worse. It is more likely to reflect a big change in business ideas of what is good advertising.

Among particular ad campaigns which got high marks among this particular American business group were those for Volkswagen and Alka-Seltzer. Large numbers found objectionable some ads for cigarettes, household cleaning products, and personal hygiene products.

Particularly disliked were the ads for Winston cigarettes ("Winston tastes good, like a cigarette should").

It's worth noting that this dislike for the style of cigarette ads has already been reflected in restrictive legislation by some North American governments, with still more to come.

Also worth pondering — and it indicates a real problem — is the fact that the Winston campaign appears to have been relatively effective. This means many businessmen want to change certain varieties of advertising even though they may prove relatively successful in selling products.

Fifty per cent of those surveyed, however, felt that most of the money spent for advertising is not well spent. A better job could be done. Only 28 per cent felt that most advertising money was wisely spent.

Remember that this is executive opinion, not a vague feeling among consumers. At a guess, consumers might be less critical.

There is little disagreement with the need for and the potential benefits of advertising — although a good many felt that today's ads sometimes cause people to buy things they neither need nor want.

In summary, the executives believe that advertising is, in itself, valuable and productive for society. But they want to see it changed. That means it is likely to change. Now, if only we could achieve this kind of success with some of society's more pressing problems. . . .[13]

More general indictments of the advertising industry come from a variety of sources. A fairly typical example of the kind of sweeping denunciations which appear in many quarters turned up in the union journal *Canadian Transport* some years ago:

Unlike informative advertising which tells us something about a product, persuasive advertising is directed to our subconscious and to our emotions. Sex, fear, prestige and conformity are exploited in persuasive advertising. No useful product information is given.

Although the main function of persuasive advertising is to mould conforming, docile consumers, it does help sell some products sometimes. This does not happen as often as we might think. Cigarettes and alcohol serve as an example.

It is accepted as a fact by many people that advertising leads to an increased consumption of cigarettes, beer and liquor. This explains the running battle between producers of these products and temperance people whose efforts have been devoted to controlling the advertising of the 'evil products'. But if we compare per capita consumption of these products in countries (such as Canada and the U.S.A.) where they are widely

---

[13] Jack McArthur, "The Business World Seeks Improvement in U.S. Ad Industry", Toronto *Star*, May 18, 1971.

advertised, with consumption in countries (such as the U.S.S.R.) where they are hardly advertised, it seems that advertising makes little, if any, difference. Perhaps this is not a proper comparison, but you will also find that liquor and cigarette consumption in areas of Canada not reached by T.V., and almost untouched by other forms of advertising, is no less than in other parts of the country. . . .

On the other hand, it seems that advertising does sell patent medicines. Last year Anacin spent almost 14½ million dollars on T.V. ads in the U.S. Not far behind was Bayer Aspirin. Both companies sell a fantastic number of headache pills, even though any drug store can supply pills with the same pain-relieving ingredients at a fraction of the cost of these advertised brands.

This is not the worst form of medicine advertising. At least these pills do help us through the problem of the morning after. Many other medicines are advertised as treatments for illnesses which do not exist. 'Tired blood' is a good example of this. Others claim to cure problems such as the common cold, although doctors are practically unanimous in stating that there is no cure for a cold except time. Among the worst ads are those for laxatives which, far from curing anyone, are frequently the cause of illness.

Persuasive advertising is also used to get customers to switch brands. Success with this varies from company to company, but the customer always loses as the price he pays includes the cost of persuading him to 'switch over' or 'come back' to some brand.

Related to the brand-switching game is the development of 'customer loyalty'. This concept, so revered by advertisers, makes me shudder. Developing customer loyalty refers to indoctrinating customers so that they will stick with a company's products through all model changes, new improved versions, price increases, and competitors' attempts to make them switch. The effectiveness of advertising is often measured by the extent to which it develops 'loyalty'. Of course, it is most effective when the process begins with children, as a well-indoctrinated child will be loyal to his companies for life.

No one, not in the pay of advertisers, can imagine that our almost unrestricted advertising is desirable. The advertisers justify it by saying that customers should be free to choose the products they want, and to do this they need information about the products. Advertising, they claim, gives customers that information.

This is true of some informative advertising which describes such things as the features and price of a product. Many women examine the grocery store ads which appear in most papers on Wednesdays. Although some stores waste a great deal of space on persuasive or gimmick ads, most now give factual and useful information on food prices.

Similarly, we tend to watch the newspaper ads for information when we are considering any large purchase, but it is difficult to imagine anyone watching T.V. ads in the hope of getting information. This probably explains why a number of studies have indicated that people place more faith in newspaper ads than in radio or T.V. ads.

Most critics of advertising concentrate their attacks on persuasive advertising and suggest controlling it by heavy taxation. (At present there are no limits on the amount of advertising expenses which can be deducted for income tax purposes. This means that taxpayers pay, through higher taxes, about 50 percent of all business advertising.) To this suggestion, the other side replies by pointing out that it is very difficult to distinguish between informative and persuasive advertising. I am not sure if this is an indication of their deceit or their stupidity, but either way this argument can be dismissed. They then turn to the argument that advertising restrictions would hurt our economy and cause unemployment.

They are right. Our economic system depends upon advertising.

But I cannot help thinking that something is wrong with our system when we can drive a new car to college and then be turned away because the college is over-crowded; when we can rent a luxurious hotel room but can't get a hospital bed; when we can get a bachelor apartment on the tenth floor of an air-conditioned building, but not a house with a bit of ground for children to play on; when we can see all signs of prosperity while one-fifth of our population lives in poverty. And I cannot help thinking that something is wrong when the content of our newspapers and the programs on our private radio and T.V. stations are determined by what is considered acceptable to the advertisers. If that's the kind of society you want, you're welcome to it. But don't try to bring honesty into advertising or the system will crumble.

If you want to live in a society which place more importance on education, housing, health and an end to poverty, rather than on a new brand of soap or hair cream, don't expect to achieve this by tinkering with the present system. It can only be achieved by a government which directs capital into socially desirable projects and quality goods. This would mean that the capital needed to support massive advertising campaigns which make it possible to sell junk and model changes, simply would not be available for that purpose. We haven't so much capital that we can use if for industries resting entirely on massive advertising and still have enough left over for proper housing, hospitals, and basic human needs.

The choice is ours. We can sit back waiting for the better life promised by the advertisements or we can use our democratic processes to create a better society ourselves.[14]

Probably nothing galls the critics of advertising more than advertisers' attempt to persuade children to pressure their parents into buying this, that or the other thing. Especially on television, both the volume of such advertising and the thinking that lies behind it are quite frightening, as this item from *Business and Society Review/Innovation* emphasizes:

Since it first flexed its muscles around 1950, television has come to occupy a staggering proportion of the waking hours of the average child. The child who watches TV only "moderately" sees over 1,000 hours of television a year — certainly more than he sees of his elementary school teacher and in many cases more than he sees of his father. In many families the TV set may even be the babysitter.

Any parent who has watched as much as an hour of children's television on Saturday or Sunday morning is probably aware of and disturbed by the numbing plot and character standardization, the massive doses of violence and aggression, and the sexual and racial sterotypes in the programs themselves. But what may be even more forcefully apparent is the

[14] Harold B. Wilson, "Advertising or Brainwashing?: People Pressured to Buy—Buy—Buy", *Canadian Transport*, October 15, 1968, p. 6.

sheer volume of the commercial barrage. An average of twenty-two messages per hour is pumped out over the airwaves during children's viewing hours, adding up to 220 minutes of pure commercials seen by the average television-watching child in one week: This is 22,000 to 25,000 commercials a year. What is being touted to children? How? What does this avalanche of ads do to children? And who decides what's fair and what's foul in the game of luring kids to buy, buy, buy?

Between 55 percent and 85 percent of the products advertised to children are for ostensibly edible products, the majority of which are of questionable or negligible nutritional worth. Snacks, cereals, soft drinks, and candy predominate. Fruits, vegetables, meats (except hot dogs and lunch meats) are seldom mentioned. Sugar, sweetness, and sparkle are peddled as a sort of Holy Grail, with cartoon and fantasy salesmen usually making the pitch.

The share accounted for by "food" products falls to 55 percent just before Christmas, when toy and game selling reaches its frantic peak. The TV hucksters ballyhoo slick, plastic, motorized, mechanized, do-everything monsters and machines to the boys; and to the girls, dolls that talk, walk, sing, maintain four-season wardrobes complete with accessories, and in general leave little to their owners beyond the chance to give Barbie a push on her way down her own "Miss America ramp."

Children's television, in its broadest sense, is also selling danger. Children under thirteen watch more TV after school than on weekend mornings. Over 5 million children watch ten well-known weekday evening prime-time shows, and a recent monitoring effort found the following ten products advertised on these programs: Geritol Tablets, Anacin, Dristan, Lysol Deodorizing Cleansers, Mennen E Deodorant, Arrid Extra Dry, Alka Seltzer, Bayer Aspirin, Gillette Soft and Dry, and Foot Guard Foot Spray. On the labels of each of these products and these or similar words: "WARNING! Keep Out of Reach of Children." But no such cautionary announcement appears in the advertisements of these products, which are viewed with interest by millions of children around the country. A child can easily become overfamiliar with these products after seeing them advertised, and experimentation can have hazardous and deadly effects. Each month H.E.W. records between 300 and 400 aerosol accidents that require emergency room treatment, and over a hundred deaths have resulted from inhalation of aerosol sprays in recent years.

However, it is the commercials intentionally aimed at the "children's market," and meant to sell the eat-'em-ups that substitute for food and the plug-'em-ins that replace play, that most clearly show how the child is manipulated by an industry whose lodestar is the direction of the profit curve. Up to $30,000 may be spent by advertising agencies on behalf of their industry clients to produce a single thirty-second children's commercial. The production of an advertisement is a sophisticated, all-out effort by a team of cartoonists, child actors, photographers, scripwriters, child psychiatrists, and child psychologists. The techniques used include the use of star filters, zoom lenses, canned laughter, wide-angle lenses, and simulated motion.

One candid assessment of the reasons for the effectiveness of this battery of techniques comes from a surprising source. A report called "Children's Television Commercials — A Content Analysis," prepared in 1973 by the National Association of Broadcasters, their employees, and student sociologists under the direction of Professor Charles Winick, contains this statement:

> ... Animation is effective with children ... [probably] because the technique is used in programs, so that the transition from program to commercial is minimally jarring to young viewers.

We may assume that the other paraphernalia of cartoon techniques are also "minimally jarring" — or to put it more bluntly, that they effectively blur the distinction in the young child's mind between entertainment and commercial message. Winnick and company offer strong circumstantial evidence that the content, as well as the technique, of children's commercials is intended to fuzz the line between the program and the sell. Direct testimonials from fictional characters occur in about one-fifth of the commercials, a cartoon or fantasy character is spokesman in over two-fifths of the commercials, and fantasy, as an aspect of a setting or story that could not exist in the real world, is employed in about three-fifths of the commercials.

Many large advertisers employ motivational research houses, which, with the aid of hidden microphones and cameras, one-way mirrors, electronic sensors, and child psychologists, delve into the minds of five-to-twelve-year-old children to find out the most effective methods they can use to sell products to other children and their mothers. (Parents and schools are often not told by research recruiters what these children are being used for) One ironic result of this massive research effort seems to be an appreciation by the ad agencies of the good sense of the older child, or in Winick's academic prose:

> ... Children's reactions to commercials may be presumed to reflect their comparative emotional and cognitive development. One study of children concluded that the smallest drop in their attention to commercials is from ages 5-7, and the greatest drop at ages 11-12.

The result of this insight, as might have been anticipated, has been the exploitation of younger children. Winick provides a distillation of the wisdom of the motivational researchers on how best to sell the innocent:

> ... The age group from 6-9 is probably the one most sensitive to peer group and emulation pressures. It is moving into game activities and beginning to learn the "rules of the game" and develop consensual validation of its precepts. Showing such children could be influential not only on the members of the 6-9 age group but also on the younger children who want to emulate the next oldest group.

> ... Because the preschooler is probably at home most of the time, he is likely to accompany his mother to the store and to exert a considerable role at the point of purchase. He is usually especially influential in terms of "free" premiums that are obtained with the purchase of products. As a relatively new member of the family group, he often is catered to more actively at meals by the parents than older children. Also, in a family with several children, the youngest is often the most "influential."

The United States is one of only five countries in the world which sell products to children via television. Many countries consider sales efforts aimed at children as an immoral activity. In this country, children are protected by laws against assault, pornography, and binding contracts. There are laws governing school attendance and statutory rape. No such laws exist with regard to television. Perhaps one of the reasons we have failed to enact such legislation is that we have little hard evidence on what television commercials do to our children.

A child eventually learns that there may be a big difference between the item advertised on the tube and the insert which comes with the perfumed glop in his cereal bowl. But in the process, does he become a burned skeptic? Does he extend his impressions of TV salesmen who exaggerate or lie to all people who sell things? Does private enterprise come into ridicule? Does the child conclude that our economic system naturally includes lying, exaggerating, and cheating even to children? Does the picture tube radiate scarring doses of sexism and racism? How does commercial emphasis on things, things, things affect cultural values?

Social scientists in the academic world have generally steered away from trying to answer these questions. This may be due to the inherent difficulty in separating the effects of ads from the effects of so many other influences on a child's development. It may also stem from the possibility that some social scientists have an elitist bias which causes them to depreciate the impact of this ever-present instrument on their own lives and on the lives of their children.[15]

As implied in one of the foregoing quotes, perhaps the only comforting thing to be derived from all of this is that many children have come to distrust TV advertising. This in itself is disturbing however, as it could have a spillover effect leading children to feel equal contempt for the contributions of related or other institutions deserving of a better reputation. Nevertheless, it is encouraging to realize that children really do begin to see through it all for what it actually is. As *Canadian Transport* states:

Talk about frank "consumerists"! Business associations and corporations currently expanding their consumer education activities in the schools will have their work cut out for them when they encounter some of today's grammar school kids.

The businessmen, and teachers under their influence, may well find that they have to deal with a generation of youngsters already skeptical of advertising, mainly because of long exposure to unbelievable TV claims, but also because of their own early experiences.

By courtesy of Professor Richard L. D. Morse of Kansas State University, a leading consumer-education authority, we got hold of a set of student opinions on labeling and advertising collected by an enterprising fifth-grade teacher.

The project came about during a science class discussion of synthetic and real sponges. One of the fifth-grade boys declared, "you can't trust a label. The manufacturer would probably lie and say it was real when it wasn't." Most of the other students expressed similar distrust, Dr. Morse reports. Several days later, as part of a discussion of the difference between factual and opinionated material, the students were assigned to write their opinions about labeling and advertising.

Their opinions may irritate or delight you, depending on your own view of advertising practices. But they will inform you as to these kids' reactions and attitudes.

Especially interesting are their reactions to TV. This is a group that

[15] Robert B. Choate, "How Television Grabs Kids for Fun and Profit", *Business & Society Review/Innovation*, Autumn 1973, No. 7, pp. 21-23.

has never known a world without TV, and has gotten most of its impressions from the big eye. But TV apparently has not really brainwashed them. In some ways it seems to have made them more skeptical. In the comments below note also the real resentment of cigarette commercials, distrust of soap commercials, and widespread disillusionment about baseball mitts. The more polite comments are from girls.

— "My opinion is about a racing track. The label on the box said that the hand controls would not bust. But they did. And they said that the power pack was guaranteed for a half a year. But it was three weeks before it ran down. I hate that darn smelly store."

— "I needed a glove. It cost 30 dollars and there was one that was on sale and it really cost 25 dollars but we got it for 10 dollars and it was guaranteed. But the first day all the strings broke."

— "I think if they would take off about smoking and say something right about it like that one they say about cancer so people don't smoke because it takes away your life. Like I don't see why they put it on TV when you can go to a store and get it."

— "Sometimes labeling is wrong and some is right. Like on baseball mitts. My brother has one that says pure leather, but it's not."

— "Some people just put advertising on TV because they want you to buy it. Like Tide. They think it's great. But I think it's terrible. And on smoking, one advertisement says you should not smoke and on another they say how good some cigarettes are."

— "I wouldn't give a penny for some things. Like the finky baseballs. Last time I bought one it said non-tear covering, and the second week I had it the covering came off."

— "I think labels are sometimes wrong. For instance, different kinds of labels on laundry products that you can get stains out. I end up with more stains than you started with."

— "I think they should take off bad advertising. They shouldn't pay so much to a famous person when a normal person can do it just as well."

— "My opinion on labeling things, they should tell what it is made of or what's in it. Otherwise should not sell them because people get gypped. They tell lies on TV all the time. They try to urge you to buy stupid junk that is no good. It looks like it came from the dump in one week. They must have a lot of nerve to make dumb-stupid stuff that is no good. They come to your house and act crazy for nothing, like an ape."

— "I don't think they should spend all of that money to advertise it when people can see it in a store."

— "On baseball goods or something like that they put it genuine leather but some isn't. Sometimes they don't put the prices on everything."

— "On detergents they say it will get stains out but it doesn't. And they say some cigarettes are lowest in tar but it isn't. And on cigarette packs they say: 'Caution, cigarettes may be a hazard for your health'."

— "A lot of advertisers try to prove that their product will work by going on TV. And some of them cheat just to get people to buy it."

— "They advertise too much. And they take too long and disrupt TV shows. Some spend too much money on people they want to go on the show. Most commercials could never be true."

— "On diet foods they should not lie about it just to get more money. It is really cheating. When you are going on a diet and are trying to lose weight all you do is gain it."

— "When advertising house to house to sell something big like a dishwasher sometimes they will cry to you."

— "I feel they shouldn't write on the labels like best equipment you can buy. The laundry products don't show the washing of the clothes, only the finished product. The way they advertise about things like soap when they should tell the people about stopping smoking and world affairs. They keep changing the celebrities so people think because they use it they themselves should use it."

— "I don't think the companies should put labels on dresses like they will not shrink or will last a long time. Then they shrink or unravel. I think they should tell the truth like pure cowhide or fake cowhide."

Quite apparently business organizations are going to waste a lot of time and money with their intensified school-program plans. Like the American Retail Federation. (The kids have me talking like them.) The retailers waged one of the angriest, stubborn fights against the new "truth in lending" law and successfully delayed its passage for several years. Now they are taking a new tack of doing consumer "education" and are conducting a pilot program in the Rochester, N.Y., public schools, starting with kindergarten.

Kindergarten may already be too late. In any case, if businessmen want to get kids to believe what they say about their products, they would do better to educate the manufacturers of baseball mitts, soap and cigarettes.[16]

A final listing in this catalogue of advertising disorders is the effect it has on the media. Since this issue will resurface again in a later chapter, one or two points will suffice for the moment. The first concerns the extent to which advertising interests have subverted the media to suit the purposes of the establishment they represent. This basic critique comes from comments in the Toronto *Star* by a top advertising man:

A Toronto advertising executive told the Senate committee on mass media today that the trouble with newspapers, radio and television is that they depend too much on advertising.

Jerry Goodis, president of Goodis, Goldberg, Soren Ltd., said the media ignore poor people, minorities, the old and the young "to build an audience of affluent consumers to serve up to the advertisers.

"We don't have mass media, we have class media," he said. "Media for the middle and upper classes."

Because newspapers get 75 per cent of their money from advertising, and broadcasting stations between 86 and 96 per cent, he said, the reader, viewer and listener are free riders and the advertiser the paying customer.

"In any conflict of interest," Goodis said, "the paying customer comes first and the free rider takes second place."

Inevitably, he said, editorial content of the media comes to serve the interest of the paying customer by appealing to "the right audience."

"The poor, the old, the young, the Indian, the Eskimo, the blacks are virtually ignored. It is as if they didn't exist."

There are more stories and pictures about charity balls than about poor people, he said. And stories on poverty present the views of remote experts.

"What we don't see in the mass media is how the poor feel about

16 Sydney Margolis, "Kids No Longer Kidded by TV", *Canadian Transport*, 1969.

themselves or what they think could be done to improve their condition," he said.

Indians show up in the media in a scramble of disconnected stories of brawls in bars, court cases over hunting rights and confusing reports of Indian reaction to government policies, Goodis said.

"But who," he asked, "reports the cause and extent of Indian poverty, the appalling state of Indian educational facilities, and the injustices inflicted on native Canadians through government actions and our general apathy or prejudice?"

Goodis said the media ignore young people's idealism, their continual questioning of the establishment, their bitterness and frustration with adult hypocrisy to zoom in on "some strange or shocking example of young behavior, usually to do with sex or dope — like '15-year-old pusher supports his own habit' or 'Yorkville Village crash pads spread hepatitis, VD'."

Goodis said the underground press, created by young people out of desperation, shows their real interests and voices their criticism of social injustice and hopes for a better society.

Although he found newspapers lacking, Goodis said "the problem is most acute in broadcasting where advertising accounts for essentially all the income.

The main occupation of radio stations is "to create audiences for advertising," he said, and on television most Canadians see the results of wholesale importing of American programming because "this is the cheapest way to build an audience for TV commercials and to fill in the spaces between them."

Canadian television stations buy American programs because this is cheaper than producing their own.

The result is that "television, the principal educator of our children and many of our adults, has been virtually abandoned to U.S. programming."

"I think it's noteworthy that it's in the single medium where there is no advertising, where the audience pays the whole shot," Goodis said. "It is in books that positive, serious social criticism must start."

He said the media had left it to Harold Cardinal, president of the Alberta Indian Brotherhood, to tell the Indians' story in his book, The Unjust Society; to Ralph Nader to expose unsafe cars; to Rachel Carson, in Silent Spring, to expose the threat of pollution 10 years ago.[17]

There is a somewhat ironic sequel to all of this. So much emphasis has been placed on TV advertising instead of programming, that at least one observer, appeearing in the Toronto Star, came to the revealing conclusion, as long ago as 1969, that the quality of the ads had surpassed that of the shows they were sponsoring:

We seem to have reached the ultimate in sensation, illogic and idiocy. It may all be downhill from now on.

This makes it hard for the columnist to find new and exciting material.

Naturally, therefore, one turns to that never-ending source of sensation, illogic and the idiotic, the TV commercial. The corporation's effort

[17] Stan McDowell, "Ad Man Attacks Media's Stress on Advertising", Toronto Star, February 18, 1970.

to woo the public on television has been a never-failing reservoir from which to draw scathing comment.

But a recent personal survey of television advertising reveals something which appears to have escaped the most eminent TV critics: The commercials are better than the programs. One is tempted to open another beer or head for the washroom BETWEEN the commercials, not during them.

Of course, it has long been obvious that the technical competence inherent in commercials has been greater than that of the programs.

But now the content of the commercials is also superior.

Just think for a moment of the increasingly terrible serials — radio soap operas were better; bring back Dr. Brent! — of the ghastly situation comedies, all situation, no comedy; of the incredibly dull talk programs, in which controversy is avoided like the smallpox. Of course, the commercials are more entertaining. No wonder sports and movies are taking over the medium.

There surely is no doubt that the "funny" commercials are often genuinely humorous. An increasing number of sponsors — realizing that particular brands of shaving cream, cereal and beer aren't that important to people — are kidding themselves, their product and their customers. Maybe that way, they seem to reason, a particular product will stick in the mind of the bored consumer long enough for him to decide that he might as well buy it as some other. Gillette has proven that.

A very intelligent approach it is. But why is it that a high proportion of commercials aimed at males are of this lighthearted type, while so many for females still are deadly serious? Messages about cooking to please your husband, for example, are likely to imply that a new happier marriage relationship can result from a new sauce for the meat loaf. In fact, it is more likely to result in the grunted question: "Whyinhell didn't you ever make this before?"

Another oddity is the earnest style of presenting commercials for pet food. If a foreigner were to judge by our television, he would decide that North Americans worry more about shovelling meaty-tasting vitamins into their dogs than about their own diet. Maybe he would be right. We do have a strange set of values. Canada's most expensive field crop is lawn grass, and Canadians cheerfully pay more and more for stuff to make it greener and thicker while creating a terrible fuss any time the price of wheat threatens to make bread more costly.

There are, of course, some bad TV commercials. There's the shampoo that (gasp) allows a woman to "dare" to swing her head, presumably ending forever our chronic problem with stiff-necked women. There's the mouth wash which produces matrimony as a byproduct. There's a cheese which is used by the bucketful where a half-slice seems logical.

But TV commercials, though they may not be enthralling, are at least more interesting than most of the stuff in which they are inserted. And they are brief. Sponsors aren't faced with the horrible problem of spinning out one slim idea for 30 or 60 minutes. They have 30 or 60 seconds and on many occasions manage to sustain interest for that long. . . .

Some one some day may develop a theory which goes like this: The TV commercial's effectiveness varies inversely with the quality of the program which surrounds it. The less memorable the program, the more memorable the commercial.

That may explain the present trend but it doesn't promise much for TV in the future, does it?[18]

To summarize what has been said thus far in this section, no better word could be found to describe the nature of advertising than "manipulation." The problem in this regard would appear to be that it is extremely difficult to get away from this practice since it has become so deeply embedded. *The Globe and Mail* reports:

The premise that advertising's unfavorable public image stems from people's distaste for manipulation should not surprise the business.

In a recent address to the American Marketing Association, Marshall McLuhan of the University of Toronto was quoted as saying "the community is horrified at advertising because it is dedicated to manipulating people."

The manipulative nature of much advertising has been obscured to a considerable degree by the emphasis on eliminating deceptive and "offensive" promotional material.

Governments may legislate "truth in advertising" measures indefinitely and the business itself may sharply accelerate its self-regulatory efforts, but these moves are unlikely to touch more than the surface of advertising manipulation — an underlying factor some observers believe prompted widespread consumer resentment that led to pressures for government controls and increased advertising self-policing measures.

Resentment about advertising manipulation has rarely been clearly articulated by consumers. Records of the Canadian Advertising Standards Council — the regulatory arm of the Canadian Advertising Advisory Board — will reveal scores of ill-defined complaints from consumers. Groping for reasons for their resentment, and failing to narrow complaints to specifics, consumers often lash out at advertising in general.

Manipulation has not been the issue — at least ostensibly — in the successive controls imposed on advertising practices in Canada and elsewhere. Yet an appraisal of curbs will show there is a relationship between controls and the fear of manipulative abuses. This is true of controls on advertising to children, cigaret promotions, alcoholic beverage advertising, and claims dealing with products and services. It is possible for advertising to meet existing regulations on truth and "good taste" and still be manipulative as, for example, in personal hygiene and cosmetic product advertising.

In defence of advertising it may be asked whether manipulation should be considered as something to be abhorred when it is practiced daily across a wide area of society. Is it possible the community dislikes what it sees in itself through advertising?

. . . Professor Stephen Greyser of the Harvard Business School said: "Traditional concern on the part of managers and creative people has focused on how to 'turn on' the audience. Now the issue of advertising irritation seems to be promoting into importance the matter of how to avoid 'turning off' the audience."

[18] Jack McArthur, "It Had to Happen TV Commercials Top the Programs", Toronto *Star*, April 26, 1969.

Other U.S. and British studies noted that soap, detergent, personal hygiene and cosmetic advertising provoked strong consumer dislike where irritation about advertising was a factor.

It is interesting that the two products drawing the strongest negative reaction were soap and detergents the advertising of which is almost totally aimed at women. This points to the evident blindness of many admen to changes that have occurred and are under way in the attitudes of women to their position in society.

Advertising alienates much of this audience by inane stereotyping. Although a sizeable number of women may still be indifferent to the way they are frequently portrayed in advertising, the issue — and it includes manipulation — is likely to emerge as much more serious than the industry seems prepared to concede or is willing to resolve.[19]

A PRESCRIPTION FOR THE ADVERTISING PROBLEM

Proposals for coming to grips with the challenges posed by advertising range over a host of possibilities. Most extreme are those who would ban, curtail, restrict or tax advertising. Then there are the self-regulators and the government regulators. There are also some who put a lot of faith in the more effective organization of consumer groups to rate consumer products, sponsor counter advertisements, pursue class action suits and so on.

A compelte ban on advertising is probably out of the question for the time being even though some advertising executives fearing the worst have tried to speculate on the supposed disaster which would overcome society if their allegedly critical role was eliminated. The following appeared in *The Financial Post*:

Naturally, the whole idea went through Parliament like shibboleth through a goose. By using various legal devices, the government avoided the usual first, second and final readings and got the thing into effect from midnight that night.

Advertising was made unlawful and thus, with a stroke of the pen, more than $1000 million was eliminated from gross national product . . . about $50 a year was "saved" per capita. The terrible burden of 7¢ a day was removed from every man, woman, and child in Canada. Public response was staggering. Crowds gathered on Parliament Hill to cheer. Motocycle brigades swept across the countryside chopping down billboards. One zealot got a concussion when a 24-sheet poster board fell on him. It read, "Wear your safety helmet."

People built huge bonfires of direct mail literature from Time, Reader's Digest, Playboy. Cosmopolitan burned very fast. Hot stuff. The heat from department store catalogues alone made the daffodils bloom in Queen's Park.

On the third day, people across the country hastened to their favorite newstands to get a newspaper and find out what was happening.

David Lewis went to the cigar store and asked for the Ottawa Citizen.

"I kept one for you, Mr. Lewis. That'll be two bucks."

[19] Nicholas Cotter, "Manipulation Issue Cannot Be Dismissed", *The Globe and Mail*, Toronto, March 28, 1973.

"Two bucks!" Lewis shouts. "What kind of a corporate ripoff is this?"

"It's a publisher's ripoff," says the dealer. "They're charging me a buck ninety a copy. I had to lay out $330 in cash for my papers today.

"The Citizen guy told me that 75% of their revenue comes from advertising and with no ads, the cost of publishing the paper is two bucks a copy."

"But this paper is only eight pages," says Lewis. "I use the Ottawa Citizen to wrap the garbage in — this isn't thick enough to wrap an order of fish and chips in."

"My wife will be bloody mad on Thursday," the news dealer told the great statesman. "She loves to plow through those supermarket ads to see where the best bargains are. The Citizen guy told me statistics show that just as many women read the Eaton's and Simpsons' ads as read the front-page news."

The ad ban really wrecked the television industry. More than 90% of a private station's income is from commercials.

The CBC ran National Film Board releases until people called up to say they were sick of watching Eskimos. Then two Eskimos called and said: "Where the hell is 'All in the Family'?"

The CBC brass was in a real sweat because the corporation takes in more than $35 million a year in ad revenues. Budgeting had to be adjusted. Hundreds of people were let go.

The mandarins had decided to go all-out on the ad ban. Instructions were given to the Department of Transport and, by Day Three, weird-looking tin shacks were being put up at key points along the world's longest undefended border.

A highly efficient jamming apparatus went into action and all commercials beamed from U.S. stations were converted into a kind of pink snow on color sets. People sat during these bleak moments and yelled at one another.

There are just so many times when you can go to the bathroom.

Over in Place Bonaventure, Montreal, thousands of members of ACTRA (the actors and actresses) from across Canada gathered to protest the advertising ban. The residuals had stopped coming in. Mrs. Fred Davis had to get rid of her dog.

Actors and actresses were reduced to consuming the free products they had taken home for years after making commercials.

Pierre Berton, who won't do commercials but who allows his show to be sponsored by all kinds of people like Quaker Oats, Vick's, Alberto Culver and Ponds — he threatened to write another book — on the CNR.

Artists and photographers who couldn't exist without advertising pulled up tripods and left.

Advertising contains a bit of the pride of the manufacturer in every ad. They do brag a bit.

On the morning of Day Five, a meeting was being held in Procter & Gamble's board room. A young genius in the product research department had discovered a new detergent that would get clothes cleaner than Tide, whiter than Cheer and once used, would actually make water algae-free without antipollution devices.

"Boy, oh boy," the research man chortled. "Just wait until our brand men hear about this one. We'll kill Lever and Colgate."

Well, they put on a big demonstration at this meeting for the brand men. There was no reaction. The men were fidgeting, making excuses to actually leave the room to take telephone calls.

In the middle of the demonstration, one of the top men announced that he had just accepted a job in Holland. Shortly after that, another brand man said he had taken a post at York University to teach the history of competition in business.

With no advertising, you see, there was no more need for brand men, product managers and the rest. For product labels all you need is a good lawyer.

The research and development men were stunned. They had always believed, along with Ralph Waldo Emerson, "if you build a better mousetrap, the world will beat a path to your door."

No dice, P & G's president explained to the eager research people: "You have a great new product, boys, but experience teaches us that we must bring new products to the attention of the consumer or she will never think of changing her normal buying patterns. If you relied on word of mouth it would take years. Not worth the investment."

Canadian Manufacturers' Association sent a cable to the Prime Minister. (It got into the Guinness Book of Records as the world's longest.)

It reminded him of all the new ideas of great value to the public which were introduced over the years — nylons in place of silk stockings, frozen foods, toothpaste with fluoride, Metrecal, J-cloths, anti-histamines, cake mixes, automatic gear shifts on the 1947 Oldsmobile, Shell gasoline with TCP, radial tires, the snowmobile, instant coffee, no-defrost refrigerators, self-cleaning ovens, travelers' cheques, electric typewriters, the Xerox machine, Band-Aides, the computer, packaged vacations for ordinary working people and the Volkswagen.

None of those things would have been economically feasible for the creators, the producers, the manufacturers to introduce without the impetus and the sales continuity made possible by advertising.

Postmaster General André Ouellette was upset and told his colleagues so.

"We've banned advertising and we've just thrown away about $50 million in revenues from direct mail," he said. "As a matter of fact, the incongruity of this whole bloody thing is that we've been telling Canadians about the $50 million and the jobs it creates in a series of advertisements in Time magazine."

Members of the cabinet were subdued — especially when they had to approve an immediate increase in postage for first-class mail from 8¢ to 12¢ to cover the deficit.

The only people who weren't particularly bothered by the advertising ban were the agencies. Some of the writers and artists caught planes for South America where there is booming growth and a ravenous appetite for good creative people. The account executive quickly went to work for Information Canada or used car dealers.

People expected a fantastic drop in prices when advertising stopped. All those university professors keep yelling about the high cost of advertising so who can doubt it? But it turned out that for gasolines when you canceled *all* the contests, the giveaways and the advertising, it came to less than half a cent a gallon.

On detergents — everybody's pet beef — if you took all the money

278

spent on all the brands and gave it back to people, it would amount to about 50¢ a year per person.

Bud Drury, Treasury Board boss, told the PM that in some communities food prices were actually *rising*. Without the food ads shouting competitive prices, the supermarket operators could ease the price up a little here and there because people couldn't compare prices in the papers.

They formed a ministry for the suppression of advertising. The debate began: what is advertising? They had a representation from Health Minister Marc Lalonde. They were advertising that cigarette smoking is harmful to the health. The ministry ruled that you had to take the bad with the good and cancelled the campaign.

They felt that the right color for all packages would be gray, with type only — all the same style like highway signs. They banned all store signs. King St. in Hamilton looked like the parade ground of the Kingston Penitentiary.

Labor Minister John Munro had a lineup of delegations waiting to see him.

First came spokesmen for the Papermakers' Union.

"Our industry employs and supports the families of about 75,000 Canadians," he said. "We were hurt years ago — when TV came on the scene and killed hundreds of newspapers all over North America — there used to be 10 in New York alone and now there are three. The Telegram was killed in Toronto, too, and lots of papers died in Britain — papers using our products. Now, you've just about destroyed our industry and most of our jobs. How many people does it take to make Kleenex and toilet paper?"

Lobbyists spoke for 10,000 of their colleagues in the printing and distribution trades and another group stood to speak for some 19,000 people who were collecting their pink slips from the television and radio industry.

There were delegations from the ink makers, from the film manufacturers, from the engraving industry, from the typesetters and metal shippers and processing trades as well as a lady who spoke for a company that makes balloons to sell beer.

The Minister of Labor went back to the cabinet meeting.

"I have to tell you lads that when we banned advertising we cut gross national product by a billion dollars. But we also seem to have eliminated about one billion dollars' worth of jobs. Not to mention at least $200 million in tax revenues from individual taxpayers, and I haven't started to calculate the loss of corporation taxes. . . .

All right, let's stop there. Of course, I'm not seriously suggesting that the world would come to a stop if advertising were to be eliminated.

What I have tried to illustrate is that advertising is a working part of our economic ecology. Sure, some advertising is silly. Some of it is irritating. But most advertising is efficient and informative. It serves the purpose of stimulating competition, of keeping things moving. It does help to generate sales, work and jobs in many service and product categories.

I am constantly told that advertising creates unnecessary desires and wants. Well, what's unnecessary? The man who prints the detergent packages needs his wage just as much as anybody else. I challenge anyone to show me and prove to me that a particular product or service has been

279

forced on him or her personally — by advertising — more than once. Maybe you can fool the consumer once, not twice.

Our world is far from perfect. It is still one of the most prosperous, growing countries in the world. A small part of the mix is the part played by advertising. It seems to be part of the whole marketing ecology. Advertising is far from perfect.

The world *with* advertising may be glittery, noisy, and brash. The world *with* advertising may be upward-moving, ambitious, the world *with* advertising may be a bit gaudy and playful.

The world *without* advertising is Russia.[20]

The reasons why at least a partial ban on advertising cannot be ruled out should be obvious. There are several circumstances under which such a proposition should receive serious consideration. The first of these is a no-growth situation which is not as speculative today as it once was. Indeed, one experienced American diplomat has gone so far as to suggest that the world may actually be heading into a state of falling instead of rising expectations:

During the '60's we used to hear a great deal about "the revolution of rising expectations." What was usually meant was the growing recognition among the populations of poor countries that, thanks to technology, they no longer needed to be as poor as they had been, and the national and social revolutions to which this recognition gave rise.

To some extent the term could have been also applied, though in a more pacific sense, to the rising expectations and increasing satisfactions of both white- and blue-collar classes in rich countries, whose standard of living was of course rising far more rapidly than those of the peoples of poor countries.

Today there seems all too solid reason to fear that this decade, in contrast with the '60's, may be characterized by widespread "revolutions of falling expectations," affecting both developed and less-developed countries, but most seriously the latter.[21]

Today, with shortages in a variety of key materials, including many sources of energy, a strong case can be made either for severe restraints on the advertising of such materials or for a drastic reorientation of such advertising in the direction of conservation. In this spirit, the Province of Ontario's Minister of Energy has called upon the advertising industry to adopt a "conservation ethic." *The Globe and Mail* reports:

Ontario Energy Minister Darcy McKeough believes the advertising business must accept a "conservation ethic" if it is to contribute to a restoration of "lost (public) confidence" in industry.

Mr. McKeough is upset by the superficial approach represented in some current energy-related advertising.

"There's no sense whatever in vast government campaigns to educate and inform the public . . . to counter incomplete, misleading information from other sources," he said, adding advertising and public relations have a key role to play in providing balanced and accurate information.

[20] John S. Straiton, "The Day Canada Banned Advertising. . .', *The Financial Post*, February 17, 1973.
[21] Charles W. Yost, "Revolutions of Falling Expectations", *The Christian Science Monitor*, April 4, 1974.

280

Mr. McKeough's department launched a $300,000 crash advertising program on energy conservation last fall as potential fuel problems loomed. The campaign was prepared by Foster Advertising Ltd. of Toronto.

Now, the department is preparing a new, over-all energy conservation program, for which advertising is being considered.

The minister has strong views about the way energy-related advertising is being presented by some areas of the private sector.

He suggests that conservation advertising by utilities and by governments has been negated to some extent by other forms of advertising that exhort consumers to buy heavy energy-consuming products.

Mr. McKeough cites as "misleading" and "irresponsible" advertising aimed at potential car buyers to get them to stay with large, energy-consuming cars.

"This kind of ethic that this represented is precisely the opposite to what we need to solve not only our energy problems, but many of society's other problems."

A major objective of the new conservation program will be the development of a conservation ethic. "It's something our ancestors had and, after our orgy of consumption over the past 20 or 30 years, I think we need it again. . . ."[22]

There are two other areas where there is a case for putting some restraints on traditional advertising practices, and these areas tend to overlap. The first is industries where there is little to differentiate the products except for ad-induced brand preferences and any resulting shifts in market shares make no difference in terms of costs or prices. The beer and cigarette industries provide excellent examples of this sort of situation. Then there are cases where advertising has come to assume such a significant proportion of the total costs of the product or service that the consumer might be better off were all advertising to be ruled out or drastically cut back.

One of the standard arguments raised against any kind of a ban on advertising should be dismissed almost out of hand. This is the school that stresses how much the cost of most of the media would go up if the advertising revenue was cut off. That is true enough on the face of it, but the point is that the consumer ultimately pays the price anyway. After all, it is the customer who bears the expense of advertising when he buys products, so that when it comes to the media, he either pays for it directly or indirectly. Given the choice, many a reader or viewer of the media would probably prefer to pay more directly for that media if it were to be free of interfering ads. He would undoubtedly have an even stronger preference in this respect if he could also be assured of paying less for media indirectly through lower prices for those products otherwise bearing a large component of media promotion costs.

Short of an outright ban on advertising, one authority, in *Business and Society Review/Innovation*, has identified four possibilities not including regulation of the content of advertising — another approach to be dealt with here.

As for direct regulation itself, there are four possible forms, each with particular advantages and disadvantages:

1. Direct limitation on advertising expenditures;
2. Economic penalties for advertising;

[22] Nicholas Cotter, "Energy Minister Urges Advertising Industry to Adopt 'Conservation Ethic' for Public Good", *The Globe and Mail*, Toronto, May 15, 1974.

3. Economic incentives for reduced advertising; and
4. Reduced access to the media.

Each proposal is worth examining in detail.

DIRECT LIMITATION ON ADVERTISING EXPENDITURES

The most direct way of regulating advertising expenditure is to establish a ceiling on absolute dollar expenditures, advertising expenditure increases, advertising-sales ratios, or some other variable. Specifically, three alternative types of limitation are possible.

The first is an advertising freeze, in which companies are not allowed to spend more (in absolute or percentage terms) than they are currently spending on advertising. . . . The second is an advertising growth ceiling in which companies are allowed to increase their annual advertising budget up to a certain amount or percentage. . . . The third is an advertising reduction in which companies are required to trim advertising budgets by a specified amount or percent a year. . . .

It is hard to conceive of circumstances that might justify any of these forms of direct limitation as a permanent measure across all industries. . . .

If, instead of an advertising freeze, advertising was allowed to rise (or required to fall) by a certain amount or rate a year, further inequities would rise. If the regulated variable was advertising dollars, a small company could increase its budget by the same number of dollars as a company many times its size, a situation which might bring forth cries of inequity from the large companies. On the other hand, consider what would happen if the regulated variable was a percentage. If, for example, companies were allowed to increase their advertising expenditures by up to 2 percent, a company spending $10 million a year could spend another $200,000 but a company spending $1 million a year could only spend another $20,000. The large company could buy ten times as much additional advertising exposure as the smaller firm.

These economic objections to a limitation on advertising expenditures are substantial enough to warrant avoiding it as an across-the-board solution for all industries.

There may be less drastic solutions than placing a direct limit on total advertising. The use of economic disincentives or incentives, industry self-regulation, and consumer education may be more feasible. We would conclude that direct limitation of advertising expenditures should not normally be used as a first line of defense against advertising inflation.

ECONOMIC PENALTIES

"Excessive" advertising expenditures may be effectively discouraged through the creation of economic disincentives. Companies remain free to spend what they wish on advertising but pay a price for doing this.

Economic disincentives can take two basic forms. The first is an advertising tax. A tax can be placed on all advertising expenditures or on advertising expenditures above a certain amount or percentage.

The second form of economic disincentive is an income tax disallowance. At present in the United States, all advertising expenditure is treated as a current expense against sales revenue. Consequently, company profits are reduced exactly by the amount spent on advertising. Thus advertising expenditures cost a firm only 50 cents instead of a dollar because of the 50 percent tax on corporate income. This has led to the suggestion that the income tax treatment of advertising expense be tightened up. An extreme proposal is to disallow advertising altogether as a tax-deductible expense. This would be an unprecedented treatment of a normal business expense, placing it in the category of dividends or charitable contributions which come out of profits. A more modest proposal is to allow companies to expense only part of their current advertising expenditures.

Either form of economic disincentive — the advertising tax or the income tax disallowance — would probably have to be enacted on an all-industry basis. It would be hard to imagine requiring the detergent industry to pay a tax on advertising but not the auto industry. Such treatment would be declared unconstitutional as discriminatory legislation. It is more conceivable that the economic disincentive could apply to all industries but be varied by industry in the case of, say, a depreciation requirement. The depreciation rate for an industry would depend on how much advertising it devoted to long-run image building (a lower rate of depreciation) versus stimulating immediate sales (a higher rate of depreciation).

Certain undesirable economic consequences could be expected as a result of penalizing advertising expenditures. First, there would be a tendency of companies to switch funds to nonregulated forms of promotion. . . .

Second, an advertising tax would discriminate against companies which are advertising-intensive rather than sales force-intensive.

Third, corporations rarely end up as the actual payers of taxes. Instead, they shift part of the tax backward to suppliers and forward to consumers.

ECONOMIC INCENTIVES

Economic incentives to encourage the reduction of advertising are another possibility. No specific economic incentive schemes have been proposed to reduce advertising expenditures, although it is not hard to conceive of possible proposals. For example, companies in an industry that manage to reduce their advertising expense in a particular year might be granted a tax credit equal to, say, half the reduced advertising expenditure. Or they might receive a special tax break if they manage to bring down their advertising expenses for a few years in a row.

Economic incentives, like economic disincentives, raise certain questions of efficiency and equity. Firms can be assumed to have a natural incentive to bring down the costs of advertising without requiring an added incentive.

REDUCTION OF MEDIA AVAILABILITY

A fourth means of direct regulation would be government action to reduce the media time or space available to advertisers.

A less extreme form of regulation would be to require the media to reduce the time or space they allot to commercial messages.

The result of reducing a particular medium's availability would be to push up the costs of using that medium and shift advertising to the less expensive media. Presumably this will decrease advertising efficiency, since advertisers would have made the shift freely had it been efficient. Furthermore, total advertising costs would not fall proportionately because of the higher levels of advertising costs per time or space unit.

In short, it would make little sense to apply any of the approaches to direct regulation across-the-board to all industries because of these unwanted consequences. Nonetheless, some form of direct regulations as well as some of the other broad approaches to limiting advertising mentioned earlier might be appropriate to specific industries. For example, if an industry's deficiency lay in providing inadequate information about its product, consumer education would be the appropriate remedy. An industry-by-industry rather than across-the-board approach is called for. The main need, therefore is for a means of identifying and ranking problem industries so that the worst offenders against the consumer could be singled out first by antitrust agencies.[23]

As to the content of permitted advertising, the rallying cry of the industry, not surprisingly, is self-regulation. Judging by the progress which some groups have made in this matter, this is not an alternative to be dismissed lightly. The Canadian Advertising Advisory Board has made considerable progress, as this item from the Toronto Star suggests:

The image-makers of Canada's $1.3-billion-a-year advertising industry are straining to make self-policing work, now that the government is breathing down their corporate necks.

"We still feel that self-regulation is best and there is a very real concern about the proliferation of government regulations," said J.S. Crosbie, vice-chairman of the Canadian Advertising Advisory Board (CAAB).

Prosecutions under the Combines Investigation Act are growing more numerous and Quebec has moved into regulation of advertising.

Advertisers also felt a chill when the former Social Credit government of B.C. banned all tobacco and alcoholic-beverage advertising in that province. The New Democratic government has promised to repeal it.

In its efforts to control false, misleading and bad-taste presentations, the industry has killed lingerie ads showing a man's hands around a girl's bare waist, made a manufacturer withdraw an "anti-colic statement" on packages of baby-feeding nipples and generally tried to raise standards all round.

Competition being what it is, red-hot, and the ingenuity of copywriters almost boundless, self-policing isn't easy.

It was five years ago that the advertisers looked into the mirror, grimaced and formed a self-regulating group. This policeman is the Advertising Standards Council, a child of the 14-year-old Canadian Advertising Advisory Board.

The board represents the advertising community and is financed by the advertisers themselves, the agencies who prepare the campaigns, and the newspapers, radio and TV stations that transmit them to the public.

The advisory board's annual budget is $180,000, roughly half of which is spent on the work of the standards council. The council has no statutory authority, but does carry considerable clout.

[23] Philip Kotler, Fred C. Allvine, and Paul N. Bloom, "It's Time to Cut Down on Advertising Waste", Business & Society Review/Innovation, Winter 1972-73, No. 4, pp. 11-14.

The billy and the handcuffs of the ad policeman are the Canadian Code of Advertising Standards and the Broadcast Code for Advertising to Children.

When complaints come in, R. E. Oliver, full-time president of the advisory board, finds his staff can settle 80 per cent of them. The tough ones are passed to the 16-member standards council.

Four members of the council are from the public, two of them nominated by the powerful Consumers' Association of Canada.

If the council decides a particular printed ad or a radio or TV commercial violates the code, it asks the advertiser for his point of view and considers it. If the council's views remain unchanged, the advertiser is asked to amend or withdraw the ad.

If he refuses, the council shows its disapproval by asking newspapers, radio and TV stations to reject it. They have always gone along with the council.

If a big campaign is involved, huge sums of money can go down the drain, especially if the agency handling the account hasn't an alternate campaign ready to go.

Oliver says the council always deals with the advertiser, not the agency, "because it's his product, his money and he's best qualified to judge whether or not he can substantiate his advertised claims."

Ninety per cent of the complaints reaching the standards council come from the public, with the rest from trade associations and competitors. In 1969-70, there were 1,500 complaints, of which 140 were sustained and action taken. In 1970-71, there were 1,005, with 105 sustained. For 1971-72, the total was down to 376, of which 80 were upheld, a much higher percentage.

It's impossible to tell from the totals whether the standards council is winning or losing in its policing job. Oliver attributes the decline in last year's figures to the fact that the advisory board joined the Canadian Chamber of Commerce in a campaign promoting national unity. The campaign, in which print and broadcast media contributed free space and time, replaced the usual campaign inviting complaints about misleading ads and commercials.[24]

That the incentive for such self-regulatory bodies is not altogether altruistic is suggested by two articles. Excerpts from the first, which appeared in *Business Week*, indicate what induced Madison Avenue to move as quickly and on as many fronts as it has:[25]

If there is one thing that Madison Avenue frets about with considerable regularity, it is the "image" that advertising has in most people's minds. To the admen their profession is perfectly respectable. But they are nevertheless always worried that some organ of government will impair the right of their clients to advertise what they please, when they please, and how they please.

Each time there is a danger that new restrictive legislation is about to be enacted, Madison Avenue whips up a campaign defending its virtue, its good citizenship, and its inalienable right to exist.[25]

[24] Ron Lowman, "Canada's Advertisers Start Setting Their House in Order", Toronto *Star*, November 22, 1972.
[25] "Madison Avenue Hurries to Mend Its Fences". Reprinted from the October 23, 1971 issue of *Business Week* by special permission. Copyright 1971 by McGraw-Hill, Inc.

The second article draws on British as well as North American experience to reveal how the real motivation for self-regulation is fear of further state intervention:

Self-regulation in the advertising industry may be difficult and restrictive, but it is far better than the alternative "straight-jacket" of government legislation.

This advice to the advertising industry — from Roger A. Purdon, vice-president and director of the National Advertising Division of the Council of Better Business Bureaus of the United States — was really the keynote of yesterday's International Symposium on Advertising Self-Regulation, held in Toronto.

Other speakers at the meeting included John Braun, secretary, Advertising Standards Authority of Britain; Ole Falck, secretary, Danish Advertising Tribunal; and R. B. Collett, secretary of the Advertising Standards Council, the regulatory arm of the Canadian Advertising Advisory Board (CAAB).

The CAAB organized the seminar believed to be the first of its kind.

Advertisers throughout much of the world face similar problems in their relations with government and consumers. The advertising industry's response to these problems has been the same in many countries — establishment of self-regulatory industrial bodies.

Mr. Purdon said advertisers have "crossed over into a strange new land where the permissiveness of government and the patience of the consumer may be things of the past.

"And if we don't regulate ourselves to meet the new challenges that exist in this strange new land, very possibly someone else is going to do it for us (in government).

Mr. Braun said the concern about advertising regulation by many governments is indicated by a resolution adopted by the ministers of the Council of Europe in March on the need for adequate legislation to control misleading advertising, and calling upon member states to encourage the establishment of professional organizations to develop fair advertising practices, to encourage the establishment of self-disciplinary bodies and to make similar moves to eliminate advertising abuses.

The Canadian Advertising Advisory Board falls between the British and U.S. systems in its approach, according to Mr. Collett.

"Our operation has deliberately cut away as much detail as possible to get to the core problem: find the unethical advertisements and get rid of them.

"In doing so, we have inevitably raised some hackles; we have also demonstrated the capacity of this industry to police itself by positive action to remove unacceptable advertising quickly and effectively."

The policing work is done through the Advertising Standards Council, the ethics arm of the board. The council was originally made up solely of industry professionals, but one-third of the members now represent the public.

If a request for changes in an advertisement is ignored by the advertiser, the council asks the media to stop accepting it.

Mr. Collett said that despite the existence of these self-regulatory bodies, legislation continues to be passed that restricts advertising.

"What we can do is exert an important influence on the amount and the content of government regulation. We can help turn what are often impractical, unnecessary and unduly restrictive proposals into practical and reasonable regulations with which the industry can live."[26]

As effective as self-regulation has proven in some instances, in general it suffers from two major deficiencies. In the first place, it tends to be introduced only after public pressure for some sort of government intervention has risen to the point that something has to be done; more often than not, self-regulation emerges as a desperate last-minute effort to forestall more vigorous state policing of whatever has raised the consumers' ire to fever pitch. Second, and in the long run far more significant, is the problem of enforcement. No voluntary codes or guidelines can ever be as rigorously imposed as those put into effect by government. In 1973, for example, the Province of Quebec's Minister of Financial Affairs criticized the aforementioned Canadian Advertising Advisory Board and other similar groups for their inability to enforce their edicts:

If advertisers can't create their own code of ethics, then we'll do it for them.
That's the challenge laid down recently by Quebec's minister of Financial Institutions, William Tetley.
And he's not bluffing. His department has already taken a firm regulatory step by laying down strict guidelines in the Consumer Protection Act for advertising directed to children.
This time, he's aiming his barrage at four major industry sectors: credit and finance companies, banks, manufacturers of drugs and patent medicines, and carpet manufacturers and dealers.
His plan points up the limited effectiveness of the Canadian Advertising Advisory Board (CAAB), a self-regulatory body which has been trying to police the ad industry for the past few years.
Since 1967, the Advertising Standards Council (ASC — the branch of the CAAB set up to adjudicate complaints) has received about 3,000 complaints and sustained about 350 of them.
All the ads deemed to violate the Canadian Code of Advertising Standards were either adjusted or withdrawn.
In no case yet has it been necessary to discipline an advertiser, says ASC Director Robert Marvin. If an advertiser did refuse to comply with the ruling, the CAAB could ask the media to suspend the offending ads.
The ASC also adjudicates a voluntary Broadcast Code for Advertising to Children, which came into effect Jan. 1, 1972, a few months before Quebec's regulations.
But Tetley feels that many existing codes of ethics are frequently useless because they're not firmly enforced, and in the case of many offenders, can't be because the wrongdoers are not subject to the group that established the code.
"The Canadian Carpet Institute has a code of advertising ethics," he says, "but not all the advertisers are members.
"You have rug companies calling themselves distributors when they're really retailers."
Tetley's initiative in introducing provincial regulations alarms most advertisers, who feel the job should be in Ottawa's lap.

[26] John Simpson, "Self-Regulation in Advertising Industry Is Considered Restrictive, but Better than Government Legislation", The Globe and Mail, Toronto, November 22, 1972.

So far, however, the federal government has scrupulously avoided regulating the content of ads, preferring simply to press criminal charges against false or misleading representations.

Since 1960, when misleading advertising was switched from the Criminal Code to the Combines Investigation Act, 348 prosecutions against misleading advertising have been launched, leading to 237 convictions.

The pace has speeded up considerably in the past three years, says Misleading Advertising division chief J. W. Fell.

Figures for the latest fiscal year ended March 31 show that 131 prosecutions were launched under Sections 36 and 37. Eighty-one cases were completed during the year, and 50 are still before the courts.

Fell's investigative staff in Ottawa and the six regional offices tend to have a background in police work, because of the criminal-law element involved. They initiate their own investigations or follow up on complaints from consumers, working on an average of 20-25 cases at a time.

Like the CAAB, the Misleading Advertising division gets many more complaints than it acts on.

The complaints, which bulge sharply around Christmas, average about 300 a month.

"We just don't have the manpower to go after all the situations that come to our attention, which, if investigated far enough, might disclose evidence of an offense," says Fell.

"We have to make a decision on which ones we should go after."

Documenting a case usually takes about four months, since the investigator is working on several cases at a time.

The Combines Investigation Act contains a unique provision allowing a group of six citizens to make a formal complaint and force the government to launch an inquiry.

However, this provision is rarely used.

"We get maybe 20 formal complaints a year, so it's usually up to the director to decide if there's reason to draw up an inquiry."

In one definite area of consumer dissatisfaction, however, the ad industry has jumped the gun on the regulators — and it seems to be successful. That's in the ticklish question of advertising "clutter."

Acting together, eight TV stations and three networks in Canada's richest markets worked out a Clutter Code, which came into effect April 2 after a one-year warning period.

The code's main provision is a ban on 30-second commercials in which more than one distinct product or service is advertised.[27]

Whatever the cause, government intervention in the advertising arena is increasing at a rapid rate, particularly in Canada, which, for a long time, was well behind the United States in this field. As for the latter, the most intriguing recent developments have surrounded the ad substantiation program under which advertising agencies and their clients can be summoned before the Federal Trade Commission to validate claims made in their ads. Failure to back up their assertions give rise to a variety of remedies including mandatory corrective advertisements. Together with his consideration of other developments taking place in the consumer protection field in the United States, one author-

[27] Ellen Roseman, "Quebec Pushes Advertisers to Enforce Code of Ethics", *The Financial Post*, May 19, 1973, p. 14.

ity concludes his exhaustive analysis of the ad substantiation program on a fairly optimistic note:

So long as there are advertisers, there will be unsubstantiated advertisements if there is no effective regulation. Thus, there is a continuing need for a substantiation program. The FTC program, as it stands now, has problems and is subject to many criticisms, but improvements can be made as the program continues and areas for improvement become more obvious. The Truth in Advertising Act would correct some, but not nearly all the flaws. Other measures, such as a private right of action may correct more. Newer programs, presently unformulated, may close more of the problem areas. Whatever happens, a positive beginning has been made to insure that the consumer no longer will be misled.[28]

Meanwhile in Canada, both the federal and provincial governments are moving forward in a number of areas of concern to consumers. In the works for some time now at the federal level has been a new Competition Act which is hoped to substantially tighten up on advertisers in terms of their standards of truthfulness. Indicative of the depth of concern this and other features of the new bill have evoked among advertisers is a *Globe and Mail* account of their initial reaction to the first draft bill which, despite some more recent revisions, still does not begin to meet their objections:

The proposed federal Competition Act has been attacked in a brief from the Canadian Advertising Advisory Board for its wide-sweeping language and its restrictive effects on business in general and advertising in particular.

The brief was presented by the board to the Department of Consumer and Corporate Affairs.

It makes special note of the "credulous man" test for determining what is misleading advertising as proposed by the competition bill. The bill stipulates that advertising will be deemed misleading if "a credulous man would be misled" by it.

"The bill seems to regard representations which are misunderstood by a careless or foolish reader — and yet create no hardship or damage — as reprehensible as representations which are in fact untrue," the brief says. "We doubt if this was the intent; if it was, we profoundly disagree."

The brief makes reference to a legal opinion on the subject of the credulous man from a lawyer who purports to have found no dictionary reference to the word "credulous" that would have any legal meaning.

The brief quotes the lawyer as saying that for the word "credulous" could be substituted the word "stupid", in the context of the proposed Competition Act.

In a telephone interview, George Orr, director of the trade practices branch of the Department of Consumer and Corporate Affairs, said the purpose of the credulous man reference is not intended to preclude all puffery in advertising.

"As I have said previously, we have no intention of prosecuting an advertiser because the little green men do not emerge from the can when it is opened," said Mr. Orr.[29]

---

[28] "The F.T.C. Ad Substantiation Program", *The Georgetown Law Journal*, Vol. 61, July 1973, p. 1452.
[29] "Competition Act Wording, Curbs Decried by Advertising Group", *The Globe and Mail*, Toronto, December 16, 1971.

At the provincial level in Canada, Ontario has been as active as any province in the promulgation of new legislation to protect consumers from undesirable advertising and marketing practices. A review of the Ontario situation reveals that, while much has already been done, more remains, and there are some nagging doubts about enforcement.

The introduction by the Ontario Government of Bill 55, the Business Practices Act, adds an important new dimension to the province's consumer protection program and could, if effectively deployed, become one of the most promising bulwarks against the manipulation of consumers by dishonest and unscrupulous businessmen.

In the long run it should also engender greater confidence in the market-place by ridding it of disreputable elements and therefore prove beneficial to the great proportion of merchants who carry on business with honesty and integrity.

Until now the principal thrust of Ontario's consumer protection legislation has been in two directions. On the one hand, by the adoption of licencing requirements the province has attempted to regulate entry into abuse-prone trades and occupations by weeding out individuals with unsavory records and subjecting licencees to a more or less strict regime of supervision. On the other hand, the Consumer Protection Act, first adopted in 1967, was designed to deal with a variety of abuses in door-to-door sales and consumer credit transactions.

Both approaches have their weaknesses. It is not practical to licence every trade or business just to eliminate the abuses of a few. Nor, in view of its limited reach, is the Consumer Protection Act capable of dealing with the many unethical or deceptive practices not associated with itinerant sellers or credit transactions. It would have been theoretically possible to amend the act each time a new abuse came to light, and indeed it has been frequently amended, but this process is time-consuming and merely invites the unscrupulous merchant to dream up new devices to circumvent the act.

The Business Practices Bill seeks to resolve this impasse by imposing an omnibus prohibition on all unfair practices and empowering the director of the business practices division of the Ministry of Consumer and Commercial Relations to obtain a prohibitory order from the Commercial Registration Appeal Tribunal (CRAT).

Unfair practices are divided into two principal classes, those involving "false, misleading or deceptive consumer representations" and those involving an element of unconscionability by taking advantage of a consumer's physical, educational or economic disabilities, or other inability to bargain effectively. The bill enumerates specific types of unfair practices under each of these headings and also empowers the government to add to the shopping list by regulation. The flexibility introduced by these means are part of the great strength of the bill and also, as seen by some business observers, a source of potential danger, but more about this later.

There is no novelty about the first class of prohibited practices. False and misleading representations and advertisements are already prohibited in Sections 36 and 37 of the federal Combines Investigation Act, but the federal provisions are exclusively criminal in character and long experience has shown that the criminal law is not always an appropriate route for enjoining misleading representations. Here lies another important strength in the Ontario bill. It clearly envisages the CRAT's injunctive power as the primary vehicle of enforcement, and since this device involves no retroactive penalty it is likely to attract much less business hostility than the stigma of a criminal prosecution.

Business objections to date have focused on the broad criteria of unconscionable practices set forth in Section 2(b) of the bill. They are indeed wide and if the director were the judge of unconscionability in a particular setting there would be cause for concern. But he is not. The Tribunal is, and from the Tribunal there is a full right of appeal to the regular courts. The courts have long been accustomed to dealing with issues of unconscionability. One of the earliest functions of the Lord Chancellor in England was to grant relief against harsh bargains in the name of equity and good conscience.

This process was temporarily arrested in the nineteenth century, in the face of laissez-faire economics, but has resumed its career during the present century. Increasingly the courts have appreciated that there is no genuine equality of bargaining power between the average consumer and the professional supplier of goods and services who relies on a standardized contract in small print whose contents the consumer cannot be expected to understand and would be powerless to change if he did.

So, once again, it will be seen that the bill does not innovate. It merely sets its stamp of approval on a doctrine which the courts have long sought to articulate, sometimes directly and more often indirectly. And moreover it is a doctrine which the Ontario Legislature (in common with the other provincial legislatures) embraced as early as 1912 when it empowered the courts to reopen lending transactions if the court found that the cost of the loan was excessive and unconscionable.

Though the main thrust of the bill is to be warmly welcomed, it is not free of defects. One of its most controversial features is Section 18(2) which imposes criminal penalties on a person who knowingly engages in an unfair practice.

This is objectionable on several grounds. First, so far as it involves deceptive representations, it duplicates the provisions in the Combines Act and may be unconstitutional. Secondly, it unnecessarily muddies the waters and may discourage reputable merchants from cooperating with the director to eliminate undesirable practices.

Also, there appears to be no precedent for punishing unconscionable practices which do not involve an element of deception. If the meaning of unfairness was clearly defined so that its application to specific situations could be easily determined, that would be one thing. Some of the criteria of unfairness in Section 2(b) are so broad that honest minds may differ as to their applicability in a given setting. It would not be fair to punish a businessman for guessing wrongly.

The regulation-making powers in the bill are also unsatisfactory. They are too narrow because it is not clear to what extent they may be used to give specificity to the broad categories of deceptive and other unfair practices enumerated in Section 2. They are too broad because the Government can apparently add to the list without giving prior notice or affording interested parties an adequate opportunity to make submissions before the regulations come into force. In practice, the Government will no doubt observe standards of due process, but the obligation to do so should be spelled out clearly.

In some respects the bill is also inadequate from the consumer's point of view. As we have seen, the CRAT may enjoin a supplier for continuing to engage in an unfair practice. The bill also confers a private remedy on aggrieved consumers by entitling them to avoid an agreement induced by an unfair practice.

This may be an appropriate remedy in some cases, but not in all. It may be too late for the consumer to avoid the transaction (as, for example, where he has received the benefit of the services or the goods have been consumed, or are no longer in his possession) and in other situations the consumer may wish to affirm the agreement but seek relief from an oppressive clause or an abatement in the price.

Another difficulty is that the bill requires the consumer to exercise his remedy within an unreasonably short period (three or six months depending on the nature of the unfair practice) and that it makes no provision for consumer class actions. This is a serious omission. Long experience has shown that consumers have a healthy distaste for litigation.

It is true that the bill does confer power on the CRAT to attach "terms and conditions" to the making of an order, but it is not clear whether these words include a full restitutionary power in favor of a class of consumers or the power to award damages and other forms of relief.[30]

Not to be neglected in any assault on the practices of advertisers is the role of organized consumer groups. Individually, customers are usually at an impossible disadvantage when tackling a large corporation which they believe to have taken unfair advantage of them. But collectively, a band of disgruntled consumers, even if organized on an *ad hoc* basis, can gain the attention of the highest level corporate officers if they threaten enough public furor over their complaints. In regard to consumer organization on a more continuing basis, a number of groups come to mind, especially in the United States which seems to have a somewhat longer and more varied history of consumer activism than Canada, except perhaps in the field of consumer cooperatives.

Probably the two most critical consumer groups in North America are the Consumers' Union in the United States and the Consumers' Association of Canada. Between them they publish *Consumer Reports*, which although basically an American consumer products rating service, also rates some Canadian equivalents. The Consumers Union of the U.S. has had widespread impact, although its reports have not always had a favourable reception:

For all the criticism, CU has had a definite impact on sales and product quality, many manufacturers believe. Westinghouse credits a favorable rating for a 20% jump in washing machines sales last year. Several years ago a Norge executive said flatly: "CU put us in the washing machine business."

Countless manufacturers have improved their products because of a CU rating. Some examples: Clevite eliminated a shock hazard in a stereo headphone, Remington corrected a tendency for its electric knife to jam, and Westinghouse improved the design of its electric boiler. "Smart

[30] Jacob S. Ziegel, "Enforcing a Consumer Bill", *The Globe and Mail*, Toronto, May 23, 1974.

manufacturers," says Dr. Robert Entenberg, professor of Marketing at the University of Denver, "use Consumer Reports to see if they can improve their products."[31]

The Consumers' Association of Canada depends primarily on voluntary memberships for its treasury but for the past few years has had to rely heavily on a subsidy from the Federal Government as well. This raises some intriguing questions, one or two of which will be dealt with here. The first concerns whether or not the government should engage in product testing on its own rather than leaving it to a voluntary association of consumers. Actually, where public health and safety are involved, the government does do a good deal of testing in its own laboratories. Beyond these areas, there would seem to be no reason why it should not help fund groups like the CAC. The other side of the coin is, of course, whether such groups should accept this funding. Although sometimes they virtually have no other choice, this does not really answer the question. It might be preferable if a tax were to be placed on advertising with a pre-designated share of the revenue derived going to the C.A.C. and similar organizations engaged in objective product rating, counter advertising and the like. If something like this were done, then bodies like the CAC could really work for the consumer. First of all, this would require continuing and much more extensive testing of products. Secondly, there would have to be an effective dissemination program to ensure that the results of such tests were readily available to the consumer. In Canada there is no reason why a regular nightly program could not be arranged to deal with comparative product ratings on a well scheduled basis. Thirdly, but only where necessary because of the failure of industry- or government-imposed regulations, there is every reason for a group like the CAC to engage in counter advertising where the original ad is so distasteful, unethical or dishonest as to require a rebuttal. Finally, groups like the CAC should be in the forefront of class action suits aimed at bringing corporations to financial task for any irresponsible actions affecting the consumer.

To end this prescriptive section, a minor point might be made about the hypocrisy which surrounds personal endorsements of products. Just how bad the situation has become in this sordid area of advertising is brought out in the following article:

When a movie star or baseball player waltzes grinning onto a TV screen to praise a product he knows nothing about, and fails to mention that he's getting paid $25,000 for his act, is it consumer fraud?

"Yes," says Betty Furness, New York city's commissioner of consumer affairs.

Maureen Stapleton disagrees. "As for associating my name with a product, well, everybody knows it's a big con game," she says. "But it's certainly not the same as throwing a ball game."

That's right, says Miss Furness, everybody does know it is a con game, so what does that say for American advertising and the manufacturers who hire these stars? And what does it say for celebrities' attitudes toward the consumer if they will endorse anything that pays them well enough?. . . .

Miss Furness says there is a strong distinction between the types of commercials in which celebrities appear. She should know, having been

31 "Consumers Union Puts on Muscle". Reprinted from the December 23, 1967 issue of *Business Week* by special permission. Copyright 1967 by McGraw-Hill, Inc.

synonymous with the Westinghouse refrigerator in the early days of television.

In one type of commercial, the star appears only as a performer, a vehicle for showing off the product. In the other the star actually endorses the product. And in 95 per cent of these cases, Miss Furness says, the star knows nothing about the product.

Miss Furness insists that she never endorsed Westinghouse refrigerators and that, for most of the time that she was showing them off, she never even owned one. "I was a performer," she recalls. "I was never concerned with the product. I was the hired help."

Now there is a new generation of commercial typified by the "Chet Huntley for American Airlines" spots that have appeared in recent months. Not only is it rare for a person who once called himself a newsman to make it big in commercials, but also, in his most recent commercial since leaving NBC News, Huntley sits in a set that resembles that of a TV news show.

"That's dirty pool," says Miss Furness.

The eagerness of stars to get into the commercial-endorsement business makes it sometimes seem like the capstone of their careers.

The very day after the New York Mets won their first World Series, an ad appeared in the New York Times announcing that pitcher Tom Seaver and his wife were taking offers to do commercials.

This shocked even Madison Avenue, since no one could remember people running commercials to do commercials. But the Seavers were soon in the TV big league, up there with Joe Namath and Henry Fonda and Raquel Welch, who reportedly got $30,000 to $40,000 to speak two lines in a Motorola commercial.

While many actors, particularly the more established ones, have shunned commercial work as undignified, many of them eventually succumbed late in their careers. The Claudette Colbert-Edward G. Robinson coffee commercial of the early 1960s was part of a trend that saw more serious actors plying wares. Now some of the bigger names actually talk about commercials as being "good exposure." That's the reason Henry Fonda gave for selling his services to GAF.

Ordinary mortals such as housewives and the like, also get paid to do commercial endorsements but they usually get peanuts compared to what the stars get.

Take the case of Larry Shelton, a retired meat cutter from San Diego. One day he just started off to walk across the country. When he got to St. Charles, Mo., he found an abandoned shopping cart and decided it would be good for carrying his belongings. Somewhere between St. Charles and New York a photographer took his picture and an official of the United Steel and Wire Co. of Battle Creek, Mich., spotted it in a newspaper. Recognizing it as one of its carts, the company scoured the east until it finally tracked Shelton down in New York.

Now Shelton appears in ads for United Wire and Steel shopping carts under the headline, "The most unusual shopping cart endurance test ever."

The company paid Shelton $200.

But then Shelton isn't Raquel Welch.[32]

One way to partially alleviate the hypocrisy which is involved in the

[32] "Those Star-Endorsed TV Ads Called a Fraud on the Viewer", Toronto *Star*, August 2, 1973.

practice of personal endorsements would be to require a little message at the end of these endorsements which would have to be read or signed by the endorser and which would say something like the following: "I (or We) are being paid . . . for saying such nice things about this product." Some will argue that to carry the case against the sordid world of advertising this far is absurd. That could well be so, but not if one believes that the immoral practices which pervade the advertising industry are more than symbolic of what afflicts many other parts of North American society.

SUMMARY AND CONCLUSION

Marketing, as earlier defined, will undoubtedly continue to have a legitimate role to play in the North American economy because the reduction of the cost of getting products and services from their source to the consumer will always have a role to play. So too will advertising, although conceivably to a much smaller extent — therefore making it a much more vulnerable target for attack.

As has been indicated here and elsewhere, the advertising industry, from its manipulation of children to its assault on society's underlying value system, has left itself exposed on all flanks. In a variety of hasty last-ditch efforts to stave off further public encroachment on its domain, the industry can be said to be trying to put its own house in order primarily through one form of supposed self-regulation or another. In these efforts, it is being prodded along not only by more and more critical governments, but by increasingly active consumer groups.

Self-policing cannot curb all the abuse, and state regulation is still bound to increase. At the same time, organized consumer vigilance, in the form of public interest groups, will develop at a similar, if not more intensive, pace, especially if supported by public funds as it should be.

The net result of all of these self-induced and external pressures for reforms will be an era of change in the advertising world which will last for some time to come:

Advertising is going through the most interesting period in its history.

If challenge is accepted as a valid stimulant to creativity — and creativity is the core of advertising — current and recent pressures on the international advertising business should precede interesting new creative directions.

This is a question not so much of evolving improved techniques as of change — a swift and direct break with advertising's traditional laissez-faire approach to the consumer market.

It is evident that advertising must do more than stay abreast of, or adapt to, new or shifting expectations. The problem of defining these expectations — not to mention anticipating what lies ahead — is a major challenge in itself.

Consider briefly some of the factors that are keeping the Canadian and, in part, the international advertising business in ferment:

— Continuing pressure by consumer groups demanding equal time, financed by public money, to counter the effects of some types of broadcast commercials could lead to similar demands for other media.

— The varying degrees of restrictiveness of government controls and the probability of more controls are still generating uncertainty and even confusion.

— An increasing government encroachment on media generally is prompted by an assumed concern about the direction of existing and emerging communications techniques and systems. The electronics communications sector, which is subject to tough licencing and regulatory controls, is an example. Provincial and federal government squabbling about jurisdiction over broadcast communications will continue;

— Despite recent nostaglia themes, there is less general consumer preoccupation with unrealistic glamor — still a hallmark of much advertising;

— Justified or not, there is continuing disillusionment with "progress", considered by many to be as much a contributor to social ills as a panacea;

This disillusionment, which may stem from unrealistic expectations, raises the question whether progress — a word with many interpretations — in any era has been considered a cure-all for prevailing social shortcomings:

— Disparities within society are emphasized by advertising. It is highly improbable that a decline in advertising appeals to status would change the situation one iota, but that is not the issue;

— The credibility of advertising generally is low. Whether it is at record low, as some suggest, cannot be determined in the absence of acceptable data on other decades;

— The volume of advertising directed at consumers daily threatens to make advertising a self-defeating process. It is estimated the "average" North American urbanite is exposed to more than 500 advertising messages daily through print, broadcast, billboards and direct mail.

People, it is suggested, are being turned off by advertising, by the so-called clutter of commercials on television and by the heavy ad content of some print media.

— Charges and test court cases involving false or deceptive advertising are besmirching both advertisers and advertising generally, whether or not they result in convictions;

— The move toward truth in advertising poses one of the toughest problems facing the business: untruth by omission.

These and other factors are, of course, known to many in advertising. A difficulty in coping with them effectively lies in the structure and nature of the business itself. It is segmented but national and retail advertising are lumped together by many consumers with unsightly posters, give-away sheets, unattractive neon advertising signs, and with the noise pollution that accompanies some urban sales and political propaganda.

Advertising is not a tight, homogenous entity to which effective, over-all policy approaches can be easily applied. The fragmented efforts under way to meet changing conditions reflect the structure of the business — agressive, individualistic and competitive.

It also raises some questions about the prevalent chatter in the advertising business about "social and moral consciousness and responsibility." This is related to the believability factor that admen desperately want to project.

The business will find that, to be believed, it will have to reflect these virtues through all its work and not through part of it or through laudable philanthropic causes. A blanket assumption by advertising of noble virtues is just as distorting as a blanket condemnation of all advertising as immoral and irresponsible.[33]

Just how far these changes may take the industry is a matter for speculation. Sometimes the speculation seems pretty far-reaching:

A new Puritanism — posing a potentially large array of problems and constraints — awaits the advertising community, if trends currently taking shape in Canada continue along their way.

That was the less than attractive future predicted by lawyer Reuben M. Bromstein at the Association of Canadian Advertisers' conference in Toronto last week.

Key indicators, Bromstein listed as:

● An increasing emphasis on antitrust measures designed to control marketing, and in particular to control the impact of high-volume advertising which is considered to lead to unusually high profits and domination of an industry by a few firms.

● An increasing pressure to minimize, or completely eliminate, advertising expenditures by controlling the number of available competing products, by banning advertising in certain product sectors, and by limiting advertising expenditures in certain product areas by one or more government techniques.

● Pressure to create moral standards (as opposed to truth standards) which advertising shall not breach.

Bromstein believes certain conditions already exist that will provide a fertile breeding ground for this new morality:

■ Commodity shortages combined with a society which is geared to consumption and which has paid little attention to the environment and waste.

■ A growing government influence in all areas of life combined with young idealist (or older) activists who concentrate their efforts on influencing government legislation.

■ A scapegoat (advertising is the scapegoat, Bromstein says).

The New Puritans will say government must protect people from themselves, that choices must be made for people who do not know how to make choices, and that consumers should no longer be able to choose between competing products, says Bromstein. They will decide which information concerning a product is permissible in advertising and which is not, and how much information should be supplied.

Bromstein acknowledges some of the above are extremes that, indeed, may not ensue. But he notes also the tendency for legislation based on legitimate grievances to assume, over time, wider application than that originally intended.

Why permit advertising of brand names when all gasolines are alike? Doesn't this waste newsprint? Why allow so many gasoline stations when land is in short supply? Why have two airlines on competing flight schedules when one can do the job and save gasoline?

These are just some of the questions the New Puritans will increasingly pose to the advertising community, says Bromstein, and which are already finding receptive ears in government circles.

[33] Nicholas Cotter, "Pressures Create Ferment in Advertising", The Globe and Mail, Toronto, November 22, 1972.

In addition, priorities may be established by decree, regardless of established consumer preferecnes. The emphasis on maximizing production and consumption, with its many benefits to the free market system, is falling into disrepute, he says. An emphasis on use, frugality, temperance and other puritan virtues may well come to the fore.

Thus, there will be increased emphasis on provable consumer needs and uses as opposed to discretionary consumer needs and uses. And there will be partisan efforts to influence the decision about what is needed or useful — since such decisions involve questions of judgment.

"By removing these decisions from the effects of competition and the marketplace, new weapons will be available to those who see advertising as evil and wasteful," Bromstein says.

"Legislation designed to create more competition is much more desirable than legislation that attempts to legislate attitudes and morality and which is inherently socialist in nature.

"The marketplace, if properly directed, can achieve the more legitimate aims required by contemporary society with less harmful side effects. However, even competition legislation can be misdirected and harmful if it is aimed solely at protecting consumers and not at protecting competitors."

Some of the contemporary issues concerning the effect of law and government on advertising Bromstein noted were:

• Government is now the largest single advertiser in the country. There will be more government advertising and these expenditures will influence media, advertisers and agencies. Informed observers are concerned about the dangerous implications of such massive spending power.

• More government corporations such as Petrocan will be marketing and will influence the advertising scene.

• New counter-advertising bodies will be created and funded by government and citizens' groups.

• The demand for informative copy will increase.

• The demands for substantiation of product claims will accelerate and be incorporated in different legislation at the federal and provincial levels.

• Consumer advocates will press for more meaningful remedies, which will include refunds, restitution and corrective advertising to take the profit out of cheating.

• There will be more class actions, such as the $5 million Firenza class action which breaks new legal ground.

• The issue over who has the right to control cable broadcasting raises the whole question of federal-provincial and constitutional jurisdiction that has yet to be resolved.

• If the provincial government's involvement in regulation of broadcasting increases, there will be more legislation such as the new Quebec rules on advertising that bans cartoons in children's advertising.

"There is no doubt that many of the problems which critics of advertising are attempting to deal with must be solved," Bromstein says, and "marketers and advertisers must share the responsibility for the current crisis."

And while "more legislation affecting advertising is inevitable, time has not run out," he says.

While advertisers can't prevent more legislation, they can directly affect the type of legislation that will be passed. They can become involved with government, with consumers, with lawyers and with other businessmen in developing legislation that solves the real problems of the contemporary marketing scene.

If the advertising industry develops a system of professionalism with built-in regulatory procedures designed to create a new sense of respect for the advertising practitioner, advertisers may still retain some measure of control over their industry, Bromstein says.[34]

What is perhaps most disturbing of all is the fact that it will take years to fully clean house in the advertising industry, if, indeed, that can ever be accomplished:

The fact remains, neither self-regulation nor government action alone, can successfully eliminate misleading advertising. What is needed, and what will continue to be needed for many years to come, is a multi-level approach encompassing all levels of government and individual and collective industry and consumer action to wrestle with this hydra-headed monster![35]

[34] Brian Roger, "How 'New Puritanism' May Affect Advertising Industry", *The Financial Post*, May 18, 1974, p. 9.
[35] Jacob S. Ziegel, "Advertising Debate", *Canadian Consumer*, August 1973.

8

THE PROFESSIONS
AND
THE TRADE UNIONS

This chapter attempts to come to grips with some of the more serious challenges posed by two increasingly significant groups in society. The first of these includes the traditional self-regulating professions such as law and medicine but also embraces the growing number of pseudo- or quasi-professional bodies which are emerging in every occupation from investment dealing to real estate. The second category covers individual unions and the labour movement as a whole, a category that hardly requires any elaboration.

The intriguing feature about these two sets of interest groups is that the distinctions which have conventionally set them apart are gradually receding into the background. Professional groups of one kind or another are slowly but surely acquiring more and more of the trappings of the typical trade union. Although not without some internal controversy, even as conservative and staid an organization as the American Medical Association is beginning to openly aspire to some of the same goals and objectives as the labour movement. Equally revealing is the fact that such an organization is now willing to resort on a less convert basis to some of the same strategies and tactics as the trade unions:

A major dispute is developing within the ranks of the American Medical Association over new guidelines that have been denounced as a big step toward unionization of all doctors and defended as a means of halting the association's loss of young doctors.

The guidelines, approved by the AMA board of trustees deal with the relationships between hospitals on one hand and interns and resident physicians in training, on the other.

The guidelines are presented as an outline of basic principles to be applied to contracts between hospital housestaff and the institution in which they serve.

Housestaff means interns, residents and other young physicians in training. They are employees of the hospital and participate in patient care but they are also being trained. Indeed the educational aspects of their programs are of prime importance.

The issue of contention rests on the following question: To what extent are educational programs for doctors amenable to contracts of the union-management type?

Opponents of the guidelines appear to be unhappy with repeated references to collective bargaining and the statement that collective bargaining contracts are recommended.

Dr. Henry D. McIntosh, chairman of the department of medicine at the Baylor College of Medicine and president of the American College of Cardiology, considers the guidelines a step toward unionization of doctors.

If the objective were to achieve unionization of doctors within 10 years, there could be no better way to achieve it than this, he has said. Dr. McIntosh argues that the attitudes developed by doctors during this crucial phase of training are likely to be permanent and that therefore a collective bargaining relationship during internship might be influential on the doctor's attitudes toward unionization for the rest of his career.

The doctor said he planned to testify against the guidelines during the AMA meeting. Whether he will do so as a department head at a major medical school or as president of the American College of Cardiology, has not yet been decided, a spokesman for the college said yesterday.[1]

Not surprisingly, some professional and quasi-professional groups are now trying to seek the best of both worlds. Teachers in Ontario have recently been condemned for pursuing just such a dual advantage:

Ontario's teachers have argued, with some logic, that they should be allowed to organize and bargain collectively with school boards and be considered a union in all respects, including the right to strike.

Fair enough. But if the Ontario Teachers Federation pursues a proposal adopted at the weekend, it will be asking for nothing less than sovereignty in the certification of teachers.

The federation wants the provincial government — the one elected by the citizenry at large, by the way — to relinquish the right to certify teachers. The federation wants teachers to have the same self-governing powers as the province's doctors and lawyers. If the plan is carried through, the federation, not the provincial government, would devise standards, set examinations and grant or withhold licenses.

Assertions that the public would have some voice in decision-making through an ill-defined advisory council are not reassuring. Allegiance to the profession has a way of supplanting concern for the service offered, in self-governing agencies.

Besides, teachers are not like doctors and lawyers. They deal with an entire segment of Ontario's population, the young. Doctors and lawyers deal with people on a need basis and are paid, wholly or in part, accordingly. Teachers are paid entirely out of general taxes.

If Ontario teachers want to be members of a professional union then they must grant their ultimate employer, the provincial government, certain management functions, one being the certification of teachers.

The provision of qualified teachers and their certification should remain right where it is, in the Ministry of Education, a department whose minister must stand in the Legislature to give an accounting.

The teachers federation cannot expect to be union, management and licensing authority all at once.[2]

That the professions are now in as much hot water with the public as unionized workers is reflected in growing government attempts to deal with

[1] "AMA Members Split Over New Guidelines", *The Globe and Mail*, Toronto, June 24, 1974. © 1974 by The New York Times Company. Reprinted by permission.
[2] "The Teachers Can't Have It Both Ways", *Toronto Star*, April 9, 1974.

their privileged position. Sometimes the reactions and counterreactions to these assaults on the professional bastions become quite vitriolic.

To hear John Farris tell it, if the bill before the Quebec National Assembly is passed, we will revert 350 years to the time when courts were ruled by politics and judges such as Lord Coke spent whole careers fighting for judicial independence.

Mr. Farris is president of the Canadian Bar Association and his startling view was delivered to the Canadian Club in Toronto. The effect of the proposed Professions Act in Quebec would be to jeopardize the independence of both bench and bar, he said.

The purpose of the bill is to protect the public against the fraud, malpractice and incompetence of members of 34 professions in Quebec including lawyers, doctors, dentists and architects. Most of the professions are governed under separate laws. The Professions Act is an attempt to centralize regulation.

The bill would turn Quebec's Interprofessional council into a legal entity to counsel the Government on the running of the professions; it would establish a three-member professions board to oversee the ethics, finances, bill-collecting procedures and indemnity arrangements of professional groups; and for each profession it would create a three-member disciplinary board which, in all professions, would be headed by a Government-appointed lawyer. There would be an appeal from a ruling of a disciplinary board to a panel of three Superior Court judges.

The Government would set down criteria by which "professional corporations" could be established and membership in a corporation would be required before a person could practice as a professional. Professions which did not have enough funds to meet their obligations or which showed a deficit would be placed under control of the Government board.

Generally speaking, the bill would allow the Government to maintain stricter control over the activities, disciplinary measures and fee schedules of the 34 professions named.

According to Mr. Farris, transferring responsibility for discipline from the governing body of a profession to what he calls a Government-dominated group, will compromise the political independence of lawyers and, since judges are appointed from among lawyers, will threaten the independence of the bench.

There are indeed aspects of the Quebec bills to which objections should be taken. But by predicting a cataclysm Mr. Farris risks rendering himself absurd. Mere Government presence does not, of itself, spell the end of independence. For instance, judges are all political appointments. Yet would Mr. Farris argue that they are therefore incapable of independence?

What Mr. Farris fails to recognize is that the public has grown apprehensive over its relations with professionals. It sees how lawyers stick together defensively when the subject of judicial involvement in plea and sentence bargaining comes up. It worries that coroners should have difficulty obtaining the ready co-operation of The College of Physicians and Surgeons of Ontario in investigations of medical mistakes resulting in death. It meets dentists who would whip denturists from the marketplace and so preserve the field of expensive dental plates for themselves.

None of these things would justify passage of Quebec's Professions Act. What they do is create a skepticism toward the professions that for a long time had been lacking. A skepticism that asks why there should not be more public involvement in the running of the professions.[3]

Given the new attention being devoted to the professions and their self-governing activities, it seems appropriate to start this chapter with a discussion of developments in their jurisdiction. There then follows a brief consideration of some widely debated issues concerning the position and power of the labour movement.

THE PROFESSIONS & THEIR REGULATION

No effort will be made here to try to define the term, "professional" or determine which groups are worthy of bearing that once august, but now somewhat commonplace and tarnished, title. On a fairly humorous note, it can at least be reported that the image of the professional is still so bright that it is widely sought after:

"I would like my daughter to marry a professional man."

How about a school custodian, lady? An opthalmic dispenser perhaps? Maybe even a public relations man?

"What's the matter, you don't know any nice doctors or lawyers? I'll even settle for a chartered accountant.

"To me, he's got to be independent, respected and give my Tessie — I mean Theresa — a fine house on . . .So, what's a school custodian?"

Remember the caretaker at John A. Beaverbook Public School? Later they called him "janitor," then superintendent . . . But this title is now "custodian."

"So, he's a professional man?"

Well, custodians may not be accepted as a profession by the public just yet. But they're trying awfully hard.

"Like the opthalmic watchamacallits?"

Why yes, they are legally recognized by the Ontario government through a provincial act. It sets up a licensing body which is supposed to watch over them to see that they protect the public. And if one is incompetent or unethical he's severely reprimanded. A professional is supposed to be personally liable to the public for errors.

"Aren't the opth . . . uh, these professionals eye doctors?"

No, actually they're not qualified to examine eyes. They're trained to fill prescriptions and dispense eye glasses to a doctor's specifications.

"Like my Joey, the pharmacist!"

Yes, lady, there have been a lot of new professions cropping up lately. That's due to new technology — opening up new advanced fields that need highly intelligent and trained people.

"I thought the computers were supposed to take over the world . . . My sister's son-in-law, he's a programmer. He says his 'profession' is going to be the most important. Do you think they'll replace chartered accountants?"

Oh, there'll be some professions that will have to change or be swept

[3] "Not Their Private Preserve", *The Globe and Mail*, Toronto, April 15, 1972.

away. Some have set up "professional status" committees like the engineers. And remember the old press agent. He's a professional public relations man now.

He's better educated, sophisticated, uses more ingenious techniques than the old huckster.

"I know, he takes special courses to use fancier words."

Ontario's industrial commissioners are asking for a university course that will give them "special training, established professional status and set terms of reference in order to avoid control by the political structure. . ."

"They're the ones bringing in all those dirty smoke-stacks into the suburbs."

But lady, we are emerging into a new socio-economic structure in which everyone is becoming a specialist. Menial and routine tasks are being handled by machines, releasing white-collar manpower to achieve greater heights.

"That means they'll make more money?"

Ah yes, and once they earn more they'll want professional status. Everyone tries to improve his image — for the public good, of course.

Unprofessional undertakers become professional funeral directors, hire a professional public relations man to write them a code of ethics and spread the news to the Fourth Estate.

"Where's that?"

That's the professional name for journalists.

"Those guzzling nogoodniks?"

Even investment dealers are calling themselves professionals.

"I thought a professional is someone who dedicates himself to his job. Making money is supposed to be secondary."

Well, lady, they're not that interested in making money for themselves. They do it for others and besides I guess they're more interested in the methods of making money than money itself, just like professional management.

"You don't say. I guess they only allow the best people in the professions to protect the public. My niece's husband, Trevor, tried to become a chartered accountant some years ago, but he flunked out and became a certified public accountant.

"But then a year later, he became a CA. He said the CPA's were 'wiped out' because too many of them were flooding the market and taking work away from the chartered ones."

Well, the CA's were only thinking of building the profession. The absorbing of the lower-echelon CPA into the profession was a first step in raising the qualifications of the whole field. There are no more CPA courses.

"I see. Maybe Theresa should marry a union man. Workers these days are becoming strong, getting good pay. And they seem to be looking for more money, not like the professionals who think of their obligation to society first."

Oh, but the professionals are getting organized too. Teachers have federations, journalists have guilds. They can threaten to strike.

"They've got unions?"

They're not actually called unions.

Engineers, for example, hate unions. Because their associations are made up of employees, independents and company management, they don't want someone like the Teamsters coming in splitting them up. After all, they can't be expected to associate with truck drivers.

But their employee group finally won collective bargaining approval from the governing body. This right will become law. It's looked upon as a formality. Others such as librarians, municipal recreation directors, nurses and civil service administrators are fighting for this right.

"Will the engineers be allowed to strike?"

Good heavens, no madam. They're professionals. They will negotiate like gentlemen and the last resort will be an arbitration board.

"What about that doctor's strike in Saskatchewan?"

That wasn't legal, lady. Doctors don't have a union.

"You know, this is all very confusing."

Be patient, lady. The new socio-economic structure is coming. It may take a generation to straighten out.

"I'm sorry, but my Theresa can't wait that long. I want for her to become a professional Manager of Household Operations."[4]

One of the more disparate groups seeking professional status of late has been the consulting fraternity, which has for some time been taking this quest quite seriously:

Marvin Bower, CMC, came to the Harvard Business School last week to sell an idea: Management consulting is a profession, not a business.

The CMC stands for Certified Management Consultant. The initials may be used by members of the Institute of Management Consultants, Inc. IMC, established in 1969, is trying to upgrade the management-consultant business — oops, profession. Mr. Bower, who is currently the institute's president, noted that consulting "still lacks the sanction of government licensing as required in the medical, legal, and accounting professions."

Pending the development of some kind of legal sanction (probably by state regulation) IMC hopes to establish certain standards in the profession. Meanwhile, incompetents, charlatans, and "retired executives who want to keep busy" are all free to hold forth as management consultants.

The men attracted into consulting today, he says, come with the same motivations as a lawyer or accountant: to become experts of their trade.

He sees his industry at a crossroads today. It will either seek recognition as and become a true profession, or it will yield to "commercialism." As he sees it, the professional can be held accountable to no one except the principals of his own firm.

The Institute of Management Consultants estimates there are 35,000 to 40,000 consultants today. No one has an accurate fix on the total, since there are many in the business part-time, and the lack of standards lets anyone call himself a consultant. But of that number, IMC says only 10,000 meet the licensing standards it has imposed: five years' practice, a check on character, performance, and reputation, and an oral exam. Somewhere in the future lurks a written examination also.[5]

[4] Paul Goldstein, "Fancy Titles, New Jobs, They All Want to Be Professionals", Toronto Star, December 19, 1966.
[5] Richard A. Nenneman, "Consulting Status", The Christian Science Monitor, April 20, 1971.

Reflecting appropriate mounting government resistance to the creation of further islands of professional self-government, some bodies seeking such a sanctuary have been compelled to reveal publicly the variety of incentives lying behind their quest:

— The real estate industry in Canada is still a business and not a profession because of blocks imposed by government, according to H.P. Bell-Irving, president of the Canadian Real Estate Association.

Speaking to the 900 delegates assembled here for the group's annual convention, he said the CREA has been working for some time toward a system of self-regulation akin to that in the engineering and law professions, but has been foiled by government.

"In the past 20 years in Canada we have made significant strides towards the attainment of professional standards of practice.

"Significant improvements in our licencing laws and in our standards of performance have been initiated in most if not every case within our association. They have not been imposed on us by government.

"In spite of this history, our attempts to achieve actual professional status, self-regulation, have been blocked by provincial governments, I believe, on the pretext that this would be contrary to the interests of free enterprise.

"Thus we are still a business and not a profession."

Mr. Bell-Irving's speech seemed primarily to be a fence-mender, designed to placate dissident groups both within and outside the association. Since he became CREA president a year ago there have been confrontations between employers and salesmen over unionization, continued overcrowding in the industry, complaints about the group's accumulated surplus of funds, high dues, federal legislation and externally imposed regulation.

As a business — in some cases big business — we are in some instances engaging salesmen in numbers far in excess of the best public interest. Eventual survival of the fittest may perhaps be a benefit at some stage but the intervening chaos is, in my opinion, too big a price to pay."

Overcrowding in the industry is a point picked up by unions in their attempts to organize salesmen. They would reduce the number of salesmen, leaving a larger share of available sales to those remaining.

Mr. Bell-Irving suggests that solving the overcrowding problem may be the key to convincing governments the industry should be self-regulating.[6]

To understand the issues involved in professional self-regulation, one has to appreciate the pros and cons of such an approach and consider how the public interest can best be protected.

The Case For and Against Professional Self-Regulation

Given the long-standing nature of government-sanctioned professional self-regulation, there is presumably a strong case to be made for it. Indeed there is, if one assumes that the professions in question have as their exclusive, or even primary, concern the advancement and protection of the public interest.

[6] Terrence Belford, "Provincial Governments Charged with Foiling Real Estate's Moves to Professional Self-Regulation", *The Globe and Mail*, Toronto, October 4, 1972.

Granted that assumption, there is no one better qualified than the membership of a given profession to establish and maintain the minimum standards required of those practicing that profession. This is the essence of the case for self-regulation, since only through effective licensing arrangements, it is argued, can an appropriate level of service be sustained. Of course if this were the central goal or objective of any profession, there would be periodic re-examination of those in that profession to ensure that they continued to merit the right to practice. Unfortunately, this is much more the exception than the rule, although efforts by professional bodies to police those already in their ranks do come to the surface periodically:

The soaring costs and sometimes deteriorating quality of medical care that followed the introduction of medicare insure that Congress will never again pass a major health bill without controls on the cost and quality of care. Sponsors of every national health insurance proposal, including the American Medical Assn., agree on the need for controls. The only question that remains is that of means — in less dignified terms, who will bell the cat?

One possible answer lies in the peer review system of San Joaquin and three adjacent California counties. There the cats have belled the cat. Since 1954, an arm of the local medical society has policed medical treatment as part of the nonprofit San Joaquin Foundation for Medical Care.

Under the San Joaquin system, panels of local doctors review the medical services provided by 96% of the area's physicians to 150,000 patients covered by 12 private health insurance plans, the federal government's medicare, and California's Medi-Cal, a program for the medically indigent. In effect, that is just about everyone in the area. The formula has been effective enough to inspire 17 imitators in California alone (and one as far away as Hawaii) and to draw observers from political camps as diverse as President Nixon's and Senator Edward Kennedy's.

By chance. San Joaquin's celebrated innovation began almost by chance, as the byproduct of an attempt to retain a medical market. In 1954 local doctors faced the possibility that San Joaquin members of the independent International Longshoremen's & Warehousemen's Union might contract with the giant Kaiser-Permanente Health Plan for the health insurance provided in their new union agreement with the Pacific Maritime Assn. This would mean that private physicians would immediately lose patients to Kaiser's salaried doctors. It would also give the Kaiser plan an entering wedge in San Joaquin County.

To stave off this threat, the San Joaquin physicians formed a nonprofit foundation under the direction of Dr. Donald Harrington, a gynecologist and long-time advocate of medical foundations. They won the ILWU contract with a competing insurance package that included a maximum fee schedule for routine medical treatments.

Soon after it went into effect, the doctors decided to review claims to make sure of equitable administration. They formed review panels of respected local doctors, expert in each field. The same system was applied to other groups as they signed San Joaquin Foundation contracts. Later, federal and state government programs arranged to use the foundation's review facilities.

Peer review. Veteran foundation members still recall with amazement their first experiences with peer review. Says Boyd Thompson, executive secretary of the foundation: "A panel would look at a claim and say, "This can't be. Old Joe can't still be giving that treatment for that condition.' We realized we had to educate Old Joe."

The effort to educate Old Joe eventually produced a handbook of standard treatments for common disorders, now used routinely by the trained reviewers who scan the 13,000 insurance claims submitted each month. The reviewers computerize all claims, pay most of them, and set aside the roughly 15% that raise doubts. These claims go to the physician review boards, which may authorize payment or ask the doctor to explain the "variance," foundation jargon for a departure from the medical or financial norm. The most common variances involve overuse or misuse of medical services rather than excessive fees.

"The doctors the federal government talks about, who make $10,000 a year on medicare — well, that's really over-utilization of office visits at $5 a visit and injections at $3 an injection," says Dr. Harrington. "Their fees aren't out of line. It's just that they give an injection for anything."

Says Mrs. Cecelia J. Richards, executive claims officer: "The first thing people from Washington always ask us is how much do you save on fees. Really, we don't save much on fees through review, only about 1.5%. Cutting down overutilization saves between 12% and 15%" The computer is invaluable in spotting overutilization, she says.

Professional judgment. Medical quality is harder to measure, but measuring it is an important part of the review process. "I ask the doctor why he gave a particular treatment if it's an unusual one," says Dr. John I. Morozumi, a panel member. "I check for underutilization as well as over-utilization — perhaps why something was omitted. If someone is giving lots of physical examinations — five or six a day — I question that. He's not doing a good job if he charges the rate for a full physical for only a 15-minute one."

Panel members are usually familiar with the medical quirks of the doctors in the area. Such local knowledge and control are essential to the San Joaquin system. Dr. Harrington believes. He is not at all sure it would work in a big city such as Chicago. "There's just too much there," he says.

The payoff. A study recently conducted by the University of California at Los Angeles suggests that the system works fine in San Joaquin County. A comparison of Medi-Cal costs in San Joaquin County and Ventura County (which contains roughly the same population mix but has no foundation coverage) produced an average annual patient cost of $51.72 in San Joaquin compared with $62.84 in Ventura. Some 54% of those eligible received medical care in San Joaquin County, compared with 47% in Ventura.

To Dr. Harrington, such figures are secondary to what he regards as the system's major value: its ability to mandate complete medical coverage for the patients it serves. In San Joaquin County, that means everyone except the self-employed and the employees of national companies that maintain their own policies. Nearly every other industrial and agricultural employee is covered by a foundation-policed policy, and the foundation will not handle policies that do not meet its coverage requirements. Since nearly all county doctors are members of the sponsoring county medical society, this leaves little margin for policies that offer coverage below the foundation standard.

Even if the details of the San Joaquin system are not universally applicable, its underlying principle is, Dr. Harrington tells medical conventions, Congressional committees, and the scores of other audiences currently eager to hear him. "Coverage should go out to the people and experiment in new ideas," he says. "Any way out of the current medical chaos, anything meaningful, must be based on doctors' enlightened self-interest. It cannot come from the ivory tower."[7]

While it may not be so apparent, a strong defence can also be made for some aspects of the fee-setting activities of different professional associations. The author himself has, to some extent, been party to such a defence as it may be applied to some of the professions:

Regardless of their other motivations, most of the groups surveyed argued that the main purpose of their fee schedules was to protect professional standards. Obviously, this is the most appealing case for them to make, and accordingly its validity is difficult to assess. Yet, just as clearly, there is something to the view that price-cutting can lead to sub-standard performance. Where the client is unable to assess standards of performance, this can be a very telling consideration. There are other means, however, of ensuring a minimum quality of service. Appropriate codes and disciplinary measures can serve to reduce the risks of inferior performance, although admittedly, only after the damage is done. Nonetheless, such measures seem to provide a far greater assurance of minimum standards of care to patients of the medical profession than do any of its fee schedules. Undoubtedly this is why one hears less about this particular justification for such schedules in the medical field. In other areas, in contrast, the power to license and, in the final analysis, to de-license, appears to afford less protection to the client, if only because he is less able to judge the quality of the service provided. In the case of architects, engineers and land surveyors, for example, it may well be that one of the surest ways of ensuring high performance standards is to insist on a level of fees which will underwrite them. The relationship between fees and standards is emphasized in the case of architects, whose fee schedules invariably spell out in some detail what the client is to receive at various stages in the project for the fees charged. In Ontario for example, the architects' fee schedule is entitled "Conditions of Engagement and Schedule of Minimum Professional Charges."

In effect, groups such as this are taking the position that competition in their cases should be of the non-price variety. Otherwise, they insist, the basic quality of the service will suffer. For anyone who believes that non-price competition is not only insufficient, but often wasteful as well, this view is difficult to accept. Nonetheless, it must be acknowledged that the argument is more persuasive in most of the fields dealt with in this study than it is in the typical market for manufactured goods. This is because the old adage of "let the buyer beware" simply is not as viable a proposition in the former as in the latter areas.[8]

Turning to the negative side of the professional self-regulatory issue — the side which is bound to be emphasized in this analysis — there is growing public concern about potential, if not actual, abuse of this power. This concern

[7] "Where the Doctors Police the Doctors". Reprinted from the September 4, 1971 issue of *Business Week* by special permission. Copyright 1971 by McGraw-Hill, Inc.
[8] John Crispo, "Fee-Setting by Independent Practitioners, a Study for the Prices and Incomes Commission" (Ottawa, Information Canada, 1972) pp. 7-8. Reproduced by permission of Information Canada.

covers such a broad array of questions that one can begin almost anywhere. Underscoring all complaints in this general area, however, is the questionable supposition that professional bodies operate solely, or even firstly, in the public interest. Although this may once have been the case, there are doubts about its applicability in more and more instances as time goes by. Given the fact that selfishness is so pervasive in North America, it is really asking too much of any group that it relegate its own interests to a secondary position vis-a-vis any other group or the public at large.

Not only is there increased public awareness of the potential power of the self-governing professions, but also, accurately or inaccurately, there is a growing feeling that in actuality, self-governing professions are using their ability to license to reduce numbers and thereby restrict competition. This suspicion has received greater credence in Canada because of the results of a major study of entrance requirements for a number of occupations:

Excessive educational requirements have created "barriers to entry" to many trades and professions in Canada and resulted in unnecessarily high costs to the public, an economist concludes in a study released today by the Economic Council of Canada.

Prof. David Dodge of Queen's University says a wide range of licensing bodies use their power to set artificial education standards, with two results: The incomes of participants are much higher than they would otherwise be; and estimates of the value of education to society are distorted.

Dodge claims there is little evidence that increases in the education levels required by professions in the last 20 years have made members of the professions more effective or productive.

He says the situation causes "misallocation of human resources" and artificial scarcities in licensed occupations as qualified young people are turned away by the costs, time and academic standings demanded for admission to training courses.

Dodge's study forms part of a publication called Canadian Higher Education in the Seventies released today in Ottawa by the federal government's economic advisory body.

In one of his calculations, he compared the incomes of 24 trades and professions, some of them licensed by professional associations or government agencies and some of them unregulated.

"There are significantly more licensed occupations with higher-than average wages and significantly fewer unlicensed occupations with higher-than-average wages than would be expected on the basis of chance," he says.

Occupational groups considered by Dodge to be "licensed by autonomous or semi-autonomous agencies" include: doctors, dentists, lawyers, accountants, pharmacists, optometrists, architects, school teachers, engineers, nurses and surveyors:

"By withdrawing the self-regulating power of all trades and professions and instituting a system of state certification in its place," he says, "the allocation of resources may be improved and the public provided with adequate information on which to base rational choice of services."[9]

One especially disturbing — and uneconomical — manifestation of professional control over their own ranks relates to the frequent opposition to the

[9] " 'Artificial' Standards Create Job Barriers, Study Finds", Toronto Star, August 10, 1972.

employment of para-professional technicians and technologists. Although severe professional manpower shortages in some areas have reduced this resistance, and though professionals in some jurisdictions, such as engineers in Ontario, have facilitated and welcomed the emergence of these new categories, too many professions have placed every conceivable roadblock in the way. The result has been a continuing public outcry in leading editorial criticism going back several years:

If Health Minister A.B.R. Lawrence looks over the massive studies that have been made of health care in Canada and Ontario, if he talks to those who are knowledgeable and concerned about the provision of health-care services to the public, he will find a great deal of unanimity on one point: that many health experts, and particularly doctors and dentists, spend far too much of their time working below their level of competence, doing jobs that could be done just as well, or better, by less expensively trained health personnel at lower cost to the public.

If Mr. Larence then looks at the report on civil rights prepared by the former Chief Justice of the High Court in Ontario, J.C. McRuer, he will discover that one of the strongest points made by Mr. McRuer was that the primary purpose of such self-governing bodies as medical and dental colleges should be to serve the public interest, not to shore up the monopolistic position of a profession.

Having informed himself on these very basic principles (and we suspect that he has been doing so), Mr. Lawrence could then address himself usefully to the matter of the dental clinics, run by dental technicians, which have this week been raided by investigators for the Royal College of Dental Surgeons of Ontario and the Ontario Provincial Police.

According to existing provincial law such dental technicians can manufacture dentures only on the prescription of a dentist. In this area, Ontario lags behind Manitoba, Alberta and British Columbia, which all have legislation permitting registered dental technicians to sell directly to the public.

There are several reasons why this direct dealing makes sense. Perhaps the most important is that a properly trained dental technician whose entire work is concentrated in the field of taking impressions and bite registrations, designing, fabricating and repairing partial and complete dentures, and fitting them, is likely to become a great deal more expert in the business than is a dentist who functions over the whole range of dentistry. To put it simply, you are likely to be more proficient at a job if you do it all day of every day than if you do it only once or twice a week.

The other important reason for permitting properly qualified dental technicians to deal directly with the public is that it would save the public a lot of money — perhaps as much as two-thirds of the cost of a set of dentures. Often the dentist is nothing more than a costly middleman between the patient and the man who actually does the work.

Finally, even the dentists themselves admit that there are not enough dentists in Ontario to give the whole population adequate dental care. Some of them have actually used this fact as an argument against the introduction of a government dental care insurance plan.

There is a proper procedure which should be used, not only in the case of dental technicians but in the case of all health-care personnel who are to be given a legally defined role. This involves, first, defining very clearly, with the protection of the public fully in mind, the precise work which the technician is to be allowed to do. . . .

The role of the dental technician must therefore be defined in legislation, with penalties for those who operate beyond their role. This would not be as lengthy or as difficult a task as might appear on the surface. Ontario could take advantage of the experience already gained by Manitoba, Alberta and British Columbia; but, in fact, a considerable body of experience has already been amassed in Ontario itself. Many dental technicians, however illegally, have been treating patients in Ontario directly for years.

The public interest, as Mr. McRuer emphasized, must predominate. It is not in the public interest to compel patients to deal through dentists, at great cost, for a service which can safely and adequately be provided without dentists. The Government has no business protecting a monopoly for the dental industry; its only business in the area is to ensure that the public is protected from malpractice by dental technicians.

Mr. Lawrence knows — as do all people in the health-care field who are more concerned with the welfare of patients than with dollars — that a great many different kinds of technicians are going to have to be given a legal role in health care if Ontarians are to be able to afford complete health care. The field cannot remain the private preserve of doctors and dentists.[10]

Although often verging on personal envy, criticisms aimed at the fees charged and incomes derived by many professionals reflect the levels of some of these fees and incomes and emphasize the fact that these amounts are often established and set by the professions themselves without being subject to any outside scrutiny, let alone control. The result is that more and more searching questions are being asked about the propriety of both the process and the outcome of these kinds of activities. Both in the United States and Canada, for example, attention is continuing to focus on the fee schedules promulgated by bar associations:

Government antitruster, hear it nearly every time they bring price-fixing charges against someone.

"It's usually something like, 'When the hell are you gonna get the lawyers?' " says a top official in the Justice Department's antitrust division. "My response is that law enforcement takes time."

Apparently, the time has come. Tired of complaints that lawyers get preferential treatment, the department is changing its long-held view that the legal profession is exempt from prosecution under U.S. antitrust laws. It has begun investigations of minimum-fee schedules maintained by local, county and state bar associations across the country. These schedules list flat charges for legal services, such as $75 for drafting a simple will, and the bar associations, to varying degrees, expect their members to charge no less.

At some point, the department almost certainly will file a price-fixing suit challenging this time-honored method of charging clients. That's chilling news for the legal profession, already shaken by the success of a private suit against fee-fixing by some Virginia attorneys, and it's having widespread effects.

10 "End Dentists' Monopoly", The Globe and Mail, Toronto, May 8, 1971.

Some state bar associations have already dropped their fee schedules, and dozens of local versions are also disappearing. Some bar groups are considering less rigid "value guides" as possible safe substitute methods, and others are switching to straight hourly charges. But some attorneys, resenting the department's change of mind, are urging the profession not to panic.

The turn of events pleases potential clients who would like to price-shop for lawyers to draw wills and handle divorces and perform other services often controlled by set fees. In Virginia, there already are signs that certain real estate settlement fees may be declining.

Thus far, the antitrust division has taken only preliminary steps. It has sent informal questionnaires to bar associations in New Jersey, California and several other states asking about their pricing practices. It has also issued formal investigative orders to bar groups in Massachusetts and Louisiana demanding documents on minimum-fee schedules that have existed there.

But the highest-ranking antitrust officials publicly have warned lawyers that a price-fixing suit may be ahead.

"I think the legal profession has been given sufficient warning," says Thomas E. Kauper, assistant attorney general in charge of the antitrust division. "Fee-fixing by lawyers can run afoul of the antitrust laws. It may well be that our next warning will be in the form of a complaint."

Traditionally, the department has assumed that lawyers' minimum-fee schedules didn't affect interstate commerce and so weren't subject to federal regulation. Moreover, fraternal bonds have seemed to deter the government prosecutors from attacking their fellow lawyers. But in recent years the courts have broadened their interpretation of interstate commerce, and the department has brought price-fixing charges against other businesses that call themselves professions, including accountants, architects and civil engineers. The actions have raised pressure for a parallel assault on lawyers' minimum fees.

The schedules surfaced as early as 1872 (in Sedgwick County in Kansas) but didn't begin to flourish until the 1950s. The basic idea was to provide lawyers with adequate compensation and discourage them from soliciting business by discounting prices. Frequently, lawyers could be disciplined by the bar for undercutting the minimum-fee tables.

That rigid aspect has gradually eased. Many schedules now are described as suggested guides and note that it's up to the individual lawyer to determine what a reasonable fee is for a particular service. Still, many lawyers feel an informal compulsion not to undercut the rate schedules. And a few note that lawyers who try to increase their business by "intentionally and regularly" charging less than the minimum may be disciplined by the bar for unethical solicitation.

A schedule may suggest fees for everything from handling a minor traffic case to drafting a complicated pension and profit-sharing plan. The now-abandoned tables issued by bar associations in Alexandria, Va., and in neighboring Arlington and Fairfax counties specified such minimums as $350 for an uncontested divorce and $600 for a contested one; $75 for drafting a "short-form" will and $100 for a longer version; and a scale of 5% for handling probate of an estate valued up to $25,000 (with a minimum fee of $250), 4% of the next $50,000; 3% of the next $100,000; 2% of the next $250,000, and 1% of all above $425,000.

It was this schedule, plus one issued by the Virginia State Bar, that drew a private anti-trust lawsuit from Lewis Goldfarb, a Virginia resident who is a lawyer with the Federal Trade Commission. The suit was prompted by Mr. Goldfarb's experience in buying a home. To obtain a mortgage, he had to retain a Virginia attorney to conduct a title search. Nineteen lawyers quoted him a fee of $522.50 for the title search on his $54,500 home; all refused to undercut that price, so he paid it.

Represented by Alan B. Morrison, a lawyer in one of Ralph Nader's organizations, Mr. Goldfarb then sued in U.S. district court in Alexandria. He argued that the Virginia bar groups had illegally fixed home-buying settlement costs at an artificially high level, in violation of antitrust laws. On behalf of himself and other buyers, he asked for treble damages of $1.2 million.

The bar associations in Alexandria and Arlington County agreed to abolish their minimum schedules, but the state bar and the Fairfax County Bar contested the suit. In January, District Judge Albert V. Bryan Jr. struck down the county schedule, ruling that "minimum-fee schedules are a form of price-fixing"; the county bar is appealing that decision. However, the judge didn't abolish the state fee table, implying that the state bar is an arm of the state government and thus immune from antitrust prosecution. That part of the ruling is being appealed by Mr. Goldfarb and the question of damages has been delayed.

The decision already has affected settlement costs. One Washington lawyer buying a home in Virginia was recently quoted a title-search fee of ¾ of 1% on the purchase price of his house. The prior fee schedule had specified 1% of the first $50,000 of the loan amount or purchase price (whichever was greater), and ½ of 1% of the amount between $50,000 and $100,000.

The benefits are mixed. On a $50,000 home, the title-search fee would be $375, compared with $500 before. On a $100,000 home, the fee would be $750 in either case. With no minimum schedule, however, the homebuyer may turn up another lawyer who is willing to do the job cheaper.

Of broader significance is the national impact of the Virginia case and the Justice Department's muscle-flexing. At least five states — Florida, Georgia, Tennessee, Delaware and Massachusetts — have dropped their fee schedules, and several others, including Louisiana, are considering it. Massachusetts withdrew its schedule in January after receiving the department's "Notice of Civil Investigative Demand," seeking all the state's fee-schedule records dating from June 1, 1967.

"We just couldn't endanger the funds of the association by continuing it," says Carl A. Modecki, executive director of the Massachusetts Bar Association, referring to the possibility of a damage suit. He says many local and county bar groups in the state are following. Fee schedules also have been abandoned in Atlanta, Cleveland, Philadelphia and Pittsburgh, and by numerous county bar associations in New York and New Jersey.

"I think they're going to fall, one by one, all over the country," says David Webster, an attorney who represented the Arlington County Bar in the Goldfarb suit.

"What we're coming to is a situation where charges will be made on the basis of time," says Mr. Modecki, the Massachusetts bar director, adding that lawyers will have to do much more to justify their fees.

"Lawyers always used to send out bills saying things like 'for professional services — $13,000.' Now they'll have to explain it."[11]

In Canada fee-setting by the legal profession now is subject to more careful scrutiny because of the development of legal aid plans under provincial government sponsorship:

It is the form that catches our interest more than the content, the unruffled smoothness with which lawyers working under Ontario's legal aid plan have achieved their pay raise. Very smooth. The Law Society of Upper Canada, which administers legal aid as well as governs Ontario's 8,500 lawyers, draws up its recommendations for fee increases. The recommendations go before Attorney-General Dalton Bales, whose department pays out $10.9-million of legal aid's $12-million annual cost. Mr. Bales says, yes, everything seems reasonable and fair. He makes an announcement and that's it — no fuss, no acrimony, no unseemly public debate. Perhaps . . . too smooth. But we'll come back to that; for the moment, let's examine the content.

The fee increases may be reasonable. They are the first since legal aid was started in Ontario in 1967. Lawyers' costs have risen in six years. The average increase of 40 per cent for criminal law work comes out to an annual rise of slightly less than 7 per cent which is not out of line with other increases.

To a layman, good sense may be made of the recommendations. The daily fees, for example, for lawyers acting in extradition cases are doubled — from $150 to $800 — which reflects one aspect of the changing face of legal work in the past few years. The fee for uncontested divorces, on the other hand, goes down: from $400 to $320. Another change in the right direction. Since Parliament liberalized the grounds for divorce in Canada, the number of divorces has soared, becoming the single most costly item under the legal aid plan — nearly $3-million worth a year. Yet uncontested actions largely involve paper work done by the lawyers' secretaries and very, very brief appearances in court. The charge could be reduced again.

At the expensive end of the scale, lawyers will now receive a maximum of $1,700 for defending a client on a capital murder charge, compared to $1,500 under the old schedule. Non-capital murder proceedings are raised to $1,150 from $1,000. Manslaughter, attempted murder, rape and criminal negligence cases will be worth $850, instead of $750. When consideration is given to the money and resources available to the state to prosecute on these offences, the fees paid to the defence counsel seem no less than fair value for the work he must do.

Even with the lawyers continuing their curious practice of taking only 75 per cent of the legal aid fee — an arrangement which confuses reason — the increases are expected to add $2.1-million to legal aid's annual bill. Most, and probably all, of the increase will be covered by the interest earned on lawyers' trust accounts. The annual value of this interest, which formerly went to the banks and trust companies by default, is estimated at anywhere between $1-million and $11-million. Its be-

[11] Wayne E. Green, "A Legal Question", The Wall Street Journal, April 11, 1973. Reprinted with permission of The Wall Street Journal © Dow Jones & Company, Inc., 1973.

latedness apart, a fine decision by Mr. Bales earlier this year redirected 75 per cent of this trove to legal aid. In addition, $3.5-million in federal money will be available to the plan under an agreement signed by Ottawa and Ontario.

What has taken place is that a self-governing profession has raised its own pay — pay provided by the public — with the acquiescence of government. We have said the fee increases seem reasonable. But we don't know; perhaps they are not high enough.

Unfortunately, it's unlikely to be a matter with which the public will become too concerned — largely, we suppose, because the money for legal aid comes out of general taxation revenue and not from a source closer to the taxpayer, such as property taxes or, more to the point, premiums. Which brings us to the doctors.

Here we have a self-governing profession that must be wondering what kind of moxie the lawyers have. When the Ontario Medical Association raises its tariffs, the public is given a ringside seat for what seems to be the inevitable namecalling and slanging exchanged by the doctors and the politicians.

Doctors unquestionably are much more under the public microscope these days than lawyers; they are being told how many operations they can charge for in a year; they are being told what services they can offer; they are hearing their qualifications publicly debated.

We are not suggesting that any profession whose fees and services are paid out of public funds should go unmonitored. We are suggesting, however, equity. The public will expect that lawyers also should be subject to careful scrutiny. For that reason, Mr. Bales' announcement of an independent committee to study the effectiveness and future of legal aid is welcome. We would expect the committee to examine the whole matter of fee schedules to see that both public and lawyers are getting fair value.[12]

To be fair, it should be acknowledged that even more embarrassing questions could be asked about fee-setting arrangements in some of the new professions, if one can call them that. Real estate commissions and other fees associated with purchasing a home provide key cases in point because they are based on a percentage of the value of the property being bought (or some portion of the value), thus ensuring rapidly escalating income as long as real estate booms as it has.

Any initiatives by the real estate industry — including a voluntary reduction in fees and commissions — that might help contain the latest outbreak of inflationary increases in urban house prices would be welcome, Ontario Housing Minister Sidney Handleman says.

Mr. Handleman and industry leaders were responding to a growing body of public opinion that questions the validity of a sales commission of $2,036.40, based on 5 per cent of the new average price. The commission on a $60,000 sale — a figure well below the average Toronto price of a newly built detached house — is $3,000.

The commission charged when a house is sold through the real estate board's multiple listing service is 6 per cent.

These fixed-rate commissions — high though they may be in total, compared with those of three years ago — are only a part of the rising

12 "No Questions Asked", The Globe and Mail, Toronto, September 11, 1973.

costs, beginning with the land, built into the end purchase price.

Added to the agents' commission — and to the end price — is 1.25 per cent in legal fees. This amounts to $509.10 on a house valued at $40,728 or $750 on a $60,000 house.

In addition, the province imposes land transfer tax calculated on the basis of $3 per $1,000 up to $35,000 and $6 on each $1,000 beyond that level.

An appraisal fee, usually about $75, is charged by most of the major mortgage lenders when property appraisal is necessary. A number of smaller companies and individual appraisers have been increasing this fee, in some cases to $175 or more, as inflation progresses.

Set-up fees in an average range of $400 to $800 on a single mortgage are overlaid on the financing package by some mortgage brokers. These fees are for arranging financing with major lenders — arrangements that often could be made directly by the purchaser, without a middleman.

Brokerage fees are usually between 1 and 3 per cent of the value of the mortgage but can rise, in some cases, to 4 per cent, higher if the broker is not a member of the Ontario association and not bound by its fee schedule.

[Leonard] Rosenberg, who is a director of the provincial association, said that although brokers may seem expensive or unnecessary to the uninitiated, they usually save the buyer more money than their services cost.

Spokesmen for some of the major lending institutions say the mortgage brokers overstate their case. The trust companies prefer to deal directly with mortgage applicants and often find that an applicant with a perfectly sound deal is paying a full brokerage fee for little more than a telephone call from the broker to the trust company.

The buyer, whatever route he follows, finds expert hands outstretched for percentages at every turn. In times like these, when the rise in house prices far outstrips general inflation, the specialists' incomes — tied as they are to percentages fixed in periods of stability — also rise at the higher-than-normal rate.[13]

What is most bothersome about the whole professional fee-setting business is that there often seems to be no rhyme or reason for what goes on. As the author noted in the aforementioned study:

. . . The most disturbing feature to emerge from this study concerns the inability of the various groups involved to identify exactly the bases for their conclusions that their members' services are worthy of their target net levels of remuneration. More disturbing in some cases was the reluctance to divulge, or even speak in terms of, the actual earnings of the practitioners in question. A spokesman for one group not only hinted that this was nobody else's business, but that it was not terribly pertinent to the issue at hand. It should be added that this was an exceptional reaction. More typical was a kind of squeamishness about coming to grips with what most of the interviewees clearly recognized as central to the whole process of fee-setting.

The general impression left was one of another set of groups not

[13] James Purdie, "Handleman Would Welcome Cuts in Real Estate Commissions, Fees", *The Globe and Mail*, Toronto, April 16, 1974.

unlike the trade unions. Just as organized workers seem to develop a sense of disturbance about their relative positions in the hierarchy of the personal income structure, and a feeling that it is time to improve those positions, so also may a similar metabolism be at work among groups of independent practitioners. Perhaps, along with almost everyone else in the country, they are looking rather jealously at the inordinate gains being scored by plumbers and electricians and simply using these break-throughs as justification for another round of increases for themselves.[14]

Even harder for advocates of professional self-government to defend are signs of failure among bodies so empowered to maintain high ethical standards of practice. In some cases there are no codes of behaviour or weak ones. In others there is laxity in their enforcement. Again, fairly or unfairly, the legal profession has come in for a good deal of criticism in recent years. Considering what the legal profession is supposed to stand for, such criticism is not surprising. Sometimes, indeed, the charges are so blatant and long-standing that one wonders at the prospects for integrity in the very profession where it should be uppermost. Take the matter of real estate insurance kickbacks in the U.S. — a serious blight that has gone uncorrected for years:

... Kickbacks are a shady practice, and they are particularly unbecoming to a profession that always has proclaimed its dedication to the highest standards of justice and ethics.

It is a little surprising, therefore, that the American Bar Assn. and the various state associations have made no real efforts to stop the kickbacks. . . .

It is time for the bar association to spit the mush out of its mouth, take a firm stand on kickbacks, and enforce it rigorously. In doing so, it would not only give the homebuyer the fair treatment he is entitled to expect, but it would also serve notice on the legal profession that it must practice the ethics it preaches.[15]

On a broader plane, a former U.S. Supreme Court Justice has chastised his profession for its general reluctance to discipline unethical lawyers:

Self-policing in the legal profession has come a long way since Watergate. However, in the eyes of some, it is nothing compared to the distance yet to be traveled.

To retired Supreme Court Justice Tom C. Clark, for instance, there has been far more progress in structure than in attitude.

Lawyers, he says, are still much too reluctant to "stand up and be counted." His view is particularly important since he is the author of a hard-hitting 1970 American Bar Association report which termed lawyer disciplinary procedures in most states "scandalous."

Mr. Clark reasons that attorneys are in a better position than anyone else to know about misconduct on the part of their colleagues, yet "they won't what they call 'snitch' on another lawyer.

"They turn their heads, just like the public, because they don't want

[14] John Crispo, "Fee-Setting by Independent Practitioners, a Study for the Prices and Incomes Commission" (Ottawa, Information Canada, 1972) pp. 29-30. Reproduced by permission of Information Canada.
[15] "The Bar's Ethical Blind Spot". Reprinted from the April 20, 1974 issue of *Business Week* by special permission. Copyright 1974 by McGraw-Hill, Inc.

to get involved. They seem to think it's below their dignity, but this involves their life blood and they ought to take an interest in it."

The consequence, says Mr. Clark, is that it's "like pulling teeth" to get enough information on a lawyer to disbar or even to reprimand him.

Given that standard obstruction, it is perhaps the more remarkable that lawyers have taken a leadership position in the move to disbar former Vice-President Spiro T. Agnew in Maryland and, in other jurisdictions, the several attorneys involved in the Watergate affair. To Mr. Clark, these are like "rays of light" shining through his generally gloomy assessment.

Most lawyers like to stress how few of their 375,000 colleagues in the United States actually need disciplining.

"We're talking about maybe half of one percent that are an embarrassment to the profession and a detriment to the consumer," declares Richard H. Senter, president of the American Bar Association's National Organization of Bar Counsel.

In 1972, the last year for which computed figures are available, there were 357 lawyers across the country who received some kind of reprimand of suspension from state courts. Some 122 of them were disbarred.

Generally, a client begins the process by complaining about his lawyer to the grievance committee of a state bar association. From there, a lengthy investigation follows, replete with screening of the complaints, hearings, transcripts, review of the hearings, a ruling by the state appeals court, and often the lawyer himself appealing the finding to a higher court.

One major factor in whether and how fast the profession itself moves to police its ranks is the seemingly unimportant matter of whether or not membership in that state's bar association is mandatory or voluntary.

In more than half the states, membership is mandatory, with the result that the budget for disciplinary proceedings is usually well-stocked and the responsibility for action clearly placed. California, for instance, spends more than $1 million a year on disciplinary matters.

Also, communication among states is much stronger that it was. The ABA set up a national discipline data bank so that each state may keep tabs on discipline problems of the others.

Lawyers whose conduct has been questioned in one state have had a resilient tendency to show up elsewhere. Coordinating this information flow and providing resource help and occasional training courses is the ABA's new national center for professional discipline, headed by Mr. Forshee.

If lawyer attitude can be brought along to match all this operational machinery, says Mr. Clark, the legal profession will be in very good shape.

"Our problem is that the only way we'll be able to get effective disciplinary action is for the lawyers who advise these state boards we set up to be willing to stand up and be counted."[16]

That there is hope for the legal profession is suggested by the aftermath of Watergate and all that it stands for, an appalling series of episodes in which lawyers played all too major a part:

[16] Lucia Mouat, "Gains Seen Since Watergate, but Much More Asked: Clark Finds Bar Reluctant to Discipline Fellow Lawyers", *The Christian Science Monitor*, February 25, 1974.

The question of ethics is receiving new attention from the U.S. legal profession in the wake of Watergate.

State bar groups move to better enforce ethical standards, law schools place more stress on proper legal conduct, low cost public interest law firms are springing up, and a drive is on to promote public understanding of the U.S. legal system.

Among the new moves stirring throughout the U.S.:

• State bar groups are starting to face the professional ethics question head on, aware that of 25 men convicted or under indictment in Watergate related cases, 11 are practicing lawyers.

For instance, Maryland's bar association is urging that former Vice-President Spiro T. Agnew be disbarred for violating a position of public trust by evading income taxes when he was governor of Maryland. This matter will be heard by a state court of appeals April 2.

California's bar is probing possible misconduct by six lawyers involved in Watergate. President Nixon heads the list which also includes John D. Ehrlichman, Herbert W. Kalmbach, Robert C. Mardian, Donald H. Segretti, and Gordon C. Strachan. Under California law, recommendations to the State Supreme Court could result in punishment ranging from private reprimand up to disbarment.

Convicted Watergate conspirator G. Gordon Liddy already has been disbarred in New York State. Egil (Bud) Krogh Jr., former White House staffer who headed the so-called "plumbers squad" and has pleaded guilty to a civil-rights violation in connection with the break-in to the office of Daniel Ellsberg's psychiatrist, has been suspended from practice in Washington State. And ex-White House counsel John W. Dean III has lost his license in Virginia and had his right to practice law in Washington, D.C., suspended.

• Law schools are also starting to stress ethics to a greater degree than ever before. In response to an American Bar Association (ABA) mandate, almost all now offer courses in ethics. Many schedule symposia and informal seminars on the issue with judges, lawyers, and others in the legal community.

Here in California, those seeking admission to the state bar, starting in 1975, will have to answer a question on ethics in the bar examination. Such a question has not surfaced since the late 1930s.

• There is renewed professional interest in rules of conduct for both lawyers and judges. Among other things, these deal with conflict of interest, courtroom demeanor, and attorney-client relationships. Most states now subscribe to broad ABA canons of professional responsibility. And some states now are urging more specific spelling out of rules of conduct.

• Public backlash against high legal fees is resulting in the springing up of cut-rate law firms and para-professional legal clinics in many areas of the U.S. and state bar groups are scrupulously watching these firms for evidences of unprofessional conduct.

Some lawyers say this is actually placing new pressures on traditional lawyers to police their own ethical tactics.

• There are greater efforts to train lawyers in actual courtroom procedures before they practice on their own. For example, McGeorge School of Law in Sacramento, Calif., now features a modern "courtroom of the future" to give students firsthand trial experience and teach legal techniques. Other law schools contemplate similar projects.

• More attention is being paid to promoting greater public understanding of the U.S. legal system. For example, there are some experiments under way which bring television cameras right into the courtroom to film actual trial proceedings.

Storefront public-interest legal groups are popping up in ghetto and underprivileged areas to apprise residents of their legal rights. And volunteer groups, such as the lawyers' wives of Los Angeles, regularly conduct school tours of courts — visiting judges, staging "mock" trials, and briefing youngsters on their rights as citizens under the judicial system.

Dorothy Nelson, dean of the law school at the University of Southern California, says that while the public may be "turning off" lawyers, students are far from turning away from the law.

Is ethics a real issue among law students?

"A lot of discussions go on that didn't go on before. Now it's OK to talk about 'honesty' and 'ethics.' Before [Watergate] it was felt you shouldn't speak about these things," Dean Nelson says.

"And there is talk about such things as responsibility to those other than one's own clients. . . . They want to know at what point you must stop and say 'no,' " the USC dean explains.[17]

Another criticism that can be levelled at professional associations hits hardest at the group of which the author is a member. Although university professors are not self-governing in the same sense as doctors or lawyers, they have refined their own guild system into something that may be corrosive and dangerous from a social point of view. Like their counterparts at the public and high school level, teachers in postsecondary institutions, and especially universities, have placed a great deal of emphasis on job security. In many universities this has led to the perversion of tenure from a legitimate measure to ensure academic freedom into a general shield which protects against dismissal on virtually any ground:

The misuse of tenure as a more or less general form of job security could compromise its most vital function, that of ensuring academic freedom. Allowing the concept of tenure to be distorted to the point where it is almost unthinkable to question the performance of those with such exalted status has risked its more legitimate and important long-term role in the preservation of our universities as havens for free-thinking individuals. As a result, there is a pressing need to clarify the basic meaning of tenure and to ensure its proper application.

The academic freedom of tenured professors at the University of Toronto, as elsewhere in academia, seems well protected. If anything, the problem may be that it is too difficult to dismiss a tenured staff member for any reason, let alone for possible abuse of his academic freedom. The arduous and even invidious procedures for dismissing a tenured professor are so protective that only a very bold and confident dean or chairman could ever be expected to try to institute them.

Tenure is a two-edged sword. It has an indispensable part to play in

---

[17] Curtis J. Sitomer, "Lawyer Ties to Watergate Put Fresh Emphasis on Legal Ethics", *The Christian Science Monitor*, March 25, 1974.

giving academics unlimited scope to engage in a continuing search for their particular versions of the truth, especially in sensitive areas of public controversy. Without tenure, faculty members might hold back that critical analysis and dissent which is so essential to a free and vibrant university for fear of alienating some vested interest group, whether within or beyond the University, that could use its influence to undermine their positions. At the same time, inadvertently or by design, tenure may serve as a shield behind which may hide some who are not living up to their obligations to the university.

The challenge is to preserve the legitimate role of tenure while preventing its abuse for other purposes. Tenure, as it is now interpreted, should be granted only after the most careful scrutiny of the candidate's credentials. This appears to be current practice, although for a time the tightness of the academic market-place no doubt disposed many departments in many universities to offer tenure prematurely, in order to recruit or hold staff that were in short supply. Even more essential is an adequate review procedure to ensure that the performance of those who have obtained tenure at least meets some reasonable minimum standard. Such a review should not take place only when an individual is thought to have so neglected his obligations as to warrant termination. Rather, there should be a formal process whereby the performance of tenured faculty members can be reviewed periodically, so that they can be told where they are not up to standard.

Nothing is sacrosanct on this planet, least of all in the changing world of the universities. Everything associated with tenure will quite properly be re-thought in the years ahead. Unless faculty members take the initiative in this re-assessment, our valid concerns may go by the board by default. For this reason alone, faculty members, whether or not they share my view of the need, should support the undertaking of such a re-assessment. In so doing, however, they should be mindful of the possible results. One consideration that comes to mind is the desirability of a complete divorce of the issues of academic freedom and job security. Tenure would thus be given to all members of the university community in the name of academic freedom, while varying degrees of job security would be reserved for those of proven and continuing ability, on the basis of a separate and distinct formula.[18]

As distorted and misused as the original concept of tenure may have become, there are two points which should be made by way of reminders, if not rejoinders. In the first place, something like tenure will always be required to protect academic freedom, the absence of which would destroy a major *raison d'etre* of the universities as havens for freethinking individuals engaged in the search for their particular version of the truth. Secondly, to the extent that something beyond the preservation of academic freedom has become part and parcel of tenure, it is discouraging to have to report that that feature of tenure, even if removed, could be replaced by something just as harmful:

If, as seems quite possible, the tenure laws are declared unconstitutional, repealed, or otherwise weakened, teachers will have to rely upon their organizations more than ever for protection from arbitrary dismissal.

[18] John Crispo, "Academic Tenure: Necessary Evil or Academic Shield", *Trinity Convocation Bulletin*, March 1971, p. 8-9.

In fact, in cases other than those involving special circumstances, such as a civil rights complaint, teacher organizations would normally offer the only practical protection for teachers contesting their dismissal. Of course, teacher organization leaders cannot reduce their public opposition to weakening the tenure laws, even though their organizations would be strengthened. Nevertheless, many of them will not be unhappy.

As a matter of fact, teachers themselves may conclude that repeal of tenure laws is essential to facilitate contractual protection against unfair dismissals. The laws providing bargaining rights for teachers were typically enacted without regard for other state legislation and are frequently inconsistent in philosophy and practice with state tenure laws.

If the price of contractual protection for unjust dismissal is the end of legislative protection, will teachers be willing to pay the price? I believe they will. A leading teacher association strategist in tenure and collective bargaining is Robert H. Chanin, the National Education Association's dynamic general counsel. Chanin is, naturally, trying to retain both legislative and contractual protections. From his standpoint and that of teacher organizations generally, there is no reason to make a choice unless it is necessary to do so. Nevertheless, it is doubtful that the choice can be avoided much longer or that the existing tenure laws will continue to prevail when the final choice is made.

In the first place, the substantive protections provided by the tenure laws are vastly exaggerated; teachers are protected more by incompetent management than by the laws. In the second place, as tenure laws are repealed, we can expect effective efforts by teacher organizations to negotiate tenure protection in the collective agreements. As long as tenure is covered by legislation, school boards have practical as well as legal arguments for refusing to bargain over it. Once tenure legislation is repealed, school boards will no longer have this excuse. Therefore, administrators may have more to fear than teachers do from the repeal of tenure laws. At present, administrators frequently cite the tenure laws as the reason they are unable to remove incompetent teachers. These assertions are typically just rhetoric; if a teacher is incompetent, an able administrator will be able to document the fact in a way that the courts will sustain. More important, few teachers would legally contest an adequately documented charge of incompetence. Nevertheless, it is easy to convince school boards and the public that the tenure laws are an insuperable obstacle. Since few persons read the laws, it is easy to perpetuate the fiction that they constitute an impregnable defense against charges of incompetence.

Actually, administrators concerned about the tenure laws should join teacher organizations in efforts to substitute negotiated procedures for statutory ones in cases involving the dismissal of tenured teachers. Certainly, the negotiated procedures would remove the threat or burden of legal proceedings in most dismissal cases. If the tenure laws are an unreasonable burden on management, and if there ought to be fair and expeditious procedures to challenge dismissals, why not authorize teacher organizations and boards of education to negotiate these procedures together? Whatever the alternatives, this is what is likely to happen in the 1970s.[19]

[19] Myron Lieberman, "Why Teachers Will Oppose Tenure Laws", *Saturday Review*, March 4, 1972, pp. 55-56. © 1972 *Saturday Review*.

Other aspects of professionalism which sometimes run counter to the public interest cover a gamut of considerations ranging from unduly restrictive covenants directed against advertising of services to jurisdictional disputes between such groups as architects and engineers over control of work assignments. As a final example of some of the problems that plague the professions, however, it is undoubtedly appropriate to come back to the lawyers. In the name of protecting the public interest they have been granted extensive self-governing powers. It is therefore somewhat ironic, although quite understandable, that they should put not only their own, but their individual clients', interests before the general public interest when the matter of accountability and responsibility is brought to the fore:

Lawyers are scrambling for copies of an SEC complaint charging National "Student Marketing Corp. and numerous other defendants with violations of federal securities law. They are keenly interested — and deeply shaken — by the fact that two of the defendants are prestigious law firms: White & Case, a New York firm that ranks sixth in the country in size, and the Chicago firm of Lord, Bissell & Brook. The attack on these law firms is believed to be unprecedented.

The SEC complaint, described by one lawyer as, "The best-read document since 'Gone With the Wind,' " essentially accuses the two firms of violating federal securities law by failing to publicly disclose certain adverse information that they learned about National Student Marketing in connection with a 1969 merger plan they were involved in. Both firms deny the specific charges and decline to comment on the broader questions raised by the case.

The case is the latest in a series of SEC actions designed to bring lawyers, accountants and bankers within the framework of securities regulations traditionally aimed at stock traders, brokers and publicly held companies. In the past two years, the commission has brought probably a dozen cases aimed at least partly at forcing those professions, in representing their individual clients in securities matters, to consider the interests of public investors.

"After all," says SEC Chairman William J. Casey, "the whole investment process, that of fair presentation of information to investors, can depend on professionals."

The case involving the two law firms, filed in federal district court here on Feb. 3 is probably the most significant brought so far against lawyers, accountants or bankers. It poses more sharply than ever before the fundamental question of how much duty a securities lawyer owes the investing public and how much he owes his own client.

Most securities lawyers say they're likely to be supercautious from now on, demanding more documentation of client companies' statements, taking more time — and, some promise, charging higher fees. They say they'll also be more selective in choosing their clients, shunning representation of speculative companies, for example. And some say they'll think twice before allowing their firm's name to be placed behind, say, a merger, as it was in this case.

SEC officials refuse to talk about the National Student Marketing case while it's pending in court. However, the agency has for some time felt that federal securities laws impose on lawyers an obligation beyond simply giving clients legal advice and then letting them do what they want. As the SEC sees it, a lawyer must tell his client whether certain conduct will violate federal securities law; if the client wants to go ahead anyway, the lawyer must withdraw from the case and even tell the SEC that a violation is about to be committed. If he doesn't, according to the SEC's view, then the lawyer also is violating the law.

The violations charged against the lawyers and Peat-Marwick centre on a so-called "comfort letter," a prerequisite for the merger. The letter was supposed to state that Peat-Marwick had no reason to believe that an unaudited interim financial statement by National Student Marketing wasn't properly prepared. The letter also was supposed to state that the company hadn't suffered any material adverse change in its financial position or operating results since the statement was issued.

In fact, the SEC alleges, the auditing firm recommended to National Student Marketing and both law firms that "significant" adjustments be made in the financial statement. But the merger was closed anyway, it charges, without disclosure of the letter's contents to the shareholders of the merging companies and to the investing public in general. The SEC says there was no disclosure even though National Student Marketing, White & Case, Lord-Bissell and certain officials in those firms "knew shareholder approval of the merger had been obtained on the basis of materially false and misleading financial statements" of National Student Marketing for the period ended May 31, 1969.

As part of the "fraudulent scheme," the SEC alleges, both law firms issued legal opinions — at the direction of certain of their partners involved in the merger — stating that the merger was being consummated validly and that they didn't know of any law their clients had violated. The commission contends the two firms — whose lawyers are said to have been aware of the Peat-Marwick recommendation — should have refused to issue the opinions and should have insisted that the financial statements be revised. Failing that, the SEC says, the firms should have withdrawn from the case and "under the circumstances" notified the SEC about the misleading nature of the statements. Peat-Marwick should have followed similar procedures, the SEC contends.

While the naming of law firms is a new development, the SEC has in recent months been filing a stream of actions involving public accounting firms, banks and individual lawyers. In some cases, the SEC has charged the party with active participation in an illegal stock scheme. But perhaps more important, SEC attorneys say, the SEC has also been holding those professions responsible if they let themselves be used as tools for the execution of a stock fraud.

What bothers lawyers about the National Student Marketing case is that it suggests law firms have the same public responsibilities as auditing firms. Attorneys view themselves first and foremost as advocates for their clients' cause, not as representatives of the public. In contrast, they argue, public accounting firms represent themselves as independent entities on which the public can rely for an objective evaluation of their clients' financial statements. Moreover, they contend, lawyers usually are passing on highly technical questions of whether a transaction fits within the law, not on whether it's sound and would make a good investment.

Attorneys also argue that the SEC's stand will put a severe strain on the confidential attorney-client relationship because the commission says attorneys should snitch on clients who are about to violate the law. A few lawyers say some clients now may feel impelled to withhold crucial information from their legal counsel. Carrying their argument to the extreme, they maintain this secrecy would defeat the SEC's basic aim, which is to rely on lawyers to keep their clients honest.

Other attorneys say that's ridiculous. They insist the American Bar Association's ethical code already obligates lawyers, in cases where a client is about to commit a crime, to withdraw from the case and possibly report it to proper authorities. Moreover, these attorneys contend, most clients are simply too dependent on lawyers in complicated securities cases to risk jeopardizing a business venture by withholding important information.

What's apparently bothering the SEC is a growing feeling that too many securities lawyers have lost sight of everything but their obligation to be an advocate. As one SEC official put it recently, "The securities bar is getting to be like the tax bar; it's specializing in finding loopholes in the law."[20]

The Public Interest and Self-Regulation

Logically, the easiest way to resolve any differences between the public interest and that of any self-regulating profession would be to completely eliminate such internal governing procedures. Certainly there should be strong resistance to the granting of such powers to any new professional or pseudo- or quasi-professional groups. Moreover, there are doubtless cases, such as that cited below, where existing powers of this kind should be rescinded:

Why are funeral directors allowed the right of self-government anyway?

That's the first question [which] comes to mind in considering allegations that an unidentified Toronto funeral director has been burying unclaimed bodies on the cheap without providing the minimum necessities for which he was being paid by welfare authorities. Spokesmen for Ontario's embalmers and funeral directors have announced that disciplinary proceedings have been commenced against the director in question. They refuse to identify him because, they say, his business may be hurt by the publicity the case is getting.

James McRuer, former Chief Justice of the Ontario High Court, had a good deal to say about self-governing occupations in his report on civil rights a few years ago. "Disciplinary powers are penal powers," he said. ". . . The private disciplinary justice meted out by self-governing bodies is, in a very real sense, an anachronism the survival of which can only be justified if all the interests concerned are better protected by this method than they could be by any other. . . .

"A perusal of the relevant statutes indicates that the powers of self-government appear to have been extended to bodies where the technical competence of their members could well be controlled by licencing, without extending to them the monopolistic attributes of self-government."

[20] Wayne E. Green, "Irate Attorneys: a Bid to Hold Lawyers Accountable to Public Stuns, Angers Firms", The Wall Street Journal, 1972. Reprinted with permission of The Wall Street Journal © Dow Jones & Company, Inc., 1972.

In any list of occupations from which the right of self-government ought to be removed, surely embalmers and funeral directors would take a prominent place. What really is achieved through self-government that couldn't be achieved better through a system of outside licencing? The fact that there hasn't been a disciplinary hearing in at least 15 years leads to the suspicion that embalmers and funeral directors may not have been particularly vigorous in policing their occupation. After all, they really can't be that much more virtuous than lawyers and doctors whose professions have several disciplinary hearings each year.

That being said, however, it becomes necessary to consider the facts of this particular case. Although the system should be changed, it would be unfair to do it retroactively.

Nevertheless, even within the context of a bad system, the matter is not being handled in a manner to inspire any sort of confidence. Everything is being done behind closed doors. The embalmers and funeral directors will look after their own. The public need not worry.

But this case goes far beyond the situation where the public may not be getting adequate service. It involves the allegation that the public has been bilked. That public funds were paid to procure decent burials and that what was delivered was a shoddy imitation.

What is required is assurance that the crown attorney's office has looked at the matter to see whether charges are appropriate — charges that would require a trial in a public courtroom. And that the Metro Welfare Department has investigated the possibility of civil action to recover funds that may be owing.

Only if the public is satisfied that there are no grounds for criminal charges and no justification for seeking civil recovery of funds can it accept disciplinary procedures as a correct resolution of the matter.

And only if the right to self-government is revoked can it have any real confidence in the future supervision of embalmers and funeral directors.[21]

Nonetheless, there are instances — such as law and medicine — where a strong case can be made for self-regulation if only because none but the professionals in question can really decide on the minimum standard of proficiency which should apply in their occupations. Bearing this in mind, the challenge then becomes that of ensuring that any such self-governing powers are exercised strictly in the public interest. This is not an easy task although there are a variety of techniques that can be utilized to bring about this objective. In most cases what is required is a combination of checks and balances and/or public participation in the self-regulatory procedures which are permitted. A number of steps that can be taken to make self-regulating professional bodies more responsive to the public interest are explored in the following article which incorporates some of the author's own thinking on this subject:

In this age of consumerism, a curious phenomenon has been the relative immunity from fundamental scrutiny so far enjoyed by many service industries, and especially the professions.

While questions of the accessibility of medical, legal and other professional services to all who need these services have attracted the concern of policy-makers, rarely has an attempt been made to move beyond the

[21] "Wrong from the Beginning", *The Globe and Mail*, Toronto, October 7, 1972.

question of access to a general re-evaluation of the role and structure of the professions in contemporary society.

However, there are many indications that consumerism is starting to fix a firm focus on the professions.

In the medical profession, the recent Pickering report commissioned by the Ontario Medical Association found that more than three-quarters of the people surveyed had serious complaints about doctors, most of them about the service and human relations aspects of medical services.

In the legal profession, the Prevost Commission in Quebec several years ago again found in surveys that a majority of citizens have negative attitudes about lawyers.

More specifically, the federal Minister of Urban Affairs, Ron Basford, has recently charged that inflated legal fees are a significant factor in the high costs involved in buying a house. The high costs of undefended divorces and other routine legal processes have also attracted fire. The expense, delays, unpleasantness and often organizational chaos of our court system have been widely documented.

In the pharmacy profession, criticisms are being voiced about the high cost of prescription drugs and the dubious value of many patent medicines sold by pharmacies.

In the dentistry profession, we are witnessing in Ontario an acrimonious confrontation between dentists and denturists. In the past few days, the provincial Minister of Health, Dr. Richard Potter, has voiced concern about some of the professional practices of chiropractors. At the same time, both levels of government has promised investigations into alleged price-fixing and monopolistic practices in the optical industry. Funeral directors have been attacked for shortcut burials of indigents, furtive disciplinary proceedings and fee-gouging. Mr. Pickering rightly concluded in his report (his remark can be applied to all professions):

"There is no reason to believe that the medical profession is any more likely to escape the pressures and demands of consumerism than any other profession or business which charges a fee for a service rendered or a price for a product sold. Consumerism is not in the slightest degree interested in maintaining the status quo of the establishment. A well-informed, inquisitive and concerned public is increasingly making its demands known."

Until now, the approach in Ontario to the kind of problems outlined has been to react (to the extent there has been a reaction at all) to each of them specifically. However, this form of ad hocery ignores the more fundamental need to construct a general regime of public accountability which will contain within itself the capacity to respond, in a rational and objective way, to legitimate demands that are made by consumers of professional services.

In Quebec, the Castonguay Commissions' report on the professions and the Professional Code subsequently enacted from it, in Ontario the McRuer Commission's inquiry into civil rights and, in Alberta, the current select committee inquiry into the professions, all recognize the importance of evolving a master policy in relation to the professions.

In evolving such a policy, the critical relationships that fail to be resolved are those between (a) self-regulation, e.g. what professions warrant the grant of the privilege of self-regulation and to what extent? (b) competition policy, e.g. to what extent should the right of entry into a profession and the setting of professional fees be subject to the usual competitive norms? (c) public participation, in the government of the professions, e.g. should there be public participation in professional decision-making processes pertaining to right of entry, fee-setting and disciplinary proceedings. How extensive should this participation be and what are the appropriate structures for it?

With reports out of Queen's Park that the Government is considering transferring some licencing functions which it now discharges in relation to, for example, insurance and mortgage brokers, car dealers, collection agents, door-to-door salesmen, to the industries concerned for self-administration, many of the issues that arise with the self-governing professions may shortly take on an even more urgent and expanded character.

However, confining the present observations, for the most part, to the traditional self-governing professions, I suggest that a master policy on the professions must meet the following touch-stones:

(1) No profession or industry should be conceded any self-governing rights whatever unless there pre-exists a comprehensive, cohesive, professional or trade association which commands the adherence of most members of the relevant profession or industry.

In addition, where the track record of the profession or industry fails to reflect a minimum acceptable level of responsiveness to legitimate public complaints or demands, this again should act as a disqualification, at least for the time being, from self-governing privileges.

(2) No self-governing profession or industry should be entitled, alone, to define standards to be met for entry to that profession or industry.

McRuer, the Quebec Professional Code, the Economic Council of Canada and the recent Crispo report on the professions to the now-defunct Prices and Incomes Commission, all favor, as a solution, a substantial public presence on the governing council of each profession.

Crispo recommends a percentage of one-third, with various constituencies such as the Consumers Association of Canada, the Chamber of Commerce, trade unions, universities and anti-poverty groups being given a right to nominate a designated number of representatives, a procedure designed to ensure a measure of independence both from the profession and government in the appointment process. As an additional safeguard, admission standards proposed by a professional body should, as McRuer suggests, be subject to final voting by the Government (preferably through one ministry only) before regulations are passed embodying them.

(3) Some public presence is required on each profession's committee of discipline to ensure that the profession's code of ethics is enforced with proper vigor.

This is provided for in the Quebec Professional Code, although there the Government-appointed member must also be a member of the profession in question. The public's interest would seem better safeguarded if the public representative was not also drawn from the profession. Election could be by the lay representatives on the governing body of each profession.

In addition, there is a strong argument for requiring all disciplinary committee proceedings to be public. The arguments of McRuer against this — that a professional person stands to be prejudiced more by adverse publicity than other classes of persons — is not persuasive.

(4) No profession or industry should be permitted to set minimum fee schedules. At most, only suggested fee schedules, which individual professionals should be free to depart from as they wish, should be permitted. . . .

However, banning minimum fee schedules is not enough. In addition advertising of fees for routine services should be permitted, rather than prohibited, as in usual at present.

In the pharmacy profession in the United States, where pharmacy chains have defied the ban on advertising of prescription drug prices, savings of up to 35 per cent to consumers have resulted.

In short, in the area of fee-setting, what is needed is a substantial public presence in the drawing up of suggested fee schedules (where even these are thought desirable) and visible, vigorous, price competition. As Pickering writes, "any unilateral system of fee-setting under present conditions is anachronistic and is no longer socially or politically defensible."

The assumption which underlies the present regime of professional self-government is that professionals are totally lacking in self-interest and, without exception, infused with a nobility of spirit and a sense of public service that other economic animals in our free enterprise system can only admire but never emulate. Thus, it has been assumed that external disciplines on fee-setting and other conduct are redundant.

Needless to say, there is no evidence to support the view that professionals walk among us as a special breed of ascetic philosopher kings. Indeed, their incomes, between 1963 and 1970, increased one-third faster than workers in the manufacturing sector.

(5) Every self-governing profession should be required to develop a mandatory continuing education program which, whether it involves formal, periodic recertification or not, provides minimum assurance to consumers of those professional services that each member of that profession has kept properly in tune with advances in his field of expertise. In an age of dramatic knowledge obsolescence, certification 20 or 30 years prior to the provision of a service provides no guarantee of continuing expertise.

(6) No self-governing profession should have statutory control over others who are not members of that profession — dentists over denturists, lawyers over law clerks, pharmacists over pharmacy technicians.

This form of paternalism tends to freeze professions in established, unitary molds and inhibits the development of para-professionals or sub-professionals who, because of lower educational overheads and scale economies, may be capable of performing certain routine professional services for the public at much reduced prices.

George Bernard Shaw once observed that "all professions are conspiracies against the laity." Because people usually go to professionals with troubles of one sort of another, inevitably their mental associations with them will often not be warm ones.

However, unnecessary mistrust, misconceptions and contrived mystique can be dispelled if the professions can be persuaded (or, if necessary, compelled) to abandon their medieval guild mentality, open up the doors of their secret societies and face up squarely to legitimate public scrutiny.[22]

On the anticombines or antitrust front it is encouraging to note positive developments in both the U.S. and Canada. The U.S. has been testing the government's use of this means to cope with abuses among the professions for several years now:

Justice Dept. antitrusters are about to drop a blockbuster on their fellow professionals. The Antitrust Div. will shortly file suit against a local bar association — as yet unnamed — charging that the minimum fee schedules commonly circulated by such groups are a form of unlawful price-fixing.

The Antitrust Div. usually prepares new prosecutions in close-mouthed secrecy, unveiling them only when suits are actually filed in court. But this suit, which would have caused shock waves in the legal community if brought just a few years ago, should cause no surprise now. For two years, department brass have been widely and publicly advertising their belief that such price-fixing is illegal and that they would move to stop it.

The suit, and the campaign preceding it, are part of a deliberate Justice Dept. policy aimed at ending practices used by various professional groups to protect themselves from price competition. Many state bar associations, for example, have long believed that "deliberate fee cutting for the purpose of soliciting business is an unethical practice." Although codes of ethics are not usually legally enforceable, as a practical matter the professional's failure to abide by them may result in sanctions against him by his professional association. Such sanctions as censure, suspension or disbarment can cripple or destroy his ability to work. Accountants, architects, engineers, and real estate men are among those already attacked, and department lawyers are now considering whether there are grounds to move against West Coast physicians in private practice who have unionized to negotiate with hospitals for uniform fee schedules.

A former Justice Dept. antitruster says that the idea of attacking lawyers' minimum fee schedules "has been kicking around for 20 years." In the mid-1960s, the government moved against restrictive practices in the funeral industry and also began to take a dim view of the restrictions placed on retail drug price advertising. The spade work for the cases against accountants and real estate men was done during the final months of the Johnson Administration.

A broader umbrella. But the current systematic assault on professionals is really a development of the past five years. When Richard W. McLaren was Justice's antitrust chief, he spotlighted professional codes of ethics that inhibit price competition as one of the important factors causing consumer bills to soar. Thomas E. Kauper, the current division head, agrees. "Price-fixing by professional organizations is not immune from the antitrust laws. We seek a competitive climate in the delivery of those services to the public," Kauper says.

This concentrated attention on the professions stems partly from developments in the law — most recently, civil rights prosecutions — that

[22] M.J. Trebilcock, "Making Professions Accountable to the Public", The Globe and Mail, Toronto, January 4, 1974.

have greatly broadened the definition of what constitutes interstate commerce and thus, at least by implication, what practices can be attacked under the federal antitrust laws. It stems also from the increasingly important role played by the service industries in the national economy. Twenty-five years ago, only 30% of the dollars spent by consumers went for services. Today, services account for more than 40% of those dollars. Bruce Wilson, who as an aide to McLaren and now as Deputy Assistant Attorney General has been overseeing the cases against professionals, says that "price-fixing and other anticompetitive conduct in the service area have direct and adverse impacts on the consumer's pocketbook."

So far, the Justice Dept. has had notable success in its prosecutions against professionals. Except for the National Society of Professional Engineers (NSPE), which is now fighting the antitrust Div. in court, none of the other cases has required a trial. Each of the groups has signed a consent decree promising to change operating procedures. Architects, for example, are now free to bid competitively on a job and real estate men to negotiate sales commission rates directly with their clients.

Once the investigation of lawyers' fees began, several state bar associations, including those in Florida, Michigan, and Massachusetts, dropped their fee schedules. Bar associations have shown an increased willingness to forego their schedules since a federal district court ruled last spring in a private suit brought by an FTC attorney that a Virginia local bar association's fee schedule violated the Sherman Act. That case is being appealed.

A direct appeal. In the government's suit against the NSPE, the courts may eventually decide just how much power the Antitrust Div. has to rewrite professional codes of conduct. Lee Loevinger, head of the division from 1961 to 1963, and now chief defense counsel for the NSPE, argues that "the antitrust laws were never intended to cover professional activities." Based on an almost casual comment in an 1834 Supreme Court decision, many lawyers have maintained over the years that the "learned professions" are not trades subject to regulation under the federal antitrust laws. In 1939, when the government challenged attempts by the American Medical Assn. and other doctor groups to stop the development of prepaid group practice, the Supreme Court sidestepped the issue and ruled against the AMA on the ground that the unlawful activity involved a corporate hospitalization scheme, not medical practice per se.

The NSPE is also claiming that its ban on members competing for jobs on a price basis is not price-fixing and is in the public interest as a means of insuring high standards. "If we lose, the ABA canons of ethics and virtually every other profession will be destroyed," Loevinger says. "What they apparently want is ads in the paper saying cut-rate engineering services and cut-rate legal services," he adds.

A pretrial hearing in the NSPE case has been called by the federal district court in Washington for Jan. 14, and a trial date for later in 1974 may be set then. Whatever the decision, a direct appeal to the Supreme Court seems likely.[23]

Meanwhile in Canada, the still-to-be-enacted Competition Act promises a range of action to be taken against similar groups:

[23] "Antitrust Hits the Professions". Reprinted from the December 8, 1973 issue of *Business Week* by special permission. Copyright 1973 by McGraw-Hill, Inc.

Doctors, lawyers, bankers, stock brokers, real estate and insurance agents and other professional and service industry groups are trying to determine the effect of the new draft Competition Act on what they charge for their services.

The bill, which will replace the Combines Investigation Act, extends the prohibitions against price fixing in the combines act to the professions and service industries. It also broadens the general scope of the present legislation.

Section 16 of the draft clearly outlaws any agreement to fix, in any manner whatever, the price or any other term of condition of a service (or commodity). However, there are exceptions. Section 92 exempts any agreement sanctioned by federal or provincial legislation.

This means that if a professional or service industry association can get a province to pass a law authorizing it to set fees or prices, there would be no breach of the Competition Act.

Here is a look at the apparent effect of the draft on some professional and service groups.

Doctors

The way provincial medicare plans work, it is uncertain whether the fee schedules set by provincial medical associations would constitute a violation of the Competition Act.

All payments made under medicare plans are based on the fee schedules set by the doctors in the particular province. These schedules, therefore, have at least the tacit approval of the provincial government.

Most medicare plans provide for consultation between the doctors and the government in the establishment of the fee schedules.

Fees set by medical associations are intended as a guide to what to charge for "normal services under normal circumstances." Doctors may charge either more or less than the tariff. However, membership in the associations obliges a doctor to inform a patient if he intends to charge more than the tariff.

Lawyers

Various local or county law associations establish tariffs they suggest as reasonable charges for various nonlitigious services (i.e., not involving court actions). These associations are voluntary and have no disciplinary or enforcement powers.

Most lawyers use the tariff as a guide to setting their fees. If a client thinks he has been overcharged, he can have this bill reviewed, or "taxed," by an officer of the court. The taxing officer can order the bill reduced if he finds it unjustifiably high.

Despite the lack of real control over fees by the law associations, the broad wording of the Competition Act could rule out the present recommended tariffs, in the absence of provincial legislation empowering the associations to set a suggested fee scale.

Where litigation is involved, costs, including fees, may be approved by the court and the new act would seem to have no bearing on such charges.

Real estate agents

Real estate boards across the country set commissions that member agents charge for selling houses. In many areas, the commission is 5% for an exclusive listing, 6% for a multiple listing.

With some boards, charging the recommended commission is a mandatory condition of membership. In other cases, commission rates are simply suggested. Some boards enforce their recommended rates by expelling those who don't adhere to the charges: others don't enforce their suggested rates.

It is clear the draft bill would mean the end of the present commission-selling practices.

Stock brokers

The present practice of the stock exchanges in fixing minimum commissions for brokers would be a breach of Section 16 of the draft bill. (Commissions on transactions above $500,000 are open to negotiation.)

Since stock exchanges are subject to the provincial securities commissions, the fixing of minimum commissions has the implied blessing of a government agency. It would be a short step for a provincial legislature officially to sanction the fixing of commission rates by an exchange through an amendment to the Securities Act.

General agents

The fixing of maximum commission rates for agents by insurance companies would be a violation of the draft bill. The Canadian Underwriters' Association sets such rates now on behalf of its member companies.

Banks

The draft bill also contains provisions to amend the Bank Act making it illegal for the banks to agree on service charges, as well as on interest rates on loans and deposits.[24]

The danger in all of these areas is that no more than token gestures will be made to guard against the pursuit of professional interests as opposed to those of the public. The risk of tokenism is particularly acute when it comes to public participation in the pertinent licensing bodies, the most appropriate model for which may well be akin to that suggested for major corporate boards in a previous chapter. That tokenism can plague every effort designed to make self-regulatory bodies more accountable and responsible is a threat which is not to be minimized:

A major dilemma, among many which exist in the field of health care, is how to determine the balance between self-regulation and public regulation of professional bodies such as dentists and doctors. The Health Disciplines Act, currently before the Ontario Legislature, is the Government's response to this dilemma and to concomitant problems in professional law and relations among various health disciplines.

While the act provides some new controls, it reflects none of the recent interest in changed concepts in the health care field, and it fails lamentably to permit any significant degree of public regulation of community input. The participation of the consumer in the five health profes-

---

[24] Robert Catherwood, "How Competition Act May Affect Professionals, Service Groups", *The Financial Post*, August 21, 1971.

sions — dentistry, medicine, nursing, optometry and pharmacy — remains minimal. All that's offered is the creation of a Health Disciplines Board.

The board would consist of five to seven members appointed by Cabinet. No civil servants or anyone who is or has been registered in the health disciplines could be a board member. Would the board provide sufficiently for public participation?

The original Health Disciplines Board as envisaged in the 1972 proposal would have been a reasonably strong board with definite over-all powers, which would have counterbalanced the strong professional bias of the professional governing councils. Had this been implemented it would have been able to break the protective chain which stretches from the profession through the Ontario Medical Association and the Royal College of Physicians all the way to the Ministry of Health and the minister himself.

However, the Health Disciplines Board, as envisaged in this 1974 Act, is an eviscerated and emasculated body largely deprived of any substantial authority. And the proposal to appoint three to five persons to the Royal College of Physicians just makes sure that they would be lost and outvoted amid the much stronger body of elected professionals. Only a significant number of intelligent, informed lay people, approaching 50 per cent of the composition of the council, can have a chance of exerting some countervailing force to the existing professional power structure.

Another major flaw in the whole general area is the assumption that a high standard of service is ensured because incompetent or inadequate practitioners are weeded out through complaints by the public. This assumption is undoubtedly the largest single delusion in the act. It is well known that citizens are hesitant to approach large bureaucratic official bodies. They often need help in making their point so that they do not feel intimidated. There should be provision in this act for a "patient advocate" — someone who will know where the complaint should go and how to present it. A system of self-government which depends on written complaints from a grieved patient is doomed to fail. What is required is something along the lines of New Zealand's ombudsman dealing exclusively with health matters.

But as it is, the lack of teeth in the Health Disciplines Board and the rigid codification of the existing powers and responsibilities of the profession means that the board will be ineffectual in dealing with many of the problems outlined. Physicians will continue to have too much control in the health care system. The new act should have had some of this tight control loosened, making it possible for other members of the health team to participate more in patient care. The act fails to recognize that a different type of professional may be delivering health care in addition to, concurrently with or in substitution for, the doctor.

The proposed Health Disciplines Board is designed in such a way that it can only remain ineffectual and tokenistic, since no attempt except in a window-dressing fashion is made to include the public and the community in health cure decisions. And that is a pity.[25]

[25] Jan Dikszta, "Proposed Health Body: Toothless Tokenism", *The Globe and Mail*, Toronto, May 14, 1974.

A particularly strong case can be made for more effective public participation in police work, a field which, if not already considered professional, should be. Here the need is for a public review board, first and foremost to protect the average citizen in the street from police abuses, but second, and hardly very far behind, to defend and justify necessary police action when such action is so easily distorted by those with ulterior motives. The police function is difficult under the best of circumstances, but it has never been more difficult than it is in North American cities today — cities suffering from overcrowded ghettos, and near-ghettos, and mixed populations whose values change faster than outmoded laws can keep up with.

The case for a police public review board is strong even in Metropolitan Toronto which is a relatively crime-free and peaceful city and which has, by most standards, one of the finest police forces in the world:

There's a brief in the desk of Terry Meagher, executive secretary of the Labor Council of Metropolitan Toronto. Next week, it will go to the council's executive and then start the trip on to Metro Council. It will put the Labor Council into one of the longest-standing hassels in this — or any other — city:

Who polices the police?

Where does Joe Citizen, the little guy, go to complain if he feels himself a victim of poor service or nastiness or assault or harassment by the police?

The Labor Council brief will ask for establishment of a civilian review board to investigate complaints against policemen. (A review board, if it follows the example of the few established in the U.S., hears both sides of the story in a complaint against a policeman, then makes recommendations to the chief of police. It has no power to discipline a policeman or anyone else.)

The Labor Council will be joining the Canadian Civil Liberties Association in its long campaign for a review board.

CCLA chairman Sydney Midanik wrote Magistrate C.O. Bick, chairman of the Metro Police Commission, two weeks ago asking for talks about a new procedure for investigating complaints. Midanik pointed out that his association "is not wedded to this alternative but suggest this as one approach."

If the Labor Council wonders about Magistrate Bick's reaction to a review board suggestion, it can get a pretty good idea from his reply to the Midanik letter at Thursday's police commission meeting: "I sometimes wonder whether these people know what they are talking about."

He dismissed the Midanik letter with one of the nastiest phrases in police talk: ". . . only a pitch for a review board."

Former mayor Phil Givens, a member of the Metro Police Commission for three years, says the idea "has all the future of a snowball on a hot stove."

Magistrate Bick asks: "What do they think we are? There's five of us. We're civilians. We review the actions of the police."

Maybe so, says lawyer and long-time civil liberties expert Irving Himel, but "the police commission is the employer of the policemen and it's just not possible for a commission like that to conduct an investigation into its own department and come up with a report that will inspire public confidence.

"I don't think there's as much opposition to the independent review board concept now as there used to be. A lot of policemen, if they don't actually seek a review board, certainly aren't opposed to the principle."

Constable Syd Brown, president of the Metro Police Association and spokesman for Toronto's 3,200 policemen, wants a change in the present police commission set-up although "we're against the review board system because of the disastrous experience they've had with it where it's been tried in the States.

The present commission there consists of a doctor and three businessmen, representing every major ethnic group in the community.

"Our men certainly don't oppose better systems for investigation of complaints, either against us or by us," says Brown. "That's something we're been after for years. The present commission's policy of secret hearings certainly doesn't do us any good. But we need an improvement of the present system, not one more body in the policeman-investigating business."

There certainly are plenty of bodies that currently oversee the police. There are the courts, criminal and civil. The case of an east-end juvenile who claims he was shot by a plainclothesman has to go before the criminal courts following a charge of criminal negligence against the policeman.

Any citizen who thinks he has been badly treated by anyone can sue, but the civil courts are notoriously slow. Last week a Church St. club owner had his case thrown out when he sued a policeman over what he claimed was false arrest. That incident occurred in December, 1965.

Two weeks ago a former policeman paid an out-of-court settlement to a youth who said he was roughed up and forced to kiss the policeman's boots — in 1964.

The police commission can investigate the actions of any policeman. It also acts as an appeal board for any policeman who feels he hasn't been fairly treated in a department hearing by Chief James Mackey.

The Ontario Police Commission, a supercommission that oversees all the police commissions in the province, can act as an appeal.

"Down there every policeman in a review board city walked the beat with the feeling that someone wsa looking over his shoulder all the time. The men, instead of reacting fast to situations, stopped and figured that if they do anything they might have to explain it to a board some day. If they do nothing, they don't have to explain anything. You don't have law and order in a city where the policemen do nothing.

"The solution lies in a change in the present commission system. Right now, three of our present commissioners — Magistrate Bick, the chairman, Judge Ian Macdonnell and Chief Magistrate Arthur Klein — are, in effect, on the job for life. If their appointments were for a term such as three years perhaps they'd be more sensitive to outside ideas, from both the public and the men."

The Bick, Klein and Macdonnell appointments were made by the provincial government. Metro Council appoints the other two members, Metro Chairman William Allen and York Mayor Jack Mould. That makes Mould the only one of the five who holds office by election.

The best system, says Brown, is in Los Angeles where a five-man commission runs the police force, each commissioner being appointed for a three-year term by city council.[26]

One possible model for a police public review board would be as follows: a seven man lay body, with three members selected by the police association or union, none, of course, to be drawn from their own ranks; three others selected by leading members of the media, such as the editors of the area's major papers; and the seventh, the chairman, to be selected by the other six. Such a body could hear complaints from both citizens and police, pass judgment on individual cases, and issue an annual report on the state of citizen-police relations in the community.

A final note about professional accountability and responsibility is in order. This point was raised in a more general sense in an earlier chapter in the context of the conscientious employee who informs on his employer for activities he believes to be contrary to the public interest. This poses a challenge of individual rights which should be of special concern to professional associations. The problems involved in shifting auditors in the accounting profession in order to avoid an adverse audit provide an excellent case in point. Perhaps such shifts should be barred in the absence of a valid reason sanctioned by the governing body of the accounting profession. As long as the public is well represented on such a body, such a bar would seem to have many advantages and few disadvantages, especially in terms of raising the quality of auditing standards.

Some of the problems entailed for individual professionals who choose to stand for ethics and integrity are brought out in the following article which indicates that a lot remains to be done, particularly by professional associations, to protect such high standards of behaviour.

If you're convinced your boss is putting out an unsafe product or wasting taxpayer money through mis-management, can you speak up candidly without losing your job?

Rarely, according to the case studies of those who have dared.

However, slowly but steadily the situation is improving, say researchers at Ralph Nader's Clearinghouse for Professional Responsibility. Apparently legal protection and colleague support for those who do blow the whistle on government or industry in the name of the public interest is coming.

One well-publicized case which recently took a turn that is proving inspiring to many who have been reticent to speak their piece is that of A. Ernest Fitzgerald.

He is the former civilian cost analyst for the Air Force who, calmly and accurately, predicted in testimony on Capitol Hill four years ago that the cost overrun on the C5A would amount to more than $2 billion.

Shortly afterward, he was dismissed from his $26,000 a year job, though ostensibly not for political reasons.

After a lengthy and costly legal fight, financed in large part by the American Civil Liberties Union, which took an interest in the case, Mr. Fitzgerald this fall was ordered reinstated to a position with the Air Force and deemed eligible to collect back pay.

One of those extremely pleased by this turn of events — "I'm very happy for Ernie, he's an outstanding American" — is Henry Durham of

[26] Robert Johnstone, "Who Should Police Our Police?", Toronto Star, April 27, 1968.

Marietta, Ga., another whistle-blower whose experience was a particularly difficult one.

Mr. Durham was a former production control supervisor at Lockheed Aircraft's Marietta plant. When he witnessed what he calls "gross mismanagement," including what he charged was falsification of company records to trigger certain installment payments due the company, he took his complaint through the industry ranks on up to the president and the chairman of the board. The responsiveness, he says, was nil.

Eventually he left the company, and, still concerned, spelled out the problem publicly before a congressional committee. A General Accounting Office report, researched shortly afterward, confirmed the substance of his findings.

All this has taken a heavy toll on Mr. Durham and his family. "I've lost almost everything I had fighting this thing," he admitted in a telephone interview with the Monitor from Florida where he is still, three years after the event, looking for work.

He came close to taking one job, but the board of directors of the firm said the "repercussions from Lockheed" would be too great for them to take him on.

At one point during his whistle-blowing experience, he was receiving so many threatening phone calls that he and his family asked for protection of federal marshals, who subsequently set up house in the Durhams' home for two months.

However, despite all this and the fact that he has still not found a satisfactory job after 19 years of work for Lockheed, he says of his whistle-blowing action: "I'd do it a thousand times over, despite the hardships. . . . I have a strong feeling that it's more patriotic to do something about things that are wrong, even though it may rock the boat, than to sit back and do nothing."

The impact of Mr. Durham's action on Lockheed? "Nothing has changed," he says. "They've lost a lot of work. The C5A contract is gone, of course. People blame me for it."

Mr. Durham says he has had letters from many other company workers around the country equally convinced their speaking out would be in the public interest but who are afraid to because of the job consequences. That's why he stresses the need for more legislative safeguards to protect such employees.

Current laws protecting government employees are stronger than those aiding workers in private industry. An employee in the public sector, says Fritzie Cohen of Mr. Nader's Clearinghouse, is at least entitled to a day in court — if he has the money to support the fight.

"In private industry, if your employer doesn't like your politics, he can fire you," says Mrs. Cohen. "You lose certain constitutional rights when you take the job."

Currently on the books are provisions in the Occupational Safety and Health Act and the Water Pollution Control Act which afford some protection for workers who report violations of those laws. However, Clearinghouse workers consider the present path of recourse — to seek reinstatement via the Labor Department — unsatisfactory, since the government agency could conceivably choose to do nothing.

Certainly an important potential prod for stronger legislation and a rich possible source of moral support for the blue collar or professional whistle blower is the union or the association to which the employee may belong.

Unfortunately unions have traditionally been reluctant to wade into this muddy-water area and, indeed, many collective bargaining agreements specifically label the product of a company as management's concern.

To date, professional associations have not been much more progressive in supporting the professional and public responsibilities of their members, either. Currently far ahead of the others is the American Chemical Society, which recently elected as president a candidate who had strongly made known his concerns in this area. That group, some 110,000 members strong, is in the process of setting up a legal defense fund to help those fighting job dismissals where the society deems a fight justified.

Also, Chemical Society members have drafted and are backing an employee bill of rights amendment to the National Labor Relations Act.

Peter Petkas of the Clearinghouse, hopes the example may spur other associations to follow suit. He puts the situation bluntly: "If professional societies or unions, or both, don't do anything, nothing will ever be done."[27]

To conclude this chapter some brief thoughts are in order with respect to the role of unions in North America. First, and perhaps foremost, is the need to consider the dilemma of those who believe in democratic and responsive unions on one hand, and in accountable and responsible unions on the other. For the most part, this dilemma arises because democracy and responsiveness must be viewed in terms of a union's membership, while accountability and responsibility are usually considered in the context of the body politic and society at large. Were accountability and responsibility also visualized in terms of a union's membership, there would be little or no difficulty involved in reconciling these two competing sets of goals.

Assuming unions are going to reflect their members' aspirations, values and wants, they are almost bound to engage in conduct and seek ends that run counter to what many would deem to be in the public interest. The fact that this happens — often or seldom, depending on one's perspective and point of view — has led to the allegation that unions are held accountable and responsible for neither their means nor their ends. That there is considerable truth in this allegation is borne out by evidence that, like so many other individuals and institutions that violate the law in North America, unions too are often able to avoid answering for their transgressions. There are, however, two stages in the analysis which leads to such a conclusion. The first concerns the question of whether they can be called to account, and the second the issue of why, if this is possible, it does not happen more often.

As to the first question, there is no doubt that, for the most part, both in the United States and Canada, unions can be punished for engaging in illegal activities. Regarding violations of the applicable regulatory statutes, such as the Taft-Hartley Act in the United States and the Canadian Industrial Relations Act in Canada, it is true that the American law is better enforced than its Canadian equivalent. The reason is that under the National Labour Relations Board setup in the United States there is a separate and reasonably indepen-

[27] Lucia Mouat, "Help for Workers Who Blow the Whistle on Employers", The Christian Science Monitor, November 19, 1973.

dent Office of General Counsel, which can proceed on its own initiative with prosecutions for violations of the applicable legislation, whereas there is no such body in Canada. As a result, Canadian labour relations law — except for some facets of the Criminal Code — is in general self-enforcing in the sense that an aggrieved or offended party must take action on his own to protect his rights. The problem with this approach is that such a party, the employer in this case, may not dare to do so for fear of even more harmful retaliatory action which, though still more illegal, could put him out of business before he could achieve recourse.

Thus many charges of illegal union conduct are not even filed in Canada, or, if filed, are traded off as part of an out-of-court settlement to end the illegal behaviour. This disquieting situation should be alleviated, if not corrected, by moving towards the American Office of General Counsel arrangement. Even this avenue has its limitations, however, as interested parties may dissuade that body from pursuing a complaint in order to avoid further trouble. Nevertheless, the existence of such an office does tend to ensure that flagrant or persistent violations of industrial relations legislation are subject to prosecution, an assurance which is now completely lacking in Canada.

As for violations of outstanding collective agreements, Canada is, if anything, better off than the United States in terms of available remedies. With few exceptions, Canada imposes mandatory arbitration of disputes arising during the life of a collective agreement, whereas this is a much more voluntary process in the United States and not as universal. In both countries, however, arbitrators have become increasingly prone to levy damages against unions for infractions of the collective agreement for which they are clearly culpable. For the most part, this means illegal walkouts in which union officials have taken a leading part or have done little or nothing to disavow or terminate. Here again, however, the aggrieved employer must seek damages through arbitration, something he may choose not to do in return for a quick end to the strike. Perhaps then, this is another area where something like an Office of General Counsel should be empowered to take some action on its own, particularly if a pattern of harassment through illegal strikes appears to be emerging.

The point is that, within fairly wide limits, recourse is now available to hold unions more accountable and responsible for any unlawful behaviour. If there is a problem, it does not lie in the lack of available remedies, but in the failure to resort to them. As a consequence, the real question is how far the state should go, through some independent prosecuting office, to ensure more respect for the labour relations statutes it now has on the books. As in the case of many other areas of law, there is a fine line to be drawn between what might be termed appropriate and what might be deemed over-zealous enforcement of the law. What is suggested here is that more effective public enforcement mechanisms can and should be put in effect without crossing this fine line.

Regardless of the enforcement procedures followed, there is the related question of how to best punish unions and their leaders and members for infractions of the law. By and large, the answer does not lie in jail sentences, since they tend to make martyrs of those incurring them. Union leaders and members should only be jailed for serious criminal offenses or flagrant or persistent civil disobedience. The major recourse for legal infractions on the union side should lie in damages and fines, since significant monetary penalties are generally of much more lasting concern to labour than are jailings. It should be added, of course, that just the reverse tends to apply on the employer side, a point which should not go unnoted when it comes to law enforcement directed against illegal employer practices.

So far this discussion of union accountability and responsibility has been largely in terms of the procedural side of labour-management relations and the strikes to which it can give rise. Equally tough questions can be raised about the terms which unions strive for and often achieve, especially in consideration of their possible inflationary impact. Since many other institutions examined in this volume engage in activities which have potentially inflationary effects, this is an aspect of union accountability and responsibility which is better left to the concluding chapter where a proposal is advanced to undercut all questionable activity of such groups.

To return to the theme outlined at the beginning of this section, there is one facet of union behaviour that does require more attention, if not in the United States, at least in Canada. At issue is the relationship between a union and its members. Although created to advance and protect the interests of its members, unions sometimes find themselves at variance with the views and wishes of some of those whom they are authorized to represent. This can give rise to some ticklish situations — as a few Ontario teachers discovered to the public embarrassment of all concerned when they were threatened with discipline by their own federation for criticizing its leadership:

Ontario high school teachers who publicly criticized Donald Felker, general secretary of the Ontario Secondary School Teachers Federation, have been called before the OSSTF's relations and discipline committee to defend their action.

At least one teacher was told by the committee that he had violated a regulation under the Teaching Profession Act. This regulation forbids any teacher to make "an adverse report" on another OSSTF member without giving it to him in writing within three days.

The teacher was Douglas Dunn, math instructor at Eastern High School of Commerce, who said he was censured as a result of a letter published in The Globe and Mail last Dec. 15.

His letter said, in part:

"I see in the Dec. 11 Globe and Mail an advertisement in the form of a column written by Dr. Donald Felker, general secretary of the Ontario Secondary School Teachers Federation. . . . I would be delighted if Dr. Felker would outline some of the things he has done to help the poor teacher who must go into the classroom and teach.

"He did send a telegram congratulating William Davis on being elected Premier. I was fascinated because due to Mr. Davis's budget cuts my classroom had not been swept out twice that week, and we have been teaching in Toronto all through September, and October, without supply teachers. . . .

"I can point out many instances where, under Dr. Felker's administration, teachers have lost financial opportunity. Possibly he could come up with one instance where he has been any help. . ."

Mr. Dunn said yesterday: "He (Dr. Felker) brought me up in front of the committee on grounds that I had not given it to him in writing in three days, a bit of an attempt to bully me into keeping quiet."

He stood before the relations and discipline committee in March, and the committee supported Dr. Felker's complaint. This committee rules on unprofessional conduct by OSSTF members, and it can recommend that a teacher's certificate be suspended. But both the Minister of Education and the OSSTF's board of governors may overrule the committee. The minister has final say.

In Mr. Dunn's case the matter was apparently dropped after the committees found he had violated the regulation. He still has his teaching certificate.

Mr. Dunn said his defense was that the criticism was in the public domain and accessible to Dr. Felker within three days.

He said he can laugh about it now, but it wasn't so funny when he stood before the committee. "I would like to see a few doors and windows opened in the upper regions of the federation . . . And I think, for the money, we deserve better."[28]

In another Ontario case, the union involved eventually felt compelled to drop pending charges against over 400 of its members for crossing its own picket lines during a protracted strike:

During last year's strike against Ontario Hydro, 400 members of Local 1000 of the Canadian Union of Public Employees crossed their fellow workers' picket lines. In so doing, they violated their union's constitution, their local's bylaws, and the oath they took when they became members.

The fate of these 400 workers has been widely publicized in the wake of the recent arbitration board report imposing a final settlement of the dispute.

Hydro management had requested the board to prohibit any retaliatory action by the union against the strikebreakers. This the board declined to do. However, it admitted it had given the matter "long and anxious consideration" and opined that it would be "tragic" for the union to engage in "punitive retaliation and retribution."

"We are convinced," the report added, "that solidarity is retarded, not advanced . . . by the vindictive punishment of dissenters."

This emotive language, which obscures rather than illuminates the issue, has been echoed by management spokesmen and editorial writers. They deplore what they call "union vengeance," "reprisals," and "the harrassment of employees who acted within their legal rights."

Such a lofty moral tone might be justified if the union's disciplinary intent had a vengeful or vindictive purpose. But surely what is at stake is the fundamental question of whether any union can allow any member to flout its constitution with impunity.

Only when a union seeks to discipline its members is any outcry heard — and then only if their offence has been to undermine a strike. Had the Hydro 400 been charged instead with slandering union officers or joining another union, few outside voices would be raised on their behalf.

But no, they merely decided to work and collect their pay while their co-workers conducted a legal strike. For that their employer and the editorial writers would give them medals, but understandably their union mates feel somewhat less kindly disposed toward them.

It is worth noting, too, that managerial concern about the power of unions to control their members is never voiced when that control is aimed at enforcing the terms of a contract. Indeed, employers often complain loudly if unions don't penalize workers who loaf, malinger, or take part in wildcat strikes.

[28] Loren Lind, "Critics of OSSTF Official Are Hauled on to Carpet", *The Globe and Mail*, Toronto, April 14, 1972.

To demand that kind of tight internal discipline when the employers' interests are threatened, but not when the union's welfare is at stake, is as hyprocritical as it is illogical.

For the union to overlook their behavior and impose no penalties would be tantamount to scraping the constitution and giving 150,000 CUPE members across the country the go-ahead to work during a strike.

To refrain from penalizing the Hydro 400 would — contrary to the arbitration board's warning — promote and perpetuate much more internal division than would a general amnesty. Union trials, after all, are not kangaroo courts. Accused members are given every right they would enjoy in a court of law and penalties are seldom draconian. In any case, Ontario law prevents unions from requiring that an employee be discharged because he has been suspended or expelled from the union.

The worst that can happen to a "convicted" union member in Ontario, apart from expulsion, is a stiff fine; and presumably those who choose to work while their co-workers are on strike can afford to forfeit a few hundred dollars of their strikebreaking pay.[29]

The following extract from the *Report of the Prime Minister's Task Force on Labour Relations*, of which task force the author was a member, expands on the previous examples, raises the larger issues involved, and reveals again how public participation can help solve a problem involving conflicting private and public interests:

Trade unions originated as voluntary unincorporated associations or craftsmen who banded together to set rates at which they agreed to sell their services and secure job opportunities for their members. Today, many interests of trade unions are vested in the legal framework of collective bargaining, including monopoly bargaining rights. They can no longer claim the status of private associations whose internal affairs are solely their concern. They have become quasi-public bodies, if not public institutions, and the public has acquired an interest in their internal operations.

We note in Part Four that union abuse of power over their members is rare. Nonetheless, because of the possibility of abuses and the severity of their impact on individual rights, we make certain recommendations. There are four areas in which the individual is entitled to protection. The first relates to access to employment as it is affected by the operation of hiring halls, the regulation of standards of competency of job performance, and financial barriers to union membership. The second relates to the right to continuation in employment as that may be affected by continuing union membership. The third relates to the right to union membership to protect interests other than an interest in employment. The fourth relates to rights of "union citizenship".

We recommend that where a hiring hall operates in an industry as the effective avenue to employment in that industry, it should be operated by the Canada Manpower Service with the assistance and co-operation of the affected employers and union or unions through a joint labour-management advisory committee.

Where access to a particular trade, occupation or industry is conting-

[29] Ed Finn, "Should Union Punish the 400 Who Crossed Own Picket Lines?" Toronto *Star*, April 30, 1973.

ent upon the attainment of certain minimum standards of competency in order to protect the public interest, we recommend the standards be set and administered by a tribunal in which there is public participation and from whose decision there is a right to appeal. In other words, licensing should be performed by some body other than a union, in order that this function, and waiting periods associated with it, may not be used as a device for controlling the intake of members. The fact that a union may consider it has good reason to close its membership rolls in the interests of the economic security of its present members, or for any other reason, is not in our view valid reason for denying a non-member a certificate of qualification in a trade to which he would otherwise have a claim. External control of competency ratings need not preclude the operation of the seniority rule in hiring halls.

Where professional bodies have exclusive licensing powers, a case may be made for public participation in the licensing function and for a right of appeal. These are appropriate matters for the study of the activities of self-employed professional groups which we recommend earlier.

In the previous section we recommend the adoption of the agency shop as the basic form of union security. Under the protections attached to the agency shop the individual has a right to continue in employment as long as he stands willing to pay regular and reasonable dues and allied assessments. Under both the agency shop and higher forms of union security, there must be protection for employees in respect of the size of these dues and assessments. We recommend that either a Public Review Board of the type we recommend shortly or the Canada Labour Relations Board be empowered to hear and determine a petition from an employee or person seeking employment that such dues and assessments are unreasonable. We also recommend that one or other of these tribunals have jurisdiction to determine the reasonableness of initiation fees as possible financial barriers to union membership and thus to employment. The latter recommendation is more relevant to the union shop, the closed shop and other higher forms of union security than to the agency shop.

We recommend that legislation prescribe basic procedural rights in internal union affairs, including the right to be heard, to be tried by an impartial body, to be represented by counsel, to be protected against double jeopardy, to have access to a speedy trial and appeal, and to receive reasoned decision.

We recommend further that legislation guarantee to members the right to run for union office in elections held at regular intervals, to nominate candidates, to vote in union affairs, to attend and participate in union meetings, and to have equal access to union facilities, including the union newspaper, especially during election campaigns. We recommend further that legislation guarantee the right of union members to audited statements of union financial affairs and to possession of the union constitution, and the right of all employees in the bargaining unit to possession of any collective agreement affecting their employment.

Where a person's union membership is to be suspended or terminated by the union against the will of the member, we recommend that the constitution of the union provide machinery for appeal and review. The culmination of this appeal and review procedure should be a Public Review Board constituted in such a way that a decisive voice lies with persons drawn from outside the labour movement. . . . Rules should not be such as to preclude union members from engaging in otherwise lawful conduct unless that conduct seriously undermines the union's position as a bargaining agent. Thus, for example, dual unionism would not be a legitimate cause for union discipline, especially where one union cannot supply a worker with regular employment opportunities, unless a member is actively engaged in trying to supplant one union by another.

To avoid short-circuiting internal union appeal procedures, a member should be denied access to either a Public Review Board or the Canada Labour Relations Board until he has exhausted internal procedures, unless he can show that the resulting costs or delay will cause undue hardship. In determining whether such hardship would ensue, it would be relevant for the Public Review Board or the Canada Labour Relations Board to consider the fact that under our previous recommendation no person would lose his job for reasons other than non-payment of dues and assessments until he has exhausted appeal procedures.

We recommend further that either the Public Review Board or the Canada Labour Relations Board be empowered to review, in the manner of the Ontario legislation, union trusteeships where a parent union must notify the Ontario Labour Relations Board of a trusteeship over a subordinate unit and of the terms of the trusteeship as required by that Board, and a twelve month limitation period is placed on trusteeships without the consent of the Board.

In respect of industrial relations, we recommend that legislation guarantee a duty of fair representation, particularly in the handling of rights acquired under a collective agreement. We recommend that a member who is of the view that he has been denied fair representation have an appeal to the Public Review Board or, in the absence of such a board, to the Canada Labour Relations Board, and that a burden be placed on the union to establish that it considered the rights and interests of the individual and that it acted in good faith and in the interests of the bargaining unit as a whole.

A special onus of fair representation arises where two bargaining units are merged into a single unit. We recommend that the Canadian Labour Relations Board be empowered to review any arrangements made to resolve competing claims to seniority within the emergent unit upon the application of the bargaining agent in either of the predecessor units.

We recommend that there be no appeal on the merits in any of these areas from decisions made by either the Public Review Board or the Canada Labour Relations Board.[30]

As useful as the above-cited approaches may be in the context in which they were advanced, it should be acknowledged that some similar American approaches are now subject to criticism of a nature similar to that touched upon earlier. It is fitting, therefore, to end this section by referring to some recent American misgivings and reservations about their famous, or infamous, *Landrum-Griffith Act*, which goes to the heart of trying to reconcile the need for both democratic and responsive and accountable and responsible unions:

Is too much union democracy bad for collective bargaining? The National Commission for Industrial Peace raised that question last week

[30] A.W.R. Carrothers, et al., *Canadian Industrial Relations: Report of the Prime Minister's Task Force on Labour Relations* (Ottawa, Information Canada, 1968) p. 485-99. Reproduced by permission of Information Canada.

in its final report to President Nixon. In doing so, the commission unamimously recommended that "an objective and comprehensive review" be made of the 1959 Landrum-Griffin Act, particularly Title I, the "Bill of Rights" clause. The purpose: "to ascertain the effect it has had on the ability of labor organizations to engage in responsible and constructive labor relations." The commission also urged government to stay out of bargaining disputes wherever possible.

Appointed by President Nixon in 1972, the commission, headed by arbitrator David Cole, was charged with seeking solutions to collective bargaining problems. It is the first official body to question publicly the amount of democracy granted union members under the Act. Since passage of the so-called "Bill of Rights of members of labor organizations." business has been critical, and protests have been increasing largely because as many as 12% of the contracts negotiated each year have been rejected by rank-and-file unionists in ratification votes.

Objectives. Title I guarantees individuals a voice in union decisions, the right to argue with leadership policies, and the right to go to court for "reasonable" remedies if they believe their rights have been violated. Earlier this year a small group of United Steelworkers members sought to block the union-industry no-strike bargaining plan because, they argued unsuccessfully, it took away their guaranteed right to strike in a contract dispute. Commission members conceded that the objectives of Title I are valid and have forced the end of undemocratic practices in some unions, but labor members argued persuasively during deliberations over the past year that it has been used by union dissidents in ways that hinder effective bargaining.

The labor members have held, said the commission, that unions and their officers "have been attacked in legal proceedings so many times that they have tended to become shy and have not exercised the leadership and general responsibility necessary in this controversial area." This made it possible for minorities "to impose their wills on majorities" and for relatively small numbers of dissidents "to prevent settlements and cause unwarranted turmoil."[31]

[31] "Democracy's Impact on Union Bargaining". Reprinted from the May 18, 1974 issue of *Business Week* by special permission. Copyright 1974 by McGraw-Hill, Inc.

9

THE MEDIA AND THE MESSAGE

Last, but hardly least significant, of the institutions to be examined in this volume is the mass media. This is no easy task as the so-called "fourth estate" is today the subject of so much criticism and controversy. Nonetheless, it has such an essential role to play in society that a careful assessment of its place in the total scheme of things is unavoidable in a study of this kind.

Although this chapter will touch briefly on other aspects of the media, its role in the gathering and dissemination of news will be featured. It is largely in this capacity that the media has found itself in so much difficulty of late. The very credibility of the institution is presently under attack perhaps as never before. As the following book review reveals, even insiders are not publically voicing their skepticism concerning the accuracy and validity of much of the media's new coverage:

Writers who work on newsmagazines normally labor under a blanket of anonymity while colleagues on other magazines, newspapers, and television reap bylines and often become celebrities. Newsmagazines are the ultimate practitioners of group journalism, and readers are rarely aware of the gifted scriveners who toil there.

This book is a delight because it strips the veil from one veteran newsmagazine writer and reveals a man of considerable wisdom, charm, and compassion who deserves greater recognition. Thomas Griffith's book is a series of provocative essays on the state of American journalism, into which the author, 58, weaves his personal recollections as a member of the craft.

Griffith began as a newspaper reporter in his home state of Washington, became a Nieman Fellow at Harvard and joined Time in 1943. Despite strong ideological differences with Henry Luce, he has had a dazzling career in the Luce empire: senior editor in charge of national affairs and later of foreign news; assistant managing editor; senior staff editor of all Time Inc. publications; and editor of Life during its final years.

From this vantage, he has important observations on the business of bringing news to the public, provoked by the furious attacks against the press during the tumultuous 1960s and early 1970s. "The disquiet inside and outside the craft of journalism about its performance cannot be disregarded," he says, "and those who celebrate the advantages of robust free thought shouldn't mind a little buffeting."

Griffith himself has unkind things to say about television reporting ("expensively produced, marginally informative news snippet service, efficient in what it does but in no way adequate to the complexity and richness of events"), about the so-called school of New Journalism (which has a "strong streak of show biz and a frank admiration for the techniques of fiction"), and the deficiencies of the press in reporting white working-class discontent (the result of newsmen's tendency to "gravitate toward the articulate").

The author, however, is essentially defensive about journalism. But rather than employ the standard cliches to defend it, he expounds on what journalists to, what can rightfully be expected of them, and how newsmen affect the times they set out to record. In short, his book is a brilliant if rambling effort to win the sympathetic understanding of non-journalists.

On the much-debated question of objectivity in the press, Griffith says that readers must assume that newsmen have views and sympathies: "Journalists are not eunuchs." But good journalists, he notes, are alert skeptics, ready to put prejudices aside in considering evidence. Griffith tells his readers to "suspect the indifference that calls itself impartiality; it is the pedestrian asset of second-raters."

Then Griffith eloquently presents his own biases: "I find it difficult to write understandably about the banal, the brutal, the greedy, and the craven; hard to sympathize with people who have everything and are discontent; hardest of all to give sympathy to those who give no sympathy to others."

For the deteriorating quality of newspapers, Griffith levels most of the blame at absentee owners who have little commitment to the communities they serve. These owners, he argues, know little about what is going on and probably would not want to disturb things even if they did learn.

Two years ago, another former senior editor and assistant managing editor of *Time*, James Keogh, wrote a book, *President Nixon and the Press*, denouncing journalists for their hostility to the Administration. Keogh, who had taken a leave of absence from the magazine to serve as a Presidential assistant, argued angrily that Richard Nixon has been unable to get a fair break from the major media.

Griffith blames the President himself and his top aides for the Administration's tribulations. In a devastating critique, he says: "Because Nixon's key subordinates came out of lawyering and advertising, his Administration became a fatal mix of special pleading, artfully calculated strategies, sloganized explanations of positions endlessly repeated, and systematic manipulation of opinion. Its best policies were rarely honestly proclaimed, and the worst were hidden or lied about. The Administration showed an aversion to general debate ... it wanted its own version of events accepted as truth, and believed that the public could be made to distrust and discount everything else."

Still, Griffith takes no pleasure in Nixon's present discomfort. "Even in the victory of Watergate," he writes, "after a moment's savoring of triumph, many journalists I think disliked being cast in the role of relentless antagonists to the President." The fundamental reason is that when the press seems to win, it is most in danger of losing. "For when any President seeks to prove the press its determined enemy, and not to be trusted because of that, his case must not be rendered provable to unprejudiced minds."

Griffith loses his cool only when discussing the demise of *Life*. He notes bitterly that the three television networks spent almost as much in one night to report the unsuspenseful news of Nixon's landslide win over McGovern than all of his magazine's annual editorial expenses.

He laments that "those who preside over America's most respected corporations are almost to a man upright, Republican, conservative, alarmed by a collapse of values in American life, disturbed about their children. They put their advertising dollars in *Playboy*, and after business hours cluck about a national decline in moral standards."

Griffith makes no dramatic proposals to improve the press. He calls for more newspapers willing to court unpopularity by shaking up community complacency and young journalists who do "not regard responsibility as a hindrance to their own creativity and abhorrent to their readership." Says he: "Perhaps such a union of opposites — a respect for facts, married to imagination and passion — is not to be dreamed of; certainly it is rarely to be found. But it's the kind of journalism I stand and cheer for."

With engaging candor, sparkling writing, and a refreshing streak of idealism, Griffith comes across as a social commentator who I stand and cheer for.[1]

The reason why the media is currently in so much trouble is brought out in an assessment by another commentator who concludes his comments with a reference to a subject to which this chapter will return at some length later on:

Politicians are in trouble with voters and they know it.

Union leaders are in trouble with public opinion and they know it.

Corporation executives are in trouble with consumers and they know it.

The media are in trouble with their viewers and readers and don't seem to know it.

They illegally publish leaks from grand jury proceedings, thereby condemning a person before he is accused. They unethically publish leaks from prosecution assistants who want to try their case in the press before they take it to court. They demand a total constitutional shield for the privacy of their sources even when the shield conflicts with the equal constitutional right of a fair trial. They assert the unlimited right to publish anything, true or false, critical of anybody, but often do not concede even a limited right of reply.

There is a pervasive criticism and hostility toward the press which go beyond anything I have observed in many years in the profession. It embraces far more dissatisfaction and distrust than Adlai Stevenson's pained complaint about the unfairness of "the one-party press" in the 1952 campaign.

The reason I say that the media do not realize the extent of their trouble is that they usually blame others for their loss of viewer and reader credibility and rarely look in the mirror. The polls show that the credibility of the media is lower than that of congressmen who rank lower than the president.

The tendency in much of the media is to account for this by arguing that the bad image of the press stems from the attacks of a beleaguered president and from viewers and readers who, they say, get sore at us because we give them too much bad news.

The dissatisfied readers and viewers and listeners don't want to undermine the First Amendment guaranteeing freedom of the press; they

---

[1] Morton A. Reichek, "A Skeptic's Guide to Believing the News". Reprinted from the June 8, 1974 issue of *Business Week* by special permission. Copyright 1974 by McGraw-Hill, Inc.

want redress from what they consider an uneven and often unfair performance by the media. They don't want to diminish the First Amendment; they want a bigger share of the First Amendment. They don't want to see the press less vigorous in serving their "right to know"; they want the press to be more open to their "right to reply."

This very issue is now before the U.S. Supreme Court on appeal by the Miami Herald from the Florida supreme court which upheld a state statute requiring newspapers to offer those they criticize the opportunity to answer back.

Two days before the 1972 run-off election the Miami Herald denounced Pat Tornillo, a candidate for the state Legislature, as a "czar" and argued that his election would be "inexcusable." Tornillo prepared a reply; it was rejected. He went to court and won.

The central contention made by Tornillo's attorneys is that a statue requiring the opportunity to reply "is not a restraint on freedom of expression, but in fact encourages and implements freedom of expression" by opening the media to additional points of view. The Florida supreme court added this point:

"The right of the public to know all sides of a controversy and from such information to be able to make an enlightened choice is being jeopardized by a growing concentration of ownership of mass media into fewer hands, resulting in a form of private censorship."

For myself I think such a statute is unwise and probably unconstitutional. It would set up the courts as the arbiter of what the media should carry and this would imperil the freedom of the press. I believe that to preserve a free press, we must preserve its constitutional right to be wrong, even to be unfair.

But this doesn't end the matter. The public deserves fuller access to the media and the media, whatever their legal rights, have a moral duty to respect voluntarily the moral right to reply. If the media do not voluntarily concede this right more equitably in practice, then they will almost certainly bring down their own house.

There is a mounting public demand for fuller access to the media. It is more often than not a fair demand, a reasonable demand. If the media are to safeguard their guaranteed right to criticize everything and everybody, do they not have a duty to respect the rights of their listeners and their readers to hear and read what those who are criticized have to say in response?

The opportunity to reply is the moral equivalent of the right to criticize and unless the press more equitably respects that moral right it will bring on legal restrictions it would like to avoid.[2]

INVESTIGATIVE REPORTING AND THE CRITICAL ROLE OF THE MEDIA

What is most worrisome about what seem to be mounting attacks on the media is the risk that, warranted or unwarranted, these assaults may dissuade their target from pursuing what has become one of its most basic contributions. Under the banner of "investigative reporting" the media has recently come to play an almost irreplaceable part in the ferreting out of illegal, improper and

[2] Roscoe Drummond, "Why the Media Are in Trouble", The Christian Science Monitor, May 8, 1974.

unethical conduct at every level and in all manner of institutions in North American society.

The classic example of just how critical the media's role can be in this process is provided by Watergate. Had it not been for *The Washington Post* and two of its junior reporters, it is questionable when, if ever, some of the most damaging revelations surrounding Watergate, would have surfaced. These two reporters have told their story in a book which brings out the best of investigative reporting:

More than once in the taped conversations he released on Apr. 30, Richard Nixon observes — sourly, it seems — "I don't want the *Washington Post* to break this case." He had two good reasons to fear that the *Post* might know as much as he did about the Watergate affair: An unlikely pair of young reporters from the newspaper's workaday metropolitan staff — rather than its glamorous national reporting team — who were assigned to cover the break-in at the Democratic National Committee back when it was still a third-rate burglary, and who helped turn it into Nixon's worst crisis.

The Watergate case probably would have come unraveled even without the drumfire of *Post* stories by Carl Bernstein and Bob Woodward. There were, after all, other reporters on the case — although at first, not so tenaciously. And there was, after all, Judge John J. Sirica, a tough law-and-order man, who most likely would have goaded everyone involved in last year's first Watergate trial to punch through the cover-up even if he had not been reading about it for months in his morning paper.

But Bernstein and Woodward certainly had a lot to do with making the system work. They broke the story that Nixon campaign contributions had ended up in the Miami bank account of Watergate burglar Bernard L. Barker. They uncovered the secret intelligence-gathering fund kept by the Committee for the Re-Election of the President. They disclosed a "massive house-cleaning" at the CRP, including destruction of records, that took place immediately after the Watergate burglars were caught. They introduced campaign saboteur Donald Segretti to the world. They reported that John N. Mitchell controlled the intelligence fund while he was still Attorney General — and included in their story one of the least restrained denials in newspaper history, when Mitchell exploded: "JEEEEEEEEEEESUS, all that crap, you're putting it in the paper? It's all been denied. Katie Graham's [*Washington Post* owner Katharine Graham] going to get her [deleted] caught in a big fat wringer if that's published."

And they report, on the next to last page of this book, that their sources tell them that the briefcase of evidence passed on from the Watergate grand jury to the House Judiciary Committee in March contains evidence of "a staggering case against the President."

All the President's Men, however, is not the inside story of Watergate and its cover-up. Instead, it is the outside story of how Woodward, then 29, and Bernstein, then 28, started digging into the Watergate burglary the way any good police reporters would check into any front-page crime, and ended up at the Oval Office.

They tell little about themselves, except to make clear that they were suspicious of each other at first. Bernstein, a long-haired college dropout who started to work as a reporter at 19, "looked like one of those counterculture journalists that Woodward despised." Woodward, a Yale man and registered Republican (he decided not to vote at all when Election Day came), was in Bernstein's view "a prima donna who played heavily at office politics ... Bernstein thought that Woodward's rapid rise at the *Post* had less to do with his ability than his establishment credentials." They got over that.

They had one undeniable stroke of luck: being assigned to the Watergate burglary in the first place. (Although when he was phoned that Saturday morning, Woodward wasn't all that happy about it: He had wanted to sleep late.) But after that, their Watergate coverage was based on thorough, hard digging, often dull and sometimes dangerous.

To learn more about James McCord, the Re-Election Committee's security chief who was nabbed inside the Watergate, they looked up the other tenants in McCord's large Rockville (Md.) office building and started phoning them at home. They tracked Segretti's travels by poring over his credit card records — obtained from a cooperative, and still anonymous, employee of the credit card company. In Miami, seeking to pass the time while waiting to interview a State's Attorney's Office investigator about the Mexican checks operation, Bernstein "sat down with the Miami Yellow Pages and started calling photo shops" in a vain effort to find the one where the burglars had bought their photo equipment. Few good stories come easy.

In time, the two men developed a web of government and Re-Election Committee sources, too. One, former CRP treasurer Hugh Sloan, they identify here for the first time, with the observation that although Sirica had accused him of lying, "Sloan was the one CRP witness who had cooperated fully with the investigation."

Another, an executive branch friend of Woodward's, remains a mystery man who could be contacted — generally — only by elaborate signals, and met at night, by stealth, in out-of-the-way places such as an underground garage or a tavern on the fringe of the city. *Post* managing editor Howard Simons dubbed him "Deep Throat." Ian Fleming, James Bond's creator, never dreamed up a better double agent. Even in this book, he would be a little hard to believe if Bernstein and Woodward had not already established their credibility so firmly.

Few good books have been written about reporters. Their work generally is not the stuff of high drama. But there haven't been many stories like Watergate, and Bernstein and Woodward's account of their role in it is a crackling good tale.[3]

The frightening follow-up to their courageous work was an understandable degree of concern in the White House which led it to consider appalling forms of retaliation which in a free society would have been anything but understandable:

Reports that President Nixon threatened action to prevent the renewal of TV broadcast licenses held by the Wasington Post have drawn strong citicism here.

"It is a shocking revelation, high-handed to say the least," commented Sen. John O. Pastore (D) of Rhode Island, chairman of the Senate sub-committee on communications which oversees broadcasting.

"If it is true," said former Federal Communications Commission

[3] Bruce Agnew, "Two Reporters Tell the 'Outside' Story". Reprinted from the June 1, 1974 issue of *Business Week* by special permission. Copyright 1974 by McGraw-Hill, Inc.

chairman Newton Minnow, "it's absolutely shocking, a recognized attempt to intimidate the news media for doing its job. Regulatory agencies are by law independent and it would be highly improper for the executive to attempt to influence them in any way."

Reports of transcripts of a House Judiciary Committee tape of a Sept. 15, 1972, meeting between the President and staff aides have the President saying, "The main thing is the Post is going to have damnable, damnable problems out of this one. They have a television station and they're going to have to get it renewed."

Adds H.R. Haldeman, former chief aide, "They have a radio station, too." Mr. Nixon: "Does that come up, too?"[4]

On balance the effects of the investigative reporting in the Watergate case were healthy. Various parts of the media which had long neglected the probing aspect of their mandate began to move in this direction. Consider how the competitive impact of this growing phenomenon affected one U.S. TV network:

"At the end of this year when you say investigative reporting you will not think, 'CBS Reports' or '60 Minutes' or 'NBC White Paper.' You will think 'ABC Closeup.' "

This is how Av Westin of ABC News describes the revolution that has been taking place there. And for those of us who have long been scolding and questioning the network's apparent indifference to investigative reporting, it is a welcome revolution indeed.

For years spokesmen for the network have asked why ABC did not join NBC and CBS in developing a prestigious once-a-month news series such as "First Tuesday." They replied vaguely that ABC preferred to do "in-depth" documentaries on a "broader based" and more irregular basis. What this usually meant in actual fact was more production time, and therefore more bland generality, less punch.

Now, for various reasons, it would appear that all that is changed. Last May, Mr. Westin, executive producer of the ABC Evening News, was made vice-president and director of television documentaries and given a "mandate," as he puts it, to develop a hard-hitting, investigative news series that would air in prime time 12 times a year. The result is "ABC News Close-Up," whose first entry was the recent "West Virginia — Life, Liberty, and the Pursuit of Coal."

If this first show was any example, Mr. Westin and his producers may step right up there with Edward R. Murrow and Fred Friendly in the tradition of fine news inquiry. It was as hard-nosed and revealing a piece of investigative reporting as even the most cynical of critics could wish.

According to producer-writer-director Stephen Fleischman, who incidentally worked with Fred Friendly at CBS for several years, "I was directed to put the documents back into documentaries," and so he has. From the opening shot of the 1968 explosion of the Consolidation Coal Co.'s Farmington mine, with its black torrents of smoke signaling the death of 78 men, the program itemized the oversights, neglects or simple lack of enforcements on the part of the West Virginia coal companies and the U.S. Bureau of Mines.

To their credit, ABC did not lard the show with interpretations and explanations, although there are several biting commentaries. For the

[4] Louise Sweeney, "Report of Nixon Threats to *Post* Stirs Shock Waves", *The Christian Science Monitor*, May 17, 1974.

most part the scrupulously researched facts were left to speak for themselves. "I've had two researchers working for weeks verifying every piece
of film, every word, every gesture, every innuendo," said Mr. Fleischman.
"I was making word changes right up to the mix. It's hard to do a show
like that, because I had a beautiful track in here with great pace and all,
and would have to change it over something like just an inflection in the
reporter's voice. Our associate producer, Alice Herb, is a lawyer, and she's
been very meticulous."

Asked if he thought the ABC management's decision to commit
themselves to tough investigative reporting had anything to do with the
atmosphere of the Watergate investigation, Mr. Fleischman replied, "If
there hadn't been Watergate none of this would have happened, and I
couldn't begin to do this. Not only did journalism get a big boost, but
honesty and truth got a big boost from that."

Mr. Westin was asked why ABC stuck its neck out like this at this
particular time, "naming names and making charges," as he put it, and
why they had not done so before. "Don't forget, ABC News started 10
years later than the others," he replied. "In 1962 they were still hiring
outside news cameramen. So you can say, well, why didn't they catch up?
Frankly, top management couldn't have cared less. But under Elton Rule
[ABC president] they've discovered that news means money, particularly
to the owned-and-operated stations. Elton Rule also believes in a mature
news department. Four years ago they decided to make the news competitive, and they did. They added to the staff, and we satellited a lot.

"Harry Reasoner came over here from CBS for two reasons. He has
said publicly that he was tired of waiting for Cronkite to retire," Mr.
Westin commented, grinning, "and he realized also we were seriously
committed."

Mr. Reasoner was also given a huge money deal, but "that in itself is a
commitment" said Mr. Westin, "showing a seriousness of purpose.

"We now have the recognition that you have to have in a news organization, and the corporate commitment and the money. $150,000 a
show — they're putting their money where their mouth is. Most of these
shows will be exposes. They're all topical. I made a big point when I did
the evening news that it could not be all things to all men. It is an illustrated daily journal. But the whole news depatment altogether, can be.
You have hard documentaries, and the 'fin and feathers,' the Jacques
Cousteau type thing, and some culture documentaries. Watergate accelerated ABC's commitment here, but management already intended to do
hard documentaries."

It is possible to say that Elton Rule wishes to make himself an image
of the fearless defender of journalistic truth, clad in the mantle of CBS's
Frank Stanton, or even that he may have political aspirations — neither of
which is in the least a discreditable ambition — and it is true that the
network still refers to the series as "12 times a year" rather than once-a-
month like its network competitors. But, says Mr. Westin, "I think the
network has the right to wait and see a year."

Time will tell, but the first show is tough and controversial, and no
murmur has arisen from the corporate heads. There has indeed been a
shakeup at ABC News, and if "West Virginia — Life, Liberty, and the
Pursuit of Coal" is any sample, vive la revolution![5]

[5] Mimi Mead, " 'ABC Closeup': A Revolution in Reporting, Learning the Lesson of Watergate", The Christian Science Monitor, October 25, 1973.

That there was some limited validity to the ratings and ravings of the White House about "the anti-Nixon press" is not to be denied:

Have the American news media been unfair to President Nixon? Have television and the press presented a biased picture during these churning Watergate months?

At a televised news conference Oct. 26 Mr. Nixon said, "I have never seen such outrageous, vicious, distorted reporting in 27 years of public life." That was a pretty vigorous statement — by a man fighting for his political life. Some newsmen have, since then, sought to elicit from the White House chapter and verse on what the President was referring to.

We have witnessed a long confrontation between a tough-minded President and a tough-minded Washington press corps. Aware of how this can affect the public weal, and the reputations of both the press and the President, the newly formed National Press Council, set up by the Twentieth Century Fund, is pondering whether to make a study of the President-press issue. This would be one of its first cases as the nation's self-appointed media watchdog.

Representatives of the press council have talked to Kenneth Clawson at the White House and have looked into network tapes and commentators' comments. At a meeting Dec. 10, the council will probably decide whether or not to make the study.

As of this writing, the White House has not been prepared to supply the news council with a formal listing or documentation of what it regards as prejudiced media behavior. Ordinarily the council would not undertake a study unless some individual or organization had brought in a bill of complaint. But the 15-member council could dispense with that requirement. The subject is tremendously important. If the fledgling council launched out on this probe it would show that it is not lacking in courage and initiative.

White House officials have been friendly and courteous but, instead of supplying a list of charges, they have referred council representatives to a compilation already in being, which Mr. Clawson dubs "the press firestorm." This is a detailing of slights and instances of alleged bias and distortion — commissions and omissions which the Nixon White House says reveal media attitudes, especially in the TV networks.

Examples? It is noted that, while CBS commentator Walter Cronkite has interviewed such personalities as Daniel Ellsberg, John Dean, and Archibald Cox, he hasn't interviewed anyone who could be called a presidential admirer. Again, it is charged that, on the first weekday after special prosecutor Archibald Cox was dismissed the three TV networks carried 19 news spots "unfavorable" to the President, one neutral, and only two "favourables." This, it is alleged, created impeachment sentiment.

Again, it is contended that the networks overplayed impeachment sentiment by playing up impeachment calls from Representatives Morris Udall and Jerome Waldie — Waldie who is running for the California governorship, and Udall who is deemed not to be a representative Democrat. Again, the fact is cited that CBS alone carried the full Kissinger press conference on the day of the Middle East alert, while all three networks managed to carry, complete, the news conferences held by Messrs. Cox and Elliot Richardson. And there's more, in similar vein.

Was all of this bias, or normal news judgment? None of the instances merit being characterized as "vicious." But the news council probers might regard the sum total of coverage as not entirely even-handed.

It would be tremendously interesting if the hopefully nonpartisan press council did make a study of whether the press has been biased. . . . There does seem to be enough evidence of an anti-Nixon outlook among a limited segment of the press to warrant the conclusion that media would not get off scot free if, via the press council, they took a sharp look at their own behavior.[6]

Nonetheless, it is hard to believe that any so-called "press conspiracy" could have made so much out of what the White House alleged to be so little, had the President disclosed everything there was to be exposed at the outset. When this finally did happen, the press was vindicated and little further prodding by it was required to end the debacle.

Sometimes it is expressed in furious, profanity-laced letters with no signature, sometimes is is argued with detailed logic and illustrative examples. It is a theory of what the present crisis of American democracy is all about. The President, it holds, has done nothing wrong, will be proved innocent of any and all charges. His troubles are all traceable to a liberal, malevolent press which has always despised him.

There is something — but not everything — to the basic premise of the theory. Many of the reporters here and in California who have covered Mr. Nixon over his congressional and presidential years don't like him. His campaigns against Jerry Voorhis and Helen Gahagan Douglas were the genesis of the dislike. To many (not all of them liberals or reporters by any means) those Nixon runs for the House and Senate were unpleasant episodes. The dislike flowered through the special fund and Checkers speech episodes, the enemies lists, and tough campaigns of 1968 and 1972. To those who dislike Mr. Nixon there is something dark and incongruous between the public and the private man.

But the "press" — including broadcasting and news magazines — is not the sum of its reporters and commentators. It is also editors, publishers, the owners of broadcast stations. In 1968 and 1972 a large majority of American newspapers supported Mr. Nixon for President on their editorial pages — the other side of press controversy.

The theory of a press conspiracy against Mr. Nixon does not, thus, fully hold water on the factual record. But even if it did, its next premise — that the press can and has turned a majority of the public against the President — is hardly demonstrable over the long run. If that press malevolence has always been there as the theorists claim, it failed miserably to turn public sentiment against Mr. Nixon until Watergate.

The press conspiracy could not defeat Mr. Nixon in 1968. It would have had its most stunning reversal (had it existed) in 1972 when the President won re-election by a thunderous landslide. The press, which is the public's principal means of learning about this or any other president, could not dissuade the public from its overwhelming approval of Mr. Nixon's China and Soviet policies, his means of ending the war in Vietnam, his domestic efforts against busing, the early phases of his economic battle, and hundreds of other policies.

By and large, Mr. Nixon's public support held until Watergate burst

[6] William H. Stringer, "Winds of Change: 'Anti-Nixon Press'?" *The Christian Science Monitor*, December 5, 1973.

upon the scene of history with the shabby revelations in testimony before the Ervin committee, and the trials and conviction of former White House and campaign aides. The sharpest drop in Mr. Nixon's public support came after the so-called "Saturday night massacre" of Oct. 20, 1973.

The question that must be asked now is obvious: even if there were a widespread and highly organized press campaign against Mr. Nixon, would its existence invalidate the hard facts that have tarnished the administration? The burglary on the night of June 17, 1972, was such a fact, so was the break-in at the office of Daniel Ellsberg's psychiatrist, the skein of hard-cash transactions in campaign contributions, the resignation of an attorney general whose rectitude Mr. Nixon had publicly praised, the plea-bargaining, the tapes.

None of these facts convicts Mr. Nixon of anything, and no one — the press included — has a right to assume his guilt. But it is the demonstrable grubbiness in this nation's highest place that has brought Mr. Nixon to low esteem — not a press conspiracy.[7]

Looking beyond Watergate, the problem is that those who make the news also like to try to manage it. Any individual or institution that attracts media attention is bound to try to shape that attention to suit his own purposes. Governments are especially adept at news management:

A classic definition of public relations is "the engineering of consent." It's an Orwellian concept which helps to explain the constant state of tension existing between the press and government, or for that matter between the press and individual politicians, public figures of all kinds, institutions, businesses, impresarios, community organizations, special-interest groups, and sundry proselytizers. They all have an axe to grind, a message to communicate, a story to tell — and they'd like it to be told their way.

They succeed just as often as an unwary or complaisant press lets down its guard and accepts the assistance so eagerly offered on every hand. And to the extent that they succeed, the news is being managed.

Governments are masters at the game, a favorite and simple technique being that of the multiple announcement, or government by press release. Massive new programs, which invariably entail massive spending, are announced at the planning stage, announced when they become policy, announced in Throne Speeches and budget speeches and ministerial statements, and announced at every stage of progress. The press dutifully reports them all and the public is impressed by the intense activity of its servants.

Toronto's new waterfront park, announced just before the last federal election, is a case in point. Study of the record on Ontario highway building provides another — successive provincial administrations have achieved more mileage on the highways than the motorists have.

There was the news this week that a few miles of Highway 7 will be rerouted to give the city of Stratford a more direct connection to Highway 401. When will it be done? Some time after 1980. It's a safe bet that the Ontario public will be given that news a good many times in the next six years.

[7] Roderick MacLeish, "President and 'Press Conspiracy' ", The Christian Science Monitor, June 7, 1974.

Strategic leaks of news are helpful too. A Star reporter in Ottawa last year learned of a new federal plan to assist cities in rehabilitating their run-down central cores. Yes, it was massive. He also found that senior officials were not too reluctant to let him have the details on an exclusive basis. The result was a headline story in The Star.

Two months later the housing minister announced the scheme officially, and again it was headline news. Not much has been heard of it lately, but it will be back.

Housing in fact is a fruitful field, with ample scope for what are invariably described as "bold new initiatives." Ancients will recall that the huge Malvern land assembly scheme in Scarborough, urgently needed to provide 10,000 homes, was first announced in 1953.

In the succeeding 20 years it was the subject of more than 100 optimistic stories in The Star alone, of which one in 1967 was typical. It was a ringing declaration by the minister of the day that "we'll start in 1968." It started some three years later.

The best of all techniques, though, is the press conference, originally devised as a convenience to the news media but now skilfully exploited by the news managers. For newspapers which prefer covering the news to uncovering it, the press conference is a boon.

It works to the advantage of the news managers for two reasons. One is that the press conference is a cheap and efficient way of getting news. The reporter turns up on schedule at the hotel or conference room, accepts the press kit, makes some notes, and returns with his story.

No muss, no fuss. The story can be run at once, complete as far as it goes. If there are gaps in the information or awkward facts to be explained, that can be done later, in a succeeding story, on an inside page. Meanwhile the carefully tailored story has done its job — for the news manager.

The second reason press conferences work is that they are treated as if they were real events, not pseudo-events as Daniel Boorman has correctly described them.

Stand on a street corner and demand the abdication of the Queen, and you will only embarrass the passersby. But call yourself the Committee for the Reform of Ancient Privileges (CRAP), hire a room and hold a press conference, and you may even make page one.

The list of techniques for getting into print or on camera is almost endless: The oddball publicity stunt, the planted story, the staged confrontation, the disruptive demonstration that distracts attention from the main event and is guaranteed to show up on television.

Editors incline to be wary, increasingly watchful of the end runs. But governments are hard to cope with because they really are a major source of news. The latest Ontario Throne Speech forecasts another bold new initiative in housing. The target has a familiar ring — a million homes in 10 years — but we'll be hearing more about that.[8]

Like any other would-be news managers, politicians are bound to condemn the media when things are not going their way. Not atypical of this kind of reaction were some recent criticisms of the press by the Energy Minister of Ontario. He commented on the role some elements of Ontario's media have tried to play as a kind of unofficial opposition to the government:

[8] Borden Spears, "Governments are Masters at the Art of Managing News", Toronto Star, March 30, 1974.

I suggest we consider the occasional practice of newspapers or individual newsmen of appropriating to themselves a role of "effective opposition" particularly when the official Opposition is weak.

This is presumptuous but it is worse than presumption. It is self-righteous, but it is much more serious than mere self-righteousness. It is, in fact, antidemocratic. It borders potentially on anarchy. It recognizes only that an opposition is there to oppose, to criticize, to propose amendment and change, to represent viewpoints in the community. What it utterly fails to recognize is that a vital role that an opposition plays is to be always ready and willing and given the support of the people, capable of governing.

The Government is elected by the people and is properly responsible to the people. An identical statement describes the role of the opposition. The staff of a newspaper is appointed by corporate authority and is properly responsive to corporate direction. All corporations can gain or lose through decisions taken in the public sector. For any corporation, whether it is in publishing, mining, retailing, financial or any other, to seek for itself the power to perform any of the functions of government, whether as the administration or the opposition, is to make a raid on rights and responsibilities that belong to the people and must be exercised only by their elected representatives.[9]

Although it is understandable that politicians should want to avoid as much media scrutiny as possible — except on their own terms, it is to be hoped that the press will not back away from its new-found interest in investigative reporting. Perhaps the most basic role of the press is to keep the public as fully informed as possible on all developments that affect their daily lives. Otherwise, how can citizens vote or do anything else intelligently? In a day and age when management of the news is being attempted on all sides, it would be irresponsible for the media not to probe every conceivable source of information in order to try to get at the facts. Investigative reporting must prove to be more than just a passing fancy if the media is to continue to do anything approaching a reasonable job.

Lest anyone misconstrue the situation, however, it should be stressed that investigative reporting is only the beginning and not the end of the matter. Although the media's first duty and obligation is undoubtedly to bring out all the facts on a given issue of public concern, it also has a responsibility to ensure that the major contending points of view on that same issue are well aired. This means that it should not state only one side of a public dispute, even in its editorializing, but see to it that the strongest aspects of both sides of the question are put before its audience. Otherwise, the media could rightly be charged with using its privileged position in society to advance whichever side of a particular controversy suited its point of view. This should not be tolerated in a free society, even though the means required to put an end to such a practice may in themselves entail some inherent threats to freedom of the press. This issue goes to the heart of ensuring an appropriate role for the media in North America and is better dealt with towards the end of this chapter after a number of other sensitive questions are reviewed.

[9] Darcy McKeough, "Excerpts from Speech to the Canadian Managing Editors' Association Annual Meeting in Windsor", The Globe and Mail, Toronto, May 24, 1974.

THE MEDIA AND THE PUBLIC INTEREST

Thus far the basic premise of this chapter has been that the media can do no wrong if it pursues and publishes every fact and point of view of interest to the public at large. This is the essence of what the media is all about, but it is not to suggest that the press is free of all other responsibilities, let alone free of suspicions on a number of other grounds. There are a variety of bases for complaint and concern about the media beyond those already alluded to.

Ownership and Control

If the media has a major part to play in a completely free and open interplay of contending ideas and points of view, then it follows that in the absence of other kinds of checks and balances some variety in terms of ownership and control is desirable, if not essential. Assuming this to be the case, the situation with regard to North American media is already disturbing with current trends suggesting that it can only get worse unless some remedial steps are soon taken.

From an overall point of view Canada provides a more manageable scene to scan and yet, probably on a more general scale, is indicative of the U.S. scene as well. How concentrated ownership and control of the media is becoming in Canada was brought out in a 1969-70 Senate report, some of the most salient aspects of which were summarized in a special article in the *Columbia Journalism Review*:

Let's state the situation in the baldest possible terms by looking at the 103 Canadian communities where a daily newspaper is published or a primary TV station is located. Within these 103 communities there are 485 "units of mass communication" — daily newspapers or radio or TV stations — and slightly over half of them are controlled or partially owned by groups. Of Canada's 116 daily newspapers, seventy-seven — or 66.4 per cent — are controlled or partially owned by groups. Of the ninety-seven TV stations (including some relay stations), forty-seven — or 48.5 per cent — are controlled by groups. Of 272 radio stations, groups control or own a substantial interest in 129, or 47.4 per cent.

There are only five cities in the country where genuine competition between newspapers exists; and in all five cities some or all of these competing dailies are owned by chains. Of Canada's eleven largest cities, chains enjoy monopolies in seven. The three biggest newspaper chains — Thomson, Southam, and F.P. — today control 44.7 per cent of the circulation of all Canadian daily newspapers; a dozen years ago the total was only 25 per cent. Fully 77 per cent of the circulation of all Canadian newspapers is now controlled by chains.

. . . What matters is the fact that control of the media is passing into fewer and fewer hands, and that the experts agree this trend is likely to continue and perhaps accelerate. If the trend is allowed to continue unabated, sooner or later it must reach the point where it collides with the public interest. The Committee believes it to be in the national interest to ensure that that point is not reached.[10]

[10] Excerpts from *Report of the Special Senate Committee on Mass Media*. Reproduced by permission of Information Canada.

In some parts of Canada the media is clearly in more concentrated hands than in others. Conviction on four charges of monopolistic practices under the federal *Combines Investigation Act* has brought this issue to a head in the newspaper industry in New Brunswick. One commentary on these convictions harks back to the aforementioned Senate report and some of the remedies it proposed in just this type of situation:

The family of the great all-purpose magnate, K.C. Irving, controls all five English-language newspapers in New Brunswick, and this week the Irving interests were convicted on four counts of illegally establishing newspaper monopolies, combines or mergers. In a country known for weak anti-monopoly laws, it was the first such prosecution of newspaper owners.

Mr. Justice Albany Robichaud's decision — together with his observation that the Irving monopoly "may not appear to have actually produced any result detrimental to the public interest" — brings to mind the 1969-70 work of the Senate Special Committee on the Mass Media. Under the chairmanship of Senator Keith Davey, the committee energetically probed the ownership, finances and performance of Canada's print and electronic media. Its report was not calculated to win friends among newspaper proprietors.

Like Mr. Justice Robichaud, however, the Davey committee was ambivalent on the issue of newspaper chains. The committee proclaimed the principle that, "diverse and antagonistic sources of information promote a healthy democracy" (a principle that would seem to argue against chains). But the committee found no direct relation between concentration of ownership and editorial quality: "Some of Canada's best newspapers are owned by groups; some of the worst are owned by independents."

Although anyone who has read the wretched Irving newspapers might question the Davey committee's forbearance, it took a not unkindly view of the newspaper situation in New Brunswick. Its report quoted approvingly from a presentation by Dalton Camp who had argued — and presumably he was serious — that the daily newspapers of New Brunswick had improved more in the previous 10 years than those in any other comparable region. The report also noted that New Brunswick has more newspapers per capital than any province except Prince Edward Island.

Questions which the committee might have posed include: Could New Brunswick support five separately owned English papers if the Irving chain, with all its financial resources, were broken up? Would the province be better served with fewer newspapers but more newspaper owners? Would the quality be any better with independent owners? The questions weren't asked because they are unanswerable.

Although its conclusion did not seem to flow easily from the evidence in the report, the committee laid down its "most fundamental conclusion: that this country should no longer tolerate a situation where the public interest in so vital a field as information is dependent on the greed or goodwill of an extremely privileged group of businessmen". The time, the committee said, had come when the principle of public regulation of ownership, already well established in broadcasting, should be extended to the print media.[11]

[11] Geoffrey Stevens, "Press Monopolies", *The Globe and Mail*, Toronto, January 26, 1974.

Equally controversial is the question of common ownership and/or control extending over different parts of the media. All over North America interlocking arrangements have emerged to embrace two or more forms of the media within the same area or community. It is not uncommon in Canada, for example, to find the same corporate interests behind a newspaper, a radio station and a TV station, all in the same vicinity. This has become a matter of grave concern in the U.S. where the Federal Communications Commission is wrestling with the pros and cons of allowing this sort of intermeshing of media interests to continue:

After more than 30 years of debate, the Federal Communications Commission (FCC) is preparing to rule on the question of whether newspapers will be allowed to own television and radio stations.

Adoption of a rule proposed by the U.S. Justice Department would bar U.S. newspaper owners from buying broadcast stations in their home cities. The proposed rule also requires newspaper owners already holding local broadcast licenses to sell or trade their stations within five years.

The rule was first proposed by the Justice Department in 1968. In 1970, the FCC agreed to consider adopting the proposal. A year and a half of hearings and heated debate ensued, before dropping the issue.

But now the Justice Department has petitioned the FCC to deny television and radio license renewals to major publishers for stations in St. Louis, Des Moines, and Minneapolis St. Paul.

In response to the Justice Department's new petition, the commission has begun to restudy the proposed rule. At issue: whether newspapers should be allowed to own broadcast stations in their circulation areas. Participants in the debate have raised the following arguments:

PRO:

The FCC encouraged newspapers to take out broadcast licenses in the early 1940's (when television was first beginning), and it is totally unfair to punish those companies which developed their cities' broadcasting facilities.

While media concentration may be a fair consideration when the license is first issued, broadcasters and publishers say that re-evaluating the situation at renewal time threatens the stability of the industry and discourages broadcasters from making large-scale investments in facilities.

Finally, FCC Commissioner Robert E. Lee told Congressional Quarterly he opposes adopting the proposed rule because "in most cases, newspapers make better station owners because they live in the community, pay more attention to local problems, and devote more broadcast time to community news."

CON:

Concentration of media ownership gives one company too much control over the news and editorials communicated in a community. And in some cases, that company can exclude the views of various groups.

Groups opposed to broadcasting policies in their own communities have been among the most influential in pressuring for adoption of a rule to break up newspaper-broadcast combinations.

Maintaining a concentration of control over the media at renewal time also can "exclude new faces and new ideas from most of the major markets," argued the Rev. Everett C. Parker, director of the United Church of Christ's communications office, in testimony before a U.S. Senate committee in 1969.

Mr. Parker also said that "Negro broadcasters at present own almost no stations." The National Council of Churches also favors adopting the rule.

The basic principle against media concentration, according to Albert H. Kramer of the National Citizens Committee for Broadcasting, is "the presumption that the more diversity of voices in the media, the more likely you are to get robust debate and critical scrutiny of the media itself.[12]

Unless some of the steps suggested later in this section are taken in the near future, the author would move strongly to curb any further concentration of media ownership and control and would suggest consideration be given to dismantling some of the conglomerates which have already ensconced themselves in the industry. Otherwise, the very essence of what a free media should be could be sacrificed to the short-term profiteering instincts of the few who are coming to own or control it. That this danger is already more than present was brought out in the Canadian Senate report cited above:

We think the figures set forth are astonishing. There are a number of individual newspapers and broadcasting stations that are having trouble meeting their payrolls. But on the average media corporations are onto a very good thing indeed. If the brewing industry made profits half this large, and the people knew it, we suspect there would be sit-ins in the beer stores. Most media corporations — fortunately for them — don't have to disclose these earnings. Because their very large profits allow them to pay for expansion and acquisitions out of retained earnings, most continue as private companies. And so we are confronted with a delicious irony: an industry that is supposed to abhor secrets is sitting on one of the best-kept, least discussed secrets, one of the hottest scoops, in Canadian business — their own balance sheets!

In a few cases, the corporations concerned are making genuine efforts to deliver quality editorial content and quality programming in return for their privileged economic position. But the general pattern, we regret to say, is of newspapers and broadcasting stations that are pulling the maximum out of their communities, and giving back the minimum in return.

It's not that the companies are charging too much — but that they're spending too little. Too many newspapers and broadcasting stations, in other words, are delivering a product that is not as good as they could afford to make it. They don't try hard enough to improve their product because there is no economic incentive to do so — quite the reverse, in fact.[13]

Censorship and Freedom of the Media

In this age of corporate journalism, it is hardly surprising that the media should

[12] "Ownership Ruling Due on TV, Radio Stations", The Christian Science Monitor, March 18, 1974.
[13] Excerpts from Report of the Special Senate Committee on Mass Media. Reproduced by permission of Information Canada.

be subject to pressures from one quarter or another to censor this, that or the other thing. More often than not, such pressures come from advertisers and their clients. But sometimes they come from the owners and controllers, from publishers and editors, and now, occasionally, even from editorial and reporting staffs and other employees.

Sometimes censorship is hardly the appropriate term for what is happening. Rather it comes back to news management or promotion, something which can often be facilitated through "press junkets" and the like, a not uncommon practice in the media judging from a special CBS-TV report on the subject.

... A United States television network last night reported on the propriety of what is known as a press junket.

The junket study, on the CBS award-winning program 60 Minutes, wasn't thorough. But given the limitations of time — it ran about 17 minutes — it did a good job of spotlighting a subject that needs illumination.

What made it of particular interest and a bit worrisome to network press agents was that commentator Mike Wallace briefly pointed out that even the three major U.S. television networks hold press junkets.

They pick up the hotel and airplane expenses for certain, but certainly not all, newspaper TV writers who come here or go to Los Angeles to inspect new shows, interview TV figures and write about same.

Right now in Los Angeles there are, by CBS' count, 56 such writers — CBS says 10 are paying their own expenses — interviewing folks working on current or new shows and talking with other TV figures.

It's the first of a twice-a-year mass press visit there — the next one is in late spring — in which CBS, NBC and ABC pay all or part of the hotel or travel costs for those making the trips.

The general criteria for those invited at network expense is the circulation of their publications. Such invitees emphasize the trips mean hard work. Their city-room colleagues always agree. Honest.

But junkets aren't restricted to TV, as Wallace and his research staff amply noted. They are offered by the auto industry, by foreign countries, by sports teams and by the fashion and travel industries.

The major defence of these and other expeditions is that those paying for journalists' trips neither influence what the scribes write nor have the assurance anything will be written at all.

The major argument against the voyages is that even if the free-tripper's integrity is without question, such trips still cast lingering shadows over the free-tripper specifically and journalists generally.[14]

Blatant forms of media censorship for commercial reasons surface from time to time, but they are usually difficult to document because the people directly involved are not likely to reveal the incidents. Nonetheless, major and minor illustrations of what can happen do gain notoriety from time to time. An especially discouraging case in point arose in regard to the Corporation for Public Broadcasting in the U.S. which was at one time apparently "bought off" by one of the major oil companies:

The CBC's increasing commercialism in recent years has provoked a concurrently growing desire among many of its frustrated patrons for

[14] Jay Sharbutt, "CBS-TV Report Spotlights the Press Junkets", Toronto *Star*, January 21, 1974.

some new instrument of public broadcasting in Canada — a desire further stimulated by the emergence and expanding influence of just that sort of instrument in U.S. television.

But the bigger it becomes, the more susceptible to commercial pressures even public broadcasting is. The pressures might be more subtle, but because of that they are more insidious, and no more striking or shocking an example is needed than the current but little-publicized battle of The Nader Report.

This series, prepared by and featuring the noted auto-safety crusader Ralph Nader, was to have been one of the prize pieces in this year's schedule of the Corporation for Public Broadcasting, a new and ostensibly flak-proof umbrella for the various public TV services operating in the United States on a combination of government grants, corporate endowments and public subscription.

In fact, The Nader Report was to be the public network's showcase series, because by its very purpose and nature it would define the essential difference between public and private broadcasting. It would dare to deal with subjects the commercial networks wouldn't touch for fear of antagonizing advertisers. The only trouble is, The Nader Report has yet to get on the air because it already has antagonized a commercial network advertiser.

But for its scandalous implications, the situation would be funny.

At the very time the Corporation for Public Broadcasting was beating the drums for The Nader Report, it also announced, with appropriate enthusiasm and gratitude a grant of $1,000,000 from Mobil Oil Corp. enabling it to purchase a 39-week BBC drama series, Masterpiece Theatre; and to distribute 5,000,000 copies of its new Sesame Street magazine to slum children. And then someone took a look at the first Nader Report and found to his horror that the subject was deceptive television advertising in general and that of Mobil Oil in particular.

One would not have to be an incorrigible cynic to suspect that the timing of Mobil's largesse was not coincidental: but would soon could become less than an idealist at the mere suggestion that the Corporation for Public Broadcasting, with its lofty status and goals, would let money (even $1,000,000) dilute its integrity. Yet this is precisely what has happened.

The kindly, public-spirited folks at Mobil let it be known that they would not consider it cricket if the hand they were feeding bit them; and, incredibly, instead of telling them where to place that hand, the Corporation for Public Broadcasting has shelved the offending Nader Report.

There is a lesson in this for Canadians, and especially for those of us who have suggested from time to time a system of corporate grants for our own public network to free it from its ever-tightening commercial constrictions. Corporate grants can mean corporate censorship, and perhaps it is better, after all, to have the commercials right there on the screen and the contracts right there on the table.[15]

Then there are those little stories that seem to get buried because a major advertiser might be offended:

If anyone still believes that newspapers are free from control by their

[15] Patrick Scott, "A Lesson in Corporate Censorship", Toronto Star, November 3, 1970.

big advertisers, let him consider a recent development that came to light in the January issue of the New Lead, a publication of the Toronto Newspaper Guild.

According to the Guild article, last December, Eaton's announced to employees that 196 maintenance workers at two Toronto stores would be taken off the payroll Jan. 12. Their jobs were to be contracted out to a private concern, Consolidated Building Maintenance Ltd.

Eaton's was paying $2.50 an hour for a 38¼-hour-week, while 10 to 20 percent of the laid off employees who were expected to transfer to Consolidated would earn $2 per hour and may, if they wish, work a 48-hour week.

Previously overtime at Eaton's was on the basis of those hours worked in excess of eight in a day. At Consolidated overtime starts after 48 hours in a week.

One would have thought that the firing of 200 workers at Eaton's is news, however, the mighty coast-to-coast retail chain is one of the biggest advertisers in Canada, and this is what happened:

The first story, according to the Guild report, was squelched at the Toronto Telegram, and not surprisingly, when one learns that the Eaton family compact controls a large chunk of the Tely and Baton Broadcasting Ltd., which in turn owns TV station CFTO.

Telegram writer Marc Zwelling, who claims he received the original tip on the story from Telegram management, wrote the story last Dec. 15, based on local labor union sources. This article revealed that an organizing drive had been started by the Building Service Employees' International union and it pointed out the reduction in wages and loss of the 10 percent Eaton employee discount suffered by the transferred workers.

Two days after Zwelling handed in his story, he was told that the paper's "Eaton's censor" had vetoed it. The story didn't die, however, because one of the fired caretakers went to see Controller Margaret Campbell at city hall to enlist her assistance. While there, the former Eaton's worker related the story to members of the city hall press corps.

Again, a Tely reporter snapped at the story, but it was quickly smothered. A Toronto Star reporter also filed a story, but to date his paper, too, has refused to run it. Globe and Mail reporters were not present for the city hall story and the only report of the Eaton firings to reach the public so far appears to be a short item on CBC local TV news.[16]

The most insidious thing about this kind of censorship is that it is often difficult to detect or prove because a story is not exactly buried but simply handled in such an obscure manner that it might as well be. For years now, for example, there have been accusations that the misdeeds of industrialists get played down, whereas those of other groups less prone to advertise receive much more coverage:

Maybe it's a legacy from the time when few dared to question — out loud — the behaviour of the "ruling classes," so-called, but the unpretty fact is that we Americans still use a double standard in measuring the morality of management and labor. One of the most eloquent examples of this duality ever recorded emerged in the government's victory in the largest antitrust case ever tried.

[16] "Eaton's: Advertisers Control News Columns?" U.E. News, Toronto, February 2, 1970.

It's a safe bet that the public at large is quite unaware that in early December, 19 big manufacturers of heavy electrical equipment pleaded guilty in federal court to criminal charges of price fixing. Among the principal defendants were firms whose brand names — General Electric, Westinghouse, Allis Chalmers — are household words.

But the word of their criminality simply didn't get around as widely as it would have if a similar rap had descended on a trade union. The story was not suppressed. But by the nature of our American sense of values as measured by the information media, it just didn't get the play given, say, exposés of labor racketeering in the heyday of the McClellan committee.[17]

Fortunately, there occasionally do appear in the world of corporate journalism illustrations of what might be termed courageous attacks on groups normally the source of vast advertising outlays, and therefore presumably able to retaliate if they want to. One such illustration recently occurred in Canada when its one national private TV network exposed much of the over-the-counter drug trade for what it really is. As the following observation reveals, however, it remains to be seen whether the network will follow through on some of the harsher implications of its findings where they run counter to its own financial interests:

On Sunday night, CTV did the unbelievable. Its Inquiry investigative series spent a full hour denouncing over-the-counter drugs as potentially fatal, addictive or just plain useless — even though these drugs account for almost 20 per cent of all prime-time TV ads.

It was a commercially courageous step to take, even in these days of consumer activism. But so far it appears to have been done safely; a spokesman for Inquiry said at press time that none of the companies, whose products were denounced by name, had complained, though a number have asked for transcripts of the show.

Whether any might cancel advertisements, it is too soon to tell. So far, none have.

The program included denunciations of our gullibility for buying these non-prescription drugs just because they're advertised, and invited the viewer to scoff at TV drug ads by comparing clips from the ads with contradictory or critical statements from researchers.

The program said "most over-the-counter drugs are harmless — so harmless they're useless," which is critical enough, but it even went on to cite a number that were alleged to be dangerous, and to mention them by name.

Having made the program's drastic claims, however, CTV now has another and even more painful obligation. It surely is obliged to refuse to carry any more of those ads which the program implied were incorrect, telling only one side of the story, or plugging damaging products.[18]

Freedom of the press may also be endangered by those whom one would think should be the most solicitous in regard to it, that is professional journalists:

[17] "Misdeeds of Business Given Scant Coverage in Daily Press". Reprinted by permission of *AFL-CIO News*.
[18] Blaik Kirby, "CTV Courageous in Attacking Over-the-Counter Drugs", *The Globe and Mail*, Toronto, April 23, 1974.

— A column attacking the Parti Quebecois written by Social Credit Leader Real Caouette was killed by Ottawa's French-language paper Le Droit a few hours before it was to be published last weekend.

The column was ordered dropped after members of Le Syndicat des Journalistes d'Ottawa called a management representative in the early hours of Saturday morning to protest, and the executive agreed to stop publication.

Mr. Caouette has accused the journalists' union of killing the column because he had criticized the "crackpots" in the Parti Quebecois. "Freedom of the press does not exist at Le Droit," he said.

The column is a regular feature on the editorial page of the paper on Saturdays and is rotated among spokesmen for the four political parties.

A spokesman for the journalists' union, Pierre Allard, denied yesterday that any censorship was intended. The union protested the column because it contravened a newly signed collective agreement that prevented publication on the editorial page of material not written by the staff.

The management representative, treasurer Gaetan Cabana, said that he agreed to the union request to stop publication because the column may have technically contravened the collective agreement but he expressed skepticism about the union's motives.

Three columns by representatives of other parties have been published on the Saturday editorial page since the new collective agreement was signed.[19]

Censorship of any of the types just described must clearly be eliminated if the media is to sustain its claim to freedom of expression. Short of government regulation, the only answer would seem to lie in some kind of media council. This is a potential remedy for many concerns, a few more of which will be described before the case for such a council can be put in its strongest possible terms.

Entertainment and the Media

The quality of programming on the media has for the most part become a recent issue only in relation to TV broadcasting, although the non-advertising and non-news coverage of other forms of the press has also occasionally been an issue over the years. Nonetheless, the pervasive influence of TV, especially upon children, makes it understandable that its programming should receive so much more attention than the rest of the media.

The impact of TV on children has long been debated. As suggested in an earlier chapter on advertising and marketing, perhaps its least damaging consequence has been to make children more cynical:

Television has helped spawn cynicism among children, says a report made public by the Ontario government yesterday.

"The generation of children brought up with television has shown an intense cynicism towards the state of the world and social reality as portrayed by television," the report said.

The report, a survey of public attitudes ordered by the ministry of transportation and communications, recommends that telecommunications policy should take into account its potential effect on children

[19] Hugh Winsor, "Paper Kills Caouette Column Following Objections by Journalists' Union", *The Globe and Mail*, Toronto, October 25, 1973.

"especially the capacity of television to create cynicism."[20]

What concerns many observers most is the amount of violence that is purveyed on TV screens. In the U.S. this led to a special study, under the auspices of the Surgeon-General, which tended to play down the impact and influence of this kind of programming. Critics of the report have, however, subsequently revealed enough about this probe to suggest that far from being objective, it may even have been loaded in favour of the industry's desire to continue to air such mayhem regardless of any possible adverse social consequences:

It is the report itself. Television and Growing Up: The Impact of Televised Violence, a 19-page summary of findings and conclusions followed by nine chapters and appendices, that is being questioned and attacked. In both style and substance its critics maintain, it tends to support the television industry's position that children are not significantly affected. This, the critics say, is clearly contradicted by evidence demonstrating a stronger link.

The committee tentatively concluded "that there is a modest relationship between exposure to television violence and aggressive behavior or tendencies". It cautioned that "it must be emphasized that the causal sequence is very likely applicable only in some children who are predisposed in this direction" and that the indications of cause-and-effect were preliminary and tentative.

In an effort to uncover the roots of the controversy, The New York Times interviewed more than a dozen of those involved.

Many of the critics see it as no coincidence that the television industry was given veto power over proposed members of the advisory committee.

This right led to the vetoing of seven of the 40 names proposed — including several of the best-known specialists in the field of children and television who had previously done work that they claimed tended to illustrate the harmful potential of televised violence. The committee itself, in the report, was critical of the selection method.

Of the 12 committee members, five had links with the television industry. Two are full-time executives of networks: two others serve as consultants, and another has done so.

Carl Perian, Murphy legislative assistant, said: "It isn't a question of opinion or even judgment, it's a matter of looking at the documents, and concluding that, yes, indeed, the surgeon-general's report is misleading." Considering "the involvement of the TV industry," he said, neither he nor Mr. Murphy has any doubt "that the report is a fraud — purposeful fraud."

The report as finally released, Dr. Murray said, gives "the over-all impression . . . that the findings are trivial." Dr. Murray, who has also read all the data, said this impression is "absolutely wrong: There's no question in my mind that normal children watching a large amount of TV violence will become more aggressive. The report accedes to that, but in a very qualified way."[21]

[20] "TV Helps Spawn Children's Cynicism Ontario Reports", Toronto Star, May 31, 1974.
[21] "Misgivings Grow About U.S. Report on Impact of TV Violence", The Globe and Mail, Toronto, February 24, 1972. © 1972 by The New York Times Company. Reprinted by permission.

Consumer groups are now taking up the battle against some media programming on a growing scale, sometimes with astounding and almost frightening results:

As of Dec. 1, viewers won't be able to see Batman or Superman on the Hollywood television station KTTV.

They're too violent.

Thanks to the collective muscle of four U.S. consumer groups, at least one television station will have to take a hard look at what it broadcasts during children's viewing hours.

The groups filed with the Federal Communications Commission (FCC) in December, 1971, a petition to deny,a pending broadcast renewal license to station KTTV, a Metromedia Inc. property.

After 21 months of grappling, Metromedia and the consortium signed an agreement which dictated terms for children's programming to settle the main issue.

The agreement, which forbids certain cartoon shows of violence, was made part of an amended 1971 license application, and Metromedia promised to continue the terms when renewal time comes round again in 1974 [22]

Even more encouraging is the fact that a few advertisers have taken up the cudgels against the worst forms of TV violence. Although anything but widespread, signs of such concern among advertisers is to be welcomed:

A laundry product manufacturer told a U.S. Senate hearing that advertisers indirectly are responsible for excessive TV violence because most advertising is bought without regard to program content.

Leo S. Singer, president of Miracle White Company, a Chicago-based manufacturer of nonphosphate laundry products, told the Senate communications subcommittee, headed by Sen. John O. Pastore (D) of Rhode Island:

"Most media buyers that I have dealt with buy on sheer numbers alone. They are not interested in whether the show is a comedy hour or a dramatic violent serial; if it will give them a good cost-per-thousand ration they make the buy."

Mr. Singer's recent testimony said buying TV advertising is in reality a rating game that "you win amassing profits."

He said that two years ago he turned his advertising responsibilities over to "my marketing and advertising responsibilities directors . . . I got involved in other things. I decided to leave the advertising decisions to the experts." But he changed his mind six months ago.

What changed his mind, Mr. Singer said, was reading about the slaying of a woman in Boston who was doused with gasoline and set on fire in an incident similar to that portrayed on a network movie.

Mr. Singer said he decided his company would no longer buy advertising on sheer numbers alone.

He added: "I can't really explain what happened. I decided right there and then that the Miracle White Company would no longer advertise on any television show which features violence. I vowed that as long

[22] Sam Solomon, "U.S. Consumer Groups Win TV Violence Battle", Toronto *Star*, November 15, 1974.

as I was president of the Miracle White Company we would never advertise on another violent show again."[23]

Ultimately, of course, the issue again comes down to whether or not the
industry can clean itself up. Government regulation of TV program content is
already on the upswing, and unless the industry does more to discipline itself,
the pressure exerted by an increasing number of citizen groups could lead to
more public intervention in this area than is probably desirable.

Keeping the Media Honest

Another general problem with the media pertains to the accuracy and fairness
of both its editorializing and its reporting. The first thing to be said on this
general subject is that "truth" in the "news" as in anything else is hard to come
by:

. . . Edward Jay Epstein, in Commentary magazine . . . has written a
thoughtful analysis of the limits of journalism-as-content in this Age of
Watergate.
"Journalists," he argues, "are rarely, if ever, in a position to establish
the truth about an issue for themselves, and they are therefore almost
entirely dependent on self-interested 'sources' for the versions of reality
that they report." Journalism, he fears, is all too often a matter of calculated "leaks," of "managed" news, of "manipulation." "Even in the case
of Watergate," he points out, "which has become synonymous with '
investigative reporting,' it was the investigative agencies of the government and not the members of the press who assembled the evidence,
which was then deliberately leaked to receptive reporters."
Mr. Epstein may overestimate the success of "manipulation" — three
presidents failed to "manage" the news in Vietnam, though they tried.
But the real flaw in his reasoning could be that he blames journalists for a
condition that extends beyond journalism: the relativity of most "truths"
in the year 1974.

In another excellent new commentary on journalism, "How True: A
Skeptic's Guide to Believing the News" (Atlantic-Little, Brown, $6.95)
Thomas Griffith, formerly managing editor of Life, gives what may be the
final word on all human essays at "truth." "If editors operate with any
underlying philosophical premise at all, it is as simple as that of the
elderly judge who after a lifetime of listening to conflicting evidence was
persuaded — not that all men are liars — but of the many-sidedness of
truth."[24]

Having said this, however, it must be acknowledged that there are many
sins of commission and omission for which the media should be called to
account. Not the least of these is the failure of many parts of the media to
develop and maintain specialized reporters in critical areas of public concern.
In the author's own field of industrial relations, one can virtually count on the
fingers of one hand the number of qualified labour reporters to be found across

23 "TV Violence — Partly Due to Ad-buying Tactics", The Christian Science Monitor, April
8, 1974.
24 Melvin Maddocks, "How 'Truthful' Is the 'News'?" The Christian Science Monitor, May 2,
1974.

372

Canada. Spokesmen for the labour movement have rightly condemned this situation, especially when it is found to characterize the nation's one public broadcasting system, the Canadian Broadcasting Corporation:

The public relations advisory committee of the Canadian Labor Congress (CLC) has been trying to persuade the Canadian Broadcasting Corporation to assign one of its reporters exclusively to cover labor.

The lack of even one labor specialist among the CBC's 8,872 full-time employees has irked the congress and its affiliated unions for many years. It's part of what unions regard as generally poor coverage and interpretation of labor in the news media.

After several written and personal appeals to the CBC hierarchy, the CLC has virtually written off the publicly owned broadcasting system as being hopelessly anti-labor.

This is ironic, since the big labor congress was one of the chief founders of the Canadian Broadcasting League, an agency devoted to defending the CBC from its detractors in the business and political worlds.

At the last meeting of the CLC's public relations advisory group, Ed Cosgrove, PR director of the Ontario Federation of Labor (OFL), reported that "successive appointed executives in the CBC have stated they would establish a permanent labor reporting position, but to date they have not done so, nor does it look like they will."

Labor today is so complex that no general reporter, no matter how capable, can expect to move in to cover a news story involving union activity and do it justice.

Generally speaking, however, the standard of labor journalism — especially in TV and radio — is scandalously poor. It explains why Canadians are so notoriously ill-informed on labor matters.[25]

Those familiar with other areas of growing social concern have pointed to similar deficiencies in other parts of the media:

In calling for more and better public commentary on what goes on under the hood of a technological society, I am not suggesting that science writing should become a growth industry, nor that the media should be asked to teach every citizen the second law of thermodynamics. One can saturate any channel of communication by increasing the detail or the under the hood of a technological society, I am not suggesting that science writing should become a growth industry, nor that the media should be asked to teach every citizen the second law of thermodynamics. One can saturate any channel of communication by increasing the detail or the level of complexity. But surely science and technology and their effects should be as much part of a magazine's content as the latest movie, rock band, vacation package, or provincial premier. Surely quantitative arguments and attractive graphs or diagrams could be used judiciously where these are relevant, instead of pictures of tin cans. Surely magazines, which play a central role in our public life, could run informative and lively articles from time to time on major issues of technology from a Canadian point of view.[26]

[25] Ed Finn, "Labor Asks Better News Coverage", Toronto Star, November 19, 1973.
[26] Robert W. Morrison, "Responsibility Evaded: Reporting on Technology in the Mass Media", Science Forum, June 1973, p. 6.

If the media represented a marginal industry always on the verge of bankruptcy, the failure to develop an adequate degree of specialized reporting might be forgiven. Although there are doubtless fringe areas of the media that find themselves in such a position, earlier data presented in this chapter hardly suggest that this is the general picture. Thus there is no excuse for major components of the media neglecting vital areas of public concern through inadequate and unqualified reporting of what is taking place in those areas.

Doubtlessly related to these deficiencies are the numbers of unsigned articles and editorials that appear in printed media. If the media is to merit public confidence and trust in what it is up to, then this is a practice which should cease. Anything that is the subject of an editorial or report in the media should be featured in such a way as to identify the editorial staff writers or reporters who were responsible for it. Otherwise it is far too easy for shabby work to creep in and for professional standards to slip.

Insisting on signed articles and editorials should not be taken as an invitation to compulsory disclosure of sources of information available to members of the media. This is one aspect of disclosure that the author shies away from. Confidentiality in terms of sources of otherwise unavailable information is one thing that is critical to investigative reporting and all that it has come to stand for. Although there are risks involved in not compelling disclosure of such sources, especially where sensitive matters such as jury or national security leaks are involved, the advantages entailed in this tried and true media technique still seem to far outweigh the disadvantages. The case for such a position would become even stronger if some of the other reforms called for in this chapter were adopted. Even in their absence, however, it remains inappropriate to cut off what are vital sources of media information by making it possible for others to force the disclosure of those sources. And this is precisely the effect which such a policy would produce.

That the press is in serious trouble with regard to confidentiality, as well as facing many other problems, is not to be denied. Indicative of this fact and the growing importance of the right of rebuttal, to which the next section of this chapter is devoted, is the following catalogue of the media's varying fate at the hands of the courts in the U.S.:

Court decisions in Massachusetts and Florida bolster an alarming trend toward requiring reporters to identify confidential sources — and thus fettering their pursuit of facts. The trend must be reversed, ideally through a return to the full spirit of the First Amendment's guarantee of freedom of the press; otherwise, through an absolute federal press shield law that would not imply new limits on the press in the attempt to codify its liberty.

The overriding reason is not to protect the reporter — but to protect the public.

It is not to elevate newsmen as an elite with rights beyond those of other citizens — but to help all citizens maintain their rights through being accurately informed.

Running against the apparent trend toward whittling away confidentiality are such hopeful signs as these:

• The American public, alerted by Watergate cover-up and disclosure, seems to be recognizing its need to know by increasing its support for newsmen's confidentiality. The latest Gallup poll shows 62 percent answering "no" to the question, "Should reporters be required to reveal sources?" — up from 57 percent a year ago. The difference in those answering "yes" was even greater, dropping from 34 percent to 27 percent.

• Acting Attorney General Robert Bork has given assurances that he would maintain former Attorney General Richardson's order putting teeth into Justice Department guidelines for dealing fairly with the press.

• The Supreme Court earlier this year let stand a Chicago decision that a reporter could preserve the confidentiality of his sources in a civil suit.

By contrast — in the wake of last year's Supreme Court decision requiring reporters to reveal sources before grand juries — other events have tended to erode the First Amendment spirit:

• The Supreme Court let stand a lower court ruling in a Louisiana case — which came to the strange conclusion that reporters could be required to obey a court order that was itself judged unconstitutional.

• The Florida supreme court has upheld an old law requiring in effect that newspapers give "equal time" to political candidates criticized in their pages. Responsible papers try to be fair to all candidates, but to tell papers what they have to print becomes a remarkable inversion of censorship.

• In the crucial realm of confidentiality of sources, a St. Petersburg (Fla.) Times reporter was sentenced to five months for refusing to divulge a source under state subpoena. Now the Massachusetts supreme judicial court has ruled that a Boston-based Wall Street Journal reporter must disclose her source for a statement on which the Journal is being sued for libel. The statement, attributed to an anonymous official, had appeared in a four-inch box along with a denial by an attorney for the man who later brought the libel suit.

The difficulty of writing legislation to shield reporters is suggested by the varying views held even within a blue-ribbon panel favoring it. Such a panel was sponsored last summer in Cambridge, Mass., by the Roscoe Pound-American Trial Lawyers Association. The need for every citizen to support press freedom as he sees it is emphasized by words used in introducing that panel's recent report. This document on press freedom was "in no way concerned with the protection of journalists or news media or the enhancement of the legal profession — it was strictly for the benefit of the public."[27]

The Right of Rebuttal

Anyone who has been abused or annoyed by the media, whether individually or on a less personal basis, has some idea of the futility of attempting to fight back. Letters to the editor provide a form of remedy in the printed media, but they are never equal to original articles or editorials, nor are they intended to be. Moreover, there is seldom even this limited form of reply on either radio or TV. Sincere attempts have been made in a limited number of cases to ensure that not every side of a contentious issue is aired, but such attempts are very much the exception rather than the rule. In the U.S. the Federal Communications Commission has enunciated and tried to impose the so-called fairness doctrine amidst a great deal of controversy:

[At the hearings of the Senate subcommittee on communications] chairman Wiley, along with Commissioner Lee and other FCC staff,

[27] "For the Public's Sake", The Christian Science Monitor, November 29, 1973.

fielded questions that ranged all over the dial: on telephone rates, domestic satellites, broadcast license renewals, children's television and commercials, prime-time access, cable television, and the FCC's own voluminous backlog.

But it was an application of the "fairness doctrine" involving First Amendment rights and religious programming which took center stage on the opening day of the hearings.

The focus was on a fundamentalist radio preacher, the Rev. Carl McIntyre, who asked the subcommittee to investigate the FCC revocation of his Media, Pa., radio license two years ago on fairness-doctrine violations. (The fairness doctrine specifies that equal time must be given to opposing views on controversial issues.)

It was Mr. McIntyre who floated a "private" radio ship, which he called Radio Free America (RFA), off Cape May, N.J., to air his religious programs when he lost his land license. The FCC then immediately ordered RFA off the air.

Mr. McIntyre's position is that "the free exercise of religion involves free speech on radio and TV, that they [broadcast licensees] should have the same rights as newspapers." He argues that the fairness doctrine should be nullified.

At the hearings, the Rev. Mr. McIntyre, the president of the International Council of Christian Churches, charged that former FCC chairman Dean Burch acted as a "speech czar" depriving him of his First Amendment rights when the FCC removed his license, and also warned a meeting of religious broadcasters "to stop airing parochial programs that reach only a select few."

Chairman Wiley returned the Rev. Mr. McIntyre's attack, arguing that the preacher had lost his case against the agency previously, before the U.S. Circuit Court of Appeals for the District of Columbia. Chairman Wiley defended the FCC position, stating that the agency had not renewed the license because the Rev. Mr. McIntyre had failed to fulfill the demands of the fairness doctrine that time be given to opposing views, had failed to abide by FCC rules on personal attack, on programming representation, and meeting the needs and interests of the area served.

"Very serious allegations have been made about the abridgment of the right of free speech," said Senator Pastore. He noted that he was a strong believer in the fairness doctrine but that the subcommittee would hold special hearings on the issue "to see if it [the doctrine] should be reviewed."[28]

Not unexpectedly, the media has fought the fairness doctrine and especially the Florida State statute that compelled newspapers to provide equivalent space free of change to any political candidate they editorially attacked:

An obscure Florida statute passed in 1913 providing political candidates with the right to reply to personal attacks in newspaper columns has become a cause celebre before the Supreme Court.

The Miami Herald Publishing Company, backed in "friends of the court" briefs by dozens of the nation's leading newspapers and broadcasters, will argue Wednesday that the court should overturn a 6-1 ruling of

[28] Louise Sweeney, "FCC Defends Action on 'Fairness Doctrine'", The Christian Science Monitor, April 1, 1974.

the Florida Supreme Court and hold the statute invalid as an invasion of First Amendment guarantees of press freedom.

Pat L. Tornillo Jr., denied by the Miami Herald an opportunity to reply to editorial attacks against his 1972 candidacy for the Florida Legislature, urges that the Florida law supports rather than derogates First Amendment freedoms.

Prof. Jerome A. Barron of the George Washington University Law School, who will argue Mr. Tornillo's case, long has pushed right-to-reply and other media access statutes as an alternative to strict libel laws for purpose of ensuring free and robust debate.

The nub of the case goes to the heart of the role of large metropolitan dailies in contemporary society. Those fearful that government regulation "chills" free debate argue that a law telling newspapers what must be printed is as onerous as censorship telling them what must not be printed.

Supporters of the Florida court decision argue, on the other hand, that with the disappearance of thousand of daily newspapers during recent decades, the remaining papers have themselves become censors dictating what Americans are to know.

In the Red Lion Broadcasting Company case of 1967, the Supreme Court held constitutional the "fairness doctrine" promulgated by the Federal Communications Commission requiring broadcast licensees to provide coverage of all sides of issues of controversy and public importance.

FCC regulations also provide for the right of individuals to reply to personal campaign attacks.

But the Red Lion case was premised upon the special duties of broadcasters owning rights to limited airwaves. Most observers regard it as offering little guidance to situations involving the print media.[29]

As far as the newspaper fraternity is concerned, it was much relieved by the U.S. Supreme Court's eventual ruling that the Florida Law was unconstitutional. As *The Christian Science Monitor* editorialized on this and a number of related matters:

The Supreme Court's unanimous decision in the Tornillo case both reaffirms freedom of the press under the First Amendment and puts the burden on the press to use its freedom responsibly.

The decision declared unconstitutional a Florida law requiring newspapers to give free and equal space to political candidates who feel they have been editorially attacked. By ruling in this manner the court not only forestalled the possibility of endless litigation and practical difficulties but adhered to a democratic faith in the wisdom of the citizenry and the efficacy of freedom in making truth prevail.

As Justice White said in a concurring opinion:

"Regardless of how beneficent-sounding the purposes of controlling the press might be, we prefer the power of reason as applied through public discussion and remain intensely skeptical about those measures that would allow government to insinuate itself into the editorial rooms of this nation's press."

[29] C. Robert Zelnick, "Media Fight 'Right to Reply' as Invasion", *The Christian Science Monitor*, April 17, 1974.

The decision comes as Watergate brings special praise and criticism to the American press — and as new demands for "access" to the media have brought new facilities for it.

The establishment of the National News Council recognizes a press and public desire for fairness and accuracy along with freedom. Its executive director says the national media generally do a good job in this respect.

The Tornillo decision is a challenge to make this good work better.[30]

Even some members of the press in Canada felt called upon to eulogize the U.S. Supreme Court for its alleged wisdom in the Florida case:

Freedom of the press is always a touchy subject for a newspaper to discuss. We have an interest to declare.

But the United States Supreme Court ruling striking down a Florida law that threatened freedom of the press with serious infringement, is as important to any private citizen interested in political democracy as it is to any newspaper publisher, editor or reporter.

Under the law, which had been on the Florida books for 61 years, a newspaper could be compelled to provide free space for a reply from any politician who had been "attacked" in its pages. Fair as that might seem in principle, at first glance, it would be unworkable in practice.

What is an attack? It happens, often, that a politician is pleased with a story that is seen by others as critical of him. It also happens that one is angered by a story that others see as favorable. Some are infuriated when they are quoted accurately. Some are unhappy when they are not mentioned at all, and attribute this to a hostile conspiracy, which is surely a form of attack. The opportunities for claiming a right of reply would be endless. And, as newspaper space is limited, adequate coverage of political life would become impossible.

The Supreme Court decision is significant. Had it not been struck down, the state law had been expected to serve as a model for federal legislation planned by the Nixon Administration. In this era of Watergate, the dangers that now have been averted need little elaboration.[31]

Yet the issue will not be solved easily, as the Editor Emeritus of *The Christian Science Monitor* has observed:

The people's right of a free press was initially and magnificently affirmed in the American Constitution and has been wisely sustained by the Supreme Court almost without exception ever since. This is indeed the fact in the most recently decided cases.

But the people's right is always in danger. It is subject to profound misunderstanding by the people themselves, never more than today. Thus in the very case last week where the Supreme Court unanimously decided Pat L. Tornillo Jr. had no right to reply to newspaper editorials, Mr. Tornillo may be correct when he commented: "I think it is a decision with which the overwhelming majority of citizens do not agree. Most think that a law giving public access to the overwhelming power of newspapers is needed today."

There is extensive and acute dissatisfaction with news media in the United States today. I get around the country a lot and I meet it on every

30 "For Free — and Fair — Press", *The Christian Science Monitor*, June 27, 1974.
31 "Press Freed", *The Globe and Mail*, Toronto, June 27, 1974.

hand. It has been intensified by Watergate, but it existed before Watergate and it will continue no matter how the constitutional crises is resolved.

The Constitution's simple affirmation of a free press, and the Supreme Court's clear, unanimous perception of it, will probably prevent the public from destroying an institution that is of indispensable value to them.

But the structure of the news media today raises severe problems. I suppose it is mainly a matter of concentration of power. In the old days, when there were several actively competing newspapers in every American city of any size, most everybody could find a paper suiting his particular bias. This was true throughout the 19th century. It didn't mean the papers were paragons of accuracy or objectivity. They certainly weren't. They distorted political news atrociously. But their distortions — some pro-Republican, some pro-Democrat, or some particular faction therein — pleased portions of the public. Everybody was happy.

Mainly economic factors forced the consolidation of many American newspapers in the 20th century. Diversity of bias diminished and almost vanished in given communities. The sole remaining newspaper, if responsible, had to try to serve the whole community as best it could. Often if suited no particular bias. No doubt some rare persons exist whose political views are detached and Olympian. But most readers have sharp opinions: These may or may not agree with the newspaper. Indeed, the more detached the paper sought to be, the more likely it was not to please anybody very intensely.

The radio and television networks are also concentrated. They have to cover the news pretty tersely, and when they have opinions — as through editorials or commentators — these are thoroughly distasteful to all who disagree. And they too are accused of bias.

It cannot be denied that the function of providing news and opinion is considerably concentrated. A large part of news coverage for all the media comes through two wire services. Syndicated columns of opinion are widely used. Chain ownership of newspapers has increased. The national television networks are concentrated into three major groups.

Those who operate the media are not infallible. They must exercise judgment every hour; even the act of selection is an important editorial decision. They have views of their own difficult to sublimate. Opinion-riddled writing has become more and more fashionable. The line between background-reporting, interpreting, and editorializing is not easy to draw or to defend.[32]

Clearly the question of the right of rebuttal is most critical in the political arena, although it also applies in many other areas. In the political sphere, the challenge posed by a one-sided media can prove particularly acute for a candidate trying to oust an incumbent. After all, even without the media actively taking a position against him, such a candidate is usually at a distinct disadvantage vis-à-vis any incumbent because at many levels of government the latter often has some built-in media advantages to begin with. This is particularly true at the national level in the United States where one commentator has documented the existence of what could be termed an "incumbent broadcasting system".

[32] Erwin D. Canham, "The Press and Power", *The Christian Science Monitor*, July 1, 1974.

Under the pink fuzz of Azaleas on Capitol Hill sits a taxpayer-subsidized, $1 million broadcasting complex that gives congressional incumbents a costly advantage over challengers.

It is part of a media system so powerful that it might be called a fourth national network and given call letters: IBS, for Incumbent Broadcasting System.

The Capitol Hill complex consists of two sets of underground TV, film, and radio studios that dazzle even commercial broadcasters and are available at bargain rates for the exclusive use of sitting members of Congress.

They are known as the Senate Recording Studio, tagged at an estimated $750,000, and the House Recording Studio, with its facilities estimated at $600,000. Together they cost the taxpayer more than $50,000 annually in appropriated funds to subsidize what many members of Congress regard as an "electronic newsletter" to communicate with constituents and what critics regard as a channel for political propaganda or personal campaigning.

The question of whether it is campaign propaganda or legitimate communication is one of the gravest ones imbedded in the present system. All radio, videotape, and film productions in both studios and records of them are guarded like the gold at Fort Knox, so it is impossible to monitor them for possible abuses.

But abuses exist. An aide to one popular Northern Senator alleges that the Senator did a campaign tape in the Senate studio for one of his friends, a Midwestern Senator.

The advantage of this and other fringe benefits, part of the incumbent broadcasting system, is summed up by the legislative director of the citizen lobby Common Cause, Fred Wertheimer. He says, "Combining the [House and Senate] Recording Studios with other factors is what really presents an advantage to incumbents. The services they provide, often with added costs picked up by the campaign committees, provide a combined outlet . . . for access to the media. [This is] opposed to the challenger, who gets none of it. . . . They only pick up the costs of incumbents. [It is] an enormous advantage to the incumbents; the real imbalance is in opportunity for access to the media."

Indeed, some congressional critics feel the present system is an abuse of incumbent privileges which makes it virtually impossible for challengers to have an equal chance.

"It's a fantastic setup," says a former Senate aide who saw it all in operation. "That's why it's virtually impossible to beat an incumbent. Along with the recording studios, there's the franking privilege and an enormous paper [stationery] allowance. They borrow from each other in off years; they flood the states with mail; they say it's just telling their constituents what they're doing, not campaigning. How do any of those guys ever get beaten?"

Evidently not many do. According to Congressional Quarterly, for instance, of 330 incumbents running for re-election in the House in 1972, only 10 incumbents or 3 percent were defeated.[33]

[33] Louise Sweeney, "Influential TV, Radio 'Network' on Capitol Hill", The Christian Science Monitor, May 8, 1974.

In a later article in a series of which the above was the first, the same commentator further enlarged on the media advantages normally accruing to incumbent politicians and suggested some remedies for this unfair imbalance:

As previous parts of this series have documented, incumbent members of Congress have a vast advantage over their challengers in terms of access to broadcasting. They can count on the bargain rates of the House and Senate radio, TV and film facilities, on the additional facilities of the Republican and Democratic campaign committees, and on thousands of dollars in backing from both to pay those broadcasting bills for "communicating with their constituents." All of this is available only to incumbents.

In addition, the system offers a potential for abuse by occasional incumbents with questionable ethics who may use legitimate communications channels for campaign spots for personal politicking. And it raises conflict of interest questions when some of these same incumbents are in the position of doing favors for the broadcasters they need as much as the broadcasters need a friend in Congress.

Congress is full of honorable men who frown on the inequities of the present system and would like to see it changed. From dozens of interviews with congressional experts some ideas emerge which might help solve some of the problems of the present system:

• Set up a watchdog committee on ethics for the House and Senate recording studios, consisting of members of impartial citizens groups as well as members of both houses of Congress, who are not heavy users of the studio, to ensure that there are no abuses of the system.

• Publish rules applying to both the Senate and House recording studios making it a punishable offense to use the studios for any campaigning or personal politicking. (Their own or for friends in Congress.)

• Make public the complete records of both studios, including specific reports on the frequency and type of use by the studios of each senator and representative, as well as detailed and inclusive budgets for both studios.

• Make public a complete record of studio use by commercial broadcasters, billing them directly at full commercial rates instead of the subsidized rates charged to members of Congress.

• Require public disclosure of the location and nature of the studios, through signs and directions as well as scheduled tours available periodically to the public.

• Provide equal access to the studios at their subsidized rates by nonincumbents running for the Senate or House.

• Enforce a form of identification, a visual logo or verbal disclaimer for all radio, TV or film products of the House or Senate studios, to be run at the beginning and end of the product's airing. (The only identification at present is a sign over the House recording studio.)

• Nullify the provision in the Federal Election Campaign Act amendments bill of 1974 (originally S.3004, now in the House) which exempts members of Congress from reporting as contributions or expenditures, services furnished by the Senate Recording Studio or the House Recording Studio, or such services paid for by the Republican or Democratic Senatorial Campaign Committee, the Democratic National Congressional Committee or the National Republican Congressional Committee.[34]

Despite the risks to freedom of the media purportedly entailed, the author feels that all forms of the media would be well advised to consider granting equal prominence, space and time to those they choose to attack, whether the attack is direct or indirect. Indeed, it would probably be best if they were to try to arrange matters in such a way as to provide an opportunity for rebuttal at the same time as the planned critique. Far from harming the media, this might actually improve it. Although some of the media's editorials would doubtless be eliminated or toned down, what remained would probably be better researched and more valid. Certainly such an approach would ensure a far more educative, informative and lively media, when it did choose to take on some cause and give its spokesmen a chance to state their side of the case.

GOVERNMENT REGULATION AND THE ROLE OF MEDIA REVIEW BOARDS

Government involvement in regulation of the media is already well advanced both in the U.S. and Canada. Some of this intervention — such as in the allocation of TV channels — may well be inevitable, although even here technology may already have rendered this kind of licensing role unnecessary by making so many more outlets available. The real question concerns the appropriate degree, extent and form of government regulation of the media.

For many reasons previously cited, the pressure is on for further public intervention. Sometimes what is threatened by government is so vindictive in character, and so patently aimed at getting the media for doing what is the essence of its job, that it more than amounts to overkill. Such was clearly the case in the instance of a recent Alabama law which has yet to be fully tested in the courts:

Let's suppose an out-of-state newspaper assigns its political correspondent to do a story on Gov. George C. Wallace of Alabama.

The reporter comes to Montgomery, interviews the Governor, goes to the state Capitol press room, writes his story, and phones it to his head office.

He packs up his typewriter and notes and starts to leave — but he is stopped by a state policeman who informs him that he has just committed a felony, punishable by a fine of $10,000 and 10 years in jail.

The reporter's crime: Before he wrote his story, he failed to file a detailed statement of economic interests with the Alabama Ethics Commission.

A far-fetched scenario? Perhaps, but nonetheless it is one which could take place in Montgomery if Alabama's new ethics law is upheld by the courts and is enforced to the letter.[35]

Government regulation of the media poses all sorts of problems, not the least of which is: who should do the regulating? The in-fighting over this issue

[34] Louise Sweeney, "Broadcast Media the Key to National Elections", *The Christian Science Monitor*, May 16, 1974.
[35] "Alabama Ethics Law — Trouble for Newsmen?" *The Christian Science Monitor*, October 23, 1973.

usually comes down to a battle for the applicable regulatory positions between those in the industry and those purporting to represent its consumers:

The seven members of the Federal Communications Commission (FCC) make decisions every day that affect every U.S. citizen's life — and right now a major change in the makeup of that commission is taking place which could have a sharp impact on communications policy affecting you over the next several years.

Mr. Nixon's imprint will be felt beyond his incumbency, since FCC commissioners serve for seven years and his unprecedented naming of the total commission will mold this powerful regulatory agency.

Some critics are concerned about whether that imprint will benefit the public or the vast businesses, like the telephone, cable TV, and broadcasting industries, which the FCC is chartered to regulate.

Already critics believe the commission is moving in directions that are pro-industry, anti-consumer, with a strongly conservative Republican thrust which might be described as the "Nixonization" of the FCC.

"There's no consumer advocate on the commission now and none in sight," says a spokesman for a communications watchdog which has kept close tabs on the FCC. He is Dr. Everett C. Parker, director of the Office of Communication of the United Church of Christ, who says, "It's the first time the commission has been left without anyone who might take the side of the people." He adds, "The commission has always been controlled by the industry. . . ."

"President Nixon has clearly moved the FCC in the direction of less consumer orientation as far af his appointees are concerned," says NCCB [National Citizens Committee for Broadcasting] president Kramer. "The only countervailing pressures will have to come from the incipient and growing consumer movement in broadcasting."

"I expect the commission will take a sudden lurch to the right with Wiley in charge," says Tracy Westen, director of Public Communications, Inc., a citizens communication organization. "Under his leadership the FCC will be much more conservative and much more politically oriented."

"Wiley is an industry-oriented commissioner," says another professional commission-watcher. "He has repeatedly addressed industry groups on the subject of FCC burdens on broadcasters. He professes open-mindedness and is somewhat more fair-minded than the others. And Wiley has been a staunch administration supporter — he was also an effective, hard worker and state chairman [Illinois] for Nixon in 1968."

Commissioner Wiley, a former Chicago lawyer, has been described as "a friend of the broadcasting industry." A spokesman for the industry's National Association of Broadcasters (NAB) sees it differently: "He's a friend of the industry only in the sense that he appreciates *all* the industries he regulates and their problems," says Grover C. Cobb, senior executive vice-president of the NAB.

The NAB reflects the view widely held in all the industries overseen by the FCC: the less regulation the better — a laissez-faire approach.[36]

[36] Louise Sweeney, "Who Owns Communications in U.S.?" *The Christian Science Monitor,* March 5, 1974.

It has been one of the themes of this book that one way out of the dilemma involved in selecting the membership of public watchdog groups is to provide for appointments emanating from sources other than government. This need would appear to be especially acute in the field of media regulation because of the many political overtones involved. To the extent that public regulatory agencies must play a part in the media field, it is probably more crucial than anywhere else that at least a majority of those selected to do the regulating find their way to that position by means other than governmental, that is political, appointment.

The function of the media is so crucial to the maintenance of a free society that those now in command of the situation should be doing everything in their power to forestall the need for further government intervention in their sphere. Probably the best means to this end would be to establish an overall media review board or a series of selective review bodies such as the press councils that are now to be found in so many jurisdictions. The advantages of such councils have proven so compelling in a number of instances that one wonders why they have not spread faster. How well such councils can work is suggested by an American reviewer of the prospects of the new National News Council which has been set up in the U.S. to handle complaints about national news outlets, a review which was undertaken in the light of experience under a comparable body in Britain which is designed to serve a somewhat similar purpose in the newspaper field:

In its continuing and necessary search for reader approval and respectability, the American news media now embark on a new venture. The National News Council, set up by the prestigious Twentieth Century Fund and financed by several foundations, is beginning to function, as a special kind of watchdog, ombudsman, and defender, to the national news suppliers of the United States.

The 15-member news council is ready to receive complaints from public, private, and press sources concerning the behavior of the national news outlets — which means, not local papers but news agencies (such as AP and UPI), the radio-TV networks, the news weeklies, the national newspapers, and the supplementary syndicating news suppliers such as the Washington Post-Los Angeles Times service.

I suppose one big long-range question is whether, a year from now, this news council will have gained in approval and acceptance from the news fraternity. How will it have functioned in this contentious Watergate climate? So far, press approval has been grudging and "give it a try," at best. Members of the American Society of Newspaper Editors responded, in a poll, negatively by 4 to 1.

But a dozen years ago, when the idea of a press council was first discussed, the ratio was more nearly 15 to 1. The British Press Council, nearest approach to the American venture, has succeeded though it too was off to a doubtful start. Recent British figures show a decline in the number of complaints lodged. In the United States, without a press council, the press has apparently suffered a decline in its reputation for fairness and credibility among the general public. The press's Watergate sleuthing did not repair this much.

Much will depend on how the council handles the complaints which are lodged with it. Will the criticisms get all the heart of the public's distrust? In Britain, complaints seem lately to have fallen under three headings: invasions of privacy, violations of good taste, and overemphasis on sex.

Of course there are minor complaints. For example, a village postmaster who drove off two armed assailants objected that in the local press he was described as an "elderly invalid." While this may have been a dramatic description, the press council decided that it was inaccurate, and an invasion of privacy, and the complaint was upheld.

In a wider-ranging issue, the British council's strictures persuaded the News of the World to tone down a series of confessions by Christine Keeler, a principal in the Profumo scandal. In another case the council criticized the London Daily Mirror for being "too definitive" in fixing blame for a plane crash when an investigation was just beginning.

The expectation, at American news council headquarters, is that the first complaints may deal with alleged press bias. For example, a charge that the news organization in question reported a protest rally but failed to report that out-of-town organizers stage-managed the demonstration. Another example would be an industrial pollution story in which the reporter sought comment from Ralph Nader but not from the corporation accused of polluting.

Will the Watergate probe stir up any complaints before the news council? One can imagine someone criticizing the networks for the spectacle of television reporters virtually pursuing a Watergate witness down the street, microphones at the ready. Those who would take newspapers to task for the views in their editorials will be frustrated; the council will not deal with editorial opinion if so labeled. Nor with columnists' opinions.

The press council may occasionally criticize but it is not primarily a critic. It is a judge and an adjudicator, dealing with complaints placed before it. Often it will praise rather than blame, vindicate and defend rather than attack.

It could happen, as happened in Britain, that when a government committee was considering new legal restrictions on news reporting (to assure responsibility, it was argued), the press council argued against the plan. And the government finally decided the new rules were unnecessary. That would be real vindication for the news council![37]

How well the new National News Council may serve the media, as well as the public, is suggested by its response to Nixon's assaults on the major American television networks:

President Nixon, during his televised news conference of Oct. 26, 1973, leveled at the major American television networks the charge of "outrageous, vicious, distorted," news reporting.

Since then the White House has repeatedly been asked to press the charge, with details and specifications, before a new institution set up specifically to police the news organizations of the United States. The White House has so far failed to present any bill of particulars. The story, in detail, follows:

On July 16, last year (1973) there came into existence in New York City a National News Council. It was organized under the auspices of the

[37] William H. Stringer, "Do Press Councils Work?" The Christian Science Monitor, August 1, 1973.

Twentieth Century Fund, but became independent on incorporation. Both the fund which sponsored the council and the council are nonpartisan and nonprofit institutions. The council is forbidden by its charter from accepting funds from government or from any newspaper or radio or television news organization. It is funded by private contributions. Most of its money comes from a consortium of 10 nonprofit foundations or funds. The two largest contributors are the Twentieth Century Fund and the Merkle Fund. Its present budget is about $300,000 a year.

The council has a "grievance committee" which exists to receive complaints of inaccurate or unfair news reporting and to investigate such reports. The committee consists of "four public members and three media members." The council has an executive director, William Arthur, former managing editor of Look magazine, and an associate director, Ned Schnurman, former city editor of WCBS-TV News.

Immediately after the charges were made Arthur and Schnurman began a series of efforts to reach and discuss them with Ronald Ziegler, press secretary to the President. A meeting was arranged, and held, on Nov. 29. At that first meeting Ziegler named six areas in which he alleged that there had been unfair reporting. The six included the reporting of the President's personal finances (San Clemente, Key Biscayne, etc.). It also included reporting of the dismissal of former special Watergate prosecutor Archibald Cox.

Following this meeting Arthur and Schnurman obtained from the Vanderbilt News Archives in Nashville, Tenn., abstracts of the news reports by the three major TV networks covering the six areas mentioned by Ziegler. These were presented to Ziegler at another meeting at the White House on Jan. 17. Ziegler was invited to identify from these abstracts specific cases of allegedly "outrageous, vicious, distorted" reporting.

Ziegler promised that the abstracts would be studied and that there would be an answer before the next scheduled meeting of the council on Jan. 28.

No answer had been received by Jan. 28. No word has been received since.

The National News Council exists to hear and to investigate grievances. But unless specific charges are brought to the council there is nothing for it to investigate or to judge. The White House had made sweeping charges, but has never yet identified what particular statement or news program was ever "outrageous," or "vicious," or "distorted."

The council stands ready to judge any specific charges of bad reporting but as in any court of law there must be an accuser.

We are informed by the council that it will be pleased to receive specific accusations from any private citizen or any organization which is ready to present them. Anyone wishing to present a case is free to examine the abstracts of the various news broadcasts in the six areas mentioned by Mr. Ziegler. These may be seen at the offices of the National News Council, One Lincoln Plaza, New York City, New York, 10023.[38]

The need for such bodies is so obvious that the only question that remains is how to get on with the business of putting them into action. Preferably this can be done by industry in concert with consumer groups sufficiently represen-

---

[38] Joseph C. Harsch, "Mr. Nixon vs. the TV Nets", The Christian Science Monitor, February 12, 1974.

tative to ensure that the bodies will quickly acquire a public awareness and credibility. An alternative would be for governments to assist in this process, but this hardly seems possible without a degree of political manipulation likely to scuttle the project before it gets off the ground. Clearly, however, despite the risks involved, this form of political intervention is superior to more direct and extensive governmental regulation of those facets of the media which call for attention by someone outside its ranks.

10

SUMMARY AND CONCLUSION

There is no ready or succinct conclusion to the problems discussed in this book. Reflection on the general approach taken throughout would seem to suggest the need to highlight four major measures. The essence of each of these measures is to a large extent captured by the first of the four which is the call for a revitalized system of checks and balances across North America. Second, within this revitalized system of checks and balances, the major point to be stressed is the key role to be played by disclosure and exposure and public scrutiny. Third, and consistent with the latter point, is the strong case to be made for incomes and costs review boards, both in the United States and Canada, as a crucial element within the overall strategy for reform. Such boards would not only assist society in coming to grips with many of the problems dealt with in preceding chapters, but also with the challenge of inflation, at least in so far as it originates in, or is aggravated by, domestic as distinct from international forces. Fourth, there is a major caveat to be added at the end of this general disgnosis and prescription: the emphasis that reform in many, if not most, of the areas dealt with in this book depends, in the final analysis, upon the wisdom and courage of North America's political leadership. Unfortunately this is a discouraging qualification.

THE NEED FOR A REVITALIZED
SYSTEM OF CHECKS AND BALANCES

This book began with a resumé of the most significant signs and symptoms of the sickness which has come to characterize North American society. Manifestations of this disease were brought out in more detail in subsequent chapters dealing with major institutional components within the overall system. This emphasized that from politics down through big business, the professions, the unions, and the media, there is not one part of the total system which is not riddled with problems crying out for attention.

As bleak as this picture may appear, it is offset to a large extent not only by the material and technological advances to be credited to North America, but also, and more important, by the fact that few of the difficulties cited cannot be alleviated or resolved. Moreover, what is most encouraging of all is the fact that nothing like a revolution is required to purge the system of most of the abuses which now afflict it. A wide variety of comparatively mild reform measures is all that is needed to make a significant difference.

What is most essential is a reconstructed system of checks and balances designed to ensure that the public interest comes more to the fore than the selfish interests which so naturally tend to assert themselves among individuals and institutions. The basic problem is that the existing set of checks and balances in North American society is no longer appropriate to the task for which it was originally constructed. Obsolete as they are, these existing checks and balances have become almost enshrined because they favour those who have found such handy ways around them. The fundamental challenge is to break this self-reinforcing log jam and to set in motion the creation of a new series of reciprocal rights and responsibilities which puts the general welfare first.

In keeping with this, one can review each of the subject areas discussed here and see that both the problems involved and their potential solutions are, essentially, common to all areas. In each case the four measures outlined above persistently come to the surface as critical variables in grappling with the difficulties in question.

In the political arena, as in most of the others discussed in this book, there are both negative and positive steps required. On the more negative side, measures must be taken to reveal, and hopefully remove, the all too many and tempting conflicts of interest which often come between politicians and their public obligations. For one thing, patronage in its many lingering forms must be eliminated from the scene. Similarly, as was brought out at several points, the advantages enjoyed by incumbent elected officials must somehow be reduced to provide a better and fairer balance between the insiders and the outsiders. Short of complete public financing of election campaigns, there must be full revelation of the sources of all private financial support. In a more positive vein, steps must be taken to make politics a more attractive calling. Among the measures required in this area are much higher salaries and expenses for those choosing to dedicate themselves to this vital public service. Leaves of absence from their regular occupations should also be granted to all such individuals.

The business and corporate world has also demanded a good deal of attention. The range of remedies called for in this sphere is almost endless, partly because business and corporate ethics, or perhaps more accurately, the lack of them, have played such a central part in downgrading the moral tone of everything else in North America. The Protestant ethic has much to be said for it, but in many instances it has degenerated into something approaching the end justifying the means. Several major reforms are needed in the economic arena. Board members and senior executives must obviously be induced to have a greater appreciation for the trust relationship within which they are supposed to be functioning. Accountants and auditors must be compelled to adopt an even higher standard of public accountability and responsibility. In the past, accountants and auditors might be said in some instances to have hidden more than they revealed. That can no longer be permitted, and the hands of reputable auditors must be strengthened in every way possible to help them provide a full, honest and true account of what is going on in both private and public enterprise. In the same spirit, measures must also be taken to protect honest insiders who choose to bring institutional abuses of one kind or another to the public's attention.

The mixed free enterprise system also poses some other business or pseudo-business problems. In the case of multinational corporations, for example, there is the need to ensure that they are not manipulating intercountry transfer payments to the detriment of one country or another. Then there is the horrendous problem posed by the stock market, riddled as it is by conflicts of interest which must be eradicated before anyone can have any real confidence in its still important but fortunately, perhaps, waning role. Failure to effectively police the securities market brings to mind the shortcomings of many

389

regulatory bodies which must be induced to protect the public interest more adequately than in the past. And finally, there is that growing octopus, government itself, which has become a big business in its own right but without the disciplining effect of any kind of competition. Contracting out of public services and other measures must be taken to ensure that those services for which the government does decide to take responsibility are delivered as efficiently as possible.

Confusion surrounds the concept of corporate social responsibility and this concept must be clarified if it is to have any operational meaning. There is a plethora of corporate social responsibility models which can be devised, most of which have some validity. Basically, however, businessmen and corporations should continue to do what they presumably can do best — that is be efficient, innovative and productive in the provision of goods and services, while generating a good return on the dollars invested in their enterprises. As long as they do this within existing laws and regulations pertaining to business, this is probably all that should be expected of them.

An especially sordid branch of the business and corporate community, of which it itself is hardly proud, is the advertising and marketing fraternity. To date, literally anything and everything seems to have been accepted in the name of promoting and selling goods and services, but this day is gradually coming to an end as consumer and other groups rise up in anger, bitterness and resentment against the way in which advertising and marketing hucksters have been treating them. Aside from placing some limitations on the most blatant, excessive and dishonest of advertising and marketing practices, encouragement must be provided for consumer groups, counter ads, class action suits and other possible remedies aimed at the most damaging and demeaning of advertising and marketing abuses.

Turning to the professions and the unions, there is again considerable room for improvement. The private preserves of the self-governing professions must be pried open and subjected to much more public scrutiny than they have been in the past. Their restrictive practices must be curbed and their professional ethics and integrity shored up. Individual professionals who choose to put their personal ethics and integrity above all else must be afforded more protection.

Unions too must be held more accountable and responsible for their activities. Remedies for those damaged by illegal union conduct must be improved and the unions, like all other groups in society, must be called to account for their share of the blame in fueling the fires of inflation. In addition, especially in Canada, further steps must be taken to ensure that union members are protected from their unions, as few and far between as are the instances where such protection is required.

When it comes to the media, the challenge of improving the present situation is delicate because of legitimate fears about the erosion of media freedom resulting from any further state intervention. Some such regulation has proven inevitable and will doubtless continue to prove necessary to prevent undue concentration of control and ownership and to curb advertising clutter and other programing abuses on radio and television. Now, however, the major problem may turn out to be to forestall any more public control than is absolutely necessary. Much of the need for such interference would be obviated if the media chose voluntarily to put its own house in order by such steps as offering equal prominence, space and time for rebuttal to those they choose to attack rather than waiting for what is almost inevitable legislation to this effect. All of this and many other measures which could help improve the vital role of the media would be enhanced if credible media review boards were established.

THE ROLE OF DISCLOSURE, EXPOSURE AND PUBLIC SCRUTINY

In any revitalized system of checks and balances in North America, there is a vital place for more disclosure and exposure and public scrutiny. With respect to disclosure and exposure, it has been a recurring theme throughout this volume that much more light must be shed on the activities of virtually all of the institutions analyzed. Without factual information about precisely what is going on, it is impossible to monitor any group's activities in relation to the public interest.

Virtually every group examined herein should have to live with a great deal more public revelation of what is transpiring within its inner confines. Politicians should have to disclose any private funding they are permitted and all potential conflicts of interest. In the business arena, members of boards of directors, and senior executives should also be subject to exposure of their interlocking corporate relations and other insider activities. As was brought out earlier, this is only one of many illustrations of the need for more disclosure in the corporate field. Advertising and marketing is still another arena where the public has a right to know much more about what is taking place. Full knowledge of even so seemingly innocuous a matter as what is paid for so-called personal endorsement of goods and services should be in the public domain. Similarly, in the professions, in the unions, and in the media, many illustrations have been offered of areas where greater disclosure and exposure is in order.

The only areas in which this study has found such public revelation of information to be out of keeping with the public interest is in cases where important trade secrets, confidential sources of media information, or necessarily privileged professional-client relationships are involved. Otherwise, there are few facts and figures which private self-seeking institutions should be allowed to hide from public view.

But more disclosure and exposure in itself will not necessarily accomplish very much. It would obviously assist regulatory bodies and consumer groups to go about their tasks more effectively, and that contribution is not to be minimized. But, in many instances, if real value, in terms of advancing the public interest, is to be derived from the greater availability of information, it will have to be accompanied by more effective means of public scrutiny of that data. This is where the role of truly public members on all sorts of private and quasi-private institutional bodies is to be promoted. Whether it is on corporate boards or professional licensing bodies or on any of a variety of other newer types of agencies explored in this book, there is much to be said for such participation. It is certainly essential on media review bodies if they are to have any credibility. It is also crucial to have such representatives on government regulatory bodies for some of the same reasons.

As long as these representatives are selected by a reputable cross section of interest groups, and not by government alone, they can play an extremely crucial role, even if they have only voice and no vote on the tribunals on which they are serving. Lest anyone harbour any doubts about society's ability to find so many public-spirited citizens with the requisite qualifications, let it simply be said that the challenge involved will bring forth many volunteers who may be overeducated for, and under utilized in, the jobs they are now doing and who would welcome such an opportunity to be of public service.

However it is handled, the point is that little can be done to bring about significant reforms in North America's leading institutions unless much more is revealed about what is going on in them and some public members are placed on their governing bodies in order to keep them conscious of their public obligations. A meaningful combination of disclosure and exposure and public scrutiny can probably do as much as anything to bring about a re-vitalized system of checks and balances in North America.

THE CASE FOR AN INCOMES
AND COSTS REVIEW BOARD

Another central measure in any attempt to reform North American society should take the form of a national incomes and costs review board. A purely federal body might well suffice in the United States, but it would have to be a joint federal-provincial body in Canada since so many issues coming under its jurisdiction would fall within the provincial sphere because of Canada's decen-tralized constitutional division of powers.

An incomes and costs review board would not only complement and supplement many of the measures already called for in this volume, but could play a critical part in the fight against inflation — yet another manifestation of what has gone wrong in North America as well as many other parts of the world. The role of such a board in the inflationary battle is probably a useful context within which to visualize the part it could play. This is because, in the long run, inflation is undoubtedly aggravated by the never-ending scramble by organized interest groups for a bigger share of the national pie, the division of which is a source of continuing dissension. Admittedly, however, foreign forces, fiscal and monetary policies, and a constantly changing mix of both general and sectoral demand-pull and cost-push pressures all play a part in the inflationary process so that there are no easy answers to the problem.

Accordingly, a variety of remedies are required, including a willingness to live with some inflation, indexed social security arrangements to protect those most disadvantaged by it, and appropriate degrees of restraint in fiscal and monetary affairs. Over and above these and other measures, however, there is a desperate need for what could best be described as a pressure-point strategy aimed at delineating areas in the economy which are giving rise to strong inflationary pressures and determining what can be done to alleviate or abort them. Some of these pressure points will be found to be caused by supply bottlenecks which can only be checked by finding a way to increase the pro-duct or service in question or by dampening the demand for it. Currently of more concern are the activities of powerful interest groups which might well simply be termed boat-rockers.

Although there may be something inherently wrong with the competitive pursuit of self-interest on ethical, moral or religious grounds, economically speaking it is hard to quarrel with the efficacy of this approach as long as there are sufficient checks and balances, either market or institutional in nature, among the various contending interest groups. What has to be avoided is unrestrained power blocs, be they in labour, management, the professions, government or elsewhere. Otherwise, as is presently the case, they are able to extract monopolistic and/or monopsonistic returns, thus whetting the appetites of others for less realizeable, but perhaps equally extortionate and inflationary, demands.

This is where the role of an incomes and costs review board comes into the picture. It should be charged with the task of identifying those out-of-line groups which have acquired too much power, deciding what can be done to bring them down to size, and raising a public furor until some such action is taken. This approach makes far more sense than wage and price guidelines or controls, not only because they are unworkable in the long run (and perhaps fail on a short-term basis as well), but because it is designed to get at the cause of problems rather than their symptoms. Instead of trying to manipulate wages and prices, or any other income of cost in the total system, it makes far more sense to attack the power base of whatever groups are exacting exorbitant returns from the rest of society.

As an exercise in political economy and for operating purposes, an incomes and costs review board would have to keep a close watch on every sector of the economy. To decide where to focus its spotlight next, it might well simply operate on the basis of a rule of thumb which singled out for attention any group whose incomes or costs over a two- or three-year period were rising faster than those of roughly comparable groups. Not surprisingly, such an approach would clearly lead to an assessment of what has been taking place in a number of areas which have long merited concern. Thus, if one were to single out a group of unions which have for years been out of line — judging by the wage increases they have been realizing in relation to virtually all other unionized workers — it would be the construction unions. Investigation of their power base would quickly reveal the kind of steps which should be taken to reduce their undue leverage. The building trades' potentially discriminating use of the hiring hall and restrictive use of apprenticeship is reason enough to force them to yield ground in these areas. Steps would have to be taken as well to strengthen the employer side of the bargaining table in that industry because of the disarray and division which has so long characterized it. Finally, to put an end to leapfrogging and whipsawing, the degree of community-by-community and trade-by-trade fragmentation which persists in construction negotiations would have to be remedied by moving toward more area-wide multitrade bargaining.

Analogous remedies could be found for any other out-of-line group within the economic system. Among the professions the same sort of fee and income tests could be employed as for the unions and similar corrective approaches could be fashioned. Examination of income trends among the professions would show some moving ahead faster than others over a period of several years, thus suggesting either a bottleneck or some boat-rocking. Again, investigation doubtlessly would reveal the true source of the problem and what could be done to arrest it. Some of the means to this end have already been explored in an earlier chapter.

On the business and corporate front the analysis involved could prove a little more tricky. The first step would be to compare return on investment in different industries over a four- or five-year period. An industry or series of industries consistently leading the profit parade would bear examination. The problem in this type of case is to determine whether a higher-than-average rate of return is deserved or not. Clearly it will often be due to one kind of anticompetitive practice or another in which event it is not socially desirable, and remedial action is called for. In many cases, however, there may be above-average risks involved, or the firms or industries in question may have pioneered in a new product, service or technique, in which event they probably warrant higher-than-usual returns for some time. Even in these situations, of course, an incomes and costs review board could play an extremely useful role by educating the public about some of the basic facts of economic life.

Such a board should also keep a watchful eye on what is taking place in the public and quasi-public sectors of the economy. Subject as they are to little or no competition, and enjoying seemingly endless and even rampant growth, these ought to be primary targets for anyone concerned about inflation, since unduly costly public services contribute as much to rising prices as anything else. The problem in these areas will be to devise a means both of identifying those elements of the public and quasi-public service most prone to waste and of doing something effective about it. The challenge is far from hopeless, however, as was indicated in a discussion of the public service in a previous chapter.

One important aspect of the concept of an incomes and costs review board is that it would have to entail a real exercise in political economy if it were ever to succeed. It would thus be important, especially at the outset, to zero in on trouble spots in all areas of the economy. If nothing else, this book should have indicated that that should be no problem. The North American economy, both north and south of the border, is so riddled with offenders that the real problem would be to select the worst of them in each sector. To begin, one could readily suggest the building trades, the doctors or dentists, the oil and gas industry or some facet of the food industry, the stock exchanges, the Defence Department in the U.S.A., the Department of Manpower and Immigration in Canada, and just about any large university one might care to name.

Before terminating this brief discussion of the kind of contribution which an incomes and costs review board could make both to the wider purposes discussed in this book and to the fight against inflation, it is well to stress some of the key assumptions upon which it rests. To begin with, such an approach assumes that pressure points in the form of unduly strong power blocks are to be found in every sector of the economy and do present serious problems. The concept of such a review board also assumes that unduly strong and out-of-line groups in all areas of society do have powers and do engage in activities which they would not like to see subjected to public scrutiny, let alone control. It further assumes that after a cross section of such offending groups did have the skeletons in their closets exposed to general view and dealt with, others would think twice about continuing or initiating actions which would invite similar treatment. Essentially, this whole strategy assumes — and here the reference might be to all the reforms called for in this volume and not only to that of an incomes and costs review board — that the best way to ensure that any interest group, or individual, for that matter, behaves in the public interest is to make them actuely aware that it is in their own self-interest to do so.

The final assumption underlying this approach really relates to the concluding section of this book. Suffice it to put it this way: no incomes and costs review board of the calibre outlined here has any hope of achieving its purpose unless government leaders — that is, politicians — are prepared to appoint to it competent, diligent, dedicated and nonpartisan personnel, and then to heed their advice and counsel even when it goes against the grain of the various power brokers which they are so accustomed to playing off against each other, usually at little expense to anyone but the public.

A MAJOR CAVEAT

As negative as this book has doubtless appeared at many points, the author's underlying intentions and purposes have been positive. Much is wrong with North America, but nothing yet so wrong that it cannot be alleviated or corrected without a revolution or anything like one. In the long run, however, that is what will be invited unless the need for reform is taken seriously and society begins to move along the path of reform at a brisker rate than it has to date.

Although the vested interests standing in the way of reform are influential and strong, the forces being mounted against them are becoming ever more powerful. Perhaps because it is a little sicker than its northern neighbour, the United States has spawned so many new public interest groups in the last few years that it is hard to keep up with them. All over North America consumers and other victims of entrenched interest groups are starting to stand up and be counted. In these new reform groups may lie North America's greatest hope.

At the other end of the spectrum — and here is the major caveat — lie too many of those in political power. Either because they have been bought — figuratively or otherwise — or because they lack the intelligence or insight necessary to appreciate the challenge, let alone the conviction and intestinal fortitude to confront it, there is an appalling dearth of politicians prepared to lead in any meaningful battle to begin to reform North America. Watergate may have changed the situation, but that seems increasingly unlikely as time passes.

Perhaps the politicians will begin to demonstrate some real reform instincts when they realize that the reforms which are now more incessantly being demanded of them should also be imposed on the leaders of many other institutions. Politics may be more in need of reform than other leading institutions in North America, but that is hardly the basic point of this book. Yet little or nothing of true long-run significance is likely to happen unless the political processes of North America start to produce politicians with more intelligence, convictions, ethics, and leadership, and until the public begins to listen to them. In the author's view, the public is more than ready — it is the politicians who are now sadly lagging behind.